The Western Heritage

SIXTH EDITION

The Western Heritage

Volume I: To 1715

SIXTH EDITION

DONALD KAGAN
Yale University

STEVEN OZMENT
Harvard University

FRANK M. TURNER
Yale University

Prentice Hall, Upper Saddle River, New Jersey 07458

Library of Congress Cataloging–in–Publication Data

The Library of Congress has catalogued the one volume edition as follows:

Kagan, Donald
The Western heritage/ Donald Kagan, Steven Ozment, Frank M. Turner. —6th ed.
p. cm.
Includes bibliographical references and index.
ISBN 0-13-617383-7
1. Civilization, Western. I. Ozment, Steven E. II. Turner, Frank M. (Frank Miller). (Date). III. Title
CB245.K28 1998 97-23706
909′.09812—dc21 CIP

Editorial Director: Charlyce Jones Owen
Editor-in-Chief, Development: Susanna Lesan
Development Editor: Roberta Meyer
Director of Production and Manufacturing: Barbara Kittle
Production Editor: Barbara DeVries
Executive Manager, New Media: Alison Pendergast
Manufacturing Manager: Nick Sklitsis
Prepress and Manufacturing Buyer: Lynn Pearlman
Creative Design Director: Leslie Osher
Interior and Cover Designer: Maria Lange
Supervisor of Production Services: Lori Clinton
Electronic Page Layout: Rosemary Ross
Photo Director: Lorinda Morris-Nantz
Photo Research: Barbara Salz
Cartographer: Maryland Cartographics
Line Art Coordinator: Michele Giusti
Copy Editor: Susan Saslow

Cover Art: *Aragonese fleet returns to Naples after victorious battle of Ischia*, F. Pagano, 15th century. E. T. Archive/Capodimonte Museum, Naples.

This book was set in 10/12 Trump Mediaeval by the HSS in-house formatting and production services group and was printed and bound by RR Donnelley & Sons. The cover was printed by The Lehigh Press, Inc.

Time Line photo credits appear on page xxvii and constitute a continuation of the copyright page.

Printed in the United States of America
10 9 8 7 6 5 4 3 2 1

ISBN 0-13-617424-8

Prentice-Hall International (UK) Limited, *London*
Prentice-Hall of Australia Pty. Limited, *Sydney*
Prentice-Hall Canada Inc., *Toronto*
Prentice-Hall Hispanoamericana, S.A., *Mexico*
Prentice-Hall of India Private Limited, *New Delhi*
Prentice-Hall of Japan, Inc. *Tokyo*
Simon & Schuster Asia Pte. Ltd., *Singapore*
Editora Prentice-Hall do Brasil, Ltda., *Rio de Janeiro*

BRIEF CONTENTS

VOLUME I

DETAILED CONTENTS

DOCUMENTS

MAPS

THE WEST & THE WORLD

POLITICAL TRANSFORMATIONS

PREFACE

The heritage of Western civilization has perhaps never been the focus of so much interest and controversy as it is today. Many commentators criticize it, many praise it, but for all it is a subject of intense discussion. *The Western Heritage,* sixth edition, is designed to allow teachers to introduce students to the subject of that discussion. It presents an overview of Western civilization, including its strengths, its weaknesses, and the controversies surrounding it.

On campus after campus, every aspect of Western civilization has become an object of scrutiny and debate. Many participants in this debate fail to recognize that such self-criticism is characteristic of Western civilization and an important part of its heritage. We welcome the debate and hope that this book can help raise its quality.

The collapse of Communism has left the people of half of Europe struggling to reorganize their political institutions and their social and economic lives. The choices they are making and the future they are forging will reflect in large measure their understanding of their heritage. To follow and participate in that process we too need to understand that heritage.

GOALS OF THE TEXT

Since *The Western Heritage* first appeared, we have sought to provide our readers with a work that does justice to the richness and variety of Western civilization. Events since then have only added urgency to our purpose.

Our primary goal has been to present a strong, clear narrative account of the central developments in Western history. We have also sought to call attention to certain critical themes:

- the development of political freedom, constitutional government, and concern for the rule of law and individual rights
- the shifting relations among religion, society, and the state
- the development of science and technology and their expanding impact on thought, social institutions, and everyday life
- the major religious and intellectual currents that have shaped Western culture

We believe that these themes have been fundamental in Western civilization, shaping the past and exerting a continuing influence on the present.

Balanced and Flexible Presentation In this edition as in past editions, our goal has been to present Western civilization fairly, accurately, and in a way that does justice to its great variety. History has many facets, no one of which alone can account for the others. Any attempt to tell the story of the West from a single overarching perspective, no matter how timely, is bound to neglect or suppress some important part of that story.

The Western Heritage, sixth edition, is designed to accommodate a variety of approaches to a course in Western civilization, allowing teachers to stress what is most important to them. Some teachers will ask students to read all the chapters. Others will select among them to reinforce assigned readings and lectures.

We do not believe that a history of the West should be limited to politics and international relations, but we share the conviction that internal and external political events have shaped the Western experience in fundamental and powerful ways. Recent events in central and eastern Europe and the former Soviet Union have strengthened that belief. We have also been told repeatedly by teachers that no matter what their own historical specialization, they believe that a political narrative gives students an effective tool to begin to organize their understanding of the past.

The Western Heritage also provides one of the richest accounts of the social history of the West available today, with strong coverage of family life, the roles of women, and the place of the family in relation to broader economic, political, and social developments. This coverage reflects the explosive growth in social historical research in the past quarter century, which has enriched virtually all areas of historical study.

Finally, no other survey text presents so full an account of the religious and intellectual development of the West. People may be political and social beings, but they are also reasoning and spiritual beings. What they think and believe are among the most important things we can know about them. Their ideas about God, society, law, gender, human nature, and the physical world have changed over the centuries and continue to change. We cannot fully grasp our own approach to the world without understanding the intellectual currents of the past and their influence on our thoughts and conceptual categories.

Clarity and Accessibility Good narrative history requires clear, vigorous prose. As in earlier editions, we have paid careful attention to the quality of our writing, subjecting every paragraph to critical scrutiny. Our goal was to make our presentation fully accessible to students without compromising vocabulary or conceptual level. We hope this effort will benefit both teachers and students.

Recent Scholarship As in previous editions, changes in this edition reflect our determination to incorporate the most recent developments in historical scholarship and the expanding concerns of professional historians.

Pedagogical Features This edition retains the pedagogical features of the last edition, including part-opening comparative timelines, a list of key topics at the beginning of each chapter, chapter review questions, and questions accompanying the more than 200 source documents in the text. Each of these features is designed to make the text morc accessible to students and to reinforce key concepts.

- The *part-opening timelines,* which follow the essays that open each of the six parts of the book, summarize major events in politics and government, society and economy, and religion and culture side by side. Appropriate photographs have been added to each timeline.
- *Primary source documents,* more than one third new to this edition, acquaint students with the raw material of history and provide intimate contact with the people of the past and their concerns. *Questions* accompanying the source documents direct students toward important, thought-provoking issues and help them relate the documents to the material in the text. They can be used to stimulate class discussion or as topics for essays and study groups.
- Each chapter includes an *outline,* a list of *key topics,* and an *introduction.* Together these features provide a succinct overview of each chapter.
- *Chronologies* follow each major section in a chapter, listing significant events and their dates.
- *Concluding sections* summarize the major themes of each chapter and provide a bridge to the next chapter.
- *Chapter review questions* help students review the material in a chapter and relate it to broader themes. They too can be used for class discussion and essay topics.
- *Suggested readings* lists following each chapter have been updated with new titles reflecting recent scholarship.

CHANGES IN THE SIXTH EDITION

The sixth edition retains all of the major content changes that appear in the fifth edition. In addition, Chapter 30, *"Europe and the Soviet-American Rivalry"* has been reorganized to relate the various regional conflicts occurring outside of Europe, including the Mideast, Korea, and Vietnam, more closely to the Cold War conflict between the superpowers. Chapter 31, *"Toward a New Europe and the Twenty-first Century,"* reviews recent events in Eastern Europe. As in the fifth edition, questions appear with each document and after every chapter.

New Features New to the edition are two major features designed to expand students' understanding of the heritage of the West. These are a series of illustrated essays, *The West & the World,* and a series of maps with explanations focusing on key *Political Transformations.*

The West & the World

The students reading this book are drawn from a wide variety of cultures and experiences. They live in a world characterized by highly interconnected economies and instant communication between cultures. In this emerging multicultural society it seems both appropriate and necessary to recognize the ways in which Western civilization has throughout its history interacted with other cultures, influencing other societies and being influenced by them. Examples of this two-way interaction, such as that with Islam, already appear in the main body of the text. In this new feature, we focus on six subjects, comparing Western institutions with those of other parts of the world, or discussing the ways in which developments in the West have influenced cultures in other areas of the globe. Topics for this feature are:

ANCIENT SLAVERY
Slavery has arisen as a social and economic institution in virtually every world culture. This essay compares slavery in the ancient cultures of Mesopotamia, Egypt, China, India, Greece, and Rome. It also describes the role of slavery in the economies of ancient Greece and the ante-bellum American South. The latter comparison seems especially appropriate since in both instances, ancient and modern, the surrounding political structures were democratic.

SOCIAL LIFE IN MALI (1200–1400)
Medieval Europe in many respects constituted an underdeveloped economy. Production was quite limited and was almost entirely agrarian. This essay explores the ways in which that society compares with Mali Society. It discusses Islamic influences on marriage customs, education, and daily life in the African setting, allowing students to draw comparisons with similar European institutions influenced by Christianity, as examined in the preceding chapter.

THE FAMILY IN EUROPE
AND CHINA (1400–1800)
Throughout the human experience, the family has been the most enduring of all institutions. Recent scholarship has greatly improved our understanding of the early modern European family. This essay draws upon that knowledge, enabling students to compare and contrast the European family of the era with family structures in China.

THE ABOLITION OF SLAVERY
IN THE TRANSATLANTIC ECONOMY
The abolition of chattel slavery in the transatlantic economy stands as one of the most remarkable social and economic developments of the eighteenth and nineteenth centuries. Never before had a society abolished slavery. This essay traces the history of that crusade, noting the manner in which it influenced the societies of Africa, Latin America and North America.

IMPERIALISM: ANCIENT AND MODERN
During the past two centuries no interaction of the West with the rest of the world was more important or of more enduring significance than the establishment of colonial empires in Asia and Africa. This essay recalls for students the earlier empires that were part of the Western experience, comparing the imperialism of the ancient world with that of the modern era.

GLOBAL DEMOCRATIZATION
With the collapse of communism in the past decade, democratization has made enormous gains in Europe and the former Soviet Union. This essay places the recent European experience in the context of the worldwide movement of the past half-century toward greater democratic political participation. It pays particular attention to the civil rights movement in the United States and to the movements toward democracy in Latin America.

Political Transformations

This new map feature concentrates on six highly significant moments of political transformation in the history of the West. As with *The West & the World,* most *Political Transformations* emphasize the interaction of the West with other areas of the world. Each of the features provides a brief overview of the transformation illustrated by a map as well as in an illustrative document. The features will provide opportunities for study not only by individual students, but also for class discussion. The topics for this feature are:

- Greek Colonization from Spain to the Black Sea
- Muslim Conquests and Domination of the Mediterranean to about 750
- Voyages of Discovery and the Colonial Claims of Spain and Portugal
- The Congress of Vienna Redraws the Map of Europe
- The Mandate System: 1919 to World War II
- Decolonization in Asia and Africa

Maps and Illustrations The skillful use of color in the maps greatly improves their clarity and pedagogical usefulness. All 90 maps in the text have been carefully edited for accuracy. The text also contains almost 500 color and black and white illustrations. In this edition, we have added photographs to the timelines preceding each part of the book.

A Note on Dates and Transliterations With this edition of *The Western Heritage* we shift to the use of B.C.E. (before the common era) and C.E. (common era) instead of B.C. (before Christ) and A.D. *(anno domini,* the year of the Lord) to designate dates.

Also, we have followed the most accurate currently accepted English transliterations of Arabic words. For example, today Koran is being replaced by the more accurate *Qur'an;* similarly *Muhammad* is preferable to *Mohammed* and *Muslim* to *Moslem.*

Ancillary Instructional Materials *The Western Heritage* sixth edition comes with an extensive package of ancillary materials.

For the Instructor:

- **Instructor's Manual with Test Items** prepared by Perry M. Rogers, Ohio State University. The manual includes chapter summaries, key points and vital concepts, identification questions, multiple-choice questions, essay questions, and suggested films.
- **Transparency Acetates** of the four-color maps, charts, figures, and graphs in the text provide useful instructional aids for lectures.
- **Prentice Hall Custom Test,** available in Windows, DOS, and Macintosh format, provides the questions from the printed test item file for generating multiple versions of tests.
- **Administrative Handbook** by Jay Boggis provides instructors with resources for using *The Western Heritage* with Annenberg/CPB telecourse, *The Western Tradition.*

For the Student:

- **Study Guide, Volumes I** and **II** includes commentary, definitions, identifications, map exercises, short-answer exercises, and essay questions.
- **Map Workbook** gives the student the opportunity to increase their knowledge of geography through identification exercises.
- **Documents in Western Civilization, Volumes I** and **II,** provides over 100 additional primary source readings with questions for discussion.
- **Telecourse Study Guide, Volumes I and II,** by Jay Boggis correlates *The Western Heritage* with the Annenberg/CPB telecourse, *The Western Tradition.*

Media Ancillaries:

- **The Western Heritage, Interactive Edition, Version 2.0** takes students on an interactive journey through the evolution of Western civilization and its people. With over 600 study questions, quizzes, and comprehension exercises, this unique CD-ROM provides a highly visual multimedia learning experience that will engage and captivate students' imagination. Available for IBM/Mac.
- **The World Wide Web Companion Study Guide** *(http://www.prenhall.com/kagan)* directly complements *The Western Heritage* and correlates the text to related material on the Internet. Each "chapter" corresponds to the chapter in the textbook and consists of objectives, multiple choice quizzes, essay questions, chapter chat, web destinations, and help.

Acknowledgments We are grateful to the scholars and teachers whose thoughtful and often detailed comments helped shape this revision:

Lenard R. Berlanstein, University of Virginia, Charlottesville
Stephanie Christelow, Idaho State University
Samuel Willard Crompton, Holyoke Community College
Robert L. Ervin, San Jacinto Community College
Joseph Gonzales, Moorpark College
Victor Davis Hanson, California State University, Fresno
William I. Hitchcock, Yale University
Pardaic Kenny, University of Colorado, Boulder
Raymond F. Kierstead, Reed College
Eleanor McCluskey, Palm Beach Atlantic College and Broward Community College
Robert J. Mueller, Hastings College
John Nicols, University of Oregon, Eugene
Sandra J. Peacock, State University of New York, Binghamton
John Powell, Pennsylvania State University

Robert A. Schneider, Catholic University
Hugo Schwyzer, Pasadena City College
Sidney R. Sherter, Long Island University
Roger P. Snow, College of Great Falls

Finally, we would like to thank the dedicated people who helped produce this revision: our development editor, Roberta Meyer; our production editor, Barbara DeVries; Maria Lange who created the handsome new design of this edition; Rosemary Ross who formatted the pages; Lynn Pearlman, our manufacturing buyer; and Barbara Salz, the photo researcher.

D.K.
S.O.
F.M.T.

The New York Times and **Prentice Hall** are sponsoring **Themes of the Times:** a program designed to enhance access to current information of relevance in the classroom.

Through this program, the core subject matter provided in the text is supplemented by a collection of time-sensitive articles from one of the world's most distinguished newspapers, **The New York Times**. These articles demonstrate the vital, ongoing connection between what is learned in the classroom and what is happening in the world around us.

To enjoy the wealth of information of **The New York Times** daily, a reduced subscription rate is available. For information, call toll-free: 1–800–631–1222.

Prentice Hall and **The New York Times** are proud to co-sponsor **Themes of the Times.** We hope it will make the reading of both textbooks and newspapers a more dynamic, involving process.

TIME LINE PHOTO CREDITS

Time Line I: page 2, (left) Gary Cralle/The Image Bank; (right) Winfield I. Parks, Jr./ National Geographic Image Collection; page 3, The Granger Collection; page 4, Battle of Alexander the Great at Issue. Roman mosaic. Museo Archeologico Nazionale, Naples, Italy. Scala/Art Resource, NY; page 5, Robert Frerck, Woodfin Camp & Associates.

Time Line II: page 198, New York University Institute of Fine Arts; page 199, Bayeux, Musee de l'Eveche. "With special authorization of the City of Bayeux." Giraudon/Art Resource.

Time Line III: page 306, George Gower (1540–96). "Elizabeth I, The Armada Portrait." The Bridgeman Art Library; page 307, The Granger Collection.

ABOUT THE AUTHORS

Donald Kagan is Hillhouse Professor of History and Classics at Yale University, where he has taught since 1969. He received the A.B. degree in history from Brooklyn College, the M.A. in classics from Brown University, and the Ph.D. in history from Ohio State University. During 1958–1959 he studied at the American School of Classical Studies as a Fulbright Scholar. He has received three awards for undergraduate teaching at Cornell and Yale. He is the author of a history of Greek political thought, *The Great Dialogue* (1965); a four-volume history of the Peloponnesian war, *The Origins of the Peloponnesian War* (1969); *The Archidamian War* (1974); *The Peace of Nicias and the Sicilian Expedition* (1981); *The Fall of the Athenian Empire* (1987); and a biography of Pericles, *Pericles of Athens and the Birth of Democracy* (1991); and *On the Origins of War* (1995). With Brian Tierney and L. Pearce Williams, he is the editor of *Great Issues in Western Civilization*, a collection of readings.

Steven Ozment is McLean Professor of Ancient and Modern History at Harvard University. He has taught Western Civilization at Yale, Stanford, and Harvard. He is the author of eight books. *The Age of Reform, 1250–1550* (1980) won the Schaff Prize and was nominated for the 1981 American Book Award. *Magdalena and Balthasar: An Intimate Portrait of Life in Sixteenth Century Europe* (1986), *Three Behaim Boys: Growing Up in Early Modern Germany* (1990), and *Protestants: The Birth of a Revolution* (1992) were selections of the History Book Club, as is also his most recent book, *The Bürgermeister's Daughter* (1996).

Frank M. Turner is John Hay Whitney Professor of History at Yale University, where he served as University Provost from 1988 to 1992. He received his B.A. degree at the College of William and Mary and his Ph.D. from Yale. He has received the Yale College Award for Distinguished Undergraduate Teaching. He has directed a National Endowment for the Humanities Summer Institute. His scholarly research has received the support of fellowships from the National Endowment for the Humanities and the Guggenheim Foundation. He is the author of *Between Science and Religion: The Reaction to Scientific Naturalism in Late Victorian England* (1974), *The Greek Heritage in Victorian Britain* (1981), which received the British Council Prize of the Conference on British Studies and the Yale Press Governors Award, and *Contesting Cultural Authority: Essays in Victorian Intellectual Life* (1993). He has also contributed numerous articles to journals and has served on the editorial advisory boards of *The Journal of Modern History, Isis, and Victorian Studies.*

The Western Heritage

SIXTH EDITION

The Foundations of Western Civilization in the Ancient World

The roots of Western civilization may be found in the experience and culture of the Greeks. Greek civilization itself, however, was richly nourished by older, magnificent civilizations to the south and east, especially in Mesopotamia and Egypt.

Some ten thousand years ago humans first began to live in settled, agricultural villages. In the valley of the Tigris and Euphrates rivers (Mesopotamia) and soon after in the valley of the Nile in Egypt, these agricultural societies underwent another shift to a much richer and more varied organization that we call *civilization.* The use of irrigation increased agricultural productivity, and population grew. A food surplus supported nonfarming specialists—artisans, merchants, priests, and soldiers—and made possible the earliest cities. The need for organizing this new and varied activity and for keeping records led to the invention of writing. Great advances took place in the arts and the sciences, in literature, and in the development of complex religious ideas and organizations.

The earliest civilizations produced powerful, centralized governments dominated by kings. The kings' power, bolstered by religious authority, rested on control of the economy and the ability to collect taxes. In Mesopotamia, kings were considered to be representatives of the gods; in Egypt they were considered themselves to be divine. Their control over the economy permitted them to raise, train, and support armies. This concentration of political, military, economic, and religious power resulted in societies that were rigidly divided into social classes: slaves, free commoners, priests, and aristocrats, as well as the divine or semidivine monarchs. Social mobility and individual freedom were sharply limited. Only a handful of people took part in government. As rulers vied with one another, the stronger ones forged ever larger and more powerful kingdoms and empires.

The struggle between great empires sometimes permitted smaller city-states and kingdoms to survive and flourish; two were especially important for the civilization that would some day arise in the West. The cities of Phoenicia, in what is now Lebanon, produced great sailors and traders who came into early and frequent contact with the Greeks. Through the Phoenicians, among other Eastern peoples, the Greeks learned the art of writing and were powerfully influenced by the art, technology, and mythology of the earlier cultures. Absorbed, transformed, and transmitted by the Greeks, the civilizations of Mesopotamia and Egypt became, indirectly, part of the Western heritage. Neighbors of the Phoenicians, called Hebrews or Israelites, would have a more direct influence on the civilization of the West. They conceived a religion based on belief in a single all-powerful God who ruled over all peoples and the entire universe and made strong ethical demands on human beings. This religion of the Jews, as they came to be called (from the name of one of their kingdoms, Judah) became the basis of two later religions also of great importance: Christianity and Islam.

Greek civilization arose after the destruction of the Bronze Age cultures on Crete and the Greek mainland before 1000 B.C.E. Based on the independent existence of hundreds of city-states called *poleis*, it developed in a sharply different pattern than its predecessors in Egypt and western Asia.

The *poleis* retained their autonomy for hundreds of years before being incorporated into larger units, attaining a degree of self-government, broad political participation, and individual freedom hitherto unknown. The Greeks also introduced a new way of thinking, looking on the world as the product of natural forces that could be understood through the senses and human reason, rather than as the product of supernatural forces. The result was the invention of science and philosophy as we know them. Greek literature placed humankind at the center of its concerns, adapting and inventing a great variety of literary genres, from epic, lyric, and dramatic poetry, to history, philosophy, rhetoric, and fiction in prose. The Greeks' way of thinking, their forms of art and literature, and their commitment to self-government and political freedom became and have remained central to Western civilization.

The Greeks planted cities from Spain to the Black Sea. Ceaseless quarrels and wars among *poleis*, however, eventually so weakened the Greeks that they fell under the control of their Macedonian cousins to the north. Alexander the Great of Macedon, using Greek troops as well as his own, swiftly conquered the Persian Empire. After his death in 323 B.C.E. the vast territory he had come to control was divided among his successors to form the three great Hellenistic kingdoms. Anyone speaking Greek could move comfortably from city to city within these kingdoms and find a familiar and common Hellenistic culture, a culture that combined Greek elements with elements native to the peoples Alexander had conquered. In the last two centuries before the Christian era this world succumbed to Roman conquest.

The Romans were originally tough farmers who inhabited a small town on the Tiber river in west-central Italy. After deposing their king in about 500 B.C.E., they invented a republican constitution and a code of law that provided a solid foundation for a stable and effective political order. Constantly at war with their neighbors, the Romans achieved military discipline and skills that allowed them to fight off attacks and to gain control of most of Italy by about 270 B.C.E. They developed an ingenious way of organizing the lands they conquered that made the peoples of those lands allies and even fellow citizens rather than subjects. From 264 until well into the first century B.C.E., the Romans extended their conquests overseas until they had conquered the Carthaginians in the west and defeated all the great Hellenistic powers, dominating the shores of the Mediterranean and beyond.

The Romans were fine engineers and road builders, but in art, literature, and philosophy they had barely made a start when they came into contact with the advanced Greek civilization of the Hellenistic world. In these areas the Romans became eager students, and as the Roman poet Horace put it, "Captive Greece took Rome captive." Roman culture put its own stamp on the Greek legacy and passed it on.

Rome's conquest of most of the known world created many problems for its republican constitution, which had been designed to govern only a small collection of farmers. Competition for eminence, power, and wealth within the Roman aristocracy led to struggles and civil wars that ravaged Italy and the empire as well. Finally, Gaius Julius Caesar defeated his opponents, put an end to the republic, and established himself as dictator for life. Rumor had it that he meant to be installed as king, and he was assassinated in 44 B.C.E. as the result of an aristocratic plot.

His assassination, however, failed to reestablish the republic. Civil war ensued and Caesar's nephew Octavian, later called Augustus, emerged as the commander of all Rome's armed forces and as the effective ruler of the Roman Empire. His new constitution tried to conceal the death of the republic and its replacement by what was really an imperial monarchy. This disguised monarchy flourished for almost two centuries, but after the death of the emperor Marcus Aurelius in 180 C.E., Rome's decline became obvious. Pressure from barbarian tribes on the frontiers, economic troubles at home, weak and incompetent emperors, and civil wars all strained Rome's resources, human and material. By the fifth century C.E., the Roman Empire in the west had collapsed and was shared out among various Germanic tribes. The eastern portion of the empire, known to us as the Byzantine Empire, with its capital at Constantinople, was to survive for a thousand years more. Before Rome's fall the empire had abandoned paganism and had adopted Christianity as its official religion. The heritage that the ancient world passed on to its medieval successor in western Europe was a combination of cultural traditions, including those coming from Egypt, Mesopotamia, Israel, Greece, Rome, and the German tribes that ultimately destroyed the Roman Empire. ✦

	POLITICS AND GOVERNMENT	SOCIETY AND ECONOMY	RELIGION AND CULTURE
1,000,000–3500 B.C.E.		ca. 1,000,000–10,000 B.C.E. **Paleolithic Age** ca. 8,000 B.C.E. **Earliest Neolithic settlements**	ca. 30,0000–6000 B.C.E. **Paleolithic art**
3500–2200 B.C.E.	ca. 3100–2700 B.C.E. **Egyptian Early Dynastic Period; unification of Upper and Lower Egypt** ca. 2800–2340 B.C.E. **Sumerian city-states' early dynastic period** 2700–2200 B.C.E. **Egyptian Old Kingdom** ca. 2370 B.C.E. **Sargon established Akkadian Empire**	ca. 3500 B.C.E. **Earliest Sumerian settlements** ca. 3000 B.C.E. **First urban settlements in Egypt and Mesopotamia; Bronze Age begins in Mesopotamia and Egypt** ca. 2900–1150 B.C.E. **Bronze Age Minoan society on Crete; Helladic society on Greek mainland**	ca. 3000 B.C.E. **Invention of writing** ca. 3000 B.C.E. **Temples to gods in Mesopotamia; development of ziggurat temple architecture** 2700–2200 B.C.E. **Building of pyramids for Egyptian god-kings, development of hieroglyphic writing in Egypt**
2200-1600 B.C.E.	2200–2052 B.C.E. **Egyptian First Intermediate Period** 2052–1786 B.C.E. **Egyptian Middle Kingdom** 1792–1760 B.C.E. **Reign of Hammurabi; height of Old Babylonian Kingdom; publication of Code of Hammurabi** 1786–1575 B.C.E. **Egyptian Second Intermediate Period** ca. 1700 B.C.E. **Hyksos' invasion of Egypt**	ca. 2000 B.C.E. **Hittites arrive in Asia Minor** ca 1900 B.C.E. **Amorites at Babylon**	2200–1786 B.C.E. **Rise of Amon-Re as chief Egyptian god** ca. 1900 B.C.E. **Traditional date for Hebrew patriarch Abraham**
1600–1100 B.C.E.	ca. 1600 B.C.E. **Fall of Old Babylonian Kingdom** 1575–1087 B.C.E. **Egyptian New Kingdom (or Empire)** ca. 1400–1200 B.C.E. **Height of Hittite Empire** ca. 1400–1200 B.C.E. **Height of Mycenaean power** 1367–1350 B.C.E. **Reign of Amenhotep IV (Akhnaton) in Egypt** ca. 1250 B.C.E. **Sack of Troy (?)** 1087–30 B.C.E. **Egyptian Post-Empire Period**	1400–1200 B.C.E. **Hittites introduce iron-smelting** ca. 1200 B.C.E. **Hebrews arrive in Palestine**	1367–1360 B.C.E. **Religious revolution led by Akhnaton makes Aton chief Egyptian god** 1347–1339 B.C.E. **Tutankhamen restores worship of Amon-Re**

Sumerian clay tablet

Queen Nefertiti

	POLITICS AND GOVERNMENT		SOCIETY AND ECONOMY		RELIGION AND CULTURE	
1100–500 B.C.E.	ca. 1000–961 B.C.E.	Reign of King David in Israel	ca. 1100–750 B.C.E.	Greek "Dark Ages"		
	ca. 961–922	Reign of King Solomon in Israel	ca. 1000 B.C.E.	Italic peoples enter Italy		
	ca. 1100–615 B.C.E.	Assyrian Empire	ca. 800 B.C.E.	Etruscans enter Italy		
	ca. 800–400 B.C.E.	Height of Etruscan culture in Italy	ca. 750–700 B.C.E.	Rise of *Polis* in Greece	ca. 750 B.C.E.	Hebrew prophets teach monotheism
	ca. 650 B.C.E.	Spartan constitution formed	ca. 750–600 B.C.E.	Great age of Greek colonization	ca. 750 B.C.E.	Traditional date for Homer
	722 B.C.E.	Israel (northern kingdom) falls to Assyrians	ca. 700 B.C.E.	Invention of hoplite phalanx	ca. 750 B.C.E.	Greeks adapt Semitic script and invent the Greek alphabet
	ca. 700–500 B.C.E.	Rise and decline of tyranny in Greece				
	621 B.C.E.	First written law code in Athens			ca. 750–600 B.C.E.	Panhellenic shrines established at Olympia, Delphi, Corinth, and Nemea; athletic festivals attached to them
	612–539 B.C.E.	Neo-Babylonian (Chaldean) Empire				
	594 B.C.E.	Solon's constitutional reforms, Athens	ca. 600–550 B.C.E.	Spartans adopt new communitarian social system	ca. 700 B.C.E.	Traditional date for Hesiod
	586 B.C.E.	Destruction of Jerusalem; fall of Judah (southern kingdom); Babylonian Captivity	ca. 600–500 B.C.E.	Athens develops commerce and a mixed economy	ca. 675–500 B.C.E.	Development of Greek lyric and elegiac poetry
					ca. 570 B.C.E.	Birth of Greek philosophy in Ionia
	ca. 560–550 B.C.E.	Peloponnesian League begins			ca. 550 B.C.E.	Oracle of Apollo at Delphi grows to great influence
	559–530 B.C.E.	Reign of Cyrus the Great in Persia			ca. 550 B.C.E.	Cult of Dionysus introduced to Athens
	546 B.C.E.	Persia conquers Lydian Empire of Croesus, including Greek cities of Asia Minor			539 B.C.E.	Restoration of temple in Jerusalem; return of exiles
	539 B.C.E.	Persia conquers Babylonia; temple at Jerusalem restored; exiles return from Babylonia				
	521–485 B.C.E.	Reign of Darius in Persia				
	509 B.C.E.	Kings expelled from Rome; Republic founded				
	508 B.C.E.	Clisthenes founds Athenian democracy				
500–336 B.C.E.	490 B.C.E.	Battle of Marathon	ca. 500–350 B.C.E.	Spartan population shrinks	ca. 500–400 B.C.E.	Great age of Athenian tragedy
	485–465 B.C.E.	Reign of Xerxes in Persia	ca. 500–350 B.C.E.	Rapid growth in overseas trade	469–399 B.C.E.	Life of Socrates

Hercules taming Cerberus, Greek, 530 B.C.E.

500–336 B.C.E. (cont.)

POLITICS AND GOVERNMENT

- 480–479 B.C.E. **Xerxes invades Greece**
- 478–477 B.C.E. **Delian League founded**
- ca. 460–445 B.C.E. **First Peloponnesian War**
- 450–449 B.C.E. **Laws of the Twelve Tables, Rome**
- 431–404 B.C.E. **Great Peloponnesian War**
- 404–403 B.C.E. **Thirty Tyrants rule at Athens**
- 400–387 B.C.E. **Spartan war against Persia**
- 398–360 B.C.E. **Reign of Agesilaus at Sparta**
- 395–387 B.C.E. **Corinthian War**
- 392 B.C.E. **Romans defeat Etruscans**
- 378 B.C.E. **Second Athenian Confederation**
- 371 B.C.E. **Thebans end Spartan hegemony**
- 362 B.C.E. **Battle of Mantinea; end of Theban hegemony**
- 338 B.C.E. **Philip of Macedon conquers Greece**

SOCIETY AND ECONOMY

- 477–431 B.C.E. **Vast growth in Athenian wealth**
- 431–400 B.C.E. **Peloponnesian War casualties cause decline in size of lower class in Athens, with relative increase in importance of upper and middle classes**

RELIGION AND CULTURE

- ca. 450–400 B.C.E. **Great influence of Sophists in Athens**
- ca. 450–385 B.C.E. **Great age of Athenian comedy**
- 448–432 B.C.E. **Periclean building program on Athenian acropolis**
- 429–347 B.C.E. **Life of Plato**
- ca. 425 B.C.E. **Herodotus' history of the Persian Wars**
- ca. 400 B.C.E. **Thucydides' history of the Peloponnesian War**
- ca. 400–325 B.C.E. **Life of Diogenes the Cynic**
- 386 B.C.E. **Foundation of Plato's Academy**
- 384–322 B.C.E. **Life of Aristotle**

336–31 B.C.E.

POLITICS AND GOVERNMENT

- 336–323 B.C.E. **Reign of Alexander III (the Great)**
- 334 B.C.E. **Alexander invades Asia**
- 330 B.C.E. **Fall of Persepolis; end Achaemenid rule in Persia**
- 323–301 B.C.E. **Ptolemaic Kingdom (Egypt), Seleucid Kingdom (Syria), and Antigonid Dynasty (Macedon) founded**
- 287 B.C.E. **Laws passed by Plebeian Assembly made binding on all Romans; end of Struggle of the Orders**
- 264–241 B.C.E. **First Punic War**
- 218–202 B.C.E. **Second Punic War**
- 215–168 B.C.E. **Rome establishes rule over Hellenistic world**

SOCIETY AND ECONOMY

Alexander the Great & Darius III

- ca. 300 B.C.E.–150 C.E. **Growth of international trade and development of large cities in Hellenistic/Roman world**
- ca. 218–135 B.C.E. **Decline of family farm in Italy; growth of tenant farming and cattle ranching**

RELIGION AND CULTURE

- 336 B.C.E. **Foundation of Aristotle's Lyceum**
- 342–271 B.C.E. **Life of Epicurus**
- 335–263 B.C.E. **Life of Zeno the Stoic**
- ca. 287–212 B.C.E. **Life of Archimedes of Syracuse**
- ca. 275 B.C.E. **Foundation of museum and library make Alexandria the center of Greek intellectual life**
- ca. 250 B.C.E. **Livius Andronicus translates the *Odyssey* into Latin**
- 106–43 B.C.E. **Life of Cicero**

336–31 B.C.E. (cont.)

Politics and Government

- 154–133 B.C.E. **Roman wars in Spain**
- 133 B.C.E. **Tribunate of Tiberius Gracchus**
- 123–122 B.C.E. **Tribunate of Gaius Gracchus**
- 82 B.C.E. **Sulla assumes dictatorship**
- 60 B.C.E. **First Triumvirate**
- 46–44 B.C.E. **Caesar's dictatorship**
- 43 B.C.E. **Second Triumvirate**

Society and Economy

- ca. 150 B.C.E. **Growth of slavery as basis of economy in Roman Republic**

The Roman Forum

Religion and Culture

- ca. 99–55 B.C.E. **Life of Lucretius**
- 86–35 B.C.E. **Life Sallust**
- ca. 84–54 B.C.E. **Life Catullus**
- 70–19 B.C.E. **Life of Vergil**
- 65–8 B.C.E. **Life of Horace**
- 59 B.C.E.–17 C.E. **Life of Livy**
- 43 B.C.E.–18 C.E. **Life of Ovid**

31 B.C.E.–400 C.E.

Politics and Government

- 31 B.C.E. **Octavian and Agrippa defeat Anthony at Actium**
- 27 B.C.E.–14 C.E. **Reign of Augustus**
- 14–68 C.E. **Reigns of Julio-Claudian Emperors**
- 69–96 C.E. **Reigns of Flavian Emperors**
- 96–180 C.E. **Reigns of "Good Emperors"**
- 180–192 C.E. **Reign of Commodus**
- 284–305 C.E. **Reign of Diocletian; reform and division of Roman Empire**
- 306–337 C.E. **Reign of Constantine**
- 330 C.E. **Constantinople new capital of Roman Empire**
- 361–363 C.E. **Reign of Julian the Apostate**
- 379–395 C.E. **Reign of Theodosius**
- 376 C.E. **Visigoths enter Roman Empire**

Society and Economy

- ca. 150–400 C.E. **Decline of slavery and growth of tenant farming and serfdom in Roman Empire**
- ca. 250–400 C.E. ***Coloni* (Roman tenant farmers) increasingly tied to the land**
- 301 C.E. **Edict of Maximum Prices at Rome**

Religion and Culture

- 9 B.C.E. **Ara Pacis dedicated at Rome**
- ca. 4 B.C.E. **Birth of Jesus of Nazareth**
- ca. 30 C.E. **Crucifixion of Jesus**
- 64 C.E. **Christians persecuted by Nero**
- 66–135 C.E. **Romans suppress rebellions of Jews**
- ca. 70–100 C.E. **Gospels written**
- ca. 150 C.E. **Ptolemy of Alexandria establishes canonical geocentric model of the universe**
- ca. 250–260 C.E. **Severe persecutions by Decius and Valerian**
- 303 C.E. **Persecution of Christians by Diocletian**
- 311 C.E. **Galerius issues Edict of Toleration**
- 312 C.E. **Constantine converts to Christianity**
- 325 C.E. **Council of Nicaea**
- 348–420 C.E. **Life of St. Jerome**
- 354–430 C.E. **Life of St. Augustine**
- 395 C.E. **Christianity becomes official religion of Roman Empire**

CHAPTER 1

A detail from the throne of King Tutankhamen (r. 1347–1339 B.C.E.) of Egypt and his queen Ankhesenamen. The king's magnificent tomb was discovered, almost fully intact, in 1922. The throne is carved wood covered with gold and inlaid with silver, faience and semiprecious stones. [Robert Frerck]

The Birth of Civilization

KEY TOPICS

- The earliest history of humanity, including the beginnings of human culture in the Paleolithic Age, the agricultural revolution and the shift from food gathering to food production, and the emergence of civilization in the great river valleys of the Near East and Asia
- The ancient civilizations of Mesopotamia and Egypt
- The Assyrians and the first great Near Eastern empires
- The emergence of Judaism
- The difference in outlook between ancient Near Eastern civilization and ancient Greek civilization

History, in its two senses—as the events of the past that make up the human experience on earth and as the written record of those events—is a subject of both interest and importance. We naturally want to know how we came to be who we are and how the world we live in came to be what it is. But beyond its intrinsic interest, history provides crucial insight into present human behavior. To understand who we are now, we need to know the record of the past and to try to understand the people and forces that shaped it.

For hundreds of thousands of years after the human species emerged, people lived by hunting, fishing, and collecting wild plants. Only some 10,000 years ago did they learn to cultivate plants, herd animals, and make airtight pottery for storage. These discoveries transformed them from gatherers to producers and allowed them to grow in number and to lead a settled life. About 5,000 years ago humans learned how to control the waters of great river valleys, making possible much richer harvests and supporting a further increase in population. The peoples of these river valley societies created the earliest civilizations. They invented writing, which, among other things, enabled them to keep inventories of food and other resources. They discovered the secret of smelting metal to make tools and weapons of bronze far superior to the stone implements of earlier times. They came together in towns and cities, where industry and commerce flourished. Complex religions took form, and social divisions increased.

Kings—considered to be representatives of the gods or to be themselves divine—emerged as rulers, assisted by priests and defended by well-organized armies.

The first of these civilizations appeared among the Sumerians before 3000 B.C.E. *in the Tigris–Euphrates Valley that we call Mesopotamia. From the Sumerians to the Assyrians, a series of peoples ruled Mesopotamia, each shaping and passing along its distinctive culture, before the region fell under the control of great foreign empires.*

A second early civilization took shape in the Nile Valley around 3000 B.C.E. *Egyptian civilization developed largely in isolation from the outside world, protected from invasion and influence by the formidable deserts and seas that surround the valley. Thus the character of the civilization, which took shape early, changed little for more than 1,000 years. The shock of invasion in the seventeenth century* B.C.E. *by a mysterious people called the Hyksos ended Egypt's isolation, bringing it in contact with neighboring states and prompting military reforms. Egyptian armies subsequently pushed into Palestine and Syria, establishing an Egyptian Empire.*

By the fourteenth century B.C.E. *several powerful empires had arisen and were vying for dominance in regions that included Egypt, Mesopotamia, and Asia Minor. Northern warrior peoples, among them the Hittites, the Kassites, and the Mitannians, conquered and ruled more civilized peoples in various areas. The Hittites dominated in Asia Minor, the Kassites in southern Mesopotamia, and the Mitannians in northern Mesopotamia. For two centuries, the Hittite and Egyptian Empires struggled with each other for control of Palestine. By about 1200* B.C.E.*, however, both these empires had collapsed, to be replaced by the mighty new Assyrian Empire. The Assyrians arose in northern Mesopotamia and ultimately ruled all the fertile lands from Egypt to southern Mesopotamia. They were dominant until the seventh century* B.C.E.*, when they fell to a combination of enemies. Their vast empire would soon become only a small part of the enormous empire of Persia.*

Among all these great empires nestled a people called the Israelites, who maintained a small independent kingdom in the region between Egypt and Syria for several centuries. This kingdom ultimately fell to the Assyrians and later remained subject to other conquerors. The Israelites possessed little worldly power or wealth, but they created a powerful religion, Judaism, the first certain and lasting worship of a single god in a world of polytheism. Judaism was the seedbed of two other religions that have played a mighty role in the history of the world: Christianity and Islam. The great empires have collapsed, their power forgotten for millennia until the tools of archaeologists uncovered their remains, but the religion of the Israelites, in itself and through its offshoots, has endured as a powerful force.

Early Humans and Their Culture

Scientists estimate that the earth may be as many as six billion years old and that creatures very much like humans appeared perhaps three to five million years ago, probably in Africa. Some one to two million years ago, erect and tool-using early humans spread over much of Africa, Europe, and Asia. Our own species, *Homo sapiens*, probably emerged some 200,000 years ago, and the earliest remains of fully modern humans date to about 90,000 years ago.

Humans, unlike other animals, are cultural beings. *Culture* may be defined as the ways of living built up by a group and passed on from one generation to another. It includes behavior such as courtship or child-rearing practices; it includes material things such as tools, clothing, and shelter; and it includes ideas, institutions, and beliefs. Language, apparently a uniquely human trait, lies behind our ability to create ideas and institutions and to transmit culture from one generation to another. Our flexible and dexterous hands enable us to hold and make tools and so to create the material artifacts of culture. Because culture is learned and not inherited, it permits more rapid adaptation to changing conditions than biological evolution, making possible the spread of humanity to almost all the lands of the globe.

The Paleolithic Age

Anthropologists designate early human cultures by their tools. The earliest period—the Paleolithic (from Greek, "old stone")—dates from the earliest use of stone tools some one million years ago to about 10,000 B.C.E. During this immensely long period, people were hunters, fishers, and gatherers, but not producers, of food. They learned to make and use increasingly sophisticated tools of stone and of perishable materials like wood; they learned to make

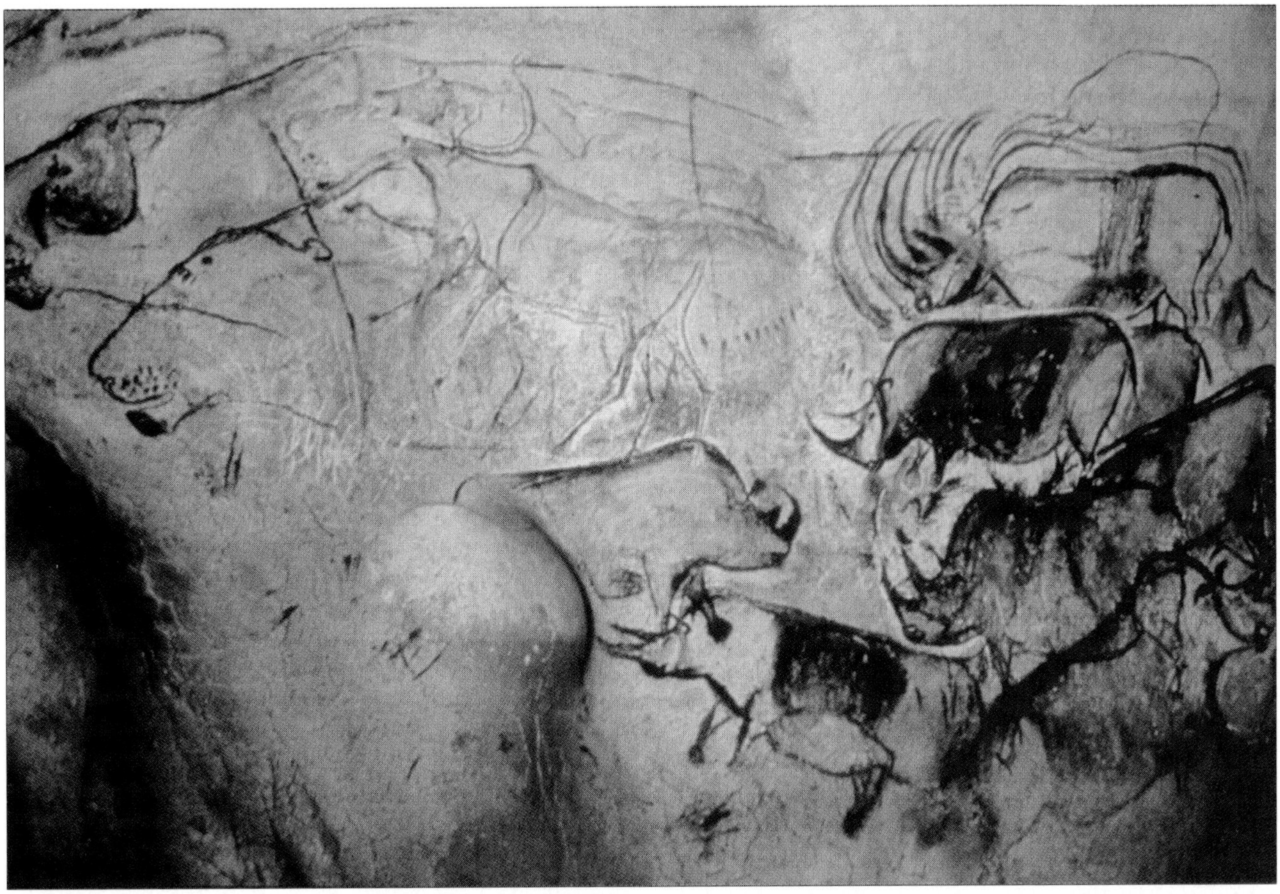

In Chauvet cave, near Avignon, France, Paleolithic artists decorated the walls with exquisite drawings of animals. [Sygma]

and control fire; and they acquired language and the ability to use it to pass on what they had learned.

These early humans, dependent on nature for food and vulnerable to wild beasts and natural disasters, may have developed responses to the world rooted in fear of the unknown—of the uncertainties of human life or the overpowering forces of nature. Religious and magical beliefs and practices may have emerged in an effort to propitiate or coerce the superhuman forces thought to animate or direct the natural world. Evidence of religious faith and practice, as well as of magic, goes as far back as archaeology can take us. Fear or awe, exultation, gratitude, and empathy with the natural world must all have figured in the cave art and in the ritual practices, such as burial, that we find evidenced at Paleolithic sites around the globe. The sense that there is more to the world than meets the eye—in other words, the religious response to the world—seems to be as old as humankind.

The style of life and the level of technology of the Paleolithic period could support only a sparsely settled society. If hunters were too numerous, game would not suffice. In Paleolithic times, people were subject to the same natural and ecological constraints that today maintain a balance between wolves and deer in Alaska.

Evidence from paleolithic art and from modern hunter–gatherer societies suggests that human life in the Paleolithic Age was probably characterized by a division of labor by sex. Men engaged in hunting, fishing, making tools and weapons, and fighting against other families, clans, and tribes. Women, less mobile because of childbearing, gathered nuts, berries, and wild grains, wove baskets, and made clothing. Women gathering food probably discovered how to plant and care for seeds. This knowledge eventually made possible the coming of the Age of Agriculture—the Neolithic revolution.

The Neolithic Age

Only a few Paleolithic societies made the initial revolutionary shift to agriculture, and anthropologists and archaeologists disagree as to why. However it happened, some 10,000 years ago parts of what we now call the Near East began to shift from a hunter–gatherer culture to a settled agricultural one. Because the shift to agriculture coincided with advances in stone tool technology—the development of precise carving and grinding—this period is called the Neolithic Age (from Greek, "new stone"). Animals as well as food crops were domesticated. The important invention of pottery made it possible to store surplus liquids, just as the invention of baskets had earlier made it possible to store dry foods. Cloth came to be made from flax and wool. Crops required constant care from planting to harvest, and so the Neolithic people built permanent buildings, usually in clusters near the best fields.

Throughout the Paleolithic Age, the human population had been small and relatively stable. The shift from food gathering to food production may not have been associated with an immediate change in population, but over time in the regions where agriculture and animal husbandry appeared, the number of human beings grew at an unprecedented rate. The Neolithic revolution was a major step in human control of nature, and it was a vital precondition for the emergence of civilization. The earliest Neolithic societies appeared in the Near East about 8000 B.C.E., in China about 4000 B.C.E., and in India about 3600 B.C.E. The Neolithic revolution in the Near East and India was based on wheat; in China, on millet and rice; in Mesoamerica, several millennia later, it would be based on corn. The wild forebears of the plants and animals that provided the foundation for the early civilizations of the Near East were native to the foothills of the mountains north and east of the Tigris and Euphrates river valleys. It was apparently in these foothill regions that they were first domesticated, later to be carried into the river valleys.

The Bronze Age and the Birth of Civilization

Neolithic agricultural villages and herding cultures gradually replaced Paleolithic culture in much of the world. Then another major shift occurred, first in the valley of the Tigris and Euphrates Rivers in the region called Mesopotamia (modern Iraq), later in the valley of the Nile River in Egypt, and somewhat later still in the Indus Valley in India and the Yellow River basin in China. This shift was marked by the appearance of urban centers, the mastery of smelting and with it the techniques for making metal tools and weapons, and the invention of writing. These traits—urbanism, metallurgy, and writing—are defining characteristics of the form of human culture called *civilization*. At about the time the earliest civilizations were emerging, some-

This mound is part of the remains of the ancient city of Jericho. Located on an oasis in ancient times, it is the site of one of the earliest Neolithic settlements in the Near East. [© Zev Radovan, Jerusalem, Israel]

one discovered how to smelt tin and copper to make a stronger and more useful material—bronze. The importance of this technological development is reflected in the term *Bronze Age*.

Early Civilizations to About 1000 B.C.E.

About 4,000 years before the Christian era, people began to move in large numbers into the river-watered lowlands of Mesopotamia and Egypt. By about 3000 B.C.E., when the invention of writing gave birth to history, urban life and the organization of society into centralized states was established in the valleys of the Tigris and Euphrates Rivers in Mesopotamia and of the Nile River in Egypt.

Much of the population of cities consists of people who do not grow their own food, and so urban life is possible only where farmers can produce a substantial surplus beyond their own needs. The fertile alluvial plains where civilization began made such a surplus possible. Efficient farming of alluvial plains, however, requires intelligent management of water resources for irrigation. According to one influential theory, urban life and the first centralized states, and with them civilization, arose in the great river valleys of China, India, Mesopotamia, and Egypt in response to the need for a strong authority capable of constructing irrigation and flood control systems and managing the distribution of water. This control and management, the theory goes, led to the need for record keeping and, therefore, writing as well as other important innovations of early civilizations. Recent research, however, has challenged this theory.

Evidence now suggests that in Mesopotamia irrigation was controlled locally rather than by central authorities at the time of the earliest city-states, implying that water management was not crucial to their development. Water management, moreover, does not figure in the earliest written records in Mesopotamia. These tend rather to deal with the care of animals, land management, and trade. The large temple complexes that were central to Mesopotamian cities generated religious texts as well as documents to keep track of the lands they owned, the offerings they received, the services they performed, and the people they employed. As city governments became larger and more complex, they, too, had many needs for writing: to record acts of the government, laws, and different kinds of literature.

This widely varied use of writing reflects the complex culture of the urban centers in the river valleys. Commerce was important enough to support a merchant class. The great need for record keeping created a class of scribes, because the picture writing and complicated scripts of these cultures took many years to learn and could not be mastered by many. To deal with the gods, great temples were built, and many priests worked in them. The collection of all these people into cities gave the settlements an entirely new character. Unlike Neolithic villages, they were communities established for purposes other than agriculture. The city served as an administrative, religious, manufacturing, entertainment, and commercial center.

The logic of nature pointed in the direction of the unification of an entire river valley. Central control would put the river's water to the most efficient use, and the absence of central control would lead to warfare, chaos, and destruction. As a result, these civilizations produced unified kingdoms under powerful monarchs who came to be identified with divinity.

The typical king in a river valley civilization was regarded either as a god or as the delegate of a god. Around him developed a rigid class structure. Beneath the monarch was a class of hereditary military aristocrats and a powerful priesthood. Below them were several kinds of freemen, mostly peasants, and at the bottom were many slaves. The population inhabited numerous peasant villages as well as the urban centers that were the locus of administrative, commercial, religious, and military activity. Most of the land was owned or controlled by the king, the nobility, and the priests. These were traditional, conservative societies. Their cultural patterns formed early and changed only slowly and grudgingly.

Mesopotamian Civilization

The first civilization appears to have arisen in the valley of the Tigris and Euphrates Rivers, an area the later Greeks and Romans called Mesopotamia. The region is naturally divided into two ecological zones, the south (Sumer), where irrigation is vital, and the north (Assyria), where agriculture depends on rainfall and wells. The oldest Mesopotamian cities seem to have been founded by a people called the Sumerians, around 3000 B.C.E. Sumerian civilization is generally associated with the southern part of the Tigris and Euphrates Valleys, close to

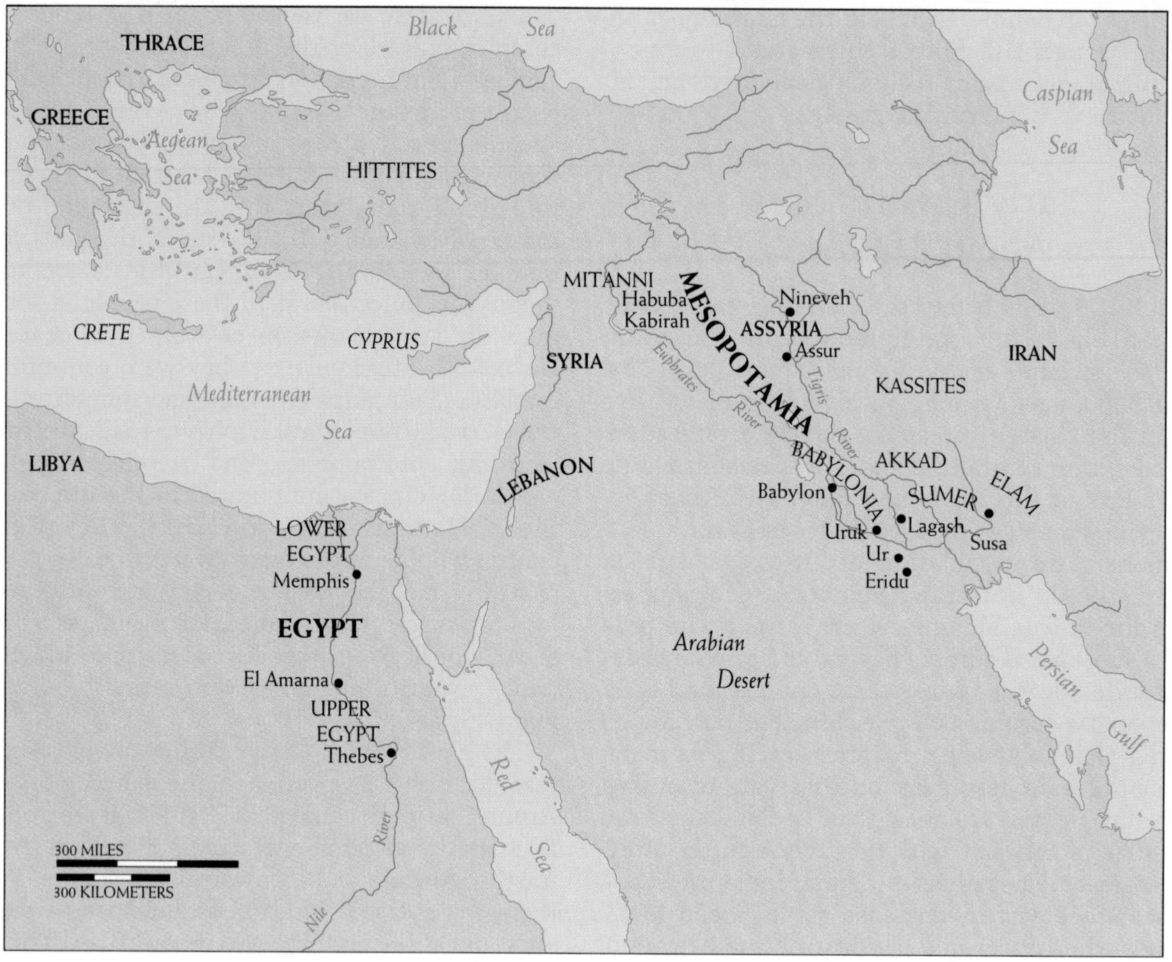

MAP 1–1 THE ANCIENT NEAR EAST *There were two ancient river valley civilizations. While Egypt early was united into a single state, Mesopotamia was long divided into a number of city-states.*

the head of the Persian Gulf, and the earliest city had long been thought to be Uruk, which lies in that region. (See Map 1–1.) Recent discoveries, however, have revealed Sumerian cities dating to the Uruk period in northern Syria, notably at Habuba Kabirah, suggesting that we still have much to learn about the earliest civilization of Mesopotamia.

From about 2800 to 2370 B.C.E., in what is called the early dynastic period, several Sumerian city-states, each controlling about 100 square miles, dotted the landscape of southern Mesopotamia. Among these cities, as revealed to us by archaeologists, are Ur, Uruk, Lagash, and Eridu. Quarrels over water rights and frontiers led to incessant fighting, and in time, stronger towns conquered weaker ones and expanded to form larger units, usually kingdoms.

The region immediately upstream from the principal Sumerian city-states was occupied mostly by people who probably originally came from North Syria and who, unlike the Sumerians, spoke a Semitic language (that is, a language in the same family as Arabic and Hebrew). These people absorbed Sumerian culture and established their own kingdom, with its capital at Akkad, near the site of a later city known to us as Babylon. Under their most famous king, Sargon, the Akkadians conquered the Sumerian cities and created an empire that extended in every direction. Sargon's name became legendary, and he is said to have conquered the "cedar forests" of Lebanon, far to the west, near the coast of the Mediterranean Sea. He ruled from about 2370 B.C.E. and established a family, or dynasty, of Semitic kings that ruled Sumer and Akkad for two centuries.

This statue of the seated King Gudea of Lagash was found in the mound of Telloh in modern Iraq, near the ancient Sumerian city of Lagash. Helping his city recover from defeat, he dedicated huge temples, expanded the irrigation system and increased foreign trade. [Giraudon/Art Resource]

External attack and internal weakness destroyed Akkad. About 2125 B.C.E. the Sumerian city of Ur rose to dominance, and the rulers of the Third Dynasty of Ur established a large empire. About 2000 B.C.E., however, it was swept aside by another invasion.

The Code of Hammurabi, the most famous ruler of the Old Babylonian Dynasty, reveals much about ancient Mesopotamian society. In the relief carving at the top of the stele on which the code is inscribed, Hammurabi receives the law from the sun god. [The Oriental Institute, University of Chicago]

The fall of the Third Dynasty of Ur put an end to Sumerian rule and to the Sumerians as an identifiable group. The Sumerian language survived only in writing, as a kind of sacred language known only to priests and scribes, preserving the cultural heritage of Sumer. For about a century after the fall of Ur, dynastic chaos reigned. Then, about 1900 B.C.E. a people called the Amorites gained control of the region, establishing their capital at Babylon.

The Amorite, or Old Babylonian, dynasty dominated Mesopotamia for about 300 years. Its high point was the reign of its most famous king, Hammurabi (r. ca. 1792–1750 B.C.E.), best known for the law code that bears his name. Codes of law existed as early as the Sumerian period, and Hammurabi's plainly owed much to earlier models. His is the fullest and best-preserved legal code we have from ancient Mesopotamia, however. The Code of Hammurabi reveals a society strictly divided by class; there were nobles, commoners, and slaves, and the law did not treat them equally. In general, punishments were harsh, based literally on the principle of "an eye for an eye, a tooth for a tooth." The prologue to the code makes it clear that law and justice came from the gods through the king.

The Reforms of a Sumerian King

Urukagina ruled the Sumerian city-state of Lagash from about 2415 to 2400 B.C.E. The following selections describe reforms that he claimed to have enacted, in the process revealing some of the social and economic problems of the time. Enlil was the chief among the Sumerian gods and Ningirsu one of his fellow deities.

✦ *What were the problems facing Lagash that King Urukagina claims to have solved?*
✦ *What does he state is the source and basis for his reforms?*
✦ *On what basis does his claim to legitimate authority rest? Why should the people of Lagash obey him and his laws?*

Formerly, from days of yore, from (the day) the seed (of man) came forth, the man in charge of the boatmen seized the boats. The head shepherd seized the donkeys. The head shepherd seized the sheep. The man in charge of the fisheries seized the fisheries. The barely rations of the *guda*-priests were measured out (to their disadvantage) in the Ashte (presumably the storehouse of the *ensi*). The shepherds of the wool-bearing sheep had to pay silver (to the *ensi*) for (the shearing of) the white sheep. The man in charge of field surveyors, the head *gala*, the *agrig*, the man in charge of brewing, (and) all of the *ugula's* had to pay silver for the shearing of the *gaba*-lambs. The oxen of the gods plowed the onion patches of the *ensi*, (and) the onion (and) cucumber fields of the *ensi* were located in the god's best fields. The *birra*-donkeys (and) the prize oxen of the *sanga's* were bundled off (presumably as taxes for the *ensi*). The attendants of the *ensi* divided the barley of the *sanga's* (to the disadvantage of the *sanga's*). The wearing apparel (here follows a list of fifteen objects, principally garments, most of which are unidentifiable) of the *sanga's* were carried off as a tax (to the palace of the *ensi*). The *sanga* (in charge) of the food (supplies) felled the trees in the garden of the indigent mother and bundled off the fruit.

These were the (social) practices of former days.

(But) when Ningirsu, the foremost warrior of Enlil, gave the kingship of Lagash to Urukagina, (and) his (Ningirsu's) hand had grasped him out of the multitude (literally, "36,000 men"); then he (Ningirsu) enjoined upon (literally, "set up for") him the (divine) decrees of former days.

He (Urukagina) held close to the word which his king (Ningirsu) spoke to him. He banned (literally "threw off") the man in charge of the boatmen from (seizing) the boats. He banned the head shepherds from (seizing) the donkeys and sheep. He banned the man in charge of the fisheries from (seizing) the fisheries. He banned the man in charge of the storehouse from (measuring out) the barley ration of the *guda*-priests. He banned the bailiff from (receiving) the silver (paid for the shearing) of the white sheep and of the *gaba*-lambs. He banned the bailiffs from the tax of (that is, levied on) the *sanga's* which (used to be) carried off (to the palace).

He made Ningirsu king of the houses of the *ensi* (and) of the field of the *ensi*. He made Bau queen of the houses of the (palace) harem (and) of the fields of the (palace) harem. He made Shulshaggana king of the houses of the (palace) nursery (and) of the fields of the (palace) nursery. From the borders of Ningirsu to the sea, there was no tax collector.

Trans. by S. N. Kramer, The Sumerians *(Chicago: University of Chicago Press, 1963), pp. 317–319.*

About 1600 B.C.E. the Babylonian kingdom fell apart under the impact of invasions from the north and east by the Hittites and the Kassites. The Hittites came as raiders, plundering what they could and then returned to Asia Minor. The Kassites stayed, ruling Mesopotamia for five centuries.

Government From the earliest historical records it is clear that the Sumerians were ruled by monarchs in some form. Some scholars have thought they could detect a "primitive democracy" in early Sumer, but the evidence, which is sketchy and hard to interpret, shows no more than a limited check on royal power even in early times. The first historical city-states had kings or priest-kings who led the army, administered the economy, and served as judges and as intermediaries between their people and the gods. At first, the kings were thought of as favorites and representatives of the gods; later, on some occasions and for relatively short periods, they instituted cults and were worshiped as divine.

This union of church and state (to use modern terminology) in the person of the king reflected the centralization of power typical of Mesopotamian life. The economy was managed from the center by the priests and the king and was planned very carefully. Each year the land was surveyed, fields were assigned to specific farmers, and the amount of seed to be used was designated. The government estimated the size of the crop and planned its distribution even before it was planted.

This process required a large and competent staff, the ability to observe and record natural phenomena, a good knowledge of mathematics, and, for all of this, a system of writing. The Sumerians invented the writing system known as *cuneiform* (from the Latin *cuneus*, "wedge") because of the wedge-shaped stylus with which they wrote on clay tablets. The writing also came to be used in beautifully cut characters in stone. The Sumerians also began the development of a sophisticated system of mathematics. The calendar they invented had twelve lunar months. To make it agree with the solar year and to make possible accurate designation of the seasons, they introduced a thirteenth month about every three years.

Religion The Sumerians and their successors worshiped gods with human forms, each of whom was usually identified with some natural phenomenon. They were pictured as frivolous, quarrelsome, selfish, and often childish, differing from humans only in their greater power and their immortality. They each appear to have begun as local deities. The people of Mesopotamia had a vague and gloomy picture of the afterworld. Their religion dealt with problems of this world, and they used prayer, sacrifice, and magic to achieve their ends. Expert knowledge was required to reach the perfection in wisdom and ritual needed to influence the gods, and so the priesthood flourished. A high percentage of the cuneiform writing we now have is devoted to religious texts: prayers, incantations, curses, and omens.

This clay tablet from the Chaldean period (612–539 B.C.E.) shows a map of the world as seen by the Babylonians. The "Salt Sea" is shown as a circle. An arc inside it is labeled "Mountains." Below it is a rectangular box marked "Babylon," and to the right of the box is a small circle marked "Assyria." [Courtesy of the Trustees of the British Museum]

The Babylonians, in an effort to discover the will and intentions of the gods, cultivated several methods of divination. Seeking evidence of divine action in the movements of the heavenly bodies, they gave birth to astrology. They also sought to discover the divine will by examining the entrails of sacrificial animals for abnormalities. All of this religious activity required armies of scribes to keep great quantities of records, as well as learned priests to interpret them.

This eighth-century B.C.E. *alabaster relief of Gilgamesh, the godlike hero of an ancient Sumerian epic poem, was found in the ruins of the palace of the Assyrian king Sargon II and is now in the Louvre. [Giraudon/Art Resource, N.Y.]*

Religion, in the form of myth, played a large part in the literature and art of Mesopotamia. In poetic language, the Babylonians told tales of the creation of the world, of a great flood that almost destroyed human life, of an island paradise from which the god Enki was expelled for eating forbidden plants, of a hero named Gilgamesh who performed great feats in his travels, and many more.

Religion was also the inspiration for the most interesting architectural achievement in Mesopotamia: the ziggurat. The ziggurat was an artificial stepped mound surmounted by a temple. Neighbors and successors of the Sumerians adopted the style, and the eroded remains of many of these monumental structures, some partly restored, still dot the Iraqi landscape.

Society Tens of thousands of texts from the mid-third millennium B.C.E. to the end of cuneiform writing give us a very full and detailed picture of the way people in ancient Mesopotamia conducted their lives and of the social conditions in which they lived. The evidence from the time of the reign of Hammurabi—including more than fifty royal letters, many business contracts, and especially the Code of Hammurabi—is particularly good. It reveals a society that was legally divided into three classes: nobles, commoners, and slaves. Punishment for crimes committed against freemen was harsher than for those against slaves, and likewise crimes committed against nobles were held to be more serious than those against commoners.

Categorizing the Code of Hammurabi according to the aspects of life with which it deals reveals much about Babylonian society. The third largest category is commerce, and the many sections of the Code devoted to such issues as debts, rates of interest, security, and default indicate the importance and sophistication of Babylonian commercial life. Sections also deal with the regulation of builders, surgeons, and other professionals. The second largest category deals with land tenure, as is not surprising in a society based so heavily on agriculture. The largest category relates to the family and its maintenance and protection.

Marriages were arranged by the parents, and betrothal was followed by the signing of a marriage contract. The husband-to-be made a bridal payment, and the father of the bride-to-be agreed to a dowry for his daughter. A marriage started out monogamous, but a husband whose wife was childless or ill for a long time could take a second wife. Extra-marital relations between the husband and concubines, female slaves, and prostitutes were common and accepted.

The wife did not have similar privileges, but she seems to have been treated as an individual with rights protected by the law. Divorce was relatively easy and not entirely inequitable. Women divorced by their husbands without good cause received their dowry back. A woman seeking divorce could also recover her dowry if her husband could not convict her of wrongdoing. On the other hand, a woman's place was thought distinctly to be in the home. One law states that if a wife "has made up her mind to leave in order to engage in business, thus neglecting her house and humiliating her husband, he may divorce her without compensation."

For most of Mesopotamian history slavery arose from debt. Parents could sell their children into slavery or pledge themselves and their entire family as surety for a loan. In case of default, they would all become slaves of the creditor for a stated period of time. Although the practice of enslaving foreign war captives dates to early periods, and native Babylonians could be enslaved for certain crimes—kicking one's mother or striking an elder brother, for example—true chattel slavery did not become common until late in Mesopotamian history, in the Neo-Babylonian period (612–539 B.C.E.). Some slaves worked for the king and the state, others for the temple and the priests, and still others for private citizens. Their tasks varied accordingly. Most temple slaves appear to have been women, who were probably used to spin thread, weave cloth, and grind flour. Sometimes the royal slaves did the heavy work of building palaces, canals, and fortifications. Private owners used their slaves chiefly as domestic servants. Some female slaves were used as concubines.

Although laws against fugitive slaves or slaves who denied their masters were harsh, in some respects Mesopotamian slavery appears enlightened compared with other slave systems in history. Slaves could engage in business and, with certain restrictions, hold property. They could marry free men or women, and the resulting children would be free. A slave who acquired the necessary wealth could buy his or her freedom. Children of a slave by the master might be allowed to share his property after his death. Nevertheless, slaves were property, were subject to their master's will, and had little legal protection. For a comparative discussion of slavery in the ancient world, see The West and the World, Chapter 4.

Key Events and People in Mesopotamian History

ca. 3500 B.C.E.	Earliest Sumerian settlements
ca. 2800–2370 B.C.E.	Sumerian city-states' early dynastic period
ca. 2370 B.C.E.	Sargon establishes Semitic dynasty at Akkad
ca. 2125–2027 B.C.E.	Third Dynasty of Ur
ca. 1900 B.C.E.	Amorites at Babylon, beginning of Old Babylonian dynasty
1792–1750 B.C.E.	Reign of Hammurabi
ca. 1600 B.C.E.	Invasion by Hittites and Kassites; end of Old Babylonian dynasty

Egyptian Civilization

As Mesopotamian civilization arose in the valley of the Tigris and Euphrates, another great civilization emerged in Egypt. The center of Egyptian civilization was the Nile River. From its source in central Africa the Nile runs north some 4,000 miles to the Mediterranean, with long navigable stretches broken by several cataracts. Ancient Egypt included the 750 miles of the valley from the First Cataract to the sea and was shaped like a funnel with two distinct parts. Upper (southern) Egypt consisted of the narrow valley of the Nile. Lower (northern) Egypt consisted of the broad, triangular delta, which branches out about 150 miles along the Mediterranean coast. (See Map 1–1.)

The Nile alone made life possible in Egypt's almost rainless desert. Each year the river flooded and covered the land, and when it receded it left a fertile mud that could produce two crops a year. The construction and maintenance of irrigation ditches to preserve the river's water, with careful planning and organization of planting and harvesting, produced agricultural prosperity unmatched in the ancient world.

The Nile also served as a highway connecting the long, narrow country and encouraging its unification. Upper and Lower Egypt were, in fact, already united into a single kingdom at the beginning of our

The Babylonian Story of the Flood

This passage is part of the Babylonian Epic of Gilgamesh, which may have been written before 2000 B.C.E. Its hero, after many adventures, becomes aware of his own mortality when his friend and companion dies. Gilgamesh then seeks the secret of immortality from Utnapishtim. This man and his wife were the sole survivors of a great flood that destroyed the rest of humanity and the only two mortals known to have been granted eternal life. It is interesting to note the similarities between this tale and the biblical story of Noah, as well as the important differences between them.

✦ *How is this tale similar to the story of Noah in the Book of Genesis in the Hebrew Bible? How is it different? How does the presence of many divinities shape this story differently from the one in Genesis?*

"For six days and (seven) nights the wind blew, and the flood and the storm swept the land. But the seventh day arriving did the rainstorm subside and the flood which had heaved like a woman in travail; there quieted the sea, and the storm-wind stood still, the flood stayed her flowing. I opened a vent and the fresh air moved over my cheek-bones. And I looked at the sea; there was silence, the tide-way lay flat as a roof-top—but the whole of mankind had returned unto clay. I bowed low: I sat and I wept: o'er my cheek-bones my tears kept on running.

"When I looked out again in the directions, across the expanse of the sea, mountain ranges had emerged in twelve places and on Mount Nisir the vessel had grounded. Mount Nisir held the vessel fast nor allowed any movement. For a first day and a second, fast Mount Nisir held the vessel nor allowed of any movement. For a third day and a fourth day, fast Mount Nisir held the vessel nor allowed of any movement. For a fifth day and a sixth day, held Mount Nisir fast the vessel nor allowed of any movement.

"On the seventh day's arriving, I freed a dove and did release him. Forth went the dove but came back to me: there was not yet a resting-place and he came returning. Then I set free a swallow and did release him. Forth went the swallow but came back to me: there was not yet a resting-place and he came returning. So I set free a raven and did release him. Forth went the raven—and he saw again the natural flowing of the waters, and he ate and he flew about and he croaked, and came not returning.

historical record, about 3100 B.C.E. Nature helped protect and isolate the ancient Egyptians from outsiders. The cataracts, the sea, and the desert made it difficult for foreigners to reach Egypt for either friendly or hostile purposes. Egypt knew far more peace and security than Mesopotamia. This security, along with the sunny, predictable climate, gave Egyptian civilization a more optimistic outlook than the civilizations of the Tigris and Euphrates, which were always in fear of assault from storm, flood, earthquake, and hostile neighbors.

The more than 3,000-year span of ancient Egyptian history is traditionally divided into thirty-one royal dynasties, from the first, founded by Menes, the unifier of Upper and Lower Egypt, to the last, established by Alexander the Great, who conquered Egypt (as we shall see in Chapter 3) in 332 B.C.E. The dynasties are conventionally arranged into periods (see the accompanying chronology). The unification of Egypt was vital, for more than in Mesopotamia the entire river valley benefitted from the central control of irrigation. By the time of the Third Dynasty, Egypt's kings had achieved full supremacy. Ruling from their capital at Memphis, in Upper Egypt, just above the opening of the delta, they had imposed internal peace and order, and their kingdom enjoyed great prosperity.

An Egyptian king was no mere representative of the gods but a god himself. The land was his own personal possession, and the people were his ser-

"So all set I free to the four winds of heaven, and I poured a libation, and scattered a food-offering, on the height of the mountain. Seven and seven did I lay the vessels, heaped into their incense-basins sweet-cane, cedarwood and myrtle. And the gods smelled the savour, the gods smelled the sweet savour, the gods gathered like flies about the priest of the offering.

"Then, as soon as the Mother-goddess arrived, she lifted up the great jewels which (in childhood, her father) Anu had made as a plaything for her: 'O ye gods here present, as I still do not forget these lapis stones of my neck, so shall I remember these days—shall not forever forget them! If it please now the gods to come here to the offering, never shall Enlil come here to the offering, for without any discrimination he brought on the deluge, even (the whole of) my people consigned to destruction.'

"But as soon as Enlil arrived, he saw only the vessel—and furious was Enlil, he was filled with anger against the (heaven) gods, the Igigi: 'Has aught of livingkind escaped? Not a man should have survived the destruction!'

"Ninurta opened his mouth and spake unto warrior Enlil:

'Who except Ea could have designed such a craft? For Ea doth know every skill of invention.'

"Then Ea opened his mouth and spake unto warrior Enlil:

'O warrior, thou wisest among gods, how thus indiscriminately couldst thou bring about this deluge? (Had thou counselled): On the sinner lay his sin, on the transgressor lay his transgression: loosen (the rope) that his life be not cut off, yet pull tight (on the rope) that he do not [escape]: then instead of thy sending a Flood would that the lion had come and diminished mankind: instead of thy sending a Flood that the wolf had come and diminished mankind: instead of thy sending a Flood would that a famine had occurred and impoverished mankind: instead of thy sending a Flood would that a pestilence had come and smitten mankind. And I, since I could not oppose the decision of the great gods, did reveal unto the Exceeding-Wise a (magic) dream, and thus did he hear the gods' decision. Wherefore now take thee counsel concerning him.'

"Thereupon Enlil went up into the vessel: he took hold of my hand and made me go aboard, he bade my wife go aboard and made her kneel at my side. Standing between us, he touched our foreheads and did bless us, saying: 'Hitherto Utnapishtim has been but a man; but now Utnapishtim and his wife shall be as gods like ourselves. In the Far Distance, at the mouth of the Rivers, Utnapishtim shall dwell.'

"So they took me and did make me to dwell in the Far Distance, at the mouth of the Rivers. . . ."

Trans. by J. V. Kinnier Wilson in Documents from Old Testament Times, *D. Winton Thomas, ed. (London: Thomas Nelson and Sons, Ltd., 1958), lines 145–198, pp. 22–24.*

vants. Nothing better illustrates the extent of royal power than the three great pyramids built as tombs by the kings of the Fourth Dynasty. The largest, that of Khufu, was originally 481 feet high and 756 feet long on each side; it was made up of 2,300,000 stone blocks averaging 2.5 tons each. The Greek historian Herodotus, writing some 2,000 years later in history, records claims that 100,000 men spent twenty years building it. The pyramids are remarkable for the great technical skill they demonstrate, but even more for the concentration of resources they represent. They give evidence that the Egyptian kings controlled vast wealth, had the power to focus enormous human effort on a personal project, and possessed the confidence to undertake one of such a long duration. There were earlier pyramids and many were built later, but those of the Fourth Dynasty were never surpassed.

THE OLD KINGDOM (2700–2200 B.C.E.) In the Old Kingdom royal power was absolute. The pharaoh, as the king was later called (the term originally meant *great house* or *palace*), governed his kingdom through his family, appointing and removing officials at his pleasure. The peasants were carefully regulated, their movement was limited, and they were taxed heavily, perhaps up to as much as one fifth of what they produced. Luxury accompanied the king in life and death, and he was raised to a remote and exalted level by his people. The

The great pyramids of Egypt, located at Giza, near Cairo, are the colossal tombs of three pharaohs of the Fourth Dynasty (ca. 2620–2480 B.C.E.): Menkaure (left), Khafre (center), and Khufu (right). The smaller tombs in the foreground may have been those of the pharaohs' wives and courtiers. [Pictor/Uniphoto Picture Agency]

Egyptians worked for the king and obeyed him because he was a living god on whom their lives, safety, and prosperity depended. He was the direct source of law and justice, and so Egypt needed no law codes.

In such a world, government was merely one aspect of religion, and religion dominated Egyptian life. The gods of Egypt had many forms: animals, humans, and natural forces. In time, Re, the sun god, came to have a special and dominant place, but for centuries there seems to have been little clarity or order in the Egyptian pantheon.

Periods in Ancient Egyptian History (Dynasties in Roman Numerals)

ca. 3100–2700 B.C.E.	Early Dynastic Period (I–II)
2700–2200 B.C.E.	Old Kingdom (III–VI)
2200–2052 B.C.E.	First Intermediate Period (VII–X)
2052–1786 B.C.E.	Middle Kingdom (XI–XII)
1786–1575 B.C.E.	Second Intermediate Period (XIII–XVII)
ca. 1700 B.C.E.	Hyksos invasion
1575–1087 B.C.E.	New Kingdom (or Empire)(XVIII–XX)
1087–30 B.C.E.	Post-Empire (XXI–XXXI)

Unlike the Mesopotamians, the Egyptians had a rather clear idea of an afterlife. They took great care to bury their dead according to convention and supplied the grave with things that the departed would need for a pleasant life after death. The king and some nobles had their bodies preserved as mummies. Their tombs were beautifully decorated with paintings; food was provided at burial and even after. Some royal tombs were provided with full-sized ships for the voyage to heaven. At first, only kings were thought to achieve eternal life; then, nobles were included; finally, all Egyptians could hope for immortality. The dead had to be properly embalmed, and the proper spells had to be written and spoken.

The Egyptians developed a system of writing not much later than the Sumerians. Though the idea of writing may have come from Mesopotamia, Egyptian script developed independently. It began as picture writing and later combined pictographs with sound signs. The result was a difficult and complicated script that the Greeks later called *hieroglyph*, "sacred carvings". Most Egyptian writing was done with pen and ink on a fine paper made from the papyrus reed found in the delta; much of

This painting from a royal Egyptian tomb shows a noble family on a boat on a trip to hunt birds in the afterlife, just as they enjoyed doing in their lives on earth. [Courtesy of the Trustees of the British Museum]

what was preserved long enough to be available to us, however, is found on wall paintings and carvings. Egyptian literature was more limited in depth and imagination than that of Mesopotamia. Hymns, myths, magical formulas, tales of travel, and "wisdom literature," or bits of advice to help one get on well in the world, have been preserved. But the Egyptian world, happier and simpler than the Mesopotamian, produced nothing as serious and probing as the Mesopotamian story of Gilgamesh.

THE MIDDLE KINGDOM (2052–1786 B.C.E.) The power of the kings of the Old Kingdom waned as priests and nobles gained more independence and influence. The governors of the regions of Egypt, called *nomes*, gained hereditary claim to their offices, and their families acquired large estates. About 2200 B.C.E. the Old Kingdom collapsed and gave way to the decentralization and disorder of the First Intermediate Period (ca. 2200–2052 B.C.E.). The nomarchs (governors) of Thebes in Upper Egypt eventually gained control of the country and established the Middle Kingdom, its capital initially at Thebes, about 2052 B.C.E.

The rulers of the Twelfth Dynasty restored the pharaoh's power over the whole of Egypt, though

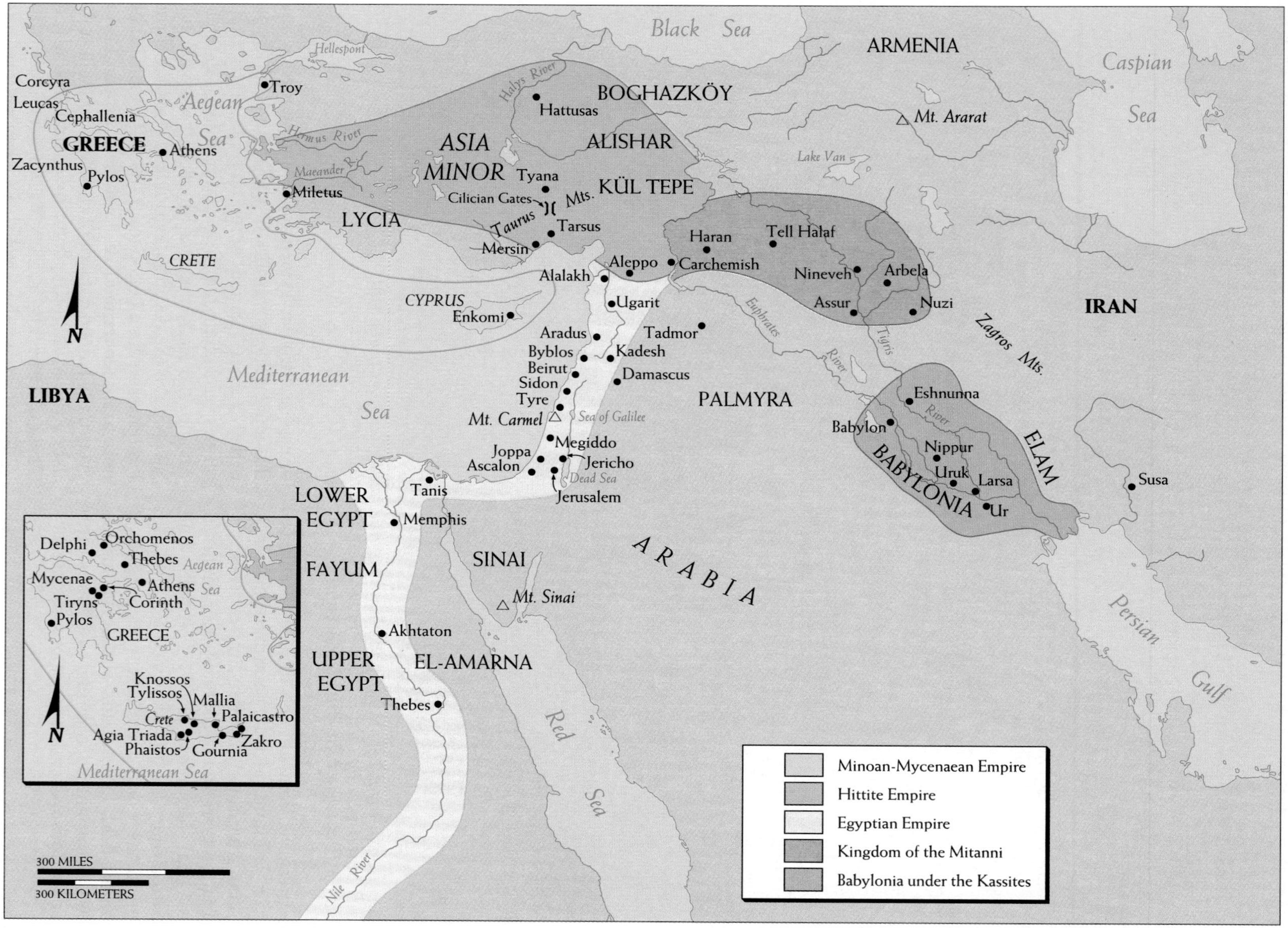

Map 1–2 The Near East and Greece About 1400 B.C.E. *About 1400 B.C.E. the Near East was divided among four empires. Egypt went south to Nubia and north through Palestine and Phoenicia. Kassites ruled in Mesopotamia, Hittites in Asia Minor, and the Mitannians in Assyrian lands. In the Aegean the Mycenaean kingdoms were at their height.*

they could not completely control the nobles who ruled the nomes. Still, they brought order, peace, and prosperity after the troubles of the First Intermediate Period. They encouraged trade and extended Egyptian power and influence northward toward Palestine and southward toward Ethiopia. They moved the capital from Thebes back to the more defensible site of Memphis, but gave great prominence to Amon, a god especially connected with Thebes. Amon became identified with Re, emerging as Amon-Re, the main god of Egypt.

The kings of this period seem to have emphasized their role as dispensers of justice. Statues often show them burdened with care, presumably concerned for their people. Tales of the period stress the king's interest in right and in the welfare of his people.

THE NEW KINGDOM (OR EMPIRE) (1575–1087 B.C.E.) AND AFTER The resurgent power of the local nobility and the erosion of central authority in the Thirteenth Dynasty mark the end of the Middle Kingdom and the beginning of the Second Intermediate Period (1786–1575 B.C.E.) About 1700 B.C.E., Egypt suffered an invasion. Tradition speaks of a people called the Hyksos who came from the east and conquered the Nile Delta. They seem to have been a collection of Semitic peoples from the area of Palestine and Syria at the eastern end of the Mediterranean. Egyptian nationalism reasserted itself about 1575 B.C.E., when a dynasty from Thebes drove out the Hyksos and reunited the kingdom, opening the New Kingdom, or Empire Period. In reaction to the humiliation of the Second Intermediate Period, the pharaohs of the Eighteenth Dynasty, the most prominent of whom was Thutmose III (r. 1490–1436 B.C.E.), built a powerful army, imposed an absolute government, and forged an empire that extended far beyond the Nile Valley. (See Map 1–2.)

From the Hyksos the Egyptians had learned new military techniques and obtained new weapons. Combining these with determination, a fighting spirit, and an increasingly militarized society, they pushed their southern frontier back a long way and extended their power into Palestine, Syria, and beyond to the upper Euphrates River. They were not checked until they came into conflict with the powerful Hittite Empire of Asia Minor. The ensuing struggle between these powers weakened both. Egypt survived, but by the end of the Twentieth Dynasty, the last dynasty of the New Kingdom, its period of glory had passed. Throughout the Post-Empire period (1087–30 B.C.E.) it again fell victim to periodic foreign invasion and rule.

This fresco painting is of Queen Nefertari of the Twentieth Dynasty, the last dynasty of the New Kingdom period. [Courtesy of the Trustees of the British Museum]

The Egyptians believed in the possibility of life after death through the god Osiris. The character of each person's life had to be tested by 42 assessor-gods before the person could be presented to Osiris. In this scene from an illustration of the Book of the Dead *the deceased and his wife (on the left) watch the scales of justice weighing his heart (on the left side of the scales) against the feather of truth. The jackal-faced god Anubis also watches the scales, while the ibis-headed god Thoth keeps the record. [Courtesy of the Trustees of the British Museum]*

Toward the end of the Eighteenth Dynasty, after the New Kingdom empire had reached its greatest extent, Egypt witnessed an interesting religious struggle. One result of the successful imperial ventures was to increase the power of the priests of Amon, making them a threat to the position of the pharaoh. When young Amenhotep IV (r. 1367–1350 B.C.E.) came to the throne, he apparently determined to resist the priesthood of Amon. Supported by his family and advisers, he ultimately made a clean break with the worship of Amon-Re, devoting himself instead to the worship of the god Aton, the physical disk of the sun. He changed his name to Akhnaton ("it pleases Aton") and moved his capital from Thebes, the center of Amon worship, to an entirely new city—Akhtaton—about 300 miles to the north at a place now called El Amarna.

The new god was different from any that had come before him, for he was believed to be universal, not merely Egyptian. Unlike the other gods, he had no cult statue but was represented in painting and relief sculpture as the sun disk.

The universal claims for Aton led to religious intolerance of the worshipers of the other gods. Their temples were shut down, and the name of Amon-Re was chiseled from monuments on which it was carved. The old priests, of course, were deprived of their posts and privileges; the pharaoh selected new people, sometimes even foreigners, to serve him. The new religion, moreover, was more remote than the old. Only the pharaoh and his family worshiped Aton directly, and the people worshiped the pharaoh.

Akhnaton's interest in religious reform apparently led him to ignore foreign affairs, which proved disastrous. The Asian possessions of Egypt fell away, and this imperial decline and its economic consequences presumably caused further hostility to the new religion. When the king died, a strong counterrevolution swept away his life's work.

His chosen successor was soon put aside and replaced by Tutankhamen (r. 1347–1339 B.C.E.), the young husband of one of the daughters of Akhnaton and his beautiful wife, Nefertiti. The new pharaoh restored the old religion and wiped out as much as he could of the memory of the worship of Aton. He restored Amon to the center of the Egyptian pantheon, abandoned El Amarna, and returned the capital to Thebes. His magnificent tomb, remarkably, survived almost fully intact until its discovery in 1922.

The end of the El Amarna age restored power to the priests of Amon and to military officers. A general named Horemhab became king (r. 1335–1308? B.C.E.). He restored order and recovered much of the lost empire. He referred to Akhnaton as "the criminal of Akhtaton" and erased his name from the records. Akhnaton's city and memory disappeared for over 3,000 years, to be rediscovered only by chance about a century ago.

Following Akhnaton, Egypt returned to its traditional gods and culture, but its mood had turned gloomy. *The Book of the Dead*, a product of this late period, was a collection of spells to help the dead reach the next world safely, avoiding destruction by a hideous monster. Egypt itself would soon be devoured by powerful empires no less menacing.

Ancient Near Eastern Empires

In the time of the Eighteenth Dynasty in Egypt, new groups of peoples had established themselves in the Near East: the Kassites in Babylonia, the Hittites in Asia Minor, and the Mitannians in northern Mesopotamia. The Kassites and Mitannians were warrior peoples who ruled as a minority over more civilized folk and absorbed their culture without changing it. The Hittites established a kingdom of their own and forged an empire that lasted some 200 years.

The Hittites

The Hittites arrived in Asia Minor about 2000 B.C.E. By about 1500 B.C.E. they had established a strong, centralized government with a capital at Hattusas (near Ankara, the capital of modern Turkey). Between 1400 and 1200 B.C.E. they contested Egypt's control of Palestine and Syria. By about 1265 B.C.E. they were strong enough to achieve a dynastic marriage with the daughter of the powerful Nineteenth Dynasty pharaoh, Ramses II. The Hittite kingdom was gone by 1200 B.C.E., swept away by the arrival of new, mysterious Indo-Europeans. Neo-Hittite centers flourished in Asia Minor and Mesopotamia for a few centuries longer, however.

In most respects the Hittites reflected the influence of the dominant Mesopotamian culture of the region. Their government, however, was different. Their kings did not claim to be divine or even to be the chosen representatives of the gods. In the early period the king's power was checked by a council of nobles, and the assembled army had to ratify his succession to the throne. The Hittites appear to have been responsible for a great technological advance, the smelting of iron. They also played an important role in transmitting the ancient cultures of Mesopotamia and Egypt to the Greeks, who lived on their frontiers.

The Assyrians

The fall of the Hittites was followed by the rise of the Assyrians, who established the first of a succession of powerful empires that dominated the Near East's ancient civilizations and even extended them to new areas. The homeland of the Assyrians was in the valleys and hills of northern Mesopotamia and the area east of the Tigris River. They had a series of capitals, of which the great city of Nineveh (modern Mosul, Iraq) is perhaps the best known. They spoke a Semitic language and, from early on, were culturally a part of Mesopotamia.

Akkadians, Sumerians, Amorites, and Mitannians had each in turn dominated Assyria. When the Hittites defeated the Mitannians in the fourteenth century B.C.E., they effectively liberated the Assyrians, allowing them to establish themselves as an independent state. After 1000 B.C.E. the Assyrians began a period of steady expansion, and by 665 B.C.E. they controlled all of Mesopotamia, much of Asia Minor, Syria, Palestine, and Egypt to its southern frontier. They succeeded thanks to a large, well-disciplined army and a society that powerfully valued the military virtues. Fierce and cruel, they boasted of their own brutality, at least in part to terrorize real and potential enemies.

Unlike earlier empires, the Assyrian Empire systematically and profitably exploited the area it held. The Assyrians used various methods of control, ranging from the mere collection of tribute to the stationing of garrisons in conquered territory to the scattering of entire populations away from their homelands, as befell the people of the kingdom of Israel. Because of their military and administrative

A reconstruction drawing of Nimrud, one of the capitals of the Assyrian Empire. Some elements of this drawing may be fanciful, but it gives a sense of what an Assyrian city looked like. [Courtesy of the Trustees of the British Museum]

skills, the Assyrians were able to hold vast areas even as they absorbed the teachings of the older cultures under their sway.

In addition to maintaining their empire, the Assyrians had to defend it against the incursions of barbarians on its frontiers. In the seventh century B.C.E. this task so drained the overextended empire that it was left vulnerable to internal rebellion. A new dynasty in Babylon threw off Assyrian rule, joined with the rising kingdom of Media to the east (in modern Iran), and defeated the Assyrians, destroying Nineveh in 612 B.C.E. The successor kingdoms, the Chaldean—or Neo-Babylonian—and the Median, did not last long. By 539 B.C.E., they were swallowed by yet another great Eastern empire, that of the Persians. We shall return to the Persians in Chapter 2.

Key Events in the History of Ancient Near Eastern Empires

ca. 1400–1200 B.C.E.	Hittite Empire
ca. 1100 B.C.E.	Rise of Assyrian power
732–722 B.C.E.	Assyrian conquest of Palestine–Syria
671 B.C.E.	Assyrian conquest of Egypt
612 B.C.E.	Destruction of Assyrian capital at Nineveh
612–539 B.C.E.	Neo-Babylonian (Chaldean) Empire

Palestine

None of the powerful kingdoms of the ancient Near East had as much influence on the future of Western civilization as the small stretch of land between Syria and Egypt, the land called Palestine for much of its history. The three great religions of the modern world outside the Far East—Judaism, Christianity, and Islam—trace their origins, at least in part, to the people who arrived there a little before 1200 B.C.E. The book that recounts their experiences is the Hebrew Bible.

The Canaanites and the Phoenicians

Before the Israelites arrived in their promised land, it was inhabited by groups of people speaking a Semitic language called Canaanite. The Canaanites lived in walled cities and carried on a version of Mesopotamian culture that included the worship of many gods. The arrival of the Israelites probably forced them northward to settle among similar people who inhabited the coastal land of Phoenicia.

The Phoenicians were a people who had played an important role in commerce from a very early time. Their writing system is among the earliest decipherable examples of a nearly alphabetic script, a simplified form of writing in which the symbols represent the individual letters of a language. They founded colonies throughout the Mediterranean as far west as Spain. The most famous of these was Carthage, near modern Tunis in North Africa. Sitting astride all trade routes, the Phoenician cities were important sites for the transmission of culture and knowledge from east to west.

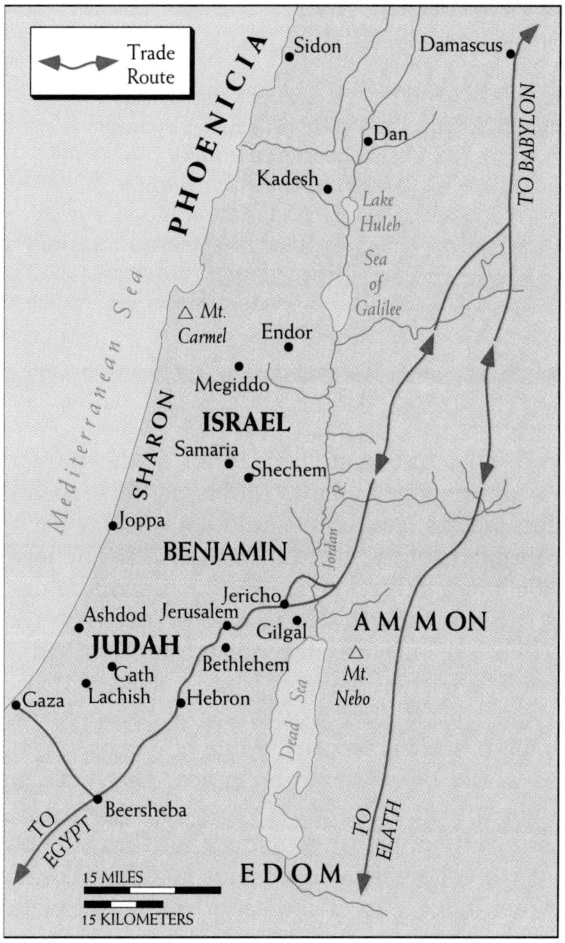

Map 1–3 Ancient Palestine *The Hebrews established a unified kingdom in Palestine under Kings David and Solomon in the tenth century B.C.E. After the death of Solomon, however, the kingdom was divided into two parts—Israel in the north and Judah, with its capital, Jerusalem, in the south. North of Israel were the great commercial cities of Phoenicia.*

The Israelites

The history of the Israelites must be pieced together from various sources. They are mentioned only rarely in the records of their neighbors, and so we must rely chiefly on their own account, the Hebrew Bible. This is not a history in our sense, but a complicated collection of historical narrative, wisdom literature, poetry, law, and religious witness. Scholars of an earlier time tended to discard it as a historical source, but the most recent trend is to take it seriously while using it with caution.

According to tradition the patriarch Abraham came from Ur about 1900 B.C.E. and wandered west to tend his flocks in the land of the Canaanites. Some of his people settled there and others wandered into Egypt, perhaps with the Hyksos. By the thirteenth century B.C.E., led by Moses, they had left Egypt and wandered in the desert until they reached Canaan. They established a united kingdom that reached its peak under David and Solomon in the tenth century B.C.E. The sons of Solomon could not maintain the unity of the kingdom, and it split into two parts: Israel in the north and Judah, with its capital at Jerusalem, in the south. (See Map 1–3.) The rise of the great empires brought disaster to the Israelites. The northern kingdom fell to the Assyrians in 722 B.C.E., and its people—the "ten lost tribes"—were scattered and lost forever. Only the kingdom of Judah remained. It is from this time that we may call the Israelites Jews.

In 586 B.C.E. Judah was defeated by the Neo-Babylonian king Nebuchadnezzar II. He destroyed the great temple built by Solomon and took thousands of hostages off to Babylon. When the Persians defeated Babylonia, they ended this Babylonian Captivity of the Jews and allowed them to return to their homeland. After that, the area of the old kingdom of the Jews in Palestine was dominated by foreign peoples for some 2,500 years until the establishment of the State of Israel in 1948 C.E.

The Jewish Religion

The fate of this small nation of Israel would be of little interest were it not for its unique religious achievement. The great contribution of the Jews is the idea of monotheism, the existence of one uni-

The Israelites

ca. 1000–961 B.C.E.	Reign of King David
ca. 961–922 B.C.E.	Reign of King Solomon
722 B.C.E.	Assyrian conquest of Israel (northern kingdom)
586 B.C.E.	Destruction of Jerusalem; fall of Judah (southern kingdom); Babylonian Captivity
539 B.C.E.	Restoration of temple; return of exiles

versal God, the creator and ruler of the universe. This idea may be as old as Moses, as the Jewish tradition asserts, and it certainly dates as far back as the prophets of the eighth century B.C.E. The Jewish God is not a natural force nor like human beings or any other creatures; He is so elevated that those who believe in Him may not picture Him in any form. The faith of the Jews is given special strength by their belief that God made a covenant with Abraham that his progeny would be a chosen people who would be rewarded for following God's commandments and the law He revealed to Moses.

A novelty of Jewish religious thought is the powerful ethical element it introduced. God is a severe but just judge. Ritual and sacrifice are not enough to achieve His approval. People must be righteous, and God Himself appears to be bound to act righteously. The Jewish prophetic tradition was a powerful ethical force. The prophets constantly criticized any falling away from the law and the path of righteousness. They placed God in history, blaming the misfortunes of the Jews on God's righteous and necessary intervention to punish the people for their misdeeds. The prophets also promised the redemption of the Jews if they repented, however. The prophetic tradition expected the redemption to come in the form of a Messiah who would restore the house of David. Christianity, emerging from this tradition, holds that Jesus of Nazareth was that Messiah.

Jewish religious ideas influenced the future development of the West, both directly and indirectly. The Jews' belief in an all-powerful creator (who is righteous Himself and demands righteousness and obedience from humankind) and a universal God (who is the father and ruler of all peoples) is a critical part of the Western heritage.

General Outlook of Near Eastern Cultures

Our very brief account of the history of the ancient Near East so far reveals that its various peoples and cultures were different in many ways. Yet the distance between all of them and the emerging culture of the Greeks (Chapter 2) is striking. We can see this distance best by comparing the approach of the other cultures with that of the Greeks on several fundamental human problems: What is the relationship of humans to nature? To the gods? To other humans? These questions involve attitudes toward religion, philosophy, science, law, justice, politics, and government in general.

Humans and Nature

For the peoples of the Near East there was no simple separation between humans and nature or even between animate creatures and inanimate objects. Humanity was part of a natural continuum, and all things partook of life and spirit. These peoples imagined the universe to be dominated by gods more or less in the shape of humans, and the world they ruled was irregular and unpredictable, subject to divine whims. The gods were capricious because nature seemed capricious.

One Egyptian text speaks of humans as "the cattle of god." The Babylonian story of creation makes it clear that humanity's function is merely to serve the gods. The creator Marduk says:

> I will create Lullu "man" be his name,
> I will form Lullu, man.
> Let him be burdened with the toil of the gods, that they may freely breathe.[1]

In a world ruled by powerful deities of this kind, human existence was precarious. Even disasters that we would think human in origin the Mesopotamians saw as the product of divine will. Thus a Babylonian text depicts the destruction of the city of Ur by invading Elamites as the work of the gods, carried out by the storm god Enlil:

> Enlil called the storm.
> The people mourn.
> Exhilarating winds he took from the land.

[1]Henri Frankfort et al., *Before Philosophy* (Baltimore: Penguin, 1949), p. 197.

The people mourn.
Good winds he took away from Sumer.
The people mourn.
He summoned evil winds.
The people mourn.
Entrusted them to Kingaluda, tender of storms.
He called the storm that will annihilate the land.
The people mourn.
He called disastrous winds.
The people mourn.
Enlil—choosing Gibil as his helper—
Called the (great) hurricane of heaven.
The people mourn.[2]

The helpless position of humankind in the face of irrational divine powers is clearly shown in both the Egyptian and the Babylonian versions of the story of the flood. In one Egyptian tale, Re, the god who had created humans, decided to destroy them because of some unnamed evil that the god had suffered. He sent the goddess Sekhmet to accomplish the deed, and she was in the midst of her task, enjoying the work and wading in a sea of blood, when Re changed his mind. Instead of ordering a halt, he poured 7,000 barrels of blood-colored beer in Sekhmet's path. She quickly became drunk, stopped the slaughter, and preserved humanity. In the Babylonian story, the motive for the destruction of humanity is more obvious:

In those days the world teemed, the people multiplied, the world bellowed like a wild bull, and the great god was aroused by the clamour. Enlil heard the clamour and he said to the gods in council, "The uproar of mankind is intolerable and sleep is no longer possible by reason of the babel." So the gods in their hearts were moved to let loose the deluge.[3]

The gods repented to a degree and decided to save one family, Utnapishtim and his wife, but they seem to have chosen him because he was friendly with Enki, the god of wisdom, who helped him to survive by a trick.

In such a universe humans could not hope to understand nature, much less control it. At best, they could try by magic to use some mysterious forces against others. An example of this device is provided by a Mesopotamian incantation to break a sorcerer's spell. The sufferers tried to use the magical powers inherent in ordinary salt to fight the witchcraft, addressing the salt as follows:

O Salt, created in a clean place,
For food of gods did Enlil destine thee.
Without thee no meal is set out in Ekur,
Without thee god, king, lord, and prince do not smell incense.
I am so-and-so, the son of so-and-so,
Held captive by enchantment,
Held in fever by bewitchment.
O Salt, break my enchantment! Loose my spell!
Take from me the bewitchment!—and as my Creator
I shall extol thee.[4]

Humans and the Gods, Law, and Justice

Human relationships to the gods were equally humble. There was no doubt that the gods could destroy humankind and might do so at any time for no good reason. Humans could—and, indeed, had to—try to win the gods over by prayers and sacrifices, but there was no guarantee of success. The gods were bound by no laws and no morality. The best behavior and the greatest devotion to the cult of the gods were no defense against the divine and cosmic irrationality.

In the earliest civilizations, human relations were guided by laws, often set down in written codes. The basic question about law concerned its legitimacy: Why, apart from the lawgiver's power to coerce obedience, should anyone obey the law? For the Egyptians the answer was simple: The law came from the king and the king was a god. For the Mesopotamians the answer was almost the same: The king was a representative of the gods, so that the laws he set forth were equally divine. The prologue to the most famous legal document in antiquity, the Code of Hammurabi, makes this plain:

I am the king who is preeminent among kings;
my words are choice; my ability has no equal.
By the order of Shamash, the great judge of heaven and earth,
may my justice prevail in the land;
by the word of Marduk, my lord,
may my statutes have no one to rescind them.[5]

The Hebrews introduced some important new ideas. Their unique God was capable of great anger

[2]Frankfort et al., p. 154.

[3]*The Epic of Gilgamesh,* trans. by N. K. Sandars (Baltimore: Penguin, 1960), p. 105.

[4]Frankfort et al., p. 143.

[5]James B. Pritchard, *Ancient Near Eastern Texts,* 2nd ed. (Princeton: Princeton University Press, 1955), pp. 164–180.

The Second Isaiah Defines Hebrew Monotheism

The strongest statement of Hebrew monotheism is found in these words of the anonymous prophet whom we call the Second Isaiah. He wrote during the Hebrew exile in Babylonia, 597–539 B.C.E.

✦ *In what ways is the deity in this passage different from the deities of the Mesopotamian and Egyptian societies? Are there any similarities? Many peoples have claimed that a single god was the greatest and the ruler over all others. What is there in this selection that claims a different status for the deity of the Hebrews?*

42

5Thus says God, the Lord
who created the heavens and stretched them out,
who spread forth the earth and what comes from it,
who gives breath to the people upon it and spirit
to those who walk in it:
6"I am the Lord, I have called you in righteousness,
I have taken you by the hand and kept you;
I have given you as a covenant to the people, a light to the nations,
7to open the eyes that are blind,
to bring out the prisoners from the dungeon,
from the prison those who sit in darkness.
8I am the Lord, that is my name;
my glory I give to no other,
nor my praise to graven images.
9Behold, the former things have come to pass, and new things I now declare;
before they spring forth I tell you of them."

44

6Thus says the Lord, the King of Israel and his Redeemer, the Lord of hosts:
"I am the first and I am the last; besides me there is no god.
7Who is like me? Let him proclaim it,
let him declare and set it forth before me.
Who has announced of old the things to come?
Let them tell us what is yet to be.
8Fear not, nor be afraid;
have I not told you from of old and declared it?
And you are my witnesses!
Is there a God besides me?
There is no Rock; I know not any."

49

22Thus says the Lord God:
"Behold, I will lift up my hand to the nations,
and raise my signal to the peoples;
and they shall bring your sons in their bosom,
and your daughters shall be carried on their shoulders
23Kings shall be your foster fathers,
and their queens your nursing mothers.
With their faces to the ground they shall bow down to you,
and lick the dust of your feet.
Then you will know that I am the Lord;
those who wait for me shall not be put to shame."
24Can the prey be taken from the mighty, or the captives of a tyrant be rescued?
25Surely, thus says the Lord:
"Even the captives of the mighty shall be taken,
and the prey of the tyrant be rescued,
for I will contend with those who contend with you
and I will save your children.
26I will make your oppressors eat their own flesh,
and they shall be drunk with their own blood as with wine.
Then all flesh shall know
that I am the Lord your Savior,
and your Redeemer, the Mighty One of Jacob."

Bible, Revised Standard Version (*New York: Division of Christian Education, National Council of Churches*, 1952).

and destruction, but He was open to persuasion and subject to morality. He was therefore more predictable and comforting, for all the terror of His wrath. The biblical version of the flood story, for instance, reveals the great difference between the Hebrew God and the Babylonian deities. The Hebrew God was powerful and wrathful, but He was not arbitrary. He chose to destroy His creatures for their moral failures, for the reason that

> the wickedness of man was great in the earth, and that every imagination of the thought of His heart was evil continually . . . the earth was corrupt in God's sight and the earth was filled with violence.[6]

When He repented and wanted to save someone, He chose Noah because "Noah was a righteous man, blameless in his generation."[7]

That God was bound by His own definition of righteousness is neatly shown in the biblical story of Sodom and Gomorrah. He had chosen to destroy these wicked cities but felt obliged first by His covenant to inform Abraham.[8] In this passage Abraham calls on God to abide by His own moral principles, and God sees Abraham's point.

In such a world there is the possibility of order in the universe and on this earth. There is also the possibility of justice among human beings, for the Hebrew God had provided His people with law. Through his prophet Moses, He had provided humans with regulations that would enable them to live in peace and justice. If they would abide by the law and live upright lives, they and their descendants could expect happy and prosperous lives. This idea was quite different from the uncertainty of the Babylonian view, but like it and its Egyptian partner, it left no doubt of the centrality of the divine. Cosmic order, human survival, and justice were all dependent on God.

Toward the Greeks and Western Thought

Greek thought offered different approaches and answers to many of the concerns we have been discussing. Calling attention to some of those differences will help convey the distinctive outlook of the Greeks and the later cultures within Western civilization that have drawn heavily on Greek influence.

It is important to recognize that Greek ideas had much in common with the ideas of earlier peoples. The Greek gods had most of the characteristics of the Mesopotamian deities; magic and incantations played a part in the lives of most Greeks; and Greek law, like that of earlier peoples, was usually connected with divinity. Many, if not most, Greeks in the ancient world must have lived their lives with notions similar to those held by other peoples. The surprising thing is that some Greeks developed ideas that were strikingly different and, in so doing, set a part of humankind on an entirely new path.

As early as the sixth century B.C.E., some Greeks living in the Ionian cities of Asia Minor raised questions and suggested answers about the nature of the world that produced an intellectual revolution. In their speculations, they made guesses that were completely naturalistic and made no reference to supernatural powers. One historian of Greek thought, discussing the views of Thales, the first Greek philosopher, put the case particularly well:

> In one of the Babylonian legends it says: "All the lands were sea . . . Marduk bound a rush mat upon the face of the waters, he made dirt and piled it beside the rush mat." What Thales did was to leave Marduk out. He, too, said that everything was once water. But he thought that earth and everything else had been formed out of water by a natural process, like the silting up of the Delta of the Nile. . . . It is an admirable beginning, the whole point of which is that it gathers into a coherent picture a number of observed facts without letting Marduk in.[9]

By putting the question of the world's origin in a naturalistic form, Thales, in the sixth century B.C.E., may have initiated the unreservedly rational investigation of the universe and, in so doing, initiated both philosophy and science.

The same relentlessly rational approach was used even in regard to the gods themselves. In the same century as Thales, Xenophanes of Colophon expressed the opinion that humans think of the gods as resembling themselves, that like themselves they were born, that they wear clothes like theirs, and that they have voices and bodies like theirs. If oxen, horses, and lions had hands and could paint like humans, Xenophanes argued, they would paint

[6]Genesis 6:5–11.

[7]Genesis 6:9.

[8]Genesis 18:20–33.

[9]Benjamin Farrington, *Greek Science* (London: Penguin, 1953), p. 37.

gods in their own image; the oxen would draw gods like oxen and the horses like horses. Thus Africans believed in flat-nosed, black-faced gods, and the Thracians in gods with blue eyes and red hair.[10] In the fifth century B.C.E. Protagoras of Abdera went so far in the direction of agnosticism as to say, "About the gods I can have no knowledge either that they are or that they are not or what is their nature."[11]

This rationalistic, skeptical way of thinking carried over into practical matters as well. The school of medicine led by Hippocrates of Cos (about 400 B.C.E.) attempted to understand, diagnose, and cure disease without any attention to supernatural forces or beings. One of the Hippocratics wrote of the mysterious disease epilepsy:

> It seems to me that the disease is no more divine than any other. It has a natural cause, just as other diseases have. Men think it divine merely because they do not understand it. But if they called everything divine which they do not understand, why, there would be no end of divine things.[12]

By the fifth century B.C.E. it was also possible for the historian Thucydides to analyze and explain the behavior of humans in society completely in terms of human nature and chance, leaving no place for the gods or supernatural forces.

The same absence of divine or supernatural forces characterized Greek views of law and justice. Most Greeks, of course, liked to think that, in a vague way, law came ultimately from the gods. In practice, however, and especially in the democratic states, they knew very well that laws were made by humans and should be obeyed because they represented the expressed consent of the citizens. Law, according to the fourth century B.C.E. statesman Demosthenes, is "a general covenant of the whole State, in accordance with which all men in that State ought to regulate their lives."[13]

✦

The statement of these ideas, so different from any that came before the Greeks, opens the discussion of most of the issues that appear in the long history of Western civilization and that remain major concerns in the modern world: What is the nature of the universe, and how can it be controlled? Are there divine powers, and, if so, what is humanity's relationship to them? Are law and justice human, divine, or both? What is the place in human society of freedom, obedience, and reverence? These and many other matters were either first considered or elaborated on by the Greeks.

The Greeks' sharp departure from the thinking of earlier cultures marked the beginning of the unusual experience that we call Western civilization. Nonetheless, they built on a foundation of lore that people in the Near East had painstakingly accumulated over millennia. From ancient Mesopotamia and Egypt they borrowed important knowledge and skills in mathematics, astronomy, art, and literature. From Phoenicia they learned the art of writing. The discontinuities, however, are more striking than the continuities.

The great civilizations of the river valleys were ruled by hereditary monarchies surrounded and elevated by the aura of divinity. The rulers amassed great wealth with which they could pay large armies to dominate their own people. Powerful priesthoods presented yet another bastion of privilege that stood between the ordinary person and the knowledge and opportunity needed for freedom and autonomy. The world of the ancient Near East, in the petty kingdoms and city-states of Palestine, Phoenicia, and Syria just as in the great empires of Egypt and Mesopotamia, was dominated by religion. The secular, reasoned questioning that sought understanding of the world in which people lived, that tried to find explanations in the natural order of things rather than in the supernatural acts of the gods, was not characteristic of the older cultures. Nor would it appear in similar societies at other times in other parts of the world. The new way of looking at things was uniquely the product of the Greeks. We now need to see whether there was something special in their experience that made them raise fundamental questions in the way that they did.

[10]Frankfort et al., pp. 14–16.

[11]Hermann Diels, *Fragmente der Vorsokratiker*, 5th ed., ed. by Walter Kranz (Berlin: Weidmann, 1934–38), Frg. 4.

[12]Diels, Frgs. 14–16.

[13]Demosthenes, *Against Aristogeiton*, 16.

Review Questions

1. How would you define "history"? What different academic disciplines do historians rely on and why is the study of history important?
2. How was life during the Paleolithic Age different from that in the Neolithic Age? What

advancements in agriculture and human development had taken place by the end of the Neolithic era? Is it valid to speak of a "Neolithic Revolution"?

3. What general conclusions can you draw about the differences in the political and intellectual outlooks of the civilizations of Egypt and Mesopotamia? Compare especially Egyptian and Mesopotamian religious views. In what ways did the regional geography influence the religious outlooks of these two civilizations?
4. How did the monotheism of Akhnaton differ from that of the Hebrews? To what extent did the Hebrew faith bind the Jews politically? Why was the concept of monotheism so radical for Near Eastern civilizations?
5. Why were the Assyrians so successful in establishing their Near Eastern empire? How did their empire differ from that of the Hittites or Egyptians? In what ways did this empire benefit the civilized Middle East? Why did the Assyrian Empire ultimately fail to survive?
6. In what ways did Greek thought develop along different lines from that of Near Eastern civilizations? What new questions about human society were asked as a result of Greek influence?

Suggested Readings

W. F. ALBRIGHT, *From the Stone Age to Christianity* (1957). An original and interesting interpretive study.

V. G. CHILDE, *What Happened in History* (1946). A pioneering study of human prehistory and history before the Greeks from an anthropological point of view.

R. DE VAUX, *Ancient Israel: Its Life and Institutions* (1961). A fine account of social institutions.

M. EHRENBERG, *Women in Prehistory* (1989). An account of the role of women in early times.

H. FRANKFORT ET AL., *Before Philosophy* (1949). A brilliant examination of the mind of the ancients from the Stone Age to the Greeks.

A. GARDINER, *Egypt of the Pharaohs* (1961). A sound narrative history.

O. R. GURNEY, *The Hittites* (1954). A good general survey.

W. W. HALLO AND W. K. SIMPSON, *The Ancient Near East: A History* (1971). A fine survey of Egyptian and Mesopotamian history.

D. C. JOHNSON AND M. R. EDEY, *Lucy: The Beginnings of Mankind* (1981). A study of the first human creatures based on remains found in Africa.

S. N. KRAMER, *The Sumerians: Their History, Culture and Character* (1963). A readable general account of Sumerian history.

S. LLOYD, *The Archaeology of Mesopotamia*, revised edition (1984). An account of the material remains of Mesopotamia and their meaning from the Old Stone Age to the Persian Conquest.

D. OATES AND J. OATES, *The Rise of Civilization*, (1976). A study of the emergence of urban life in southern Mesopotamia placed in a broad context and well illustrated with photographs.

J. OATES, *Babylon*, revised edition (1986). An introduction to the history and archaeology of Babylonia revised to make use of newly discovered evidence.

J. N. POSTGATE, *The First Empires* (1977). A fine account of Mesopotamian history from the dawn of history to the Persian conquest.

J. N. POSTGATE, *Early Mesopotamia* (1992). An excellent study of Mesopotamian economy and society from the earliest times to about 1500 B.C.E., helpfully illustrated with drawings, pictures, and translated documents.

J. B. PRITCHARD (ED.), *Ancient Near Eastern Texts Relating to the Old Testament* (1969). A good collection of documents in translation with useful introductory material.

D. B. REDFORD, *Akhenaten* (1987). A new study of the controversial religious reformer.

C. L. REDMAN, *The Rise of Civilization* (1978). An attempt to use the evidence provided by anthropology, archaeology, and the physical sciences to illuminate the development of early urban society.

W. F. SAGGS, *The Greatness That Was Babylon* (1962). An excellent narrative account of Mesopotamian history.

W. F. SAGGS, *Everyday Life in Babylonia and Assyria* (1965).

W. F. SAGGS, *The Might That Was Assyria* (1984). A history of the northern Mesopotamian Empire and a worthy companion to the author's account of the Babylonian Empire in the south.

N. K. SANDARS, *The Sea Peoples* (1985). A lively account of the collection of peoples who disrupted established Mediterranean civilizations in the thirteenth century B.C.E.

K. C. SEELE, *When Egypt Ruled the East* (1965). A study of Egypt in its imperial period.

B. G. TRIGGER ET AL., *Ancient Egypt: A Social History* (1982).

J. A. WILSON, *Culture of Ancient Egypt* (1956). A fascinating interpretation of the civilization of ancient Egypt.

CHAPTER 2

The ruins of the sanctuary of Apollo at Delphi, dating from the sixth century B.C.E. *Greeks and foreigners traveled great distances to worship Apollo and to consult the famous Delphic oracle for clues to the future. [Jose Fuste Raga, The Stock Market]*

The Rise of Greek Civilization

KEY TOPICS

- The Bronze Age civilizations that ruled the Aegean area before the development of Hellenic civilization
- The rise, development, and expansion of the *polis*, the characteristic political unit of Hellenic Greece
- The early history of Sparta and Athens
- The wars between the Greeks and the Persians

About 2000 B.C.E., Greek-speaking peoples settled the lands surrounding the Aegean Sea and established a style of life and formed a set of ideas, values, and institutions that spread far beyond the Aegean corner of the Mediterranean Sea. Preserved and adapted by the Romans, Greek culture powerfully influenced the society of western Europe in the Middle Ages and dominated the Byzantine Empire in the same period. It would ultimately spread across Europe and in time cross the Atlantic to the Western Hemisphere.

At some time in their history, the Greeks of the ancient world founded cities on every shore of the Mediterranean Sea. Pushing on through the Dardanelles, they placed many settlements on the coasts of the Black Sea in southern Russia and as far east as the approaches to the Caucasus Mountains. The center of Greek life, however, has always been the Aegean Sea and the islands in and around it. This location at the eastern end of the Mediterranean very early put the Greeks in touch with the more advanced and earlier civilizations of Mesopotamia, Egypt, Asia Minor, and Syria–Palestine.

The Greeks acknowledged the influence of these predecessors. A character in one of Plato's dialogues says, "Whatever the Greeks have acquired from foreigners they have, in the end, turned into something finer."[1] *This is a proud statement, but it also shows the Greeks were aware of how much they had learned from other civilizations.*

The Bronze Age Minoan culture of Crete contributed to Greek civilization, and the mainland Mycenaean culture, which conquered Minoan Crete, contributed even more. Both these cultures, however, had more in common with the cultures of the Near East than with the new Hellenic culture established by the Greeks in the centuries after the end of the Bronze Age in the twelfth century B.C.E.

The rugged geography of the Greek peninsula and its nearby islands isolated the Greeks of the early Iron Age from their richer and more culturally advanced neighbors, shaping, in part, their way of life, and permitting them to develop that way of life on their own. The aristocratic world of the "Greek Dark Ages" (1150–750 B.C.E.*) produced impressive artistic achievements, especially in the development of painted pottery and most magnificently in the epic poems of Homer. In the eighth century* B.C.E.*, social, economic, and military changes profoundly influenced the organization of Greek political life; the Greek city-state, the* polis, *came into being and thereafter dominated the cultural development of the Greek people.*

This change came in the midst of turmoil, for the pressure of a growing population led many Greeks to leave home and establish colonies far away. Those who remained often fell into political conflict, from which tyrannies sometimes emerged. These tyrannies, however, were in all cases transitory, and the Greek cities emerged from them as self-governing polities, usually ruled by an oligarchy, broad or narrow. The two most important states, Athens and Sparta, developed in different directions. Sparta formed a mixed constitution in which a very small part of the population dominated the vast majority and Athens developed the world's first democracy.

The Bronze Age on Crete and on the Mainland to About 1150 B.C.E.

The Bronze Age civilizations in the region that the Greeks would rule arose on the island of Crete, on the islands of the Aegean, and on the mainland of Greece. Crete was the site of the earliest Bronze Age settlements, and modern scholars have called the civilization that arose there *Minoan*, after the legendary king of Crete. A later Bronze Age civilization was centered at the mainland site of Mycenae and is called *Mycenaean*.

The Minoans

With Greece to the north, Egypt to the south, and Asia to the east, Crete was a cultural bridge between the older civilizations and the new one of the Greeks. The Bronze Age came to Crete not long after 3000 B.C.E., and the Minoan civilization, which powerfully influenced the islands of the Aegean and the mainland of Greece, arose in the third and second millennia B.C.E.

Scholars have established links between stratigraphic layers at archaeological sites on Crete and

(a) The Minoan-period Palace at Cnossus on the island of Crete. (b) A fresco painting from the east wing of the palace. The fresco shows acrobats leaping over a charging bull. It is not known whether such acrobatic displays were only for entertainment or part of some religious ritual. [(a) D.A. Harissiadis, Athens; (b) Scala/Art Resource, N.Y.]

(a)

(b)

[1]Plato, *Epinomis*, 987 d.

specific styles of pottery and other artifacts found in the layers. On this basis they have divided the Bronze Age on Crete into three major periods—Early, Middle, and Late Minoan—with some subdivisions. Dates for Bronze Age settlements on the Greek mainland, for which the term *Helladic* is used, are derived from the same chronological scheme.

During the Middle and Late Minoan periods in the cities of eastern and central Crete, a civilization developed that was new and unique in its character and its beauty. Its most striking creations are the palaces uncovered at such sites as Phaestus, Haghia Triada, and, most important, Cnossus. Each of these palaces was built around a central court surrounded by a labyrinth of rooms. Some sections of the palace at Cnossus were as tall as four stories high. The basement contained many storage rooms for oil and grain, apparently paid as taxes to the king. The main and upper floors contained living quarters as well as workshops for making pottery and jewelry. There were sitting rooms and even bathrooms, to which water was piped through excellent plumbing. Lovely columns, which tapered downward, supported the ceilings, and many of the walls carried murals showing landscapes and seascapes, festivals, and sports. The palace design and the paintings show the influence of Syria, Asia Minor, and Egypt, but the style and quality are unique to Crete.

In contrast to the Mycenaean cities on the mainland of Greece, Minoan palaces and settlements lacked strong defensive walls. This evidence that the Minoans built without defense in mind has raised questions and encouraged speculation. Some scholars, pointing also to evidence that Minoan religion was more matriarchal than the patriarchal religion of the Mycenaeans and their Greek descendants, have argued that the civilizations of Crete, perhaps reflecting the importance of women, were inherently more tranquil and pacific than others. An earlier and very different explanation for the absence of fortifications was that the protection provided by the sea made them unnecessary. The evidence is not strong enough to support either explanation, and the mystery remains.

Along with palaces, paintings, pottery, jewelry, and other valuable objects, excavations have revealed clay writing tablets like those found in Mesopotamia. The tablets, preserved accidentally when a great fire that destroyed the royal palace at Cnossus hardened them, have three distinct kinds of writing on them: a kind of picture writing called *hieroglyphic*, and two different linear scripts called Linear A and Linear B. The languages of the other two scripts remain unknown, but Linear B proved to be an early form of Greek. The contents of the tablets, primarily inventories, reveal an organization centered on the palace and ruled by a king who was supported by an extensive bureaucracy that kept remarkably detailed records.

A linear B tablet from Pylos, dated about 1200 B.C.E. First discovered late in the nineteenth century, Linear B was not deciphered until 1952, when a brilliant young Briton, Michael Ventris, demonstrated that it was an early Greek dialect. This tablet is part of a palace inventory. It survived because it was hardened in a fire when the palace at Pylos was destroyed by invaders. [Hirmer Verlag, Munich]

This sort of organization is typical of early civilizations in the Near East but, as we shall see, is nothing like that of the Greeks after the Bronze Age. Yet the inventories were written in a form of Greek. If they controlled Crete throughout the Bronze Age, why should Minoans, who were not Greek, have written in a language not their own? This question raises the larger one of what the relationship was between Crete and the Greek mainland in the Bronze Age and leads us to an examination of mainland, or Helladic, culture.

The Mycenaeans

In the third millennium B.C.E.—the Early Helladic Period—most of the Greek mainland, including many of the sites of later Greek cities, was settled by people who used metal, built some impressive houses, and traded with Crete and the islands of the Aegean. The names they gave to places, names that were sometimes preserved by later invaders, make it clear that they were not Greeks and that they spoke a language that was not Indo-European (the language family to which Greek belongs).

Not long after the year 2000 B.C.E., many of the Early Helladic sites were destroyed by fire, some were abandoned, and still others appear to have yielded peacefully to an invading people. These signs of invasion probably signal the arrival of the Greeks.

All over Greece, there was a smooth transition between the Middle and Late Helladic periods. The invaders succeeded in establishing control of the entire mainland. The shaft graves cut into the rock at the royal palace-fortress of Mycenae show that they prospered and sometimes became very rich. At Mycenae, the richest finds come from the period after 1600 B.C.E. The city's wealth and power reached their peak during this time, and the culture of the whole mainland during the Late Helladic Period goes by the name *Mycenaean*.

The presence of the Greek Linear B tablets at Cnossus suggests that Greek invaders also established themselves in Crete, and there is good reason to believe that at the height of Mycenaean power (1400–1200 B.C.E.), Crete was part of the Mycenaean world. Although their dating is still controversial, the Linear B tablets at Cnossus seem to belong to Late Minoan III, so what is called the great "palace period" at Cnossus would have followed an invasion by Mycenaeans in 1400 B.C.E. These Greek invaders ruled Crete until the end of the Bronze Age.

MYCENAEAN CULTURE The excavation of Mycenae, Pylos, and other Mycenaean sites reveals a culture influenced by, but very different from, the Minoan culture. Mycenae and Pylos, like Cnossus, were built some distance from the sea. It is plain, however, that defense against attack was foremost in the minds of the founders of the Mycenaean cities. Both were built on hills in a position commanding the neighboring territory. The Mycenaean people were warriors, as their art, architecture, and weapons reveal. The success of their campaigns and the defense of their territory required strong central authority, and all available evidence shows that the kings provided it. Their palaces, in which the royal family and its retainers lived, were located within the walls; most of the population lived outside the walls. Usually paintings covered the palace walls, as on Crete; but instead of peaceful scenery and games, the Mycenaean murals depicted scenes of war and boar hunting.

About 1500 B.C.E. the already impressive shaft graves were abandoned in favor of *tholos* tombs. These large, beehivelike chambers were built of enormous, well-cut, and fitted stones, and approached by an unroofed passage (*dromos*) cut horizontally into the side of the hill. The lintel block alone of one of these tombs weighs over one hundred tons. Only a strong king whose wealth was great, whose power was unquestioned, and who commanded the labor of many people could undertake such a project. His wealth probably came from plundering raids, piracy, and trade. Some of this trade went westward to Italy and Sicily, but most of it was with the islands of the Aegean, the coastal towns of Asia Minor, and the cities of Syria, Egypt, and Crete. The Mycenaeans sent pottery, olive oil, and animal hides in exchange for jewels and other luxuries.

Tablets containing the Mycenaean Linear B writing have been found all over the mainland; the largest and most useful collection was found at Pylos. These tablets reveal a world very similar to the one shown by the records at Cnossus. The king, whose title was *wanax*, held a royal domain, appointed officials, commanded servants, and kept a close record of what he owned and what was owed to him. This evidence confirms all the rest; the Mycenaean world was made up of several independent, powerful, and well-organized monarchies.

THE RISE AND FALL OF MYCENAEAN POWER At the height of their power (1400–1200 B.C.E.), the Mycenaeans were prosperous and active. They enlarged their cities, expanded their trade, and even established commercial colonies in the East. They are mentioned in the archives of the Hittite kings of Asia Minor. They are named as marauders of the Nile Delta in Egyptian records. Sometime about 1250 B.C.E. they probably sacked Troy, on the coast of northwestern Asia Minor, giving rise to the epic

Map 2–1 The Aegean Area in the Bronze Age *The Bronze Age in the Aegean area lasted from about 1900 to about 1100 B.C.E. Its culture on Crete is called Minoan and was at its height about 1900–1400 B.C.E. Bronze Age Helladic culture on the mainland flourished from about 1600 to 1200 B.C.E.*

poems of Homer, the *Iliad* and the *Odyssey*. (See Map 2–1.) Around 1200 B.C.E., however, the Mycenaean world showed signs of great trouble, and by 1100 B.C.E. it was gone. Its palaces were destroyed, many of its cities were abandoned, and its art, its pattern of life, and its system of writing were buried and forgotten.

What happened? Some recent scholars, noting evidence that the Aegean island of Thera (modern Santorini) suffered a massive volcanic explosion in the middle to late second millennium B.C.E., have suggested that this natural disaster was responsible. According to one version of this theory, the explosion occurred around 1400 B.C.E., blackening and poisoning the air for many miles around and sending a monstrous tidal wave that destroyed the great palace at Cnossus and, with it, Minoan culture. According to another version, the explosion took place about 1200 B.C.E., destroying Bronze Age culture throughout the Aegean. This second version conveniently accounts for the end of both Minoan and Mycenaean civilizations in a single blow, but the evidence does not support it. The Mycenaean towns were not destroyed all at once; many fell around 1200 B.C.E., but some flourished for another century, and the Athens of the period was never destroyed or abandoned. No theory of natural disaster can account for this pattern, leaving us to seek less dramatic explanations for the end of Mycenaean civilization.

THE DORIAN INVASION Some scholars have suggested that piratical sea raiders destroyed Pylos and, perhaps, other sites on the mainland. The Greeks themselves believed in a legend that told of the Dorians, a rude people from the north who spoke a Greek dialect different from that of the Mycenaean peoples. According to the legend, the Dorians joined with one of the Greek tribes, the Heraclidae, in an attack on the southern Greek peninsula of Peloponnesus, which was repulsed. One hundred years later they returned and gained full control. Recent historians have identified this legend of "the return of the Heraclidae" with a Dorian invasion.

Archaeology has not provided material evidence of a single Dorian invasion or a series of them, and it is impossible as yet to say with any certainty what happened at the end of the Bronze Age in the Aegean. The chances are good, however, that Mycenaean civilization ended gradually over the century between 1200 B.C.E. and 1100 B.C.E. Its end may have been the result of internal conflicts among the Mycenaean kings combined with continuous pressure from outsiders, who raided, infiltrated, and eventually dominated Greece and its neighboring islands. There is reason to believe that Mycenaean society suffered internal weaknesses due to its organization around the centralized control of military force and agricultural production. This rigid organization may have deprived it of flexibility and vitality, leaving it vulnerable to outside challengers. In any case, Cnossus, Mycenae, and Pylos were abandoned, their secrets to be kept for over 3,000 years.

The Greek "Middle Ages" to About 750 B.C.E.

The immediate effects of the Dorian invasion were disastrous for the inhabitants of the Mycenaean world. The palaces and the kings and bureaucrats who managed them were destroyed. The wealth and organization that had supported the artists and merchants were likewise swept away by a barbarous people who did not have the knowledge or social organization to maintain them. Many villages were abandoned and never resettled. Some of their inhabitants probably turned to a nomadic life, and many perished. The chaos resulting from the collapse of the rigidly controlled palace culture produced severe depopulation and widespread poverty that lasted for a long time.

Greek Migrations

Another result of the invasion was the spread of the Greek people eastward from the mainland to the Aegean islands and the coast of Asia Minor. The Dorians themselves, after occupying most of the Peloponnesus, swept across the Aegean to occupy the southern islands and the southern part of the Anatolian coast.

These migrations made the Aegean a Greek lake. Trade with the old civilizations of the Near East, however, was virtually ended by the fall of the advanced Minoan and Mycenaean civilizations; nor was there much internal trade among the different parts of Greece. The Greeks were forced to turn inward, and each community was left largely to its own devices. The Near East was also in disarray at this time, and no great power arose to impose its ways and its will on the helpless people who lived about the Aegean. The Greeks were allowed time to recover from their disaster and to create their unique style of life.

Our knowledge of this period in Greek history rests on very limited sources. Writing disappeared after the fall of Mycenae, and no new script appeared until after 750 B.C.E., so we have no contemporary author to shed light on this period. Excavation reveals no architecture, sculpture, or painting until after 750 B.C.E.

The Age of Homer

For a picture of society in these "Dark Ages," the best source is Homer. His epic poems, the *Iliad* and the *Odyssey*, emerged from a tradition of oral poetry whose roots extend into the Mycenaean Age. Through the centuries bards had sung tales of the heroes who had fought at Troy, using verse arranged in rhythmic formulas to aid the memory. In this way some very old material was preserved into the eighth century B.C.E., when the poems attributed to Homer were finally written down. Although the poems tell of the deeds of Mycenaean Age heroes, the world they describe clearly differs from the Mycenaean world. Homer's heroes are not buried in *tholos*

The "Trojan Horse," depicted on a seventh-century B.C.E. *Greek vase. According to legend, the Greeks finally defeated Troy by pretending to abandon their siege of the city, leaving a giant wooden horse behind. Soldiers hidden in the horse opened the gates of the city to their compatriots after the Trojans had brought it within their walls. Note the wheels on the horse and the Greek soldiers holding weapons and armor who are hiding inside it. [Greek 10th–6th* B.C.E. *Trojan Horse and Greek Soldiers. Relief from neck of an earthenware amphora (640* B.C.E.*) from Mykanos, ht. 120 cm. Archeological Museum, Mykanos, Greece. Erich Lessing/Art Resource]*

tombs but are cremated; they worship gods in temples, whereas the Mycenaeans had no temples; they have chariots but do not know their proper use in warfare. Certain aspects of the society described in the poems appear rather to resemble the world of the tenth and ninth centuries B.C.E., and other aspects appear to belong to the poet's own time, when population was growing at a swift pace and prosperity was returning, thanks to important changes in Greek agriculture, society, and government.

GOVERNMENT In the Homeric poems the power of the kings is much less than that of the Mycenaean rulers. Homeric kings were limited in their ability to make important decisions by the need to consult a council of nobles. The nobles felt free to discuss matters in vigorous language and in opposition to the king's wishes. In the *Iliad*, Achilles does not hesitate to address Agamemnon, the "most kingly" commander of the Trojan expedition, in these words: "you with a dog's face and a deer's heart." Such language may have been impolite, but it was not treasonous. The king, on the other hand, was free to ignore the council's advice, but it was risky for him to do so.

The right to speak in council was limited to noblemen, but the common people could not be ignored. If a king planned a war or a major change of policy during a campaign, he would not fail to call the common soldiers to an assembly; they could listen and express their feelings by acclamation, though they could not take part in the debate. Homer shows that even in these early times the Greeks, unlike their predecessors and contemporaries, practiced some forms of limited constitutional government.

SOCIETY Homeric society, nevertheless, was sharply divided into classes, the most important division being the one between nobles and everyone else. We do not know the origin of this distinction, but we cannot doubt that at this time Greek society was aristocratic. Birth determined noble status, and wealth usually accompanied it. Below the nobles were three other classes: *thetes*, landless laborers, and slaves. We do not know whether the *thetes* owned the land they worked outright (and so were free to sell it) or worked a hereditary plot that belonged to their clan (and was therefore not theirs to dispose of as they chose).

The worst condition was that of the free but landless hired agricultural laborer. The slave, at least, was attached to a family household and so was protected and fed. In a world where membership in a settled group gave the only security, the free laborers were desperately vulnerable. Slaves were few in number and were mostly women, who served as maids and concubines. Some male slaves worked as shepherds. Few, if any, worked in agriculture, which depended on free labor throughout Greek history.

HOMERIC VALUES The Homeric poems reflect an aristocratic code of values that powerfully influenced all future Greek thought. In classical times Homer was the schoolbook of the Greeks. They memorized his texts, settled diplomatic disputes by citing passages in them, and emulated the behavior and cherished the values they found in them. Those values were physical prowess; courage; fierce protection of one's family, friends, property, and, above all, one's personal honor and reputation. Speed of foot, strength, and, most of all, excellence at fighting make a man great, and all these attributes serve to promote personal honor. The great hero of the *Iliad*, Achilles, refuses to fight in battle, allowing his fellow Greeks to be slain and almost defeated, because Agamemnon has wounded his honor by taking away his battle prize. He returns not out of a sense of duty to the army but to avenge the death of his dear friend Patroclus. Odysseus, the hero of the *Odyssey*, returning home after his wanderings, ruthlessly kills the many suitors who had, in his long absence, sought to marry his wife Penelope; they had dishonored him by consuming his wealth, wooing Penelope, and scorning his son.

The highest virtue in Homeric society was *arete*—manliness, courage in the most general sense, and the excellence proper to a hero. This quality was best revealed in a contest, or *agon*. Homeric battles are not primarily group combats, but a series of individual contests between great champions. One of the prime forms of entertainment is the athletic contest, and the funeral of Patroclus is celebrated by such a contest.

The central ethical idea in Homer can be found in the instructions that Achilles' father gives him when he sends him off to fight at Troy: "Always be the best and distinguished above others." The father of another Homeric hero has given his son exactly the same orders and has added to them the injunction: "Do not bring shame on the family of your fathers who were by far the best in Ephyre and in wide Lycia." Here in a nutshell we have the chief values of the aristocrats of Homer's world: to vie for individual supremacy in *arete* and to defend and increase the honor of the family. These would remain prominent aristocratic values long after Homeric society was only a memory.

WOMEN IN HOMERIC SOCIETY In the world described by Homer the role of women was chiefly to bear and raise children, but the wives of the heroes also had a respected position, presiding over the household , overseeing the servants, and safeguarding the family property. They were prized for their beauty, constancy and skill at weaving. All these fine qualities are combined in Penelope, the wife of Odysseus, probably the ideal Homeric woman. For the twenty years of her husband's absence, she put off the many suitors who sought to marry her and take his place, remained faithful to him, reserved his property and protected the future of their son. Far different was the reputation of Agamemnon's wife, Clytemnestra who betrayed her husband while he was off fighting at Troy and murdered him on his return. Homer contrasts her with the virtuous Penelope in a passage that reveals a streak of hostility to women that can be found throughout the ancient history of the Greeks:

> Not so did the daughter of Tyndareus fashion her evil
> deeds, when she killed her wedded lord, and a song of loathing
> will be hers among men, to make evil the reputation
> of womankind, even for those whose acts are virtuous.[2]

The *Polis*

The characteristic Greek institution was the *polis*. The common translation of that word as "city-state" is misleading, for it says both too much and too little. All Greek *poleis* began as little more than agricultural villages or towns, and many stayed that way, so the word "city" is inappropriate. All of them were states, in the sense of being independent political units, but they were much more than that. The *polis* was thought of as a community of relatives; all its citizens, who were theoretically descended from a common ancestor, belonged to subgroups, such as fighting brotherhoods or *phratries*, clans, and tribes, and worshiped the gods in common ceremonies.

Aristotle argued that the *polis* was a natural growth and that the human being was by nature "an animal who lives in a *polis*." Humans alone have the power of speech and from it derive the ability to distinguish good from bad and right from wrong, "and the sharing of these things is what makes a household and a *polis*." Therefore, humans who are incapable of sharing these things or who are so self-sufficient that they have no need of them are not humans at all, but either wild beasts or gods. Without law and justice human beings are the worst and most dangerous of the animals. With them humans can be the best, and justice exists

[2]*Odyssey* 24.199–202, trans. by Richmond Lattimore (Chicago: University of Chicago Press, 1965).

Kingship in Ithaca

Homer's Odyssey *tells the tale of Odysseus, king of Ithaca, who, after departing to fight at Troy, is unable to return home for twenty years. During this time his infant son Telemachus has grown to manhood and the nobles of Ithaca, thinking Odysseus dead, have paid suit to his wife Penelope, wasting his wealth and insulting his family. In this passage from the First Book of the Odyssey, Telemachus calls for an assembly. The ensuing debate tells us much about the peculiar nature of Homeric kingship.*

✦ *If the kingship of Ithaca belongs to Telemachus by hereditary right and Odysseus is thought to be dead, why isn't Telemachus king? What does Telemachus mean when he says there are many kings in Ithaca? What does this passage reveal about the nature of kingship in the world of Homer?*

Meanwhile in the shadowy hall the Suitors burst into uproar, and each man voiced the hope that he might share her bed.

But the wise Telemachus called them to order, 'from you who court my mother, this is sheer insolence. For the moment, let us dine and enjoy ourselves—quietly, I insist, for it is a lovely thing to listen to a minstrel such as we have here, with a voice like a god. But in the morning I propose that we all take our places in assembly, so that I can give you formal notice to quit my palace. Yes, you can feast yourselves elsewhere, and eat your own provisions in each other's homes. But if you think it a sounder scheme to destroy one man's estate and go scot-free yourselves, then eat your fill, while I pray to the immortal gods for a day of reckoning, when I can go scot-free though I destroy you in this house of mine.'

It amazed them all that Telemachus should have the audacity to adopt this tone, and they could only bite their lips. But at last Antinous, Eupeithes' son, spoke up in answer: 'It seems that the gods are already helping you, Telemachus, by teaching you this bold and haughty way of speaking. Being your father's son, you are heir to this island realm. Heaven grant that you may never be its king!'

But Telemachus was not at a loss. 'Antinous,' he answered, 'it may disappoint you to learn that I should gladly accept that office from the hands of Zeus. Perhaps you argue that nothing worse could happen to a man? I, on the contrary, maintain that it is no bad thing to be a king—to see one's house enriched and one's authority enhanced. However, the Achaeans are not short of princes; young and old they swarm in sea-girt Ithaca. And since the great Odysseus is dead, one of them must surely succeed him. But I intend at least to be master of my own house and the servants whom my royal father won for me in war.'

The Odyssey, *trans. by E. V. Rieu (Harmondsworth: Penguin Books, Ltd., 1946), pp. 34–35.*

only in the *polis*. These high claims were made in the fourth century B.C.E., hundreds of years after the *polis* came into existence, but they accurately reflect an attitude that was present from the first.

Development of the Polis

Originally the word *polis* referred only to a citadel, an elevated, defensible rock to which the farmers of the neighboring area could retreat in case of attack. The Acropolis in Athens and the hill called Acrocorinth in Corinth are examples. For some time such high places and the adjacent farms comprised the *polis*. The towns grew gradually and without planning, as their narrow, winding, and disorderly streets show. For centuries they had no walls. Unlike the city-states of the Near East, they were not placed for commercial convenience on rivers or the sea. Nor did they grow up around a temple to serve the needs of priests and to benefit from the needs of worshipers. The availability of farmland and of a natural fortress determined their location. They were placed either well inland or far enough away from the sea to avoid piratical raids. Only later and gradually did the *agora*—a marketplace and civic center—appear within the *polis*. The *agora* was to become the heart of the Greeks' remarkable social life, distinguished by conversation and argument carried on in the open air.

Some *poleis* probably came into existence early in the eighth century B.C.E. The institution was certainly common by the middle of the century, for all the colonies that were established by the Greeks in the years after 750 B.C.E. took the form of the *polis*. Once the new institution had been fully established, true monarchy disappeared. Vestigial kings survived in some places, but they were almost always only ceremonial figures without power. The original form of the *polis* was an aristocratic republic dominated by the nobility through its council of nobles and its monopoly of the magistracies.

About 750 B.C.E., coincident with the development of the *polis*, the Greeks borrowed a writing system from one of the Semitic scripts and added vowels to create the first true alphabet. This new Greek alphabet was easier to learn than any earlier writing system, leading to much wider literacy.

The Hoplite Phalanx

A new military technique was crucial to the development of the *polis*. In earlier times the brunt of fighting had been carried on by small troops of cavalry and individual "champions" who first threw their spears and then came to close quarters with swords. Toward the end of the eighth century B.C.E., however, the hoplite phalanx came into being and remained the basis of Greek warfare thereafter.

The hoplite was a heavily armed infantryman who fought with a spear and large shield. These soldiers were formed into a phalanx in close order, usually at least eight ranks deep. So long as the hoplites fought bravely and held their ground, there would be few casualties and no defeat; but if they gave way, the result was usually a rout. All depended on the discipline, strength, and courage of the individual soldier. At its best the phalanx could withstand cavalry charges and defeat infantries not as well protected or disciplined. Until defeated by the Roman legion, it was the dominant military force in the eastern Mediterranean.

The usual hoplite battle in Greece was between the armies of two *poleis* quarreling over a piece of land. One army invaded the territory of the other when the crops were almost ready for harvest. The defending army had no choice but to protect its fields. If the army was beaten, its fields were captured or destroyed and its people might starve. In every way, the phalanx was a communal effort that relied not on the extraordinary actions of the individual but on the courage of a considerable portion of the citizenry. This style of fighting produced a single decisive battle that reduced the time lost in fighting other kinds of warfare; it spared the houses, livestock, and other capital of the farmer-soldiers who made up the phalanx, and it reduced the number of casualties, as well. It perfectly suited the farmer-soldier-citizen, who was the backbone of the *polis*, and, by keeping wars short and limiting their destructiveness and expense, it helped the *polis* prosper.

The phalanx and the *polis* arose together, and both heralded the decline of the kings. The phalanx, however, was not made up only of aristocrats. Most of the hoplites were farmers working small holdings. The immediate beneficiaries of the royal decline were the aristocrats, but because the existence of the *polis* depended on small farmers, their wishes could not long be wholly ignored. The rise of the hoplite phalanx created a bond between the aristocrats and the yeomen family farmers who fought in it. This bond helps explain why class conflicts were muted for some time. It also guaranteed, however, that the aristocrats, who dominated at first, would not always be unchallenged.

The Importance of the Polis

The Greeks looked to the *polis* for peace, order, prosperity, and honor in their lifetime. They counted on it to preserve their memory and to honor their descendants after death. Some of them came to see it not only as a ruler, but as the molder of its citizens. Knowing this, we can understand the pride and scorn that underlie the comparison made by the poet Phocylides between the Greek state and the capital of the great and powerful Assyrian Empire: "A little *polis* living orderly in a high place is stronger than a block-headed Nineveh."

Expansion of the Greek World

From the middle of the eighth century B.C.E. until well into the sixth century B.C.E., the Greeks vastly expanded the territory they controlled, their wealth, and their contacts with other peoples. A burst of colonizing activity placed *poleis* from Spain to the Black Sea. A century earlier a few Greeks had established trading posts in Syria. There they had learned new techniques in the arts and crafts and much more from the older civilizations of the Near East.

Magna Graecia

Syria and its neighboring territory were too strong to penetrate, and so the Greeks settled the southern coast of Macedonia and the Chalcidic peninsula. (see Political Transformations, p. 46.) These regions were sparsely settled, and the natives were not well enough organized to resist the Greek colonists. Southern Italy and eastern Sicily were even more inviting areas. Before long there were so many Greek colonies in Italy and Sicily that the Romans called the whole region *Magna Graecia*, "Great Greece". The Greeks also put colonies in Spain and southern France. In the seventh century B.C.E. Greek colonists settled the coasts of the northeastern Mediterranean, the Black Sea, and the straits connecting them. About the same time they established settlements on the eastern part of the North African coast. The Greeks now had outposts throughout the Mediterranean world.

The Greek Colony

The Greeks did not lightly leave home to join a colony. The voyage by sea was dangerous and uncomfortable, and at the end of it were uncertainty and danger. Only powerful pressures like overpopulation and land hunger drove thousands from their homes to establish new *poleis*. See Political Transformations.

Colonization had a powerful influence on Greek life. By relieving the pressure of a growing population, it provided a safety valve that allowed the *poleis* to escape civil wars. By confronting the Greeks with the differences between themselves and the new peoples they met, colonization gave them a sense of cultural identity and fostered a Panhellenic ("all-Greek") spirit that led to the establishment of a number of common religious festivals. The most important ones were at Olympia, Delphi, Corinth, and Nemea.

Colonization also encouraged trade and industry. The influx of new wealth from abroad and the increased demand for goods from the homeland stimulated a more intensive use of the land and an emphasis on crops for export, chiefly the olive and the wine grape. The manufacture of pottery, tools, weapons, and fine artistic metalwork as well as perfumed oil, the soap of the ancient Mediterranean world, was likewise encouraged. New opportunities allowed some men, sometimes outside the nobility, to become wealthy and important. The newly enriched became a troublesome element in the aristocratic *poleis*, for, although increasingly important in the life of their states, they were barred from political power, religious privileges, and social acceptance by the ruling aristocrats. These conditions soon created a crisis in many states.

The Tyrants (About 700–500 B.C.E.)

In some cities, perhaps only a small percentage of the more than 1,000 Greek *poleis*, the crisis produced by new economic and social conditions led to or intensified factional divisions within the ruling aristocracy. In the years between 700 and 500 B.C.E., the result was often the establishment of a tyranny.

THE RISE OF TYRANNY A tyrant was a monarch who had gained power in an unorthodox or unconstitutional but not necessarily wicked way and who exercised a strong one-man rule that might well be beneficent and popular.

The founding tyrant was usually a member of the ruling aristocracy who either had a personal grievance or led an unsuccessful faction. He often rose to power because of his military ability and support from the hoplites. He generally had the support of the politically powerless group of the newly wealthy and of the poor farmers. When he took power, he often expelled many of his aristocratic opponents and divided at least some of their land among his supporters. He pleased his commercial and industrial supporters by destroying the privileges of the old aristocracy and by fostering trade and colonization.

The tyrants presided over a period of population growth that saw an increase especially in the

POLITICAL TRANSFORMATIONS

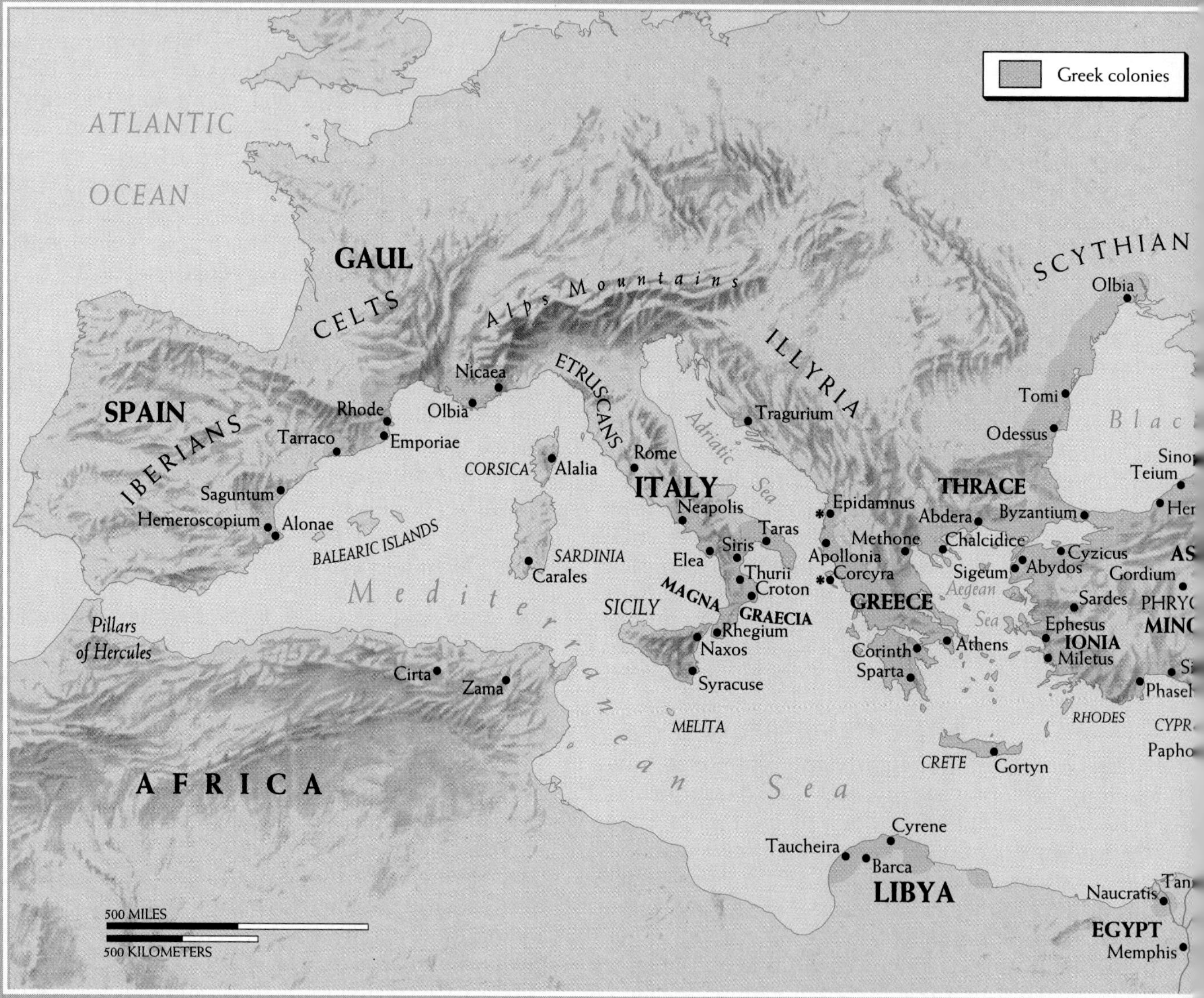

Map 2–2

Greek Colonization from Spain to the Black Sea

During the height of Greek expansion, from the middle of the eighth century B.C.E. to the middle of the sixth century B.C.E., colonies stretched from the Mediterranean coast of Spain in the west to the Black Sea coast of Asia Minor in the east. The colony, although sponsored by the mother city, was established for the good of the colonists rather than for the benefit of those whom they left behind. The colonists tended to divide the land they settled into equal shares, reflecting an egalitarian tendency inherent in the ethical system of the yeoman farmers in the mother cities. They often copied their home constitution, worshiped the same gods as the people of the mother city at the same festivals in the same way, and carried on a busy trade with the mother city. Most colonies, though independent, were friendly with their mother cities. Each might ask the other for aid in time of trouble and expect to receive a friendly hearing, although neither was obligated to help the other.

The Athenians had colonies of this typical kind, but introduced innovations during their imperial period (478–404 B.C.E.). At one point they began to treat all the members of their empire as though they were Athenian settlements, requiring them to bring an offering of a cow and a suit of armor to the Great Panathenaic festival, just like true Athenian colonies. The goal may have been to cloak imperial rule in the more friendly garb of colonial family attachment.

The best known exception tot he general rule of friendly relations between colony and mother-city was the case of Corinth and its colony Corcyra, who quarreled and fought over more than two centuries. Thucydides tells of a fateful conflict between them that played a major role in causing the Peloponnesian War.

Corcyra: An Exceptional Colony

In 435 B.C.E., the people of Epidamnus, a colony of Corcyra torn by civil war, asked the Corinthians to accept them as their own colony. In the excerpt below, Thucydides explains why the Corinthians agreed.

> The Corinthians undertook the task . . . through hatred of the Corcyraeans, because they, although colonists of Corinth, neglected their mother-city. They would not grant the customary privileges to Corinthians at their common festivals nor allow a Corinthian representative precedence in beginning the ritual at sacrifices, as the other colonies did, but treated them with contempt.

(Thucydides, *History of the Peloponnesian War,* 1.25)

The ruins of the Temple of Apollo at Corinth. The colony of Corcyra failed to show customary respect to its mother-city of Corinth. [Anne van der Vaeren/The Image Bank]

number of city dwellers. They responded with a program of public works that included the improvement of drainage systems, care for the water supply, the construction and organization of marketplaces, the building and strengthening of city walls, and the erection of temples. They introduced new local festivals and elaborated the old ones. They were active in the patronage of the arts, supporting poets and artisans with gratifying results. All this activity contributed to the tyrant's popularity, to the prosperity of his city, and to his self-esteem.

In most cases the tyrant's rule was secured by a personal bodyguard and by mercenary soldiers. An armed citizenry, necessary for an aggressive foreign policy, would have been dangerous, so the tyrants usually pursued a program of peaceful alliances with other tyrants abroad and avoided war.

THE END OF THE TYRANTS By the end of the sixth century B.C.E. tyranny had disappeared from the Greek states and did not return in the same form or for the same reasons. The last tyrants were universally hated for the cruelty and repression they employed. They left bitter memories in their own states and became objects of fear and hatred everywhere.

Besides the outrages committed by individual tyrants, there was something about the very concept of tyranny that was inimical to the idea of the *polis*. The notion of the *polis* as a community to which every member must be responsible, the connection of justice with that community, and the natural aristocratic hatred of monarchy all made tyranny seem alien and offensive. The rule of a tyrant, however beneficent, was arbitrary and unpredictable. Tyranny came into being in defiance of tradition and law, and the tyrant governed without either. He was not answerable in any way to his fellow citizens.

From a longer perspective, however, the tyrants made important contributions to the development of Greek civilization. They encouraged economic changes that helped secure the future prosperity of Greece. They increased communication with the rest of the Mediterranean world and cultivated the crafts and technology, as well as the arts and literature. Most important of all, they broke the grip of the aristocracy and put the productive powers of the most active and talented of its citizens fully at the service of the *polis*.

The Major States

Generalization about the *polis* becomes difficult not long after its appearance, for though the states had much in common, some of them developed in unique ways. Sparta and Athens, which became the two most powerful Greek states, had especially unusual histories.

Sparta

At first Sparta seems not to have been strikingly different from other *poleis*. About 725 B.C.E., however, the pressure of population and land hunger led the Spartans to launch a war of conquest against their western neighbor, Messenia. (See Map 2–3.) The First Messenian War gave the Spartans as much land as they would ever need. The reduction of the Messenians to the status of serfs, or Helots, meant that the Spartans need not even work the land that supported them.

The turning point in Spartan history came about 650 B.C.E., when, in the Second Messenian War, the Helots rebelled with the help of Argos and other Peloponnesian cities. The war was long and bitter and at one point threatened the existence of Sparta. After the revolt had been put down, the Spartans were forced to reconsider their way of life. They could not expect to keep down the Helots, who outnumbered them perhaps ten to one, and still maintain the old free-and-easy habits typical of most

Chronology of the Rise of Greece

ca. 2900–1150 B.C.E.	Minoan period
ca. 1900 B.C.E.	Probable date of the arrival of the Greeks on the mainland
ca. 1600–1150 B.C.E.	Mycenaean period
ca. 1250 B.C.E.	Sack of Troy (?)
ca. 1200–1150 B.C.E.	Destruction of Mycenaean centers in Greece
ca. 1100–750 B.C.E.	"Greek Dark Ages"
ca. 750–500 B.C.E.	Major period of Greek colonization
ca. 725 B.C.E.	Probable date when Homer flourished
ca. 700 B.C.E.	Probable date when Hesiod flourished
ca. 700–500 B.C.E.	Major period of Greek tyranny

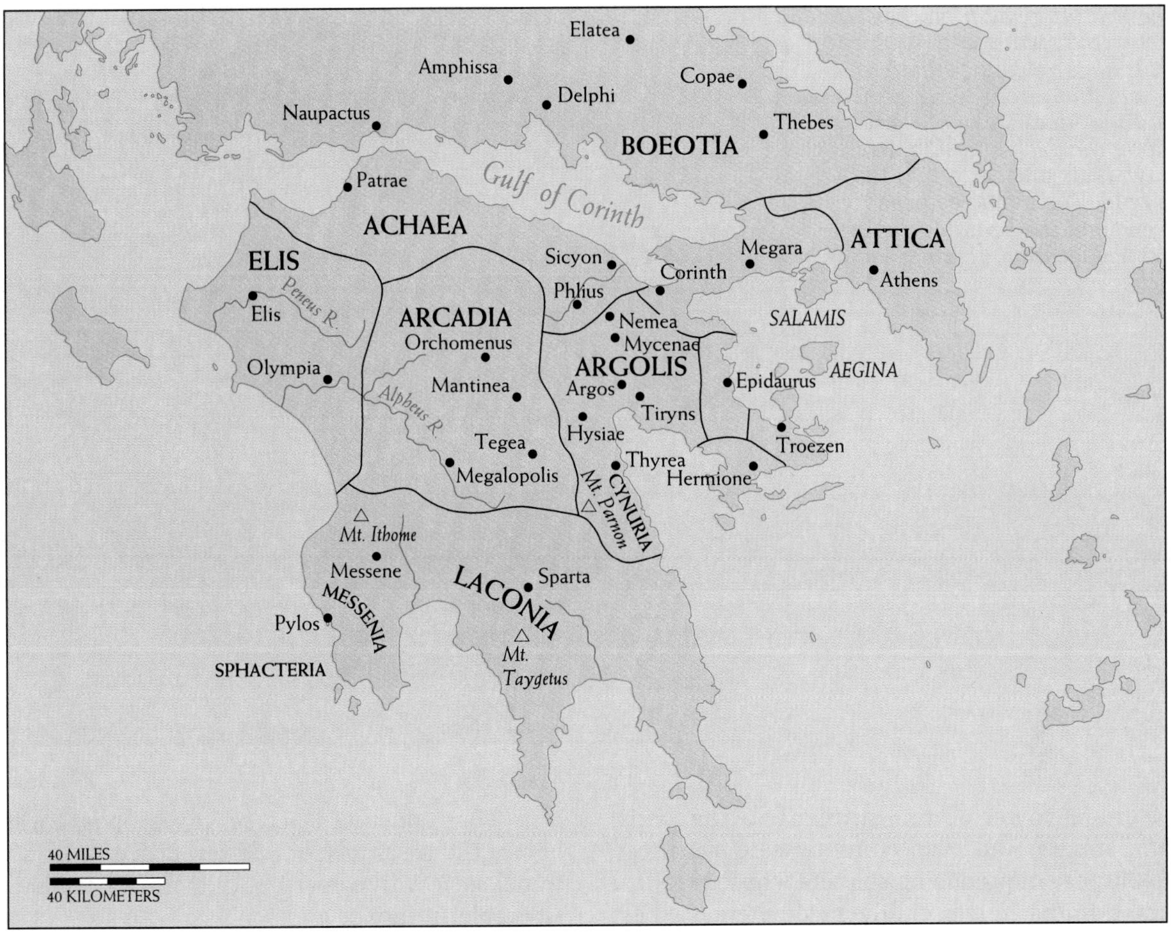

MAP 2–3 THE PELOPONNESUS *Sparta's region, Laconia, was in the Peloponnesus. Nearby states were members of the Peloponnesian League under Sparta's leadership.*

Greeks. Faced with the choice of making drastic changes and sacrifices or abandoning their control of Messenia, the Spartans chose to introduce fundamental reforms that turned their city forever after into a military academy and camp.

SPARTAN SOCIETY The new system that emerged late in the sixth century B.C.E. exerted control over each Spartan from birth, when officials of the state decided which infants were physically fit to survive. At the age of seven the Spartan boy was taken from his mother and turned over to young instructors. He was trained in athletics and the military arts and taught to endure privation, to bear physical pain, and to live off the country, by theft if necessary. At twenty the Spartan youth was enrolled in the army and lived in barracks with his companions until the age of thirty. Marriage was permitted, but a strange sort of marriage it was, for the Spartan male could visit his wife only infrequently and by stealth. At thirty he became a full citizen, an "equal." He took his meals at a public mess in the company of fifteen comrades. His food, a simple diet without much meat or wine, was provided by his own plot of land, worked by Helots. Military service was required until the age of sixty; only then could the Spartan retire to his home and family.

This educational program extended to women, too, although they were not given military training. Female infants were examined for fitness to survive in the same way as males. Girls were given gymnastic training, were permitted greater freedom of movement than among other Greeks, and were equally indoctrinated with the idea of service to Sparta.

The entire system was designed to change the natural feelings of devotion to family and children

A large Spartan plate from the second quarter of the sixth century B.C.E. *It shows traders weighing silphium, a medicinal plant from North Africa, before King Arcesilas of Cyrene, seated on the deck of a ship. Below them, workers pile cargo into the ship's hold. The monkey at the top of the scene and the lizard at the left suggest the location. [Hirmer Verlag, Munich]*

into a more powerful commitment to the *polis*. Privacy, luxury, and even comfort were sacrificed to the purpose of producing soldiers whose physical powers, training, and discipline made them the best in the world. Nothing that might turn the mind away from duty was permitted. The very use of coins was forbidden lest it corrupt the desires of Spartans. Neither family nor money were allowed to interfere with the only ambition permitted to a Spartan male: to win glory and the respect of his peers by bravery in war.

SPARTAN GOVERNMENT The Spartan constitution was mixed, containing elements of monarchy, oligarchy, and democracy. There were two kings, whose power was limited by law and also by the rivalry that usually existed between the two royal houses. The origins and explanation of this unusual dual kingship are unknown, but both kings ruled together in Sparta and exercised equal powers. Their functions were chiefly religious and military. A Spartan army rarely left home without a king in command.

The oligarchic element was represented by a council of elders consisting of twenty-eight men over the age of sixty, elected for life, and the kings. These elders had important judicial functions, sitting as a court in cases involving the kings. They also were consulted before any proposal was put before the assembly of Spartan citizens. In a traditional society like Sparta's, they must have had considerable influence.

The Spartan assembly consisted of all males over thirty. Theoretically they were the final authority, but in practice, debate was carried on by magistrates, elders, and kings alone, and voting was usually by acclamation. Therefore, the assembly's real function was to ratify decisions already taken or to decide between positions favored by the leading figures. In addition, Sparta had a unique institution, the board of *ephors*. This consisted of five men elected annually by the assembly. Originally, boards of *ephors* appear to have been intended to check the power of the kings, but gradually they gained other important functions. They controlled foreign policy, oversaw the generalship of the kings on campaign, presided at the assembly, and guarded against rebellions by the Helots.

The whole system was remarkable both for the way in which it combined participation by the citizenry with significant checks on its power and for its unmatched stability. Most Greeks admired the Spartan state for these qualities and also for its ability to mold citizens so thoroughly to an ideal. Many political philosophers, from Plato to modern times, have based utopian schemes on a version of Sparta's constitution and educational system.

THE PELOPONNESIAN LEAGUE By about 550 B.C.E. the Spartan system was well established, and its limitations were made plain. Suppression of the Helots required all the effort and energy that Sparta had. The Spartans could expand no further, but they could not allow unruly independent neighbors to cause unrest that might inflame the Helots.

When the Spartans defeated Tegea, their northern neighbor, they imposed an unusual peace. Instead of taking away land and subjugating the defeated state, Sparta left the Tegeans their land and their freedom. In exchange they required the Tegeans to follow the Spartan lead in foreign affairs and to supply a fixed number of soldiers to Sparta on demand. This became the model for Spartan relations with the other states in the Peloponnesus. Soon Sparta was the leader of an alliance that included every Peloponnesian state but Argos; modern scholars have named this alliance the Peloponnesian League. It provided the Spartans with the security they needed, and it also made Sparta the most powerful *polis* in Hellenic history. By 500 B.C.E. Sparta and the league had given the Greeks a force capable of facing mighty threats from abroad.

Athens

Athens was slow to come into prominence and to join in the new activities that were changing the more advanced states. The reasons were several. Athens was not situated on the most favored trade routes of the eighth and seventh centuries B.C.E., its large area (about 1,000 square miles) allowed population growth without great pressure, and the unification of the many villages and districts within this territory into a single *polis* was not completed until the seventh century B.C.E. (See Map 2–4.)

MAP 2–4 ATTICA AND VICINITY *Citizens of all towns in Attica were also citizens of Athens.*

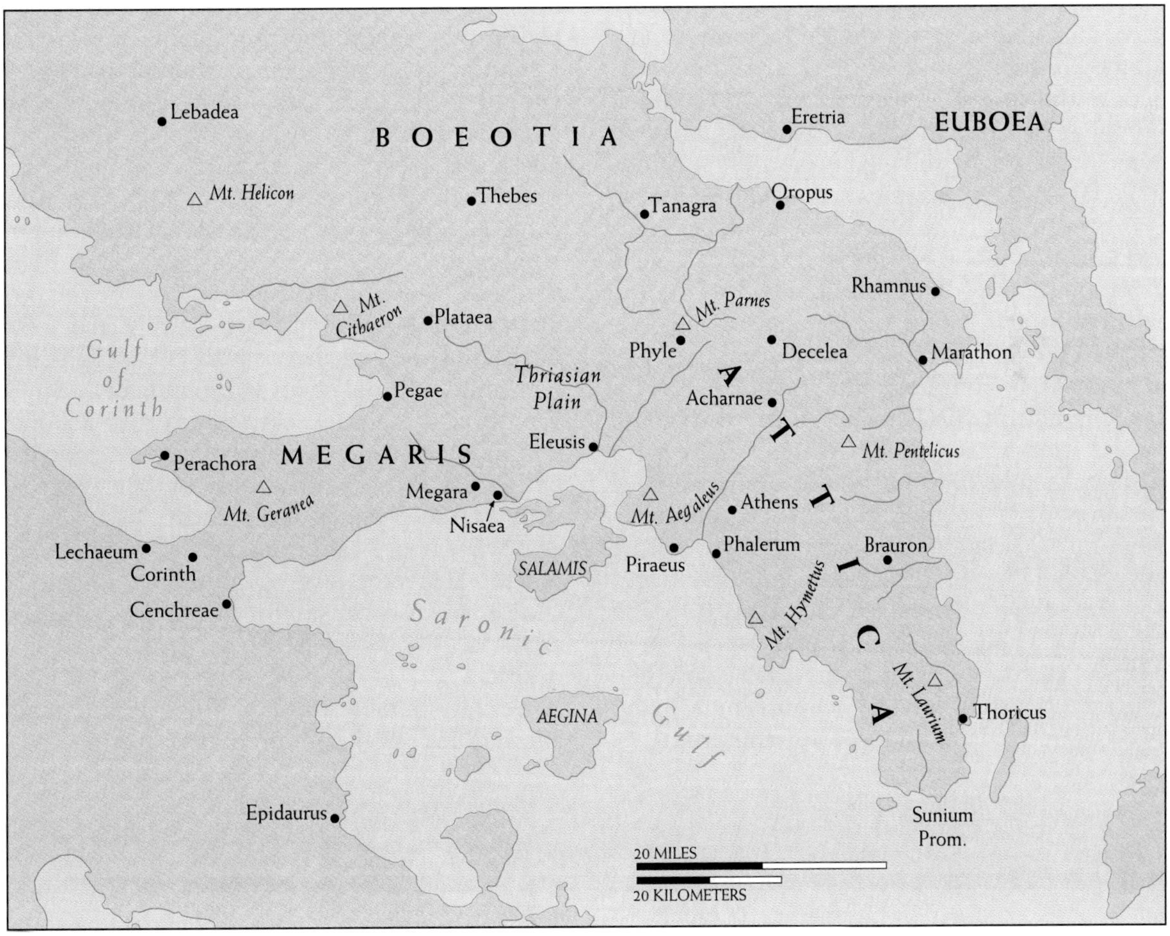

The Greek and Persian Ways of War—Autocracy versus Freedom Under the Law

The Greek historian Herodotus, who wrote his account of the wars between the Greeks and Persians more than half a century after they ended, was very interested in the differences between the ways of the Greeks and other peoples of the world. In the following passage he describes a conversation between Demaratus, an exiled king of Sparta, and Xerxes, the Great King of Persia. Demaratus had come to Xerxes' court after his exile. Xerxes received him kindly and made him a royal adviser.

✦ *On what does Xerxes rely for Persian military success? What is the source of Demaratus's confidence in the Spartans? Does the claim he makes hold for other Greeks as well as the Spartans? How is it possible to reconcile freedom with obedience to the laws?*

'How is it possible that a thousand men, or ten thousand, or fifty thousand, should stand up to an army as big as mine, especially if they were not under a single master, but all perfectly free to do as they pleased? Suppose them to have five thousand men: in that case we should be more than a thousand to one! If, like ours, their troops were subject to the control of a single man, then possibly for fear of him, in spite of the disparity in numbers, they might show some sort of factitious courage, or let themselves be whipped into battle; but, as every man is free to follow his fancy, it is not conceivable that they should do either. Indeed, my own opinion is that even on equal terms the Greeks could hardly face the Persians alone. We, too, have this thing that you were speaking of—I do not say it is common, but it does exist; for instance, amongst the Persians in my bodyguard there are men who would willingly fight with three Greeks together. But you know nothing of such things, or you could not talk such nonsense.'

'My lord,' Demaratus answered, 'I knew before I began that if I spoke the truth you would not like it. But, as you demanded the plain truth and nothing less, I told you how things are with the Spartans. Yet you are well aware that I now feel but little affection for my countrymen, who robbed me of my hereditary power and privileges and made me a fugitive without a home—whereas your father welcomed me at his court and gave me the means of livelihood and somewhere to live. Surely it is unreasonable to reject kindness; any sensible man will cherish it. Personally I do not claim to be able to fight ten men—or two; indeed I should prefer not even to fight with one. But should it be necessary—should there be some great cause to urge me on—then nothing would give me more pleasure than to stand up to one of those men of yours who claim to be a match for three Greeks. So it is with the Spartans; fighting singly, they are as good as any, but fighting together they are the best soldiers in the world. They are free—yes—but not entirely free; for they have a master, and that master is Law, which they fear much more than your subjects fear you. Whatever this master commands they do; and his command never varies: it is never to retreat in battle, however great the odds, but always to stand firm, and to conquer or die. If, my lord, you think that what I have said is nonsense—very well; I am willing henceforward to hold my tongue. This time I spoke because you forced me to speak. In any case, I pray that all may turn out as you desire.'

Xerxes burst out laughing at Demaratus' answer, and goodhumouredly let him go.

From Herodotus, The Histories, *trans. by Aubrey de Selincourt (Harmondsworth: Penguin Books, 1976), pp. 476–477.*

Aristocratic Rule In the seventh century B.C.E. Athens was a typical aristocratic *polis*. Its people were divided into four tribes and into several clans and brotherhoods (*phratries*). The aristocrats held the most land and the best land and dominated religious and political life. There was no written law, and decisions were rendered by powerful nobles on the basis of tradition and, most likely, self-interest. The state was governed by the Areopagus, a council of nobles deriving its name from the hill where it held its sessions. Annually the council elected nine magistrates, called *archons*, who joined the Areopagus after their year in office. Because the *archons* served for only a year, were checked by their colleagues, and looked forward to a lifetime as members of the Areopagus, it is plain that the aristocratic Areopagus, not the *archons*, was the true master of the state.

Pressure for Change In the seventh century B.C.E. the peaceful life of Athens experienced some disturbances, caused in part by quarrels within the nobility and in part by the beginnings of an agrarian crisis. In 632 B.C.E. a nobleman named Cylon attempted a coup to establish himself as tyrant. He was thwarted, but the unrest continued.

In 621 B.C.E. a man named Draco was given special authority to codify and publish laws for the first time. In later years Draco's penalties were thought to be harsh; hence the saying that his laws were written in blood. (We still speak of unusually harsh penalties as *Draconian*.) Draco's work was probably limited to laws concerning homicide and was aimed at ending blood feuds between clans, but it set an important precedent. The publication of laws strengthened the hand of the state against the local power of the nobles.

The root of Athens' troubles was agricultural. Many Athenians worked family farms, from which they obtained most of their living. It appears that they planted wheat, the staple crop, year after year without rotating fields or using enough fertilizer. Shifting to more intensive agricultural techniques and to the planting of trees and vines required capital, leading the less successful farmers to acquire excessive debt. To survive, some farmers had to borrow from wealthy neighbors to get through the year. In return, they promised one sixth of the next year's crop. The deposit of an inscribed stone on the entailed farms marked the arrangement. As their troubles persisted, debtors had to pledge their wives, their children, and themselves as surety for new loans. Inevitably, many Athenians defaulted and were enslaved. Some were even sold abroad. Revolutionary pressures grew among the poor, who began to demand the abolition of debt and a redistribution of the land.

Reforms of Solon In the year 594 B.C.E., as tradition has it, the Athenians elected Solon as the only *archon*, with extraordinary powers to legislate and revise the constitution. Immediately, he attacked the agrarian problem by canceling current debts and forbidding future loans secured by the person of the borrower. He helped bring back many Athenians enslaved abroad and freed those in Athens enslaved for debt. This program was called the "shaking off of burdens." It did not, however, solve the fundamental economic problem, and Solon did not redistribute the land.

In the short run, therefore, Solon did not put an end to the economic crisis, but his other economic actions had profound success in the long run. He forbade the export of wheat and encouraged that of olive oil. This policy had the initial effect of making wheat more available in Attica and encouraging the cultivation of olive oil and wine as cash crops. By the fifth century B.C.E. the cultivation of cash crops had become so profitable that much Athenian land was diverted from grain production, and Athens became dependent on imported wheat. Solon also changed the Athenian standards of weights and measures to conform with those of Corinth and Euboea and the cities of the East. This change also encouraged commerce and turned Athens in the direction that would lead it to great prosperity in the fifth century B.C.E. He also encouraged industry by offering citizenship to foreign artisans, and his success is reflected in the development of the outstanding Attic pottery of the sixth century B.C.E.

Solon also significantly changed the constitution. Citizenship had previously been the privilege of all male adults whose fathers were citizens; to their number he added those immigrants who were tradesmen and merchants. All these Athenian citizens were divided into four classes on the basis of wealth, measured by annual agricultural production. The two highest classes alone could hold the *archonship*, the chief magistracy in Athens, and sit on the Areopagus.

Men of the third class were allowed to serve as *hoplites*. They could be elected to a council of 400

The Rule of the Tyrant Pisistratus

Although tyranny came to have a bad reputation, the first tyrants were often popular because they broke the unchallenged domination of the aristocrats. Their careers were sometimes remembered fondly because their achievements contrasted favorably with those of their successors. So it was with the Athenian view of the reign of their first tyrant, Pisistratus, as suggested by this passage from Aristotle's Athenian Constitution, written two centuries after the events described.

✦ *What were the bases of Pisistratus's power? If he was a tyrant, why is his rule portrayed as a golden age? If it was a golden age, why did the Athenians after his death pass a law against the establishment of tyranny? What was the relation between the tyranny at Athens and the rule of law?*

Such was the origin and such the vicissitudes of the tyranny of Pisistratus. His administration was temperate, as has been said before, and more like constitutional government than a tyranny. Not only was he in every respect humane and mild and ready to forgive those who offended, but, in addition, he advanced money to the poorer people to help them in their labours, so that they might make their living by agriculture. In this he had two objects, first that they might not spend their time in the city but might be scattered over all the face of the country, and secondly that, being moderately well off and occupied with their own business, they might have neither the wish nor the time to attend to public affairs. At the same time his revenues were increased by the thorough cultivation of the country, since he imposed a tax of one tenth on all the produce. For the same reasons he instituted the local justices, and often made expeditions in person into the country to inspect it and to settle disputes

chosen by all the citizens, 100 from each tribe. Solon seems to have meant this council to serve as a check on the Areopagus and to prepare any business that needed to be put before the traditional assembly of all adult male citizens. The *thetes* made up the last class. They voted in the assembly for the *archons* and the council members and on any other business brought before them by the *archons* and the council. They also sat on a new popular court established by Solon. This new court was recognized as a court of appeal, and by the fifth century B.C.E. almost all cases came before it.

PISISTRATUS THE TYRANT Solon's efforts to avoid factional strife failed. Within a few years contention reached such a degree that no *archons* could be chosen. Out of this turmoil emerged the first Athenian tyranny. Pisistratus, a nobleman, faction leader, and military hero, briefly seized power in 560 B.C.E. and again in 556 B.C.E., but each time his support was inadequate and he was driven out. At last, in 546 B.C.E. he came back at the head of a mercenary army from abroad and established a successful tyranny. It lasted beyond his death, in 527 B.C.E., until the expulsion of his son Hippias in 510 B.C.E.

In many respects Pisistratus resembled the other Greek tyrants. His rule rested on the force provided by mercenary soldiers. He engaged in great programs of public works, urban improvement, and religious piety. Temples were built and religious centers expanded and improved. Poets and artists were supported to add cultural luster to the court of the tyrant.

Pisistratus sought to increase the power of the central government at the expense of the nobles. The newly introduced festival of Dionysus and the improved and expanded Great Panathenaic festival helped fix attention on the capital city, as did the new temples and the reconstruction of the *agora* as the center of public life. Circuit judges were sent out into the country to hear cases, weakening the power of the local barons. All this time Pisistratus made no formal change in the Solonian constitu-

between individuals, that they might not come into the city and neglect their farms. It was in one of these progresses that, as the story goes, Pisistratus had his adventure with the man of Hymettus, who was cultivating the spot afterwards known as "Tax-free Farm." He saw a man digging and working at a very stony piece of ground, and being surprised he sent his attendant to ask what he got out of this plot of land. "Aches and pains," said the man; "and that's what Pisistratus ought to have his tenth of." The man spoke without knowing who his questioner was; but Pisistratus was so pleased with his frank speech and his industry that he granted him exemption from all taxes. And so in matters in general he burdened the people as little as possible with his government, but always cultivated peace and kept them in all quietness. Hence the tyranny of Pisistratus was often spoken of proverbially as "the age of gold"; for when his sons succeeded him the government became much harsher. But most important of all in this respect was his popular and kindly disposition. In all things he was accustomed to observe the laws, without giving himself any exceptional privileges. Once he was summoned on a charge of homicide before the Areopagus, and he appeared in person to make his defense; but the prosecutor was afraid to present himself and abandoned the case. For these reasons he held power long, and whenever he was expelled he regained his position easily. The majority alike of the upper class and of the people were in his favour; the former he won by his social intercourse with them, the latter by the assistance which he gave to their private purses, and his nature fitted him to win the hearts of both. Moreover, the laws in reference to tyrants at that time in force at Athens were very mild, especially the one which applies more particularly to the establishment of a tyranny. The law ran as follows, "These are the ancestral statutes of the Athenians; if any persons shall make an attempt to establish a tyranny, or if any person shall join in setting up a tyranny, he shall lose his civic rights, both himself and his whole house."

Aristotle, Athenian Constitution, *16, trans. by Henry G. Dakyns, Vol. 2, ed. by F. R. B. Godolphin, in* The Greek Historians *(New York: Random House, 1942).*

tion. Assembly, councils, and courts met; magistrates and councils were elected. Pisistratus merely saw to it that his supporters dominated these bodies. The intended effect was to blunt the sharp edge of tyranny with the appearance of constitutional government, and it worked. The rule of Pisistratus was remembered as popular and mild. The unintended effect was to give the Athenians more experience in the procedures of self-government and a growing taste for it.

SPARTAN INTERVENTION Pisistratus was succeeded by his oldest son, Hippias, who followed his father's ways at first. In 514 B.C.E., however, his brother Hipparchus was murdered as a result of a private quarrel. Hippias became nervous, suspicious, and harsh. The Alcmaeonids, one of the noble clans that Hippias and Hipparchus had exiled, won favor with the influential oracle at Delphi and used its support to persuade Sparta to attack the Athenian tyranny. Led by their ambitious king, Cleomenes I, the Spartans marched into Athenian territory in 510 B.C.E. and deposed Hippias, who went into exile to the Persian court. The tyranny was over.

The Spartans must have hoped to leave Athens in friendly hands, and indeed Cleomenes' friend Isagoras, a rival of the Alcmaeonids, held the leading position in Athens after the withdrawal of the Spartan army. Isagoras, however, faced competitors, chief among them Clisthenes of the restored Alcmaeonid clan. Clisthenes lost out in the initial political struggle among the noble factions. Isagoras seems then to have tried to restore a version of the pre-Solonian aristocratic state. As part of his plan, he carried through a purification of the citizen lists, removing those whom Solon or Pisistratus had enfranchised and any others thought to have a doubtful claim.

Clisthenes then took an unprecedented action—he turned to the people for political support and won it with a program of great popular appeal. In response, Isagoras called in the Spartans again; Cleomenes arrived and allowed Isagoras to expel Clisthenes and many of his supporters. But the fire

Aristogeiton and Harmodius were Athenian aristocrats slain in 514 B.C.E. after assassinating Hipparchus, brother of the tyrant Hippias. After the overthrow of the Pisistratids in 510 B.C.E., the Athenians erected a statue to honor their memory. This is a Roman copy. [Scala/Art Resource, N.Y.]

of Athenian political consciousness, ignited by Solon and kept alive under Pisistratus, had been fanned into flames by the popular appeal of Clisthenes. The people refused to tolerate an aristocratic restoration and drove out the Spartans and Isagoras with them. Clisthenes and his allies returned, ready to put their program into effect.

CLISTHENES, THE FOUNDER OF DEMOCRACY A central aim of Clisthenes' reforms was to diminish the influence of traditional localities and regions in Athenian life, for these were an important source of power for the nobility and of factions in the state. He immediately restored to citizenship those Athenians who had supported him whom Isagoras had disenfranchised, and he added new citizens to the rolls. In 508 B.C.E. he made the *deme*, the equivalent of a small town in the country or a ward in the city, the basic unit of civic life. The *deme* was a purely political unit that elected its own officers. The distribution of *demes* in each tribe guaranteed that no region would dominate any of them. Because the tribes had common religious activities and fought as regimental units, the new organization also increased devotion to the *polis* and diminished regional divisions and personal loyalty to local barons.

A new council of 500 was invented to replace the Solonian council of 400. The council's main responsibility was to prepare legislation for discussion by the assembly, but it also had important financial duties and received foreign emissaries. Final authority in all things rested with the assembly of all adult male Athenian citizens. Debate in the assembly was free and open; any Athenian could submit legislation, offer amendments, or argue the merits of any question. In practice political leaders did most of the talking. We may imagine that in the early days the council had more authority than it did after the Athenians became more confident in their new self-government.

It is fair to call Clisthenes the father of Athenian democracy. He did not alter the property qualifications of Solon, but his enlargement of the citizen rolls, his diminution of the power of the aristocrats, and his elevation of the role of the assembly, with its effective and manageable council, all give him a firm claim to that title.

As a result of the work of Solon, Pisistratus, and Clisthenes, Athens entered the fifth century B.C.E. well on the way to prosperity and democracy. It was much more centralized and united than it had been, and it was ready to take its place among the major states that would lead the defense of Greece against the dangers that lay ahead.

Life in Archaic Greece

Society

As the "Dark Ages" ended, the features that would distinguish Greek society thereafter took shape. The roles of the artisan and the merchant grew

Key Events in the Early History of Sparta and Athens

ca. 725–710 B.C.E.	First Messenian War
ca. 650–625 B.C.E.	Second Messenian War
632 B.C.E.	Cylon tries to establish a tyranny at Athens
621 B.C.E.	Draco publishes legal code at Athens
594 B.C.E.	Solon institutes reforms at Athens
ca. 560–550 B.C.E.	Sparta defeats Tegea: Beginning of Peloponnesian League
546–527 B.C.E.	Pisistratus reigns as tyrant at Athens (main period)
510 B.C.E.	Hippias, son of Pisistratus, deposed as tyrant of Athens
ca. 508–501 B.C.E.	Clisthenes institutes reforms at Athens

This terra-cotta figurine from Boeotia is a rare ancient Greek representation of the lives of ordinary people. It shows Boeotian women laundering clothes. [Louvre, Paris]

more important as contact with the non-Hellenic world became easier. The great majority of people, however, continued to make their living from the land. Wealthy aristocrats with large estates, powerful households, families, and clans led very different lives from those of the poorer countryfolk and the independent farmers who had smaller and less fertile fields.

FARMERS Ordinary country people rarely leave a written record of their thoughts or activities, and we have no such record from ancient Greece. The poet Hesiod (ca. 700 B.C.E.), however, was certainly no aristocrat. He presented himself as a small farmer, and his *Works and Days* gives some idea of the life of such a farmer. The crops included grain, chiefly barley but also wheat; grapes for the making of wine; olives for food, but mainly for oil, used for cooking, lighting, and washing; green vegetables, especially the bean; and some fruit. Sheep and goats provided milk and cheese. The Homeric heroes had great herds of cattle and ate lots of meat, but by Hesiod's time land fertile enough to provide fodder for cattle was needed to grow grain. He and small farmers like him tasted meat chiefly from sacrificial animals at festivals.

These farmers worked hard to make a living. Although Hesiod had the help of oxen and mules and one or two hired helpers for occasional labor, his life was one of continuous toil. The hardest work came in October, at the start of the rainy season, the time for the first plowing. The plow was light and easily broken, and the work of forcing the iron tip into the earth was backbreaking, even with the help of a team of oxen. For the less fortunate farmer, the cry of the crane that announced the time of year to plow "bites the heart of the man without oxen." Autumn and winter were the time for cutting wood, building wagons, and making tools. Late winter was the time to tend to the vines, May the time to harvest the grain, July to winnow and store it. Only at the height of summer's heat did Hesiod allow for rest, but when September came, it was time to harvest the grapes. No sooner was that task done than the cycle started again. The work went on under the burning sun and in the freezing cold.

Hesiod wrote nothing of pleasure or entertainment, but his poetry displays an excitement and pride that reveals the new hopes of a rural population more dynamic and confident than we know of anywhere else in the ancient world. Less austere farmers than Hesiod gathered at the blacksmith's shop for warmth and companionship in winter, and even he must have taken part in religious rites and festivals that were accompanied by some kind of entertainment. Nonetheless, the lives of yeoman farmers were certainly hard and their pleasures few.

ARISTOCRATS Most aristocrats were rich enough to employ many hired laborers, sometimes sharecroppers and sometimes even slaves, to work their extensive lands. They were therefore able to enjoy leisure for other activities. The center of aristocratic social life was the drinking party, or *symposium*. This activity was not a mere drinking bout, meant to remove inhibitions and produce oblivion. The

This scene on an Attic jar from late in the sixth century B.C.E. shows how olives, one of Athens' most important crops, were harvested. [Courtesy of the Trustees of the British Museum]

Greeks, in fact, almost always mixed their wine with water, and one of the goals of the participants was to drink as much as the others without becoming drunk.

The *symposium* was a carefully organized occasion, with a "king" chosen to set the order of events and to determine that night's mixture of wine and water. Only men took part; they ate and drank as they reclined on couches along the walls of the room. The sessions began with prayers and libations to the gods. Usually there were games, such as dice or *kottabos*, in which wine was flicked from the cups at different targets. Sometimes dancing girls or flute girls offered entertainment. Frequently the aristocratic participants provided their own amusements with songs, poetry, or even philosophical disputes. Characteristically these took the form of contests, with some kind of prize for the winner, for aristocratic values continued to emphasize competition and the need to excel, whatever the arena.

This aspect of aristocratic life appears in the athletic contests that became widespread early in the sixth century. The games included running events; the long jump; the discus and javelin throws; the *pentathlon*, which included all of these; boxing; wrestling; and the chariot race. Only the rich could afford to raise, train, and race horses, and so the chariot race was a special preserve of aristocracy. Wrestling, however, was also especially favored by the nobility, and the *palaestra*, or fields, where they practiced became an important social center for the aristocracy. The contrast between the hard, drab life of the farmers and the leisured and lively one of the aristocrats could hardly have been greater.

Religion

Like most ancient peoples, the Greeks were polytheists, and religion played an important part in their lives. A great part of Greek art and literature was closely connected with religion, as was the life of the *polis* in general.

OLYMPIAN GODS The Greek pantheon consisted of the twelve gods who lived on Mount Olympus. These were

- Zeus, the father of the gods
- Hera, his wife

Zeus's siblings

- Poseidon, his brother, god of the seas and earthquakes
- Hestia, his sister, goddess of the hearth
- Demeter, his sister, goddess of agriculture and marriage

and his children

- Aphrodite, goddess of love and beauty
- Apollo, god of the sun, music, poetry, and prophecy
- Ares, god of war
- Artemis, goddess of the moon and the hunt
- Athena, goddess of wisdom and the arts
- Hephaestus, god of fire and metallurgy
- Hermes, messenger of the gods, connected with commerce and cunning

These gods were seen as behaving very much as mortal humans behaved, with all the foibles of humans, except that they were superhuman in these as well as in their strength and immortality.

Hesiod's Farmer's Almanac

Hesiod was a farmer and poet who lived in a village in Greece about 700 B.C.E. His poem Works and Days *contains wisdom on several subjects, but its final section amounts to a farmer's almanac, taking readers through the year and advising them on just when each activity is demanded. Hesiod painted a picture of a very hard life for Greek farmers, allowing rest only in the passage that follows.*

✦ *What might be Hesiod's purposes in writing this poem? What can be learned from this passage about the character of Greek farming? How did it differ from other modes of agriculture? What are the major virtues Hesiod associates with farming? How do they compare with the virtues celebrated by Homer?*

But when House-on-Back, the snail, crawls from the ground up
the plants, escaping the Pleiades, it's no longer time for vine-digging;
time rather to put an edge to your sickles, and rout out your helpers.
Keep away from sitting in the shade or lying in bed till the sun's up
in the time of the harvest, when the sunshine scorches your skin dry.
This is the season to push your work and bring home your harvest;
get up with the first light so you'll have enough to live on.
Dawn takes away from work a third part of the work's measure.
Dawn sets a man well along on his journey, in his work also,
dawn, who when she shows, has numerous people going their ways; dawn who puts the yoke upon many oxen.
But when the artichoke is in flower, and the clamorous cricket
sitting in his tree lets go his vociferous singing, that issues
from the beating of his wings, in the exhausting season of summer,
then is when goats are at their fattest, when the wine tastes best,
women are most lascivious, but the men's strength fails them
most, for the star Seirios shrivels them, knees and heads alike,
and the skin is all dried out in the heat; then, at that season,
one might have the shadow under the rock, and the wine of Biblis,
a curd cake, and all the milk that the goats can give you,
the meat of a heifer, bred in the woods, who has never borne a calf,
and of baby kids also. Then, too, one can sit in the shadow
and drink the bright-shining wine, his heart satiated with eating
and face turned in the direction where Zephyros blows briskly,
make three libations of water from a spring that keeps running forever
and has no mud in it; and pour wine for the fourth libation.

Hesiod, Works and Days, *trans. by Richmond Lattimore (Ann Arbor: University of Michigan Press, 1959), pp. 87, 89. Reprinted by permission.*

On the other hand, Zeus, at least, was seen as a source of human justice, and even the Olympians were understood to be subordinate to the Fates. Each *polis* had one of the Olympians as its guardian deity and worshiped that god in its own special way, but all the gods were Panhellenic. In the eighth and seventh centuries B.C.E. common shrines were established at Olympia for the worship of Zeus, at

Delphi for Apollo, at the Isthmus of Corinth for Poseidon, and at Nemea once again for Zeus. Each held athletic contests in honor of its deity, to which all Greeks were invited and for which a sacred truce was declared.

IMMORTALITY AND MORALITY Besides the Olympians, the Greeks also worshiped countless lesser deities connected with local shrines. They even worshiped human heroes, real or legendary, who had accomplished great deeds and had earned immortality and divine status. The worship of these deities was not a very emotional experience. It was a matter of offering prayer, libations, and gifts in return for protection and favors from the god during the lifetime of the worshiper. There was no hope of immortality for the average human, and these devotions involved little moral teaching.

Most Greeks seem to have held to the commonsense notion that justice lay in paying one's debts. They thought that civic virtue consisted of worshiping the state deities in the traditional way, performing required public services, and fighting in defense of the state. To them, private morality meant to do good to one's friends and harm to one's enemies.

This Attic cup from the fifth century B.C.E. shows the two great poets from the island of Lesbos, Sappho (right) and Alcaeus. [Hirmer Verlag, Munich]

THE CULT OF DELPHIAN APOLLO In the sixth century B.C.E. the influence of the cult of Apollo at Delphi and of his oracle there became very great. The oracle was the most important of several that helped satisfy human craving for a clue to the future. The priests of Apollo preached moderation; their advice was exemplified in the two famous sayings identified with Apollo: "Know thyself" and "Nothing in excess." Humans needed self-control (*sophrosynē*). Its opposite was arrogance (*hubris*), brought on by excessive wealth or good fortune. Hubris led to moral blindness and finally to divine vengeance. This theme of moderation and the dire consequences of its absence was central to Greek popular morality and appears frequently in Greek literature.

THE CULT OF DIONYSUS AND THE ORPHIC CULT The somewhat cold religion of the Olympian gods and of the cult of Apollo did little to assuage human fears or satisfy human hopes and passions. For these needs the Greeks turned to other deities and rites. Of these the most popular was Dionysus, a god of nature and fertility, of the grape vine and drunkenness and sexual abandon. In some of his rites the god was followed by *maenads*, female devotees who cavorted by night, ate raw flesh, and were reputed to tear to pieces any creature they came across.

The Orphic cult, named after its supposed founder, the mythical poet Orpheus, provided its followers with more hope than did the worship of the twelve Olympians. Cult followers are thought to have refused to kill animals or eat their flesh and to have believed in the transmigration of souls, which offered the prospect of some form of life after death.

Poetry

The great changes sweeping through the Greek world were also reflected in the poetry of the sixth century B.C.E. The lyric style—poetry meant to be

Sappho the Poet

Sappho was born at Mytilene on the island of Lesbos about 612 B.C.E. After a period of exile in Sicily, she returned and became a central figure in a thiastos, *a company of revelers who sang and danced in honor of a god. Sappho's group was made up of young girls who gave honor to Aphrodite and the Muses, the goddesses of the fine arts. They lived together intimately and affectionately. Sappho wrote poems to and about them and to celebrate their marriages. Her poems were highly admired in antiquity, winning her a position among the greatest lyric poets, but they are preserved only in fragments. The following selection illustrates one type of her poetry.*

✦ *How does the mood and style of the poem compare with the excerpts from Homer and Hesiod in this chapter? Since we have little reliable information about Sappho outside the fragments of her poems, what does the selection tell us about her life and activities?*

Fragment 94

'and honestly I want to die'
—so sobbing, many times, she left me
and she said this [to me]
'My god! what awful things are happening to us:
Sappho, I swear I am leaving you against my will.'
And I replied to her in these words:
'Go with a light heart, and with memories
of me, for you know how we cherished you.
And if not, then I want to
remind you [ ]
[ ] and we had good times
For ma[ny garland]s of violets
and roses [ ] together
and [ ] you put on beside me
And many garlands
woven from flowers about your soft neck
[ ] fashioned
And with m[uch] myrrh
from rich flowers [ ]
and royal you rubbed your skin
And on soft beds
tender [ ]
you would satisfy desire [ ]
And there was no [ ] nothing
holy nor [ ]
from which [we] kept away
No grove [ ]
[ ] sound
[ ]'

Sappho, Fragment 94, trans. by Ewen Bowie, in J. Boardman, J. Griffin, and O. Murray, The Oxford History of the Classical World *(Oxford and New York: Oxford University Press, n.d.), p. 104.*

sung, either by a chorus or by one person—predominated. Sappho of Lesbos, Anacreon of Teos, and Simonides of Cos composed personal poetry, often relating the pleasure and agony of love. Alcaeus of Mytilene, an aristocrat driven from his city by a tyrant, wrote bitter invective.

Perhaps the most interesting poet of the century from a political point of view was Theognis of Megara. He was an aristocrat who lived through a tyranny, an unusually chaotic and violent democracy, and an oligarchy that restored order but ended the rule of the old aristocracy. Theognis was the spokesperson for the old, defeated aristocracy of birth. He divided everyone into two classes, the noble and the base; the former were the good, the latter bad. Those nobly born must associate only with others like themselves if they were to preserve their virtue; if they mingled with the base, they became base. Those born base, on the other hand, could never become noble. Only nobles could aspire

Theognis of Megara Gives Advice to a Young Aristocrat

Theognis was born about 580 B.C.E. and lived to see his native city Megara torn by social upheaval and civil war. His poems present the political and ethical ideas of the Greek aristocracy.

- ✦ *What does Theognis claim is the source of virtue among human beings?*
- ✦ *What role does he give to education in improving the character of people?*
- ✦ *What does he mean by "judgment"?*
- ✦ *What are the political and constitutional implications of his way of thinking?*

Do not consort with bad men, but always hold to the good. Eat and drink with them. You will learn good from good men, but if you mingle with the bad you will lose such wisdom as you already have. Therefore consort with the good and one day you will say that I give good advice to my friends.

We seek thoroughbred rams asses and horses, Cyrnus, and a man wants offspring of good breeding. But in marriage a good man does not decline to marry the bad daughter of a bad father, if he gives him much wealth. Nor does the wife of a bad man refuse to be his bedfellow if he be rich, preferring wealth to goodness. For they value possessions and a good man marries a woman of bad stock and the bad a woman of good. Wealth mixes the breed. So do not wonder, son of Polypaus, that the race of your citizens is obscured since bad things are mixed with good.

It is easier to beget and rear a man than to put good sense into him. No one has ever discovered a way to make a fool wise or a bad man good. If God had given the sons of Asclepius the knowledge to heal the evil nature and mischievous mind of man, great and frequent would be their pay. If thought could be made and put into a man, the son of a good man would never become bad, since he would obey good counsel. But you will never make the bad man good by teaching.

The best thing the gods give to men, Cyrnus, is judgment; judgment contains the ends of everything. O happy is the man who has it in his mind; it is much greater than destructive insolence and grievous satiety. There are no evils among mortals worse than these—for every evil, Cyrnus, comes out of them.

Trans. by Donald Kagan in *Sources in Greek Political Thought*, ed. by D. Kagan (New York: Free Press, 1965), pp. 39–40.

to virtue, and only nobles possessed the critical moral and intellectual qualities, respect or honor and judgment. These qualities could not be taught; they were innate. Even so they had to be carefully guarded against corruption by wealth or by mingling with the base. Intermarriage between the noble and the base was especially condemned. These were the ideas of the unreconstructed nobility, whose power had been destroyed or reduced in most Greek states by this time. These ideas remained alive in aristocratic hearts throughout the next century and greatly influenced later thinkers, Plato among them.

The Persian Wars

The Greeks' period of fortunate isolation and freedom ended in the sixth century B.C.E. They had established colonies along most of the coast of Asia Minor from as early as the eleventh century B.C.E. The colonies maintained friendly relations with the mainland but developed a flourishing economic and cultural life independent of their mother cities and of their eastern neighbors. In the middle of the sixth century B.C.E., however, these Greek cities of Asia Minor came under the control of Lydia and its king, Croesus (ca. 560–546 B.C.E.). Lydian rule

The Rise of Persia

559–530 B.C.E.	Reign of Cyrus the Great
546 B.C.E.	Persians conquer Lydia
530–522 B.C.E.	Reign of Cambyses
522–521 B.C.E.	Civil war in Persia
521–485 B.C.E.	Reign of Darius
485–465 B.C.E.	Reign of Xerxes

seems not to have been very harsh, but the Persian conquest of Lydia in 546 B.C.E. brought a less pleasant subjugation.

The Persian Empire

The Persian Empire had been created in a single generation by Cyrus the Great, the founder of the Achaemenid dynasty. In 559 B.C.E. he came to the throne of Persia, then a small kingdom well to the east of the lower Mesopotamian Valley. He unified Persia under his rule; made an alliance with Babylonia; and led a successful rebellion toward the north against the Medes, the overlords of Persia. (See Map 2–5.) In succeeding years he expanded his empire in all directions, in the process defeating Croesus and occupying Lydia. Most of the Greek cities of Asia Minor sided with Croesus and resisted the Persians. By about 540 B.C.E., however, they had all been subdued. The western part of Asia Minor was divided into three provinces, each under its own *satrap*, or governor.

The Ionian Rebellion

The Ionian Greeks (those living on the central part of the west coast of Asia Minor and nearby islands) had been moving toward democracy and were not pleased to find themselves under the monarchical

MAP 2–5 THE PERSIAN EMPIRE *The empire created by Cyrus had reached its fullest extent under Darius when Persia attacked Greece in 490 B.C.E. It extended from India to the Aegean and even into Europe. It included the lands formerly ruled by Egyptians, Hittites, Babylonians, and Assyrians.*

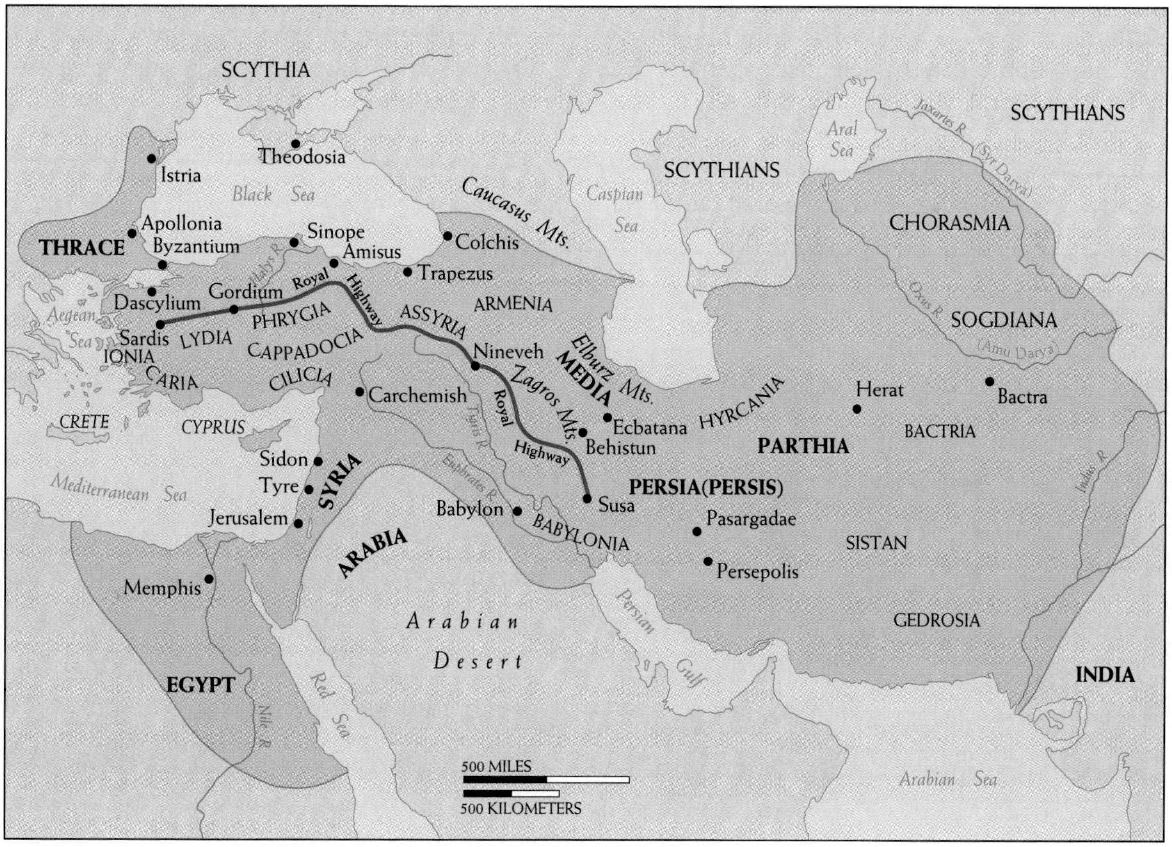

rule of Persia. That rule, however, was not overly burdensome at first. The Persians required their subjects to pay tribute and to serve in the Persian army. They ruled the Greek cities through local individuals, who governed their cities as "tyrants." Most of the "tyrants," however, were not harsh, the Persian tribute was not excessive, and the Greeks enjoyed general prosperity. Neither the death of Cyrus fighting on a distant frontier in 530 B.C.E. nor the suicide of his successor Cambyses, nor the civil war that followed it in 522–521 B.C.E. produced any disturbance in the Greek cities. When Darius emerged as Great King (as the Persian rulers styled themselves) in 521 B.C.E., he found Ionia perfectly obedient.

The private troubles of the ambitious tyrant of Miletus, Aristagoras, ended this calm. He had urged a Persian expedition against the island of Naxos; when it failed, he feared the consequences and organized the Ionian rebellion of 499 B.C.E. To gain support, he overthrew the tyrannies and proclaimed democratic constitutions. Then he turned to the mainland states for help, petitioning first Sparta, the most powerful Greek state. The Spartans, however, would have none of Aristagoras's promises of easy victory and great wealth. They had no close ties with the Ionians and no national interest in the region. Furthermore, they were terrified at the thought of leaving their homeland undefended against the Helots for a long time while their army was far off.

Aristagoras next sought help from the Athenians, who were related to the Ionians and had close ties of religion and tradition with them. Besides, Hippias, the deposed tyrant of Athens, was an honored guest at the court of Darius, and the Great King had already made it plain that he favored the tyrant's restoration. The Persians, moreover, controlled both sides of the Hellespont, the route to the grain fields beyond the Black Sea that were increasingly vital to Athens. Perhaps some Athenians already feared that a Persian attempt to conquer the Greek mainland was only a matter of time. The Athenian assembly agreed to send a fleet of twenty ships to help the rebels. The Athenian expedition was strengthened by five ships from Eretria in Euboea, which participated out of gratitude for past favors.

In 498 B.C.E. the Athenians and their allies made a surprise attack on Sardis, the old capital of Lydia and now the seat of the *satrap*, and burned it. This action caused the revolt to spread throughout the Greek cities of Asia Minor outside Ionia, but the Ionians could not follow it up. The Athenians withdrew and took no further part. Gradually the Persians reimposed their will. In 495 B.C.E. they defeated the Ionian fleet at Lade, and in the next year they wiped out Miletus. They killed many of the Miletan men, transported others to the Persian Gulf, and enslaved the women and children. The Ionian rebellion was over.

Persian nobles pay homage to King Darius in this relief from the treasury at the Persian capital of Persepolis. Darius is seated on the throne; his son and successor Xerxes stands behind him. Darius and Xerxes are carved in larger scale to indicate their royal status. [Courtesy of the Oriental Institute, the University of Chicago]

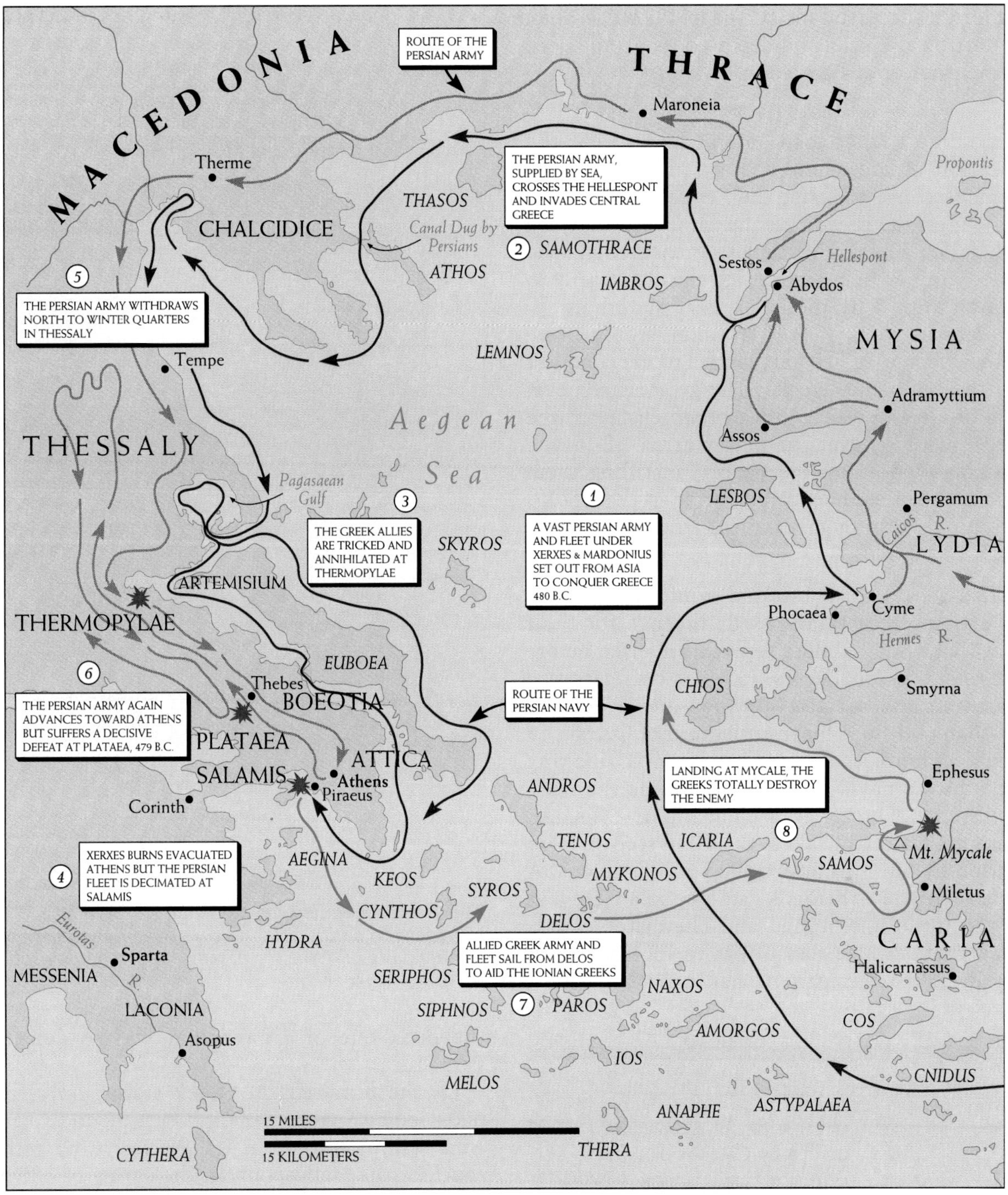

MAP 2–6 THE PERSIAN INVASION OF GREECE *This map traces the route taken by the Persian king Xerxes in his invasion of Greece in 480 B.C.E. The gray arrows show movements of Xerxes' army, the purple arrows show movements of his navy, and the green arrows show movements of the Greek army and navy.*

The War in Greece

In 490 B.C.E. the Persians launched an expedition directly across the Aegean to punish Eretria and Athens, to restore Hippias, and to gain control of the Aegean Sea. (See Map 2–6.) They landed their infantry and cavalry forces first at Naxos, destroying it for its successful resistance in 499 B.C.E. Then they destroyed Eretria and deported its people deep into the interior of Persia.

MARATHON Rather than submit and accept the restoration of the hated tyranny of Hippias, the Athenians chose to resist the Persian forces bearing down on them and risk the same fate that had just befallen Eretria. Miltiades, an Athenian who had fled from Persian service, led the city's army to a confrontation with the Persians at Marathon.

A Persian victory at Marathon would have destroyed Athenian freedom and led to the conquest of all the mainland Greeks. The greatest achievements of Greek culture, most of which lay in the future, would never have occurred. But the Athenians won a decisive victory, instilling them with a sense of confidence and pride in their *polis*, their unique form of government, and themselves.

THE GREAT INVASION Internal troubles prevented the Persians from taking swift revenge for their loss at Marathon. Almost ten years elapsed before Darius's successor, Xerxes, in 481 B.C.E., gathered an army of at least 150,000 men and a navy of more than 600 ships for the conquest of Greece. In Athens, Themistocles, who favored making Athens into a naval power, had become the leading politician. During his archonship in 493 B.C.E., Athens had already taken the first step in that direction by building a fortified port at Piraeus. A decade later the Athenians came upon a rich vein of silver in the state mines, and Themistocles persuaded them to use the profits to increase their fleet. By 480 B.C.E. Athens had over 200 ships, the backbone of a navy that was to defeat the Persians.

This bronze helmet was dedicated to Zeus by Miltiades to commemorate the Athenian victory over the Persians in 490 B.C.E. [Deutsche Archäologisches Institut, Athens]

The Greek Wars Against Persia

ca. 560–546 B.C.E.	Greek cities of Asia Minor conquered by Croesus of Lydia
546 B.C.E.	Cyrus of Persia conquers Lydia and gains control of Greek cities
499–494 B.C.E.	Greek cities rebel (Ionian rebellion)
490 B.C.E.	Battle of Marathon
480–479 B.C.E.	Xeres' invasion of Greece
480 B.C.E.	Battles of Thermopylae, Artemisium, and Salamis
479 B.C.E.	Battles of Plataea and Mycale

Of the hundreds of Greek states, only thirty-one—led by Sparta, Athens, Corinth, and Aegina—were willing to fight as the Persian army gathered south of the Hellespont. In the spring of 480 B.C.E. Xerxes launched his invasion. The Persian strategy was to march into Greece, destroy Athens, defeat the Greek army, and add the Greeks to the number of Persian subjects. The huge Persian army needed to keep in touch with the fleet for supplies. If the Greeks could defeat the Persian navy, the army could not remain in Greece long. Themistocles knew that the Aegean was subject to sudden devastating storms. His strategy was to delay the

Persian army and then to bring on the kind of naval battle he might hope to win.

The Greek League, founded specifically to resist this Persian invasion, met at Corinth as the Persians were ready to cross the Hellespont. They chose Sparta as leader on land and sea and first confronted the Persians at Thermopylae, the "hot gates", on land and off Artemisium at sea. The opening between the mountains and the sea at Thermopylae was so narrow that it might be held by a smaller army against a much larger one. The Spartans sent their king, Leonidas, with 300 of their own citizens and enough allies to make a total of about 9,000.

Severe storms wrecked many Persian ships while the Greek fleet waited safely in a protected harbor. Then Xerxes attacked Thermopylae, and for two days the Greeks butchered his best troops without serious loss to themselves. On the third day, however, a traitor showed the Persians a mountain trail that permitted them to come on the Greeks from behind. Many allies escaped, but Leonidas and his 300 Spartans all died fighting. At about the same time the Greek and Persian fleets fought an indecisive battle at Artemisium. The fall of Thermopylae, however, forced the Greek navy to withdraw.

After Thermopylae, the Persian army moved into Attica and burned Athens. If an inscription discovered in 1959 is authentic (see the document on page 68), Themistocles had foreseen this possibility before Thermopylae, and the Athenians had begun to evacuate their homeland before they sent their fleet north to fight at Artemisium.

Defeating the Persians The fate of Greece was decided in a sea battle in the narrow waters to the east of the island of Salamis to which the Greek fleet withdrew after the battle at Artemisium. The Peloponnesians were reluctant to confront the Persian fleet at this spot, but Themistocles persuaded them to stay by threatening to remove all the Athenians from Greece and settle them anew in Italy. The Spartans knew that they and the other Greeks could not hope to win without the aid of the Athenians. Because the Greek ships were fewer, slower, and less maneuverable than those of the Persians, the Greeks put soldiers on their ships and relied chiefly on hand-to-hand combat. In the ensuing battle the Persians lost more than half their ships and retreated to Asia with a good part of their army, but the danger was not over yet.

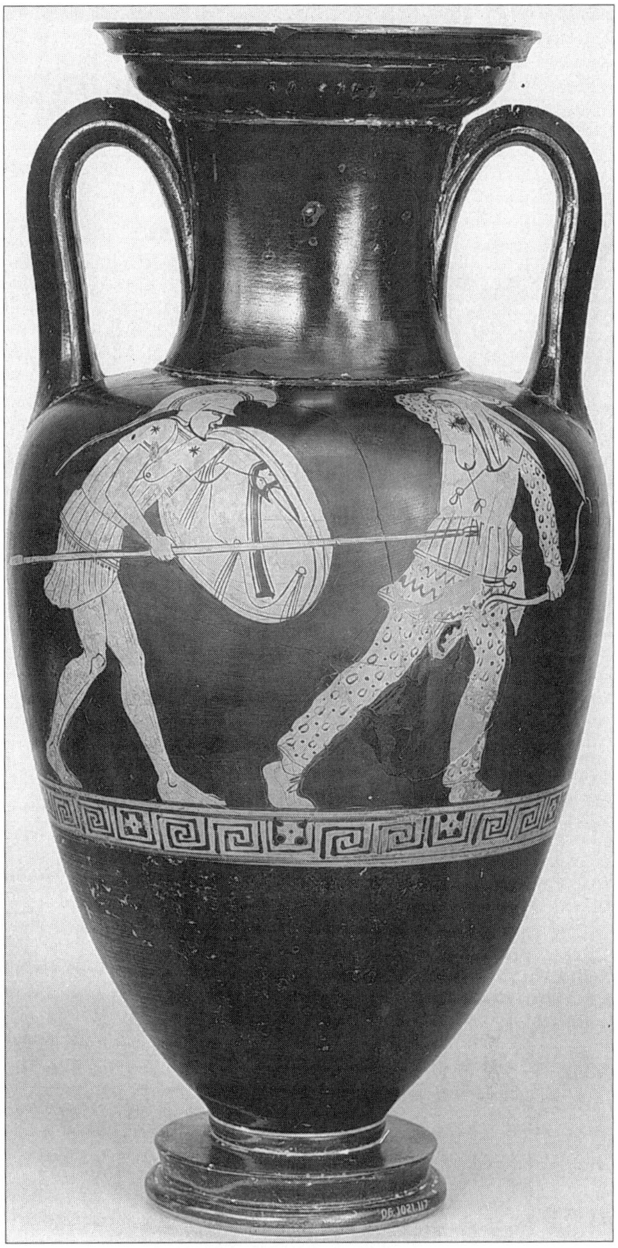

A Greek hoplite *attacks a Persian soldier. The contrast between the Greek's metal body armor, large shield, and long spear and the Persian's cloth and leather garments indicates one reason the Greeks won. This Attic vase was found on Rhodes and dates from ca. 475 B.C.E. [The Metropolitan Museum of Art, Rogers Fund, 1906 Acc. # 06.1021.117]*

The Persian general Mardonius spent the winter in central Greece, and in the spring he unsuccessfully tried to win the Athenians away from the Greek League. The Spartan regent, Pausanias, then led the largest Greek army up to that time to confront Mardonius in Boeotia. At Plataea, in the

The Athenian Assembly Passes Themistocles' Emergency Decree

The following is a translation of a portion of the Themistocles decree. It is included in an inscription from the third century B.C.E. *that purports to be an Athenian decree passed in 480* B.C.E. *Some scholars are uncertain of its authenticity, but many believe it reflects a reliable tradition.*

✦ *If this decree is authentic, where should it fit in the chronology of the Persian invasion? Who are the men who have been exiled for ten years? Why are they and those who have lost their citizen rights being recalled? Why are some ships being sent to Artemision [Artemisium] in Euboia [Euboea] and others to Salamis? How does this document help explain the strategies of the Greeks and Persians?*

The Gods

Resolved by the Council and the People
Themistocles, son of Neokles, of Phrearroi, made the motion:
To entrust the city to Athena the Mistress of Athens and to all the other Gods to guard and defend from the Barbarian for the sake of the land. The Athenians themselves and the foreigners who live in Athens are to send their children and women to safety to Troizen, their protector being Pittheus, the founding hero of the land. They are to send the old men and their movable possessions to safety on Salamis. The treasurers and priestesses are to remain on the acropolis guarding the property of the gods.
All the other Athenians and foreigners of military age are to embark on the 200 ships that are ready and defend against the Barbarian for the sake of their own freedom and that of the rest of the Greeks along with the Lakedaimonians, the Korinthians, the Aiginetans, and all others who wish to share the danger. . . .

When the ships have been manned, with 100 of them they are to meet the enemy at Artemision in Euboia, and with the other 100 they are to lie off Salamis and the coast of Attica and keep guard over the land. In order that all Athenians may be united in their defense against the Barbarian those who have been sent into exile for ten years are to go to Salamis and to stay there until the People come to some decision about them, while those who have been deprived of citizen rights are to have their rights restored. . . .

Trans. by M. H. Jameson, in "Waiting for the Barbarian," Greece and Rome, *Second Series, Vol. 8 (Oxford: Clarendon Press, 1961), pp. 5–18.*

summer of 479 B.C.E., the Persians suffered a decisive defeat. Mardonius died in battle and his army fled toward home.

Meanwhile the Ionian Greeks urged King Leotychidas, the Spartan commander of the fleet, to fight the Persian fleet at Samos. At Mycale, on the coast nearby, Leotychidas destroyed the Persian camp and its fleet offshore. The Persians fled the Aegean and Ionia. For the moment, at least, the Persian threat was gone.

✦

Hellenic civilization, that unique cultural experience at the root of Western civilization, has powerfully influenced the peoples of the modern world.

It was itself influenced by the great Bronze Age civilization of Crete called Minoan, and emerged from the collapse of the Bronze Age civilization on the Greek mainland called Mycenaean. These earlier Aegean civilizations more closely resembled other early civilizations in Egypt, Mesopotamia, Palestine–Syria, and elsewhere than the Hellenic civilization that sprang from them. They had highly developed cities; a system of writing; strong, centralized monarchical systems of government with tightly organized, large bureaucracies; hierarchical social systems; professional standing armies; and a regular system of taxation supporting all this. To a greater or lesser degree, these early civilizations tended toward cultural stability—changing little over time—and uniformity—all sharing many structural features. The striking thing about the emergence of Hellenic civilization is its sharp departure from this pattern.

The collapse of the Mycenaean world produced a harsh material and cultural decline for the Greeks. Cities were swept away and replaced by small farm villages. Trade all but ended, and communication among the Greeks themselves and between them and other peoples was sharply curtailed. The art of writing was lost for more than three centuries. During this "Dark Age," the Greeks—poor, small in number, isolated, and illiterate—were ignored by the rest of the world and left alone to develop their own society and the matrix of Hellenic civilization.

During the three and a half centuries from about 1100 to 750 B.C.E. the Greeks set the foundations for their great achievements. The crucial unit in the new Greek way of life was the polis, *the Hellenic city-state. There were hundreds of them, and each evoked a kind of loyalty and attachment by its citizens that made the idea of dissolving one's own polis into a larger unit unthinkable. The result was a dynamic, many-faceted, competitive, sometimes chaotic world in which rivalry for excellence and victory had the highest value. This agonistic, or competitive, quality marks Greek life throughout its history. Its negative aspect was constant warfare among the states. Its positive side was an extraordinary achievement in literature and art; competition, sometimes formal and organized, spurred on poets and artists.*

Kings had been swept away with the Mycenaean world and the poleis *were republics. Since the Greeks were so poor, the difference in wealth among them was relatively small. Therefore, class distinctions were less marked and important than in other civilizations. The introduction of a new mode of fighting, the* hoplite *phalanx, had further leveling effects, for it placed the safety of the state in the hands of the average farmer. Armies were made up of citizen—soldiers, who were not paid and who returned to their farms after a campaign. As a result, political control was shared with a relatively large portion of the people, and participation in political life was highly valued. There was no bureaucracy, for there were no kings and not much economic surplus to support bureaucrats. Most states imposed no regular taxation. There was no separate caste of priests and little concern with any life after death. In this varied, dynamic, secular, and remarkably free context there arose speculative natural philosophy based on observation and reason, the root of modern natural science and philosophy.*

Contact with the rest of the world increased trade and wealth and brought in valuable new information and ideas. Greek art was powerfully shaped by Egyptian and Near Eastern models that were always adapted and changed rather than copied. Changes often produced social and economic strain, leading to the overthrow of traditional aristocratic regimes by tyrants. But monarchic rule was anathema to the Greeks, and these regimes were temporary. In Athens the destruction of the tyranny brought the world's first democracy. Sparta, on the other hand, developed a uniquely stable government that avoided tyranny and impressed the other Greeks.

The Greeks' time of independent development, untroubled by external forces, ended in the sixth century, when Persia's powerful Achaemenid dynasty conquered the Greek cities of Asia Minor. When the Persian kings tried to conquer the Greek mainland, however, the leading states managed to put their quarrels aside and unite against the common enemy. Their determination to preserve their freedom carried them to victory over tremendous odds.

Review Questions

1. Describe the Minoan civilization of Crete. How did the later Bronze Age Mycenaean civilization differ from the Minoan civilization in political organization, art motifs, and military posture?

2. What are the most important historical sources for the Minoan and Mycenaean civilizations? Most particularly, what is Linear B and what problems does it raise for the reconstruction of Bronze Age history? How valuable are the Homeric epics as sources of early Greek history?
3. Define the concept of *polis*. What role did geography play in its development and why did the Greeks consider it a unique and valuable institution?
4. Compare the fundamental political, social, and economic institutions of Athens and Sparta about 500 B.C.E. Why did Sparta develop its unique form of government?
5. What were the main stages in the transformation of Athens from an aristocratic state to a democracy between 600 and 500 B.C.E.? In what ways did Draco, Solon, Pisistratus, and Clisthenes each contribute to the process?
6. Why did the Greeks and Persians go to war in 490 and 480 B.C.E.? What benefit could the Persians have derived from conquering Greece? Why were the Greeks able to defeat the Persians and how did they benefit from the victory?

Suggested Readings

A. ANDREWES, *Greek Tyrants* (1963). A clear and concise account of tyranny in early Greece.

J. BOARDMAN, *The Greeks Overseas* (1964). A study of the relations between the Greeks and other peoples.

A. R. BURN, *The Lyric Age of Greece* (1960). A discussion of early Greece that uses the evidence of poetry and archaeology to fill out the sparse historical record.

A. R. BURN, *Persia and the Greeks*, 2nd ed. (1984). A thorough narrative and analysis of the conflict between the Persians and the Greeks down to 479 B.C.E.

J. CHADWICK, *The Mycenaean World* (1976). A readable account by an author who helped decipher Mycenaean writing.

E. R. DODDS, *The Greeks and the Irrational* (1955). An excellent account of the role of the supernatural in Greek life and thought.

R. DREWS, *The Coming of the Greeks* (1988). A fine study of the arrival of the Greeks as part of the movement of Indo-European peoples.

V. EHRENBERG, *The Greek State* (1964). A good handbook of constitutional history.

V. EHRENBERG, *From Solon to Socrates* (1968). An interpretive history that makes good use of Greek literature to illuminate politics.

J. V. A. FINE, *The Ancient Greeks* (1983). An excellent survey that discusses historical problems and the evidence that gives rise to them.

M. I. FINLEY, *World of Odysseus*, rev. ed. (1965). A fascinating attempt to reconstruct Homeric society.

W. G. FORREST, *The Emergence of Greek Democracy* (1966). A lively interpretation of Greek social and political developments in the archaic period.

W. G. FORREST, *A History of Sparta, 950–192 B.C.E.* (1968). A brief but shrewd account.

P. GREEN, *Xerxes at Salamis* (1970). A lively and stimulating history of the Persian wars.

V. D. HANSON, *The Western Way of War* (1989). A brilliant and lively discussion of the rise and character of the hoplite phalanx and its influence on Greek society.

V. D. HANSON, *The Other Greeks* (1995). A revolutionary account of the invention of the family farm by the Greeks and the central role of agrarianism in shaping the Greek city-state.

C. HIGNETT, *A History of the Athenian Constitution* (1952). A scholarly account, somewhat too skeptical of the ancient sources.

C. HIGNETT, *Xerxes' Invasion of Greece* (1963). A valuable account, but too critical of all sources other than Herodotus.

J. M. HURWIT, *The Art and Culture of Early Greece* (1985). A fascinating study of the art of early Greece in its literary and cultural context.

S. ISAGER AND J. E. SKYDSGAARD, *Ancient Greek Agriculture: An Introduction* (1993). A new study of a fundamental subject.

D. KAGAN, *The Great Dialogue: A History of Greek Political Thought from Homer to Polybius* (1965). A discussion of the relationship between the Greek historical experience and political theory.

H. D. F. KITTO, *The Greeks* (1951). A personal and illuminating interpretation of Greek culture.

W. K. LACEY, *The Family in Ancient Greece* (1984).

P. B. MANVILLE, *The Origins of Citizenship in Ancient Athens* (1990). An examination of the origins of the concept of citizenship in the time of Solon of Athens.

O. MURRAY, *Early Greece* (1980). A lively and imaginative account of the early history of Greece to the end of the Persian War.

A. T. OLMSTEAD, *History of the Persian Empire* (1960). A thorough survey.

H. W. PARKE, *Festivals of the Athenians* (1977). A fine discussion of the religious practices of the Athenians.

G. M. A. RICHTER, *Archaic Greek Art* (1949).

C. ROEBUCK, *Ionian Trade and Colonization* (1959). An introduction to the history of the Greeks in the East.

R. SALLARES, *The Ecology of the Ancient Greek World* (1991). A valuable study of the Greeks and their environment.

D. M. SCHAPS, *Economic Rights of Women in Ancient Greece* (1981).

B. SNELL, *Discovery of the Mind* (1960). An important study of Greek intellectual development.

A. M. SNODGRASS, *The Dark Age of Greece* (1972). A good examination of the archaeological evidence.

C. G. STARR, *Origins of Greek Civilization 1100–650 B.C.E.* (1961). An interesting interpretation based largely on archaeology and especially on pottery styles.

C. G. STARR, *The Economic and Social Growth of Early Greece, 800–500 B.C.E.* (1977).

E. VERMEULE, *Greece in the Bronze Age* (1972). A study of the Mycenaean period.

A. G. WOODHEAD, *Greeks in the West* (1962). An account of the Greek settlements in Italy and Sicily.

W. J. WOODHOUSE, *Solon the Liberator* (1965). A discussion of the great Athenian reformer.

D. C. YOUNG, *The Olympic Myth of Greek Athletics* (1984). A lively challenge to the orthodox view that Greek athletes were amateurs.

CHAPTER 3

The Winged Victory of Samothrace. This is one of the great masterpieces of Hellenistic sculpture. It appears to be the work of the Rhodian sculptor Pythokritos, about 200 B.C.E. The statue stood in the sanctuary of the Great Gods on the Aegean island of Smothrace on a base made in the shape of a ship's prow. The goddess is seen as landing on the ship to crown its victorious commander and crew. [Erich Lessing/Art Resource]

Classical and Hellenistic Greece

KEY TOPICS

- The Peloponnesian War and the struggle between Athens and Sparta
- Democracy and empire in fifth-century B.C.E. Athens
- Culture and society in Classical Greece
- The struggle for dominance in Greece after the Peloponnesian War
- The Hellenistic world

The Greeks' remarkable victory over the Persians in 480–479 B.C.E. won them another period of freedom and autonomy. They used this time to carry their political and cultural achievement to its height. In Athens, especially, it produced a great sense of confidence and ambition.

Spartan withdrawal from active leadership against the Persians left a vacuum that was filled by the Delian League, which soon turned into the Athenian Empire. At the same time as it tightened its hold over the Greek cities in and around the Aegean Sea, Athens developed an extraordinarily democratic constitution at home. Fears and jealousies of this new kind of state and empire created a split in the Greek world; this led to a series of major wars that impoverished Greece and left it vulnerable to conquest. In 338 B.C.E. Philip of Macedon conquered the Greek states, putting an end to the age of the polis.

Aftermath of Victory

The unity of the Greeks had shown strain even in the life-and-death struggle against the Persians. Within two years of the Persian retreat it gave way almost completely and yielded to a division of the Greek world into two spheres of influence, dominated by Sparta and Athens. The need of the Ionian Greeks to obtain and defend their freedom from Persia and the desire of many Greeks to gain revenge and financial reparation for the Persian attack brought on the split.

The Delian League

Sparta had led the Greeks to victory, and it was natural to look to the Spartans to continue the campaign against Persia. But Sparta was ill suited to the task, which required both a long-term commitment far from the Peloponnesus and continuous naval action.

Athens had become the leading naval power in Greece, and the same motives that led the Athenians to support the Ionian revolt prompted them to try to drive the Persians from the Aegean and the Hellespont. The Ionians were at least as eager for the Athenians to take the helm as the Athenians were to accept the responsibility and opportunity.

In the winter of 478–477 B.C.E. the islanders, the Greeks from the coast of Asia Minor and from some other Greek cities on the Aegean, met with the Athenians on the sacred island of Delos and swore oaths of alliance. As a symbol that the alliance was meant to be permanent, they dropped lumps of iron into the sea; the alliance was to hold until these lumps of iron rose to the surface. The aims of this new Delian League were to free those Greeks who were under Persian rule, to protect all against a Persian return, and to obtain compensation from the Persians by attacking their lands and taking booty. League policy was determined by a vote of an assembly in which each state, including Athens, had one vote. Athens, however, was clearly designated the leader.

MAP 3–1 CLASSICAL GREECE *Greece in the Classical period (ca. 480–338 B.C.E.) centered on the Aegean Sea. Although there were important Greek settlements in Italy, Sicily, and all around the Black Sea, the area shown in this general reference map embraced the vast majority of Greek states.*

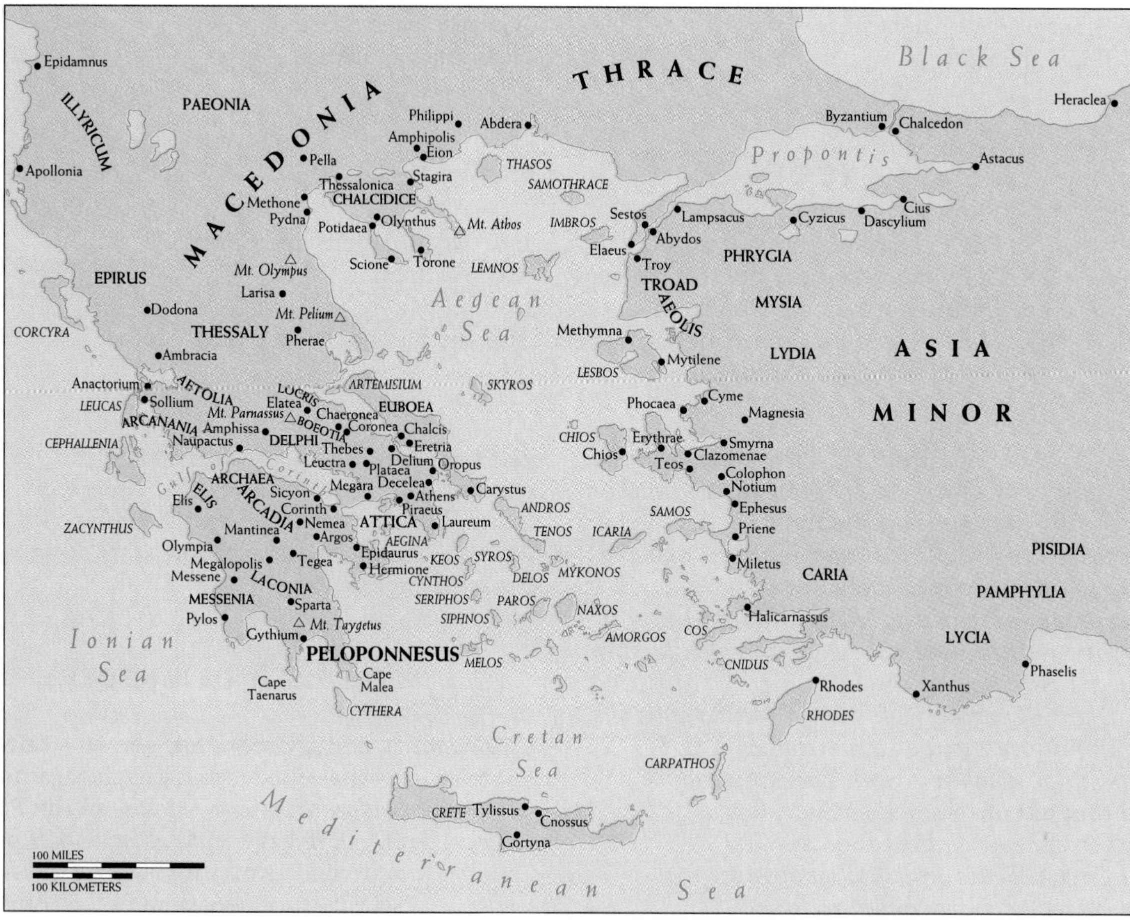

From the first, the league was remarkably successful. The Persians were driven from Europe and the Hellespont, and the Aegean was cleared of pirates. Some states were forced into the league or were prevented from leaving. The members approved coercion because it was necessary for the common safety. In 467 B.C.E. a great victory over the Persians at the Eurymedon River in Asia Minor routed the Persians and added several cities to the league.

The Rise of Cimon

Cimon, son of Miltiades, the hero of Marathon, became the leading Athenian soldier and statesman soon after the war with Persia. Themistocles appears to have been driven from power by a coalition of his enemies. Ironically, the author of the Greek victory over Persia of 480 B.C.E. was exiled and ended his days at the court of the Persian king. Cimon, who was to dominate Athenian politics for almost two decades, pursued a policy of aggressive attacks on Persia and friendly relations with Sparta. In domestic affairs Cimon was conservative. He accepted the democratic constitution of Clisthenes, which appears to have become somewhat more limited after the Persian war. Defending this constitution and this foreign policy, Cimon led the Athenians and the Delian League to victory after victory, and his own popularity grew with his successes.

The First Peloponnesian War: Athens Against Sparta

The Thasian Rebellion

In 465 B.C.E. the island of Thasos rebelled from the Delian League, and Cimon put it down after a siege of more than two years. The revolt of Thasos is the first recorded instance in which Athenian interests alone seemed to determine league policy, a significant step in the league's evolution into the Athenian Empire.

When Cimon returned to Athens from Thasos, he was charged with taking bribes for having refrained from conquering Macedonia, although conquering Macedonia had not been part of his assignment. He was acquitted; the trial was only a device by which his political opponents tried to reduce his influence. Their program at home was to undo the gains made by the Areopagus and to bring about further changes in the direction of democracy. In foreign policy, these enemies of Cimon wanted to break with Sparta and to contest its claim to leadership over the Greeks. They intended at least to establish the independence of Athens and its alliance. The head of this faction was Ephialtes. His supporter, and the person chosen to be the public prosecutor of Cimon, was Pericles, a member of a distinguished Athenian family. He was still young, and his defeat in court did not do lasting damage to his career.

The Breach with Sparta

When the Thasians began their rebellion, they asked Sparta to invade Athens the next spring, and the *ephors*, the annual magistrates responsible for Sparta's foreign policy, agreed. An earthquake, however, accompanied by a rebellion of the Helots that threatened the survival of Sparta, prevented the invasion. The Spartans asked their allies, the Athenians among them, for help, and Cimon persuaded the Athenians to send it.

The results of this policy were disastrous for Cimon and his faction. While Cimon was in the Peloponnesus helping the Spartans, Ephialtes stripped the Areopagus of almost all its power. The Spartans, meanwhile, fearing "the boldness and revolutionary spirit of the Athenians," ultimately sent them home. In 462 B.C.E. Ephialtes was assassinated and Pericles replaced him as leader of the democratic faction. In the spring of 461 B.C.E. Cimon was ostracized, and Athens made an alliance with Argos, Sparta's traditional enemy. Almost overnight Cimon's domestic and foreign policies had been overturned.

The Division of Greece

The new regime at Athens, led by Pericles and the democratic faction, was confident and ambitious. When Megara, getting the worst of a border dispute with Corinth, withdrew from the Peloponnesian League, the Athenians accepted the Megarians as allies. This alliance gave Athens a great strategic advantage, for Megara barred the way from the Peloponnesus to Athens. Sparta, however, resented the defection of Megara to Athens, leading to the outbreak of the First Peloponnesian War, the first phase in a protracted struggle between Athens and Sparta. The Athenians conquered Aegina and gained

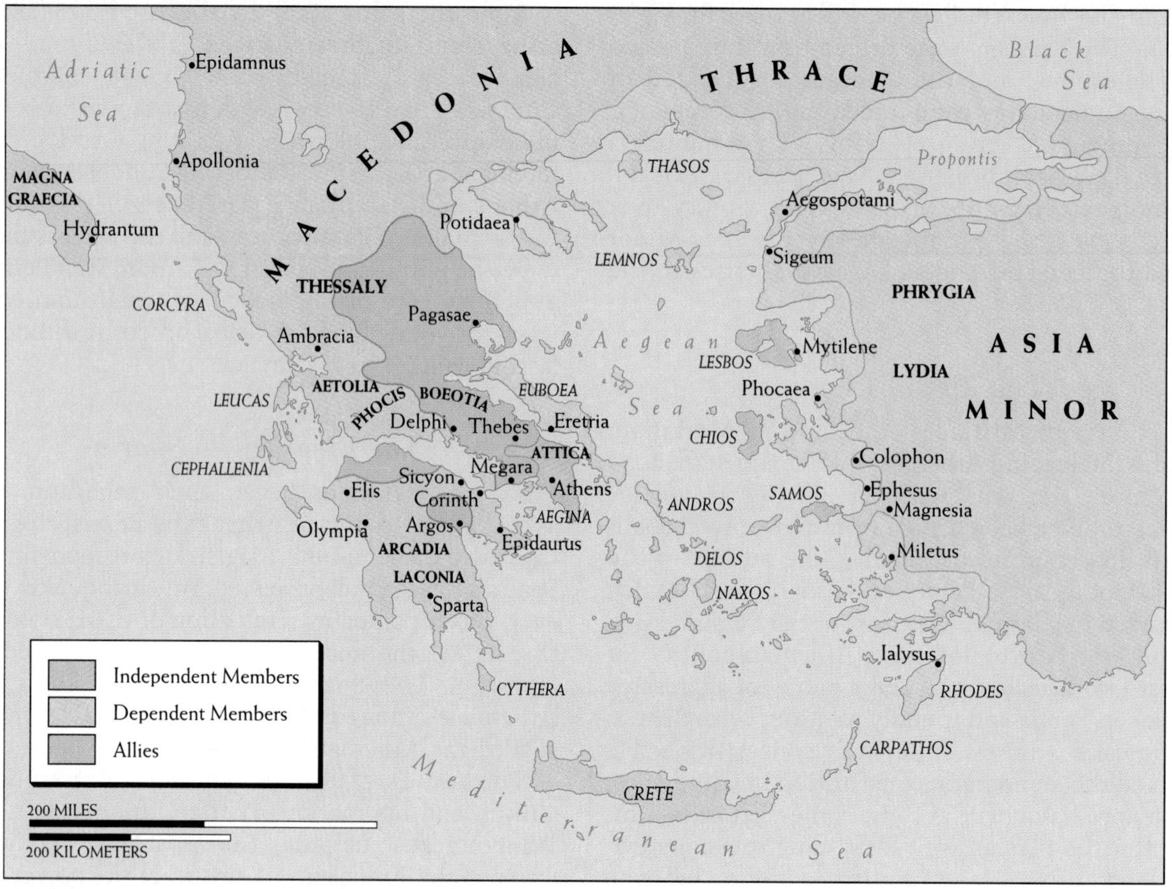

MAP 3–2 THE ATHENIAN EMPIRE ABOUT 450 B.C.E. *The Athenian Empire at its fullest extent shortly before 450 B.C.E. We see Athens and the independent states that provided manned ships for the imperial fleet but paid no tribute, dependent states that paid tribute, and states allied to but not actually in the empire.*

control of Boeotia. At this moment Athens was supreme and apparently invulnerable, controlling the states on its borders and dominating the sea. (See Map 3–2).

About 455 B.C.E., however, the tide turned. A disastrous defeat met an Athenian fleet that had gone to aid an Egyptian rebellion against Persia. The great loss of men, ships, and prestige caused rebellions in the empire, forcing Athens to make a truce in Greece to subdue its allies in the Aegean. In 449 B.C.E. the Athenians ended the war against Persia.

In 446 B.C.E. the war on the Greek mainland broke out again. Rebellions in Boeotia and Megara removed Athens' land defenses and brought a Spartan invasion. Rather than fight, Pericles, the commander of the Athenian army, agreed to a peace of thirty years by the terms of which he abandoned all Athenian possessions on the Greek mainland outside of Attica. In return, the Spartans gave formal recognition to the Athenian Empire. From then on Greece was divided into two power blocs: Sparta with its alliance on the mainland, and Athens ruling its empire in the Aegean.

Classical Greece

The Athenian Empire

After the Egyptian disaster the Athenians moved the Delian League's treasury to Athens and began to keep one-sixtieth of the annual revenues for themselves. Because of the peace with Persia there seemed no further reason for the allies to pay tribute, and so the Athenians were compelled to find a new justification for their empire. They called for a Panhellenic congress to meet at Athens to discuss rebuilding the temples destroyed by the Persians

Key Events in Athenian History Between the Persian War and the Great Peloponnesian War

478–477 B.C.E.	Delian League founded
ca. 474–462 B.C.E.	Cimon leading politician
467 B.C.E.	Victory over Persians at Eurymedon River
465–463 B.C.E.	Rebellion of Thasos
462 B.C.E.	Ephialtes murdered; Pericles rises to leadership
461 B.C.E.	Cimon ostracized
461 B.C.E.	Reform of Areopagus
ca. 460 B.C.E.	First Peloponnesian War begins
454 B.C.E.	Athens defeated in Egypt; crisis in the Delian League
449 B.C.E.	Peace with Persia
445 B.C.E.	Thirty Years' Peace ends First Peloponnesian War

and to consider how to maintain freedom of the seas. When Sparta's reluctance to participate prevented the congress, Athens felt free to continue to collect funds from the allies, both to maintain its navy and to rebuild the Athenian temples. Athenian propaganda suggested that henceforth the allies would be treated as colonies and Athens as their mother city, the whole to be held together by good feeling and common religious observances.

There is little reason, however, to believe that the allies were taken in or were truly content with their lot. Nothing could cloak the fact that Athens was becoming the master and its allies mere subjects. By 445 B.C.E., when the Thirty Years' Peace gave formal recognition to an Athenian Empire, only Chios, Lesbos, and Samos were autonomous and provided ships. All the other states paid tribute. The change from alliance to empire came about because of the pressure of war and rebellion and largely because the allies were unwilling to see to their own defense. Although the empire had many friends among the lower classes and the democratic politicians in the subject cities, it came to be seen more and more as a tyranny. Athenian prosperity and security, however, had come to depend on the empire, and the Athenians were determined to defend it at any cost.

Athenian Democracy

Even as the Athenians were tightening their control over their empire, they were expanding democracy at

(a)

(b)

*An Athenian silver four-*drachma *coin (*tetradrachm*) from the fifth century B.C.E. (440–430 B.C.E.). On the front (a) is the profile of Athena and on the back (b) is her symbol of wisdom, the owl. The silver from which the coins were struck came chiefly from the state mines at Sunium in southern Attica. [Hirmer Verlag, Munich]*

home. Under the leadership of Pericles, they evolved the freest government the world had yet seen.

DEMOCRATIC LEGISLATION Legislation was passed making the *hoplite* class eligible for the *archonship*, and in practice no one was thereafter prevented from serving in this office on the basis of property class. Pericles himself proposed a law introducing pay for jury members, opening that important duty to the poor. Circuit judges were reintroduced, a policy making swift impartial justice available even to the poorest residents in the countryside.

Finally, Pericles himself introduced a bill limiting citizenship to those who had two citizen parents. From a modern perspective this measure might be seen as a step away from democracy, and, in fact, it would have barred Cimon and one of Pericles' ancestors. In Greek terms, however, it was quite natural. *Democracy* was defined as the privilege of those who held citizenship, making citizenship a valuable commodity. The decision to limit it would have increased its value. Thus, this bill must have won a large majority. Women, resident aliens, and slaves were also denied participation in government in all the Greek states.

How Did the Democracy Work? Within the citizen body, the extent of Athenian democracy was remarkable. Every decision of the state had to be approved by the popular assembly—a collection of the people, not their representatives. Every judicial decision was subject to appeal to a popular court of not fewer than 51 and as many as 1,501 citizens, chosen from an annual panel of jurors widely representative of the Athenian population. Most officials were selected by lot without regard to class. The main elected officials, such as the ten generals (the generalship was an office that had both political and military significance) and the imperial treasurers, were generally nobles and almost always rich men, but the people were free to choose otherwise. All public officials were subject to scrutiny before taking office and could be called to account and removed from office during their tenure. They were held to compulsory examination and accounting at the end of their term. There was no standing army, no police force, open or secret, and no way to coerce the people.

Pericles was elected to the generalship fifteen years in a row and thirty times in all, not because he was a dictator but because he was a persuasive speaker, a skillful politician, a respected military leader, an acknowledged patriot, and patently incorruptible. When he lost the people's confidence, they did not hesitate to depose him from office. In 443 B.C.E., however, he stood at the height of his power. The defeat of the Athenian fleet in the Egyptian

The Acropolis was both the religious and civic center of Athens. In its final form it is the work of Pericles and his successors in the late fifth century B.C.E. *This photograph shows the Parthenon and to its left the Erechtheum. [Meredith Pillon, Greek National Tourist Organization]*

The Delian League Becomes the Athenian Empire

In the years after its foundation in the winter of 478–477 B.C.E., the Delian League gradually underwent changes that finally justified calling it the Athenian Empire. In the following selection, the historian Thucydides explains why the organization changed its character.

✦ *Why did some allies choose to pay money rather than supply ships and men? Since membership in the league was originally voluntary, why did the allies refuse to meet their obligations? Who was responsible for converting a voluntary league of allies into the Athenian Empire?*

The causes which led to the defections of the allies were of different kinds, the principal being their neglect to pay the tribute or to furnish ships, and, in some cases, failure of military service. For the Athenians were exacting and oppressive, using coercive measures towards men who were neither willing nor accustomed to work hard. And for various reasons they soon began to prove less agreeable leaders than at first. They no longer fought upon an equality with the rest of the confederates, and they had no difficulty in reducing them when they revolted. Now the allies brought all this upon themselves; for the majority of them disliked military service and absence from home, and so they agreed to contribute a regular sum of money instead of ships. Whereby the Athenian navy was proportionally increased, while they themselves were always untrained and unprepared for war when they revolted.

Thucydides, The Peloponnesian War, Vol. 2, *trans. by Benjamin Jowett, in* The Greek Historians, *ed. by F. R. B. Godolphin (New York: Random House, 1942), p. 609.*

campaign and the failure of Athens's continental campaigns had persuaded him to favor a conservative policy, seeking to retain the empire in the Aegean and live at peace with the Spartans. It was in this direction that he led Athens's imperial democracy in the years after the First Peloponnesian War.

The Women of Athens—Two Views

Greek society, like most societies all over the world throughout history, was dominated by men. This was true of the democratic city of Athens in the great days of Pericles, in the fifth century B.C.E., no less than of other Greek cities. The actual position of women in classical Athens, however, has been the subject of much controversy.

SUBJECTION The bulk of the evidence, coming from the law, from philosophical and moral writings, and from information about the conditions of daily life and the organization of society, shows that women were excluded from most aspects of public life. They could not vote, could not take part in the political assemblies, could not hold public office, and could not take any direct part in politics at all. Since Athens was one of the few places in the ancient world where male citizens of all classes had these public responsibilities and opportunities, the exclusion of women was all the more significant.

The same sources show that in the private aspects of life women were always under the control of a male guardian—a father, a husband, or some other male relative. Women married young, usually between the ages of twelve and eighteen, whereas their husbands were typically over thirty. In many ways, women's relationships with men were similar to father–daughter relationships. Marriages were arranged; women normally had no choice of husband, and their dowries were con-

Athenian Democracy: An Unfriendly View

The following selection comes from an anonymous pamphlet thought to have been written in the midst of the Peloponnesian War. Because it has come down to us among the works of Xenophon but cannot be his work, it is sometimes called "The Constitution of the Athenians" by Pseudo-Xenophon. It is also common to refer to the unknown author as "The Old Oligarch"—although neither his age nor his purpose is known—because of the obviously antidemocratic tone of the work. Such opinions were common among members of the upper classes in Athens late in the fifth century B.C.E. *and thereafter.*

✦ *What are the author's objections to democracy? Does he describe the workings of the Athenian democracy accurately? How would a defender of the Athenian constitution and way of life meet his complaints? Is there any merit in his criticisms?*

Now, in discussing the Athenian constitution, I cannot commend their present method of running the state, because in choosing it they preferred that the masses should do better than the respectable citizens; this, then, is my reason for not commending it. Since, however, they have made this choice, I will demonstrate how well they preserve their constitution and handle the other affairs for which the rest of the Greeks criticise them.

Again, some people are surprised at the fact that in all fields they give more power to the masses, the poor and the common people than they do to the respectable elements of society, but it will become clear that they preserve the democracy by doing precisely this. When the poor, the ordinary people and the lower classes flourish and increase in numbers, then the power of the democracy will be increased; if, however, the rich and the respectable flourish, the democrats increase the strength of their opponents. Throughout the world the aristocracy are opposed to democracy, for they are naturally least liable to loss of self control and injustice and most meticulous in their regard for what is respectable, whereas the masses display extreme ignorance, indiscipline and wickedness, for poverty gives them a tendency towards the ignoble, and in some cases lack of money leads to their being uneducated and ignorant.

It may be objected that they ought not to grant each and every man the right of speaking in the Ekklesia and serving on the Boule, but only the ablest and best of them; however, in this also they are acting in their own best interests by allowing the mob also a voice. If none but the respectable spoke in the Ekklesia and the Boule, the result would benefit that class and harm the masses; as it is, anyone who wishes rises and speaks, and as a member of the mob he discovers what is to his own advantage and that of those like him.

But someone may say: 'How could such a man find out what was advantageous to himself and the common people?' The Athenians realise that this man, despite his ignorance and badness, brings them more advantage because he is well disposed to them than the ill-disposed respectable man would, despite his virtue and wisdom. Such practices do not produce the best city, but they are the best way of preserving democracy. For the common people do not wish to be deprived of their rights in an admirably governed city, but to be free and to rule the city; they are not disturbed by inferior laws, for the common people get their strength and freedom from what you define as inferior laws.

Aristotle and Xenophon on Democracy and Oligarchy, *trans. with introductions and commentary by J. M. Moore (Berkeley and Los Angeles: University of California Press, 1975), pp. 37–38.*

trolled by male relatives. Divorce was difficult for women to obtain, for they needed the approval of a male relative who was willing to serve as guardian after the dissolution of the marriage. In case of divorce, the dowry returned with the woman but was controlled by her father or the appropriate male relative.

The main function and responsibility of a respectable Athenian woman of a citizen family was to produce male heirs for the *oikos*, or household, of her husband. If, however, her father's *oikos* lacked a male heir, the daughter became an *epikleros*, the "heiress" to the family property. In that case, she was required by law to marry a relative on her father's side in order to produce the desired male offspring. In the Athenian way of thinking, women were "lent" by one household to another for bearing and raising a male heir to continue the existence of the *oikos*.

Because the pure and legitimate lineage of the offspring was important, women were carefully segregated from men outside the family and were confined to the women's quarters in the house. Men might seek sexual gratification outside the house with prostitutes of high or low style, frequently recruited from abroad. Respectable women stayed home to raise the children, cook, weave cloth, and oversee the management of the household. The only public function of women—an important one—was in the various rituals and festivals of the state religion. Apart from these activities, Athenian women were expected to remain at home out of sight, quiet and unnoticed. Pericles told the widows and mothers of the Athenian men who died in the first year of the Peloponnesian War only this: "Your great glory is not to fall short of your natural character, and the greatest glory of women is to be least talked about by men, whether for good or bad."

POWER The picture of the legal status of women derived from these sources is largely accurate. It does not fit well, however, with other evidence from mythology, from pictorial art, and from the tragedies and comedies by the great Athenian dramatists. These often show women as central characters and powerful figures in both the public and the private spheres, suggesting that the role played by Athenian women may have been more complex than their legal status suggests. In Aeschylus's tragedy Agamemnon, for example, Clytemnestra arranges the murder of her royal husband and establishes the tyranny of her lover, whom she dominates.

This red-figure kalyx crater, or wine bowl, was painted by the Dokimasia painter about 470–465 B.C.E. It shows the murder of King Agamemnon on his return from the sack of Troy, by his wife, Clytemnestra, and her lover, Aegisthus. In red-figure painting, the red color of the fired clay is used for the foreground (figure) and a black pigment for the background. [Museum of Fine Arts, Boston]

As a famous speech in Euripides' tragedy *Medea* makes clear, we are left with an apparent contradiction. In this speech (see the document on the next page), Medea paints a bleak picture of the subjugation of women as dictated by their legal status. Yet Medea, as depicted by Euripides, is herself a powerful and terrifying figure who negotiates with kings. She is the central figure in a tragedy bearing her name, produced at state expense before most of the Athenian population, and written by one of Athens' greatest poets and dramatists. She is a cause of terror to the audience and, at the same time, an object of their pity and sympathy as a victim of injustice. She is certainly not "least talked about by men, whether for good or for bad."

Slavery

The Greeks had some form of slavery from the earliest times, but true chattel slavery was initially

Medea Bemoans the Condition of Women

In 431 B.C.E. Euripides (ca. 485–406 B.C.E.) presented his play Medea *at the Festival of Dionysus in Athens. The heroine is a foreign woman who has unusual powers. Her description of the condition of women in the speech that follows, however, appears to be an accurate representation of the condition of women in fifth-century B.C.E. Athens.*

✦ *Apart from participation in politics, how did the lives of men and women differ in ancient Athens? How well or badly did that aspect of Athenian society suit the needs of the Athenian people and the state in the Classical Age? Since men had a dominant position in the state and the presentation of tragedies was managed and financed by the state, how do you explain the sympathetic account of the condition of women Euripides puts into the mouth of Medea?*

Of all things which are living and can form a judgment
We women are the most unfortunate creatures.
Firstly, with an excess of wealth it is required
For us to buy a husband and take for our bodies
A master; for not to take one is even worse.
And now the question is serious whether we take
A good or bad one; for there is no easy escape
For a woman, nor can she say no to her marriage.
She arrives among new modes of behavior and manners,
And needs prophetic power, unless she has learned at home,
How best to manage him who shares the bed with her.
And if we work out all this well and carefully,
And the husband lives with us and lightly bears his yoke,
Then life is enviable. If not, I'd rather die.
A man, when he's tired of the company in his home,
Goes out of the house and puts an end to his boredom
And turns to a friend or companion of his own age.
But we are forced to keep our eyes on one alone.
What they say of us is that we have a peaceful time
Living at home, while they do the fighting in war.
How wrong they are! I would very much rather stand
Three times in the front of battle than bear one child.

Euripides, Medea, *in* Four Tragedies, *trans. by Rex Warner (Chicago: University of Chicago Press, 1955), pp. 66–67.*

rare. The most common forms of bondage were different kinds of serfdom in relatively backward areas such as Crete, Thessaly, and Sparta. As noted in Chapter 2, the Spartans conquered the natives of their region and reduced them to the status of Helots, subjects who belonged to the Spartan state and worked the land for the benefit of their Spartan masters. Another early form of bondage—involving a severe but rarely permanent loss of freedom—resulted from default in debt. In Athens, however, about 600 B.C.E., such bondsmen, called *hektemoroi*, were sold outside their native land as true slaves until the reforms of Solon put an end to debt-bondage entirely.

True chattel slavery began to increase about 500 B.C.E. and remained important to Greek society thereafter. For a fuller discussion of Greek slavery and how it compared with slavery in other ancient societies, see The West and the World, in Chapter 4.

The Great Peloponnesian War

During the first decade after the Thirty Years' Peace of 445 B.C.E., the willingness of each side to respect the new arrangements was tested and not found wanting. About 435 B.C.E., however, a dispute in a remote and unimportant part of the Greek world ignited a long and disastrous war that shook the foundations of Greek civilization.

Causes

The spark that ignited the conflict was a civil war at Epidamnus, a Corcyraean colony on the Adriatic. This civil war caused a quarrel between Corcyra and her mother city and traditional enemy, Corinth, an ally of Sparta. The Corcyraean fleet was second in size only to that of Athens, and the Athenians feared that its capture by Corinth would change the balance of power at sea and seriously threaten Athenian security. As a result, they made an alliance with the previously neutral Corcyra, angering Corinth and leading to a series of crises in the years 433–432 B.C.E. that threatened to bring the Athenian Empire into conflict with the Peloponnesian League.

In the summer of 432 B.C.E. the Spartans met to consider the grievances of their allies. Persuaded, chiefly by the Corinthians, that Athens was an insatiably aggressive power seeking to enslave all the Greeks, they voted for war. The treaty of 445 B.C.E. specifically provided that all differences be submitted to arbitration, and Athens repeatedly offered to arbitrate any question. Pericles insisted that the Athenians refuse to yield to threats or commands and that they uphold the treaty and the arbitration clause. Sparta refused to arbitrate, and in the spring of 431 B.C.E. its army marched into Attica, the Athenian homeland.

Strategic Stalemate

The Spartan strategy was traditional: to invade the enemy's country and threaten the crops, forcing the enemy to defend them in a *hoplite* battle. Such a battle the Spartans were sure to win because they had the better army and they outnumbered the Athenians at least two to one. Any ordinary *polis* would have yielded or fought and lost. Athens, however, had an enormous navy, an annual income from the empire, a vast reserve fund, and long walls that connected the fortified city with the fortified port of Piraeus.

The Athenians' strategy was to allow devastation of their own land to prove that Spartan invasions could not hurt Athens. At the same time, the Athenians launched seaborne raids on the Peloponnesian coast to show that Sparta's allies could be hurt. Pericles expected that within a year or two, three at most, the Peloponnesians would become discouraged and make peace, having learned their lesson. If the Peloponnesians held out, Athenian resources were inadequate to continue for more than four or five years without raising the tribute in the empire and running an unacceptable risk of rebellion.

The plan required restraint and the leadership only a Pericles could provide. In 429 B.C.E., however, in the wake of a devastating plague and a political crisis that had challenged his authority, Pericles died. After his death, no dominant leader emerged to hold the Athenians to a consistent policy. Two factions vied for influence: one, led by Nicias, wanted to continue the defensive policy, and the other, led by Cleon, preferred a more aggressive strategy. In 425 B.C.E. the aggressive faction was able to win a victory that changed the course of the war. Four hundred Spartans surrendered. Sparta offered peace at once to get them back. The great victory and the prestige it brought Athens made it safe to raise the imperial tribute, without which Athens could not continue to fight. The Athenians indeed wanted to continue, for the Spartan peace offer gave no adequate guarantee of Athenian security.

In 424 B.C.E. the Athenians undertook a more aggressive policy. They sought to make Athens safe by conquering Megara and Boeotia. Both attempts failed, and defeat helped discredit the aggressive policy, leading to a truce in 423 B.C.E. Meanwhile, Sparta's ablest general, Brasidas, took a small army to Thrace and Macedonia. He captured Amphipolis, the most important Athenian colony in the region. Thucydides was in charge of the Athenian fleet in

The Great Peloponnesian War

435 B.C.E.	Civil war at Epidamnus
432 B.C.E.	Sparta declares war on Athens
431 B.C.E.	Peloponnesian invasion of Athens
421 B.C.E.	Peace of Nicias
415–413 B.C.E.	Athenian invasion of Sicily
405 B.C.E.	Battle of Aegospotami
404 B.C.E.	Athens surrenders

those waters and was held responsible for the city's loss. He was exiled and was thereby given the time and opportunity to write his famous history of the Great Peloponnesian War. In 422 B.C.E. Cleon led an expedition to undo the work of Brasidas. At Amphipolis both he and Brasidas died in battle. The removal of these two leaders of the aggressive factions in their respective cities paved the way for the Peace of Nicias, named for its chief negotiator, which was ratified in the spring of 421 B.C.E.

The Fall of Athens

The peace, officially supposed to last fifty years and, with a few exceptions, guarantee the status quo, was in fact tenuous. Neither side carried out all its commitments, and several of Sparta's allies refused ratification. In 415 B.C.E. Alcibiades persuaded the Athenians to attack Sicily to bring it under Athenian control. This ambitious and unnecessary undertaking ended in disaster in 413 B.C.E. when the entire expedition was destroyed. The Athenians lost some two hundred ships, about 4,500 of their own men, and almost ten times as many allies. It shook Athenian prestige, reduced the power of Athens, provoked rebellions, and brought the wealth and power of Persia into the war on Sparta's side.

It is remarkable that the Athenians could continue fighting in spite of the disaster. They survived a brief oligarchic coup in 411 B.C.E. and won several important victories at sea as the war shifted to the Aegean. Their allies rebelled, however, and were sustained by fleets paid for by Persia. The Athenians saw their financial resources shrink and finally disappear. When their fleet was caught napping and was destroyed at Aegospotami in 405 B.C.E., they could not build another. The Spartans, under Lysander, a clever and ambitious general who was responsible for obtaining Persian support, cut off the food supply through the Hellespont, and the Athenians were starved into submission. In 404 B.C.E. they surrendered unconditionally; the city walls were dismantled, Athens was permitted no fleet, and the empire was gone. The Great Peloponnesian War was over.

Competition for Leadership in the Fourth Century B.C.E.

The defeat of Athens did not bring domination to the Spartans. Instead, the period from 404 B.C.E. until the Macedonian conquest of Greece in 338 B.C.E. was a time of intense rivalry among the Greek cities, each seeking to achieve leadership and control over some or all of the others. Sparta, a recovered Athens, and a newly powerful Thebes were the main competitors in a struggle that ultimately weakened all the Greeks and left them vulnerable to outside influence and control.

The Hegemony of Sparta

The collapse of the Athenian Empire created a vacuum of power in the Aegean and opened the way for Spartan leadership, or hegemony. Fulfilling the contract that had brought them the funds to win the war, the Spartans handed the Greek cities of Asia Minor back to Persia. Under the leadership of Lysander, the Spartans went on to make a complete mockery of their promise to free the Greeks by stepping into the imperial role of Athens in the cities along the European coast and the islands of the Aegean. In most of the cities Lysander installed a board of ten local oligarchs loyal to him and supported them with a Spartan garrison. Tribute brought in an annual revenue almost as great as that the Athenians had collected.

Limited population, the Helot problem, and traditional conservatism all made Sparta a less than ideal state to rule a maritime empire. The increasing arrogance of Sparta's policies alienated some of its allies, especially Thebes and Corinth. In 404 B.C.E. Lysander installed an oligarchic government in Athens, and the outrageous behavior of its leaders earned them the title "Thirty Tyrants." Democratic exiles took refuge in Thebes and Corinth and created an army to challenge the oligarchy. Sparta's conservative king, Pausanias, replaced Lysander, arranging a peaceful settlement and ultimately the restoration of democracy. Thereafter Athenian foreign policy remained under Spartan control, but otherwise Athens was free.

In 405 B.C.E. Darius II of Persia died and was succeeded by Artaxerxes II. His younger brother, Cyrus, contested his rule and received Spartan help in recruiting a Greek mercenary army to help him win the throne. The Greeks marched inland as far as Mesopotamia, where they defeated the Persians at Cunaxa in 401 B.C.E., but Cyrus was killed in the battle. The Greeks were able to march back to the Black Sea and safety; their success revealed the potential weakness of the Persian Empire.

The Greeks of Asia Minor had supported Cyrus and were now afraid of Artaxerxes' revenge. The Spartans accepted their request for aid and sent an army into Asia, attracted by the prospect of prestige, power, and money. In 396 B.C.E. the command of Sparta's army was given to a new king, Agesilaus. This leader dominated Sparta throughout its period of hegemony and until his death in 360 B.C.E. Some have argued that his consistent advocacy of aggressive policies that provided him with opportunities to display his bravery in battle may have been motivated by a psychological need to compensate for his physical lameness and his disputed claim to the throne.

Agesilaus collected much booty and frightened the Persians. They sent a messenger with money and promises of further support to friendly factions in all of the Greek states likely to help them against Sparta. By 395 B.C.E. Thebes was able to organize an alliance that included Argos, Corinth, and a resurgent Athens. The result was the Corinthian War (395–387 B.C.E.), which put an end to Sparta's Asian adventure. In 394 B.C.E. the Persian fleet destroyed Sparta's maritime empire. Meanwhile the Athenians took advantage of events to rebuild their walls, to enlarge their navy, and even to recover some of their lost empire in the Aegean. The war ended when the exhausted Greek states accepted a peace dictated by the Great King of Persia.

The Persians, frightened now by the recovery of Athens, turned the management of Greece over to Sparta. Agesilaus broke up all alliances except the Peloponnesian League. He used or threatened to use the Spartan army to interfere in other *poleis* and put friends of Sparta in power within them. Sparta reached a new level of lawless arrogance in 382 B.C.E., when it seized Thebes during peacetime without warning or pretext. In 379 B.C.E. a Spartan army made a similar attempt on Athens. That action persuaded the Athenians to join with Thebes, which had rebelled from Sparta a few months earlier, to wage war on the Spartans.

In 371 B.C.E. the Thebans, led by their great generals Pelopidas and Epaminondas, defeated the Spartans at Leuctra. The Thebans encouraged the Arcadian cities of the central Peloponnesus to form a league, freed the Helots, and helped them found a city of their own. They deprived Sparta of much of its farmland and of the people who worked it and hemmed it in with hostile neighbors. Sparta's population had shrunk so that it could put fewer than 2,000 men into the field at Leuctra. Sparta's aggressive policies had led to ruin. The Theban victory brought the end of Sparta as a power of the first rank.

The Hegemony of Thebes: The Second Athenian Empire

Thebes's power after the its victory at Leuctra lay in its democratic constitution, its control over Boeotia, and its two outstanding and popular generals. One of these generals, Pelopidas, died in a successful attempt to gain control of Thessaly. The other, Epaminondas, consolidated his work, making Thebes dominant over all Greece north of Athens and the Corinthian Gulf and challenging the reborn Athenian Empire in the Aegean. All this activity provoked resistance, and by 362 B.C.E. Thebes faced a Peloponnesian coalition as well as Athens. Epaminondas, once again leading a Boeotian army into the Peloponnesus, confronted this coalition at the Battle of Mantinea. His army was victorious, but Epaminondas himself was killed. With both its great leaders now dead, Theban dominance ended.

The Second Athenian Confederation, which Athens had organized in 378 B.C.E., was aimed at resisting Spartan aggression in the Aegean. Its constitution was careful to avoid the abuses of the Delian League, but the Athenians soon began to repeat them anyway. This time, however, they did not have the power to put down resistance. When the collapse of Sparta and Thebes and the restraint of Persia removed any reason for voluntary membership, Athens's allies revolted. By 355 B.C.E. Athens had to abandon most of the empire. After

The Spartan and Theban Hegemonies

404–403 B.C.E.	"Thirty Tyrants" rule at Athens
401 B.C.E.	Expedition of Cyrus, rebellious prince of Persia; Battle of Cunaxa
400–387 B.C.E.	Spartan War against Persia
398–360 B.C.E.	Reign of Agesilaus at Sparta
395–387 B.C.E.	Corinthian War
382 B.C.E.	Sparta seizes Thebes
378 B.C.E.	Second Athenian Confederation founded
371 B.C.E.	Thebans defeat Sparta at Leuctra; end of Spartan hegemony
362 B.C.E.	Battle of Mantinea; end of Theban hegemony

Xenophon Recounts How Greece Brought Itself to Chaos

Confusion in Greece in the fourth century B.C.E. *reached a climax with the inconclusive Battle of Mantinea in 362. The Theban leader Epaminondas was killed, and no other city or person emerged to provide the needed general leadership for Greece. Xenophon, a contemporary, pointed out the resulting near chaos in Greek affairs—tempting ground for the soon-to-appear conquering Macedonians under their king Philip II.*

✦ *What does this passage reveal about the nature of ancient Greek warfare and the customs surrounding it? How decisive were most battles in ancient Greece? Before the Macedonian conquest of Greece in 338* B.C.E. *why was no state able to impose its rule over the others? Why was that possible elsewhere?*

The effective result of these achievements was the very opposite of that which the world at large anticipated. Here, where well-nigh the whole of Hellas was met together in one field, and the combatants stood rank against rank confronted, there was no one who doubted that, in the event of battle, the conquerors this day would rule; and that those who lost would be their subjects. But god so ordered it that both belligerents alike set up trophies as claiming victory, and neither interfered with the other in the act. Both parties alike gave back their enemy's dead under a truce, and in right of victory; both alike, in symbol of defeat, under a truce took back their dead. And though both claimed to have won the day, neither could show that he had thereby gained any accession of territory, or state, or empire, or was better situated than before the battle. Uncertainty and confusion, indeed, had gained ground, being tenfold greater throughout the length and breadth of Hellas after the battle than before.

Xenophon, Hellenica, *trans. by H. G. Dakyns, in* The Greek Historians, *ed. by F. R. B. Godolphin (New York: Random House, 1942), p. 221.*

two centuries of almost continuous warfare, the Greeks returned to the chaotic disorganization that characterized the time before the founding of the Peloponnesian League.

The Culture of Classical Greece

The repulse of the Persian invasion released a flood of creative activity in Greece that was rarely, if ever, matched anywhere at any time. The century and a half between the Persian retreat and the conquest of Greece by Philip of Macedon (479–338 B.C.E.) produced achievements of such quality as to justify the designation of that era as the Classical Period. Ironically, we often use the term *classical* to suggest calm and serenity, but the word that best describes the common element present in Greek life, thought, art, and literature in this period is *tension*.

The Fifth Century B.C.E.

Two sources of tension contributed to the artistic outpouring of fifth-century B.C.E. Greece. One arose from the conflict between the Greeks' pride in their accomplishments and their concern that overreaching would bring retribution. Friction among the *poleis* intensified during this period as Athens and Sparta gathered most of them into two competing and menacing blocs. The victory over the Persians brought a sense of exultation in the capacity of humans to accomplish great things and a sense of confidence in the divine justice that had brought low the arrogant pride of Xerxes. But the

The Theatre of Dionysus in Athens, seen from the Acropolis. It was here, in contests held in honor of Dionysus, that the great Attic tragedies and comedies were performed for the citizens of Athens. [Meredith Pillon, Greek National Tourist Organization]

Greeks recognized that the fate that had met Xerxes awaited all those who reached too far, creating a sense of unease. The second source of tension was the conflict between the soaring hopes and achievements of individuals and the claims and limits put on them by their fellow citizens in the *polis*. These tensions were felt throughout Greece. They had the most spectacular consequences, however, in Athens in its Golden Age, the time between the Persian and the Peloponnesian wars.

ATTIC TRAGEDY Nothing reflects these concerns better than Attic tragedy, which emerged as a major form of Greek poetry in the fifth century B.C.E. The tragedies were presented in a contest as part of the public religious observations in honor of the god Dionysus. The festivals in which they were shown were civic occasions.

Each poet who wished to compete submitted his work to the *archon*. Each offered three tragedies (which might or might not have a common subject) and a *satyr play*, or comic choral dialogue with Dionysus, to close. The three best competitors were each awarded three actors and a chorus. The actors were paid by the state. The chorus was provided by a wealthy citizen selected by the state to perform this service as *choregos*, for the Athenians had no direct taxation to support such activities. Most of the tragedies were performed in the theater of Dionysus on the south side of the Acropolis, and as many as 30,000 Athenians could attend. Prizes and honors were awarded to the author, the actor, and the *choragus* voted best by a jury of Athenians chosen by lot.

Attic tragedy served as a forum in which the poets raised vital issues of the day, enabling the Athenian audience to think about them in a serious yet exciting context. On rare occasions the subject of a play might be a contemporary or historic event, but almost always it was chosen from mythology. Until late in the century the tragedies always dealt solemnly with difficult questions of religion, politics, ethics, morality, or some combination of these. The plays of the dramatists Aeschylus and Sophocles, for example, follow this pattern. The plays of Euripides written toward the end of the century are less solemn and more concerned with individual psychology.

OLD COMEDY Comedy was introduced into the Dionysian festival early in the fifth century B.C.E. Cratinus, Eupolis, and the great master of the genre called Old Comedy, Aristophanes (ca. 450–385 B.C.E.), the only one from whom we have complete plays, wrote political comedies. They were filled with scathing invective and satire against such contemporary figures as Pericles, Cleon, Socrates, and Euripides.

ARCHITECTURE AND SCULPTURE The great architectural achievements of Periclean Athens, as much as Athenian tragedy, illustrate the magnificent results of the union and tension between religious and civic responsibilities on the one hand and the transcendent genius of the individual artist on the other. Beginning in 448 B.C.E. and continuing to the outbreak of the Great Peloponnesian War, Pericles undertook a great building program on the Acrop-

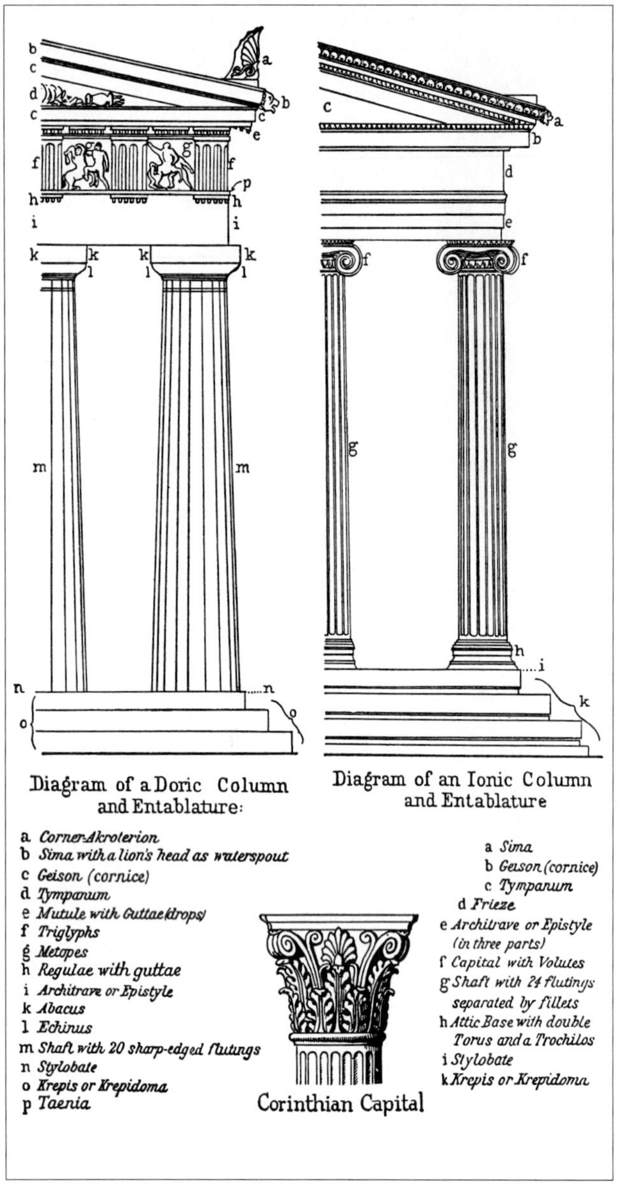

The three orders of Greek Architecture, Doric, Ionic, and Corinthian, have had an enduring impact on Western architecture.

The porch of the maidens is part of the Erechtheum on the Athenian Acropolis near the Parthenon. Built between 421 and 409 B.C.E., the Erechtheum housed the shrines of three different gods. In place of the usual fluted columns, the porch uses the statues of young girls taking part in a religious festival. [Meredith Pillon, Greek National Tourist Organization]

olis. (See Map 3–3.) The funds were provided by the income from the empire. The new buildings included temples to honor the city's gods and a fitting gateway to the temples. Pericles' main purpose seems to have been to represent visually the greatness and power of Athens, but in such a way as to emphasize intellectual and artistic achievement—civilization rather than military and naval power. It was as though these buildings were tangible proof of Pericles' claim that Athens was "the school of Hellas," that is, the intellectual center of all Greece.

PHILOSOPHY The tragic dramas, architecture, and sculpture of the fifth century B.C.E. are all indications of an extraordinary concern with human beings—their capacities, their limits, their nature, their place in the universe. The same concern is clear in the development of philosophy.

To be sure, some philosophers continued the speculation about the nature of the cosmos (as opposed to human nature) that began with Thales in the sixth century B.C.E. Parmenides of Elea and his pupil Zeno, in opposition to the earlier philosopher, Heraclitus, argued that change was only an illusion of the senses. Reason and reflection showed that reality was fixed and unchanging because it seemed evident that nothing could be created out of nothingness. Empedocles of Acragas further advanced such fundamental speculations by identifying four basic elements: fire, water, earth, and air. Like Parmenides, he thought that reality was permanent, but he thought it not immobile; the four elements, he contended, were moved by two primary forces, love and strife—or, as we might say, attraction and repulsion.

Empedocles' theory is clearly a step on the road to the atomic theory of Leucippus of Miletus and Democritus of Abdera. According to this theory, the world consists of innumerable tiny, solid, indivisible, and unchangeable particles—or "atoms"—that move about in the void. The size of the atoms and the arrangements they form when joined produce the secondary qualities that our senses perceive, such as color and shape. These secondary qualities are merely conventional—the result of human interpretation and agreement—unlike the atoms themselves, which are natural.

Previous to the atomists, Anaxagoras of Clazomenae, an older contemporary and a friend of Pericles, had spoken of tiny fundamental particles called *seeds*, which were put together on a rational basis by a force called *nous*, or "mind." Anaxagoras was thus suggesting a distinction between matter and mind. The atomists, however, regarded "soul," or mind, as material and believed that everything was guided by purely physical laws. In these conflicting positions we have the beginning of the enduring philosophical debate between materialism and idealism.

These speculations were of interest to very few people, and in fact, most Greeks were suspicious of them. A far more influential debate was begun by a group of professional teachers who emerged in the mid-fifth century B.C.E. Called *Sophists*, they traveled about and received pay for teaching such practical techniques of persuasion as rhetoric, dialectic, and argumentation. (Persuasive skills were much valued in democracies like Athens, where so many issues were resolved through open debate.) Some Sophists claimed to teach wisdom and even virtue. Reflecting the human focus characteristic of fifth-century thought, they refrained from speculations about the physical universe, instead applying reasoned analysis to human beliefs and institutions. In doing so they identified a central problem of human social life and the life of the *polis*, the conflict between nature and custom, or law. The more traditional among them argued that law itself was in accord with nature

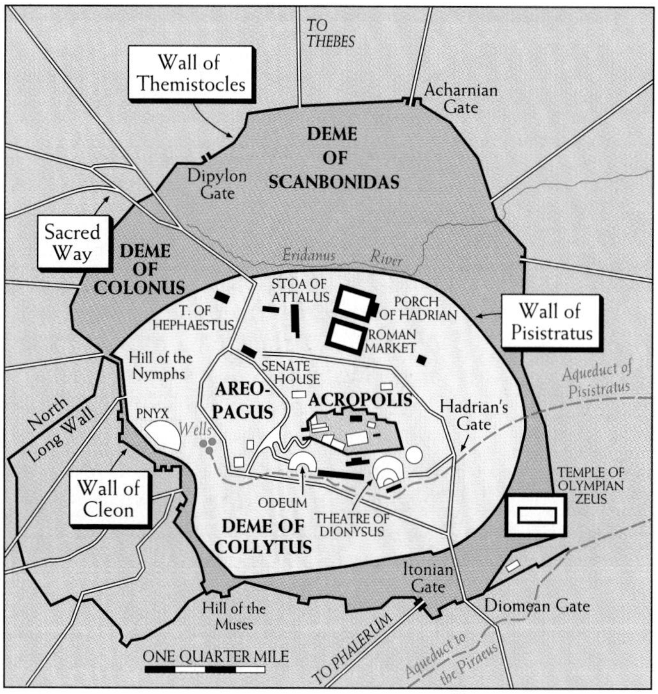

Map 3–3 Ancient Athens *This sketch locates some of the major features of the ancient city of Athens that have been excavated and are visible today. It includes monuments ranging in age from the earliest times to the period of the Roman Empire. The geographical relation of the Acropolis to the rest of the city is apparent, as is that of the Agora, the Areopagus (where the early council of aristocrats met), and the Pnyx (site of assembly for the larger, more democratic meetings of the entire people).*

and of divine origin, a view that fortified the traditional beliefs of the *polis*.

Others argued, however, that laws were merely the result of convention—an agreement among people—and not in accord with nature. The laws could not pretend to be a positive moral force but merely had the negative function of preventing people from harming each other. The most extreme Sophists argued that law was contrary to nature, a trick whereby the weak control the strong. Critias, an Athenian oligarch and one of the more extreme Sophists, went so far as to say that the gods themselves had been invented by some clever person to deter people from doing what they wished. Such ideas attacked the theoretical foundations of the *polis* and helped provoke the philosophical responses of Plato and Aristotle in the next century.

History The first prose literature in the form of history was an account of the Persian War written

Lysistrata Ends the War

Aristophanes, the greatest of the Athenian comic poets, presented the play Lysistrata *in 411 B.C.E., two decades into the Great Peloponnesian War. The central idea of the plot is that the women of Athens, led by Lysistrata, tired of the privations imposed by the war, decide to take matters into their own hands and bring the war to an end. The device they employ is to get the women on both sides to deny their marital favors to their husbands, a kind of sexual strike that quickly achieves its purpose. Before the following passage, Lysistrata has set the terms the Spartans must accept. Next she turns to the Athenians. The play is a masterful example of Athenian Old Comedy, which was almost always full of contemporary and historical political satirical references and sexual and erotic puns and jokes. The references to "Peace" in the stage directions are to an actor playing the goddess Peace.*

✦ *To what historic event does the passage concerning "the Tyrant's days" refer? To what does the "Promontory of Pylos" refer? What was the real role of women in Athenian political life, and what does the play tell us about it? What is the relationship between humor and reality in this play?*

LYSISTRATA
(*Turning to the Athenians*)
—Men of Athens, do you think I'll let you off?
Have you forgotten the Tyrant's days, when you wore
the smock of slavery, when the Spartans turned to the spear,
cut down the pride of Thessaly, despatched the friends
of tyranny, and dispossessed your oppressors?
Recall:
On that great day, your only allies were Spartans;
your liberty came at their hands, which stripped away
your servile garb and clothed you again in Freedom!

SPARTAN
(*Indicating Lysistrata*)
Hain't never seed no higher type of woman.

KINESIAS
(*Indicating Peace*)
Never saw one I wanted so much to top.

LYSISTRATA
(*Oblivious to the byplay, addressing both groups*)
With such a history of mutual benefits conferred
and received, why are you fighting? Stop this wickedness!
Come to terms with each other! What prevents you?

SPARTAN
We'd a heap sight druther make Peace, if we was indemnified with a plumb strategic location.
(*Pointing at Peace's rear*)

by Herodotus. "The father of history," as he has been deservedly called, was born shortly before the outbreak of the war. His account goes far beyond all previous chronicles, genealogies, and geographical studies and attempts to explain human actions and to draw instruction from them.

Although his work was completed about 425 B.C.E. and shows a few traces of Sophist influence, its spirit is that of an earlier time. Herodotus accepted the evidence of legends and oracles, although not uncritically, and often explained human events in terms of divine intervention. Human arrogance and divine vengeance are key forces that help explain the defeat of Croesus by Cyrus as well as Xerxes' defeat by the Greeks. Yet the *History* is typical of its time in celebrating the crucial role of human intelligence as exemplified by Miltiades at Marathon and Themistocles at Salamis. Nor was Herodotus unaware of the importance of institutions. There is no mistaking his pride in the

We'll take thet butte.

LYSISTRATA

Butte?

SPARTAN

The Promontory of Pylos—Sparta's Back Door.
We've missed it fer a turrible spell.
(Reaching)
Hev to keep our hand in.

KINESIAS

(Pushing him away)
The price is too high—you'll never take that!

LYSISTRATA

Oh, let them have it.

KINESIAS

What room will we have left for maneuvers?

LYSISTRATA

Demand another spot in exchange.

KINESIAS

(Surveying Peace like a map as he addresses the Spartan)
Then you hand over to us—uh, let me see—
let's try Thessaly—
(Indicating the relevant portions of Peace)
First of all, Easy Mountain . . .
then the Maniac Gulf behind it . . .
and down to Megara for the legs . . .

SPARTAN

You cain't take all of thet! Yore plumb
out of yore mind!

LYSISTRATA

(To Kinesias)
Don't argue. Let the legs go.
(Kinesias nods. A pause, general smiles of agreement)

KINESIAS

(Doffing his cloak)
I feel an urgent desire to plow a few furrows.

SPARTAN

(Doffing his cloak)
Hit's time to work a few loads of fertilizer in.

LYSISTRATA

Conclude the treaty and the simple life is yours.
If such is your decision, convene your councils,
and then deliberate the matter with your
allies.

KINESIAS

Deliberate? Allies?
We're over-extended already!
Wouldn't every ally approve of our position—
Union Now?

SPARTAN

I know I kin speak for ourn.

KINESIAS

And I for ours.
They're just a bunch of gigolos.

LYSISTRATA

I heartily approve.
Now first attend to your purification,
then we, the women, will welcome you to the Citadel
and treat you to all the delights of a home-cooked banquet.
Then you'll exchange your oaths and pledge your faith,
and every man of you will take his wife
and depart for home.

Aristophanes, Lysistrata, *trans. by Douglass Parker, in* Four Comedies by Aristophanes, *ed. by W. Arrowsmith (Ann Arbor: University of Michigan Press, 1969), pp. 79–81.*

superiority of the Greek *polis* and the discipline it inspired in its citizen soldiers and his pride in the superiority of the Greeks' voluntary obedience to law over the Persians' fear of punishment.

Thucydides, the historian of the Peloponnesian War, was born about 460 B.C.E. and died a few years after the end of the Great Peloponnesian War. He was very much a product of the late fifth century B.C.E.. His work, which was influenced by the secular, human-centered, skeptical rationalism of the Sophists, also reflects the scientific attitude of the school of medicine named for his contemporary, Hippocrates of Cos.

The Hippocratic school, known for its pioneering work in medicine and scientific theory, placed great emphasis on an approach to the understanding, diagnosis, and treatment of disease that combined careful observation with reason. In the same way Thucydides took great pains to achieve factual accuracy and tried to use his evidence to discover meaningful patterns of human behavior. He believed that human nature was essentially unchanging, so that a wise person equipped with the understanding provided by history might accurately foresee events and thus help to guide them. He believed, however, that only a few had the ability to understand history and to put its lessons to good use. He thought that even the wisest could be foiled by the intervention of chance, which played a great role in human affairs. Thucydides focused his interest on politics, and in that area his assumptions about human nature do not seem unwarranted. His work has proved to be, as he hoped, "a possession forever." Its description of the terrible civil war between the two basic kinds of *poleis* is a final and fitting example of the tension that was the source of both the greatness and the decline of Classical Greece.

The Fourth Century B.C.E.

Historians often speak of the Peloponnesian War as the crisis of the *polis* and of the fourth century B.C.E. as the period of its decline. The war did bring powerfully important changes: the impoverishment of some Greek cities and with it an intensification of class conflict; the development of professionalism in the army; and demographic shifts that sometimes reduced the citizen population and increased the numbers of resident aliens. The Greeks of the fourth century B.C.E. did not know, however, that their traditional way of life was on the verge of destruction. Still, thinkers could not avoid recognizing that they lived in a time of troubles, and they responded in various ways. Some looked to the past and tried to shore up the weakened structure of the *polis*; others tended toward despair and looked for new solutions; and still others averted their gaze from the public arena altogether. All of these responses are apparent in the literature, philosophy, and art of the period.

DRAMA The tendency of some to turn away from the life of the *polis* and inward to everyday life, the family, and their own individuality is apparent in the poetry of the fourth century B.C.E. A new genre, called Middle Comedy, replaced the political subjects and personal invective of the Old Comedy with a comic-realistic depiction of daily life, plots of intrigue, and mild satire of domestic situations. Significantly, the role of the chorus, which in some way represented the *polis*, was very much diminished. These trends all continued and were carried even further in the New Comedy. Its leading playwright, Menander (342–291 B.C.E.), completely abandoned mythological subjects in favor of domestic tragicomedy. His gentle satire of the foibles of ordinary people and his tales of lovers temporarily thwarted before a happy and proper ending would not be unfamiliar to viewers of modern situation comedies.

Tragedy faded as a robust and original form. It became common to revive the great plays of the previous century. No tragedies written in the fourth century B.C.E. have been preserved. The plays of Euripides, which rarely won first prize when first produced for Dionysian festival competitions, became increasingly popular in the fourth century and after. Euripides was less interested in cosmic confrontations of conflicting principles than in the psychology and behavior of individual human beings. Some of his late plays, in fact, are less like the tragedies of Aeschylus and Sophocles than forerunners of later forms such as the New Comedy. Plays like *Helena*, *Andromeda*, and *Iphigenia in Tauris* are more like fairy tales, tales of adventure, or love stories than tragedies.

SCULPTURE The same movement away from the grand, the ideal, and the general and toward the ordinary, the real, and the individual is apparent in the development of Greek sculpture. To see these developments, one has only to compare the statue of the Striding God of Artemisium (ca. 460 B.C.E.), thought to be either Zeus on the point of releasing a thunderbolt or Poseidon about to throw his trident, or the Doryphoros of Polycleitus (ca. 450–440 B.C.E.) with the Hermes of Praxiteles (ca. 340–330 B.C.E.) or the Apoxyomenos attributed to Lysippus (ca. 330 B.C.E.).

Philosophy and the Crisis of the Polis

SOCRATES Probably the most complicated response to the crisis of the *polis* may be found in the life and teachings of Socrates (469–399 B.C.E.). Because he wrote nothing, our knowledge of him comes chiefly from his disciples Plato and Xenophon and from later tradition. Although as a young man he was interested in speculations about the physical world, he later turned to the investigation of ethics and morality; as Cicero put it, he brought philosophy down from the heavens. Socrates was committed to

The striding god from Artemisium is a bronze statue dating from about 460 B.C.E. It was found in the sea near Artemisium, the northern tip of the large Greek island of Euboea, and is now on display in the Athens archaeological museum. Exactly whom he represents is not known. Some have thought him to be Poseidon holding a trident; others believe that he is Zeus hurling a thunderbolt. In either case he is a splendid representative of the early Classical period of Greek sculpture. [National Archaeological Museum, Athens]

the search for truth and for the knowledge about human affairs that he believed could be discovered by reason. His method was to go among men, particularly those reputed to know something, such as craftsmen, poets, and politicians, to question and cross-examine them.

The result was always the same. Those Socrates questioned might have technical information and skills but seldom had any knowledge of the fundamental principles of human behavior. It is understandable that Athenians so exposed should be angry with their examiner, and it is not surprising that they thought Socrates was undermining the beliefs and values of the *polis*. Socrates' unconcealed contempt for democracy, which seemingly relied on ignorant amateurs to make important political decisions without any certain knowledge,

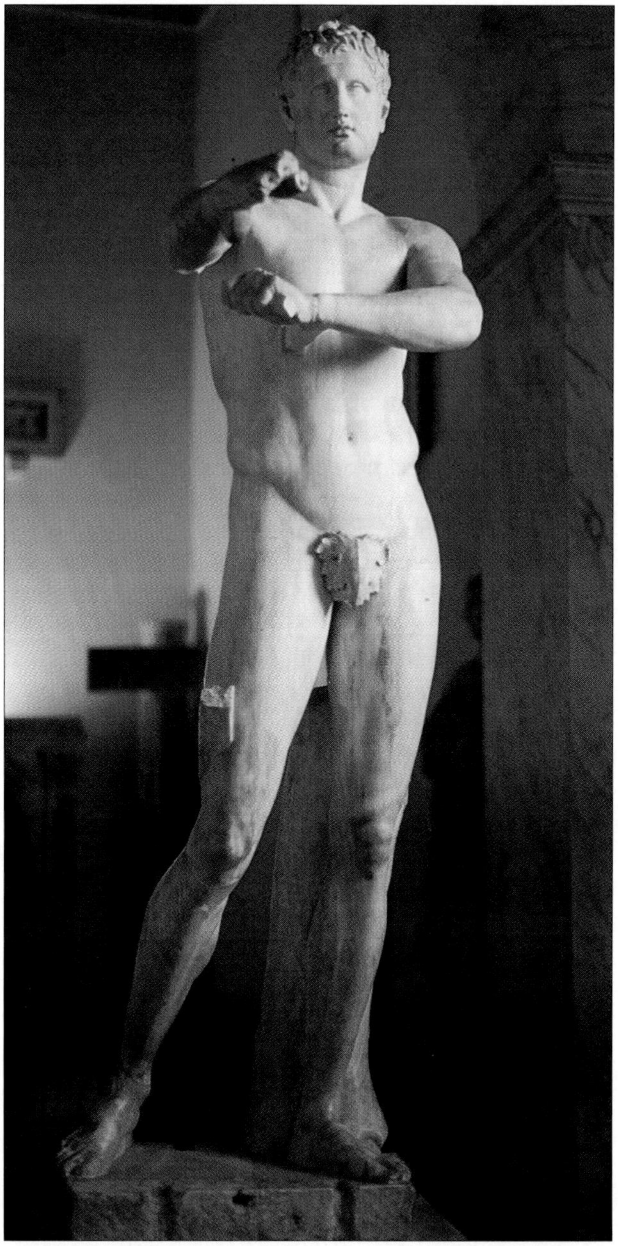

This is a Roman copy of the Apoxyomenos *(the scraper) by Lysippus of Sicyon. It shows a young athlete scraping from his body the oil used for cleansing after exertion. The original was made about 330 B.C.E. [Robert Miller]*

created further hostility. Moreover, his insistence on the primacy of his own individualism and his determination to pursue philosophy even against the wishes of his fellow citizens reinforced this hostility and the prejudice that went with it.

But Socrates, unlike the Sophists, did not accept pay for his teaching; he professed ignorance and denied that he taught at all. His individualism, moreover, was unlike the worldly hedonism of some of the Sophists. It was not wealth or pleasure or power that he urged people to seek, but "the greatest improvement of the soul." He differed also from the more radical Sophists in that he denied that the *polis* and its laws were merely conventional. He thought, on the contrary, that they had a legitimate claim on the citizen, and he proved it in the most convincing fashion.

In 399 B.C.E. he was condemned to death by an Athenian jury on the charges of bringing new gods into the city and of corrupting the youth. His dialectical inquiries had angered many important people. His criticism of democracy must have been viewed with suspicion, especially as Critias and Charmides, who were members of the Thirty Tyrants, and the traitor Alcibiades had been among his disciples. He was given a chance to escape but, as we are told in Plato's *Crito*, he refused to do so because of his veneration of the laws. Socrates' career set the stage for later responses to the travail of the *polis*. He recognized its difficulties and criticized its shortcomings, and he turned away from an active political life, but he did not abandon the idea of the *polis*. He fought as a soldier in its defense, obeyed its laws, and sought to put its values on a sound foundation by reason.

THE CYNICS One branch of Socratic thought—the concern with personal morality and one's own soul, the disdain of worldly pleasure and wealth, and the withdrawal from political life—was developed and then distorted almost beyond recognition by the Cynic school. Antisthenes (ca. 455–360 B.C.E.), a follower of Socrates, is said to have been its founder, but its most famous exemplar was Diogenes of Sinope (ca. 400–325 B.C.E.). Because Socrates disparaged wealth and worldly comfort, Diogenes wore rags and lived in a tub. He performed shameful acts in public and made his living by begging to show his rejection of convention. He believed that happiness lay in satisfying natural needs in the simplest and most direct way; because actions to this end, being natural, could not be indecent, they could and should be done publicly.

Socrates questioned the theoretical basis for popular religious beliefs; the Cynics, in contrast, ridiculed all religious observances. As Plato said, Diogenes was Socrates gone mad. Beyond that, the way of the Cynics contradicted important Socratic beliefs. Socrates, unlike traditional aristocrats such as Theognis, believed that virtue was a matter not of birth but of knowledge and that people do wrong only through ignorance of what is virtuous. The Cynics, on the other hand, believed that "virtue is an affair of deeds and does not need a store of words and learning."[1] Wisdom and happiness come from pursuing the proper style of life, not from philosophy.

They moved even further away from Socrates by abandoning the concept of the *polis* entirely. When Diogenes was asked about his citizenship, he answered that he was *kosmopolites*, a citizen of the world. The Cynics plainly had turned away from the past, and their views anticipated those of the Hellenistic Age.

PLATO Plato (429–347 B.C.E.) was by far the most important of Socrates' associates and is a perfect example of the pupil who becomes greater than his master. He was the first systematic philosopher and therefore the first to place political ideas in their full philosophical context. He was also a writer of genius, leaving us twenty-six philosophical discussions. Almost all are in the form of dialogues, which somehow make the examination of difficult and complicated philosophical problems seem dramatic and entertaining. Plato came from a noble Athenian family, and he looked forward to an active political career until the excesses of the Thirty Tyrants and the execution of Socrates discouraged him from that pursuit. Twice he made trips to Sicily in the hope of producing a model state at Syracuse under the tyrants Dionysius I and II, but without success.

In 386 B.C.E. he founded the Academy, a center of philosophical investigation and a school for training statesmen and citizens. It had a powerful impact on Greek thought and lasted until it was closed by the emperor Justinian in the sixth century C.E.

Like Socrates, Plato firmly believed in the *polis* and its values. Its virtues were order, harmony, and justice, and one of its main objects was to produce good people. Like his master, and unlike the radical Sophists, Plato thought that the *polis* was in accord with nature. He accepted Socrates' doctrine of the identity of virtue and knowledge. He made it plain what that knowledge was: *episteme*, science, a body of true and unchanging wisdom open to only a few philosophers, whose training, character, and intellect allowed them to see reality. Only such

[1] *Diogenes Laertius*, Life of Antisthenes, *6.11.*

people were qualified to rule; they would prefer the life of pure contemplation but would accept their responsibility and take their turn as philosopher kings. The training of such an individual required a specialization of function and a subordination of that individual to the community even greater than that at Sparta. This specialization would lead to Plato's definition of *justice*: that each man should do only that one thing to which his nature is best suited.

Plato saw quite well that the *polis* of his day suffered from terrible internal stress, class struggle, and factional divisions. His solution, however, was not that of some Greeks, that is, conquest and resulting economic prosperity. For Plato the answer was in moral and political reform. The way to harmony was to destroy the causes of strife: private property, the family—anything, in short, that stood between the individual citizen and devotion to the *polis*.

Concern for the redemption of the *polis* was at the heart of Plato's system of philosophy. He began by asking the traditional questions: What is a good man, and how is he made? The goodness of a human being belonged to moral philosophy, and when goodness became a function of the state, it became political philosophy. Because goodness depended on knowledge of the good, it required a theory of knowledge and an investigation of what kind of knowledge was required for goodness. The answer must be metaphysical and so required a full examination of metaphysics. Even when the philosopher knew the good, however, the question remained how the state could bring its citizens to the necessary comprehension of that knowledge. The answer required a theory of education. Even purely logical and metaphysical questions, therefore, were subordinate to the overriding political questions. In this way Plato's need to find a satisfactory foundation for the beleaguered *polis* contributed to the birth of systematic philosophy.

ARISTOTLE Aristotle (384–322 B.C.E.) was a pupil of Plato's and owed much to the thought of his master, but his very different experience and cast of mind led him in some new directions. He was born at Stagirus in the Chalcidice, the son of the court doctor of neighboring Macedon. As a young man he went to Athens to study at the Academy, where he stayed until Plato's death. Then he joined a Platonic colony at Assos in Asia Minor, and from there he moved to Mytilene. In both places he did research in marine biology, and biological interests played a large part in all his thoughts. In 342 B.C.E. Philip, the king of Macedon, appointed him tutor to his son, the young Alexander. (See the following section.)

Sixth century B.C.E. marble head of Aristotle. [Erich Lessing/Art Resource, NY]

In 336 B.C.E. he returned to Athens, where he founded his own school, the Lyceum, or the Peripatos, as it was also called because of the covered walk within it. In later years its members were called *Peripatetics*. On the death of Alexander in 323 B.C.E., the Athenians rebelled from Macedonian rule, and Aristotle found it wise to leave. He died at Chalcis in Euboea in the following year.

The Lyceum was a very different place from the Academy. Its members took little interest in mathematics and were concerned with gathering, ordering, and analyzing all human knowledge. Aristotle wrote dialogues on the Platonic model, but none survive. He and his students also prepared many collections of information to serve as the basis for scientific works. Of these only the *Constitution of the Athenians*, one of 158 constitutional treatises, remains. Almost all of what we possess is in the form of philosophical and scientific studies, whose

Plato Reports the Claims of the Sophist Protagoras

Plato (429–347 B.C.E.) remains to many the greatest of the ancient philosophers. Protagoras, the famous Sophist from Leontini in Sicily, came to Athens in 427 B.C.E. and created great excitement. In the following passage from the dialogue Protagoras, *Plato's spokesman, Socrates, introduces a young man who wishes to benefit from Protagoras's skills.*

✦ *From reading this selection why do you think Plato chose to present his philosophical ideas in the form of a dramatic dialogue? In what ways is Protagoras typical of the Sophists? In what ways is he different from Socrates? What role did the Sophists play in Athenian society? What was their importance? How would you compare the kind of education offered by Protagoras with that offered by other Sophists, by Socrates, and with your own?*

When we were all seated, Protagoras said: Now that the company are assembled, Socrates, tell me about the young man of whom you were just now speaking.

I replied: I will begin again at the same point, Protagoras, and tell you once more the purport of my visit: this is my friend Hippocrates, who is desirous of making your acquaintance; he would like to know what will happen to him if he associates with you. I have no more to say.

Protagoras answered: Young man, if you associate with me, on the very first day you will return home a better man than you came and better on the second day than on the first, and better every day than you were on the day before.

When I heard this, I said: Protagoras, I do not at all wonder at hearing you say this; even at your age, and with all your wisdom, if any one were to teach you what you did not know before, you would become better no doubt: but please to answer in a different way—I will explain how by an example. Let me suppose that Hippocrates, instead of desiring your acquaintance, wished to become acquainted with the young man Zeuxippus of Heraclea, who has lately been in Athens, and he had come to him as he has come to you, and had heard him say, as he has heard you say, that every day he would grow and become better if he associated with him: and then suppose that he were to ask him, "In what shall I become better, and in what shall I grow?" Zeuxippus would answer, "In painting." And suppose that he went to Orthagoas the Theban, and heard him say the same thing, and asked him, "In what shall I become better day by day?" he would reply, "In flute-playing." Now I want you to make the same sort of answer to this young man and to me, who am asking questions on his account. When you say that on the first day on which he associates with you he will return home a better man, and on every day will grow in like manner,—in what, Protagoras, will he be better? and about what?

When Protagoras heard me say this, he replied: You ask questions fairly, and I like to answer a question which is fairly put. If Hippocrates comes to me he will not experience the sort of drudgery with which other Sophists are in the habit of insulting their pupils; who, when they have just escaped from the arts, are taken and driven back into them by these teachers, and made to learn calculation, and astronomy, and geometry, and music (he gave a look at Hippias as he said this); but if he comes to me, he will learn that which he comes to learn. And this is prudence in affairs private as well as public; he will learn to order his own house in the best manner, and he will be able to speak and act for the best in the affairs of the state.

Plato, Protagoras, *trans. by Benjamin Jowett, in* The Dialogues of Plato, *Vol. 1 (New York: Random House, 1937), pp. 88–89.*

loose organization and style suggest that they were lecture notes. The range of subjects treated is astonishing, including logic, physics, astronomy, biology, ethics, rhetoric, literary criticism, and politics.

In each field the method is the same. Aristotle began with observation of the empirical evidence, which in some cases was physical and in others was common opinion. To this body of information he applied reason and discovered inconsistencies or difficulties. To deal with these, he introduced metaphysical principles to explain the problems or to reconcile the inconsistencies.

His view on all subjects, like Plato's, was teleological; that is, both Plato and Aristotle recognized purposes apart from and greater than the will of the individual human being. Plato's purposes, however, were contained in ideas, or forms that were transcendental concepts outside the experience of most people. For Aristotle the purposes of most things were easily inferred by observation of their behavior in the world. Aristotle's most striking characteristics are his moderation and his common sense. His epistemology finds room for both reason and experience; his metaphysics gives meaning and reality to both mind and body; his ethics aims at the good life, which is the contemplative life, but recognizes the necessity for moderate wealth, comfort, and pleasure.

All these qualities are evident in Aristotle's political thought. Like Plato, he opposed the Sophists' assertion that the *polis* was contrary to nature and the result of mere convention. His response was to apply the teleology he saw in all nature to politics as well. In his view matter existed to achieve an end, and it developed until it achieved its form, which was its end. There was constant development from matter to form, from potential to actual. Therefore, human primitive instincts could be seen as the matter out of which the human's potential as a political being could be realized. The *polis* made individuals self-sufficient and allowed the full realization of their potentiality. It was therefore natural.

It was also the highest point in the evolution of the social institutions that serve the human need to continue the species—marriage, household, village, and finally, *polis*. For Aristotle the purpose of the *polis* was neither economic nor military, but moral. According to Aristotle, "The end of the state is the good life" (*Politics* 1280b), the life lived "for the sake of noble actions" (1281a), a life of virtue and morality.

Characteristically, Aristotle was less interested in the best state—the utopia that required philosophers to rule it—than in the best state practically possible, one that would combine justice with stability. The constitution for that state he called *politeia*, not the best constitution, but the next best, the one most suited to and most possible for most states. Its quality was moderation, and it naturally gave power to neither the rich nor the poor, but to the middle class, which must also be the most numerous. The middle class possessed many virtues; because of its moderate wealth it was free of the arrogance of the rich and the malice of the poor. For this reason it was the most stable class.

The stability of the constitution also came from its being a mixed constitution, blending in some way the laws of democracy and of oligarchy. Aristotle's scheme was unique because of its realism and the breadth of its vision. All the political thinkers of the fourth century B.C.E. recognized that the *polis* was in danger, and all hoped to save it. All recognized the economic and social troubles that threatened it. Isocrates, a contemporary of Plato and Aristotle, urged a program of imperial conquest as a cure for poverty and revolution. Plato saw the folly of solving a political and moral problem by purely economic means and resorted to the creation of utopias. Aristotle combined the practical analysis of political and economic realities with the moral and political purposes of the traditional defenders of the *polis*. The result was a passionate confidence in the virtues of moderation and of the middle class and the proposal of a constitution that would give it power. It is ironic that the ablest defense of the *polis* came soon before its demise.

The Hellenistic World

The term *Hellenistic* was coined in the nineteenth century to describe the period of three centuries during which Greek culture spread far from its homeland to Egypt and far into Asia. The new civilization formed in this expansion was a mixture of Greek and Near Eastern elements, although the degree of mixture varied from time to time and place to place. The Hellenistic world was larger than the world of Classical Greece, and its major political units were much larger than the city-states, though these persisted in different forms. The new political and cultural order had its roots in the rise to power of a Macedonian dynasty that conquered Greece and the Persian Empire in the space of two generations.

The Macedonian Conquest

The quarrels among the Greeks brought on defeat and conquest by a new power that suddenly rose to eminence in the fourth century B.C.E., the kingdom of Macedon. The Macedonians inhabited the land to the north of Thessaly (see Map 3–1), and through the centuries they had unknowingly served the vital purpose of protecting the Greek states from barbarian tribes further to the north.

By Greek standards Macedon was a backward, semibarbaric land. It had no *poleis* and was ruled loosely by a king in a rather Homeric fashion. He was chosen partly on the basis of descent, but the acclamation of the army gathered in assembly was required to make him legitimate. Quarrels between pretenders to the throne and even murder to secure it were not uncommon. A council of nobles checked the royal power and could reject a weak or incompetent king. Hampered by constant wars with the barbarians, internal strife, loose organization, and lack of money, Macedon played no great part in Greek affairs up to the fourth century B.C.E.

The Macedonians were of the same stock as the Greeks and spoke a Greek dialect, and the nobles, at least, thought of themselves as Greeks. The kings claimed descent from Heracles and the royal house of Argos. They tried to bring Greek culture into their court and won acceptance at the Olympic games. If a king could be found to unify this nation, it was bound to play a greater part in Greek affairs.

PHILIP OF MACEDON That king was Philip II (r. 359–336 B.C.E.), who, while still under thirty, took advantage of his appointment as regent to overthrow his infant nephew and make himself king. Like many of his predecessors, he admired Greek culture. Between 367 and 364 B.C.E. he had been a hostage in Thebes, where he learned much about Greek politics and warfare under the tutelage of Epaminondas. His talents for war and diplomacy and his boundless ambition made him the ablest king in Macedonian history. Using both diplomatic and military means, he was able to pacify the tribes on his frontiers and make his own hold on the throne firmer. Then he began to undermine Athenian control of the northern Aegean. He took Amphipolis, which gave him control of the Strymon Valley and of the gold and silver mines of Mount Pangaeus. The income allowed him to found new cities, to bribe politicians in foreign towns, and to reorganize his army into the finest fighting force in the world.

THE MACEDONIAN ARMY Philip put to good use what he had learned in Thebes and combined it with the advantages afforded by Macedonian society and tradition. His genius created a versatile and powerful army that was at once national and professional, unlike the amateur armies of citizen-soldiers who fought for the individual *poleis*.

The infantry was drawn from among Macedonian farmers and the frequently rebellious Macedonian hill people. In time these two elements were integrated to form a loyal and effective national force. Infantrymen were armed with thirteen-foot pikes instead of the more common nine-foot pikes and stood in a more open phalanx formation than the *hoplite* phalanx of the *poleis*. The effectiveness of this formation depended more on skillful use of the pike than the weight of the charge. In Macedonian tactics, the role of the phalanx was not to be the decisive force but to hold the enemy until a massed cavalry charge could strike a winning blow on the flank or into a gap. The cavalry was made up of Macedonian nobles and clan leaders, called Companions, who lived closely with the king and developed a special loyalty to him.

Philip also employed mercenaries who knew the latest tactics used by mobile light-armed Greek troops and were familiar with the most sophisticated siege machinery known to the Greeks. With these mercenaries, and with draft forces from among his allies, he could expand on his native Macedonian army of as many as 40,000 men.

THE INVASION OF GREECE So armed, Philip turned south toward central Greece. Since 355 B.C.E. the Phocians had been fighting against Thebes and Thessaly. Philip gladly accepted the request of the Thessalians to be their general, defeated Phocis, and treacherously took control of Thessaly. Swiftly he turned northward again to Thrace and gained domination over the northern Aegean coast and the European side of the straits to the Black Sea. This conquest threatened the vital interests of Athens, which still had a formidable fleet of 300 ships.

The Athens of 350 B.C.E. was not the Athens of Pericles. It had neither imperial revenue nor allies to share the burden of war on land or sea, and its

Demosthenes Denounces Philip of Macedon

Demosthenes (384–322 B.C.E.) was an Athenian statesman who urged his fellow citizens and other Greeks to resist the advance of Philip of Macedon (r. 359–336 B.C.E.). This passage is from the speech we call the First Philippic, delivered probably in 351 B.C.E.

✦ *Whom does Demosthenes blame for the danger facing Athens?*
✦ *What hope does he see of stopping Philip's advance?*
✦ *How important is Philip himself, according to Demosthenes, as a source of the menace to Athens and the rest of Greece?*

Do not imagine, that his empire is everlastingly secured to him as a god. There are those who hate and fear and envy him, Athenians, even among those that seem most friendly; and all feelings that are in other men belong, we may assume, to his confederates. But now they are cowed, having no refuge through your tardiness and indolence, which I say you must abandon forthwith. For you see, Athenians, the case, to what pitch of arrogance the man has advanced, who leaves you not even the choice of action or inaction, but threatens and uses (they say) outrageous language, and, unable to rest in possession of his conquests, continually widens their circle, and whilst we dally and delay, throws his net all around us. When then, Athenians, when will ye act as becomes you? In what event? In that of necessity, I suppose. And how should we regard the events happening now? Methinks, to freemen the strongest necessity is the disgrace of their condition. Or tell me, do ye like walking about and asking one another:—is there any news? Why, could there be greater news than a man of Macedonia subduing Athenians, and directing the affairs of Greece? Is Philip dead? No, but he is sick. And what matters it to you? Should anything befall this man, you will soon create another Philip, if you attend to business thus. For even he has been exalted not so much by his own strength, as by our negligence.

Demosthenes, *The Olynthiac and Other Public Orations of Demosthenes* (London: George Bell and Sons, 1903), pp. 62–63.

own population was smaller than in the fifth century B.C.E. The Athenians, therefore, were reluctant to go on expeditions themselves or even to send out mercenary armies under Athenian generals, for they had to be paid out of taxes or contributions from Athenian citizens.

The leading spokesman against these tendencies and the cautious foreign policy that went with them was Demosthenes (384–322 B.C.E.), one of the greatest orators in Greek history. He was convinced that Philip was a dangerous enemy to Athens and the other Greeks. He spent most of his career urging the Athenians to resist Philip's encroachments. He was right, for beginning in 349 B.C.E. Philip attacked several cities in northern and central Greece and firmly planted Macedonian power in those regions. The king of "barbarian" Macedon was elected president of the Pythian Games at Delphi, and the Athenians were forced to concur in the election.

In these difficult times it was Athens's misfortune not to have the kind of consistent political leadership that Cimon or Pericles had offered a century earlier. Many, perhaps most, Athenians accepted Demosthenes' view of Philip, but few were willing to run the risks and make the sacrifices necessary to stop his advance. Others, like Eubulus, an outstanding financial official and conservative political leader, favored a cautious policy of cooperation with Philip in the hope that his aims were limited and no real threat to Athens.

Not all Athenians feared Philip. Isocrates (436–338 B.C.E.), the head of an important rhetorical and philosophical school in Athens, looked to him to provide the unity and leadership needed for a

Panhellenic campaign against Persia. He and other orators had been urging such a campaign for some years. They saw the conquest of Asia Minor as the solution to the economic, social, and political problems that had brought poverty and civil war to the Greek cities ever since the Peloponnesian War. Finally, there seem to have been some Athenians who were in the pay of Philip, for he used money lavishly to win support in all the cities.

The years between 346 B.C.E. and 340 B.C.E. were spent in diplomatic maneuvering, each side trying to win strategically useful allies. At last, Philip attacked Perinthus and Byzantium, the life line of Athenian commerce; in 340 B.C.E. he besieged both cities and declared war. The Athenian fleet saved both, and so in the following year Philip marched into Greece. Demosthenes performed wonders in rallying the Athenians and winning Thebes over to the Athenian side. In 338 B.C.E., however, Philip defeated the allied forces at Chaeronea in Boeotia. The decisive blow in this great battle was a cavalry charge led by the eighteen-year-old son of Philip, Alexander.

THE MACEDONIAN GOVERNMENT OF GREECE The Macedonian settlement of Greek affairs was not as harsh as many had feared, although in some cities the friends of Macedon came to power and killed or exiled their enemies. Demosthenes remained free to engage in politics. Athens was spared from attack on the condition that it give up what was left of its empire and follow the lead of Macedon. The rest of Greece was arranged in such a way as to remove all dangers to Philip's rule. To guarantee his security, Philip placed garrisons at Thebes, Chalcis, and Corinth.

In 338 B.C.E. Philip called a meeting of the Greek states to form the federal League of Corinth. The constitution of the league provided for autonomy, freedom from tribute and garrisons, and suppression of piracy and civil war. The league delegates would make foreign policy in theory without consulting their home governments or Philip. All this was a facade; not only was Philip of Macedon president of the league, he was its ruler. The defeat at Chaeronea ended Greek freedom and autonomy. Although it maintained its form and way of life for some time, the *polis* had lost control of its own affairs and the special conditions that had made it unique.

Philip did not choose Corinth as the seat of his new confederacy simply from convenience or by accident. It was at Corinth that the Greeks had gathered to resist a Persian invasion almost 150 years earlier. And it was there in 337 B.C.E. that Philip announced his intention to invade Persia in a war of liberation and revenge as leader of the new league. In the spring of 336 B.C.E., however, as he prepared to begin the campaign, Philip was assassinated.

In 1977 a mound was excavated at the Macedonian village of Vergina. The structures that were revealed and the extraordinarily rich finds associated with them have led many scholars to conclude that this is the royal tomb of Philip II, and the evidence seems persuasive that they are right. Philip certainly deserved so distinguished a resting place. He found Macedon a disunited kingdom of semibarbarians, despised and exploited by the Greeks. He left it a united kingdom, master and leader of the Greeks, rich, powerful, and ready to undertake the invasion of Asia.

Alexander the Great

Philip's first son, Alexander III (356–323 B.C.E.), later called Alexander the Great, succeeded his father at the age of twenty. Along with the throne, the young king inherited his father's daring plans for the conquest of Persia.

THE CONQUEST OF THE PERSIAN EMPIRE The Persian Empire was vast and its resources enormous. The usurper Cyrus and his Greek mercenaries, however, had shown it to be vulnerable when they penetrated deep into its interior in the fourth century B.C.E. Its size and disparate nature made it hard to control and exploit. Its rulers faced constant troubles on its far-flung frontiers and constant intrigues within the royal palace. Throughout the fourth century B.C.E. they had called on Greek mercenaries to suppress uprisings. At the time of Philip II's death in 336 B.C.E., Persia was ruled by a new and inexperienced king, Darius III. Yet with a navy that dominated the sea, a huge army, and vast wealth, it remained a formidable opponent.

In 334 B.C.E. Alexander crossed the Hellespont into Asia. His army consisted of about 30,000 infantry and 5,000 cavalry; he had no navy and little money. These facts determined his early strategy—he must seek quick and decisive battles to gain money and supplies from the conquered territory; he must move along the coast to neutralize the Persian navy by depriving it of ports. Memnon, the

This sculpture of Alexander the Great, king of Macedon and conqueror of the Persian Empire, was made in the second century B.C.E. and found at the ancient city of Magnesia in Asia Minor. Alexander's conquests spread Greek culture far from its homeland, laying the foundation of the Hellenistic world. [Erich Lessing/Art Resource, N.Y.]

commander of the Persian navy, recommended the perfect strategy against this plan: to retreat, to scorch the earth and deprive Alexander of supplies, to avoid battles, to use guerrilla tactics, and to stir up rebellion in Greece. He was ignored. The Persians preferred to stand and fight; their pride and courage were greater than their wisdom.

Alexander met the Persian forces of Asia Minor at the Granicus River, where he won a smashing victory in characteristic style (See Map 3–4.) He led a cavalry charge across the river into the teeth of the enemy on the opposite bank. He almost lost his life in the process, but he won the devotion of his soldiers. That victory left the coast of Asia Minor open. Alexander captured the coastal cities, thus denying them to the Persian fleet.

In 333 B.C.E., Alexander marched inland to Syria, where he met the main Persian army under King Darius at Issus. Alexander himself led the cavalry charge that broke the Persian line and sent Darius fleeing into central Asia Minor. He continued along the coast and captured previously impregnable Tyre after a long and ingenious siege, putting an end to the threat of the Persian navy. He took Egypt with little trouble and was greeted as liberator, pharaoh, and son of Re (an Egyptian god whose Greek equivalent was Zeus). At Tyre, Darius sent Alexander a peace offer, yielding his entire empire west of the Euphrates River and his daughter in exchange for an alliance and an end to the invasion. But Alexander aimed at conquering the whole empire and probably whatever lay beyond.

In the spring of 331 B.C.E. Alexander marched into Mesopotamia. At Gaugamela, near the ancient Assyrian city of Nineveh, he met Darius, ready for a last stand. Once again Alexander's tactical genius and personal leadership carried the day. The Persians were broken, and Darius fled once more. Alexander entered Babylon, again hailed as liberator and king.

In January of 330 B.C.E. he came to Persepolis, the Persian capital, which held splendid palaces and the royal treasury. This bonanza ended his financial troubles and put a vast sum of money into circulation, with economic consequences that lasted for centuries. After a stay of several months, Alexander burned Persepolis to dramatize the destruction of the native Persian dynasty and the completion of Hellenic revenge for the earlier Persian invasion of Greece.

The new regime could not be secure while Darius lived, and so Alexander pursued him eastward. Just south of the Caspian Sea, he came upon the corpse of Darius, killed by his relative Bessus. The Persian nobles around Darius had lost faith in him and had joined in the plot. The murder removed Darius from Alexander's path, but now he

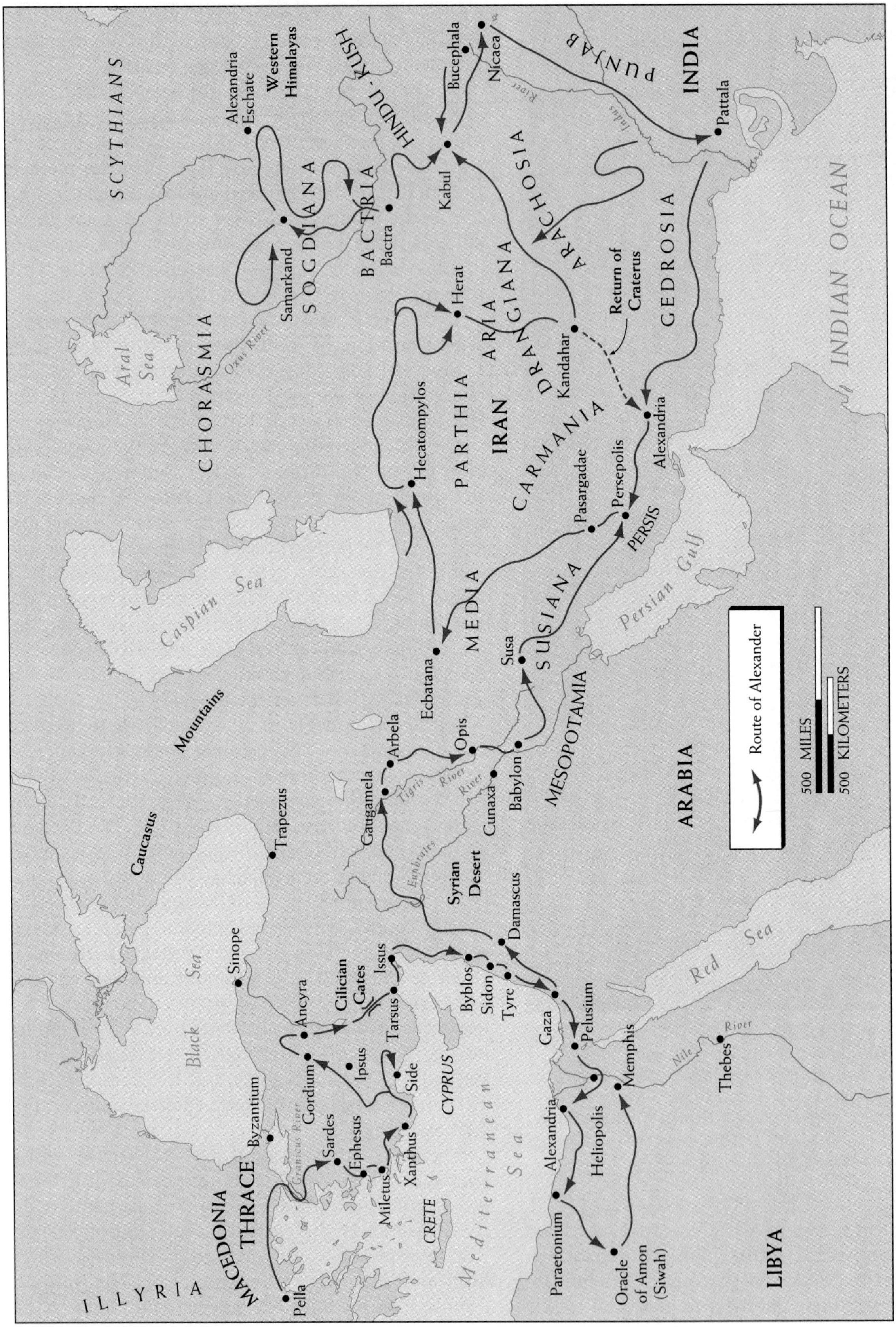

Map 3–4 Alexander's Campaigns *The route taken by Alexander the Great in his conquest of the Persian Empire, 334–323 B.C.E. Starting from the Macedonian capital at Pella, he reached the Indus Valley before being turned back by his own restive troops. He died of fever in Mesopotamia.*

had to catch Bessus, who proclaimed himself successor to Darius. The pursuit of Bessus (who was soon caught), combined with his own great curiosity and longing to go to the most distant places, took Alexander to the frontier of India.

Near Samarkand, in the land of the Scythians, he founded Alexandria Eschate ("Furthest Alexandria"), one of the many cities bearing his name that he founded as he traveled. As part of his grand scheme of amalgamation and conquest, he married the Bactrian princess Roxane and enrolled 30,000 young Bactrians into his army. These were to be trained and sent back to the center of the empire for use later.

In 327 B.C.E. Alexander took his army through the Khyber Pass in an attempt to conquer the lands around the Indus River (modern Pakistan). He reduced its king, Porus, to vassalage but pushed on in the hope of reaching the river called Ocean that the Greeks believed encircled the world. Finally, his weary men refused to go on. By the spring of 324 B.C.E. the army was back at the Persian Gulf and celebrated in the Macedonian style, with a wild spree of drinking.

THE DEATH OF ALEXANDER Alexander was filled with plans for the future: for the consolidation and organization of his empire; for geographical exploration; for building new cities, roads, and harbors; perhaps even for further conquests in the West. There is even some evidence that he asked to be deified and worshiped as a god, although we cannot be sure if he really did so or why. In June of 323 B.C.E., however, he was overcome by a fever and died in Babylon at the age of thirty-three. His memory has never faded, and he soon became the subject of myth, legend, and romance. From the beginning, estimates of him have varied. Some have seen in him a man of grand and noble vision who transcended the narrow limits of Greek and Macedonian ethnocentrism and sought to realize the solidarity of humankind in a great world state. Others have seen him as a calculating despot, given to drunken brawls, brutality, and murder.

The truth is probably somewhere in-between. Alexander was one of the greatest generals the world has seen; he never lost a battle or failed in a siege, and with a modest army he conquered a vast empire. He had rare organizational talents, and his plan for creating a multinational empire was the only intelligent way to consolidate his conquests. He established many new cities—seventy, according to tradition—mostly along trade routes. These cities had the effect of encouraging commerce and prosperity as well as of introducing Hellenic civilization into new areas. It is hard to know if even Alexander could have held together the vast new empire he had created, but his death proved that only he would have had a chance to succeed.

The Rise of Macedon

359–336 B.C.E.	Reign of Philip II
338 B.C.E.	Battle of Chaeronea; Philip conquers Greece
338 B.C.E.	Founding of League of Corinth
336–323 B.C.E.	Reign of Alexander III, the Great
334 B.C.E.	Alexander invades Asia
333 B.C.E.	Battle of Issus
331 B.C.E.	Battle of Gaugamela
330 B.C.E.	Fall of Persepolis
327 B.C.E.	Alexander reaches Indus Valley
323 B.C.E.	Death of Alexander

The Successors

Nobody was prepared for Alexander's sudden death in 323 B.C.E., and affairs were further complicated by a weak succession: Roxane's unborn child and Alexander's weak-minded half-brother. His able and loyal Macedonian generals at first hoped to preserve the empire for the Macedonian royal house, and to this end they appointed themselves governors of the various provinces of the empire. The conflicting ambitions of these strong-willed men, however, led to prolonged warfare among various combinations of them. In these conflicts three of the original number were killed, and all of the direct members of the Macedonian royal house were either executed or murdered. With the murder of Roxane and her son in 310 B.C.E., there was no longer any focus for the enormous empire, and in 306 and 305 B.C.E. the surviving governors proclaimed themselves kings of their various holdings.

Three of these Macedonian generals founded dynasties of significance in the spread of Hellenistic culture:

- Ptolemy I, 367?–283 B.C.E.; founder of the Thirty-First Dynasty in Egypt, the Ptolemies, of whom Cleopatra, who died in 30 B.C.E., was the last
- Seleucus I, 358?–280 B.C.E.; founder of the Seleucid Dynasty in Mesopotamia

- Antigonus I, 382–301 B.C.E.; founder of the Antigonid Dynasty in Asia Minor and Macedon

For the first seventy-five years or so after the death of Alexander, the world ruled by his successors enjoyed considerable prosperity. The vast sums of money that he and they put into circulation greatly increased the level of economic activity. The opportunities for service and profit in the East attracted many Greeks and relieved their native cities of some of the pressure of the poor. The opening of vast new territories to Greek trade, the increased demand for Greek products, and the new availability of desired goods, as well as the conscious policies of the Hellenistic kings, all helped the growth of commerce.

The new prosperity, however, was not evenly distributed. The urban Greeks, the Macedonians, and the Hellenized natives who made up the upper and middle classes lived in comfort and even luxury, but the rural native peasants did not. Unlike the independent men who owned and worked the relatively small and equal lots of the *polis* in earlier times, Hellenistic farmers were reduced to subordinate, dependent, peasant status, working on large plantations of decreasing efficiency. During prosperous times these distinctions were bearable, although even then there was tension between the two groups. After a while, however, the costs of continuing wars, inflation, and a gradual lessening of the positive effects of the introduction of Persian wealth all led to economic crisis. The kings bore down heavily on the middle classes, who were skilled at avoiding their responsibilities, however. The pressure on the peasants and the city laborers became great, too, and they responded by slowing down their work and even by striking. In Greece economic pressures brought clashes between rich and poor, demands for the abolition of debt and the redistribution of land, and even, on occasion, civil war.

These internal divisions, along with international wars, weakened the capacity of the Hellenistic kingdoms to resist outside attack. By the middle of the second century B.C.E. they had all, except for Egypt, succumbed to an expanding Italian power, Rome. The two centuries between Alexander and the Roman conquest, however, were of great and lasting importance. They saw the entire eastern Mediterranean coast, Greece, Egypt, Mesopotamia, and the old Persian Empire formed into a single political, economic, and cultural unit.

Hellenistic Culture

The career of Alexander the Great marked a significant turning point in Greek thought as it was represented in literature, philosophy, religion, and art. His conquests and the establishment of the successor kingdoms put an end to the central role of the *polis* in Greek life and thought. Some scholars disagree about the end of the *polis*, denying that Philip's victory at Chaeronea put an end to its existence. They point to the continuance of *poleis* throughout the Hellenistic period and even see a continuation of them in the Roman *municipia*. These were, however, only a shadow of the vital reality that had been the true *polis*.

Deprived of control of their foreign affairs, and with their important internal arrangements determined by a foreign monarch, the post-Classical cities lost the kind of political freedom that was basic to the old outlook. They were cities, perhaps—in a sense, even city-states—but not *poleis*. As time passed, they changed from sovereign states to municipal towns merged in military empires. Never again in antiquity would there be either a serious attack on or a defense of the *polis*, for its importance was gone. For the most part, the Greeks after Alexander turned away from political solutions for their problems. Instead they sought personal responses to their hopes and fears, particularly in religion, philosophy, and magic. The confident, sometimes arrogant, humanism of the fifth century B.C.E. gave way to a kind of resignation to fate, a recognition of helplessness before forces too great for humans to manage.

Philosophy

These developments are noticeable in the changes that overtook the established schools of philosophy as well as in the emergence of two new and influential groups of philosophers, the Epicureans and the Stoics. Athens's position as the center of philosophical studies was reinforced, for the Academy and the Lyceum continued in operation, and the new schools were also located in Athens. The Lyceum turned gradually away from the universal investigations of its founder, Aristotle, even from his scientific interests, to become a center chiefly of literary and especially historical studies.

The Academy turned even further away from its tradition. It adopted the systematic Skepticism of Pyrrho of Elis. Under the leadership of Arcesilaus and Carneades, the Skeptics of the Academy became skilled at pointing out fallacies and weaknesses in the philosophies of the rival schools. They thought that nothing could be known and so consoled themselves and their followers by suggesting that nothing mattered. It was easy for them, therefore, to accept conventional morality and the world as it was. The Cynics, of course, continued to denounce convention and to advocate the crude life in accordance with nature, which some of them practiced publicly to the shock and outrage of respectable citizens. Neither Skepticism nor Cynicism had much appeal to the middle-class city dweller of the third century B.C.E., who sought some basis for choosing a way of life now that the *polis* no longer provided one ready-made.

THE EPICUREANS Epicurus of Athens (342–271 B.C.E.) formulated a new teaching, embodied in the school he founded in his native city in 306 B.C.E. His philosophy conformed to the mood of the times in that its goal was not knowledge but human happiness, which he believed could be achieved if one followed a style of life based on reason. He took sense perception to be the basis of all human knowledge. The reality and reliability of sense perception rested on the acceptance of the physical universe described by the atomists, Democritus and Leucippus. The Epicureans proclaimed that atoms were continually falling through the void and giving off images that were in direct contact with the senses. These falling atoms could swerve in an arbitrary, unpredictable way to produce the combinations seen in the world.

Epicurus thereby removed an element of determinism that existed in the Democritean system. When a person died, the atoms that composed the body dispersed so that the person had no further existence or perception and therefore nothing to fear after death. Epicurus believed that the gods existed but that they took no interest in human affairs. This belief amounted to a practical atheism, and Epicureans were often thought to be atheists.

The purpose of Epicurean physics was to liberate people from their fear of death, of the gods, and of all nonmaterial or supernatural powers. Epicurean ethics were hedonistic, that is, based on the acceptance of pleasure as true happiness. But pleasure for Epicurus was chiefly negative: the absence of pain and trouble. The goal of the Epicureans was *ataraxia*, the condition of being undisturbed, without trouble, pain, or responsibility. Ideally a man should have enough means to allow him to withdraw from the world and avoid business and public life. Epicurus even advised against marriage and children. He preached a life of genteel, restrained selfishness that might appeal to intellectual men of means, but was not calculated to be widely attractive.

THE STOICS Soon after Epicurus began teaching in his garden in Athens, Zeno of Citium in Cyprus (335–263 B.C.E.) established the Stoic school. It derived its name from the *stoa poikile*, or painted portico, in the Athenian *agora*, where Zeno and his disciples walked and talked beginning about 300 B.C.E. From then until about the middle of the second century B.C.E., Zeno and his successors preached a philosophy that owed a good deal to Socrates, by way of the Cynics. It was fed also by a stream of Eastern thought. Zeno, of course, came from Phoenician Cyprus; Chrysippus, one of his successors, came from Cilicia; and other early Stoics came from such places as Carthage, Tarsus, and Babylon.

Like the Epicureans, the Stoics sought the happiness of the individual. Quite unlike them, the Stoics proposed a philosophy almost indistinguishable from religion. They believed that humans must live in harmony within themselves and in harmony with nature; for the Stoics god and nature were the same. The guiding principle in nature was divine reason (*Logos*), or fire. Every human had a spark of this divinity, and after death it returned to the eternal divine spirit. From time to time the world was destroyed by fire, from which a new world arose.

The aim of humans, and the definition of human happiness, was the virtuous life: a life lived in accordance with natural law, "when all actions promote the harmony of the spirit dwelling in the individual man with the will of him who orders the universe."[2] To live such a life required the knowledge possessed only by the wise, who knew what was good, what was evil, and what was neither, but "indifferent." According to the Stoics, good and evil were dispositions of the mind or soul: prudence, justice, courage, temperance, and so on were good, whereas folly, injustice, cowardice, and the like were evil. Life, health, pleasure, beauty, strength, wealth, and so on, were neutral, morally indifferent, for they did not contribute either to happiness or to misery. Human misery came from an irrational mental contraction, from passion, which was

[2] *Diogenes Laertius,* Life of Zeno, *88.*

a disease of the soul. The wise sought *apatheia*, or freedom from passion, because passion arose from things that were morally indifferent.

Politically the Stoics fit well into the new world. They thought of it as a single *polis* in which all people were children of the same god. Although they did not forbid political activity, and many Stoics took part in political life, withdrawal was obviously preferable because the usual subjects of political argument were indifferent. Because the Stoics strove for inner harmony of the individual, their aim was a life lived in accordance with the divine will, their attitude fatalistic, and their goal a form of apathy. They fit in well with the reality of post-Alexandrian life. In fact, the spread of Stoicism facilitated the task of creating a new political system that relied not on the active participation of the governed, but merely on their docile submission.

Literature

The literature of the Hellenistic period reflects the new intellectual currents, the new conditions of literary life, and the new institutions created in that period. The center of literary production in the third and second centuries B.C.E. was the new city of Alexandria in Egypt. There the Ptolemies, the monarchs of Egypt during that time, founded the museum—a great research institute where royal funds supported scientists and scholars—and the library, which contained almost half a million volumes, or papyrus scrolls.

The library contained much of the great body of past Greek literature, most of which has since been lost. The Alexandrian scholars saw to it that what they judged to be the best works were copied. They edited and criticized these works from the point of view of language, form, and content and wrote biographies of the authors. Their work is responsible for the preservation of most of what remains to us of ancient literature. Much of their work proved valuable, but some of it is dry, petty, quarrelsome, and simply foolish. At its best, however, it is full of learning and perception.

The scholarly atmosphere of Alexandria naturally gave rise to work in the field of history and its ancillary discipline, chronology. Eratosthenes (ca. 275–195 B.C.E.) established a chronology of important events dating from the Trojan War, and others undertook similar tasks. Contemporaries of Alexander, such as Ptolemy I, Aristobulus, and Nearchus, wrote what were apparently sober and essentially factual accounts of his career. Most of the work done by Hellenistic historians is known to us only in fragments cited by later writers. It seems in general to have emphasized sensational and biographical detail over the kind of rigorous impersonal analysis that marked the work of Thucydides.

Architecture and Sculpture

The advent of the Hellenistic monarchies greatly increased the opportunities open to architects and sculptors. Money was plentiful, rulers sought outlets for conspicuous display, new cities needed to be built and beautified, and the well-to-do created an increasing demand for objects of art. The new cities were usually laid out on the grid plan introduced in the fifth century B.C.E. by Hippodamus of Miletus. Temples were built on the classical model, and the covered portico, or *stoa*, became a very popular addition to the *agoras* of the Hellenistic towns.

Reflecting the cosmopolitan nature of the Hellenistic world, leading sculptors accepted commissions wherever they were attractive. The result was a certain uniformity of style, although Alexandria, Rhodes, and the kingdom of Pergamum in Asia Minor developed their own distinctive stylistic characteristics. For the most part Hellenistic sculpture moved away from the balanced tension and idealism of the fifth century B.C.E. toward the sentimental, emotional, and realistic mode of the fourth century B.C.E. These qualities are readily apparent in the marble statue called the *Laocoon*, carved at Rhodes in the second century B.C.E. and afterward taken to Rome.

Mathematics and Science

Among the most spectacular and remarkable intellectual developments of the Hellenistic age were those that came in mathematics and science. The burst of activity in these subjects drew from several sources. The stimulation and organization provided by the work of Plato and Aristotle should not be ignored. To these was added the impetus provided by Alexander's interest in science, evidenced by the scientists he took with him on his expedition and the aid he gave them in collecting data.

The expansion of Greek horizons geographically and the consequent contact with Egyptian and Babylonian knowledge were also helpful. Finally,

This is a Roman copy of one of the masterpieces of Hellenistic sculpture, the Laocoon. *According to legend, Laocoon was a priest who warned the Trojans not to take the Greek's wooden horse within their city. This sculpture depicts his punishment. Great serpents sent by the goddess Athena, who was on the side of the Greeks, devoured Laocoon and his sons before the horrified people of Troy. [Robert Miller]*

Plutarch Cites Archimedes and Hellenistic Science

Archimedes (ca. 287–211 B.C.E.) was one of the great mathematicians and physicists of antiquity. He was a native of Syracuse in Sicily and a friend of its king. Plutarch discusses him in the following selection and reveals much about the ancient attitude toward applied science.

✦ *Was the attitude toward science and technology attributed to Archimedes by Plutarch common in the ancient world? How can that attitude be explained? If it was common, what were the consequences? Are distinctions between the importance of pure science and applied science made in the modern world? If so, are they the same as the ancient ones? How do you explain any similarities or differences?*

Archimedes, however, in writing to King Hiero, whose friend and near relation he was, had stated that given the force, any given weight might be moved, and even boasted, we are told, relying on the strength of demonstration, that if there were another earth, by going into it he could remove this. Hiero being struck with amazement at this, and entreating him to make good this problem by actual experiment, and show some great weight moved by a small engine, he fixed accordingly upon a ship of burden out of the king's arsenal, which could not be drawn out of the dock without great labour and many men; and, loading her with many passengers and a full freight, sitting himself the while far off, with no great endeavor, but only holding the head of the pulley in his hand and drawing the cords by degrees. . . . Yet Archimedes possessed so high a spirit, so profound a soul, and such treasures of scientific knowledge, that though these inventions had now obtained him the renown of more than human sagacity, he yet would not deign to leave behind him any commentary or writing on such subjects; but, repudiating as sordid and ignoble the whole trade of engineering, and every sort of art that lends itself to mere use and profit, he placed his whole affection and ambition in those purer speculations where there can be no reference to the vulgar needs of life.

Plutarch, "Marcellus," in Lives of the Noble Grecians and Romans, *trans. by John Dryden, rev. by A. H. Clough (New York: Random House, n.d.), pp. 376–378.*

the patronage of the Ptolemies and the opportunity for many scientists to work with one another at the museum at Alexandria provided a unique opportunity for scientific work. It is not too much to say that the work done by the Alexandrians formed the greater part of the scientific knowledge available to the Western world until the scientific revolution of the sixteenth and seventeenth centuries C.E.

Euclid's *Elements* (written early in the third century B.C.E.) remained the textbook of plane and solid geometry until recent times. Archimedes of Syracuse (ca. 287–212 B.C.E.) made further progress in geometry, established the theory of the lever in mechanics, and invented hydrostatics.

These advances in mathematics, once applied to the Babylonian astronomical tables available to the Hellenistic world, spurred great progress in the field of astronomy. As early as the fourth century Heraclides of Pontus (ca. 390–310 B.C.E.) had argued that Mercury and Venus circulate around the sun and not the Earth. He appears to have made other suggestions leading in the direction of a heliocentric theory of the universe. Most scholars, however, give credit for that theory to Aristarchus of Samos (ca. 310–230 B.C.E.), who asserted that the sun, along with the other fixed stars, did not move and that the Earth revolved around the sun in a circular orbit and rotated on its axis while doing so. The heliocentric theory ran contrary not only to the traditional view codified by Aristotle but to what seemed to be common sense.

Hellenistic technology was not up to proving the theory, and, of course, the planetary orbits are not circular. The heliocentric theory did not, therefore, take hold. Hipparchus of Nicea (b. ca. 190 B.C.E.) constructed a model of the universe on the geocentric theory; his ingenious and complicated model did a very good job of accounting for the movements of the sun, the moon, and the planets. Ptolemy of Alexandria (second century C.E.) adopted Hipparchus's system with a few improvements. It remained dominant until the work of Copernicus, in the sixteenth century C.E.

Hellenistic scientists made progress in mapping the Earth as well as the sky. Eratosthenes of Cyrene (ca. 275–195 B.C.E.) was able to calculate the circumference of the Earth within about 200 miles. He wrote a treatise on geography based on mathematical and physical reasoning and the reports of travelers. In spite of the new data that were available to later geographers, Eratosthenes' map (see Map 3–5) was in many ways more accurate than the one constructed by Ptolemy of Alexandria, which became standard in the Middle Ages.

The Hellenistic Age contributed little to the life sciences, such as biology, zoology, and medicine. Even the sciences that had such impressive achievements to show in the third century B.C.E. made little progress thereafter. In fact, to some extent, there was a retreat from science. Astrology and magic became subjects of great interest as scientific advance lagged.

✦

The Classical Age of Greece was a period of unparalleled achievement. While the rest of the world continued to be characterized by monarchical, hierarchical, command societies, in Athens democracy was carried as far as it would go before

MAP 3–5 THE WORLD ACCORDING TO ERATOSTHENES *Eratosthenes of Alexandria (ca. 275–195 B.C.E.) was a Hellenistic geographer. His map, reconstructed here, was remarkably accurate for its time. The world was divided by lines of "latitude" and "longitude," thus anticipating our global divisions.*

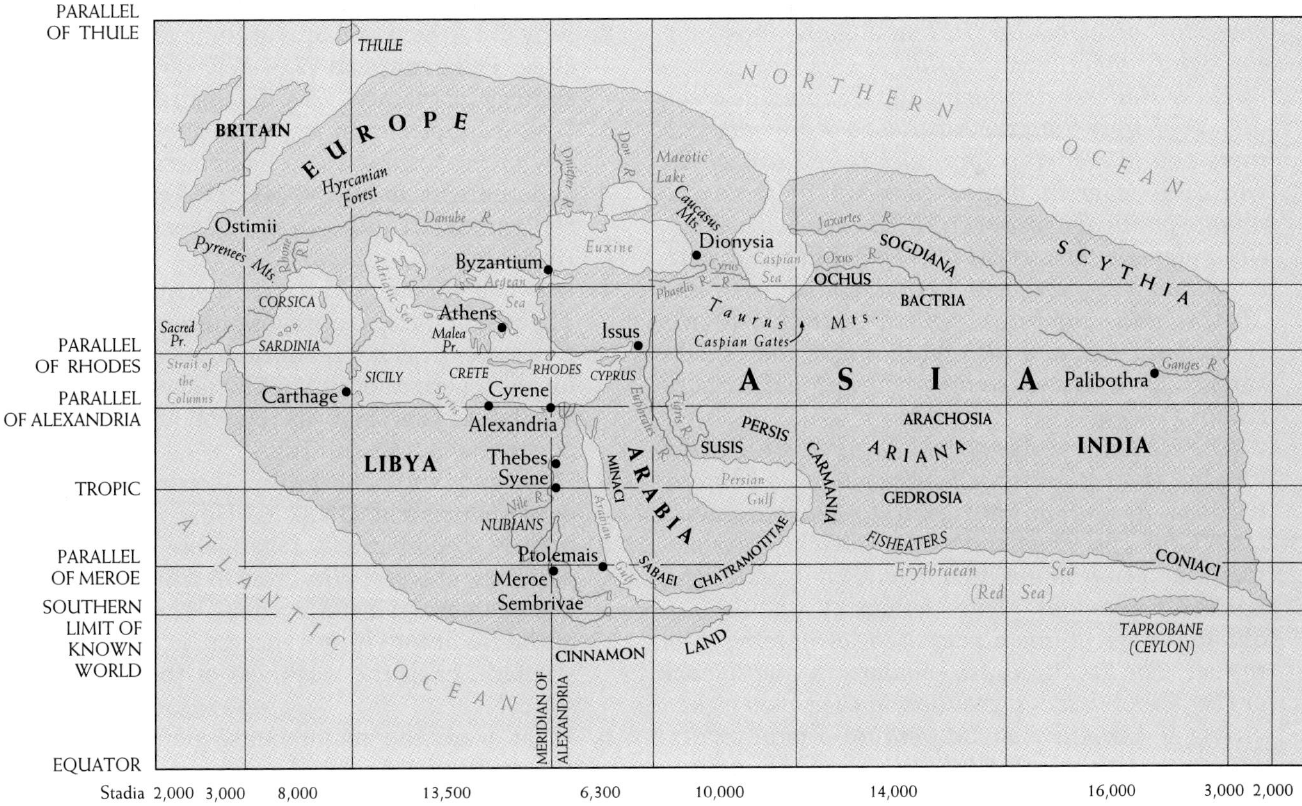

modern times. Although Athenian citizenship was limited to adult males of native parentage, citizens were granted full and active participation in every decision of the state without regard to wealth or class. Democracy disappeared late in the fourth century B.C.E. with the end of Greek autonomy. When it returned in the modern world more than two millennia later, it was broader but shallower. Democratic citizenship did not again imply the active direct participation of every citizen in the government of the state.

It was in this democratic imperial Athens that the greatest artistic, literary, and philosophical achievements of Classical Greece took place. Analytical, secular history, tragedy and comedy, the philosophical dialogue, an organized system of logic, and the logical philosophical treatise were among the achievements of the Classical Age. The tradition of rational, secular speculation in natural philosophy and science was carried forward, but more attention was devoted to human questions in medicine and ethical and political philosophy. A naturalistic style of art evolved that showed human beings first as they ideally might look, and then as they really looked, an approach that dominated Greek and Roman art until the late stages of the Roman Empire. This naturalistic style had a powerful effect on the Italian Renaissance and, through it, the modern world.

These Hellenic developments, it should be clear, diverge sharply from the experience of previous cultures and of contemporary ones in the rest of the world. To a great degree they sprang from the unique political experience of the Greeks, based on the independent city-states. That unique experience and the Classical period ended with the Macedonian conquest, which introduced the Hellenistic Age and ultimately made the Greeks subject to or part of some great national state or empire.

The Hellenistic Age speaks to us less fully and vividly than that of Classical Greece, chiefly because it had no historian to compare with Herodotus and Thucydides. We lack the clear picture that a continuous, rich, lively, and meaningful narrative provides. This deficiency should not obscure the great importance of the achievements of the age. The literature, art, scholarship, and science of the period deserve attention in their own right.

The Hellenistic Age did perform a vital civilizing function. It spread Greek culture over a remarkably wide area and made a significant and lasting impression on much of it. Greek culture also adjusted to its new surroundings to a degree, unifying and simplifying its cultural cargo to make it more accessible to outsiders. The various Greek dialects gave way to a version of the Attic tongue, the koine, *or common language.*

In the same way, the scholarship of Alexandria established canons of literary excellence and the scholarly tools with which to make the great treasures of Greek culture understandable to later generations. The syncretism of thought and belief introduced in this period also made understanding and accord more likely among peoples who were very different. When the Romans came into contact with Hellenism, they were powerfully impressed by it. When they conquered the Hellenistic world, they became, as Horace said, captives of its culture.

Review Questions

1. How was the Delian League transformed into the Athenian Empire during the fifth century B.C.E.? Did the empire offer any advantages to its subjects? Why was there such resistance to Athenian efforts to unify the Greek world in the fifth and fourth centuries B.C.E.?

2. Why did Athens and Sparta come to blows in the Great Peloponnesian War? What was each side's strategy for victory? Why did Sparta win the war?

3. Give examples from art, literature, and philosophy of the tension that characterized Greek life and thought in the Classical Age. How does Hellenistic art differ from that of the Classical Age?

4. Between 431 and 362 B.C.E., Athens, Sparta, and Thebes each tried to impose hegemony over the city-states of Greece, but none succeeded except for short periods of time. Why did each state fail? What does your analysis tell you about the components of successful rule?

5. How and why did Philip II conquer Greece between 359 and 338 B.C.E.? How was he able to turn Macedon into a formidable military and political power? Why was Athens unable to defend itself against Macedon? Where does more of the credit for Philip's success lie: in Macedon's strength, or in the weakness of the Greek city-states?

6. What were the major consequences of Alexander's death? Assess the achievement of Alexander. Was he a conscious promoter of Greek civilization, or just an egomaniac drunk with the lust of conquest?

Suggested Readings

M. Austin and P. Vidal-Naquet, *The Economic and Social History of Classical Greece* (1977). A collection of documents with commentary.

H. I. Bell, *Egypt from Alexander the Great to the Arab Conquest* (1948). A history of Hellenistic Egypt.

J. Buckler, *The Theban Hegemony, 371–362 B.C.E.* (1980). A study of Thebes at the height of its power.

W. Burkert, *Greek Religion* (1985). A fine general study.

P. Cartledge, *Agesilaus and the Crisis of Sparta* (1987). More than a biography of the Spartan king, it is a thorough study of Spartan society.

G. Cawkwell, *Philip of Macedon* (1978). A brief but learned account of Philip's career.

W. R. Connor, *The New Politicians of Fifth-Century Athens* (1971). A study on changes in political style and their significance for Athenian society.

J. M. Cook, *The Persian Empire* (1983). A solid history that makes good use of archaeological evidence.

J. K. Davies, *Democracy and Classical Greece* (1978). Emphasizes archaeological evidence and social history.

V. Ehrenberg, *The People of Aristophanes* (1962). A study of Athenian society as revealed by the comedies of Aristophanes.

J. R. Ellis, *Philip II and Macedonian Imperialism* (1976). A study of the career of the founder of Macedonian power.

J. Ferguson, *The Heritage of Hellenism* (1973). A good survey.

J. R. L. Fox, *Alexander the Great* (1973). An imaginative account that does more justice to the Persian side of the problem than is usual.

Y. Garlan, *Slavery in Ancient Greece* (1988). An up-to-date survey.

P. Green, *Alexander the Great* (1972). A lively biography.

P. Green, *From Alexander to Actium* (1990). A brilliant new synthesis of the Hellenistic period.

C. D. Hamilton, *Agesilaus and the Failure of Spartan Hegemony* (1991). An excellent biography of the king who was the central figure in Sparta during its domination in the fourth century B.C.E.

N. G. L. Hammond and G. T. Griffith, *A History of Macedonia, Vol. 2, 550–336 B.C.E.* (1979). A thorough account of Macedonian history that focuses on the careers of Philip and Alexander.

R. Just, *Women in Athenian Law and Life* (1988). A good study of the place of women in Athenian life.

D. Kagan, *Pericles of Athens and the Birth of Athenian Democracy* (1991). An account of the life and times of the great Athenian statesman.

D. Kagan, *The Outbreak of the Peloponnesian War* (1969). A study of the period from the foundation of the Delian League to the coming of the Peloponnesian War that argues that war could have been avoided.

G. B. Kerferd, *The Sophistic Movement* (1981). A fine study of these worldly thinkers of the Classical period.

H. D. F. Kitto, *Greek Tragedy* (1966). A good introduction.

B. M. W. Knox, *The Heroic Temper: Studies in Sophoclean Tragedy* (1964). A brilliant analysis of tragic heroism.

J. A. O. Larsen, *Greek Federal States* (1968). Emphasis on the federal movements of the Hellenistic era.

J. Lear, *Aristotle: The Desire to Understand* (1988). A brilliant yet comprehensible introduction to the work of the philosopher.

D. M. Lewis, *Sparta and Persia* (1977). A valuable discussion of relations between Sparta and Persia in the fifth and fourth centuries B.C.E.

G. E. R. Lloyd, *Greek Science After Aristotle* (1974).

A. A. Long, *Hellenistic Philosophy: Stoics, Epicureans, Skeptics* (1974). A solid study.

R. Meiggs, *The Athenian Empire* (1972). A fine study of the rise and fall of the empire, making excellent use of inscriptions.

J. J. Pollitt, *Art and Experience in Classical Greece* (1972). A scholarly and entertaining study of the relationship between art and history in Classical Greece, with excellent illustrations.

J. J. Pollitt, *Art in the Hellenistic Age* (1986). An extraordinary analysis that places the art in its historical and intellectual context.

M. I. Rostovtzeff, *Social and Economic History of the Hellenistic World*, 3 vols. (1941). A masterpiece of synthesis by a great historian.

B. S. Strauss, *Athens After the Peloponnesian War* (1987). An excellent discussion of Athens' recovery and of the nature of Athenian society and politics in the fourth century B.C.E.

D. Stockton, *The Classical Athenian Democracy* (1990). A brief and clear account.

W. W. Tarn, *Alexander the Great*, 2 vols. (1948). The first volume is a narrative account, the second a series of detailed studies.

W. W. Tarn and G. T. Griffith, *Hellenistic Civilization* (1961). A survey of Hellenistic history and culture.

V. Tcherikover, *Hellenistic Civilization and the Jews* (1970). A fine study of the impact of Hellenism on the Jews.

G. Vlastos, *The Philosophy of Socrates* (1971). A splendid collection of essays illuminating the problems presented by this remarkable man.

G. Vlastos, *Platonic Studies*, 2nd ed. (1981). A similar collection on the philosophy of Plato.

F. W. Walbank, *The Hellenistic World* (1981). A solid history.

A. E. Zimmern, *The Greek Commonwealth* (1961). A study of political, social, and economic conditions in fifth-century Athens.

CHAPTER 4

In the Villa of Mysteries outside Pompeii, a fresco dedicated to Dionysos decorates the walls of a central room. This segment of a larger panel depicts the education of Dionysos as a boy. [Robert Frerck/Woodfin Camp & Associates]

Rome: From Republic to Empire

KEY TOPICS

- The emergence of the Roman Republic
- The development of the republican constitution
- Roman expansion and imperialism
- The character of Roman society in the republican era
- The fall of the republic

The achievement of the Romans was one of the most remarkable in human history. The descendants of the inhabitants of a small village in central Italy, they came eventually to rule the entire Italian peninsula, then the entire Mediterranean coastline. They conquered most of the Near East and finally much of continental Europe. They ruled this vast empire under a single government that provided considerable peace and prosperity for centuries. Never before the Romans nor since has that area been united, and rarely, if ever, has it enjoyed a stable peace. But Rome's legacy was not merely military excellence and political organization. The Romans adopted and transformed the intellectual and cultural achievements of the Greeks and combined them with their own outlook and historical experience. The resulting Graeco-Roman tradition in literature, philosophy, and art provided the core of learning for the Middle Ages and pointed the way to the new paths taken in the Renaissance. It remains at the heart of Western civilization to this day.

Prehistoric Italy

The culture of Italy developed late. Paleolithic settlements gave way to the Neolithic mode of life only about 2500 B.C.E. The Bronze Age came about 1500 B.C.E. About 1000 B.C.E. bands of new arrivals, warlike peoples speaking a set of closely related languages we call *Italic*, began to infiltrate Italy from across the Adriatic Sea and around its northern end. These invaders cremated their dead and put the ashes in tombs stocked with weapons and armor. Their bronzework was of a higher quality than that of the people they displaced, and they were soon making weapons, armor, and tools of iron. By 800 B.C.E. they had occupied the highland pastures of the Apennines and within a short time they began to challenge the earlier settlers for control of the tempting western plains. It would be the descendants of these tough mountain people—Umbrians, Sabines, Samnites, and Latins—together with others soon to arrive—Etruscans, Greeks, and Celts—who would shape the future of Italy.

The Etruscans

The Etruscans exerted the most powerful external influence on the Romans. Their civilization arose in Etruria (now Tuscany), west of the Apennines between the Arno and Tiber rivers, about 800 B.C.E. (See Map 4–1.) Their origin is far from clear, but their tomb architecture, resembling that of Asia Minor, and their practice of divining the future by inspecting the livers of sacrificial animals point to an eastern origin.

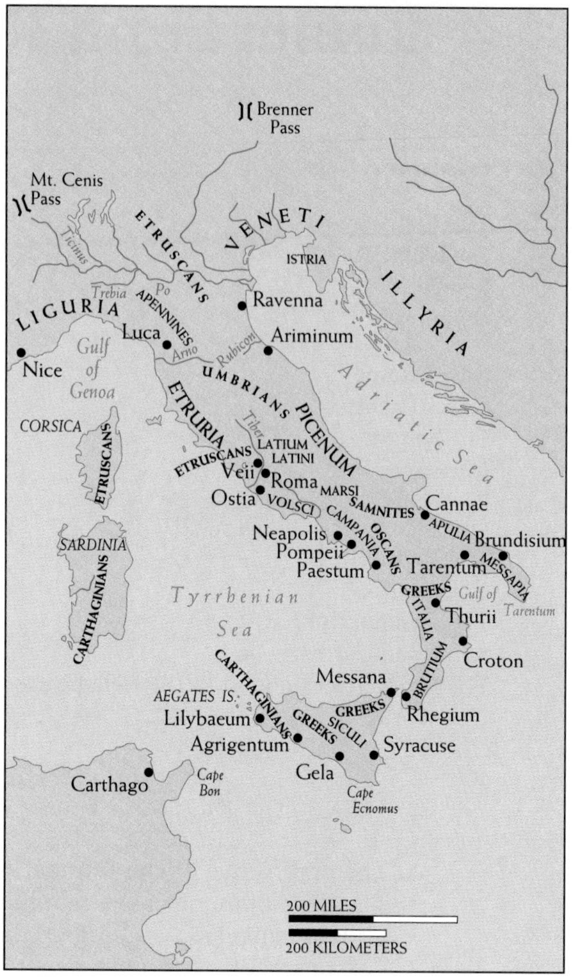

MAP 4–1 ANCIENT ITALY *This map of ancient Italy and its neighbors before the expansion of Rome shows major cities and towns as well as several geographical regions and the locations of some of the Italic and non-Italic peoples.*

Government

The Etruscans brought civilization with them. Their settlements were self-governing, fortified city-states, of which twelve formed a loose religious confederation. At first, kings ruled these cities, but they were replaced by an aristocracy of the agrarian nobles. The latter ruled by means of a council and elected annual magistrates. The Etruscans were a military ruling class that dominated and exploited the native Italians (the predecessors of the later Italic speakers), who worked the Etruscans' land and mines and served as infantry in the Etruscan armies. This aristocracy accumulated considerable wealth through agriculture, industry, piracy, and a growing commerce with the Carthaginians and the Greeks.

Religion

The Etruscans' influence on the Romans was greatest in religion. They imagined a world filled with gods and spirits, many of them evil. To deal with such demons, the Etruscans evolved complicated rituals and powerful priesthoods. Divination by sacrifice and omens in nature helped discover the divine will, and careful attention to precise rituals directed by priests helped please the gods. After a while the Etruscans, influenced by the Greeks, worshiped gods in the shape of humans and built temples for them.

Dominion

The Etruscan aristocracy remained aggressive and skillful in the use of horses and war chariots. In the seventh and sixth centuries B.C.E. they expanded their power in Italy and across the sea to Corsica and Elba. They conquered Latium (a region that included the small town of Rome) and Campania,

Much of what we know of the Etruscans comes from their funerary art. This sculpture of an Etruscan couple is part of a sarcophagus. [Erich Lessing/Art Resource, N.Y.]

where they became neighbors of the Greeks of Naples. In the north they got as far as the Po Valley. These conquests were carried out by small bands led by Etruscan chieftains who did not work in concert and would not necessarily aid one another in distress. As a result, the conquests outside Etruria were not firmly based and did not last long.

Etruscan power reached its height some time before 500 B.C.E. and then rapidly declined. About 400 B.C.E. Celtic peoples from the area the Romans called *Gaul* (modern France) broke into the Po Valley and drove out the Etruscans. They settled this land so firmly that the Romans thereafter called it *Cisalpine Gaul* (Gaul on this side of the Alps). Eventually, even the Etruscan heartland in Etruria lost its independence and was incorporated into Roman Italy. The Etruscan language was forgotten and Etruscan culture gradually became only a memory, but its influence on the Romans remained.

Royal Rome

Rome was an unimportant town in Latium until its conquest by the Etruscans, but its location—fifteen miles from the mouth of the Tiber River at the point at which the hills made further navigation impossible—gave it several advantages over its Latin neighbors. The island in the Tiber southwest of the Capitoline Hill made the river fordable, and so Rome was naturally a center for communication and trade, both east–west and north–south.

Government

In the sixth century B.C.E. Rome came under Etruscan control. Led by Etruscan kings, the Roman army, equipped and organized like the Greek phalanx, gained control of most of Latium. An effective political and social order that gave extraordinary power to the ruling figures in both public and private life made this success possible. To their kings the Romans gave the awesome power of *imperium*, the right to issue commands and to enforce them by fines, arrests, and corporal, or even capital, punishment. Although it tended apparently to remain in the same family, kingship was elective. The Roman Senate had to approve the candidate for the office, and a vote of the people in assembly formally granted the *imperium.* A basic characteristic of later Roman government—the granting of great power to executive officers contingent on the approval of the Senate and ultimately the people—was already apparent in this structure.

In theory and law the king was the commander of the army, the chief priest, and the supreme judge. He could make decisions in foreign affairs, call out the army, lead it in battle, and impose discipline on his troops, all by virtue of his *imperium*. In practice the royal power was much more limited.

The Senate was the second branch of the early Roman government. According to tradition, it originated when Romulus, Rome's legendary first king, chose 100 of Rome's leading men to advise him. The number of senators ultimately rose to 300, where it stayed through most of the history of the

Busts of a Roman couple from the period of the Republic. Although some people have identified the individuals as Cato the Younger and his daughter Porcia, no solid evidence confirms this claim. [Scala/Art Resource, N.Y.]

republic. Ostensibly the Senate had neither executive nor legislative power; it met only when summoned by the king and then only to advise him. In reality its authority was great, for the senators, like the king, served for life. The Senate, therefore, had continuity and experience, and it was composed of the most powerful men in the state. It could not lightly be ignored.

The third branch of government, the curiate assembly, was made up of all citizens as divided into thirty groups. (In early Rome citizenship required descent from Roman parents on both sides.) The assembly met only when summoned by the king; he determined the agenda, made proposals, and recognized other speakers, if any. Usually, the assembly was called to listen and approve. Voting was not by head but by group; a majority within each group determined its vote, and the decisions were made by majority vote of the groups. Group voting would be typical of all future forms of Roman assembly.

The Family

The center of Roman life was the family. At its head stood the father, whose power and authority within the family resembled those of the king within the state. Over his children the father held broad powers analogous to *imperium* in the state; he had the right to sell his children into slavery, and he even had the power of life and death over them. Over his wife he had less power; he could not sell or kill her. In practice his power to dispose of his children was limited by consultation with the family, by public opinion, and, most of all, by tradition. A wife could not be divorced except for stated serious offenses, and even then she had to be convicted by a court made up of her male blood relatives. The Roman woman had a respected position and the main responsibility for managing the household. The father was the chief priest of the family. He led it in daily prayers to the dead, which reflected the ancestor worship central to the Roman family and state.

Clientage

Clientage was one of Rome's most important institutions. The *client* was "an inferior entrusted, by custom or by himself, to the protection of a stranger more powerful than he, and rendering certain services and observances in return for this protection."[1] The Romans spoke of a client as being in the *fides*, or trust, of his patron, and so the relationship always had moral implications. The patron provided his client with protection, both physical

[1] *E. Badian,* Foreign Clientelae (264–70 B.C.E.) *(Oxford, 1958), p. 1.*

and legal. He gave him economic assistance in the form of a land grant, the opportunity to work as a tenant farmer or a laborer on the patron's land, or simply handouts. In return the client would fight for his patron, work his land, and support him politically. These mutual obligations were enforced by public opinion and tradition. When early custom was codified in the mid-fifth century B.C.E., one of the twelve tablets of laws announced: "Let the patron who has defrauded his client be accursed."

In the early history of Rome, patrons were rich and powerful whereas clients were poor and weak, but as time passed it was not uncommon for rich and powerful members of the upper classes to become clients of even more powerful men, chiefly for political purposes. Because the client–patron relationship was hereditary and was sanctioned by religion and custom, it was to play a very important part in the life of the Roman Republic.

Patricians and Plebeians

In the royal period, Roman society was divided in two by a class distinction based on birth. The wealthy patrician upper class held a monopoly of power and influence. Its members alone could conduct state religious ceremonies, sit in the Senate, or hold office. They formed a closed caste by forbidding marriage outside their own group.

The plebeian lower class must have consisted originally of poor, dependent small farmers, laborers, and artisans, the clients of the nobility. As Rome and its population grew in various ways, families that were rich but outside the charmed circle of patricians grew wealthy. From very early times, therefore, there were rich plebeians, and incompetence and bad luck must have produced some poor patricians. The line between the classes and the monopoly of privileges remained firm, nevertheless, and the struggle of the plebeians to gain equality occupied more than two centuries of republican history.

The Republic

Roman tradition tells us that the outrageous behavior of the last kings led the noble families to revolt in 509 B.C.E., bringing the monarchy to a sudden close and leading to the creation of the Roman Republic.

Constitution

THE CONSULS The Roman constitution was an unwritten accumulation of laws and customs. The Romans were a conservative people, and so they were never willing to deprive their chief magistrates of the great powers exercised by the monarchs. They elected two patricians to the office of consul and endowed them with *imperium*. They were assisted by two financial officials called *quaestors*, whose number ultimately reached eight. Like the kings, the consuls led the army, had religious duties, and served as judges. They retained the visible symbols of royalty—the purple robe, the ivory chair, and the *lictors* (minor officials), who accompanied them bearing rods and axe. The power of the consuls, however, was limited legally and institutionally as well as by custom.

The power of the consulship was granted not for life but only for a year. Each consul could prevent any action by his colleague by simply saying no to his proposal, and the religious powers of the consuls were shared with others. Even the *imperium* was limited. Although the consuls had full powers of life and death while leading an army, within the sacred boundary of the city of Rome the citizens had the right to appeal to the popular assembly all cases involving capital punishment. Besides, after their one year in office, the consuls would spend the rest of their lives as members of the Senate. It was a most reckless consul who failed to ask the advice of the Senate or who failed to follow it when there was general agreement.

The many checks on consular action tended to prevent initiative, swift action, and change, but this was just what a conservative, traditional, aristocratic republic wanted. Only in the military sphere did divided counsel and a short term of office create important problems. The Romans tried to get around the difficulties by sending only one consul into the field or, when this was impossible, allowing each consul sole command on alternate days. In really serious crises, the consuls, with the advice of the Senate, could appoint a single man, the *dictator*, to the command and could retire in his favor. The dictator's term of office was limited to six months, but his own *imperium* was valid both inside and outside the city without appeal.

These devices worked well enough in the early years of the republic, when Rome's battles were near home. Longer wars and more sophisticated oppo-

Lictors, *pictured here, attended the chief Roman magistrates when they appeared in public. The axe carried by one of the* lictors *and the bound bundle of staffs carried by the others symbolize both the power of Roman magistrates to inflict corporal punishment on Roman citizens and the limits on that power. The bound staffs symbolize the right of citizens within the city of Rome not to be punished without a trial. The axe symbolizes the power of the magistrates, as commanders of the army, to put anyone to death without a trial outside the city walls. [Alinari/Art Resource, N.Y.]*

nents, however, revealed the system's weaknesses and required significant changes. Long campaigns prompted the invention of the *proconsulship* in 325 B.C.E., whereby the term of a consul serving in the field was extended. This innovation contained the seeds of many troubles for the constitution.

The creation of the office of *praetor* also helped provide commanders for Rome's many campaigns. The basic function of the *praetors* was judicial, but they also had *imperium* and served as generals. *Praetors'* teams were also for one year. By the end of the republic, there were eight *praetors*, whose annual terms, like the consuls', could be extended for military commands when necessary.

The job of identifying citizens and classifying them according to age and property was at first the responsibility of the consuls. After the middle of the fifth century B.C.E., this job was delegated to a new office, that of *censor*. The Senate elected two *censors* every five years. They conducted a census and drew up the citizen rolls. Their task was not just clerical; the classification fixed taxation and status, and so the *censors* had to be men of reputation, former consuls. They soon acquired additional powers. By the fourth century B.C.E. they compiled the roll of senators and could strike senators from that roll not only for financial but also for moral reasons. As the prestige of the office grew, it came to be considered the ultimate prize of a Roman political career.

THE SENATE AND THE ASSEMBLY With the end of the monarchy, the Senate became the single continuous deliberative body in the Roman state, greatly increasing its influence and power. Its members were prominent patricians, often leaders of clans and patrons of many clients. The Senate soon gained control of the state's finances and of foreign policy. Its formal advice was not lightly ignored either by magistrates or by popular assemblies.

The most important assembly in the early republic was the *centuriate assembly*, which was, in a sense, the Roman army acting in a political capacity. Its basic unit was the *century*, theoretically 100 fighting men classified according to their weapons, armor, and equipment. Because each man equipped himself, this meant that the organization was by classes according to wealth.

Voting was by century and proceeded in order of classification from the cavalry down. The assembly elected the consuls and several other magistrates, voted on bills put before it, made decisions of war and peace, and also served as the court of appeal against decisions of the magistrates affecting the life or property of a citizen. In theory it had final authority, but the Senate exercised great, if informal, influence.

THE STRUGGLE OF THE ORDERS The laws and constitution of the early republic gave to the patricians almost a monopoly of power and privilege. Plebeians were barred from public office, from priesthoods, and from other public religious offices. They could not serve as judges and could not even know the law, for there was no published legal code. The only law was traditional practice, and that existed only in the minds and actions of patrician magistrates. Plebeians were subject to the *imperium* but could not exercise its power. They were not allowed to marry patricians. When Rome gained new land by conquest, patrician magistrates distributed it in a way that favored patricians. The patricians dominated the assemblies and the Senate. The plebeians undertook a campaign to achieve political, legal, and social equality, and this attempt, which succeeded after two centuries of intermittent effort, is called the *Struggle of the Orders*.

The most important source of plebeian success was the need for their military service. According to tradition, the plebeians, angered by patrician resistance to their demands, withdrew from the city and camped on the Sacred Mount. There they formed a plebeian tribal assembly and elected plebeian tribunes to protect them from the arbitrary power of the magistrates. They declared the tribune inviolate and sacrosanct; anyone laying violent hands on him was accursed and liable to death without trial. By extension of his right to protect the plebeians, the tribune gained the power to veto any action of a magistrate or any bill in a Roman assembly or the Senate. The plebeian assembly voted by tribe, and a vote of the assembly was binding on plebeians. They tried to make their decisions binding on all Romans but could not do so until 287 B.C.E.

The next step was for the plebeians to obtain access to the laws, which they accomplished by 450 B.C.E. when early Roman custom in all its harshness and simplicity was codified in the Twelve Tables. In 445 B.C.E. plebeians gained the right to marry patricians. The main prize, the consulship, the patricians did not yield easily. Not until 367 B.C.E. did legislation—the Licinian–Sextian Laws—provide that at least one consul could be a plebeian. Before long plebeians held other offices, even the dictatorship and the censorship. In 300 B.C.E. they were admitted to the most important priesthoods, the last religious barrier to equality. In 287 B.C.E. the plebeians completed their triumph. They once again withdrew from the city and secured the passage of a law whereby decisions of the plebeian assembly bound all Romans and did not require the approval of the Senate.

It might seem that the Roman aristocracy had given way under the pressure of the lower class. Yet the victory of the plebeians did not bring democracy. An aristocracy based strictly on birth had given way to an aristocracy more subtle, but no less restricted, based on a combination of wealth and birth. A relatively small group of rich and powerful families, both patrician and plebeian, known as *nobiles*, attained the highest offices in the state. The significant distinction was no longer between patrician and plebeian but between the *nobiles* and everyone else.

The absence of the secret ballot in the assemblies enabled the *nobiles* to control most decisions and elections by a combination of intimidation and bribery. The leading families were in constant competition with one another for office, power, and prestige, but they often combined in marriage and less formal alliances to keep the political plums within their own group. In the century from 233 to 133 B.C.E., for instance, twenty-six families provided 80 percent of the consuls and only ten families accounted for almost 50 percent. These same families dominated the Senate, whose power became ever greater. Rome's success brought the Senate prestige, increased control of policy, and confidence in its capacity to rule. The end of the struggle of the orders brought domestic peace under a republican constitution dominated by a capable, if narrow, senatorial aristocracy. This outcome satisfied most Romans outside the ruling group because Rome conquered Italy and brought many benefits to its citizens.

The Conquest of Italy

Not long after the fall of the monarchy in 509 B.C.E., a coalition of Romans, Latins, and Italian Greeks defeated the Etruscans and drove them out of Latium for good. Throughout the fifth century B.C.E., the powerful Etruscan city of Veii, only twelve miles north of the Tiber River, raided Roman territory. After a hard struggle and a long siege, the Romans took it in 392 B.C.E., more than doubling the size of Rome.

Roman policy toward defeated enemies used both the carrot and the stick. When the Romans made friendly alliances with some, they gained new soldiers for their army. When they treated others

The Rise of the Plebeians to Equality in Rome

509 B.C.E.	Kings expelled; republic founded
450–449 B.C.E.	Laws of the Twelve Tables published
445 B.C.E.	Plebeians gain right of marriage with patricians
367 B.C.E.	Licinian–Sextian Laws open consulship to plebeians
300 B.C.E.	Plebeians attain chief priesthoods
287 B.C.E.	Laws passed by Plebeian Assembly made binding on all Romans

more harshly by annexing their land, they achieved a similar end. Service in the Roman army was based on property, and the distribution to poor Romans of conquered land made soldiers of previously useless men. It also gave the poor a stake in Rome and reduced the pressure against its aristocratic regime. The long siege of Veii kept soldiers from their farms during the campaign. From that time on the Romans paid their soldiers, thus giving their army greater flexibility and a more professional quality.

Gallic Invasion of Italy and Roman Reaction At the beginning of the fourth century B.C.E. a disaster struck. In 387 B.C.E. the Gauls, barbaric Celtic tribes from across the Alps, defeated the Roman army and captured, looted, and burned Rome. The Gauls sought plunder, not conquest, so they extorted a ransom from the Romans and returned to their homes in the north. Rome's power appeared to be wiped out.

By about 350 B.C.E., however, the Romans were more dominant than ever. Their success in turning back new Gallic raids added still more to their power and prestige. As the Romans tightened their grip on Latium, the Latins became resentful. In 340 B.C.E. they demanded independence from Rome or full equality and launched a war of independence that lasted until 338 B.C.E. The victorious Romans dissolved the Latin League, and their treatment of the defeated opponents provided a model for the settlement of Italy.

Original Roman pavement of the Via Appia, part of the network of military roads that tied all Italy to Rome. These roads enabled Roman legions to move swiftly to enforce their control of Italy. The Via Appia dates from the fourth century B.C.E. [Scala/Art Resource, N.Y.]

Roman Policy Toward the Conquered The Romans did not destroy any of the Latin cities or their people, nor did they treat them all alike. Some near Rome received full Roman citizenship. Others farther away gained municipal status, which gave them the private rights of intermarriage and commerce with Romans but not the public rights of voting and holding office in Rome. They retained the rights of local self-government and could obtain full Roman citizenship if they moved to Rome. They followed Rome in foreign policy and provided soldiers to serve in the Roman legions.

Still other states became allies of Rome on the basis of treaties, which differed from city to city. Some were given the private rights of intermarriage and commerce with Romans and some were not; the allied states were always forbidden to exercise these rights with one another. Some, but not all, were allowed local autonomy. Land was taken from some but not from others, nor was the percentage taken always the same. All the allies supplied troops to the army, in which they fought in auxiliary battalions under Roman officers, but they did not pay taxes to Rome.

On some of the conquered land the Romans placed colonies, permanent settlements of veteran soldiers in the territory of recently defeated enemies. The colonists retained their Roman citizenship and enjoyed home rule; in return for the land they had been given, they served as a kind of permanent garrison to deter or suppress rebellion. These colonies were usually connected to Rome by a network of military roads built as straight as possible and so durable that some are used even today. The roads guaranteed that a Roman army could swiftly reinforce an embattled colony or put down an uprising in any weather.

The Roman settlement of Latium reveals even more clearly than before the principles by which Rome was able to conquer and dominate Italy for many centuries. The excellent army and the diplomatic skill that allowed Rome to separate its enemies help to explain its conquests. The reputation for harsh punishment of rebels—and the sure promise that such punishment would be delivered was made unmistakably clear by the presence of colonies and military roads—helps to account for the reluctance to revolt. But the positive side, represented by Rome's organization of the defeated states, is at least as important. The Romans did not regard the status given each newly conquered city as permanent. They held out to loyal allies the prospect of improving their status, even of achieving the ultimate prize, full Roman citizenship. In so doing, the Romans gave their allies a stake in Rome's future success and a sense of being colleagues, though subordinate ones, rather than subjects. The result, in general, was that most of Rome's allies remained loyal even when put to the severest test.

DEFEAT OF THE SAMNITES The next great challenge to Roman arms came in a series of wars with a tough mountain people of the southern Apennines, the Samnites. Some of Rome's allies rebelled, and soon the Etruscans and Gauls joined in the war against Rome. But most of the allies remained loyal. In 295 B.C.E., at Sentinum, the Romans defeated an Italian coalition, and by 280 B.C.E. they were masters of central Italy. Their power extended from the Po Valley south to Apulia and Lucania.

Now the Romans were in direct contact with the Greek cities of southern Italy. Roman intervention in a quarrel between Greek cities brought them face to face with Pyrrhus, king of Epirus. Pyrrhus, probably the best general of his time, commanded a well-disciplined and experienced mercenary army, which he hired out for profit, and a new weapon: twenty war elephants. He defeated the Romans twice but suffered many casualties. When one of his officers rejoiced at the victory, Pyrrhus told him, "If we win one more battle against the Romans we shall be completely ruined." This "Pyrrhic victory" led him to withdraw to Sicily in 275 B.C.E. The Greek cities that had hired him were forced to join the Roman confederation. By 265 B.C.E. Rome ruled all Italy as far north as the Po River, an area of 47,200 square miles. The year after the defeat of Pyrrhus, Ptolemy Philadelphus, king of Egypt, sent a message of congratulation to establish friendly relations with Rome. This act recognized Rome's new status as a power in the Hellenistic world.

Roman Expansion in Italy

392 B.C.E.	Fall of Veii; Etruscans defeated
387 B.C.E.	Gauls burn Rome
338 B.C.E.	Latin League defeated
295 B.C.E.	Battle of Sentinum; Samnites and allies defeated
275 B.C.E.	Pyrrhus driven from Italy
265 B.C.E.	Rome rules Italy south of the Po River

Rome and Carthage

The conquest of southern Italy brought the Romans face to face with the great naval power of the western Mediterranean, Carthage. (See Map 4–2.) Late in the ninth century B.C.E. the Phoenician city of Tyre had planted a colony on the coast of northern Africa near modern Tunis, calling it the New City, or Carthage. In the sixth century B.C.E. the conquest of Phoenicia by the Assyrians and the Persians left Carthage independent and free to exploit its very advantageous situation. The city was located on a defensible site and commanded an excellent harbor that encouraged commerce. The coastal plain grew abundant grain, fruits, and vegetables. An inland plain allowed sheep herding. The Phoenician settlers conquered the native inhabitants and used them to work the land.

Beginning in the sixth century B.C.E. the Carthaginians expanded their domain to include the coast of northern Africa west beyond the Straits of Gibraltar and eastward into Libya. Overseas they came to control the southern part of Spain, Sardinia, Corsica, Malta, the Balearic Islands, and western Sicily. The people of these territories, though originally allies, were all reduced to subjection like the natives of the Carthaginian home territory. They all served in the Carthaginian army or navy and paid tribute. Carthage also profited greatly from the mines of Spain and from an absolute monopoly of trade imposed on the western Mediterranean.

An attack by Hiero, tyrant of Syracuse, on the Sicilian city of Messana just across from Italy first caused trouble between Rome and Carthage. Messana had been seized by a group of Italian mercenary soldiers who called themselves *Mamertines*, the sons of the war god Mars. When Hiero defeated the Mamertines, some of them called on the Carthaginians to help save their city. Carthage agreed and sent a garrison, for the Carthaginians

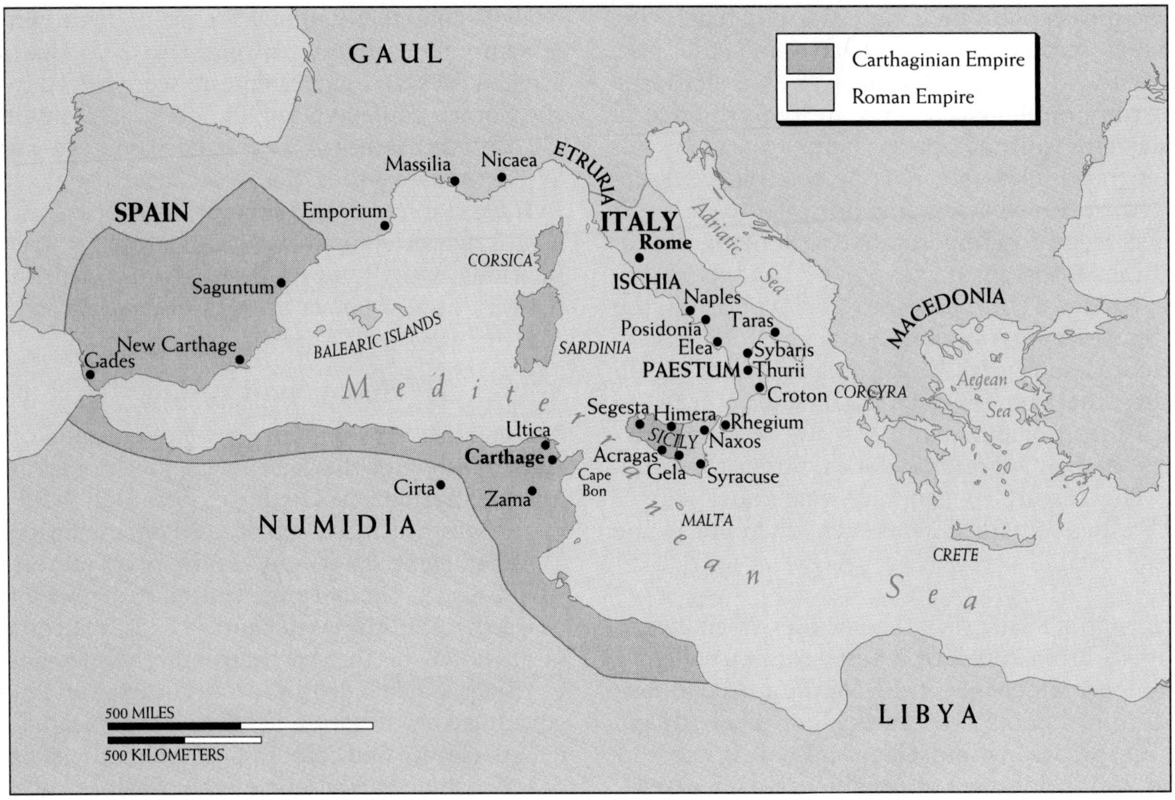

MAP 4–2 THE WESTERN MEDITERRANEAN AREA DURING THE RISE OF ROME *This map covers the theater of conflict between the growing Roman dominions and those of Carthage in the third century B.C.E. The Carthaginian Empire stretched westward from the city (in modern Tunisia) along the North African coast and into southern Spain.*

wanted to prevent Syracuse from dominating the straits. One Mamertine faction, however, fearing that Carthage might take undue advantage of the opportunity, asked Rome for help.

In 264 B.C.E. the request came to the Senate. Because a Punic garrison (the Romans called the Carthaginians *Phoenicians*; in Latin the word is *Poeni* or *Puni*, hence the adjective *Punic*) was in place at Messana, any intervention would not be against Syracuse but against the mighty empire of Carthage. Unless Rome intervened, however, Carthage would gain control of all Sicily and the straits. The assembly voted to send an army to Messana, and expelled the Punic garrison. The First Punic War was on.

THE FIRST PUNIC WAR (264–241 B.C.E.) The war in Sicily soon settled into a stalemate until the Romans built a fleet to cut off supplies to the besieged Carthaginian cities at the western end of Sicily. When Carthage sent its own fleet to raise the siege, the Romans destroyed it. In 241 B.C.E. Carthage signed a treaty giving up Sicily and the islands between Italy and Sicily; it also agreed to pay a war indemnity in ten annual installments. Neither side was to attack the allies of the other. The peace was realistic and not unduly harsh; Rome had earned Sicily, and Carthage could well afford the indemnity. If it had been carried out in good faith, it might have brought lasting peace.

A rebellion, however, broke out in Carthage among the mercenaries, newly recruited from Sicily, who now demanded their pay. In 238 B.C.E., while Carthage was still preoccupied with the rebellion, Rome seized Sardinia and Corsica and demanded that Carthage pay an additional indemnity. This was a harsh and cynical action by the Romans; even the historian Polybius, a great champion of Rome, could find no justification for it. It undid the calming effects of the peace of 241 B.C.E. without preventing the Carthaginians from recovering their strength to seek vengeance in the future.

The conquest of overseas territory presented the Romans with new administrative problems. Instead of following the policy they had pursued in Italy, they made Sicily a province and Sardinia and Corsica another. It became common to extend the term of the governors of these provinces beyond a year. The governors were unchecked by colleagues and exercised full *imperium*. New magistracies, in effect, were thus created free of the limits put on the power of officials in Rome.

The new populations were neither Roman citizens nor allies; they were subjects who did not serve in the army but paid tribute instead. The old practice of extending citizenship and, with it, loyalty to Rome, thus stopped at the borders of Italy. Rome collected taxes on these subjects by "farming" them out at auction to the highest bidder. At first, the tax collectors were natives from the same province. Later they were Roman allies, and finally Roman citizens below senatorial rank who could become powerful and wealthy by squeezing the provincials hard. These innovations were the basis for Rome's imperial organization in the future. In time they strained the constitution and traditions to such a degree as to threaten the existence of the republic.

After the First Punic War, campaigns against the Gauls and across the Adriatic distracted Rome. Meanwhile Hamilcar Barca, the Carthaginian governor of Spain from 237 B.C.E. until his death in 229 B.C.E., was leading Carthage on the road to recovery. Hamilcar sought to compensate for Carthaginian losses elsewhere by building a Punic Empire in Spain. He improved the ports and the commerce conducted in them, exploited the mines, gained control of the hinterland, won over many of the conquered tribes, and built a strong and disciplined army.

Hamilcar's successor, his son-in-law Hasdrubal, pursued the same policies. His success alarmed the Romans. They imposed a treaty in which he promised not to take an army north across the Ebro River in Spain, although Punic expansion in Spain was well south of that river at the time. Though the agreement appeared to put Rome in the position of giving orders to an inferior, it benefited both sides equally. If the Carthaginians accepted the limit of the Ebro on their expansion in Spain, the Romans would not interfere with that expansion.

THE SECOND PUNIC WAR (218–202 B.C.E.) On Hasdrubal's assassination in 221 B.C.E. the army chose as his successor Hannibal, son of Hamilcar Barca. Hannibal was at that time twenty-five years old. He quickly consolidated and extended the Punic Empire in Spain. A few years before his accession Rome had received an offer of alliance from the people of the Spanish town Saguntum (about one hundred miles south of the Ebro). The Romans accepted the friendship and the responsibilities it entailed, in the process violating at least the spirit of the Ebro treaty. At first, Hannibal was careful to avoid any action against Saguntum, but the Saguntines, confident of Rome's protection, began

A Roman warship. Rome became a naval power late in its history, in the course of the First Punic War. Roman sailors initially lacked the skill and experience in sea warfare of their Carthaginian opponents, who could maneuver their oared ships to ram the enemy. To compensate for this disadvantage, the Romans sought to make a sea battle more like an encounter on land by devising ways to grapple enemy ships and board them with armed troops. In time, they also mastered the skillful use of the ram. This picture shows a Roman ship, propelled by oars, with both ram and soldiers, ready for either kind of fight. [Vatican Museum]

to interfere with some of the Spanish tribes allied with Hannibal. When the Romans sent an embassy to Hannibal warning him to let Saguntum alone and repeating the injunction not to cross the Ebro, he ignored the warning and proceeded to besiege and capture the town. The Romans sent an ultimatum to Carthage demanding the surrender of Hannibal. Carthage refused, and Rome declared war in 218 B.C.E.

Between the close of the First Punic War and the outbreak of the Second, Rome had repeatedly provoked Carthage, taking Sardinia in 238 B.C.E. and interfering in Spain, but had taken no measures to prevent Carthage from building a powerful and dangerous empire or even to prepare defenses against a Punic attack in Spain. Hannibal saw to it that the Romans paid the price for these blunders. By September of 218 B.C.E. he was across the Alps, in Italy and among the friendly Gauls.

Hannibal defeated the Romans at the Ticinus River and crushed the joint consular armies at the Trebia River. In 217 B.C.E. he outmaneuvered and trapped another army at Lake Trasimene. The key to success, however, would be defection by Rome's allies. Hannibal released Italian prisoners without harm or ransom and moved his army south of Rome to encourage rebellion. But the allies remained firm.

Sobered by their defeats, the Romans elected Quintus Fabius Maximus dictator. His strategy was to avoid battle while following and harassing Hannibal's army. He would fight only when his army had recovered and then only on favorable ground.

In 216 B.C.E. Hannibal marched to Cannae in Apulia to tempt the Romans, under different generals, into another open fight. They sent off an army of some 80,000 men to meet him. Almost the entire Roman army was killed or captured. It was the worst defeat in Roman history. Rome's prestige was shattered, and most of its allies in southern Italy as well as Syracuse in Sicily now went over to Hannibal. For more than a decade no Roman army would dare face Hannibal in the open field.

Hannibal, however, had neither the numbers nor the supplies to besiege walled cities, nor did he have the equipment to take them by assault. To win the war in Spain, the Romans appointed Publius Cornelius Scipio (237–183 B.C.E.), later called Africanus, to the command in Spain with proconsular *imperium*. Scipio was not yet twenty-five and had held no high office. But he was a general almost as talented as Hannibal. Within a few years young Scipio had conquered all Spain and had deprived Hannibal of hope of help from that region.

In 204 B.C.E. Scipio landed in Africa, defeated the Carthaginians, and forced them to accept a peace the main clause of which was the withdrawal of Hannibal and his army from Italy. Hannibal had won every battle but lost the war, for he had not counted on the determination of Rome and the loyalty of its allies. Hannibal's return inspired Carthage to break the peace and to risk all in battle. In 202 B.C.E. Scipio and Hannibal faced each other at the Battle of Zama. The generalship of Scipio and the desertion of Hannibal's mercenaries gave the victory to Rome. The new peace terms reduced Carthage to the status of a dependent ally to Rome. The Second Punic War ended the Carthaginian command of the western Mediterranean and Carthage's term as a great power. Rome ruled the seas and the entire Mediterranean coast from Italy westward.

The Punic Wars

264–241 B.C.E.	First Punic War
238 B.C.E.	Rome seizes Sardinia and Corsica
221 B.C.E.	Hannibal takes command of Punic army in Spain
218–202 B.C.E.	Second Punic War
216 B.C.E.	Battle of Cannae
209 B.C.E.	Scipio takes New Carthage
202 B.C.E.	Battle of Zama
149–146 B.C.E.	Third Punic War
146 B.C.E.	Destruction of Carthage

The Republic's Conquest of the Hellenistic World

THE EAST By the middle of the third century B.C.E. the eastern Mediterranean had reached a condition of stability based on a balance of power among the three great Hellenistic kingdoms that allowed an established place even for lesser states. This equilibrium, however, was threatened by the activities of two aggressive monarchs, Philip V of Macedon (221–179 B.C.E.) and Antiochus III of the Seleucid kingdom (223–187 B.C.E.). Philip and Antiochus moved swiftly, the latter against Syria and Palestine, the former against cities in the Aegean, in the Hellespontine region, and on the coast of Asia Minor.

The threat that a more powerful Macedon might pose to Rome's friends and, perhaps, even to Italy was enough to persuade the Romans to intervene. Philip had already attempted to meddle in Roman affairs when he formed an alliance with Carthage during the Second Punic War, provoking a conflict known as the First Macedonian War (215–205 B.C.E.). In 200 B.C.E., in an action that began the Second Macedonian War, the Romans sent an ultimatum to Philip ordering him not to attack any Greek city and to pay reparations to Pergamum. These orders were meant to provoke, not avoid, war, and Philip refused to obey. Two years later the Romans sent out a talented young general, Flamininus, who demanded that Philip withdraw from Greece entirely. In 197 B.C.E., with Greek support, Flamininus defeated Philip in the hills of Cynoscephalae in Thessaly, ending the war. The Greek cities freed from Philip were made autonomous, and in 196 B.C.E. Flamininus proclaimed the freedom of the Greeks.

Soon after the Romans withdrew from Greece, they came into conflict with Antiochus, who was expanding his power in Asia and on the European side of the Hellespont. On the pretext of freeing the Greeks from Roman domination, he landed an army on the Greek mainland. The Romans routed Antiochus at Thermopylae and quickly drove him from Greece. In 189 B.C.E. they crushed his army at Magnesia in Asia Minor. The peace of Apamia in the next year deprived Antiochus of his elephants and his navy and imposed a huge indemnity on him. Once again, the Romans took no territory for themselves and left several Greek cities in Asia free. They continued to regard Greece, and now Asia Minor, as a kind of protectorate in which they could intervene or not as they chose.

This relatively mild policy was destined to end as the stern and businesslike policies favored by the conservative censor Cato gained favor in Rome. A new harshness was to be applied to allies and bystanders as well as to defeated opponents.

In 179 B.C.E. Perseus succeeded Philip V as king of Macedon. He tried to gain popularity in Greece by favoring the democratic and revolutionary forces in the cities. The Romans, troubled by his threat to stability, launched the Third Macedonian War (172–168 B.C.E.), and in 168 B.C.E. Æmilius Paullus defeated Perseus at Pydna. The peace that followed this war, reflecting the changed attitude at Rome, was harsh. It divided Macedon into four separate republics, whose citizens were forbidden to intermarry or even to do business across the new national boundaries. Leaders of anti-Roman factions in the Greek cities were punished severely.

When Æmilius Paullus returned from his victory, he celebrated for three days, by parading the spoils of war, royal prisoners, and great wealth through the streets of Rome. The public treasury benefited to such a degree that the direct property tax on Roman citizens was abolished. Part of the booty went to the general and part to his soldiers. New motives were thereby introduced into Roman foreign policy, or, perhaps, old motives were given new prominence. Foreign campaigns could bring profit to the state, rewards to the army, and wealth, fame, honor, and political power to the general.

THE WEST Harsh as the Romans had become toward the Greeks, they were even worse in their treatment of the people of the Iberian Peninsula, whom they considered barbarians. They committed dreadful atrocities, lied, cheated, and broke treaties to exploit and pacify the natives, who fought back fiercely in guerilla style. From 154 to 133 B.C.E. the fighting waxed, and it became hard to recruit Roman soldiers to participate in the increasingly ugly war. At last, in 134 B.C.E., Scipio Aemilianus took the key city of Numantia by siege and burned it to the ground. This put an end to the war in Spain.

Roman treatment of Carthage was no better. Although Carthage lived up to its treaty with Rome faithfully and posed no threat, some Romans refused to abandon their hatred and fear of the traditional enemy. Cato is said to have ended all his speeches in the Senate with the same sentence: *"Ceterum censeo delendam esse Carthaginem"* ("Besides, I think that Carthage must be destroyed"). At last the Romans took advantage of a

Roman Engagement Overseas

215–205 B.C.E.	First Macedonian War
200–197 B.C.E.	Second Macedonian War
196 B.C.E.	Proclamation of Greek freedom by Flamininus at Corinth
189 B.C.E.	Battle of Magnesia; Antiochus defeated in Asia Minor
172–168 B.C.E.	Third Macedonian War
168 B.C.E.	Battle of Pydna
154–133 B.C.E.	Roman wars in Spain
134 B.C.E.	Numantia taken

technical breach of the peace to destroy Carthage. In 146 B.C.E. Scipio Aemilianus took the city, plowed up its land, and put salt in the furrows as a symbol of the permanent abandonment of the site. The Romans incorporated it as the province of Africa, one of six Roman provinces, including Sicily, Sardinia–Corsica, Macedonia, Hither Spain, and Further Spain.

Civilization in the Early Roman Republic

Close and continued association with the Greeks of the Hellenistic world wrought important changes in the Roman style of life and thought. The Roman attitude toward the Greeks ranged from admiration for their culture and history to contempt for their constant squabbling, their commercial practices, and their weakness. Conservatives such as Cato might speak contemptuously of the Greeks as "Greeklings" (*Graeculi*), but even he learned Greek and absorbed Greek culture.

Before long, the education of the Roman upper classes was bilingual. In addition to the Twelve Tables young Roman nobles studied Greek rhetoric, literature, and sometimes philosophy. These studies even had an effect on education and the Latin language. As early as the third century B.C.E. Livius Andronicus, a liberated Greek slave, translated the *Odyssey* into Latin. It became a primer for young Romans and put Latin on the road to becoming a literary language.

Religion

Roman religion was influenced by the Greeks almost from the beginning. The Romans identified their own gods with Greek equivalents and incorporated Greek mythology into their own. Mostly, however, Roman religious practice remained simple and Italian, until the third century B.C.E. brought important new influences from the East.

In 205 B.C.E. the Senate approved the public worship of Cybele, the Great Mother goddess from Phrygia. Hers was a fertility cult accompanied by ecstatic, frenzied, and sensual rites that shocked and outraged conservative Romans to such a degree that they soon banned the cult. Similarly, the Senate banned the worship of Dionysus, or Bacchus, in 186 B.C.E. In the second century B.C.E. interest in Babylonian astrology also grew, and the Senate's attempt in 139 B.C.E. to expel the "Chaldaeans," as the astrologers were called, did not prevent the continued influence of their superstition.

Education

The education provided in the early centuries of the Roman Republic reflected the limited, conservative, and practical nature of that community of plain farmers and soldiers. Education was entirely the responsibility of the family, the father teaching his own son at home. It is not clear whether in these early times girls received any education, though they certainly did later on. The boys learned to read, write, and calculate, and they learned the skills of farming. They memorized the laws of the Twelve Tables; learned how to perform religious rites; heard stories of the great deeds of early Roman history and particularly those of their ancestors; and engaged in the physical training appropriate for potential soldiers. This course of study was practical, vocational, and moral. It aimed at making the boys moral, pious, patriotic, law-abiding, and respectful of tradition.

HELLENIZED EDUCATION In the third century B.C.E. the Romans came into contact with the Greeks of southern Italy, and this contact produced momentous changes in Roman education. Greek teachers introduced the study of language, literature, and philosophy, as well as the idea of a liberal education, or what the Romans called *humanitas*, the root of our concept of the humanities. The aim of education changed from the mastery of practical, vocational skills to an emphasis on broad intellectual training, critical thinking, an interest in ideas, and the development of a well-rounded person.

The new emphasis required students to learn Greek, for Rome did not yet have a literature of its own. Hereafter educated Romans were expected to be bilingual. For this purpose schools were established in which a teacher, called a *grammaticus*, taught students the Greek language and its literature, especially the poets and particularly Homer. After the completion of this elementary education, Roman boys of the upper classes studied rhetoric, the art of speaking and writing well. For the Greeks, rhetoric was a subject of less importance than philosophy. The more practical Romans took to it avidly, however, for it was of great use in legal disputes and was becoming ever more valuable in political life.

Plutarch Describes a Roman Triumph

In 168 B.C.E. L. Æmilius Paullus defeated King Perseus in the Battle of Pydna, bringing an end to the Third Macedonian War. For his great achievement the Senate granted Paullus the right to celebrate a triumph, the great honorific procession granted only for extraordinary victories and eagerly sought by all Roman generals. Plutarch described the details of Paullus's triumph.

✦ *How do you explain the particular elements displayed on each day of the triumph? What purposes do you think a triumph served? What can be learned from this selection about the values celebrated by the Romans? How are they different from the values cherished by Americans in our day? Are there any similarities?*

The people erected scaffolds in the forum, in the circuses, as they call their buildings for horse races, and in all other parts of the city where they could best behold the show. The spectators were clad in white garments; all the temples were open, and full of garlands and perfumes; the ways were cleared and kept open by numerous officers, who drove back all who crowded into or ran across the main avenue. This triumph lasted three days. On the first, which was scarcely long enough for the sight, were to be seen the statues, pictures, and colossal images which were taken from the enemy, drawn upon two hundred and fifty chariots. On the second was carried in a great many wagons the finest and richest armour of the Macedonians, both of brass and steel, all newly polished and glittering; the pieces of which were piled up and arranged purposely with the greatest art, so as to seem to be tumbled in heaps carelessly and by chance:

On the third day, early in the morning, first came the trumpeters, who did not sound as they were wont in a procession or solemn entry, but such a charge as the Romans use when they encourage the soldiers to fight. Next followed young men wearing frocks with ornamented borders, who led to the sacrifice a hundred and twenty stalled oxen, with their horns gilded, and their heads adorned with ribbons and garlands; and with these were boys that carried basins for libation, of silver and gold.

After his children and their attendants came Perseus himself, clad all in black, and wearing the boots of his country, and looking like one altogether stunned and deprived of reason, through the greatness of his misfortunes. Next followed a great company of his friends and familiars, whose countenances were disfigured with grief, and who let the spectators see, by their tears and their continual looking upon Perseus, that it was his fortune they so much lamented, and that they were regardless of their own.

After these were carried four hundred crowns, all made of gold, sent from the cities by their respective deputations to Æmilius, in honour of his victory. Then he himself came, seated on a chariot magnificently adorned (a man well worthy to be looked at, even without these ensigns of power), dressed in a robe of purple, interwoven with gold, and holding a laurel branch in his right hand. All the army, in like manner, with boughs of laurel in their hands, divided into their bands and companies, followed the chariot of their commander; some singing verses, according to the usual custom, mingled with raillery; others, songs of triumph and the praise of Æmilius's deeds; who, indeed, was admired and accounted happy by all men, and unenvied by every one that was good; except so far as it seems the province of some god to lessen that happiness which is too great and inordinate, and so to mingle the affairs of human life that no one should be entirely free and exempt from calamities; but, as we read in Homer, that those should think themselves truly blessed whom fortune has given an equal share of good and evil.

Plutarch, "Aemilius Paullus," in Lives of the Noble Grecians and Romans, *trans. by John Dryden, rev. by A. H. Clough (New York: Random House, n.d.), pp. 340–341.*

Cato Educates His Son

Marcus Porcius Cato (234–149 B.C.E.) was a remarkable Roman who rose from humble origins to the highest offices in the state. He stood as the firmest defender of the old Roman traditions at a time when Hellenic ideas were strongly influential. In the following passage Plutarch tells how Cato attended to his son's education.

✦ *What was the curriculum prepared for Cato's son? Was it suitable for the kind of life he would lead? Was his education more or less helpful and appropriate in this way than that of the average American student today? Why did Cato teach his son himself? Why did he pay so much attention to Roman history? Was he wise in doing so?*

After the birth of his son, no business could be so urgent, unless it had a public character, as to prevent him from being present when his wife bathed and swaddled the babe. For the mother nursed it herself, and often gave suck also to the infants of her slaves, that so they might come to cherish a brotherly affection for her son. As soon as the boy showed signs of understanding, his father took him under his own charge and taught him to read, although he had an accomplished slave, Chilo by name, who was a school teacher, and taught many boys. Still, Cato thought it not right, as he tells us himself, that his son should be scolded by a slave, or have his ears tweaked when he was slow to learn, still less that he should be indebted to his slave for such a priceless thing as education. He was therefore himself not only the boy's reading teacher, but his tutor in law, and his athletic trainer, and he taught his son not merely to hurl the javelin and fight in armour and ride the horse, but also to box, to endure heat and cold, and to swim lustily through the eddies and billows of the Tiber. His History of Rome, as he tells us himself, he wrote out with his own hand and in large characters, that his son might have in his own home an aid to acquaintance with his country's ancient traditions.

Plutarch, Cato Major, *20, trans. by Bernadotte Perrin (London and New York: Loeb Classical Library, William Heinemann, 1914).*

Some Romans were powerfully attracted to Greek literature and philosophy. So important and powerful a Roman aristocrat as Scipio Aemilianus, the man who finally defeated and destroyed Carthage, surrounded himself and his friends with such Greek thinkers as the historian Polybius and the philosopher Panaetius.

Equally outstanding Romans, such as Cato the Elder, were more conservative and opposed the new learning on the grounds that it would weaken Roman moral fiber. They were able on more than one occasion to pass laws expelling philosophers and teachers of rhetoric. But these attempts to go back to older ways failed. The new education suited the needs of the Romans of the second century B.C.E. They found themselves changing from a rural to an urban society and were being thrust into the sophisticated world of Hellenistic Greeks.

By the last century of the Roman Republic, the new Hellenized education had become dominant. Latin literature had come into being along with Latin translations of Greek poets, and these formed part of the course of study. But Roman gentlemen still were expected to be bilingual, and Greek language and literature were still central to the curriculum. Many schools were established. The number of educated people grew, extending beyond the senatorial class to the equestrians and outside Rome to the cities of Italy.

In the late republic, Roman education, though still entirely private, became more formal and organized. From the ages of seven to twelve, boys went

The temple of Vesta at Rome was built in the first century B.C.E. *Vesta was the Roman goddess of the hearth. Her cult included an eternal flame, which was tended by the famous Vestal Virgins.*

to elementary school accompanied by a Greek slave called a *paedagogus* (whence our term *pedagogue*), who looked after their physical well-being and their manners, and who improved their ability in Greek conversation. At school the boys learned to read and write, using a wax tablet and a stylus, and to do simple arithmetic with an abacus and pebbles (*calculi*). Discipline was harsh and corporal punishment frequent. From twelve to sixteen, boys went to a higher school, where the *grammaticus* undertook to provide a liberal education, using Greek and Latin literature as his subject matter. In addition, he taught dialectic, arithmetic, geometry, astronomy, and music. Sometimes he included the elements of rhetoric, especially for those boys who would not go on to a higher education.

At sixteen, some boys went on to advanced study in rhetoric. The instructors were usually Greek. They trained their charges by study of models of fine speech of the past and by having them write, memorize, and declaim speeches suitable for different occasions. Sometimes the serious student attached himself to some famous public speaker and followed him about to learn what he could. Sometimes a rich and ambitious Roman would support a Greek philosopher in his own home. His son could converse with the philosopher and acquire the learning and polished thought necessary for the fully cultured gentleman. Some, like the great orator Cicero, undertook what we might call postgraduate study by traveling abroad to study with great teachers of rhetoric and philosophy in the Greek world.

One result of this whole style of education was to broaden the Romans' understanding through the careful study of a foreign language and culture. It made them a part of the older and wider culture of the Hellenistic world, a world that they had come to dominate and needed to understand.

EDUCATION FOR WOMEN Though the evidence is limited, we can be sure that girls of the upper classes received an education equivalent at least to the early stages of a boy's education. They were

This carved relief from the second century C.E. *shows a schoolmaster and his pupils. The pupil at the right is arriving late. [Alinari/Art Resource, N.Y.]*

This wall painting from the first century B.C.E. *comes from the villa of Publius Fannius Synistor at Pompeii and shows a woman playing a cithera. [The Metropolitan Museum of Art, Rogers Fund, 1903 (Acc. # 03.14.5)]*

probably taught by tutors at home rather than going to school, as was increasingly the fashion among boys in the late republic. Young women did not study with philosophers and rhetoricians, for they were usually married by the age at which the men were pursuing their higher education. Still, some women found ways to continue their education. Some became prose writers and others poets. By the first century C.E. there were apparently enough learned women to provoke the complaints of a crotchety and conservative satirist:

Still more exasperating is the woman who begs as soon as she sits down to dinner, to discourse on poets and poetry, comparing Virgil with Homer; professors, critics, lawyers, auctioneers—even another woman—can't get a word in. She rattles on at such a rate that you'd think that all the pots and pans in the kitchen were crashing to the floor or that every bell in town was clanging. All by

A Women's Uprising in Republican Rome

In 195 B.C.E. Roman women staged a rare public political protest when they demanded the repeal of a law passed two decades earlier during the Second Punic War, which they judged to limit their rights unfairly. Livy (59 B.C.E.–17 C.E.) describes the affair and the response of the traditionalist Marcus Porcius Cato (234–149 B.C.E.).

✦ *Of what did the women complain? How did they try to achieve their goals? Which of Cato's objections to their behavior do you think were most important? Since women did not vote or sit in assemblies, how can the outcome of the affair be explained?*

Amid the anxieties of great wars, either scarce finished or soon to come, an incident occurred, trivial to relate, but which, by reason of the passions it aroused, developed into a violent contention. [Two] tribunes of the people, proposed to the assembly the abrogation of the Oppian law. The tribune Gaius Oppius had carried this law in the heat of the Punic War, . . . that no woman should possess more than half an ounce of gold or wear a parti-coloured garment or ride in a carriage in the City or in a town within a mile thereof, except on the occasion of a religious festival. . . . [T]he Capitoline was filled with crowds of supporters and opponents of the bill. The matrons could not be kept at home by . . . their husbands' orders, but blocked all the streets and approaches to the Forum, begging the men as they came down to the Forum that, in the prosperous condition of the state, when the private fortunes of all men were daily increasing, they should allow the woman too to have their former distinctions restored. The crowd of women grew larger day by day; for they were now coming in from the towns and rural districts. Soon they dared even to approach and appeal to the consuls, the praetors, and the other officials, but one consul, at least, they found adamant, Marcus Porcius Cato, who spoke thus in favour of the law whose repeal was being urged.

"If each of us, citizens, had determined to assert his rights and dignity as a husband with 'respect to his own spouse, we should have less trouble with the sex as a whole; as it is, our liberty, destroyed at home by female violence, even here in the Forum is crushed and trodden underfoot, and because we have not kept them individually under control, we dread them collectively. . . . But from no class is there not the greatest danger if you permit them meetings . . . and secret consultations.

I should have said, 'What sort of practice is this, of running out into the streets and blocking the roads and speaking to other women's husbands? Could you not have made the same requests, each of your own husband, at home? And yet, not even at home, if modesty would keep matrons within the limits of their proper rights, did it become you to concern yourselves with the question of what laws should be adopted in this place or repealed.' Our ancestors permitted no woman to conduct even personal business without a guardian to intervene in her behalf; they wished them to be under the control of fathers, brothers, husbands; we (Heaven help us!) allow them now even to interfere in public affairs, yes, and to visit the Forum and our informal and formal sessions. Give loose rein to their uncontrollable nature and to this untamed creature and expect that they will themselves set bounds to their licence; unless you act, this is the least of the things enjoined upon women by custom or law and to which they submit with a feeling of injustice. It is complete liberty or, rather, if we wish to speak the truth, complete licence that they desire.

"If they win in this, what will they not attempt? Review all the laws with which your forefathers restrained their licence and made them subject to their husbands; even with all these bonds you can scarcely control them. What of this? If you suffer them to seize these bonds one by one and wrench themselves free and finally to be placed on a parity with their husbands, do you think that you will be able to endure them? The moment they begin to be your equals, they will be your superiors."

The next day an even greater crowd of women appeared in public, and all of them in a body beset the doors of those tribunes, who were vetoing their colleagues' proposal, and they did not desist until the threat of veto was withdrawn by the tribunes. After that there was no question that all the tribes would vote to repeal the law. The law was repealed twenty years after it was passed.

Livy, *trans. by Evan T. Stage (Cambridge, Mass.: Harvard University Press, 1935), XXXIV, i–iii; viii, pp. 413–419, 439.*

herself she makes as much noise as some primitive tribe chasing away an eclipse. She should learn the philosopher's lesson: "moderation is necessary even for intellectuals." And, if she still wants to appear educated and eloquent, let her dress as a man, sacrifice to men's gods and bathe in the men's baths. Wives shouldn't try to be public speakers; they shouldn't use rhetorical devices; they shouldn't read all the classics—there should be some things women don't understand. I myself cannot understand a woman who can quote the rules of grammar and never make a mistake and cites obscure, long-forgotten poets—as if men cared about such things. If she has to correct somebody let her correct her girl friends and leave her husband alone.[2]

Slavery

Like most ancient peoples, the Romans had slaves from very early in their history, but among the shepherds and family-farmers of early Rome they were relatively few. Slavery became a basic element in the Roman economy and society only during the second century B.C.E., after the Romans had conquered most of the lands bordering the Mediterranean. In the time between the beginning of Rome's first war against Carthage (264 B.C.E.) and the conquest of Spain (133 B.C.E.), the Romans enslaved some 250,000 prisoners of war, greatly increasing the availability of slave labor and reducing its price. For a fuller discussion of slavery in Roman society, see The West and the World, p. 150.

Roman Imperialism: The Late Republic

Rome's expansion in Italy and overseas was accomplished without a grand general plan. (See Map 4–3.) The new territories were gained as a result of wars that the Romans believed were either defensive or preventive. Their foreign policy was aimed at providing security for Rome on Rome's terms, but these terms were often unacceptable to other nations and led to continued conflict. Whether intended or not, Rome's expansion brought the Romans an empire and, with it, power, wealth, and responsibilities. The need to govern an empire beyond the seas would severely test the republican constitution that had served Rome well during its years as a city-state and that had been well adapted to the mastery of Italy. Roman society and the Roman character had maintained their integrity through the period of expansion in Italy. But these would be tested by the temptations and strains presented by the wealth and the complicated problems of an overseas empire.

The Aftermath of Conquest

War and expansion changed the economic, social, and political life of Italy. Before the Punic wars most Italians owned their own farms, which provided the greater part of the family's needs. Some families owned larger holdings, but their lands chiefly grew grain, and they used the labor of clients, tenants, and hired workers rather than slaves. Fourteen years of fighting in the Second Punic War did terrible damage to much Italian farmland. Many veterans returning from the wars found it impossible or unprofitable to go back to their farms. Some moved to Rome, where they could find work as occasional laborers, but most stayed in the country to work as tenant farmers or hired hands. Often the land they abandoned was gathered into large parcels by the wealthy. They converted these units, later called *latifundia*, into large plantations for growing cash crops—grain, olives, and grapes for wine—or into cattle ranches.

The upper classes had plenty of capital to stock and operate these estates because of profits from the war and from exploiting the provinces. Land was cheap, and slaves conquered in war provided cheap labor. By fair means and foul, large landholders obtained great quantities of public land and forced small farmers from it. These changes separated the people of Rome and Italy more sharply into rich and poor, landed and landless, privileged and deprived. The result was political, social, and ultimately constitutional conflict that threatened the existence of the republic.

The Gracchi

By the middle of the second century B.C.E. the problems caused by Rome's rapid expansion troubled perceptive Roman nobles. The fall in status of peasant farmers made it harder to recruit soldiers and came to present a political threat as well. The patron's traditional control over his clients was weakened by their flight from their land. Even those

[2]*Juvenal,* Satires *6.434–456, trans. by Roger Killian, Richard Lynch, Robert J. Rowland, and John Sims, cited by Sarah B. Pomeroy in* Goddesses, Whores, Wives, and Slaves *(New York: Schocken Books, 1975), p. 172.*

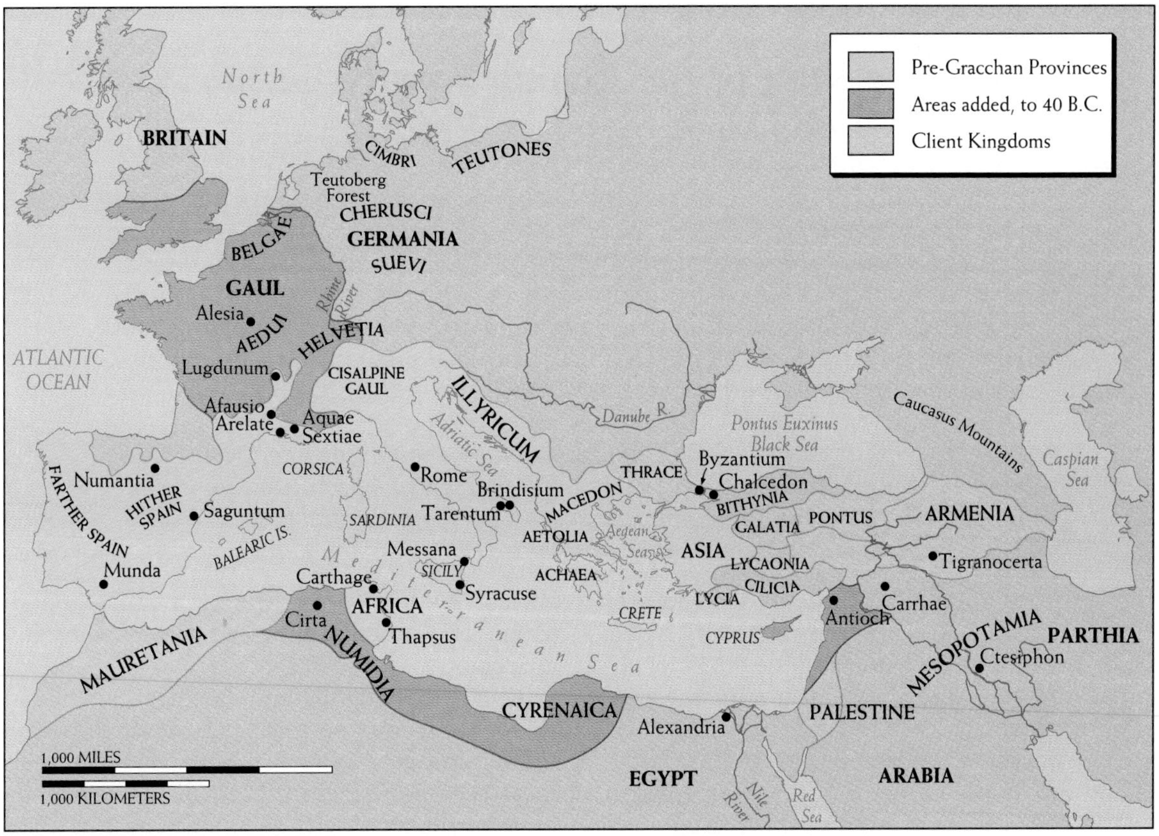

Map 4–3 Roman Dominions of the Late Roman Republic *The Roman Republic's conquest of Mediterranean lands—and beyond—until the death of Julius Caesar is shown here. Areas conquered before Tiberius Gracchus (ca. 133* b.c.e.*) are distinguished from later ones and from client areas owing allegiance to Rome.*

former landowners who worked on the land of their patrons as tenants or hired hands were less reliable. The introduction of the secret ballot in the 130s B.C.E. made them even more independent.

Tiberius Gracchus In 133 B.C.E. Tiberius Gracchus tried to solve these problems. He became tribune for 133 B.C.E. on a program of land reform; some of the most powerful members of the Roman aristocracy helped him draft the bill. They meant it to be a moderate attempt at solving Rome's problems. The bill's target was public land that had been acquired and held illegally, some of it for many years. The bill allowed holders of this land to retain as many as 300 acres in clear title as private property, but the state would reclaim anything over that. The recovered land would be redistributed in small lots to the poor, who would pay a small rent to the state and could not sell what they had received.

The bill aroused great hostility. Many senators held vast estates and would be hurt by its passage. Others thought it would be a bad precedent to allow any interference with property rights, even ones so dubious as those pertaining to illegally held public land. Still others feared the political gains that Tiberius and his associates would make if the beneficiaries of their law were properly grateful to its drafters.

When Tiberius put the bill before the tribal assembly, one of the tribunes, M. Octavius, interposed his veto. Tiberius went to the Senate to discuss his proposal, but the senators continued their opposition. Tiberius now had to choose between dropping the matter and undertaking a revolutionary course. Unwilling to give up, he put his bill before the tribal assembly again. Again Octavius vetoed. So Tiberius, strongly supported by the people, had Octavius removed from office, violating the constitution. The assembly's removal of a

The Ruin of the Roman Family Farm and the Gracchan Reforms

The independent family farm was the backbone both of the Greek polis *and the early Roman Republic. Rome's conquests, the long wars that kept the citizen-soldier away from his farm, and the availability of great numbers of slaves at a low price, however, badly undercut the traditional way of farming and with it the foundations of republican society. In the following passage Plutarch describes the process of agricultural change and the response to it of the reformer Tiberius Gracchus, tribune in 133* B.C.E.

✦ *What were the causes of the troubles faced by Roman farmers? What were the social and political consequences of the changes in agricultural life? What solution did Tiberius Gracchus propose? Can you think of any reasons, besides selfishness and greed, that people might oppose his plan?*

Of the territory which the Romans won in war from their neighbours, a part they sold, and a part they made common land, and assigned it for occupation to the poor and indigent among the citizens, on payment of a small rent into the public treasury. And when the rich began to offer larger rents and drove out the poor, a law was enacted forbidding the holding by one person of more than five hundred acres of land. For a short time this enactment gave a check to the rapacity of the rich, and was of assistance to the poor, who remained in their places on the land which they had rented and occupied the allotment which each had held from the outset. But later on the neighbouring rich men, by means of fictitious personages, transferred these rentals to themselves, and finally held most of the land openly in their own names. Then the poor, who had been ejected from their land, no longer showed themselves eager for military service, and neglected the bringing up of children, so that soon all Italy was conscious of a dearth of freemen, and was filled with gangs of foreign slaves, by whose aid the rich cultivated their estates, from which they had driven away the free citizens.

And it is thought that a law dealing with injustice and rapacity so great was never drawn up in milder and gentler terms. For men who ought to have been punished for their disobedience and to have surrendered with payment of a fine the land which they were illegally enjoying, these men it merely ordered to abandon their injust acquisitions upon being paid their value, and to admit into ownership of them such citizens as needed assistance. But although the rectification of the wrong was so considerate, the people were satisfied to let bygones be bygones if they could be secure from such wrong in the future; the men of wealth and substance, however, were led by their greed to hate the law, and by their wrath and contentiousness to hate the lawgiver, and tried to dissuade the people by alleging that Tiberius was introducing a re-distribution of land for the confusion of the body politic, and was stirring up a general revolution.

Plutarch, "Tiberius Gracchus," in Lives *8–9, vol. 10, trans. by Bernadotte Perrin and William Heinemann (London: G. P. Putnam's Sons, New York, 1921), pp. 159–167.*

magistrate implied a fundamental shift of power from the Senate to the people. If the assembly could pass laws opposed by the Senate and vetoed by a tribune, if they could remove magistrates, then Rome would become a democracy like Athens instead of a traditional oligarchy. At this point many of Tiberius's powerful senatorial allies deserted him.

Tiberius proposed a second bill, harsher than the first and more appealing to the people, for he had given up hope of conciliating the Senate. This bill, which passed the assembly, provided for a commission to carry it out. When King Attalus of Pergamum died and left his kingdom to Rome, Tiberius proposed to use the Pergamene revenue to finance the commission. This proposal challenged the Senate's control both of finances and of foreign affairs. Hereafter there could be no compromise. Either Tiberius or the Roman constitution must go under.

Tiberius understood the danger that he would face if he stepped down from the tribunate, and so he announced his candidacy for a second successive term, striking another blow at tradition. His opponents feared that he might go on to hold office indefinitely, to dominate Rome in what appeared to them a demagogic tyranny. They concentrated their fire on the constitutional issue, the deposition of the tribune. They appear to have had some success, for many of Tiberius's supporters did not come out to vote. At the elections a riot broke out, and a mob of senators and their clients killed Tiberius and some 300 of his followers and threw their bodies into the Tiber River. The Senate had put down the threat to its rule, but at the price of the first internal bloodshed in Roman political history.

The tribunate of Tiberius Gracchus brought a permanent change to Roman politics. Heretofore Roman political struggles had generally been struggles for honor and reputation between great families or coalitions of such families. Fundamental issues were rarely at stake. The revolutionary proposals of Tiberius, however, and the senatorial resort to bloodshed created a new situation. Tiberius's use of the tribunate to challenge senatorial rule encouraged imitation in spite of his failure. From then on, Romans could pursue a political career that was not based solely on influence within the aristocracy; pressure from the people might be an effective substitute. In the last century of the republic politicians who sought such backing were called *populares*, whereas those who supported the traditional role of the Senate were called *optimates* or "the best men".

These groups were not political parties with formal programs and party discipline, but they were more than merely vehicles for the political ambitions of unorthodox politicians. Fundamental questions—such as those about land reform, the treatment of the Italian allies, the power of the assemblies versus the power of the Senate, and other problems—divided the Roman people, from the time of Tiberius Gracchus to the fall of the republic. Some popular leaders, of course, were cynical self-seekers who used the issues only for their own ambitions. Some few may have been sincere advocates of a principled position. Most, no doubt, were a mixture of the two, like most politicians in most times.

GAIUS GRACCHUS The tribunate of Gaius Gracchus (brother of Tiberius) was much more dangerous than that of Tiberius. All the tribunes of 123 B.C.E. were his supporters, so there could be no veto, and a recent law permitted the reelection of tribunes. Gaius developed a program of such breadth as to appeal to a variety of groups. First, he revived the agrarian commission, which had been allowed to lapse. Because there was not enough good public land left to meet the demand, he proposed to establish new colonies: two in Italy and one on the old site of Carthage. Among other popular acts, he put through a law stabilizing the price of grain in Rome, which involved building granaries to guarantee an adequate supply.

Gaius broke new ground in appealing to the equestrian order in his struggle against the Senate. The equestrians (so called because they served in the Roman cavalry) were neither peasants nor senators. A highly visible minority of them were businesspeople who supplied goods and services to the Roman state and collected its taxes. Almost continuous warfare and the need for tax collection in the provinces had made many of them rich. Most of the time these wealthy men had the same outlook as the Senate; generally they used their profits to purchase land and to try to reach senatorial rank themselves. Still they had a special interest in Roman expansion and in the exploitation of the provinces. Toward the latter part of the second century B.C.E., they came to have a clear sense of group interest and to exert political influence.

In 129 B.C.E. Pergamum became the new province of Asia. Gaius put through a law turning over to the equestrian order the privilege of collecting its revenue. He also barred senators from serving as jurors on the courts that tried provincial governors charged with extortion. The combination was a wonderful gift for wealthy equestrian businessmen, who were now free to squeeze profits out of the rich province of Asia without much fear of interference from the governors. The results for Roman provincial administration were bad, but the immediate political consequences for Gaius were excellent. The equestrians were now given reality as a class; as a political unit they might be set against the Senate or be formed into a coalition to serve Gaius's purposes.

Gaius easily won reelection as tribune for 122 B.C.E. He aimed at giving citizenship to the Italians, both to solve the problem that their dissatisfaction presented and to add them to his political coalition. But the common people did not want to share the advantages of Roman citizenship. The Senate seized on this proposal as a way of driving a wedge between Gaius and his supporters.

The Romans did not reelect Gaius for 121 B.C.E., leaving him vulnerable to his enemies. A hostile consul provoked an incident that led to violence. The Senate invented an extreme decree ordering the consuls to see to it that no harm came to the republic; in effect, this decree established martial law. Gaius was hunted down and killed, and a senatorial court condemned and put to death without trial some 3,000 of his followers.

Marius and Sulla

For the moment the senatorial oligarchy had fought off the challenge to its traditional position. Before long, it faced more serious dangers arising from troubles abroad. The first grew out of a dispute over the succession to the throne of Numidia, a client kingdom of Rome's near Carthage.

MARIUS AND THE JUGURTHINE WAR The victory of Jugurtha, who became king of Numidia, and his massacre of Roman and Italian businessmen in Numidia, gained Roman attention. Although the Senate was reluctant to become involved, pressure from the equestrians and the people forced the declaration of what became known as the Jugurthine War in 111 B.C.E.

As the war dragged on, the people, sometimes with good reason, suspected the Senate of taking bribes from Jugurtha. They elected C. Marius (157–86 B.C.E.) to the consulship for 107 B.C.E. The assembly, usurping the role of the Senate, assigned him to the province of Numidia. This action was significant in several ways. Marius was a *novus homo*, a "new man," that is, the first in the history of his family to reach the consulship. Although a wealthy equestrian, he had been born in the town of Arpinum and was outside the closed circle of the old Roman aristocracy. His earlier career had won him a reputation as an outstanding soldier and something of a political maverick.

Marius quickly defeated Jugurtha, but Jugurtha escaped and guerilla warfare continued. Finally Marius's subordinate, L. Cornelius Sulla (138–78 B.C.E.), trapped Jugurtha and brought the war to an end. Marius celebrated the victory, but Sulla, an ambitious but impoverished descendant of an old Roman family, resented being cheated of the credit he thought he deserved. Soon rumors circulated crediting Sulla with the victory and diminishing Marius's role. Thus were the seeds planted for a personal rivalry and a mutual hostility that would last until Marius's death.

While the Romans were fighting Jugurtha, a far greater danger threatened Rome from the north. In 105 B.C.E. two barbaric tribes, the Cimbri and the Teutones, had come down the Rhone Valley and crushed a Roman army at Arausio (Orange). When these tribes threatened again, the Romans elected Marius to his second consulship to meet the danger. He served five consecutive terms until 100 B.C.E., when the crisis was over.

While the barbarians were occupied elsewhere, Marius used the time to make important changes in the army. He began using volunteers for the army, mostly the dispossessed farmers and rural proletarians whose problems had not been solved by the Gracchi. They enlisted for a long term of service and looked on the army not as an unwelcome duty but as an opportunity and a career. They became semiprofessional clients of their general and sought guaranteed food, clothing, shelter, and booty from victories. They came to expect a piece of land as a form of mustering-out pay, or veteran's bonus, when they retired.

Volunteers were most likely to enlist with a man who was a capable soldier and influential enough to obtain what he needed for them. They looked to him rather than to the state for their rewards. He, on the other hand, had to obtain these favors from the Senate if he was to maintain his power and reputation. Marius's innovation created both the opportunity and the necessity for military leaders to gain enough power to challenge civilian authority. The promise of rewards won these leaders the personal loyalty of their troops, and that loyalty allowed them to frighten the Senate into granting their demands.

THE WAR AGAINST THE ITALIAN ALLIES (90–88 B.C.E.) For a decade Rome avoided serious troubles, but in that time the Senate took no action to deal with Italian discontent. The Italians were excluded from the land bill for Marius's veterans. Their discontent was serious enough to cause the Senate to expel all Italians from Rome in 95 B.C.E. Four years later the tribune M. Livius Drusus put forward a bill to

Mithridates the Great, king of Pontus. For two decades he opposed Rome's expansion. In this sculpture from the Louvre he wears a lion's head in imitation of Hercules. [Giraudon/Art Resource]

enfranchise the Italians. Drusus seems to have been a sincere aristocratic reformer, but he was assassinated in 90 B.C.E. In frustration the Italians revolted and established a separate confederation with its own capital and its own coinage.

Employing the traditional device of divide and conquer, the Romans immediately offered citizenship to those cities that remained loyal and soon made the same offer to the rebels if they laid down their arms. Even then, hard fighting was needed to put down the uprising, but by 88 B.C.E. the war against the allies was over. All the Italians became Roman citizens with the protections that citizenship offered. However, they retained local self-government and a dedication to their own municipalities that made Italy flourish. The passage of time blurred the distinction between Romans and Italians and forged them into a single nation.

SULLA AND HIS DICTATORSHIP During the war against the allies Sulla had performed well. He was elected consul for 88 B.C.E. and was given command of the war against Mithridates, who was leading a major rebellion in Asia. At this point the seventy-year-old Marius emerged from obscurity and sought the command for himself. With popular and equestrian support, he got the assembly to transfer the command to him. Sulla, defending the rights of the Senate and his own interests, marched his army against Rome. This was the first time a Roman general had used his army against fellow citizens. Marius and his friends fled, and Sulla regained the command. No sooner had he left again for Asia than Marius joined with the consul Cinna and reconquered Rome by force. He outlawed Sulla and launched a bloody massacre of the senatorial opposition. Marius died soon after his election to a seventh consulship, for 86 B.C.E.

Cinna now was the chief man at Rome. Supported by Marius's men, he held the consulship from 87 to 84 B.C.E. His future depended on Sulla's fortunes in the East.

By 85 B.C.E. Sulla had driven Mithridates from Greece and had crossed over to Asia Minor. Eager to regain control of Rome, he negotiated a compromise peace. In 83 B.C.E. he returned to Italy and fought a civil war that lasted for more than a year. Sulla won and drove the followers of Marius from Italy. He now held all power and had himself appointed dictator, not in the traditional sense, but for the express purpose of reconstituting the state.

Sulla's first step was to wipe out the opposition. The names of those proscribed were posted in public. As outlaws they could be killed by anyone, and the killer received a reward. Sulla proscribed not only political opponents but his personal enemies and men whose only crime was having wealth and property. With the proceeds from the confiscations, Sulla rewarded his veterans, perhaps as many as 100,000 men, and thereby built a solid base of support.

Sulla had enough power and influence to make himself the permanent ruler of Rome. He was traditional enough to want a restoration of senatorial government, however, reformed so as to prevent the

Sallust on Faction and the Decline of the Republic

Sallust (86–35 B.C.E.) was a supporter of Julius Caesar and of the political faction called populares, *translated here as "the democratic party," opponents of the* optimates, *translated here as "the nobility." In this selection from his monograph on the Jugurthine War, he tries to explain Rome's troubles in the period after the destruction of Carthage in 146 B.C.E.*

✦ *Why did Sallust think the destruction of Carthage marked the beginning of the decline of the Roman Republic? Does his account of events seem fair and dispassionate? How would a member of "the nobility" have evaluated the same events? Is the existence of factions or "parties" inevitably harmful to a republic?*

The division of the Roman state into warring factions, with all its attendant vices, had originated some years before, as a result of peace and of that material prosperity which men regard as the greatest blessing. Down to the destruction of Carthage, the people and Senate shared the government peaceably and with due restraint, and the citizens did not compete for glory or power; fear of its enemies preserved the good morals of the state. But when the people were relieved of this fear, the favourite vices of prosperity—licence and pride—appeared as a natural consequence. Thus the peace and quiet which they had longed for in time of adversity proved, when they obtained it, to be even more grievous and bitter than the adversity. For the nobles started to use their position, and the people their liberty, to gratify their selfish passions, every man snatching and seizing what he could for himself. So the whole community was split into parties, and the Republic, which hitherto had been the common interest of all, was torn asunder. The nobility had the advantage of being a close-knit body, whereas the democratic party was weakened by its loose organization, its supporters being dispersed among a huge multitude. One small group of oligarchs had everything in its control alike in peace and war—the treasury, the provinces, public offices, all distinctions and triumphs. The people were burdened with military services and poverty, while the spoils of war were snatched by the generals and shared with a handful of friends. Meantime, the soldiers' parents or young children, if they happened to have a powerful neighbour, might well be driven from their homes. Thus the possession of power gave unlimited scope to ruthless greed, which violated and plundered everything, respecting nothing and holding nothing sacred, till finally it brought about its own downfall. For the day came when noblemen rose to power who preferred true glory to unjust dominion: then the state was shaken to its foundations by civil strife, as by an earthquake.

Sallust, The Jugurthine War and the Conspiracy of Catiline, The Jugurthine War *41, trans. by S. A. Handford (Baltimore and Harmondsworth: Penguin Books, 1963), pp. 77–78.*

misfortunes of the past. To deal with the decimation of the Senate caused by the proscriptions and the civil war, he enrolled 300 new members, many of them from the equestrian order and the upper classes of the Italian cities. The office of tribune, used by the Gracchi to attack senatorial rule, was made into a political dead end.

Sulla's most valuable reforms improved the quality of the courts and the entire legal system. He created new courts to deal with specified crimes, bringing the number of courts to eight. As both judge and jurors were senators, these courts, too, enhanced senatorial power. These actions were the most permanent of Sulla's reforms, laying the foundation for Roman criminal law.

Sulla retired to a life of ease and luxury in 79 B.C.E. He could not, however, undo the effect of his own example, that of a general using the loyalty of his own troops to take power and to massacre his opponents, as well as innocent men. These actions proved to be more significant than his constitutional arrangements.

The Fall of the Republic

Pompey, Crassus, Caesar, and Cicero

Within a year of Sulla's death his constitution came under assault. To deal with an armed threat to its powers, the Senate violated the very procedures meant to defend them. The Senate gave the command of the army to Pompey (106–48 B.C.E.), who was only twenty-eight and had never been elected to a magistracy. Then, when Sertorius, a Marian general, resisted senatorial control, the Senate appointed Pompey proconsul in Spain in 77 B.C.E. These actions ignored Sulla's rigid rules for office holding, which had been meant to guarantee experienced, loyal, and safe commanders. In 71 B.C.E. Pompey returned to Rome with new glory, having put down the rebellion of Sertorius. In 73 B.C.E. the Senate made another extraordinary appointment to put down a great slave rebellion led by the gladiator Spartacus. Marcus Licinius Crassus, a rich and ambitious senator, received powers that gave him command of almost all Italy. Together with the newly returned Pompey, he crushed the rebellion in 71 B.C.E. Extraordinary commands of this sort proved to be the ruin of the republic.

Crassus and Pompey were ambitious men whom the Senate feared. Both demanded special honors and election to the consulship for the year 70 B.C.E. Pompey was legally ineligible because he had never gone through the strict course of offices prescribed in Sulla's constitution, and Crassus needed Pompey's help. They joined forces, though they disliked and were jealous of each other. They gained popular support by promising to restore the full powers of the tribunes, which Sulla had curtailed. And they gained equestrian backing by promising to restore equestrians to the extortion court juries. They both won election and repealed most of Sulla's constitution. This opened the way for further attacks on senatorial control and for collaboration between ambitious generals and demagogic tribunes.

Pompey the Great (106–48 B.C.E.). He was successful in crushing rebellions against the Roman Republic. [Alinari/Art Resource, N.Y.]

In 67 B.C.E. a special law gave Pompey *imperium* for three years over the entire Mediterranean and fifty miles in from the coast. It also gave him the power to raise great quantities of troops and money to rid the area of pirates. The assembly passed the law over senatorial opposition, and in three months Pompey cleared the seas of piracy. Meanwhile a new war had broken out with Mithridates. In 66 B.C.E. the assembly transferred the command to Pompey, giving him unprecedented powers. He held *imperium* over all Asia, with the right to make war and peace at will. His *imperium* was superior to that of any proconsul in the field.

Once again Pompey justified his appointment. He defeated Mithridates and drove him to suicide. By 62 B.C.E. he had extended Rome's frontier to the Euphrates River and had organized the territories of Asia so well that his arrangements remained the basis of Roman rule well into the imperial period. When Pompey returned to Rome in 62 B.C.E., he had more power, prestige, and popular support than any Roman in history. The Senate and his personal enemies had reason to fear that he might emulate Sulla and establish his own rule.

Rome had not been quiet in Pompey's absence. Crassus was the foremost among those who had reason to fear Pompey's return. Although rich and influential, he did not have the confidence of the Senate, a firm political base of his own, or the kind of military glory needed to rival Pompey. During the 60s B.C.E., therefore, he allied himself with various popular leaders.

The ablest of these men was Gaius Julius Caesar (100–44 B.C.E.). He was a descendant of an old but politically obscure patrician family that claimed descent from the kings and even from the goddess Venus. In spite of this noble lineage, Caesar was connected to the popular party through his aunt, the wife of Marius, and through his own wife, Cornelia, the daughter of Cinna. Caesar was an ambitious and determined young politician whose daring and rhetorical skill made him a valuable ally in winning the discontented of every class to the cause of the *populares*. Though Crassus was very much the senior partner, each needed the other to achieve what both wanted: significant military commands whereby they might build a reputation, a political following, and a military force to compete with Pompey's.

The chief opposition to Crassus's candidates for the consulship for 63 B.C.E. came from Cicero (106–43 B.C.E.), a *novus homo*, or "new man," from Marius's home town of Arpinum. He had made a spectacular name as the leading lawyer in Rome. Cicero, though he came from outside the senatorial aristocracy, was no *popularis*. His program was to preserve the republic against demagogues and ambitious generals by making the government more liberal. He wanted to unite the stable elements of the state—the Senate and the equestrians—in a harmony of the orders. This program did not appeal to the senatorial oligarchy, but the Senate preferred him to Catiline, a dangerous and popular politician thought to be linked with Crassus. Cicero and Antonius were elected consuls for 63 B.C.E., Catiline running third.

Cicero soon learned of a plot hatched by Catiline. Catiline had run in the previous election on a platform of cancellation of debts; this appealed to discontented elements in general but especially to the heavily indebted nobles and their many clients. Made desperate by defeat, Catiline planned to stir up rebellions around Italy, to cause confusion in the city, and to take it by force. Quick action by Cicero defeated Catiline.

Formation of the First Triumvirate

Toward the end of 62 B.C.E. Pompey landed at Brundisium. To general surprise, he disbanded his army, celebrated a great triumph, and returned to private life. He had delayed his return in the hope of finding Italy in such a state as to justify his keeping the army and dominating the scene. Cicero's quick suppression of Catiline prevented his plan. Pompey, therefore, had either to act illegally or to lay down his arms. Because he had not thought of monarchy or revolution but merely wanted to be recognized and treated as the greatest Roman, he chose the latter course.

Pompey had achieved amazing things for Rome and simply wanted the Senate to approve his excellent arrangements in the East and to make land allotments to his veterans. His demands were far from unreasonable, and a prudent Senate would have granted them and would have tried to employ his power in defense of the constitution. But the Senate was jealous and fearful of overmighty individuals and refused his requests. Pompey was driven to an alliance with his natural enemies, Crassus and Caesar, because all three found the Senate standing in the way of what they wanted.

In 60 B.C.E. Caesar returned to Rome from his governorship of Spain. He wanted the privilege of celebrating a triumph, the great victory procession that the Senate granted certain generals to honor especially great achievements, and of running for consul. The law did not allow him to do both, however, requiring him to stay outside the city with his army but demanding that he canvass for votes personally within the city. He asked for a special dispensation, but the Senate refused. Caesar then performed a political miracle. He reconciled Crassus with Pompey and gained the support of both for his own ambitions. So was born the First Triumvirate, an informal agreement among three Roman politicians, each seeking his private goals, which further undermined the future of the republic.

Julius Caesar and His Government of Rome

Though he was forced to forgo his triumph, Caesar's efforts were rewarded when he was elected to the consulship for 59 B.C.E. His fellow consul was M. Calpernius Bibulus, the son-in-law of Cato and a conservative hostile to Caesar and the other *populares*. Caesar did not hesitate to override his colleague. The triumvirs' program was quickly

A bust of Julius Caesar. [Alinari/Art Resource, N.Y.]

enacted. Caesar got the extraordinary command that would give him a chance to earn the glory and power with which to rival Pompey: the governorship of Illyricum and Gaul for five years. A land bill settled Pompey's veterans comfortably, and his eastern settlement was ratified. Crassus, much of whose influence came from his position as champion of the equestrians, won for them a great windfall by having the government renegotiate a tax contract in their favor. To guarantee themselves against any reversal of these actions, the triumvirs continued their informal but effective collaboration, arranging for the election of friendly consuls and the departure of potential opponents.

Caesar was now free to seek the military success he craved. His province included Cisalpine Gaul in the Po Valley (by now occupied by many Italian settlers as well as Gauls) and Narbonese Gaul beyond the Alps (modern Provence).

Relying first on the excellent quality of his army and the experience of his officers, then on his own growing military ability, Caesar made great progress. By 56 B.C.E. he had conquered most of Gaul, but he had not yet consolidated his victories firmly. He therefore sought an extension of his command, but quarrels between Crassus and Pompey so weakened the Triumvirate that the Senate was prepared to order Caesar's recall.

To prevent the dissolution of his base of power, Caesar persuaded Crassus and Pompey to meet with him at Luca in northern Italy to renew the coalition. They agreed that Caesar would get another five-year command in Gaul, and Crassus and Pompey would be consuls again in 55 B.C.E. After that they would each receive an army and a five-year command. Caesar was free to return to Gaul and finish the job. The capture of Alesia in 51 B.C.E. marked the end of the serious Gallic resistance and of Gallic liberty. For Caesar it brought the wealth, fame, and military power he wanted. He commanded thirteen loyal legions, a match for his enemies as well as for his allies.

By the time Caesar was ready to return to Rome, the Triumvirate had dissolved and a crisis was at hand. At Carrhae, in 53 B.C.E., Crassus died trying to conquer the Parthians, successors to the Persian Empire. His death broke one link between Pompey and Caesar. The death of Caesar's daughter Julia, who had been Pompey's wife, dissolved another.

As Caesar's star rose, Pompey became jealous and fearful. He did not leave Rome but governed his province through a subordinate. In the late 50s B.C.E. political rioting at Rome caused the Senate to appoint Pompey sole consul. This grant of unprecedented power and responsibility brought Pompey closer to the senatorial aristocracy in mutual fear of and hostility to Caesar. The Senate wanted to bring Caesar back to Rome as a private citizen after his proconsular command expired. He would then be open to attack for past illegalities. Caesar tried to avoid the trap by asking permission to stand for the consulship in absentia.

Early in January of 49 B.C.E. the more extreme faction in the Senate had its way. It ordered Pompey to defend the state and Caesar to lay down his command by a specified day. For Caesar this meant exile or death, so he ordered his legions to cross the Rubicon River, the boundary of his province. (See Map 4–4.) This action started a civil war. In 45 B.C.E. Caesar defeated the last forces of his enemies under Pompey's sons at Munda in Spain. The war was over, and Caesar, in Shakespeare's words, bestrode "the narrow world like a Colossus."

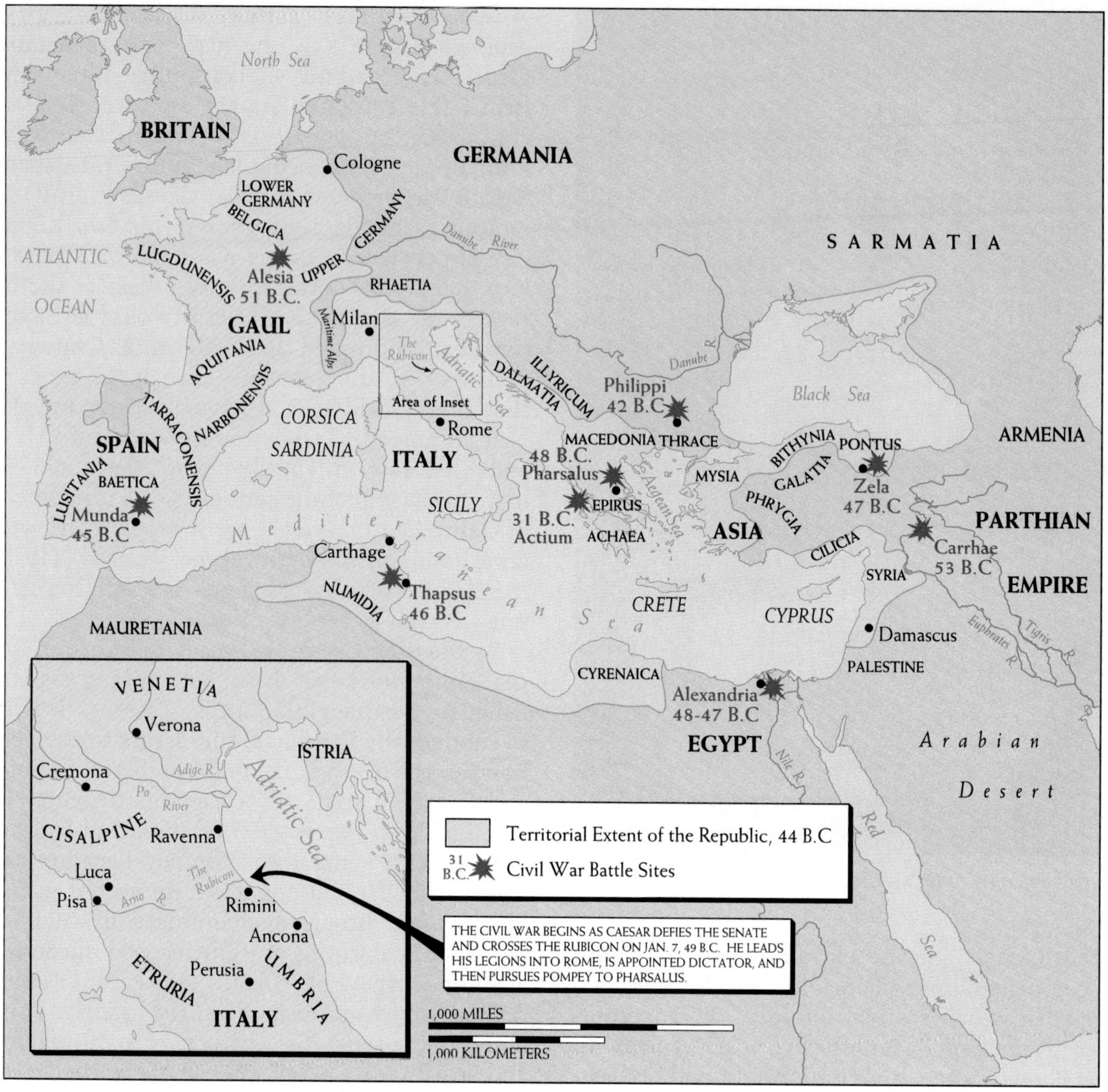

MAP 4–4 THE CIVIL WARS OF THE LATE ROMAN REPUBLIC *This map shows the extent of the territory controlled by Rome at the time of Caesar's death and the sites of the major battles of the civil wars of the late republic.*

From the beginning of the civil war until his death in 44 B.C.E., Caesar spent less than a year and a half in Rome, and many of his actions were attempts to deal with immediate problems between campaigns. His innovations generally sought to make rational and orderly what was traditional and chaotic. An excellent example is Caesar's reform of the calendar. By 46 B.C.E. it was eighty days ahead of the proper season because the official year was lunar, containing only 355 days. Using the best scientific advice, Caesar instituted a new calendar. With minor changes by Pope Gregory XIII in the sixteenth century, it is the calendar in use today.

Another general tendency of his reforms in the political area was the elevation of the role of Italians and even provincials at the expense of the old Roman families, most of whom were his political enemies. He raised the number of senators to 900 and filled the Senate's depleted ranks with Italians and even Gauls. He was free with grants of Roman citizenship, giving the franchise to

Cisalpine Gaul as a whole and to many individuals of various regions.

Caesar made few changes in the government of Rome. The Senate continued to play its role, in theory. But its increased size, its packing with supporters of Caesar, and his own monopoly of military power made the whole thing a sham. He treated the Senate as his creature, sometimes with disdain. His legal position rested on several powers. In 46 B.C.E. he was appointed dictator for ten years and in the next year for life. He also held the consulship, the immunity of a tribune (although, being a patrician, he had never been a tribune), the chief priesthood of the state, and a new position, prefect of morals, which gave him the censorial power. Usurping the elective power of the assemblies, he even named the magistrates for the next few years, because he expected to be away in the East.

The enemies of Caesar were quick to seize on every pretext to accuse Caesar of aiming at monarchy. A senatorial conspiracy gathered strength under the leadership of Gaius Cassius Longinus and Marcus Junius Brutus and included some sixty senators in all. On March 15, 44 B.C.E., Caesar entered the Senate, characteristically without a bodyguard, and was stabbed to death. The assassins regarded themselves as heroic tyrannicides but did not have a clear plan of action to follow the tyrant's death.

Plutarch Describes How Crassus Became a Millionaire

Marcus Licinius Crassus (ca. 112–53 B.C.E.) was a fine general, a powerful politician, and the richest person in Rome. There is no doubt that his wealth contributed greatly to his power. In the following selection Plutarch describes how Crassus acquired his riches.

✦ *By what devices did Crassus become rich? Why is Plutarch critical of his techniques? How would they be described and evaluated in our own time? What does this passage tell us about the ways in which Roman society had changed since the days of the early republic?*

Most of [his wealth], if one must tell the scandalous truth, he gathered by fire and war, making the public calamities his greatest source of revenue. For when Sulla seized Rome and sold the property of those put to death by him, regarding and calling it booty, and wishing to make as many influential men as he could partners in the crime, Crassus refused neither to accept nor buy such property. Moreover, observing how natural and familiar at Rome were the burning and collapse of buildings, because of their massiveness and their closeness to one another, he bought slaves who were builders and architects. Then, when he had more than 500 of these, he would buy houses that were on fire and those adjoining the ones on fire. The owners would let them go for small sums, because of their fear and uncertainty, so that the greatest part of Rome came into his hands. But though he had so many artisans, he never built any house but the one he lived in, and used to say that those that were addicted to building would undo themselves without the help of other enemies. And though he had many silver mines, and very valuable land with laborers on it, yet one might consider all this as nothing compared with the value of his slaves, such a great number and variety did he possess—readers, amanuenses, silversmiths, stewards and table-servants. He himself directed their training, and took part in teaching them himself, accounting it, in a word, the chief duty of a master to care for his slaves as the living tools of household management.

Plutarch, Life of Crassus, *trans. by N. Lewis and M. Reinhold, in* Roman Civilization, *Vol. 1 (New York: Columbia University Press, 1955), pp. 458–459. Used by permission.*

Suetonius Describes Caesar's Dictatorship

Seutonius (ca. C.E. 69–ca. 140) wrote a series of biographies of the emperors from Julius Caesar to Domitian. In the following selection he described some of Caesar's actions during his dictatorship in the years 46–44 B.C.E.

✦ *Why does Suetonius think Caesar deserved to be killed? To what group of Romans did his behavior give the greatest offense?*
✦ *How would other Romans view the pros and cons of Caesar's career?*

[Caesar's] other words and actions, however, so far outweigh all his good qualities, that it is thought he abused his power, and was justly cut off. For he not only obtained excessive honours, such as the consulship every year, the dictatorship for life, and the censorship, but also the title of emperor, and the surname of Father of His Country, besides having his statue amongst the kings, and a lofty couch in the theatre. He even suffered some honours to be decreed to him, which were unbefitting the most exalted of mankind; such as gilded chair of state in the senate-house and on his tribunal, a consecrated chariot, and banners in the Circensian procession, temples, altars, statues among the gods, a bed of state in the temples, a priest, and a college of priests dedicated to himself, like those of Pan; and that one of the months should be called by his name. There were, indeed, no honours which he did not either assume himself, or grant to others, at his will and pleasure. In his third and fourth consulship, he used only the title of the office, being content with the power of dictator, which was conferred upon him with the consulship; and in both years he substituted other consuls in his room, during the three last months; so that in the intervals he held no assemblies of the people, for the election of magistrates, excepting only tribunes and ediles of the people; and appointed officers, under the name of præfects, instead of the prætors, to administer the affairs of the city during his absence. The office of consul having become vacant, by the sudden death of one of the consuls the day before the calends of January [the 1st Jan.], he conferred it on a person who requested it of him, for a few hours. Assuming the same licence, and regardless of the customs of his country, he appointed magistrates to hold their offices for terms of years. He granted the insignia of the consular dignity to ten persons of prætorian rank. He admitted into the senate some men who had been made free of the city, and even natives of Gaul, who were semi-barbarians. He likewise appointed to the management of the mint, and the public revenue of the state, some servants of his own household; and entrusted the command of three legions, which he left at Alexandria, to an old catamite of his, the son of his freed-man Rufinus.

He was guilty of the same extravagance in the language he publicly used, as Titus Ampius informs us; according to whom he said, "The republic is nothing but a name, without substance or reality. Sylla was an ignorant fellow to abdicate the dictatorship. Men ought to consider what is becoming when they talk with me, and look upon what I say as a law."

Seutonius, *The Lives of the Twelve Caesars,* trans. by Alexander Thompson, rev. by T. Forster (London: George Bell and Sons, 1903), pp. 45–47.

No doubt they simply expected the republic to be restored in the old way, but things had gone too far for that. There followed instead thirteen more years of civil war, at the end of which the republic received its final burial.

The Second Triumvirate and the Emergence of Octavian

Caesar had had legions of followers, and he had a capable successor in Mark Antony. But the dictator

Caesar Tells What Persuaded Him to Cross the Rubicon

Julius Caesar competed with Pompey for the leading position in the Roman state. Complicated maneuvers failed to produce a compromise. In the following selection Caesar gives his side of the story of the beginning of the Roman civil war. Note that Caesar writes about himself in the third person.

✦ *This selection, of course makes the case for Caesar's actions. From your reading in this book, and from any other information you have, how do you think Pompey might have replied? On constitutional and legal grounds who had the stronger case? On grounds of practical considerations and of the welfare of the Roman state, which party, if either, deserved support? If neither did, why not?*

These things being made known to Caesar, he harangued his soldiers; he reminded them of the wrongs done to him at all times by his enemies, and complained that Pompey had been alienated from him and led astray by them through envy and a malicious opposition to his glory, though he had always favored and promoted Pompey's honor and dignity. He complained that an innovation had been introduced into the republic, that the intercession of the tribunes, which had been restored a few years before by Sulla, was branded as a crime, and suppressed by force of arms; that Sulla, who had stripped the tribunes of every other power, had, nevertheless, left the privilege of intercession unrestrained; that Pompey, who pretended to restore what they had lost, had taken away the privileges which they formerly had; that whenever the senate decreed, "that the magistrates should take care that the republic sustained no injury' (by which words and decree the Roman people were obliged to repair to arms), it was only when pernicious laws were proposed; when the tribunes attempted violent measures; when the people seceded, and possessed themselves of the temples and eminences of the city; (and these instances of former times, he showed them were expiated by the fate of Saturninus and the Gracchi): that nothing of this kind was attempted now, nor even thought of: that no law was promulgated, no intrigue with the people going forward, no secession made; he exhorted them to defend from the malice of his enemies the reputation and honor of that general under whose command they had for nine years most successfully supported the state; fought many successful battles, and subdued all Gaul and Germany." The soldiers of the thirteenth legion, which was present (for in the beginning of the disturbances he had called it out, his other legions not having yet arrived), all cry out that they are ready to defend their general, and the tribunes of the commons, from all injuries.

Having made himself acquainted with the disposition of his soldiers, Caesar set off with that legion to Ariminum, and there met the tribunes, who had fled to him for protection.

Julius Caesar, Commentaries, *trans. by W. A. McDevitte and W. S. Bosh (New York: Harper and Brothers, 1887), pp. 249–250.*

had named his eighteen-year-old grandnephew, Gaius Octavius (63 B.C.E.–C.E. 14), as his heir and had left him three quarters of his vast wealth. To everyone's surprise, the sickly and inexperienced young man came to Rome to claim his legacy. He gathered an army, won the support of many of Caesar's veterans, and became a figure of importance—the future Augustus.

At first, the Senate tried to use Octavius against Antony, but when the conservatives rejected his

(a)

(b)

A profile of Brutus, one of Caesar's assassins, appeared on this silver coin. The reverse shows a cap of liberty between two daggers and reads "Ides of March." [*H. Roger Viollet*]

request for the consulship, Octavius broke with them. Following Sulla's grim precedent, he took his army and marched on Rome. There he finally assumed his adopted name, C. Julius Caesar Octavianus. Modern historians refer to him at this stage in his career as Octavian, although he insisted on being called Caesar. In August of 43 B.C.E. he became consul and declared the assassins of Caesar outlaws. Brutus and Cassius had an army of their own, so Octavian sought help on the Caesarean side. He made a pact with Mark Antony and M. Aemilius Lepidus, a Caesarean governor of the western provinces. They took control of Rome and had themselves appointed "triumvirs to put the republic in order," with great powers. This was the Second Triumvirate and, unlike the first, it was legally empowered to rule almost dictatorially.

The need to pay their troops, their own greed, and the passion that always emerges in civil wars led the triumvirs to start a wave of proscriptions that outdid even those of Sulla. In 42 B.C.E. the triumviral army defeated Brutus and Cassius at Philippi in Macedonia, and the last hope of republican restoration died with the tyrannicides. Each of the triumvirs received a command. The junior partner, Lepidus, was given Africa, Antony took the rich and inviting East, and Octavian got the West and the many troubles that went with it.

Octavian had to fight a war against Sextus, the son of Pompey, who held Sicily. He also had to settle 100,000 veterans in Italy, confiscating much property and making many enemies. Helped by his friend Agrippa, he defeated Sextus Pompey in 36 B.C.E. Among his close associates was Maecenas, who served him as adviser and diplomatic agent. Maecenas helped manage the delicate relations with Antony and Lepidus, but perhaps equally important was his role as a patron of the arts. Among his clients were Vergil and Horace, both of whom did important work for Octavian. They painted him as a restorer of traditional Roman values, as a man of ancient Roman lineage and of traditional Roman virtues, and as the culmination of Roman destiny. More and more he was identified with Italy and the West as well as with order, justice, and virtue.

Meanwhile Antony was in the East, chiefly at Alexandria with Cleopatra, the queen of Egypt. In 36 B.C.E. he attacked Parthia, with disastrous results. Octavian had promised to send troops to support Antony's Parthian campaign but never sent them. Antony was forced to depend on the East for support, and to some considerable degree this meant reliance on Cleopatra. Octavian clearly understood the advantage of representing himself as the champion of the West, Italy, and Rome. Meanwhile he represented Antony as the man of the East, the dupe of Cleopatra, her tool in establishing Alexandria as the center of an empire and herself as its ruler. Such propaganda made it easier

The Fall of the Roman Republic

133 B.C.E.	Tribunate of Tiberius Gracchus
123–122 B.C.E.	Tribunate of Gaius Gracchus
111–105 B.C.E.	Jugurthine War
104–100 B.C.E.	Consecutive consulships of Marius
90–88 B.C.E.	War against the Italian allies
88 B.C.E.	Sulla's march on Rome
82 B.C.E.	Sulla assumes dictatorship
71 B.C.E.	Crassus crushes rebellion of Spartacus
71 B.C.E.	Pompey defeats Sertorius in Spain
70 B.C.E.	Consulship of Crassus and Pompey
60 B.C.E.	Formation of First Triumvirate
58–50 B.C.E.	Caesar in Gaul
53 B.C.E.	Crassus killed in Battle of Carrhae
49 B.C.E.	Caesar crosses Rubicon; civil war begins
48 B.C.E.	Pompey defeated at Pharsalus; killed in Egypt
46–44 B.C.E.	Caesar's dictatorship
45 B.C.E.	End of civil war
43 B.C.E.	Formation of Second Triumvirate
42 B.C.E.	Triumvirs defeat Brutus and Cassius at Philippi
31 B.C.E.	Octavian and Agrippa defeat Anthony at Actium

for Caesareans to abandon their veteran leader in favor of the young heir of Caesar. It did not help Antony's cause that he agreed to a public festival at Alexandria in 34 B.C.E., where he and Cleopatra sat on golden thrones. She was proclaimed "Queen of Kings," her son by Julius Caesar was named "King of Kings," and parts of the Roman Empire were doled out to her various children.

By 32 B.C.E. all pretense of cooperation ended. Octavian and Antony each tried to put the best face on what was essentially a struggle for power. Lepidus had been put aside some years earlier. Antony sought senatorial support and promised to restore the republican constitution. Octavian seized and published what was alleged to be the will of Antony, revealing his gifts of provinces to the children of Cleopatra. This caused the conflict to take the form of East against West, Rome against Alexandria.

In 31 B.C.E.. the matter was settled at Actium in western Greece. Agrippa, Octavian's best general, cut off the enemy by land and sea, forcing and winning a naval battle. Antony and Cleopatra escaped to Egypt, but Octavian pursued them to Alexandria, where both committed suicide. The civil wars were over, and at the age of thirty-two Octavian was absolute master of the Mediterranean world. His power was enormous, but so too was the task before him. He had to restore peace, prosperity, and confidence. All of these required establishing a constitution that would reflect the new realities without offending unduly the traditional republican prejudices that still had so firm a grip on Rome and Italy.

✦

The history of the Roman Republic was almost as sharp a departure from the common experiences of ancient civilizations as that of the Greek city-states. A monarchy in its earliest-known form, Rome quite early expelled its king, abandoned the institution of monarchy, and established an aristocratic republic somewhat like the poleis *of the Greek "Dark Ages." But unlike the Greeks, the Romans continued to be in touch with foreign neighbors, including the far more civilized urban monarchies of the Etruscans. Nonetheless, the Romans clung faithfully to their republican institutions. For a long time the Romans remained a nation of farmers and herdsmen, to whom trade was relatively unimportant, especially outside Italy.*

Over time the caste distinctions between patricians and plebeians became unimportant. They were replaced by distinctions based on wealth and, even more important, aristocracy, where the significant distinction was between noble families, who held the highest elected offices in the state, and those outside the nobility. The Roman Republic from the first found itself engaged in almost continuous warfare with its neighbors—either in defense of its own territory, in fights over disputed territory, or in defense of other cities or states who were friends and allies of Rome.

Both internally and in their foreign relations the Romans were a very legalistic people, placing great importance on traditional behavior encoded into laws. Although backed by the powerful authority of the magistrates at home and the potent Roman army abroad, the laws were based on experience, common sense, and equity. Roman law aimed at stability and fairness, and it succeeded well enough that few people who lived under it wanted to do away with it. It lived on and grew during the imperial period and beyond. During the European

Middle Ages it played an important part in the revival of the West and continued to exert an influence into modern times.

The force of Roman arms, the high quality of Roman roads and bridges, and the pragmatic character of Roman law helped create something unique: an empire ruled by a republic, first a large one on land including all of Italy, later one that commanded the shores of the entire Mediterranean and quite a distance inland in many places. Rome controlled an area that bears comparison with some of the empires of the East. It acquired that territory, wealth, and power in a state managed by annual magistrates elected by the male Roman citizens and by an aristocratic Senate, which had to take notice of popular assemblies and a published, impersonal code of law. It achieved its greatness with an army of citizens and allies, without a monarchy or a regular bureaucracy.

The temptations and responsibilities of governing a vast and rich empire, however, finally proved too much for the republican constitution. Trade grew, and with it a class of merchants and financiers—equestrians—that was neither aristocratic nor agricultural, but increasingly powerful. The influx of masses of slaves captured in war undermined the small farmers who had been the backbone of the Roman state and its army. As many of them were forced to leave their farms, they moved to the cities, chiefly to Rome, where they had no productive role. Conscripted armies of farmers serving relatively short terms gave way to volunteer armies of landless men serving as professionals and expecting to be rewarded for their services with gifts of land or money. The generals of these armies were not annual magistrates controlled by the Senate and the constitution but ambitious military leaders seeking glory and political advantage.

The result was civil war and the destruction of the republic. The conquest of a vast empire moved the Romans away from their unusual historical traditions toward the more familiar path of empire trodden by older rulers in Egypt and Mesopotamia.

Review Questions

1. In what ways did the institutions of family and clientage and the establishment of patrician and plebeian classes contribute to the stability of the early Roman Republic? How important was education to the success of the republic? the institution of slavery?
2. What was the Struggle of the Orders? What methods did plebeians use to get what they wanted? How was Roman society different after the struggle ended?
3. Discuss Rome's expansion to 265 B.C.E. How was Rome able to conquer and control Italy? In their relations with Greece and Asia Minor in the second century B.C.E., were the Romans looking for security? wealth? power? fame?
4. Explain the clash between the Romans and the Carthaginians in the First and Second Punic wars. Could the wars have been avoided? How did Rome benefit from its victory over Carthage? What problems were created by this victory?
5. What social, economic, and political problems did Italy have in the second century B.C.E.? What were the main proposals of Tiberius Gaius Gracchus? What questions about Roman society did they raise? Why did the proposals fail?
6. What were the problems that plagued the Roman Republic in the last century? What caused these problems and how did the Romans try to solve them? To what extent was the republic destroyed by ambitious generals who loved power more than Rome itself?

Suggested Readings

F. E. ADCOCK, *The Roman Art of War Under the Republic* (1940). A basic study of the subject.

E. BADIAN, *Foreign Clientelae* (1958). A brilliant study of the Roman idea of a client–patron relationship extended to foreign affairs.

E. BADIAN, *Roman Imperialism in the Late Republic*, 2nd ed. (1968).

A. H. BERNSTEIN, *Tiberius Sempronius Gracchus: Tradition and Apostasy* (1978). A new interpretation of Tiberius's place in Roman politics.

J. BOARDMAN, J. GRIFFIN, AND O. MURRAY, *The Oxford History of the Roman World* (1990). An encyclopedic approach to the varieties of the Roman experience.

P. A. BRUNT, *Social Conflicts in the Roman Republic* (1971). A fine study by a master of the subject.

T. CORNELL AND J. MATTHEWS, *Atlas of the Roman World* (1982). Much more than the title indicates, this book presents a comprehensive view of the Roman world in its physical and cultural setting.

R. M. ERRINGTON, *The Dawn of Empire: Rome's Rise to Power* (1972). An account of Rome's conquest of the Mediterranean.

M. Gelzer, *Caesar: Politician and Statesman*, trans. by P. Needham (1968). The best biography of Caesar.

E. S. Gruen, *The Last Generation of the Roman Republic* (1973). An interesting but controversial interpretation of the fall of the republic.

E. S. Gruen, *The Hellenistic World and the Coming of Rome* (1984). A new interpretation of Rome's conquest of the eastern Mediterranean.

W. V. Harris, *War and Imperialism in Republican Rome, 327–70 B.C.E.* (1975). An analysis of Roman attitudes and intentions concerning imperial expansion and war.

L. P. Homo, *Primitive Italy and the Beginning of Roman Imperialism* (1967). A study of early Roman relations with the peoples of Italy.

A. Keaveney, *Lucullus: A Life* (1992). A biography of the famous Roman epicure.

J. F. Lazenby, *Hannibal's War* (1978). An excellent military history of the Second Punic War.

F. B. Marsh, *A History of the Roman World from 146 to 30 B.C.E.*, 3rd ed., rev. by H. H. Scullard (1963). An excellent narrative account.

J. C. Meyer, *Pre-Republican Rome* (1983). A good account of early Rome.

C. Nicolet, *The World of the Citizen in Republican Rome* (1980). A valuable study of the meaning of Roman citizenship.

M. Pallottino, *The Etruscans*, 6th ed. (1974). Makes especially good use of archaeological evidence.

J. Rich and G. Shipley, *War and Society in the Roman World* (1993). A useful collection of essays on military topics.

E. T. Salmon, *Roman Colonization Under the Republic* (1970). An account of the character and importance of the Roman colony.

E. T. Salmon, *The Making of Roman Italy* (1980). The story of Roman expansion on the Italian peninsula.

H. H. Scullard, *A History of the Roman World 753–146 B.C.E.*, 4th ed. (1980). An unusually fine narrative history with useful critical notes.

H. H. Scullard, *From the Gracchi to Nero*, 5th ed. (1982). A work of the same character and quality.

A. N. Sherwin-White, *Roman Citizenship* (1939). A useful study of the Roman franchise and its extension to other peoples.

D. Stockton, *Cicero: A Political Biography* (1971). A readable and interesting study.

D. Stockton, *The Gracchi* (1979). An interesting analytical narrative.

L. R. Taylor, *Party Policies in the Age of Caesar* (1949). A fascinating analysis of Roman political practices.

B. H. Warmington, *Carthage* (1960). A good survey.

R. D. Weigel, *Lepidus: The Tarnished Triumvir* (1992). A biography of the less famous partner of Mark Antony and Augustus.

G. Williams, *The Nature of Roman Poetry* (1970). An unusually graceful and perceptive literary study.

The West & the World

ANCIENT SLAVERY

The institution of slavery existed early in the histories of the ancient civilizations of Egypt, Mesopotamia, Greece, Rome, India, and China. The ancient world knew many forms of unfree labor—serfs and bondsmen called by various names—as well as outright slaves. Slaves are property, fully under the domination of their master, and their labor is imposed by coercion. Unlike the relationship between serf and lord in medieval Europe, in which the serf retained some legal rights and the lord was bound by legal restraints and obligations (see Chapter 6), the relationship between master and slave was entirely one-sided. In many places and at many times in antiquity, however, the line between slavery and some forms of serfdom was indistinct, and the slave's position was not always the worse.

Mesopotamia. Slavery in the ancient world differed from one society to another and from time to time. In ancient Mesopotamia slaves were used chiefly as domestic servants, agricultural workers, or craftsmen. Because the average slave holder had no more than two or three slaves, he generally worked alongside them in the field or shop. In early Sumerian times slaves were chiefly captives in war but later came to include people who had defaulted on a debt or been sold as children into slavery by parents too poor to raise them. By the time of Hammurabi (ca. 1792–1760 B.C.E.), the chief source of slaves had become foreigners bought from slave traders.

In Mesopotamia, slaves were generally people of the same appearance and culture as their masters. They had been enslaved because of misfortunes to which their masters themselves were not immune, and they labored in their masters' homes or alongside them at their work. As a result, in many ways, slavery in Mesopotamia was mild. Slaves engaged in business and acquired property. With their master's permission, slaves could use their profits to buy their own freedom. Male slaves could marry free women, and the children of such marriages were free. Still, a Mesopotamian slave was a piece of property—bought, sold, leased, and exchanged, often tattooed or branded for identification and to deter escape. The Code of Hammurabi provided the death penalty for anyone who sheltered or helped a fugitive slave to escape. Finally, it appears that slaves were set free only when they could purchase their own freedom.

Egypt. In Egypt, too, slavery existed from early times, but because agricultural labor was done by a vast class of serfs, slaves did not become numerous until the spread of Egyptian imperial power in the Middle Kingdom (2052–1786 B.C.E.). During that period black Africans from Nubia to the south and Asians from Palestine-Syria and beyond to the east who were captured in war were brought back to Egypt as slaves. The great period of Egyptian imperial expansion, the New Kingdom (1575–1087 B.C.E.), brought far greater numbers of captives into slavery in Egypt. Sometimes an entire people was enslaved, as the biblical tradition portrays the Hebrews about 1400 B.C.E. They were put to work in the fields alongside the serfs, in the shops as artisans, and in homes as servants. Some worked as policemen and soldiers; many labored to erect the great temples, obelisks, and other huge monuments. As in Mesopotamia, slaves were branded for identification and to prevent escape; freeing slaves was rare.

This Egyptian wallpainting, in the tomb of Mennah, shows men carrying grain while, in the background, two slaves fight over the left-overs. Mennah was scribe of the fields and estate inspector under Pharaoh Thutmosis IV 15th century B.C.E. *(18th Dynasty). [Erich Lessing/Art Resource]*

China. Fully developed Chinese slavery resembled the slave systems of the other complex ancient civilizations. The slave population included captives in war; victims of kidnapping and slave trading; and defaulted debtors and poor men who sold themselves, their wives, and their children into bondage. Slaves were used in a wide range of occupations:

> in farming, food and handicraft industries, commerce, and perhaps in mining; as business managers, bodyguards, fighters, tomb watchers, servants, grooms, signers, dancers, and acrobats; in concubinage, luxury and display, and in reinforcing the master's power. Government bondsmen worked as servants, retainers, clerks, accountants, and petty bureaucrats; in skilled crafts, game-keeping, ranching, and . . . heavy gang labor.[1]

In the earliest dynasties, evidence suggests that slavery was punishment for criminal behavior. So it is not surprising that the Chinese term for slaves carried the sense of "base" or "ignoble," whereas the rest of the population was called "good." Later, in the Han period (206 B.C.E.–C.E. 220) and afterward, the Chinese explained slavery as the result of the criminal acts of the slaves or even of their ancestors. A document from the Han period provided that "the wives and children of criminals shall be confiscated as slaves and tattooed on the face. . . . [T]he genuine slaves of today are the descendants of criminal ancestors. Though a hundred generations pass by, they are still tattooed on the face and serve the government."[2]

This sharp distinction between slaves and normal "good" people may help explain the connection that had arisen by the time of the T'ang dynasty (C.E. 618–907) between racial prejudice and slavery. The Chinese regarded foreigners, in general, as lesser beings, so they did not hesitate to enslave Turks, Koreans, Persians, and Indonesians, all of whom they referred to as "black." Their greatest contempt was reserved for the dark-skinned, people of the islands off China's southern coast, whom them considered uncivilized and inferior. Many were enslaved and brought to Canton in the seventh and eighth centuries. Fearing "pollution," the Chinese forbade sexual intercourse between foreign slaves and Chinese women.

India. Racial discrimination and prejudice also characterized slavery in India under its Aryan rulers as late as the Vedic period (ca. 1000–500 B.C.E.). These invaders from the north were contemptuous of the Dasas, the dark-skinned people whom they had subjected. The word *dasa*, in fact, came to mean slave as well as the name of the conquered people. It was only after centuries that the word lost its strictly ethnic meaning, and restrictions on mixture between groups were relaxed. Nevertheless, sexual relations between a slave and a free woman were punished by her mutilation and the death of both parties.

Greece. The Greeks had some form of slavery from the earliest times. The epic poems of Homer show us the women of conquered cities taken

[1]C. M. Wilbur, Slavery in China During the Former Han Dynasty, 206 B.C.E.–A.D. (New York: Kraus, 1943), p. 241.

[2]Cited in E. G. Pulleyblank, "The Origins and Nature of Chattel Slavery in China," Journal of the Economic and Social History of the Orient 1 (1958): 206.

home by the victors to serve in their households as concubines. In early Greece, however, true chattel slavery appears to have been rare. The most common forms of bondage were different kinds of serfdom in relatively backward areas such as Crete, Thessaly, and Sparta. In Sparta, for instance, the ruling people conquered the natives of the region and reduced them to the status of helots, subjects who belonged to the Spartan state and worked the land for the benefit of their Spartan masters. Another form of early bondage, involving a severe but rarely permanent loss of freedom, resulted from default in debt. In Athens about 600 B.C.E. such bondsmen, called *hektemoroi*, were sold outside their native land as true slaves, until the reforms of Solon banned all debt-bondage.

True chattel slavery began to increase about 500 B.C.E. and remained an important element in society. The main sources of slaves were war captives and the captives of pirates. Like the Chinese, Egyptians, and many other peoples, the Greeks regarded foreigners as inferior, and most slaves working for the Greeks were foreigners. Greeks sometimes enslaved Greeks, but not to serve in their home territories.

The chief occupation of the Greeks, as of most of the world before our century, was agriculture. The great majority of Greek farmers worked small holdings too poor to support even one slave, but some had as many as one or two slaves to work alongside them. The upper classes had larger farms that were let out to free tenant farmers or worked by slaves, generally under an overseer who was himself a slave. Large landowners generally did not have a single great estate but several smaller farms scattered about the *polis*. This arrangement did not encourage the amassing of great numbers of agricultural slaves such as those who would later work the cotton and sugar plantations of the New World. Industry, however, was different.

Larger numbers of slaves labored in industry, especially in mining. Nicias, a wealthy Athenian of the fifth century B.C.E. owned one thousand slaves whom he rented to a mining contractor for profit, but this is by far the largest number known. Most manufacturing was on a very small scale, with shops using one, two, or a handful of slaves. Slaves worked as craftsmen in almost every trade, and, like agricultural slaves on small farms, they worked alongside their masters. A significant proportion of slaves were domestic servants, and many were shepherds. Publicly held slaves served as policemen, prison attendants, clerks, and secretaries.

The number of slaves in ancient Greece and their importance to Greek society are the subjects of controversy. We have no useful figures for the absolute number of slaves or their percentage of the free population in any city except Athens. There the evidence permits estimates for the slave population in the classical period (fifth and fourth centuries B.C.E.) that range from twenty thousand to one hundred thousand. Accepting the mean between the extremes, sixty thousand, and estimating the free population at its height at about forty thousand households, would yield a figure of fewer than two slaves per family. Estimates suggest that only a quarter to a third of free Athenians owned any slaves at all.

Some historians have noted that in the American South during the period before the Civil War—where slaves made up less than one-third of the total population and three-quarters of free Southerners had no slaves—the proportion of slaves to free citizens was similar to that of ancient Athens. Because slavery was so important to the economy of the South, these historians suggest, it may have been equally important and similarly oppressive in ancient Athens. This argument has several problems.[3] First, it is important to make a distinction between the cotton states of the American South before the Civil War, where a single cash crop, well suited for exploitation by large groups of slaves, dominated the economy and society, and Athens, where the economy was mixed, the crops varied, and the land and its distribution poorly suited to massive slavery.

Quite different, too, was the likelihood that a slave would become free. Americans rarely freed their slaves, but in Greece liberation was common. The most famous example is that of the Athenian slave Pasion, who began as a bank clerk, earned his freedom, became Athens's richest banker, and was awarded Athenian citizenship. Such cases were certainly rare, but gaining one's freedom was not.

It is important also to distinguish the American South, where skin color separated slaves from their masters, from the very different society of classical Athens. Southern masters were increas-

[3]M. I. Finley, "Was Greek Civilization Based on Slave Labor?" Historia 8 (1959): 151.

ingly hostile to freeing slaves and afraid of slave rebellions, but in Athens, slaves walked the streets with such ease that class-conscious Athenians were offended.

Even more remarkable, the Athenians sometimes considered freeing all their slaves. In 406 B.C.E., their city facing defeat in the Peloponnesian War, they freed all slaves of military age and granted citizenship to those who rowed the ships that won the battle of Arginusae. Twice more at crucial moments, similar proposals were made, although without success. No such suggestion, of course, would have been conceivable in the slave societies of the New World. (For more on American slavery and the Atlantic slave trade, see Chapter 17 and The West and the World in Part IV.)

Rome. Like most ancient peoples, the Romans had slaves from very early in their history, but slavery became a fundamental element in the Roman economy and society only during the second century B.C.E. after the Romans had conquered most of the lands bordering the Mediterranean. In the time between the beginning of Rome's first war against Charthage (264 B.C.E.) and the conquest of Spain (133 B.C.E.), the Romans enslaved some two hundred fifty thousand prisoners of war, greatly increasing the availability of slave labor and reducing its price. Many became domestic servants, feeding the Roman upper class's growing appetite for luxury; at the other end of the spectrum, many worked in the mines of Spain and Sardinia. Some worked as artisans in small factories and shops or as public clerks. Slaves were permitted to marry, and they appear to have produced sizable families. As in Greece, domestic slaves and those used in crafts and commerce were permitted to earn money, to keep it, and, in some cases, to use it to purchase their own freedom. Manumission (the freeing of slaves) was very common among the Romans. After a time a considerable proportion of the Roman people included freedmen who had been slaves themselves or whose ancestors had been bondsmen. It was not uncommon to see the son or grandson of a slave become wealthy as a freedman and the slave himself or his son become a Roman citizen.

The unique development in the Roman world was the emergence of an agricultural system that employed and depended on a vast number of slaves. By the time of Jesus there were between two and three million slaves in Italy, about 35 to 40 percent of the total population, most of them part of great slave gangs that worked the vast plantations the Romans called *latifundia*. Turning from the grain that was the chief crop of the free Roman farmer, these large estates concentrated on such cash-producing products as wool, wine, and olive oil. The life of Rome's agricultural slaves appears to have been much harder than that of other Roman slaves and of slaves in other ancient societies, with the possible exception of slaves working in mines. *Latifundia* owners sought maximum profits and treated their slaves simply as means to that end. The slaves often worked in chains, oppressed by brutal foremen, and lived in underground prisons.

Such harsh treatment led to a number of serious slave rebellions of a kind we do not hear of in other ancient societies. A rebellion in Sicily in 134 B.C.E. kept the island in turmoil for more than two years, and the rebellion of the gladiators led by Spartacus in 73 B.C.E. produced an army of seventy thousand slaves that repeatedly defeated the Roman legions and overran all of southern Italy before it was brutally crushed.

Slavery retained its economic and social importance in the first century of the imperial period, but its centrality began to decline in the second. The institution was never abolished nor did it disappear while the Roman Empire lasted, but over time it became less important. The reasons for this decline are rather obscure. A rise in the cost of slaves and a consequent reduction in their economic value seem to have been factors. More important, it appears, was a general economic decline that permitted increasing pressure on the free lower classes. More and more they were employed as *coloni*—tenant farmers—tied by imperial law to the land they worked, ostensibly free but bonded and obligated. Over centuries most agricultural slave labor was replaced by these increasingly serf-like *coloni*. Pockets of slave labor remained as late as the time of Charlemagne, but the system of ancient slavery had essentially been replaced by the time the Roman Empire fell in the West.

✦ *In which ancient societies did race play an important role in slavery? How was Athenian slavery similar to and different from slavery in America's ante-bellum south? What were the special characteristics of Roman slavery?*

CHAPTER 5

Hadrian's entry into Rome. This carved relief from the first half of the second century C.E. *shows the Emperor Hadrian at the city gates of Rome where he is greeted by the guiding spirits of the Senate and the Roman people. [Nimatallah/Art Resource]*

The Roman Empire

KEY TOPICS

- The Augustan constitution
- The organization and government of the Roman Empire
- Culture and civilization from the late republic through the imperial period
- The early history of Christianity
- The decline and fall of Rome

The victory of Augustus put an end to the deadly period of civil strife that had begun with the murder of Tiberius Gracchus. The establishment of a monarchy, at first concealed in republican forms but gradually more obvious, brought a long period of peace. Rome's unquestioned control of the entire Mediterranean permitted the growth of trade and a prosperity in the first two centuries of the Roman Empire not to be equalled for more than a millennium.

Management of the empire outside Italy became more benign and efficient. With shared citizenship, the provinces usually accepted Roman rule readily and even enthusiastically. Latin became the official language of the western part of the empire and Greek the official language in the east. This permitted the growth and spread of a common culture, today called Classical Civilization, throughout the empire. The same conditions fostered a great outburst of activity and excellence in the arts. The loss of political freedom, however, brought a decline in the vitality of the great Roman genre of rhetoric.

Christianity emerged in the first century C.E. as one of many competing Eastern cults. It continued to spread and attract converts, winning toleration and finally dominance in the fourth century. Christianity was powerfully shaped by the world of imperial Rome, absorbing and using classical culture even while fighting against it.

The third century C.E. brought serious attacks on several of Rome's fron-

tiers, causing political and economic chaos. For a time such emperors as Diocletian (r. 284–305) and Constantine (r. 306–337) instituted heroic measures to restore order. Their solutions involved increased centralization, militarization, and attempts to control closely every aspect of life. The emperors became more exalted and remote, the people increasingly burdened with heavy taxes even as the loss of economic freedom reduced their ability to pay. At last a new wave of barbarian attacks proved irresistible, and the Roman Empire in the west ended in the second half of the fifth century.

The Augustan Principate

If the problems facing Octavian after the Battle of Actium in 31 B.C.E. were great, so too were his resources for addressing them. He was the master of a vast military force, the only one in the Roman world, and he had loyal and capable assistants. Of enormous importance was the rich treasury of Egypt, which Octavian treated as his personal property. He was helped by the great eagerness of the people of Italy for an end to civil war and a return to peace, order, and prosperity. In exchange for these most people were prepared to accept a considerable abandonment of republican practices and to give significant power to an able ruler. The memory of Julius Caesar's fate, however, was still fresh in Octavian's mind. Its lesson was that it was dangerous to flaunt unprecedented powers and to disregard all republican traditions.

Octavian did not create his constitutional solution at a single stroke. It developed gradually as he tried new devices to fit his perception of changing conditions. Behind all the republican trappings and the apparent sharing of authority with the Senate, the government of Octavian, like that of his successors, was a monarchy. All real power, both civil and military, lay with the ruler—whether he was called by the unofficial title of *princeps* or "first citizen," like Octavian, the founder of the regime, or *imperator*, "emperor" like those who followed. During the civil war Octavian's powers came from his triumviral status, whose dubious legality and unrepublican character were an embarrassment. From 31 B.C.E. on, he held the consulship each year, but this circumstance was neither strictly legal nor very satisfactory.

On January 13, 27 B.C.E., he put forward a new plan in dramatic style, coming before the Senate to give up all his powers and provinces. In what was surely a rehearsed response, the Senate begged him to reconsider. At last he agreed to accept the provinces of Spain, Gaul, and Syria with proconsular power for military command and to retain the consulship in Rome. The other provinces would be governed by the Senate as before. Because the provinces he retained were border provinces that contained twenty of Rome's twenty-six legions, his true power was undiminished. The Senate, however, responded with almost hysterical gratitude, voting him many honors. Among them was the semireligious title "Augustus," which carried implications of veneration, majesty, and holiness. From this time on, historians speak of Rome's first emperor as Augustus and of his regime as the Principate. This would have pleased him, for it helps conceal the novel, unrepublican nature of the regime and the naked power on which it rested.

In 23 B.C.E. Augustus resigned his consulship and held that office only rarely thereafter. Instead he was voted two powers that were to be the base of his rule thenceforth: the proconsular *imperium maius* and the tribunician power. The former made his proconsular power greater than that of any other proconsul and permitted him to exercise it even within the city of Rome. The latter gave him the right to conduct public business in the assemblies and the Senate, gave him the power of the veto, the tribunician sacrosanctity (immunity from arrest and punishment), and a connection with the Roman popular tradition. Thereafter, with only minor changes, Augustus's powers remained those conferred by the settlement of 23 B.C.E.

Administration

Augustus made important changes in the government of Rome, Italy, and the provinces. Most of his reforms reduce inefficiency and corruption, ended the danger to peace and order from ambitious individuals, and reduced the distinction between Romans and Italians, senators and equestrians. The assemblies lost their significance as a working part of the constitution, and the Senate took on most of the functions of the assemblies. Augustus purged the old Senate of undesirable members and fixed its number at 600. He recruited its members from wealthy men of good character, who entered after serving as lesser magistrates. Augustus controlled the elections and ensured that promising young men, whatever their origin, served the state as

This statue of Emperor Augustus (r. 27 B.C.E.–14 C.E.), now in the Vatican, stood in the villa of Augustus's wife Livia. The figures on the elaborate breastplate are all of symbolic significance. At the top, for example, Dawn in her chariot brings in a new day under the protective mantle of the sky god; in the center, Tiberius, Augustus's future successor, accepts the return of captured Roman army standards from a barbarian prince; and at the bottom, Mother Earth offers a horn of plenty. [Charitable Foundation, Leonardvon Matt]

administrators and provincial governors. In this way equestrians and Italians who had no connection with the Roman aristocracy entered the Senate in great numbers. For all his power Augustus was careful always to treat the Senate with respect and honor.

Augustus divided Rome into regions and wards with elected local officials. He gave the city, with its rickety wooden tenements, its first public fire department and rudimentary police force. Grain distribution to the poor was carefully controlled and limited, and organizations were created for providing an adequate water supply. The Augustan period was one of great prosperity, based on the wealth brought in by the conquest of Egypt, on the great increase in commerce and industry made possible by general peace and a vast program of public works, and on a strong return to successful small farming by Augustus's resettled veterans.

The union of political and military power in the hands of the *princeps* made it possible for him to install rational, efficient, and stable government in the provinces for the first time. The emperor, in effect, chose the governors, removed the incompetent or rapacious, and allowed the effective ones to keep their provinces for longer periods. Also, he provided for much greater local autonomy, giving considerable responsibility to the upper classes in the provincial cities and towns and to the tribal leaders in less civilized areas.

The Army and Defense

The main external problem facing Augustus—and one that haunted all his successors—was the northern frontier. (See Map 5–1.) Rome needed to pacify the regions to the north and the northeast of Italy and to find defensible frontiers against the recurring waves of barbarians. Augustus's plan was to push forward into central Europe to create the shortest possible defensive line. The eastern part of the plan succeeded, and the campaign in the west started well. In 9 C.E., however, there was a revolt led by the German tribal leader Herrmann, or Arminius, as the Romans called him. He ambushed and destroyed three Roman legions, and the aged Augustus abandoned the campaign, leaving a problem of border defense that caused great trouble for his successors.

Under Augustus, the armed forces achieved true professional status. Enlistment, chiefly by Italians, was for twenty years, but the pay was relatively good with occasional bonuses and the promise of a pension on retirement in the form of money or a plot of land. Together with the auxiliaries from the provinces, these forces formed a frontier army of about 300,000 men. In normal times this number was barely enough to hold the line.

The army permanently based in the provinces played a vital role in bringing Roman culture to the natives. The soldiers spread their language and customs, often marrying local women and settling down in the area of their service. They attracted merchants, who often became the nuclei of new towns and cities that became centers of Roman civilization. As time passed, the provincials on the frontiers became Roman citizens who helped

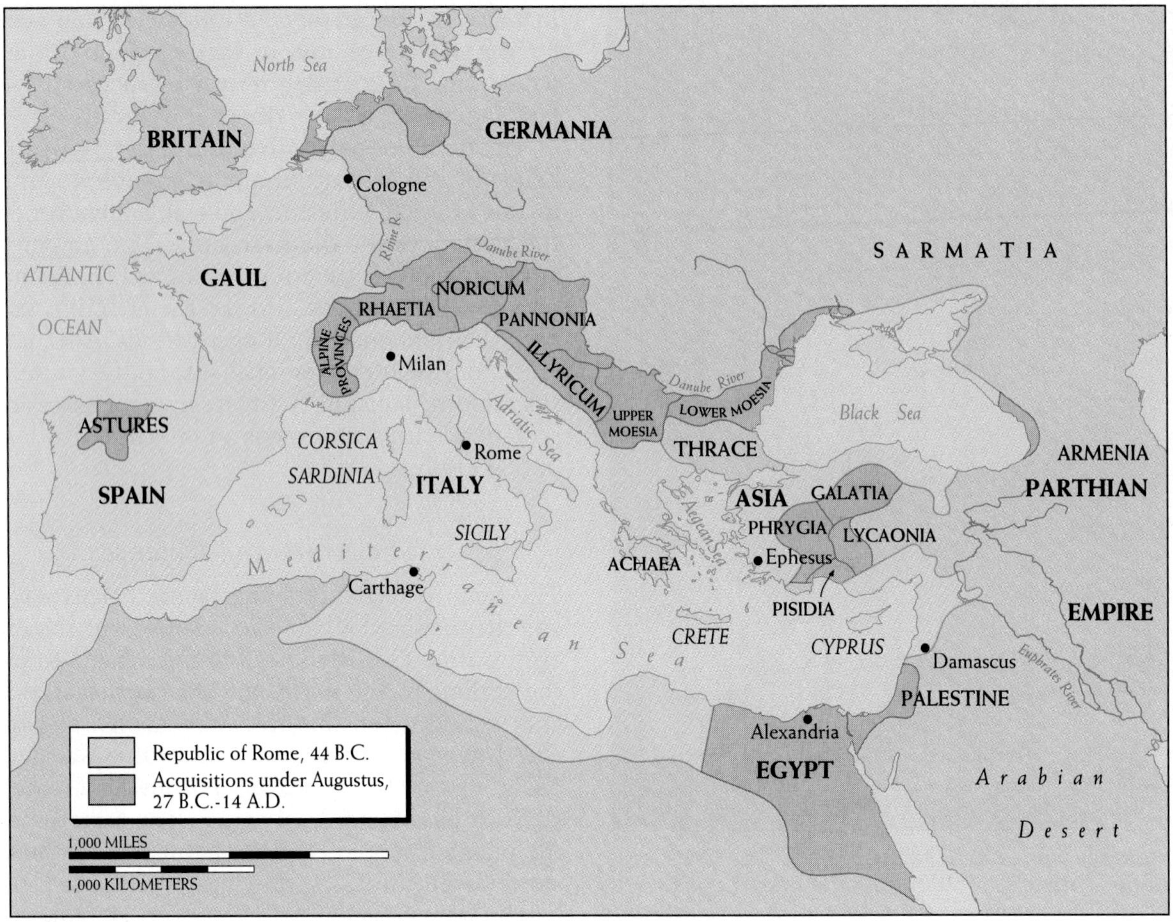

MAP 5–1 THE ROMAN EMPIRE, 14 C.E. *This map shows the growth of the empire under Augustus and its extent at his death.*

strengthen Rome's defenses against the barbarians outside.

Religion and Morality

A century of political strife and civil war had undermined many of the foundations of traditional Roman society. Augustus thought it desirable to try to repair the damage. So he undertook a program aimed at preserving and restoring the traditional values of the family and religion in Rome and Italy. He introduced laws curbing adultery and divorce and encouraging early marriage and the procreation of legitimate children. He set an example of austere behavior in his own household and even banished his daughter, Julia, whose immoral behavior had become public knowledge.

Augustus worked at restoring the dignity of formal Roman religion, building many temples, reviving old cults, and reorganizing and invigorating the priestly colleges. He banned the worship of newly introduced foreign gods. Writers whom he patronized, such as Vergil, pointed out his family's legendary connection with Venus. During his lifetime he did not accept divine honors, though he was deified after his death. As with Julius Caesar, a state cult was dedicated to his worship.

Civilization of the Ciceronian and Augustan Ages

The high point of Roman culture came in the last century of the republic and during the principate of Augustus. Both periods reflected the dominant influence of Greek culture, especially its Hellenistic mode. Upper class Romans were educated in Greek rhetoric, philosophy, and literature, which also served as the models for Roman writers and artists. Yet in spirit and sometimes in form, the art and writing of both periods show uniquely Roman qualities, though each in different ways.

The Late Republic

CICERO The towering literary figure of the late republic was Cicero (106–43 B.C.E.). He is most famous for his orations delivered in the law courts and in the Senate. Together with a considerable body of his private letters, these orations provide us with a clearer and fuller insight into his mind than into that of any other figure in antiquity. We see the political life of his period largely through his eyes. He also wrote treatises on rhetoric, ethics, and politics that put Greek philosophical ideas into Latin terminology and at the same time changed them to suit Roman conditions and values.

Cicero's own views provide support for his moderate and conservative practicality. He believed in a world governed by divine and natural law that human reason could perceive and human institutions reflect. He looked to law, custom, and tradition to produce both stability and liberty. His literary style, as well as his values and ideas, was an important legacy for the Middle Ages and, reinterpreted, for the Renaissance. He was killed at the order of Mark Antony, whose political opponent he had been during the civil wars after the death of Julius Caesar.

HISTORY The last century of the republic produced some historical writing, much of which is lost to us. Sallust (86–35 B.C.E.) wrote a history of the years 78–67 B.C.E., but only a few fragments remain to remind us of his reputation as the greatest of republican historians. His surviving work consists of two pamphlets on the Jugurthine War and on the Catilinarian conspiracy of 63 B.C.E. They reveal his Caesarean and antisenatorial prejudices and the stylistic influence of Thucydides.

Julius Caesar wrote important treatises on the Gallic and civil wars. They are not fully rounded historical accounts but chiefly military narratives written from Caesar's point of view and with propagandist intent. Their objective manner (Caesar always referred to himself in the third person) and their direct, simple, and vigorous style make them persuasive even today. They must have been most effective with their immediate audience.

LAW The period from the Gracchi to the fall of the republic was important in the development of Roman law. Before that time Roman law was essentially national and had developed chiefly by juridical decisions, case by case. Contact with foreign peoples and the influence of Greek ideas, however, forced a change. From the last century of the republic on, the edicts of the *praetors* had increasing importance in developing the Roman legal code. They interpreted and even changed and added to existing law. Quite early the edicts of the magistrates who dealt with foreigners developed the idea of the *jus gentium*, or "law of peoples," as opposed to that arising strictly from the experience of the Romans. In the first century B.C.E. the influence of Greek thought made the idea of *jus gentium* identical with that of the *jus naturale*, or "natural law," taught by the Stoics. It was this view of a world ruled by divine reason that Cicero enshrined in his treatise on the law, *De Legibus*.

POETRY The time of Cicero was also the period of two of Rome's greatest poets, Lucretius and Catullus, each representing a different aspect of Rome's poetic tradition. The Hellenistic poets and literary theorists saw two functions for the poet, as entertainer and as teacher. They thought the best poet combined both roles, and the Romans adopted the same view. When Naevius and Ennius wrote epics on Roman history, they combined historical and moral instruction with pleasure. Lucretius (ca. 99–55 B.C.E.) pursued a similar path in his epic poem *De Rerum Natura* (*On the Nature of the World*). In it he set forth the scientific and philosophical ideas of Epicurus and Democritus with the zeal of a missionary trying to save society from fear and superstition. He knew that his doctrine might be bitter medicine to the reader: "That is why I have tried to administer it to you in the dulcet strain of poesy, coated with the sweet honey of the Muses."[1]

Catullus (ca. 84–54 B.C.E.) was a thoroughly different kind of poet. He wrote poems that were personal, even autobiographical. Imitating the Alexandrians, he wrote short poems filled with learned allusions to mythology, but he far surpassed his models in intensity of feeling. He wrote of the joys and pains of love, he hurled invective at important contemporaries like Julius Caesar, and he amused himself in witty poetic exchanges with others. He offered no moral lessons and was not interested in Rome's glorious history and in contemporary politics. In a sense he is an example of the proud, independent, pleasure-

[1] *I, Lucretius,* De Rerum Natura, *lines 931ff.*

Roman Law

One of the most important achievements of Roman civilization was the establishment over a wide area of a code of law derived from experience and custom but based on principles thought to apply universally and organized according to reason. It had a powerful influence in shaping the character of Western civilization long after the fall of the empire. The following selection, from the Digest, *compiled at the order of the emperor Justinian in the sixth century* C.E., *quotes the* Institutes, *a work by Ulpian, a leading jurist of the third century* C.E. *It discusses the fundamental issues underlying the Roman conception of law in the imperial period.*

✦ *According to this document, for what reason should a Roman citizen obey the law? How does this rationale compare with the rationale for obeying the law in the Mesopotamia of Hammurabi or in democratic Athens? What is the importance of the concept of natural law? What are the consequences of rejecting such an idea?*

Justice and Law

(Ulpian *Institutes I*) When a man means to give his attention to law, he ought first to know whence the term law (*ius*) is derived. Now it is so called from justice (*iustitia*). In fact, as Celsus neatly defines it, *ius* is the art of the good and fair. Of this art we may deservedly be called the priests; we cherish justice and profess the knowledge of the good and the fair, separating the fair from the unfair, discriminating between the permitted and the forbidden, desiring to make men good, not only by the fear of penalties, but also by the incentives of rewards, affecting, if I mistake not, a true and not a simulated philosophy.

This subject comprises two categories, public law and private law. Public law is that which regards the constitution of the Roman state, private law that which looks to the interest of individuals; for some things are beneficial from the point of view of the state, and some with reference to private persons. Public law is concerned with sacred rites, with priests, with public officers. Private law is tripartite, being derived from the rules of natural law, or of the law of nations, or of civil law. Natural law is that which all animals have been taught by nature; this law is not peculiar to the human race, but is common to all animals which are produced on land or sea, and to the birds as well. From it comes the union of male and female, which we call matrimony, and the procreation and rearing of children; we find in fact that animals in general, even the wild beasts, are marked by acquaintance with this law. The law of nations is that which the various peoples of mankind observe. It is easy to see that it falls short of natural law, because the latter is common to all living creatures, whereas the former is common only to human beings in their mutual relations—

Justinian, Digest *I, i. iii–iv, trans. by Naphtali Lewis and Meyer Reinhold, in* Roman Civilization, *Vol. 2 (New York: Columbia University Press, 1955), p. 534.*

seeking nobleman who characterized part of the aristocracy at the end of the republic.

The Age of Augustus

The spirit of the Augustan Age, the Golden Age of Roman literature, was quite different, reflecting the new conditions of society. The old aristocratic order, with its system of independent nobles following their own particular interests, was gone. So was the world of poets of the lower orders, receiving patronage from any of a number of individual aristocrats. Augustus replaced the complexity of republican patronage with a simple scheme in which all patronage flowed from the *princeps*, usually through his chief cultural adviser, Maecenas.

The major poets of this time, Vergil and Horace, had lost their property during the civil wars. The patronage of the *princeps* allowed them the leisure and the security to write poetry; at the same time it made them dependent on him and limited their freedom of expression. They wrote on subjects that were useful for his policies and that glorified him and his family. These poets were not mere propagandists, however. It seems clear that mostly they were persuaded of the virtues of Augustus and his reign and sang its praises with some degree of sincerity. Because they were poets of genius, they were also able to maintain a measure of independence in their work.

VERGIL Vergil (70–19 B.C.E.) was the most important of the Augustan poets. His first important works, the *Eclogues*, or *Bucolics*, are pastoral idylls in a somewhat artificial mode. The subject of the *Georgics*, however, was suggested to Vergil by Maecenas. The model here was the early Greek poet Hesiod's *Works and Days*, but the mood and purpose of Vergil's poem are far different. It pays homage to the heroic human effort to forge order and social complexity out of an ever hostile and sometimes brutal natural environment. It was also a hymn to the cults, traditions, and greatness of Italy.

All this served the purpose of glorifying Augustus's resettlement of the veterans of the civil wars on Italian farms and his elevation of Italy to special status in the empire. Vergil's greatest work is the *Aeneid*, a long national epic that succeeded in placing the history of Rome in the great tradition of the Greeks and the Trojan War. Its hero, the Trojan warrior Aeneas, personifies the ideal Roman qualities of duty, responsibility, serious purpose, and patriotism. As the Romans' equivalent of Homer, Vergil glorified not the personal honor and excellence of the Greek epic heroes but the civic greatness represented by Augustus and the peace and prosperity that he and the Julian family had given to imperial Rome.

HORACE Horace (65–8 B.C.E.) was the son of a freeman and fought on the republican side until its defeat at Philippi. He was won over to the Augustan cause by the patronage of Maecenas and by the attractions of the Augustan reforms. His *Satires* are genial and humorous. His great skills as a lyric poet are best revealed in his *Odes*, which are ingenious in their adaptation of Greek meters to the requirements of Latin verse. Two of the *Odes* are directly in praise of Augustus, and many of them glorify the new Augustan order, the imperial family, and the empire.

OVID The career of Ovid (43 B.C.E.–18 C.E.) reveals the darker side of Augustan influence on the arts. He wrote light and entertaining love elegies that reveal the sophistication and the loose sexual code of a notorious sector of the Roman aristocracy whose values and way of life were contrary to the seriousness and family-centered life Augustus was trying to foster. Ovid's *Ars Amatoria*, a poetic textbook on the art of seduction, angered Augustus and was partly responsible for the poet's exile in 8 C.E. Ovid tried to recover favor, especially with his *Fasti,* a poetic treatment of Roman religious festivals, but to no avail. His most popular work is the *Metamorphoses*, a kind of mythological epic that turns Greek myths into charming stories in a graceful and lively style. Ovid's fame did not fade with his exile and death, but his fate was an effective warning to later poets.

HISTORY The achievements of Augustus, his emphasis on tradition, and the continuity of his regime with the glorious history of Rome encouraged both historical and antiquarian prose works. Some Augustan writers wrote scholarly treatises on history and geography in Greek. By far the most important and influential prose writer of the time, however, was Livy (59 B.C.E.–17 C.E.), an Italian from Padua. His *History of Rome* was written in Latin and treated the period from the legendary origins of Rome until 9 B.C.E. Only a fourth of his work is extant; of the rest we have only pitifully brief summaries. He based his history on earlier accounts and made no effort at original research. His great achievement was in telling the story of Rome in a continuous and impressive narrative. Its purpose was moral, and he set up historical models as examples of good and bad behavior, and, above all, patriotism. He glorified Rome's greatness and connected it with Rome's past, as Augustus tried to do.

ARCHITECTURE AND SCULPTURE Augustus was the great patron of the visual arts as he was of literature. He embarked on a building program that beautified Rome, glorified his reign, and contributed to

Ruins of the Roman Forum. From the earliest days of the city, the Forum was the center of Roman life. Augustus had it rebuilt, and it was frequently rebuilt and refurbished by his successors, so most of the surviving buildings date to the imperial period. [The Bettmann Archive]

the general prosperity and his own popularity. He filled the Campus Martius with beautiful new buildings, theaters, baths, and basilicas; the Roman Forum was rebuilt; and Augustus built a forum of his own. At its heart was the temple of Mars the Avenger, which commemorated Augustus's victory and the greatness of his ancestors. On Rome's Palatine Hill he built a splendid temple to his patron god, Apollo, in pursuit of his religious policy.

Most of the building was influenced by the Greek classical style, which aimed at serenity and the ideal type. The same features were visible in the portrait sculpture of Augustus and his family. The greatest monument of the age is the *Ara Pacis*, or "Altar of Peace," dedicated in 9 B.C.E. Set originally in an open space in the Campus Martius, its walls still carry a relief. Part of it shows a procession in which Augustus and his family appear to move forward, followed in order by the magistrates, the Senate, and the people of Rome. There is no better symbol of the new order.

A panel from the Ara Pacis *(Altar of Peace). The altar was dedicated in 9 B.C.E. It was part of a propaganda campaign—involving poetry, architecture, myth, and history—that Augustus undertook to promote himself as the savior of Rome and the restorer of peace. This panel shows the goddess Earth and her children with cattle, sheep, and other symbols of agricultural wealth. [Nimatallah/Art Resource, N.Y.]*

Imperial Rome 14–180 C.E.

The central problem for Augustus's successors was the position of the ruler and his relationship to the ruled. Augustus tried to cloak the monarchical nature of his government, but his successors soon abandoned all pretense. The ruler came to be called *imperator*—from which comes our word *emperor*—as well as *Caesar*. The latter title signified connection with the imperial house, and the former indicated the military power on which everything was based.

The Emperors

Because Augustus was ostensibly only the "first citizen" of a restored republic and his powers were theoretically voted him by the Senate and the people, he could not legally name his successor. In fact, he plainly designated his heirs by lavishing favors on them and by giving them a share in the imperial power and responsibility. Tiberius (r. 14–37 C.E.),[2] his immediate successor, was at first embarrassed by the ambiguity of his new role, but soon the monarchical and hereditary nature of the regime became patent. Gaius (Caligula, r. 37–41 C.E.), Claudius (r. 41–54 C.E.), and Nero (r. 54–68 C.E.) were all descended from either Augustus or his wife, Livia, and all were elevated because of that fact.

In 41 C.E. the naked military basis of imperial rule was revealed when the Praetorian Guard dragged the lame, stammering, and frightened Claudius from behind a curtain and made him emperor. In 68 C.E. the frontier legions learned what the historian Tacitus called "the secret of Empire . . . that an emperor could be made elsewhere than at Rome." Nero's incompetence and unpopularity, and especially his inability to control his armies, led to a serious rebellion in Gaul in 68 C.E. The year 69 saw four different emperors assume power in quick succession as different Roman armies took turns placing their commanders on the throne.

Vespasian (r. 69–79 C.E.) emerged victorious from the chaos, and his sons, Titus (r. 79–81 C.E.) and Domitian (r. 81–96 C.E.), carried forward his line, the Flavian dynasty. Vespasian was the first emperor who did not come from the old Roman

[2]*Dates for emperors give the years of their reigns, as indicated by "r."*

This cameo shows profiles of the Emperor Claudius and his wife, Agrippina the younger, superimposed over profiles of Germanicus, the nephew of the Emperor Tiberius, and his wife Agrippina the elder, mother of the wife of Claudius. [Kunsthistorisches Museum, Vienna]

nobility. He was a tough soldier who came from the Italian middle class. A good administrator and a hard-headed realist of rough wit, he resisted all attempts by flatterers to find noble ancestors for him. On his deathbed he is said to have ridiculed the practice of deifying emperors by saying, "Alas, I think I am becoming a god."

The assassination of Domitian put an end to the Flavian dynasty. Because Domitian had no close relative who had been designated as successor, the Senate put Nerva (r. 96–98 C.E.) on the throne to avoid chaos. He was the first of the five "good emperors," who included Trajan (r. 98–117 C.E.), Hadrian (r. 117–138 C.E.), Antoninus Pius (r. 138–161 C.E.), and Marcus Aurelius (r. 161–180 C.E.). Until Marcus Aurelius none of these emperors had sons, and so they each followed the example set by Nerva of adopting an able senator and establishing him as successor. This rare solution to the problem of monarchical succession was, therefore, only a historical accident. The result, nonetheless, was almost a century of peaceful succession and competent rule, which ended when Marcus Aurelius allowed his incompetent son, Commodus (r. 180–192 C.E.), to succeed him, with unfortunate results.

The genius of the Augustan settlement lay in its capacity to enlist the active cooperation of the upper classes and their effective organ, the Senate. The election of magistrates was taken from the assemblies and given to the Senate. The Senate became the major center for legislation and it exercised important judicial functions. This semblance of power persuaded some contemporaries and even some modern scholars that Augustus had established a "dyarchy," a system of joint rule by *princeps* and Senate. This was never true.

The hollowness of the senatorial role became more apparent as time passed. Some emperors, like Vespasian, took pains to maintain, increase, and display the prestige and dignity of the Senate. Others, like Caligula, Nero, and Domitian, degraded the Senate and paraded their own despotic power. But from the first the Senate's powers were illusory. Magisterial elections were, in fact, controlled by the emperors, and the Senate's legislative function quickly degenerated into mere assent to what the emperor or his representatives put before it. The true function of the Senate was to be a legislative and administrative extension of the emperor's rule.

There was, of course, some real opposition to the imperial rule. It sometimes took the form of plots against the life of the emperor. Plots and the suspicion of plots led to repression, the use of spies and paid informers, book burning, and executions. The opposition consisted chiefly of senators who looked back to republican liberty for their class and who found justification in the Greek and Roman traditions of tyrannicide as well as in the precepts of Stoicism. Plots and repression were most common under Nero and Domitian. From Nerva to Marcus Aurelius, however, the emperors, without yielding any power, again learned to enlist the cooperation of the upper class by courteous and modest deportment.

Rulers of the Early Empire

27 B.C.E.–14 C.E.	Augustus
The Julio-Claudian Dynasty	
14–37 C.E.	Tiberius
37–41 C.E.	Gaius (Caligula)
41–54 C.E.	Claudius
54–68 C.E.	Nero
69 C.E.	Year of the Four Emperors
The Flavian Dynasty	
69–79 C.E.	Vespasian
79–81 C.E.	Titus
81–96 C.E.	Domitian
The "Good Emperors"	
96–98 C.E.	Nerva
98–117 C.E.	Trajan
117–138 C.E.	Hadrian
138–161 C.E.	Antoninus Pius
161–180 C.E.	Marcus Aurelius

The Administration of the Empire

The provinces flourished economically and generally accepted Roman rule easily. (See Map 5–2.) In the eastern provinces the emperor was worshiped as a god; even in Italy most emperors were deified after their death as long as the imperial cult established by Augustus continued. Imperial policy usually combined an attempt to unify the empire and its various peoples with a respect for local customs and differences. Roman citizenship was spread ever more widely, and by 212 C.E. almost every inhabitant of the empire was a citizen. Latin became the language of the western provinces. Although the East remained essentially Greek in language and culture, even it adopted many aspects of Roman life. The spread of *Romanitis*,

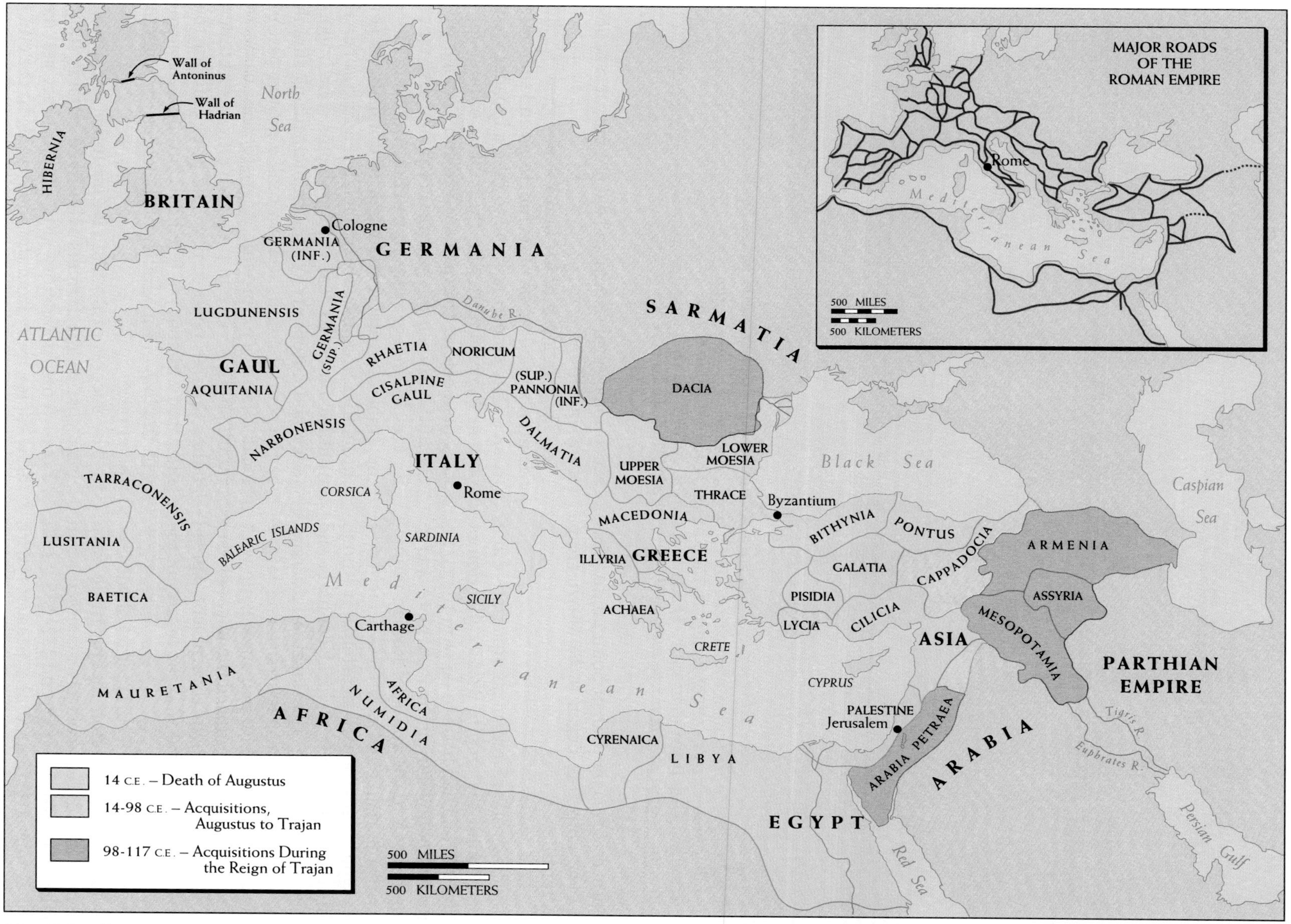

MAP 5–2 PROVINCES OF THE ROMAN EMPIRE TO 117 C.E. *The growth of the empire to its greatest extent is here shown in three stages—at the death of Augustus in 14 C.E., at the death of Nerva in 98, and at the death of Trajan in 117. The division into provinces is also shown. The insert shows the main roads that tied the far-flung empire together.*

Spoils from the temple in Jerusalem were carried in triumphal procession by Roman troops. This relief from Titus's arch of victory in the Roman Forum celebrates his capture of Jerusalem after a two-year siege. The Jews found it difficult to reconcile their religion with Roman rule and frequently rebelled. [Scala/Art Resource, N.Y.]

or "Roman-ness," was more than nominal, for senators and even emperors began to be drawn from provincial families.

LOCAL MUNICIPALITIES From an administrative and cultural standpoint the empire was a collection of cities and towns and had little to do with the countryside. Roman policy during the Principate was to raise urban centers to the status of Roman municipalities with the rights and privileges attached to them. A typical municipal charter left much responsibility in the hands of local councils and magistrates elected from the local aristocracy. Moreover, the holding of a magistracy, and later a seat on the council, carried Roman citizenship with it. Therefore, the Romans enlisted the upper classes of the provinces in their own government, spread Roman law and culture, and won the loyalty of the influential people.

There were exceptions to this picture of success. The Jews found their religion incompatible with Roman demands and were savagely repressed when they rebelled in 66–70, 115–117, and 132–135 C.E. In Egypt the Romans exploited the peasants with exceptional ruthlessness and did not pursue a policy of urbanization.

As the efficiency of the bureaucracy grew, so did the number and scope of its functions and therefore its size. The emperors came to take a broader view of their responsibilities for the welfare of their subjects than before. Nerva conceived and Trajan introduced the *alimenta*, a program of public assistance for the children of indigent parents. More and more the emperors intervened when municipalities got into difficulties, usually financial, sending imperial troubleshooters to deal with problems. The importance and autonomy of the municipalities shrank as the central administration took a greater part in local affairs. The provincial aristocracy came to regard public service in their own cities as a burden rather than an opportunity. The price paid for the increased efficiency offered by centralized control was the loss of the vitality of the cities throughout the empire.

The success of Roman civilization also came at great cost to the farmers who lived outside Italy. Taxes, rents, mandatory gifts, and military service drew capital away from the countryside to the cities

Daily Life in a Roman Provincial Town: Graffiti from Pompeii

On the walls of the houses of Pompeii, buried and preserved by the eruption of Mount Vesuvius in 79 C.E., are many scribblings that give us an idea of what the life of ordinary people was like.

✦ *How do these graffiti differ from those one sees in a modern American city? What do they reveal about the similarities and differences between the ordinary people of ancient Rome and the people of today? How would you account for the differences?*

I

Twenty pairs of gladiators of Decimus Lucretius Satrius Valens, lifetime *flamen* of Nero son of Caesar Augustus, and ten pairs of gladiators of Decimus Lucretius Valens, his son, will fight at Pompeii on April 8, 9, 10, 11, 12. There will be a full card of wild beast combats, and awnings [for the spectators]. Aemilius Celer [painted this sign], all alone in the moonlight.

II

Market days: Saturday in Pompeii, Sunday in Nuceria, Monday in Atella, Tuesday in Nola, Wednesday in Cumae, Thursday in Puteoli, Friday in Rome.

III

Pleasure says: "You can get a drink here for an *as* [a few cents], a better drink for two, Falernian for four."

IV

A copper pot is missing from this shop. 65 sesterces reward if anybody brings it back, 20 sesterces if he reveals the thief so we can get our property back.

V

The weaver Successus loves the innkeeper's slave girl, Iris by name. She doesn't care for him, but he begs her to take pity on him. Written by his rival. So long.

[Answer by the rival:] Just because you're bursting with envy, don't pick on a handsomer man, a lady-killer and a gallant.

[Answer by the first writer:] There's nothing more to say or write. You love Iris, who doesn't care for you.

VI

Take your lewd looks and flirting eyes off another man's wife, and show some decency on your face!

VII

Anybody in love, come here. I want to break Venus' ribs with a club and cripple the goddess' loins. If she can pierce my tender breast, why can't I break her head with a club?

VIII

I write at Love's dictation and Cupid's instruction;

But damn it! I don't want to be a god without you.

IX

[A prostitute's sign:] I am yours for 2 *asses* cash.

N. Lewis and M. Reinhold, Roman Civilization, *Vol. 2 (New York: Columbia University Press, 1955), pp. 359–360.*

Trajan's Column was erected at Rome about 110 C.E. to celebrate the emperor Trajan's (r. 98–117) victory over the Dacians beyond the Danube. Trajan pushed the boundaries of the Roman Empire to their farthest limits, defeating the Parthians in the east as well as the Dacians in the north. Carved in a spiraling relief, the column shows more than a thousand figures, accurately depicting people, buildings, flowers, animals, implements, and weapons. [Scala/Art Resource]

on a scale not previously seen in the Graeco-Roman world. More and more the rich life of the urban elite came at the expense of millions of previously stable farmers.

FOREIGN POLICY Augustus's successors, for the most part, accepted his conservative and defensive foreign policy. Trajan was the first emperor to take the offensive in a sustained way. Between 101 and 106 C.E. he crossed the Danube and, after hard fighting, established the new province of Dacia between the Danube and the Carpathian Mountains. He was tempted, no doubt, by its important gold mines, but he probably was also pursuing a new general strategy: to defend the empire more aggressively by driving wedges into the territory of threatening barbarians. The same strategy dictated the invasion of the Parthian Empire in the east (113–117 C.E.). Trajan's early success was astonishing, and he established three new provinces in Armenia, Assyria, and Mesopotamia. But his lines were overextended. Rebellions sprang up, and the campaign crumbled. Trajan was forced to retreat, and he died before getting back to Rome.

Hadrian's reign marked an important shift in Rome's frontier policy. Heretofore, even under the successors of Augustus, Rome had been on the offensive against the barbarians. Although the Romans rarely gained new territory, they launched frequent attacks to chastise and pacify troublesome tribes. Hadrian hardened the Roman defenses, building a stone wall in the south of Scotland and a wooden one across the Rhine–Danube triangle.

The Roman defense became rigid, and initiative passed to the barbarians. Marcus Aurelius was compelled to spend most of his reign resisting dangerous attacks in the east and on the Danube frontier.

AGRICULTURE: THE DECLINE OF SLAVE LABOR AND THE RISE OF *COLONI* The defense of its frontiers put enormous pressure on the human and financial resources of the empire, but the effect of these pressures was not immediately felt. The empire generally experienced considerable economic growth well into the reigns of "good emperors." Internal peace and efficient administration benefited agriculture as well as trade and industry. Farming and trade developed together as political conditions made it easier to sell farm products at a distance.

Small farms continued to exist, but the large estate, managed by an absentee owner and growing cash crops, became the dominant form of agriculture. At first, as in the republican period, these estates were worked chiefly by slaves, but in the first century this began to change. Economic pressures on the free lower classes forced many of them to become tenant farmers, or *coloni*, and eventually these *coloni* replaced slaves as the mainstay of agricultural labor. Typically, these sharecroppers paid rent in labor or in kind, though sometimes they made cash payments. Eventually, their movement

The Bar-Kochba *Rebellion: The Final Jewish Uprising Against Rome*

Unlike most conquered peoples the Jews found accommodation to Roman rule difficult. Their first rebellion was crushed by Vespasian's son, the future emperor Titus, in 70 C.E. At that time the Temple in Jerusalem was destroyed. A second revolt was put down in 117 C.E. Finally, when Hadrian ordered a Roman colony placed on the site of Jerusalem, Simon, who was called Bar Kochba, *or "Son of the Star," led a last uprising from 132 to 135. Dio Cassius describes the brutality of its suppression.*

✦ *Did the Romans treat the Jews differently from other people under their control? What special problems did the Roman conquest pose to the Jews? What problems did the Jews present to the Romans?*

At Jerusalem Hadrian founded a city in place of the one which had been razed to the ground, naming it Aelia Capitolina, and on the site of the temple of the god he raised a new temple to Jupiter. This brought on a war of no slight importance nor of brief duration, for the Jews deemed it intolerable that foreign peoples should be settled in their city and foreign rites planted there. . . .

At first the Romans took no account of them. Soon, however, all Judaea had been stirred up, and the Jews everywhere were showing signs of disturbance, were gathering together, and giving evidence of great hostility to the Romans, partly by secret and partly by overt acts; many outside peoples, too, were joining them through eagerness for gain, and the whole world, one might almost say, was being stirred up over the matter. Then, indeed, Hadrian sent his best generals against them. Foremost among these was Julius Severus, who was dispatched against the Jews from Britain, where he was governor. . . . [In Judaea] he was able, rather slowly . . . but with comparatively little danger, to crush, exhaust, and exterminate them. Very few of them in fact survived. Fifty of their most important strongholds and 985 of their most famous villages were razed to the ground; 580,000 men were slain in the various raids and battles, and the number of those that perished by famine, disease, and fire was past finding out.

Dio Cassius, Roman History *59.12–14, trans. by Ernest Cary (London: Loeb Classical Library and William Heinemann, 1916).*

was restricted, and they were tied to the land they worked, much as were the manorial serfs of the Middle Ages. Whatever its social costs, the system was economically efficient, however, and contributed to the general prosperity.

Although the economic importance of slavery began to decline in the second century with the rise of *coloni* labor, the institution was never abolished nor did it disappear so long as the Roman Empire lasted. Pockets of slave labor remained as late as the time of Charlemagne. (See Chapter 6.)

Life in Imperial Rome: The Apartment House

The civilization of the Roman Empire depended on the vitality of its cities. The typical city had about 20,000 inhabitants and perhaps only three or four had a population of more than 75,000. The population of Rome, however, was certainly greater than 500,000, perhaps more than a million. People coming to Rome for the first time found it overwhelming and were either thrilled or horrified by its

This is a reconstruction of a typical Roman apartment house found at Ostia, Rome's port. The ground floor contained shops, and the stories above it held many apartments. [Scala/Art Resource, N.Y.]

size, bustle, and noise. The rich lived in elegant homes called *domūs*. These were single-storied houses with plenty of space, an open central courtyard, and several rooms designed for specific and different purposes, such as dining, sitting, or sleeping, in privacy and relative quiet. Though only a small portion of Rome's population lived in them, these houses took up as much as a third of the city's space. Public space for temples, markets, baths, gymnasiums, theaters, forums, and governmental buildings took up another quarter of Rome's territory.

This left less than half of Rome's area to house the mass of its inhabitants, who were squeezed into multiple dwellings that grew increasingly tall. Most Romans during the imperial period lived in apartment buildings called *insulae*, or "islands", that rose to a height of five or six stories and sometimes even more. The most famous of them, the Insula of Febiala, seems to have "towered above the Rome of the Antonines like a skyscraper."[3]

These buildings were divided into separate apartments (*cenicula*) of undifferentiated rooms, the same plan on each floor. The apartments were cramped and uncomfortable. They had neither central heating nor open fireplaces; heat and fire for cooking came from small, portable stoves. The apartments were hot in summer, cold in winter, and stuffy and smoky when the stoves were lit. There was no plumbing, so tenants needed to go into the streets to wells or fountains for water and to public baths and latrines, or to less regulated places. The higher up one lived, the more difficult these trips, and so chamber pots and commodes were kept in the rooms. These receptacles were emptied into vats on the staircase landings or in the alleys outside; on occasion, the contents, and even the containers, were tossed out the window. Roman satirists complained of the discomforts and dangers of walking the streets beneath such windows. Roman law tried to find ways to assign responsibilities for the injuries done to dignity and person.

In spite of these difficulties, the attractions of the city and the shortage of space caused rents to rise, making life in these buildings expensive as well as uncomfortable. It was also dangerous. The houses were lightly built of concrete and brick, far too high for the limited area of their foundations, and so they often collapsed. Laws limiting the height of buildings were not always obeyed and did not, in any case, always prevent disaster. The satirist Juvenal did not exaggerate much when he wrote, "We

[3]*J. Carcopino,* Daily Life in Ancient Rome *(New Haven, Conn.: Yale University Press 1940), p. 26.*

inhabit a city held up chiefly by slats, for that is how the landlord patches up the cracks in the old wall, telling the tenants to sleep peacefully under the ruin that hangs over their heads."

Even more serious was the threat of fire. Wooden beams supported the floors, and the rooms were lit by torches, candles, and oil lamps and heated by braziers. Fires broke out easily and, without running water, were not easily put out; once started, they usually led to disaster.

When we consider the character of these apartments and compare them with the attractive public places in the city, we can easily understand why the people of Rome spent most of their time out of doors.

The Culture of the Early Empire

The years from 14 to 180 C.E. were a time of general prosperity and a flourishing material and artis-

Juvenal on Life in Rome

The satirical poet Juvenal lived and worked in Rome in the late first and early second centuries C.E. His poems present a vivid picture of the material and cultural world of the Romans of his time. In the following passages, he tells of the discomforts and dangers of life in the city, both indoors and out.

✦ *According to Juvenal what dangers awaited pedestrians in the Rome of his day? Who had responsibility for the condition of Rome? If the situation was as bad as he says, why was nothing done about it? Why did people choose to live in Rome at all and especially in the conditions he describes?*

Who, in Praeneste's cool, or the wooded
 Volsinian uplands,
Who, on Tivoli's heights, or a small town like
 Gabii, say,
Fears the collapse of his house? But Rome is
 supported on pipestems,
Matchsticks; it's cheaper, so, for the landlord to
 shore up his ruins,
Patch up the old cracked walls, and notify all
 the tenants
They can sleep secure, though the beams are in
 ruins above them.
No, the place to live is out there, where no cry
 of *Fire!*
Sounds the alarm of the night, with a neighbor
 yelling for water,
Moving his chattels and goods, and the whole
 third story is smoking.
This you'll never know: for if the ground floor is
 scared first,
You are the last to burn, up there where the
 eaves of the attic
Keep off the rain, and the doves are brooding
 over their nest eggs.
....
Look at other things, the various dangers of
 nighttime.
How high it is to the cornice that breaks, and a
 chunk beats my brains out,
Or some slob heaves a jar, broken or cracked,
 from a window.
Bang! It comes down with a crash and proves its
 weight on the sidewalk.
You are a thoughtless fool, unmindful of sudden
 disaster,
If you don't make your will before you go out to
 have dinner.
There are as many deaths in the night as there
 are open windows
Where you pass by; if you're wise, you will pray,
 in your wretched devotions,
People may be content with no more than
 emptying slop jars.

Juvenal, The Satires of Juvenal, *trans. by Rolfe Humphries (Bloomington: Indiana University Press, 1958), pp. 40, 43.*

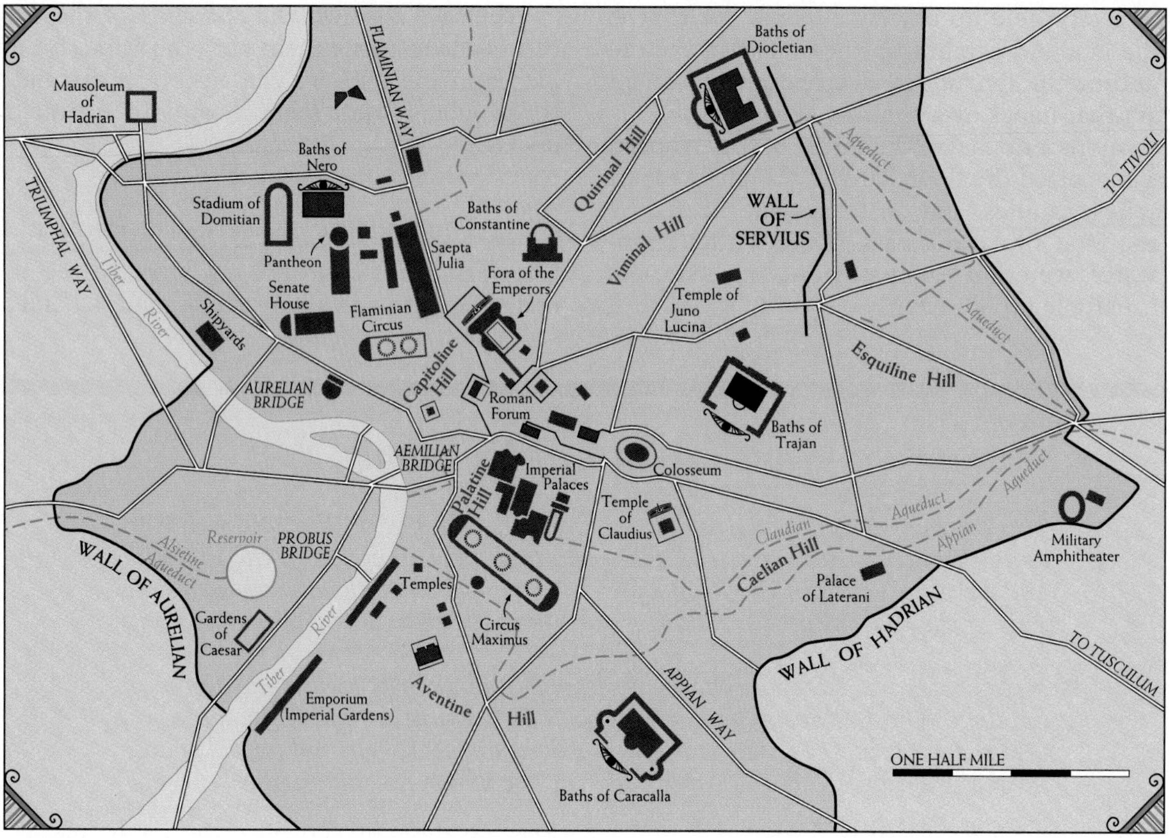

Map 5–3 Ancient Rome *This map of Rome during the late empire shows the seven hills on and around which the city was built, and the major walls, bridges, and other public sites and buildings.*

tic culture, but one not so brilliant and original as in the Age of Augustus.

Literature In Latin literature the period between the death of Augustus and the time of Marcus Aurelius is known as the Silver Age. As the name implies, this age produced work of high quality although probably not of so high a quality as in the Augustan era. In contrast to the hopeful, positive optimists of the Augustans, the writers of the Silver Age were gloomy, negative, and pessimistic. In the works of the former period, praise of the emperor, his achievements, and the world abounds; in the latter, criticism and satire lurk everywhere. Some of the most important writers of the Silver Age came from the Stoic opposition and reflected its hostility to the growing power and personal excesses of the emperors.

The writers of the second century C.E. appear to have turned away from contemporary affairs and even recent history. Historical writing was about remote periods so that there was less danger of irritating imperial sensibilities. Scholarship was encouraged, but we hear little of poetry, especially that dealing with dangerous subjects. In the third century C.E. romances written in Greek became popular and provide further evidence of the tendency of writers of the time to seek and provide escape from contemporary realities.

Architecture The main contribution of the Romans lay in two new kinds of buildings—the great public bath and a new, free-standing kind of amphitheater—and in the advances in engineering that made these large structures possible. While keeping the basic post-and-lintel construction used by the Greeks, the Romans added to it the principle of the semicircular arch, borrowed from the Etruscans. They also made good use of concrete, a building material first used by the Hellenistic Greeks and fully developed by the Romans. The arch, combined with the post and lintel, produced the great Colosseum built by the Flavian emperors. When used internally in the form of vaults and domes, the arch permitted great buildings like the baths, of which the most famous and best preserved are those of the later emperors Caracalla and Diocletian. (See Map 5–3.)

One of Rome's most famous buildings, the Pantheon, begun by Augustus's friend Agrippa and rebuilt by Hadrian, combined all these elements. Its portico of Corinthian columns is of Greek origin, but its rotunda of brick-faced concrete with its domed ceiling and relieving arches is thoroughly Roman. The new engineering also made possible the construction of more mundane but useful structures like bridges and aqueducts.

SOCIETY Seen from the harsh perspective of human history, the first two centuries of the Roman Empire deserve their reputation of a "golden age." But by the second century C.E., troubles had arisen, troubles that foreshadowed the difficult times ahead. The literary efforts of the time reveal a flight from the present, from reality, and from the public realm to the past, to romance, and to private

Dinner at Trimalchio's: A Satire on the Newly Rich at Rome

The following selection is from Trimalchio's Feast, part of a fragmentary satire called The Satyricon, *by Petronius, a writer of the first century C.E. The speaker is a guest at a lavish dinner given by Trimalchio, a former slave risen to great wealth at Rome. Included among the jibes and sneers is some useful information about life in this period.*

✦ *What is the source of Trimalchio's wealth? What sources of wealth were available at the time? What does this selection reveal about social mobility in the first century? What of the range of commerce? How do you explain the tone of the narrator?*

"As for old Trimalchio, that man's got more farms than a kite could flap over. And there's more silver plate stuffed in his porter's lodge than another man's got in his safe. As for slaves, whoosh! So help me, I'll bet not one in ten has ever seen his master. Your ordinary rich man is just peanuts compared to him; he could knock them all under a cabbage and you'd never know they were gone.

"And buy things? Not him. No sir, he raises everything right on his own estate. Wool, citron, pepper, you name it. By god, you'd find hen's milk if you looked around. Now take his wool. The home-grown strain wasn't good enough. So you know what he did? Imported rams from Tarentum, bred them into the herd. Attic honey he raises at home. Ordered the bees special from Athens. And the local bees are better for being crossbred too. And, you know, just the other day he sent off to India for some mushroom spawn. Every mule he owns had a wild ass for a daddy. And you see those pillows there? Every last one is stuffed with purple or scarlet wool. That boy's loaded!

"And don't sneer at his friends. They're all ex-slaves, but every one of them's rich. You see that guy down there on the next to last couch? He's worth a cool half-million. Came up from nowhere. Used to tote wood on his back. People say, but I don't know, he stole a cap off a hobgoblin's head and found a treasure. He's the god's fair-haired boy. That's luck for you, but I don't begrudge him. Not so long ago he was just a slave. Yes sir, he's doing all right."

Petronius, The Satyricon, *trans. by William Arrowsmith (Ann Arbor: University of Michigan Press, 1959), pp. 35–36.*

pursuits. Some of the same aspects may be seen in the more prosaic world of everyday life, especially in the decline of vitality in local government.

In the first century C.E. members of the upper classes vied with one another for election to municipal office and for the honor of doing service to their communities. By the second century C.E. it became necessary for the emperors to intervene to correct abuses in local affairs and even to force unwilling members of the ruling classes to accept public office. Magistrates and council members were held personally and collectively responsible for the revenues due. There were even some instances of magistrates fleeing to avoid their office, a practice that became widespread in later centuries.

These difficulties reflected more basic problems. The prosperity brought by the end of civil war and the influx of wealth from the east could not sustain itself beyond the first half of the second century C.E. There also appears to have been a decline in population for reasons that remain mysterious. The cost of government kept rising. The emperors were required to maintain a standing army, minimal in size but costly, to keep the people in Rome happy with "bread and circuses," to pay for an increasingly numerous bureaucracy, and to wage expensive wars to defend the frontiers against dangerous and determined barbarian enemies. The ever-increasing need for money compelled the emperors to raise taxes, to press hard on their subjects, and to bring on inflation by debasing the coinage. These elements brought on the desperate crises that ultimately destroyed the empire.

The Rise of Christianity

Christianity emerged, spread, survived, and ultimately conquered the Roman Empire in spite of its origin among poor people from an unimportant and remote province of the empire. Christianity faced the hostility of the established religious institutions of its native Judaea. It also had to compete against the official cults of Rome and the highly sophisticated philosophies of the educated classes and against such other "mystery" religions as the cults of Mithra, Isis, and Osiris. In addition to all this, the Christians faced the opposition of the imperial government and formal persecution. Yet Christianity achieved toleration and finally exclusive command as the official religion of the empire.

Jesus of Nazareth

An attempt to understand this amazing outcome must begin with the story of Jesus of Nazareth. The most important evidence about his life is in the Gospel accounts, all of them written well after his death. The earliest, by Mark, is dated about 70 C.E., and the latest, by John, about 100 C.E. They are not, moreover, attempts at simply describing the life of Jesus with historical accuracy. Rather they are statements of faith by true believers. The authors of the Gospels believed that Jesus was the son of God and that he had come into the world to redeem humanity and to bring immortality to those who believed in him and followed his way. To the Gospel writers, Jesus' resurrection was striking proof of his teachings. At the same time, the Gospels regard Jesus as a figure in history, and they recount events in his life as well as his sayings.

There is no reason to doubt that Jesus was born in the province of Judaea in the time of Augustus and that he was a most effective teacher in the tradition of the prophets. This tradition promised the coming of a Messiah (in Greek, *christos*—so *Jesus Christ* means "Jesus the Messiah"), the redeemer who would make Israel triumph over its enemies and establish the kingdom of God on earth. In fact, Jesus seems to have insisted that the Messiah would not establish an earthly kingdom but would bring an end to the world as human beings knew it at the Day of Judgment. On that day God would reward the righteous with immortality and happiness in heaven and condemn the wicked to eternal suffering in hell. Until that day (which his followers believed would come very soon), Jesus taught the faithful to abandon sin and worldly concerns; to follow him and his way; to follow the moral code described in the Sermon on the Mount, which preached love, charity, and humility; and to believe in him and his divine mission.

Jesus won a considerable following, especially among the poor, which caused great suspicion among the upper classes. His novel message and his criticism of the religious practices connected with the temple at Jerusalem and its priests provoked the hostility of the religious establishment. A misunderstanding of the movement made it easy to convince the Roman governor that Jesus and his followers might be dangerous revolutionaries. He was put to death in Jerusalem by the cruel and degrading device of crucifixion, proba-

Mark Describes the Resurrection of Jesus

Belief that Jesus rose from the dead after his Crucifixion (about 30 C.E.) was and is central to traditional Christian doctrine. The record of the Resurrection in the Gospel of Mark, written a generation later (toward 70 C.E.), is the earliest we have. The significance to most Christian groups revolves about the assurance given them that death and the grave are not final and that, instead, salvation for a future life is possible. The appeal of these views was to be nearly universal in the West during the Middle Ages. The church was commonly thought to be the means of implementing the promise of salvation; hence the enormous importance of the church's sacramental system, its rules, and its clergy.

✦ *Why are the stories of miracles such as the one described here important for the growth of Christianity? What is special and important about this miracle? Why is it important in the story that days passed between the death of Jesus and the opening of the tomb? Why might the early Christians believe this story? Why was belief in the resurrection important for Christianity in the centuries immediately after the life of Jesus? Is it still important today?*

And when evening had come, since it was the day of Preparation, that is, the day before the sabbath, Joseph of Arimathea, a respected member of the council, who was also himself looking for the kingdom of God, took courage and went to Pilate, and asked for the body of Jesus. And Pilate wondered if he were already dead; and summoning the centurion, he asked him whether he was already dead. And when he learned from the centurion that he was dead, he granted the body to Joseph. And he brought a linen shroud, and taking him down, wrapped him in the linen shroud, and laid him in a tomb which had been hewn out of the rock; and he rolled a stone against the door of the tomb. Mary Magdalene and Mary the mother of Jesus saw where he was laid.

And when the sabbath was past, Mary Magdalene, and Mary the mother of James, and Salome, bought spices, so that they might go and anoint him. And very early on the first day of the week they went to the tomb when the sun had risen. And they were saying to one another, "Who will roll away the stone for us from the door of the tomb?" And looking up, they saw that the stone was rolled back; for it was very large. And entering the tomb, they saw a young man sitting on the right side, dressed in a white robe; and they were amazed. And he said to them, "Do not be amazed; you seek Jesus of Nazareth, who was crucified. He has risen, he is not here, see the place where they laid him. But go, tell his disciples and Peter that he is going before you to Galilee; there you will see him, as he told you." And they went out and fled from the tomb; for trembling and astonishment had come upon them; and they said nothing to any one, for they were afraid.

Gospel of Mark 15:42–47; 16:1–8, Revised Standard Version of the Bible *(New York: Thomas Nelson and Sons,* 1946, 1952*).*

bly in 30 C.E. His followers believed that he was resurrected on the third day after his death, and that belief became a critical element in the religion that they propagated throughout the Roman Empire and beyond.

The new belief spread quickly to the Jewish communities of Syria and Asia Minor. There is reason to believe, however, that it might have had only a short life as a despised Jewish heresy were it not for the conversion and career of Saint Paul.

Paul of Tarsus

Paul was born Saul, a citizen of the Cilician city of Tarsus in Asia Minor. He had been trained in Hellenistic culture and was a Roman citizen. But he was also a zealous member of the Jewish sect known as the *Pharisees*, the group that was most strict in its insistence on adherence to the Jewish law. He took a vigorous part in the persecution of the early Christians until his own conversion outside Damascus about 35 C.E.

The great problem facing the early Christians was to resolve their relationship to Judaism. If the new faith was a version of Judaism, then it must adhere to the Jewish law and seek converts only among Jews. James, called the brother of Jesus, was a conservative who held to that view, whereas the Hellenist Jews tended to see Christianity as a new and universal religion. To force all converts to follow Jewish law would have been fatal to the growth of the new sect. Jewish law's many technicalities and dietary prohibitions were strange to gentiles, and the necessity of circumcision—a frightening, painful, and dangerous operation for adults—would have been a tremendous deterrent to conversion. Paul, converted and with his new name, supported the position of the Hellenists and soon won many converts among the gentiles. After some conflict within the sect, Paul won out. Consequently, the "apostle to the gentiles" deserves recognition as a crucial contributor to the success of Christianity.

Paul believed it important that the followers of Jesus be evangelists (messengers), to spread the gospel, or "good news," of God's gracious gift. He taught that Jesus would soon return for the Day of Judgment, and it was important that all who would should believe in him and accept his way. Faith in Jesus as the Christ was necessary but not sufficient for salvation, nor could good deeds alone achieve it. That final blessing of salvation was a gift of God's grace that would be granted to some but not to all.

Organization

Paul and the other apostles did their work well. The new religion spread throughout the Roman Empire and even beyond its borders. It had its greatest success in the cities and mostly among the poor and uneducated. The rites of the early communities appear to have been simple and few. Baptism by water removed original sin and permitted participation in the community and its activities. The central ritual was a common meal called the *agape*, or "love feast," followed by the ceremony of the *Eucharist*, or "thanksgiving", a celebration of the Lord's Supper in which unleavened bread was eaten and unfermented wine was drunk. There were also prayers, hymns, and readings from the Gospels.

Not all the early Christians were poor, and it became customary for the rich to provide for the poor at the common meals. The sense of common love fostered in these ways focused the community's attention on the needs of the weak, the sick, the unfortunate, and the unprotected. This concern gave the early Christian communities a warmth and a human appeal that stood in marked contrast to the coldness and impersonality of the pagan cults. No less attractive were the promise of salvation, the importance to God of each human soul, and the spiritual equality of all in the new faith. As Paul put it, "There is neither Jew nor Greek, there is neither slave nor free, there is neither male nor female; for you are all one in Christ Jesus."[4]

The future of Christianity depended on its communities' finding an organization that would preserve unity within the group and help protect it against enemies outside. At first, the churches had little formal organization. Soon, it appears, affairs were placed in the hands of boards of *presbyters*, or "elders," and *deacons*, or "those who serve." By the second century C.E., as their numbers grew, the Christians of each city tended to accept the authority and leadership of bishops (*episkopoi*, or "overseers"). Bishops were elected by the congregation to lead them in worship and to supervise funds. As time passed, the bishops extended their authority over the Christian communities in out-

[4]*Galatians 3:28*. Revised Standard Version of the Bible.

lying towns and the countryside. The power and almost monarchical authority of the bishops were soon enhanced by the doctrine of Apostolic Succession, which asserted that the powers that Jesus had given his original disciples were passed on from bishop to bishop by ordination.

The bishops kept in touch with one another, maintained communications between different Christian communities, and prevented doctrinal and sectarian splintering, which would have destroyed Christian unity. They maintained internal discipline and dealt with the civil authorities. After a time they began the practice of coming together in councils to settle difficult questions, to establish orthodox opinion, and even to expel as heretics those who would not accept it. It is unlikely that Christianity could have survived the travails of its early years without such strong internal organization and government.

The Persecution of Christians

The new faith soon incurred the distrust of the pagan world and of the imperial government. At first Christians were thought of as a Jewish sect and were therefore protected by Roman law. It soon became clear, however, that they were quite different, seeming both mysterious and dangerous. They denied the existence of the pagan gods and so were accused of atheism. Their refusal to worship the emperor was judged to be treason. Because they kept mostly to themselves, took no part in civic affairs, engaged in secret rites, and had an organized network of local associations, they were misunderstood and suspected. The love feasts were erroneously reported to be scenes of sexual scandal. The alarming doctrine of the actual presence of Jesus' body in the Eucharist was distorted into an accusation of cannibalism.

The privacy and secrecy of Christian life and worship ran counter to a traditional Roman dislike of any private association, especially any of a religious nature. Christians thus earned the reputation of being "haters of humanity." Claudius expelled them from Rome, and Nero tried to make them scapegoats for the great fire that struck the city in 64 C.E. By the end of the first century "the name alone"—that is, simple membership in the Christian community—was a crime.

But, for the most part, the Roman government did not take the initiative in attacking Christians in the first two centuries. When one governor sought instructions for dealing with the Christians, the emperor Trajan urged moderation. Christians were not to be sought out, anonymous accusations were to be disregarded, and anyone denounced could be acquitted merely by renouncing Christ and sacrificing to the emperor. Unfortunately, no true Christian could meet the conditions, and so there were some martyrdoms.

Most persecutions in this period, however, were started not by the government but by mob action. Though they lived quiet, inoffensive lives, some Christians must have seemed unbearably smug and self-righteous. Unlike the tolerant, easygoing pagans, who were generally willing to accept the new gods of foreign people and add them to the pantheon, the Christians denied the reality of the pagan gods. They proclaimed the unique rightness of their own way and looked forward to their own salvation and the damnation of nonbelievers. It is not surprising, therefore, that pagans disliked these strange and unsocial people, tended to blame misfortunes on them, and, in extreme cases, turned to violence. But even this adversity had its uses. It weeded out the weaklings among the Christians, and brought greater unity to those who remained faithful. It also provided the Church with martyrs around whom legends could grow that would inspire still greater devotion and dedication.

The Emergence of Catholicism

Division within the Christian Church may have been an even greater threat to its existence than persecution from outside. The great majority of Christians never accepted complex, intellectualized opinions but held to what even then were traditional, simple, conservative beliefs. This body of majority opinion, considered to be universal, or "catholic," was enshrined by the church that came to be called *Catholic*. The Catholic Church's doctrines were deemed *orthodox*, that is, "holding the right opinions," whereas those holding contrary opinions were heretics.

The need to combat heretics, however, compelled the orthodox to formulate their own views more clearly and firmly. By the end of the second century C.E., an orthodox canon had been shaped that included the Old Testament, the Gospels, and the Epistles of Paul, among other writings. The process of creating a standard set of holy books was not completed for at least two more centuries, but a vitally important start had been made. The ortho-

This is the Catacomb of the Jordani in Rome. The early Christians built miles of catacombs, or tunnels, in Rome. They were used as underground cemeteries and as refuges from persecution. [Charitable Foundation, Leonard von Matt]

dox declared the Catholic Church itself to be the depository of Christian teaching and the bishops to be its receivers. They also drew up creeds, or brief statements of faith to which true Christians should adhere.

In the first century all that was required of one to be a Christian was to be baptized, to partake of the Eucharist, and to call Jesus the Lord. By the end of the second century an orthodox Christian—that is, a member of the Catholic Church—was required to accept its creed, its canon of holy writings, and the authority of the bishops. The loose structure of the apostolic church had given way to an organized body with recognized leaders able to define its faith and to exclude those who did not accept it. Whatever the shortcomings of this development, there can be little doubt that it provided the clarity, unity, and discipline needed for survival.

Rome As a Center of the Early Church

During this same period the church in Rome came to have special prominence. As the center of communications and the capital of the empire, Rome had natural advantages. After the Roman destruction of Jerusalem in 135 C.E., no other city had any convincing claim to primacy in the church. Besides having the largest single congregation of Christians, Rome also benefited from the tradition that both Jesus' apostles Peter and Paul were martyred there.

Peter, moreover, was thought to be the first bishop of Rome. The Gospel of Matthew (16:18) reported Jesus' statement to Peter: "Thou art Peter [in Greek, *Petros*] and upon this rock [in Greek, *petra*] I will build my church." Eastern Christians might later point out that Peter had been leader of the Christian community at Antioch before he went to Rome. But in the second century the church at Antioch, along with the other Christian churches of Asia Minor, was fading in influence, and by 200 C.E. Rome was the most important center of Christianity. Because of the city's early influence and because of the Petrine doctrine derived from the Gospel of Matthew, later bishops of Rome claimed supremacy in the Catholic Church. But as the era of the "good emperors" came to a close, this controversy was far in the future.

The Crisis of the Third Century

Dio Cassius, a historian of the third century C.E., described the Roman Empire after the death of Marcus Aurelius as declining from "a kingdom of gold into one of iron and rust." Although we have seen that the gold contained more than a little impurity, there is no reason to quarrel with Dio's assessment of his own time. Commodus (r. 180–192 C.E.), the son of Marcus Aurelius, proved the wisdom of the "good emperors" in selecting their successors for their talents rather than for family ties. Commodus was incompetent and autocratic. He reduced the respect in which the imperial office was held, and his assassination brought the return of civil war.

Barbarian Invasions

The pressure on Rome's frontiers, already serious in the time of Marcus Aurelius, reached massive proportions in the third century. In the east a new power arising in the old Persian Empire threatened the frontiers. In the third century B.C.E. the Parthians had made the Iranians independent of the Hellenistic kings and had established an empire of their own on the old foundations of the Persian Empire. Several Roman attempts to conquer them had failed, but as late as 198 C.E. the Romans could reach and destroy the Parthian capital and bring at least northern Mesopotamia under their rule.

In 224 C.E., however, a new Iranian dynasty, the Sassanians, seized control from the Parthians and brought new vitality to Persia. They soon recovered Mesopotamia and made raids deep into Roman provinces. In 260 C.E. they humiliated the Romans by actually taking the emperor Valerian prisoner; he died in captivity.

On the western and northern frontiers the pressure came not from a well-organized rival empire but from an ever-increasing number of German tribes. Though they had been in contact with the Romans at least since the second century B.C.E., they had not been much affected by civilization. The men did no agricultural work, but confined their activities to hunting, drinking, and fighting. They were organized on a family basis by clans, hundreds, and tribes. They were led by chiefs, usually from a royal family, elected by the assembly of fighting men. The king was surrounded by a collection of warriors, whom the Romans called his *comitatus*. Always eager for plunder, these tough barbarians were attracted by the civilized delights they knew existed beyond the frontier of the Rhine and Danube rivers.

The most aggressive of the Germans in the third century C.E. were the Goths. Centuries earlier they had wandered from their ancestral home near the Baltic Sea into the area of southern Russia. In the 220s and 230s C.E. they began to put pressure on the Danube frontier. By about 250 C.E. they were able to penetrate the empire and overrun the Balkan provinces. The need to meet this threat and the one posed by the Persian Sassanids in the east made the Romans weaken their western frontiers, and other Germanic peoples—the Franks and the Alemanni—broke through in those regions. There was considerable danger that Rome would be unable to meet this challenge.

Rome's perils were caused, no doubt, by the unprecedentedly numerous and simultaneous attacks, but its internal weakness encouraged these attacks. The Roman army was not what it had been in its best days. By the second century C.E. it was made up mostly of romanized provincials. The pressure on the frontiers and epidemics of plague in the time of Marcus Aurelius forced the emperor to resort to the conscription of slaves, gladiators, barbarians, and brigands. The training and discipline with which the Romans had conquered the Mediterranean world had declined. The Romans also failed to respond to the new conditions of constant pressure on all the frontiers. A strong, mobile reserve that could meet a threat in one place without causing a weakness elsewhere might have helped, but no such unit was created.

Septimius Severus (r. 193–211 C.E.) and his successors played a crucial role in the transformation of the character of the Roman army. Septimius was a military usurper who owed everything to the support of his soldiers. He meant to establish a family dynasty, in contrast to the policy of the "good emperors" of the second century. He was prepared to make Rome into an undisguised military monarchy. Septimius drew recruits for the army increasingly from peasants of the less civilized provinces.

Economic Difficulties

These changes were a response to the great financial needs caused by the barbarian attacks. Inflation had forced Commodus to raise the soldiers' pay. Yet the Severan emperors had to double it to keep up with prices, which increased the imperial budget by as much as 25 percent. To raise money, the emperors resorted to inventing new taxes, debasing the coinage, and even selling the palace furniture. But it was still hard to recruit troops. The new style of military life introduced by Septimius—with its laxer discipline, more pleasant duties, and greater opportunity for advancement, not only in the army but in Roman society—was needed to attract men into the army. The policy proved effective for a short time but could not prevent the chaos of the late third century.

The same forces that caused problems for the army did great damage to society at large. The shortage of workers for the large farms, which had all but wiped out the independent family farm, reduced agricultural production. As external threats

A mosaic from Carthage illustrating aspects of life on the manorial estate of a certain Julian in the province of Africa. His housing, provisions, and entertainment appear to have been opulent. Social boundaries hardened in the late empire, and large fortified estates like this increasingly dominated social and economic life. [Photothèque du Musée du Bardo]

distracted the emperors, they were less able to preserve domestic peace. Piracy, brigandage, and the neglect of roads and harbors all hampered trade. So, too, did the debasement of the coinage and the inflation in general. Imperial taxation and confiscations of the property of the rich removed badly needed capital from productive use.

More and more the government was required to demand services that had been given gladly in the past. Because the empire lived hand-to-mouth, with no significant reserve fund and no system of credit financing, the emperors were led to compel the people to provide food, supplies, money, and labor. The upper classes in the cities were made to serve as administrators without pay and to meet deficits in revenue out of their own pockets. Sometimes these demands caused provincial rebellions, as in Egypt and Gaul. More typically they caused peasants and even town administrators to flee to escape their burdens. The result of all these difficulties was a weakening of Rome's economic strength when it was most needed.

The Social Order

The new conditions caused important changes in the social order. Direct attacks from hostile emperors and economic losses decimated the Senate and the traditional ruling class. Their ranks were filled by men coming up through the army. The whole state began to take on an increasingly military appearance. Distinctions among the classes by dress had been traditional since the republic; in the third and fourth centuries C.E. the people's everyday clothing had become a kind of uniform that precisely revealed status. Titles were assigned to ranks in society as to ranks in the army. The most important distinction was the one formally established by Septimius Severus, which drew a sharp line between the *honestiores* (senators, equestrians, the municipal aristocracy, and the soldiers) and the lower classes, or *humiliores*. Septimius gave the *honestiores* a privileged position before the law. They were given lighter punishments, could not be tortured, and alone had the right of appeal to the emperor.

As time passed, it became more difficult to move from the lower order to the higher, another example of the growing rigidity of the late Roman Empire. Peasants were tied to their lands, artisans to their crafts, soldiers to the army, merchants and shipowners to the needs of the state, and citizens of the municipal upper class to the collection and payment of increasingly burdensome taxes. Freedom and private initiative gave way before the needs of the state and its ever-expanding control of its citizens.

This ivory relief, carved a little after 395 C.E., shows a Vandal warrior, Stilicho, who rose to prominence in the Roman army. From the third century onward, the Roman army was composed increasingly of foreign mercenaries. [Monza Cathedral, Italy/Alinari/Art Resource, N.Y.]

Civil Disorder

Commodus was killed on the last day of 192 C.E. The succeeding year was similar to the year 69. Three emperors ruled in swift succession, Septimius Severus emerging, as we have seen, to establish firm rule and a dynasty. The death of Alexander Severus, the last of the dynasty, in 235 C.E., brought on a half century of internal anarchy and foreign invasion.

The empire seemed on the point of collapse. But the two conspirators who overthrew and succeeded the emperor Gallienus proved to be able soldiers. Claudius II Gothicus (268–270 C.E.) and Aurelian (270–275 C.E.) drove back the barbarians and stamped out internal disorder. The soldiers who followed Aurelian on the throne were good fighters who made significant changes in Rome's system of defense. Around Rome, Athens, and other cities they built heavy walls that could resist barbarian attack. They drew back their best troops from the frontiers, relying chiefly on a newly organized heavy cavalry and a mobile army near the emperor's own residence.

Hereafter the army was composed largely of mercenaries who came from among the least civilized provincials and even from among the Germans. The officers gave personal loyalty to the emperor rather than to the empire. These officers became a foreign, hereditary caste of aristocrats that increasingly supplied high administrators and even emperors. In effect, the Roman people hired an army of mercenaries, who were only technically Roman, to protect them.

The Late Empire

During the fourth and fifth centuries the Romans strove to meet the many challenges, internal and external, that threatened the survival of their empire. Growing pressure from barbarian tribes pushing against its frontier intensified the empire's tendency to smother individuality, freedom, and initiative, in favor of an increasingly intrusive and autocratic centralized monarchy. Economic and military weakness increased, and it became even harder to keep the vast empire together. Hard and dangerous times may well have helped the rise of Christianity, encouraging people to turn away from the troubles and dangers of this world to concern about the next.

The Fourth Century and Imperial Reorganization

The period from Diocletian (r. 284–305 C.E.) to Constantine (r. 306–337 C.E.) was one of reconstruction and reorganization after a time of civil war and turmoil. Diocletian was from Illyria (the former Yugoslavia). He was a man of undistinguished birth who rose to the throne through the ranks of the army. He knew that he was not a great general and that the job of defending and governing the entire empire was too great for one individual.

Diocletian therefore decreed the introduction of the *tetrarchy*, the rule of the empire by four men with power divided territorially. (See Map 5–4.) He allotted the provinces of Thrace, Asia, and Egypt to himself. His co-emperor, Maximian, shared with him the title of Augustus and governed Italy, Africa, and Spain. In addition, two men were given the subordinate title of Caesar: Galerius, who was in charge of the Danube frontier and the Balkans, and Constantius, who governed Britain and Gaul. This arrangement not only provided a good solution to the military problem but also provided for a peaceful succession.

Diocletian was recognized as the senior Augustus, but each tetrarch was supreme in his own sphere. The Caesars were recognized as successors to each half of the empire, and their loyalty was enhanced by marriages to daughters of the Augusti. It was a return, in a way, to the precedent of the "good emperors" of 96–180 C.E., who chose their successors from the ranks of the ablest men. It seemed to promise orderly and peaceful transitions instead of assassinations, chaos, and civil war.

Each man established his residence and capital at a place convenient for frontier defense, and none chose Rome. The effective capital of Italy became the northern city of Milan. Diocletian beautified Rome by constructing his monumental baths, but he visited the city only once and made his own capital at Nicomedia in Bithynia. This was another step in the long leveling process that had reduced the eminence of Rome and Italy. It was also evidence of the growing importance of the east.

In 305 C.E. Diocletian retired and compelled his co-emperor to do the same. But his plan for a smooth succession failed completely. In 310 there were five Augusti and no Caesars. Out of this chaos Constantine, son of Constantius, produced order. In 324 he defeated his last opponent and made himself sole emperor, uniting the empire once again; he reigned until 337. Mostly, Constantine carried forward the policies of Diocletian. He supported Christianity, however, which Diocletian had tried to suppress.

DEVELOPMENT OF AUTOCRACY The development of the imperial office toward autocracy was carried to the extreme by Diocletian and Constantine. The emperor ruled by decree, consulting only a few high officials whom he himself appointed. The Senate had no role whatever, and its dignity was further diminished by the elimination of all distinctions between senator and equestrian.

The emperor was a remote figure surrounded by carefully chosen high officials. He lived in a great palace and was almost unapproachable. Those admitted to his presence had to prostrate themselves before him and kiss the hem of his robe, which was purple and had golden threads going through it. The emperor was addressed as *dominus*, or "lord", and his right to rule was not derived from

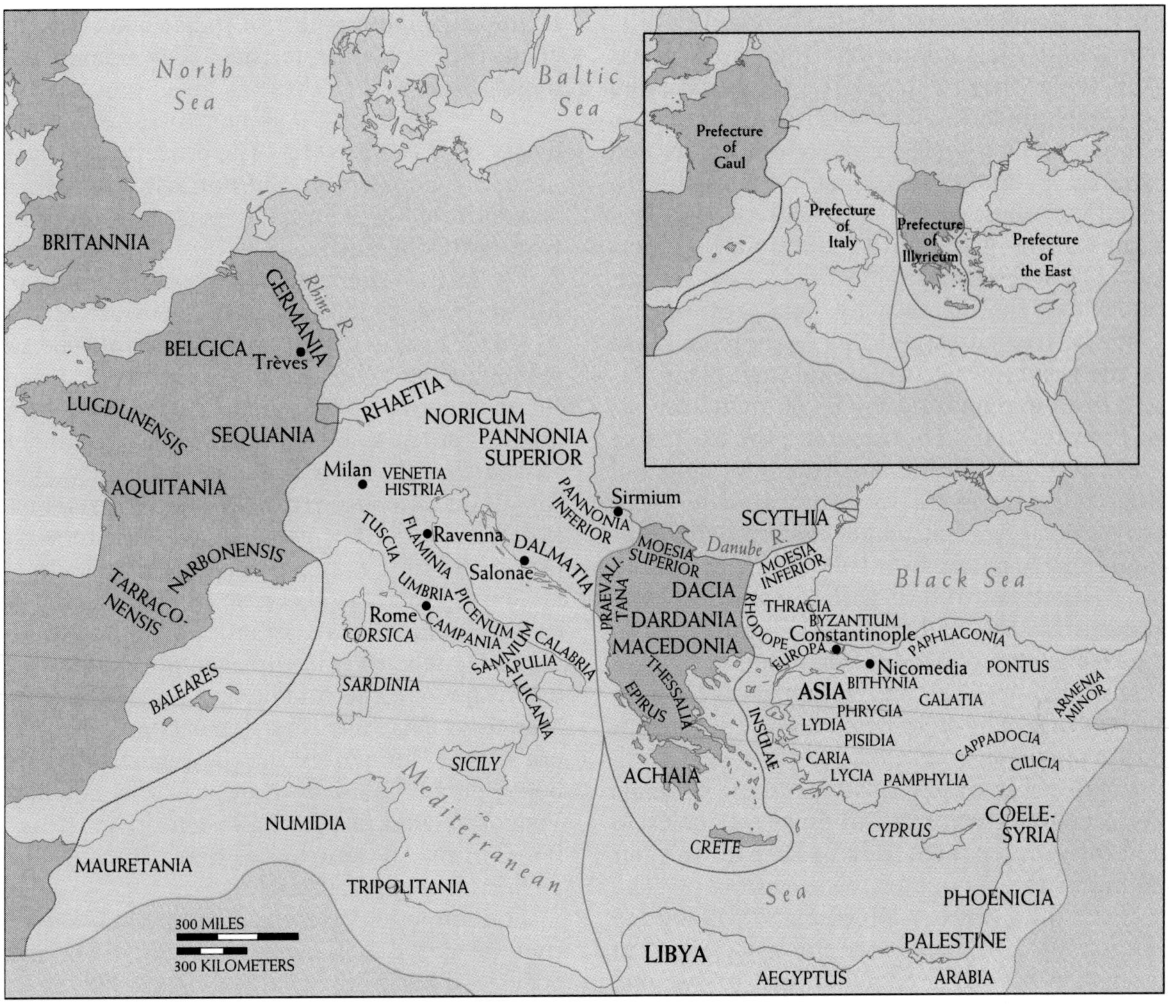

Map 5–4 Divisions of the Roman Empire Under Diocletian *Diocletian divided the sprawling empire into four prefectures for more effective government and defense. The inset map shows their boundaries, and the larger map gives some details of regions and provinces. The major division between east and west was along the line running south between Pannonia and Moesia.*

the Roman people but from heaven. All this remoteness and ceremony had a double purpose: to enhance the dignity of the emperor and to safeguard him against assassination.

Constantine erected the new city of Constantinople on the site of ancient Byzantium on the Bosporus, which leads to both the Aegean and Black seas. He made it the new capital of the empire. Its strategic location was excellent for protecting the eastern and Danubian frontiers, and, surrounded on three sides by water, it was easily defended. This location also made it easier to carry forward the policies that fostered autocracy and Christianity. Rome was full of tradition, the center of senatorial and even republican memories and of pagan worship. Constantinople was free from both, and its dedication in 330 C.E. marked the beginning of a new era. Until its fall to the Turks in 1453, it served as a bastion of civilization, the preserver of classical culture, a bulwark against barbarian attack, and the greatest city in Christendom.

The autocratic rule of the emperors was carried out by a civilian bureaucracy, carefully separated from the military to reduce the chances of rebellion by anyone combining the two kinds of power. Below the emperor's court the most important officials were the praetorian prefects, each of whom administered one of the four major areas into which the empire was divided: Gaul, Italy, Illyricum, and the Orient. The four prefectures were subdivided into twelve territorial units called *dioceses*, each under a vicar who was subordinate to the prefect. The dioceses were further divided into almost a hundred provinces, each under a provincial governor.

The operation of the entire system was supervised by a vast system of spies and secret police, without whom the increasingly rigid organization could not be trusted to perform. In spite of these efforts, the system was corrupt and inefficient.

The cost of maintaining a 400,000-man army as well as the vast civilian bureaucracy, the expensive imperial court, and the imperial taste for splendid buildings put a great strain on an already weak economy. Diocletian's attempts to establish a uniform and reliable currency failed, leading instead to increased inflation. To deal with it, he resorted to price control with his Edict of Maximum Prices in 301 C.E.. For each product and each kind of labor, a maximum price was set, and violations were punishable by death. The edict failed despite the harshness of its provisions.

Peasants unable to pay their taxes and officials unable to collect them tried to escape. Diocletian resorted to stern regimentation to keep all in their places and at the service of the government. The terror of the third century forced many peasants to seek protection in the *villa*, or "country estate," of a large and powerful landowner and to become tenant farming *coloni*. As social boundaries hardened, these *coloni* and their descendants became increasingly tied to these estates.

DIVISION OF THE EMPIRE The peace and unity established by Constantine did not last long. His death was followed by a struggle for succession that was won by Constantius II (r. 337–361 C.E.), whose death, in turn, left the empire to his young cousin Julian (r. 361–363 C.E.). Julian was called the Apostate by the Christians because of his attempt to stamp out Christianity and restore paganism. Julian undertook a campaign against Persia with the aim of putting a Roman on the throne of the Sassanids and ending the Persian menace once and for all. He penetrated deep into Persia but was killed in battle. His death put an end to the expedition and to the pagan revival.

The Germans in the West took advantage of the eastern campaign to attack along the Rhine and upper Danube rivers. And even greater trouble was brewing along the middle and upper Danube. (See Map 5–5.) That territory was occupied by the eastern Goths, known as the Ostrogoths. They were being pushed hard by their western cousins, the Visigoths, who in turn had been driven from their home in the Ukraine by the fierce Huns, a nomadic people from central Asia.

The emperor Valentinian (r. 364–375 C.E.) saw that he could not defend the empire alone and appointed his brother Valens (r. 364–378 C.E.) as co-

The Arch of Constantine, built in 315 C.E., represents a transition between classical and medieval, pagan and Christian. Many of the sculptures incorporated in it were taken from earlier works dating to the first and second centuries. Others, contemporary with the arch, reflect a new, less refined style. [Robert Miller]

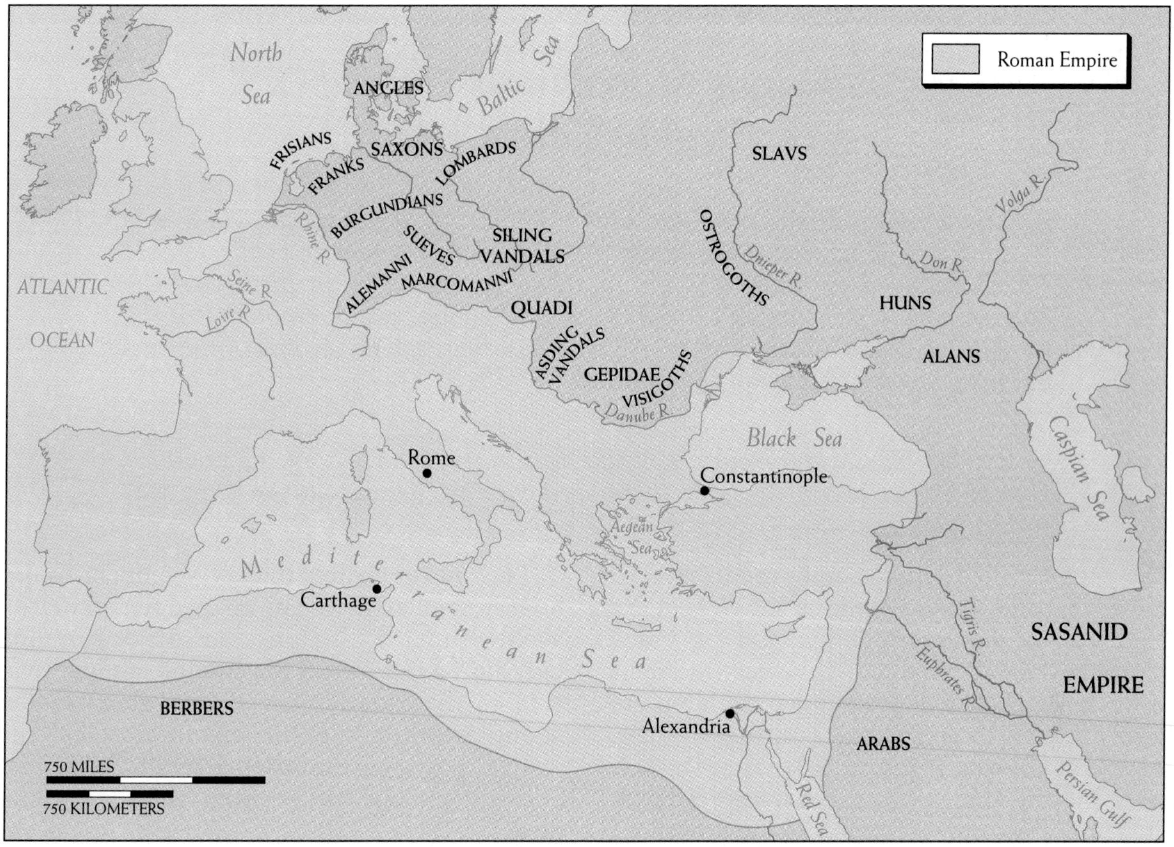

MAP 5–5 THE EMPIRE'S NEIGHBORS *In the fourth century the Roman Empire was nearly surrounded by ever more threatening neighbors. The map shows who these so-called barbarians were and where they lived before their armed contact with the Romans.*

ruler. Valentinian made his own headquarters at Milan and spent the rest of his life fighting successfully against the Franks and the Alemanni in the West. Valens was given control of the east. The empire was once again divided in two. The two emperors maintained their own courts, and the halves of the empire became increasingly separate and different. Latin was the language of the west and Greek of the east.

In 376 the Visigoths, pursued by the Huns, asked and received permission to enter the empire. Soon to be Christianized, they won rights of settlement and material assistance within the empire from the eastern emperor Valens (r. 364–378) in exchange for defending the eastern frontier as *foederati*, or special allies of the empire.

The Visigoths, however, did not keep their bargain with the Romans, retaining their weapons and plundering the Balkan provinces. Nor did the Romans comply: they treated the Visigoths cruelly, even forcing them to trade their children for dogs to eat. Valens attacked the Goths and died, along with most of his army, at Adrianople in Thrace in 378. Theodosius (r. 379–395 C.E.), an able and experienced general, was named co-ruler in the East. By a combination of military and diplomatic skills Theodosius pacified the Goths, giving them land and a high degree of autonomy and enrolling many of them in his army. He made important military reforms, putting greater emphasis on the cavalry. Theodosius tried to unify the empire again, but his death in 395 left it divided and weak.

THE RURAL WEST The two parts of the empire went their separate and different ways. The west became increasingly rural as barbarian invasions continued and grew in intensity. The villa, a fortified country estate, became the basic unit of life. There, *coloni* gave their services to the local magnate in return for economic assistance and protec-

Ammianus Marcellinus Describes the People Called Huns

Ammianus Marcellinus was born about 330 C.E. in Syria, where Greek was the language of his well-to-do family. After a military career and considerable travel, he lived in Rome and wrote an encyclopedic Latin history of the empire, covering the years 96 to 378 C.E. and giving special emphasis to the difficulties of the fourth century. Here he describes the Huns, one of the barbarous peoples pressing on the frontiers.

✦ *In what ways did the culture of the Huns differ from that of the Romans? How did their way of life give them an advantage against Rome? How was it disadvantageous?*

The people called Huns, barely mentioned in ancient records, live beyond the sea of Azof, on the border of the Frozen Ocean, and are a race savage beyond all parallel. At the very moment of birth the cheeks of their infant children are deeply marked by an iron, in order that the hair, instead of growing at the proper season on their faces, may be hindered by the scars; accordingly the Huns grow up without beards, and without any beauty. They all have closely knit and strong limbs and plump necks; they are of great size, and low legged, so that you might fancy them two-legged beasts or the stout figures which are hewn out in a rude manner with an ax on the posts at the end of bridges.

They are certainly in the shape of men, however uncouth, and are so hardy that they neither require fire nor well-flavored food, but live on the roots of such herbs as they get in the fields, or on the half-raw flesh of any animal, which they merely warm rapidly by placing it between their own thighs and the backs of their horses.

They never shelter themselves under roofed houses, but avoid them, as people ordinarily avoid sepulchers as things not fit for common use. Nor is there even to be found among them a cabin thatched with reeds; but they wander about, roaming over the mountains and the woods, and accustom themselves to bear frost and hunger and thirst from their very cradles. . . .

There is not a person in the whole nation who cannot remain on his horse day and night. On horseback they buy and sell, they take their meat and drink, and there they recline on the narrow neck of their steed, and yield to sleep so deep as to indulge in every variety of dream.

And when any deliberation is to take place on any weighty matter, they all hold their common council on horseback. They are not under kingly authority, but are contented with the irregular government of their chiefs, and under their lead they force their way through all obstacles. . . .

Ammianus Marcellinus, Res Gestae, *trans. by C. D. Yonge (London: George Bell and Son, 1862), pp. 312–314.*

tion from both barbarians and imperial officials. Many cities shrank to no more than tiny walled fortresses ruled by military commanders and bishops. The upper classes moved to the country and asserted ever greater independence of imperial authority. The failure of the central authority to maintain the roads and the constant danger from robber bands sharply curtailed trade and communications, forcing greater self-reliance and a more primitive style of life.

The new world emerging in the west by the fifth century and after was increasingly made up of iso-

Reigns of Selected Late Empire Rulers (All dates are C.E.)	
180–192	Commodus
193–211	Septimius Severus
222–235	Alexander Severus
249–251	Decius
253–260	Valerian
253–268	Gallienus
268–270	Claudius II Gothicus
270–275	Aurelian
284–305	Diocletian
306–337	Constantine
324–337	Constantine sole emperor
337–361	Constantius II
361–363	Julian the Apostate
364–375	Valentinian
364–378	Valens
379–395	Theodosius

lated units of rural aristocrats and their dependent laborers. The only institution providing a high degree of unity was the Christian Church. The pattern for the early Middle Ages in The West was already formed.

THE BYZANTINE EAST In the east the situation was quite different. Constantinople became the center of a vital and flourishing culture that we call Byzantine and that lasted until the fifteenth century. Because of its defensible location, the skill of its emperors, and the firmness and strength of its base in Asia Minor, it could deflect and repulse barbarian attacks. A strong navy allowed commerce to flourish in the eastern Mediterranean and, in good times, far beyond. Cities continued to prosper and the emperors made their will good over the nobles in the countryside. The civilization of the Byzantine Empire was a unique combination of classical culture, the Christian religion, Roman law, and eastern artistic influences.

While the west was being overrun by barbarians, the Roman Empire, in altered form, persisted in the east. While Rome shrank to an insignificant ecclesiastical town, Constantinople flourished as the seat of empire, the "New Rome." The Byzantines called themselves "Romans." When we contemplate the decline and fall of the Roman Empire in the fourth and fifth centuries, we are speaking only of the west. A form of classical culture persisted in the Byzantine East for a thousand years more.

The Triumph of Christianity

The rise of Christianity to dominance in the empire was closely connected with the political and cultural experience of the third and fourth centuries. Political chaos and decentralization had religious and cultural consequences.

RELIGIOUS CURRENTS IN THE EMPIRE In some of the provinces, native languages replaced Latin and Greek, sometimes even for official purposes. The classical tradition that had been the basis of imperial life became the exclusive possession of a small, educated aristocracy. In religion the public cults had grown up in an urban environment and were largely political in character. As the importance of the cities diminished, so did the significance of their gods. People might still take comfort in the worship of the friendly, intimate deities of family, field, hearth, storehouse, and craft, but these gods were too petty to serve their needs in a confused and frightening world. The only universal worship was of the emperor, but he was far off, and obeisance to his cult was more a political than a religious act.

In the troubled times of the fourth and fifth centuries people sought powerful, personal deities who would bring them safety and prosperity in this world and immortality in the next. Paganism was open and tolerant. It was by no means unusual for people to worship new deities alongside the old and even to intertwine elements of several to form a new amalgam by the device called *syncretism*.

Manichaeism was an especially potent rival of Christianity. Named for its founder, Mani, a Persian who lived in the third century C.E., this movement contained aspects of various religious traditions, including Zoroastrianism from Persia and both Judaism and Christianity. The Manichaeans pictured a world in which light and darkness, good and evil, were constantly at war. Good was spiritual and evil was material. Because human beings were made of matter, their bodies were a prison of evil and darkness, but they also contained an element of light and good. The "Father of Goodness" had sent Mani, among other prophets, to free humanity and gain its salvation. To achieve salvation, humans must want to reach the realm of light and to abandon all physical desires. Manichaeans led an ascetic life and practiced a simple worship guided by a well-organized Church. The movement reached its greatest strength in the fourth and fifth centuries,

Map 5–6 The Spread of Christianity *Christianity grew swiftly in the third, fourth, fifth, and sixth centuries—especially after the conversion of the emperors in the fourth century. By 600, on the eve of the birth of the new religion of Islam, Christianity was dominant throughout the Mediterranean world and most of western Europe.*

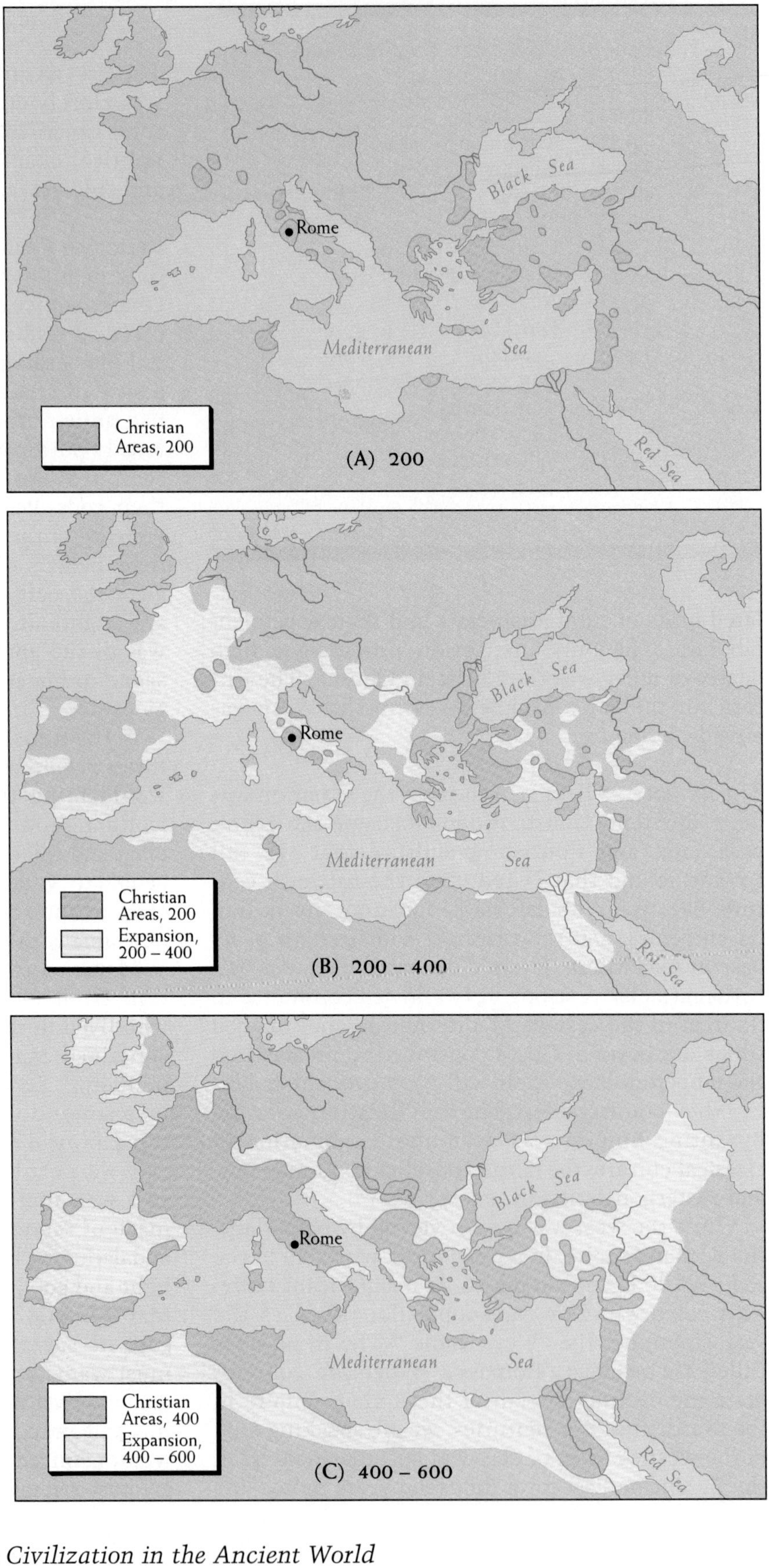

and some of its central ideas persisted into the Middle Ages.

Christianity had something in common with these cults and answered many of the same needs felt by their devotees. None of them, however, attained Christianity's universality, and none appears to have given the early Christians and their leaders as much competition as the ancient philosophies or the state religion.

Imperial Persecution By the third century Christianity had taken firm hold in the eastern provinces and in Italy. It had not made much headway in the west, however. (See Map 5–6.) Christian apologists pointed out that Christians were good citizens who differed from others only in not worshiping the public gods. Until the middle of the third century, the emperors tacitly accepted this view, without granting official toleration. As times became bad and the Christians became more numerous and visible, that policy changed. Popular opinion blamed disasters, natural and military, on the Christians.

About 250 the emperor Decius (r. 249–251 C.E.) invoked the aid of the gods in his war against the Goths and required that all citizens worship the state gods publicly. True Christians could not obey, and Decius started a major persecution. Many Christians, even some bishops, yielded to threats and torture, but others held out and were killed. Valerian (r. 253–260 C.E.) resumed the persecutions, partly to confiscate the wealth of rich Christians. His successors, however, found other matters more pressing, and the persecution lapsed until the end of the century.

By the time of Diocletian the number of Christians had grown still greater and included some high state officials. At the same time hostility to the Christians grew on every level. Diocletian was not generous toward unorthodox intellectual or religious movements. His own effort to bolster imperial power with the aura of divinity boded ill for the church, and in 303, he launched the most serious persecution inflicted on the Christians in the Roman Empire. He issued a series of edicts confiscating church property and destroying churches and their sacred books. He deprived upper-class Christians of public office and judicial rights, imprisoned clergy, and enslaved Christians of the lower classes. He placed heavy fines on anyone refusing to sacrifice to the public gods. A final decree required public sacrifices and libations. The persecution horrified many pagans, and the plight and the demeanor of the martyrs often aroused pity and sympathy.

Ancient states could not carry out a program of terror with the thoroughness of modern totalitarian governments, and so the Christians and their church survived to enjoy what they must have considered a miraculous change of fortune. In 311 Galerius, who had been one of the most vigorous persecutors, was influenced, perhaps by his Christian wife, to issue the Edict of Toleration, permitting Christian worship.

The victory of Constantine and his emergence as sole ruler of the empire changed the condition of Christianity from a precariously tolerated sect to the religion favored by the emperor. This put it on the path to becoming the official and only legal religion in the empire.

Emergence of Christianity as the State Religion The sons of Constantine continued to favor the new religion, but the succession of Julian the Apostate posed a new threat. He was a devotee of traditional classical pagan culture and, as a believer in Neoplatonism, an opponent of Christianity. Neoplatonism was a religious philosophy, or a philosophical religion, whose connection with Platonic teachings was distant. Its chief formulator was Plotinus (205–270 C.E.), who tried to combine classical and rational philosophical speculation with the mystical spirit of his time. Plotinus's successors were bitter critics of Christianity, and their views influenced Julian. Though he refrained from persecution, he tried to undo the work of Constantine by withdrawing the privileges of the church, removing Christians from high offices, and attempting to introduce a new form of pagan worship. His reign, however, was short, and his work did not last.

In 394 Theodosius forbade the celebration of pagan cults and abolished the pagan religious calendar. At his death Christianity was the official religion of the Roman Empire.

The establishment of Christianity as the state religion did not put an end to the troubles of the Christians and their church; instead it created new ones and complicated some old ones. The favored position of the church attracted converts for the wrong reasons and diluted the moral excellence and spiritual fervor of its adherents. The problem of the relationship between church and state arose, presenting the possibility that religion would become subordinate to the state, as it had been in the classical world and in earlier civilizations. In the East that is what happened to a considerable degree.

In the West the weakness of the emperors prevented such a development and permitted church leaders to exercise remarkable independence. In 390 Ambrose, bishop of Milan, excommunicated Theodosius for a massacre he had carried out, and the emperor did humble penance. This act provided an important precedent for future assertions of the church's autonomy and authority, but it did not put an end to secular interference and influence in the church.

ARIANISM AND THE COUNCIL OF NICAEA Internal divisions proved to be even more troubling as new heresies emerged. Because they threatened the unity of an empire that was now Christian, they took on a political character and inevitably involved the emperor and the powers of the state. Before long, the world would view Christians persecuting other Christians with a zeal at least as great as had been displayed against them by the most fanatical pagans.

Among the many controversial views that arose, the most important and the most threatening was Arianism. It was founded by a priest named Arius of Alexandria (ca. 280–336 C.E.) in the fourth century. The issue creating difficulty was the relation of God the Father and God the Son. Arius argued that Jesus was a created being, unlike God the Father. He was, therefore, not made of the substance of God and was not eternal. "The Son has a beginning," he said, "but God is without beginning." For Arius, Jesus was neither fully man nor fully God but something in between. Arius's view did away with the mysterious concept of the Trinity, the difficult doctrine that holds that God is three persons (the Father, the Son, and the Holy Spirit) and also one in substance and essence.

The Arian concept had the advantage of appearing to be simple, rational, and philosophically acceptable. To its ablest opponent, Athanasius, however, it had serious shortcomings. Athanasius (ca. 293–373 C.E.), later bishop of Alexandria, saw the Arian view as an impediment to any acceptable theory of salvation, to him the most important religious question. He adhered to the old Greek idea of salvation as involving the change of sinful mortality into divine immortality through the gift of "life." Only if Jesus were both fully human and fully God could the transformation of humanity to divinity have taken place in him and be transmitted by him to his disciples. "Christ was made man," he said, "that we might be made divine."

To deal with the growing controversy, Constantine called a council of Christian bishops at Nicaea, not far from Constantinople, in 325. For the emperor the question was essentially political, but for the disputants salvation was at stake. At Nicaea the view expounded by Athanasius won out, became orthodox, and was embodied in the Nicene Creed. But Arianism persisted and spread. Some later emperors were either Arians or sympathetic to that view. Some of the most successful missionaries to the barbarians were Arians; as a result, many of the German tribes that overran the empire were Arians. The Christian emperors hoped to bring unity to their increasingly decentralized realms by imposing the single religion. Over time it did prove to be a unifying force, but it also introduced divisions where none had existed before.

Arts and Letters in the Late Empire

The art and literature of the late empire reflect the confluence of pagan and Christian ideas and traditions as well as the conflict between them. Much of the literature is of a polemical nature and much of the art is propaganda.

The salvation of the empire from the chaos of the third century was accomplished by a military revolution based on and led by provincials whose origins were in the lower classes. They brought

The Triumph of Christianity

ca. 4 B.C.E.	Jesus of Nazareth born
ca. 30 C.E.	Crucifixion of Jesus
64 C.E.	Fire at Rome—persecution by Nero
ca. 70–100 C.E.	Gospels written
ca. 250–260 C.E.	Major persecutions by Decius and Valerian
303 C.E.	Persecution by Diocletian
311 C.E.	Galerius issues Edict of Toleration
312 C.E.	Battle of Milvian Bridge—conversion of Constantine to Christianity
325 C.E.	Council of Nicaea
395 C.E.	Christianity becomes official religion of Roman Empire

This late-Roman ivory plaque shows a scene from Christ's Passion. The art of the late empire was transitional between the classical past and the medieval future. [British Museum, London. The Bridgeman Art Library]

with them the fresh winds of cultural change, which blew out not only the dust of classical culture but much of its substance as well. Yet the new ruling class was not interested in leveling; it wanted instead to establish itself as a new aristocracy. It thought of itself as effecting a great restoration rather than a revolution and sought to restore classical culture and absorb it. The confusion and uncertainty of the times were tempered in part, of course, by the comfort of Christianity. But the new ruling class sought order and stability—ethical, literary, and artistic—in the classical tradition as well.

THE PRESERVATION OF CLASSICAL CULTURE One of the main needs and accomplishments of this period was the preservation of classical culture. Ways were discovered to make it available and useful to the newly arrived ruling class. Works of the great classical authors were reproduced in many copies and were transferred from perishable and inconvenient papyrus rolls to sturdier codices, bound volumes that were as easy to use as modern books. Scholars also digested long works like Livy's *History of Rome* into shorter versions and wrote learned commentaries and compiled grammars. Original works by pagan writers of the late empire were neither numerous nor especially distinguished.

CHRISTIAN WRITERS On the other hand, the late empire saw a great outpouring of Christian writings. There were many examples of Christian apologetics in poetry as well as in prose, and there were sermons, hymns, and biblical commentaries. Christianity could also boast important scholars. Jerome (348–420 C.E.), thoroughly trained in both the east and the west in classical Latin literature and rhetoric, produced a revised version of the Bible in Latin. Commonly called the Vulgate, it became the Bible used by the Catholic Church. Probably the most important eastern scholar was Eusebius of Caesarea (ca. 260–340 C.E.). He wrote apologetics, an idealized biography of Constantine, and a valuable attempt to reconstruct the chronology of important events in the past. His most important contribution, however, was his *Ecclesiastical History*, an attempt to set forth the Christian view of history. He saw all of history as the working out of God's will. All of history, therefore, had a purpose and a direction, and Constantine's victory and the subsequent unity of empire and church were its culmination.

The closeness and also the complexity of the relationship between classical pagan culture and that of the Christianity of the late empire are nowhere better displayed than in the career and writings of Augustine (354–430 C.E.), bishop of Hippo in North Africa. He was born at Carthage and was trained as a teacher of rhetoric. His father was a pagan, but his mother was a Christian and hers was ultimately the stronger influence. He passed through several intellectual way stations, skepticism and Neoplatonism among others, before his conversion to Christianity. His training and skill in pagan rhetoric and philosophy made him peerless among his contemporaries as a defender of Christianity and as a theologian.

His greatest works are his *Confessions*, an autobiography describing the road to his conversion, and *The City of God*. The latter was a response to the pagan charge that Rome's sack by the Visigoths in 410 was caused by the abandonment of the old gods and the advent of Christianity. The optimistic view held by some Christians that God's will worked its way in history and was easily comprehensible needed further support in the face of the Vigigoths' sack of Rome. Augustine sought to separate the fate of Christianity from that of the Roman Empire. He contrasted the secular world, the City of Man, with the spiritual, the City of God. The former was selfish, the latter unselfish; the former evil, the latter good.

Augustine argued that history was moving forward, in the spiritual sense, to the Day of Judgment but there was no reason to expect improvement before then in the secular sphere. The fall of Rome was neither surprising nor important. All states, even a Christian Rome, were part of the City of Man and were therefore corrupt and mortal. Only the City of God was immortal, and it, consisting of all the saints on earth and in heaven, was untouched by earthly calamities.

Though the *Confessions* and *The City of God* are Augustine's most famous works, they emphasize only a part of his thought. His treatises *On the Trinity* and *On Christian Education* reveal the great skill with which he supported Christian belief with the learning, logic, and philosophy of the pagan classics. Augustine believed that faith is essential and primary (a thoroughly Christian view), but it is not a substitute for reason (the foundation of classical thought). Instead, faith is the starting point for and liberator of human reason, which continues to be the means by which people can understand what faith reveals. His writings constantly reveal the presence of both Christian faith and pagan reason, as well as the tension between them, a legacy he left to the Middle Ages.

The Problem of the Decline and Fall of the Empire in the West

Whether important to Augustine or not, the massive barbarian invasions of the fifth century put an end to effective imperial government in the west. For centuries people have speculated about the causes of the collapse of the ancient world. Every kind of reason has been put forward, and some suggestions seem to have nothing to do with reason at all. Soil exhaustion, plague, climatic change, and even poisoning caused by lead water pipes have been suggested as reasons for Rome's decline in population, vigor, and the capacity to defend itself. Some blame the institution of slavery and a resulting failure to make advances in science and technology. Others blame excessive government interference in the economic life of the empire, and still others the destruction of the urban middle class, the carrier of classical culture.

Perhaps a simpler and more obvious explanation can be found. It might begin with the observation that the growth of so mighty an empire as Rome's was by no means inevitable. Rome's greatness had come from conquests that provided the Romans with the means to expand still further, until there were not enough Romans to conquer and govern any more peoples and territory. When pressure from outsiders grew, the Romans lacked the resources to advance and defeat the enemy as in the past. The tenacity and success of their resistance for so long were remarkable. Without new conquests to provide the immense wealth needed for the defense and maintenance of internal prosperity, the Romans finally yielded to unprecedented onslaughts by fierce and numerous attackers.

To blame the ancients and the institution of slavery for the failure to produce an industrial and economic revolution like that of the later Western world (one capable of producing wealth without taking it from another) is to stand the problem on its head. No one yet has a satisfactory explanation for those revolutions. So it is improper to blame any institution or society for not achieving what has been achieved only once in human history. Perhaps we would do well to think of the problem as Gibbon did:

> The decline of Rome was the natural and inevitable effect of immoderate greatness. Prosperity ripened the principle of decay; the cause of the destruction multiplied with the extent of conquest; and, as soon as time or accident had removed the artificial supports, the stupendous fabric yielded to the pressure of its own weight. The story of the ruin is simple and obvious; and instead of inquiring why the Roman Empire was destroyed, we should rather be surprised that it had subsisted so long.[5]

✦

Out of the civil wars and chaos that brought down the republic, Augustus brought unity, peace, order, and prosperity. As a result he was regarded with almost religious awe and attained more military and political power than any Roman before him. He ruled firmly but with moderation. He tried to limit military adventures and the costs they incurred. Augustus supported public works that encouraged trade and communication in the empire. He tried to restore and invigorate the old civic pride, and in this he had considerable success. He was less successful in promoting private morality based on family values. He patronized the arts so as to beautify Rome and glorify his reign. On his death Augustus was able to pass on the regime to his family, the Julio-Claudians.

For almost two hundred years, with a few brief interruptions, the empire was generally prosperous, peaceful, and well run. But problems were growing. Management of the many responsibilities assumed by the government required the growth of a large bureaucracy that placed a heavy and increasing burden on the treasury, required higher taxes, and stifled both civic spirit and private enterprise. Pressure from barbarian tribes on the frontiers required a large standing army, which was also very costly and led to further rises in taxation.

In the late empire Rome's rulers resorted to many devices for dealing with their problems. Policies came to include putting down internal military rebellions led by generals from different parts of the empire. More and more, the emperors' rule and their safety depended on the loyalty of the army, and so they courted the soldiers' favor with gifts of various kinds. This only increased the burden of taxes; the rich and powerful found ways to avoid their obligations, making the load on everyone else all the heavier. The government's control over the lives of its people became ever greater and the society more rigid as people tried to flee to escape the crushing load of taxes. Expedients were tried, including inflating the currency, fixing farmers to the soil as serfs or coloni, *building walls to keep the barbarians out, and bribing barbarian tribes to fight for Rome against other barbarians. Ultimately, all these measures failed. The Roman Empire in the west fell, leaving disunity, insecurity, disorder, and poverty. Like similar empires in the ancient world, it had been unable to sustain its "immoderate greatness."*

Review Questions

1. Discuss the Augustan constitution and government. What solutions did Augustus provide for the problems that had plagued the Roman Republic? Why was the Roman population willing to accept Augustus as head of the state?
2. How was the Roman Empire organized and why did it function smoothly? What role did the

[5]*Edward Gibbon,* The History of the Decline and Fall of the Roman Empire, *2nd ed., Vol. 4, ed. by J. B. Bury (London: 1909), pp. 173–174.*

emperor play in the maintenance of political stability?

3. How did the literature in the Golden Age of Augustus differ from that of the Silver Age during the first and second centuries C.E.? How did the poetry of Vergil and Horace contribute to the stability of Augustus's rule?
4. In spite of unpromising beginnings, Christianity was enormously popular by the fourth century C.E. Why were Christians persecuted by Roman authorities? What were the more important reasons for Christianity's success?
5. What were the political, social, and economic problems that beset Rome in the third and fourth centuries C.E.? How did Diocletian and Constantine deal with them? Were they effective in stemming the tide of decline and disintegration in the Roman Empire? What problems were they unable to solve?
6. Discuss three theories that scholars have advanced to explain the decline and fall of the Roman Empire. What are the difficulties involved in explaining the fall? What explanation would you give?

Suggested Readings

J. P. V. D. Balsdon, *Roman Women* (1962). A standard treatment.

T. Barnes, *The New Empire of Diocletian and Constantine* (1982). A study of the character of the late empire.

P. Brown, *Augustine of Hippo* (1967). A splendid biography.

P. Brown, *The World of Late Antiquity, C.E. 150–750* (1971). A brilliant and readable essay.

J. Burckhardt, *The Age of Constantine the Great* (1956). A classic work by the Swiss cultural historian.

C. M. Cochrane, *Christianity and Classical Culture* (1957). A study of intellectual change in the late empire.

S. Dill, *Roman Society in the Last Century of the Western Empire* (1958). A classic social history.

E. R. Dodds, *Pagan and Christian in an Age of Anxiety* (1965). An original and perceptive study.

A. Ferrill, *The Fall of the Roman Empire, The Military Explanation* (1986). An interpretation that emphasizes the decline in the quality of the Roman army.

A. Ferrill, *Caligula: Emperor of Rome* (1991). A biography of the monstrous young emperor.

E. Gibbon, *The History of the Decline and Fall of the Roman Empire*, 7 vols., ed. by J. B. Bury, 2nd ed. (1909–1914). One of the masterworks of the English language.

M. Grant, *The Fall of the Roman Empire* (1990). A lively, well-written account.

T. R. Holmes, *Architect of the Roman Empire*, 2 vols. (1928–1931). An account of Augustus's career in detail.

A. H. M. Jones, *The Later Roman Empire*, 3 vols. (1964). A comprehensive study of the period.

D. Kagan, ed., *The End of the Roman Empire: Decline or Transformation?* 3rd. ed. (1992). A collection of essays discussing the problem of the decline and fall of the Roman Empire.

M. L. W. Laistner, *The Greater Roman Historians* (1963). Essays on the major Roman historical writers.

J. Lebreton and J. Zeiller, *History of the Primitive Church*, 3 vols. (1962). The Catholic viewpoint.

H. Lietzmann, *History of the Early Church*, 2 vols. (1961). From the Protestant viewpoint.

E. N. Luttwak, *The Grand Strategy of the Roman Empire* (1976). An original and fascinating analysis by a keen student of modern strategy.

R. MacMullen, *Enemies of the Roman Order* (1966). An original and revealing examination of opposition to the emperors.

R. MacMullen, *Roman Social Relations, 50 B.C. to A.D. 284* (1981). An interesting study of social developments.

R. MacMullen, *Corruption and the Decline of Rome* (1988). A study that examines the importance of changes in ethical ideas and behavior.

R. W. Mathison, *Roman Aristocrats in Barbarian Gaul: Strategies for Survival* (1993). An unusual slant on the late empire.

F. G. B. Millar, *The Roman Empire and Its Neighbors* (1968). An analysis of Roman foreign relations in the imperial period.

F. G. B. Millar, *The Emperor in the Roman World, 31 B.C.–A.D. 337* (1977). A study of Roman imperial government.

A. Momigliano, ed., *The Conflict Between Paganism and Christianity* (1963). A valuable collection of essays.

H. M. D. Parker, *A History of the Roman World from A.D. 138 to 337* (1969). A good survey.

M. I. Rostovtzeff, *Social and Economic History of the Roman Empire*, 2nd. ed. (1957). A masterpiece whose main thesis has been much disputed.

V. Rudich, *Political Dissidence Under Nero, The Price of Dissimulation* (1993). A brilliant exposition of the lives and thoughts of political dissidents in the early empire.

E. T. Salmon, *A History of the Roman World, 30 B.C. to 138 A.D.* (1968). A good survey.

C. G. Starr, *Civilization and the Caesars* (1965). A study of Roman culture in the Augustan period.

G. E. M. de Ste. Croix, *The Class Struggle in the Ancient World* (1981). An ambitious interpretation of all of clas-

sical civilization from an idiosyncratic Marxist perspective.
R. SYME, *The Roman Revolution* (1960). A brilliant study of Augustus, his supporters, and their rise to power.
L. R. TAYLOR, *The Divinity of the Roman Empire* (1931). A study of the imperial cult.

The Middle Ages, 476–1300

During the eight centuries between the fall of Rome and the beginning of the Renaissance, the major institutions of western European civilization acquired a definite shape. These same centuries saw Eastern, or Byzantine, civilization peak and Islamic civilization rise and crest; both were militarily and culturally superior to the West. The many formative outside influences that had come upon the West from the Byzantine Empire, the migrating Germanic tribes, and the Islamic world during the early Middle Ages were folded into a distinctive Western civilization.

The Middle Ages saw the division of Christendom into two very different and opposed Christian churches: the Western church, centered in Rome, and the Byzantine Church, centered in Constantinople. The Roman Catholic Church emerged from the chaos of the Roman Empire's collapse as a major custodian of Western culture. Firmly based in the cities and directed by the pope from Rome, its broad network of loyal clergy made it the only Western institution capable of extending its influence over many diverse regions.

The Carolingian rulers came to power in the seventh century and, with the assistance of the church, brought a modest revival of Western imperial pretensions. Particularly during the long reign of Charlemagne, Christian bishops and clergy became important allies in the organization of the Carolingian Empire, both in the countryside and in the towns.

New developments in farming increased the productivity of the rural manors, where 95 percent of the population lived. By Charlemagne's time a better harness for oxen and ploughs that could cut deeply into the soil, furrowing it, improved crop yields. Rotation of crops among three fields kept land fertile and productive. These new techniques stimulated population growth and cultural development.

In the twelfth and thirteenth centuries, thanks to a great rise in mercantile activity, towns and urban culture grew rapidly. A new merchant class emerged in the towns and took its place alongside the nobility and the clergy. Rulers increasingly drew on this class for servants and administrators. This group formed a loyal bureaucracy and brain trust that allowed rulers to challenge both the nobility and the church successfully. The alliance between rulers and towns was an important factor in the rise of Europe's new secular monarchies and the creation of Europe's major nation-states.

In the twelfth and thirteenth centuries in England and France, the foundations of Western monarchies were laid. Parliaments and popular assemblies also formed to represent the growing power of the privileged classes (that is, the nobility, the clergy, and property-owning townspeople). Western capitalism was at this time in the birthing chair. The new wealth created by trade and conquest made possible the creation of universities, which multiplied to twenty in Catholic Europe by 1300.

Emperors and kings clashed repeatedly with popes during the twelfth and thirteenth centuries, when the Roman Catholic Church was still a formidable political power. At the end of the Investiture Controversy in the twelfth century, a clear distinction was drawn between the spheres of ecclesiastical and secular authority. After 1300, monarchs progressively limited the church's influence over their political and economic affairs, restricting the church to the important but less threatening spiritual and cultural sphere of influence.

The Crusades to the Holy Land attested to the church's continuing popularity in the high Middle Ages, even though these ventures had acquired a mercenary character by the thirteenth century. In an increasingly materialistic age, the rise of the Dominican and Franciscan friars signaled a new spiritual revival among the clergy that also attracted large numbers of pious laity. Until the Reformation, church reformers rallied under the banner of apostolic poverty. ✦

3 0 0 - 1 3 0 0 C.E.

	POLITICS AND GOVERNMENT	SOCIETY AND ECONOMY	RELIGION AND CULTURE
300–500	315 **Constantinople becomes new capital of Roman Empire** 410 **Visigoths sack Rome** 451–453 **Attila the Hun invades Italy** 455 **Vandals overrun Rome** 476 **Odovacer deposes the last Western emperor** 489–493 **Theodoric's Ostrogoth kingdom established in Italy**	400 **Cities and trade begin to decline in the West; Germanic (barbarian) tribes settle in the West**	312 **Constantine embraces Christianity** 325 **Council of Nicaea** 380 **Christianity becomes the official religion of the Roman Empire** 413–426 **Saint Augustine writes *City of God*** 451 **Council of Chalcedon** 496 **The Franks embrace Christianity**
500–700	527–565 **Reign of Justinian** 568 **Lombard invasion of Italy** 632–733 **Muslim expansion and conquests**	533–534 ***Corpus juris civilis* compiled by Justinian** 632–733 **Muslims disrupt western Mediterranean trade**	529 **Saint Benedict founds monastery at Monte Cassino** 537 **Byzantine Church of Hagia Sophia completed** 590–604 **Pope Gregory the Great** 622 **Muhammad's flight from Mecca (Hegira)**
700–900	734 **Charles Martel defeats Muslims at Poltiers** 768–814 **Reign of Charlemagne** 843 **Treaty of Verdun partitions Carolingian empire**	700 **Agrarian society centered around the manor predominates in the west** 700–800 **Moldboard plow and three field system in use** 700 **Islam enters its Golden Age** 800 **Byzantium enters its Golden Age** 800 **Introduction of collar harness** 850 **Muslims occupy parts of Spain** 880s **Vikings penetrate central Europe**	725–787 **Iconoclastic Controversy in East** ca. 775 ***Donation of Constantine*** 782 **Alcuin of York runs Charlemagne's palace school** 800 **Pope Leo crowns Charlemagne emperor**

Interior of Hagia Sophia

900–1100

POLITICS AND GOVERNMENT

918 Saxon Henry I becomes first non-Frankish king, as Saxons succeed Carolingians in Germany

987 Capetians succeed Carolingians in France

1066 Battle of Hastings (Norman Conquest of England)

Harold's crowning. The Bayeux Tapestry

1071 Seljuk Turks defeat Byzantine armies at Manzikert

1099 Jerusalem falls to Crusaders

SOCIETY AND ECONOMY

900 Introduction of the horseshoe

900–1100 Rise of towns, guilds, and urban culture in West

1086 *Domesday Book*

RELIGION AND CULTURE

910 Benedictine monastery of Cluny founded

980s Orthodox Christianity penetrates Russia

1054 Schism between Eastern and Western churches

1075 Pope Gregory VII condemns lay investiture

1095 Pope Urban II preaches the First Crusade

1100–1300

POLITICS AND GOVERNMENT

1152 Frederick I Barbarossa first Hohenstaufen emperor

1187 Saladin reconquers Jerusalem from West

1204 Fourth Crusade captures Constantinople

1214 Philip II Augustus defeats English and German armies at Bouvines

1215 Magna Carta

1240 Mongols dominate Russia

1250 Death of Frederick II (end of Hohenstaufen dynasty)

1257 German princes establish electoral college to elect emperor

SOCIETY AND ECONOMY

1130 Gothic architecture begins to displace Romanesque

1200 Shift from dues to rent tenancy on manors

RELIGION AND CULTURE

1122 Concordat of Worms ends Investiture Controversy

1158 First European university founded in Bologna

1210 Franciscan order founded

1216 Dominican order founded

1265 Thomas Aquinas's *Summa Theologica* begun

ca. 1275 *Romance of the Rose*

CHAPTER 6

A decorated initial from the opening page of the Gospel of St. Matthew. From the Lindisfarne Gospels, *ca. 725. [British Library, London. Bridgeman/Art Resource, N.Y.]*

The Early Middle Ages (476–1000):
The Birth of Europe

KEY TOPICS

- How the fusion of Germanic and Roman culture laid the foundation for a distinctively European society after the collapse of the western Roman Empire
- The Byzantine and Islamic empires and their impact on the West
- The role of the church in Western society during the early Middle Ages
- The political and economic features of Europe under the Franks
- The characteristics of feudal society

The early Middle Ages mark the birth of Europe. This period of recovery from the collapse of Roman civilization gave rise to forced experimentation with new ideas and institutions. Greco-Roman culture combined with the new Germanic culture and an evolving Christianity to create distinctive political and cultural forms within what had been the northern and western provinces of the Roman Empire. In government, religion, and language, as well as geography, these regions grew separate from the Eastern Byzantine world and the Islamic Arab world, which extended across North Africa from Spain to the eastern Mediterranean.

The early Middle Ages have been called, not with complete fairness, a "dark age," because during these centuries western Europe lost touch with classical, especially Greek, learning and science. People the Romans somewhat arrogantly called "barbarians"—because their origins were rural and they knew no Latin—intruded on the region from the north and east. German tribes that had been settling peacefully around the empire since the first century B.C.E. *began to migrate directly into it by the fourth century. During the fifth century, these tribes turned fiercely against their Roman hosts, largely because the Romans treated them so cruelly. To the south, Arab dominance transformed the Mediterranean into an often inhospitable "Islamic lake," greatly reducing (although by no means completely sev-*

ering) Western trade with the East and isolating Western people more than they had been before. Thus surrounded and assailed from north, east, and south, Europe understandably became somewhat insular and even stagnant.

On the other hand, being forced to manage by themselves, western Europeans also learned to develop their native resources. The reign of Charlemagne saw a modest renaissance of antiquity. And the peculiar social and political forms that emerged during this period—manorialism and feudalism—not only were successful at coping with unprecedented chaos on local levels but also proved to be fertile seedbeds for the growth of distinctive Western institutions.

On the Eve of the Frankish Ascendancy

As we have already seen, by the late third century the Roman Empire had become too large for a single sovereign to govern and was failing in many respects. The emperor Diocletian (r. 284–305) tried to strengthen the empire by dividing it between himself and a co-emperor, Maximian. The result was a dual empire with an eastern and a western half, each with its own emperor and, eventually, imperial bureaucracy. A critical shift of the empire's resources and orientation to the eastern half accompanied these changes. In 284 Diocletian moved to Nicomedia (in modern Turkey), where he remained until the last two years of his reign. As imperial rule weakened in the West and strengthened in the East, it also became increasingly autocratic.

In an attempt to end the factional strife that followed Diocletian's reign and to position himself better to meet the empire's new eastern enemies, Constantine the Great (r. 306–337) briefly reunited the empire by conquest (it would be redivided by his three sons and subsequent successors) and ruled as sole emperor of the eastern and western halves after 324. In that year he moved the capital of the empire from Rome to Byzantium, an ancient city that stood at the crossroads of the major sea and land routes between Europe and Asia Minor. On the site of this ancient city, Constantine built the new city of Constantinople, dedicated in 330. Serving as the imperial residence and the new administrative center of the empire, Constantinople gradually became a "new Rome." The "old" Rome, suffering from internal political quarrels and geographically distant from new military fronts in Syria and along the Danube River, declined in importance. The city and the western empire were actually on the wane in the late third and fourth centuries, well before the barbarian invasions in the West began. Milan had replaced Rome as the imperial residence in 286; in 402 the seat of Western government would be moved yet again, to Ravenna. When the barbarian invasions began in the late fourth century, the West was in political disarray, and imperial power and prestige had shifted decisively to Constantinople and the East.

Germanic Migrations

The German tribes did not burst in on the West all of a sudden. They were at first a token and benign presence on the fringes of the empire and even within it. Before the massive migrations from the north and the east, Roman and Germanic cultures had commingled peacefully for centuries. The Romans had "imported" barbarians as domestics, slaves, and soldiers. Barbarian soldiers rose to positions of high leadership and fame in Roman legions.

Beginning in 376 with a great influx of Visigoths, or "west Goths," into the empire, this peaceful coexistence ended. The Visigoths, accomplished horsemen and fierce warriors, were themselves pushed into the empire by the emergence of a notoriously violent people, the Huns, from the region of what is now Mongolia. The Visigoths ultimately reached southern Gaul and Spain. Soon to be Christianized, they won rights of settlement and material assistance within the empire from the eastern emperor Valens (r. 364–378) in exchange for defending the eastern frontier as *foederati,* or the emperor's "special allies."

Instead of the promised assistance, however, the Visigoths received harsh treatment from their new allies. They had arrived in the empire an impoverished people fleeing the Huns. So bad off were they that they traded their own children to the Romans for dogs to eat. The Romans, showing no mercy, charged them one child per dog. After repeated conflicts, the Visigoths rebelled and handily defeated Roman armies led by Valens at the Battle of Adrianople in 378.

After Adrianople, the Romans passively permitted the settlement of barbarians within the very heart of the western empire. The Vandals crossed the Rhine in 406 and within three decades gained control of northwest Africa and a sizable portion of

A Contemporary Description of Attila the Hun

In 448 a Roman envoy, Priscus, visited the home of Attila in a Scythian village at the base of the Danube River, three years before Attila's famous invasion of Italy. Knowing Attila's reputation for savagery, he was surprised to find him a simple and cultured man.

✦ *How would you account for the discrepancy between this portrait of Attila and his reputation? Has history falsely portrayed this fiercest of warriors? What does it say about the Huns' system of justice that Attila dispensed judgments on the street as he walked?*

Attila's residence . . . was made of polished boards, and surrounded with wooden enclosures, designed not so much for protection as for appearance's sake. . . . I entered the enclosure of Attila's palace, bearing gifts to his wife, whose name was Kreka. . . . Having been admitted by the barbarians at the door, I found her reclining on a soft couch. The floor of the room was covered with woolen mats for walking on. . . . Having approached, saluted her, and presented the gifts, I went out and walked to the other houses. . . . Attila came forth from [one of] the house[s] with a dignified strut, looking round on this side and on that. . . . Many persons who had lawsuits with one another came up and received his judgment. Then he returned into the house and received ambassadors of barbarous peoples. . . .

[We were invited to a banquet with Attila at three o'clock.] The cupbearers gave us a cup, according to the national custom, that we might pray before we sat down. Having tasted the cup, we proceeded to take our seats, all the chairs being ranged along the walls of the room on either side. Attila sat in the middle on a couch; a second couch was set behind him, and from it steps led up to his bed, which was covered with linen sheets and wrought coverlets for ornament, such as Greeks and Romans used to deck bridal beds. The places on the right of Attila were held chief in honor; those on the left, where we sat, were only second. . . .

The attendant of Attila first entered with a dish full of meat, and behind him came the other attendants with bread and viands [plates of food], which they laid on the tables. A luxurious meal, served on silver plate, had been made ready for us and the barbarian guests, but Attila ate nothing but meat on a wooden trencher [a wooden plate]. In everything else, too, he showed himself temperate; his cup was of wood, while to the guests were given goblets of gold and silver. His dress, too, was quite simple, affecting only to be clean. The sword he carried at his side, the latchets of his . . . shoes, the bridle of his horse were not adorned with gold or gems or anything costly . . . like those of the other Scythians.

[After two courses were eaten and] evening fell, torches were lit and two barbarians, coming forward in front of Attila, sang songs they had composed, celebrating his victories and deeds of valor in war.

James Harvey Robinson, ed., Readings in European History, *vol. 1 (Boston: Athenaeum, 1904), pp. 47–48.*

the Mediterranean. The Burgundians, who came on the heels of the Vandals, settled in Gaul. Most important for subsequent Western history were the Franks, who settled northern and central Gaul, some along the sea coast (the Salian Franks) and others along the Rhine, Seine, and Loire Rivers (the Ripuarian Franks).

Why was there so little Roman resistance to these Germanic tribes, whose numbers—at most 100,000 people in the largest of them—were comparatively very small? The invaders were successful because they had come upon a badly overextended western empire divided politically by ambitious military commanders and weakened by decades of

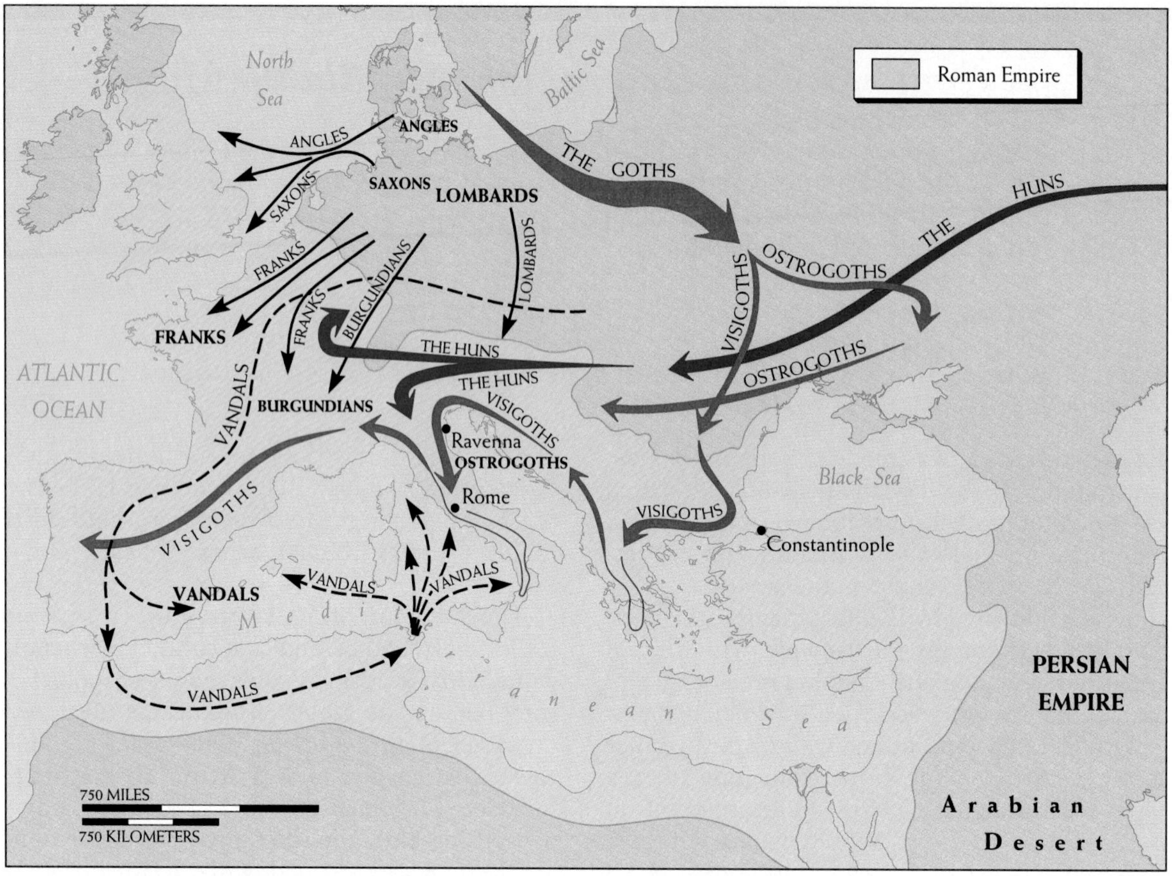

MAP 6–1 BARBARIAN MIGRATIONS INTO THE WEST IN FOURTH AND FIFTH CENTURIES *The forceful intrusion of Germanic and non-Germanic barbarians into the Roman Empire from the last quarter of the fourth century through the fifth century made for a constantly changing pattern of movement and relations. The map shows the major routes taken by the usually unwelcome newcomers and the areas most deeply affected by main groups.*

famine, pestilence, and overtaxation. By the second half of the fourth century, Roman frontiers had become too vast to manage. Efforts to do so by "barbarizing" the Roman army, that is, by recruiting many peasants into it and by making the Germanic tribes key Roman allies, only weakened it further. The eastern empire retained enough wealth and vitality to field new armies or to buy off the invaders. The western empire, in contrast, succumbed not only because of moral decay and materialism, but also because of a combination of military rivalry, political mismanagement, disease, and sheer poverty.

Fall of the Roman Empire

In the early fifth century, Italy and the "eternal city" of Rome suffered a series of devastating blows. In 410, the Visigoths, under Alaric (ca. 370–410), revolted and sacked Rome. In 452, the Huns, led by Attila—known to contemporaries as the "scourge of God"—invaded Italy. And in 455 Rome was overrun yet again, this time by the Vandals.

By the mid-fifth century, power in western Europe had passed decisively from the hands of the Roman emperors to those of barbarian chieftains. In 476, the traditional date given for the fall of the Roman Empire, the barbarian Odovacer (ca. 434–493) deposed and replaced the western emperor Romulus Augustulus. The eastern emperor, Zeno (r. 474–491), recognized Odovacer's authority in the west, and Odovacer acknowledged Zeno as sole emperor, contenting himself to serve as Zeno's western viceroy. In a later coup in 493 manipulated by Zeno, Theodoric (ca. 454–526), king of the Ostrogoths, or "east Goths," replaced Odovacer. At least until the last part of his reign, Theodoric governed with the full acceptance of the Roman people and the Christian Church.

By the end of the fifth century, barbarians had thoroughly overrun the western empire. The Ostrogoths settled in Italy, the Franks in northern Gaul, the Burgundians in Provence, the Visigoths in southern Gaul and Spain, the Vandals in Africa and the western Mediterranean, and the Angles and Saxons in England. (See Map 6–1.)

Western Europe, however, was not transformed into a savage land. Its new masters were willing to learn from the people they had conquered; barbarian military victories did not result in a great defeat of Roman culture. Except in Britain and northern Gaul, Roman language, law, and government coexisted with the new Germanic institutions. In Italy under Theodoric, Roman law gradually replaced tribal custom. Only the Vandals and the Anglo-Saxons—and, after 466, the Visigoths—refused to profess at least titular obedience to the emperor in Constantinople.

That the Visigoths, the Ostrogoths, and the Vandals entered the West as Christianized people contributed to this accommodation of cultures. They were followers, however, of the Arian creed, considered heretical in the West. Arian Christians believed that Jesus Christ was not one identical being with God the Father—a point of view the Council of Nicaea had condemned in 325. (See Chapter 5.)

In spite of the hostility their Arian Christianity provoked, the Germans themselves admired Roman culture and had no desire to destroy it, although their rural lifestyle further weakened its urban foundations. Later, around 500, the Franks, under their strong king, Clovis, converted to the orthodox, or "Catholic," form of Christianity supported by the bishops of Rome. Then, as Roman Christians, the Franks helped conquer and convert the Goths and other barbarians in western Europe.

All things considered, rapprochement and a gradual interpenetration of two strong cultures—a creative tension—marked the period of the Germanic migrations. The stronger culture was the Roman, and it became dominant in a later fusion. Despite western military defeat, the Goths and the Franks became far more romanized than the Romans were germanized. Latin language, Nicene Christianity, and eventually Roman law and government were to triumph in the West during the Middle Ages.

The Byzantine Empire

As western Europe succumbed to the Germanic invasions, imperial power shifted to the Byzantine Empire, that is, the eastern part of the Roman Empire. Emperor Constantine the Great began the rebuilding of Byzantium in 324, renaming the city Constantinople and dedicating it in 330. Constantinople became the sole capital of the empire and remained so until the successful revival of the western empire in the eighth century by Charlemagne.

Between 324 and 1453 the empire passed from an early period of expansion and splendor to a time of contraction and splintering and finally to catastrophic defeat by the Ottoman Turks. Historians commonly divide the history of the empire into three distinct periods:

1. from the rebuilding of Byzantium as Constantinople in 324 to the beginning of the Arab expansion and the spread of Islam in 632
2. from 632 to the conquest of Asia Minor by the Seljuk Turks after the fall of Manzikert in 1071, or, as some prefer, to the fall of Constantinople to western Crusaders in 1204
3. from 1071 or 1204 to the defeat of Constantinople by the Turks in 1453.

The Reign of Justinian

In terms of territory, political power, and culture, the first period of Byzantine history (324–632) was by far its greatest. The height of this period was the reign of the emperor Justinian (r. 527–565) and his brilliant wife, the empress Theodora (d. 548). (See Map 6–2.) The daughter of a bear trainer in the circus, the empress in her youth had fallen prey to the seedy side of sixth-century circus life. Her activities may have included prostitution, if the controversial *Secret History* by Justinian's court historian, Procopius, is to be believed. Her background may have given her a toughness that fully matched and even exceeded her husband's.

An influential counselor, Theodora became a major figure in imperial government. In 532, Justinian contemplated abdication following riots against his rule that left much of Constantinople in ruins and thousands dead. Theodora stiffened his resolve, reportedly insisting that he crack down ruthlessly on the rioters and firmly reestablish his authority, which he most decisively did. In doctri-

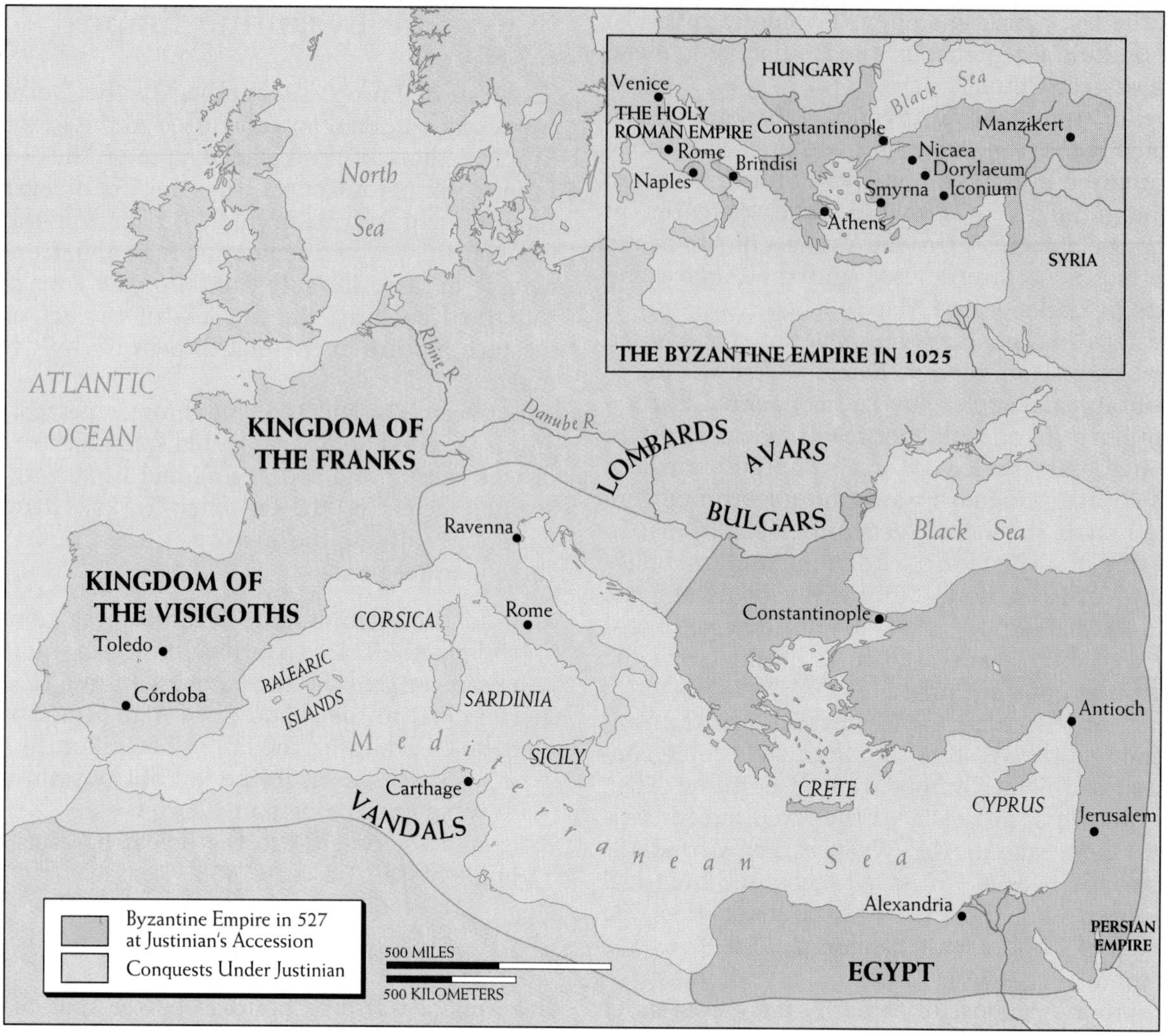

Map 6–2 The Byzantine Empire at the Time of Justinian's Death

nal matters, the empress clearly had a mind and will of her own. Whereas Justinian remained strictly orthodox in his Christian beliefs, Theodora lent her support to a Christian heresy known as Monophysitism, which taught that Jesus had only one nature, a composite divine–human one, not a fully human and fully divine dual nature, as orthodox doctrine taught. In the sixth century the Monophysites formed a separate church that had a very strong influence in the eastern provinces of the empire. The imperial government persecuted them as heretics after Theodora's death, a policy that cost the empire dearly when, in the seventh century, Persian and Arab armies besieged its eastern frontiers. Bitter over their treatment, the Monophysites offered little resistance to the invaders.

Law The imperial goal in the East—as reflected in the policy "one God, one empire, one religion"—was to centralize government and impose legal and doctrinal conformity. To this end, Justinian collated and revised Roman law. This codification had become a pressing matter because of the enormous number of often contradictory legal decrees that had piled up since the mid-second century as the empire grew increasingly Christian and imperial rule increasingly autocratic.

Justinian's *Corpus juris civilis* or "body of civil law," was a fourfold compilation undertaken by a learned committee of lawyers. The first compilation, known as the *Code*, appeared in 533. It revised imperial edicts issued since the reign of Hadrian (r. 117–138). A second compilation, the *Novellae*, or "new things," contained the decrees issued by Justinian and his immediate successors after 534. The third compilation, the *Digest*, was a summary of the major opinions of the old legal experts. The fourth compilation, the *Institutes*, was a textbook for young scholars, which drew its lessons from the *Code* and the *Digest*. These works had little immediate effect on medieval common law, but, beginning with the Renaissance, they provided the foundation for most subsequent European law down to the nineteenth century. They especially benefitted those rulers who aspired to centralize their states.

RELIGION Religion as well as law served imperial centralization. Since the fifth century, the patriarch of Constantinople had crowned emperors in Constantinople. This practice reflected the close ties between rulers and the church. In 380 Christianity had been proclaimed the official religion of the eastern empire. All other religions and sects were denounced as "demented and insane."[1] Between the fourth and sixth centuries the patriarchs of Constantinople, Alexandria, Antioch, and Jerusalem acquired enormous wealth in the form of land and gold. The church, in turn, acted as the state's welfare agency, drawing on its generous endowments from pious rich donors to aid the poor and needy. The prestige and comfort of the clergy swelled the clerical ranks of the Eastern Church.

[1]*Cyril Mango,* Byzantium: The Empire of New Rome *(New York: Charles Scribner's Sons, 1980), p. 88.*

Orthodox Christianity was not, however, the only religion within the empire with a significant following. Nor did the rulers view religion as merely a political tool. At one time or another the Christian heresies of Arianism, Monophysitism, and Iconoclasm also received imperial support. Persecution and absorption into popular Christianity served to curtail many pagan religious practices.

The empire was also home, although at times a less than hospitable one, to large numbers of Jews. Non-Christian Romans saw Jews as narrow, dogmatic, and intolerant people in comparison with Christians, and they had little love for them. Under Roman law Jews had legal protection so long as they did not proselytize among Christians, build

A sixth-century ivory panel depicting the Byzantine emperor Justinian as the champion of the Christian faith. From 500 to 1100, the Byzantine Empire was the center of Christian civilization. [Giraudon/Art Resource, N.Y.]

The Character and "Innovations" of Justinian and Theodora

According to Procopius, their court historian and biographer, Justinian and Theodora were tyrants, pure and simple. His Secret History *(sixth century), which some historians distrust as a source, had only criticism and condemnation for the two rulers. Procopius especially resented Theodora, and he did not believe that the rule of law was respected at the royal court.*

✦ *Is Procopius being fair to Justinian and Theodora? Is the* Secret History *an ancient tabloid? How does one know when a source is biased and self-serving and when it is telling the truth? What does Procopius most dislike about the queen? Was Theodora the last woman ruler to receive such criticism?*

Formerly, when the senate approached the Emperor, it paid homage in the following manner. Every patrician kissed him on the right breast; the Emperor [then] kissed the patrician on the head, and he was dismissed. Then the rest bent their right knee to the Emperor and withdrew. It was not customary to pay homage to the Queen.

But those who were admitted [in]to the presence of Justinian and Theodora, whether they were patricians or otherwise, fell on their faces on the floor, stretching their hands and feet out wide, kissed first one foot and then the other of the Augustus [i.e., the emperor], and then retired. Nor did Theodora refuse this honor; and she even received the ambassadors of the Persians and other barbarians and gave them presents, as if she were in command of the Roman Empire: a thing that had never happened in all previous time.

And formerly intimates of the Emperor called him Emperor and the Empress, Empress. . . . But if anybody addressed either of these two as Emperor or Empress without adding "Your Majesty" or "Your Highness," or forgot to call himself their slave, he was considered either ignorant or insolent, and was dismissed in disgrace as if he had done some awful crime or committed some unpardonable sin.

And [whereas] before, only a few were sometimes admitted to the palace . . . when these two came to power, the magistrates and everybody else had no trouble in fairly living in the palace. This was because the magistrates of old had administered justice and the laws according to their conscience . . . but these two, taking control of everything to the misfortune of their subjects, forced everyone to come to them and beg like slaves. And almost any day one could see the law courts nearly deserted, while in the hall of the Emperor there was a jostling and pushing crowd that resembled nothing so much as a mob of slaves.

Procopius, Secret History, *in* The Early Middle Ages 500–1000, *ed. by Robert Brentano (New York: Free Press, 1964), pp. 70–71.*

new synagogues, or try to enter sensitive public offices or professions. Justinian (the emperor most intent on religious conformity within the empire) adopted a policy of encouraging Jews to convert voluntarily. Later emperors ordered all Jews to be baptized, and granted tax breaks to those who voluntarily complied. But neither persuasion nor coercion succeeded in converting the empire's Jews.

Cities During Justinian's reign the empire's strength was its more than 1,500 cities. The largest, with perhaps 350,000 inhabitants, was Constantinople, the cultural crossroads of the Asian and European civilizations. The large provincial cities had populations of 50,000. Between the fourth and fifth centuries, councils of about 200 members, all of whom were local wealthy landowners known as

Empress Theodora and her attendants. The union of political and spiritual authority in the person of the empress is shown by the depiction on Theodora's mantle of three magi carrying gifts to the Virgin and Jesus. [Scala/Art Resource, N.Y.]

decurions, governed the cities. Decurions were the intellectual and economic elite of the empire. They were also heavily taxed, and for this reason they were not always the emperor's most docile or loyal servants. By the sixth century, special governors and bishops, appointed from the landholding classes, replaced the decurion councils and proved to be more reliable instruments of the emperor's will.

A fifth-century statistical record gives us some sense of the size and splendor of Constantinople at its peak. It lists five imperial and nine princely palaces; eight public and 153 private baths; four public forums; five granaries; two theaters; one hippodrome; 322 streets; 4,388 substantial houses; fifty-two porticoes; twenty public and 120 private bakers; and fourteen churches.[2] The most popular entertainments were the theater, frequently denounced by the clergy for nudity and immorality, and the races at the hippodrome. Many public taverns existed as well.

Eastern Influences

During the reign of Heraclius (r. 610–641) the empire took a decidedly Eastern, as opposed to Roman, direction. Heraclius spoke Greek, not Latin. He spent his entire reign resisting Persian and Islamic invasions, the former successfully, the latter in vain. Islamic armies progressively overran the empire after 632, directly attacking Constantinople for the first time in 677. Not until the reign of Leo III of the Isaurian dynasty (r. 717–740) were the Islamic armies repulsed and most of Asia Minor regained by the Byzantines.

Leo, however, offended Western Christians when he forbade the use of images in Eastern churches and tried to enforce the ban also in the West. This was an affront to Western Christianity, which had carefully nurtured the adoration of Jesus, Mary, and the saints in images and icons. Historians have speculated that Leo and his immediate successors pursued this policy under the influence of Islam, which condemned image veneration, perhaps hoping to placate the Muslims by joining them on this point of doctrine. Be that as it may, the banning of images was a major expression of eastern Caesaro-papism—the direct involvement of the emperor in religious dogma and practice as if he were both secular ruler and the head of the church—which, as we will see, the Western church always resisted. In addition to creating a new division within Christendom, the ban on images led to the destruction of much religious art until it was reversed in the late eighth century.

[2]*Mango, p. 76.*

(a)

(b)

(a) The exterior of Hagia Sophia (Holy Wisdom) is plain and ordinary compared with the interior—a reflection of the priority the Byzantines attached to the inner life. The four towering minarets were among additions made by the Turkish Muslims after they conquered Constantinople in 1453 and transformed the building into a mosque. Since 1935, it has been a national museum. [Giraudon/Art Resource, N.Y.] (b) The great church of Hagia Sophia. Built in Constantinople (now Istanbul, Turkey) by the emperor Justinian between 532 and 537, this church was one of the most influential achievements of Byzantine art and architecture. This interior view shows part of the great dome of the church (107 feet in diameter) and its rich decoration of marbles and mosaics. [Giraudon/Art Resource, N.Y.]

In 1071, the Byzantine Empire suffered a major defeat at the hands of the Muslim Seljuk Turks. Successful over Byzantine armies at Manzikert, the Turks rapidly overran the eastern provinces of the empire. This defeat was the beginning of the end of the empire, although the actual end—at the hands of the Seljuks' cousins, the Ottoman Turks—still lay centuries ahead. After two decades of steady Turkish advance, the eastern emperor Alexius I Comnenus (r. 1081–1118) invoked Western aid in 1092. Three years later the West launched the first of the Crusades. A century later (1204) the Crusaders would inflict far more damage on Constantinople and Eastern Christendom than all previous non-Christian invaders had done.

Throughout the early Middle Ages, the Byzantine Empire remained a protective barrier between western Europe and hostile Persian, Arab, and Turkish armies. The Byzantines were also a major conduit of classical learning and science into the West down to the Renaissance. While western Europeans were fumbling to create a culture of their own, the cities of the Byzantine Empire provided them a model of a civilized society.

Islam and the Islamic World

A new drama began to unfold in the sixth century with the awakening of a rival far more dangerous to the West than the German tribes: the new faith of Islam. By the time of Muhammad's death (632), Islamic armies absorbed the attention and the resources of the emperors in Constantinople and rulers in the West.

At first, the Muslims were both open and cautious. They borrowed and integrated elements of Persian and Greek culture into their own. The new religion of Islam adopted elements of Christian, Jewish, and native pagan religious beliefs and practices. Muslims tolerated religious minorities within the territories they conquered so long as these minorities recognized Islamic political rule, refrained from proselytizing among Muslims, and paid their taxes. Nonetheless, the Muslims were keen to protect the purity and integrity of Islamic religion, language, and law from any corrupting foreign influence. With the passage of time, and increased conflict with Eastern and Western Christians, this protective tendency grew stronger. Despite significant contacts and exchanges, Islamic culture would not penetrate the West as creatively as Germanic culture did, but would remain largely strange and threatening to Westerners.

Muhammad's Religion

Muhammad (570–632), an orphan, was raised by a family of modest means. As a youth, he worked as a merchant's assistant, traveling the major trade routes. When he was twenty-five, he married a wealthy Meccan widow. Thereafter, himself a wealthy man, he became a kind of social activist, criticizing Meccan materialism, paganism, and unjust treatment of the poor and needy. At about age forty a deep religious experience heightened his commitment to reform and transformed his life. He began to receive revelations from the angel Gabriel, who recited God's word to him at irregular intervals. These revelations grew into the *Qur'an* (literally, a "reciting"), which his followers compiled between 650 and 651. The basic message Muhammad received was a summons to all Arabs to submit to God's will. Followers of Muhammad's religion came to be called *Muslim* ("submissive" or "surrendering"); the name applied to the religion itself, *Islam*, has the same derivation and means "submission."

The message was not a new one. It had been reiterated by a long line of Jewish prophets going back to Noah. According to Muslims, however, this line ended with Muhammad, who, as the last of God's chosen prophets, became "the Prophet." The Qur'an also recognized Jesus Christ as a prophet, but did not view him as God's co-eternal and coequal son. Like Judaism, Islam was a monotheistic and theocentric religion, not a trinitarian one like Christianity.

Mecca was a major pagan pilgrimage site (the *Ka'ba*—a black meteorite that became Islam's holiest shrine—was originally a pagan object of worship). Muhammad's attacks on idolatry and immorality threatened the trade that flowed from the pilgrims, enraging the merchants of the city. Persecuted for their attacks on traditional religion, Muhammad and his followers fled in 622 to Medina, 240 miles to the north. This event came to be known as the *Hegira* and marks the beginning of the Islamic calendar.

In Medina, Muhammad organized his forces and drew throngs of devoted followers. He raided caravans going back and forth to Mecca. Also at this time he had his first conflicts with Medinan Jews, who were involved in Meccan trade. By 624 his army was powerful enough to conquer Mecca and make it the center of the new religion.

During these years the basic rules of Islamic practice evolved. True Muslims were expected (1) to be honest and modest in all their dealings and behavior; (2) to be unquestionably loyal to the Islamic community; (3) to abstain from pork and alcohol at all times; (4) to wash and pray facing Mecca five times a day; (5) to contribute to the support of the poor and needy; (6) to fast during daylight hours for one month each year; and (7) to make a pilgrimage to Mecca and visit the Ka'ba at least once in a lifetime. The last requirement reflects the degree to which Islam was an assimilationist religion; here it "Islamicized" a major pagan religious practice.

In another distinctive feature, Islam permitted Muslim men to have up to four wives—provided they treated them all justly and gave each equal attention—and as many concubines as they wished. A husband could divorce a wife with a simple declaration, whereas a wife, to divorce her husband, had to have a very good reason and go before an official. A wife was expected to be totally loyal and devoted to her husband. She was allowed to show her face to no man but him.

In contrast to Christianity, Islam drew no rigid distinction between the clergy and the laity. A lay scholarly elite developed, however, that held moral authority within Islamic society and formed a kind of magisterium in moral and religious matters. This elite, known as the *ulema* or "persons with correct knowledge," served a social function similar to that of a professional priesthood or rabbinate. Its members were men of great piety and obvious learning whose opinions came to have the force of law in Muslim society. They also kept a critical eye on Muslim rulers, seeing that they adhered to the letter of the Qur'an.

Muslims are enjoined to live by the divine law, or Shari'a, *and have a right to have disputes settled by an arbiter of the* Shari'a. *Here we see a husband complaining about his wife before the state-appointed judge, or* qadi. *The wife, backed up by two other women, points an accusing finger at the husband. In such cases, the first duty of the* qadi, *who should be a learned person of faith, is to try to effect a reconciliation before the husband divorces his wife, or the wife herself seeks a divorce. [Bibliothèque Nationale, Paris]*

Islamic Diversity

The success of Islam lay in its ability to unify and inspire tribal Arabs and other non-Jewish and non-Christian people. In a world where Christianity and Judaism had reigned supreme among religions, Islam must also have appealed to Arab pride, for it made Muhammad history's major religious figure and his followers God's chosen people.

As early as the seventh century, however, disputes arose among Muslims over the shape of Islamic society that left permanent divisions within it. Disagreement over the true line of succession to Muhammad—the caliphate—was one source of discord. Another, tied to the first, was disagreement on doctrinal issues involving the extent to which Islam was meant to be an inclusive religion, open to the weak as well as to the strong. Several groups emerged from these disputes. The most radical was the Kharijites, whose leaders seceded from the camp of the caliph Ali (656–661) because Ali compromised with his enemies on a matter of principle. Righteous and judgmental, the Kharijites wanted to exclude all but rigorously virtuous Muslims from the community of the faithful. In 661 one of their members assassinated Ali.

Another, more influential group was the Shi'a, or "partisans of Ali" (*Shi'at Ali*). The Shi'a looked on Ali and his descendants as the rightful successors of Muhammad not only by virtue of kinship, but also by the expressed will of the Prophet himself. To the Shi'a, Ali's assassination revealed the most basic truth of a devout Muslim life: a true *imam*, or "ruler," must expect to suffer unjustly even unto death in the world, and so too must his followers. A distinctive theology of martyrdom has ever since been a mark of Shi'a teaching. And the Shi'a, until modern times, have been an embattled minority within mainstream Islamic society.

A third group, which has been dominant for most of Islamic history, was the majority centrist Sunnis (followers of *sunna*, or "tradition"). Sunnis have always put loyalty to the community of Islam above all else and have spurned the exclusivism and purism of the Kharijites and the Shi'a.

Islamic Empires

Under Muhammad's first three successors—the caliphs Abu Bakr (r. 632–634), Umar (r. 634–644), and Uthman (r. 644–655)—Islam expanded by conquest throughout the southern and eastern Mediterranean, territories mostly still held today by Islamic states. In the eighth century Muslim armies occupied parts of Spain in the West and India in the East, producing a truly vast empire. (See Political Transformations, p. 214.) The capital of this empire moved from Mecca to Damascus, and then, in 750, to Baghdad after a civil war in which the Abbasid dynasty replaced the Umayyad dynasty in the caliphate. Thereafter, the huge Muslim Empire broke up into separate states, each with its own line of caliphs, each claiming to be the true successor of Muhammad.

These conquests would not have been so rapid and thorough had the contemporary Byzantine and Persian empires not been exhausted after a long period of war. The Muslims struck at both empires shortly after the Byzantine emperor Heraclius (r. 610–641) had recovered Egypt, Palestine, Syria, and Asia Minor from the Persians. Before Heraclius died in 641, however, Arab armies had conquered Egypt, Palestine, and Syria and by 643 had overrun most of the Persian Empire. Byzantine territory in North Africa fell by the end of the seventh century. Most of the inhabitants in the territory Heraclius had reconquered from the Persians, although Christian, were, like the Arabs, Semitic. Any religious unity

One of the reasons the Byzantines were able to repulse the Arab attack on Constantinople in 717–718 was a secret weapon: Greek fire, a highly flammable mixture of petroleum, sulphur, and pitch that would burn even on water. In this fourteenth-century manuscript, the Byzantine navy is spraying Greek fire from a copper tube onto an enemy vessel. [Amplicaciones y Reproducciones Mas (ARXIU MAS)]

POLITICAL TRANSFORMATIONS

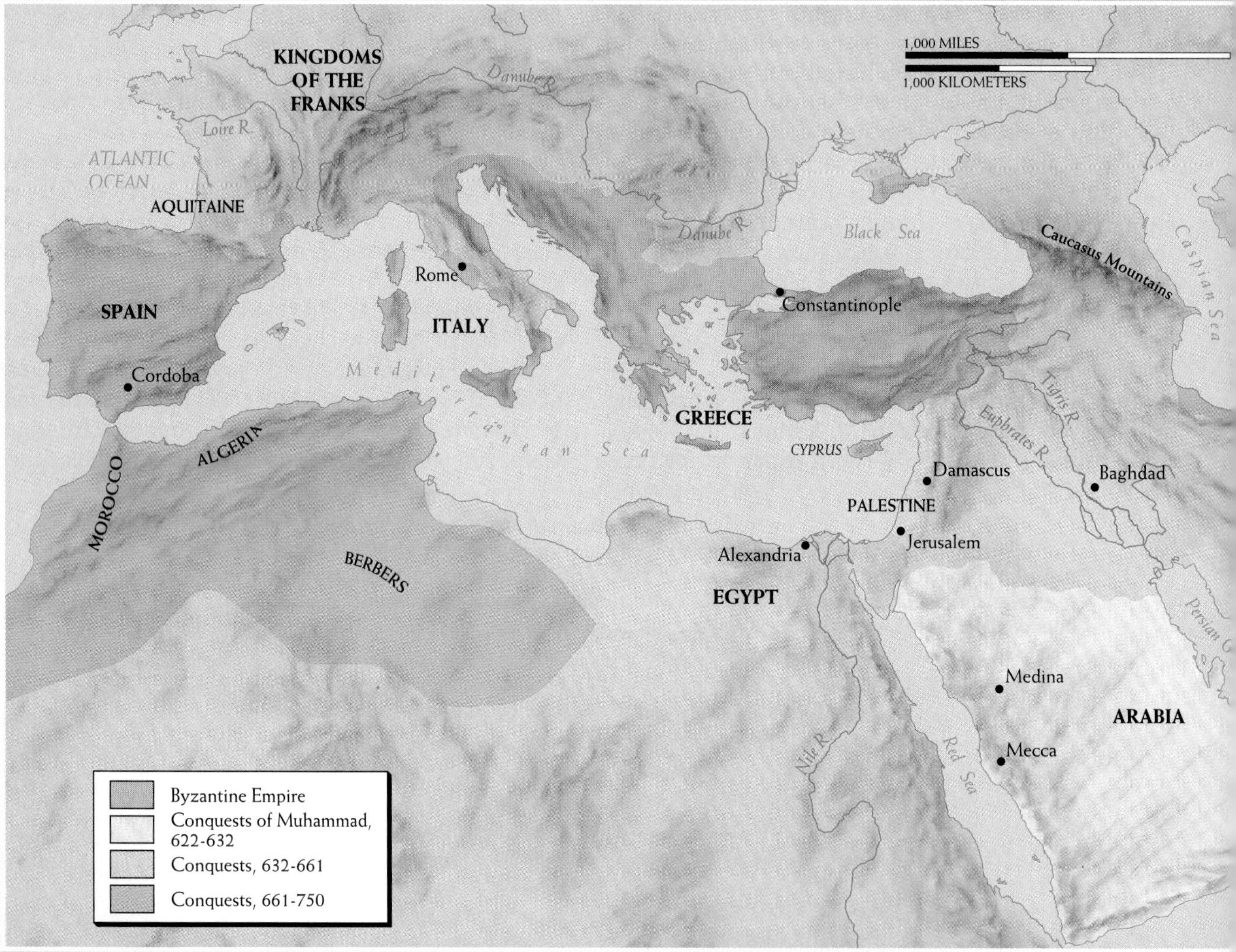

Map 6–3

Muslim Conquests and Domination of the Mediterranean to About 750

Under Muhammad's first three successors—the caliphs Abu Bakr (632–634), Umar (634–644), and Uthman (644–655)—Islam expanded by conquest throughout the southern and eastern Mediterranean. In the eighth century Muslim armies marching west through Palestine and Egypt and east through Persia and Khorasan occupied parts of Spain in the west and India in the east, producing a vast empire under an accommodating Muslim rule and tolerant popular culture, especially by comparison to Byzantine and Persian conquerors. There was especially heavy Arab Muslim immigration into Iraq and Iran, where native political elites converted early to Islam, while in North Africa and Spain, capturing political power proved to be slower and more difficult. The capital of the new empire moved from Mecca to Damascus, and then, in 750, to Baghdad after a civil war in which the Abbasid dynasty replaced the Umayyad dynasty in the caliphate. Thereafter, the Muslim Empire progressively broke up into separate states, each with its own line of caliphs claiming to be the true successor of Muhammad. With the notable exception of Spain, from which Muslims were driven in the fifteenth century, most of the occupied territories have remained under the control of Islamic states.

While scholars have debated whether fighting in God's name was one of the five Pillars of Islam, going to war for Islam or "fighting in the way of the Lord" was a fundamental Muslim duty and a key to expansion and colonization of the new Islamic Empire. As the following excerpt from the Qur'an makes clear, the conquest of disputed lands was not understood as aggression, and once an Islamic state was established, maintaining it was a holy cause.

Fight those in the way of God who fight you, but do not be aggressive: God does not like aggressors. And fight those wheresoever you find them, and expel them from the place they had turned you out from. Oppression is worse than killing. Do not fight them by the Holy Mosque unless they fight you there. If they [fight], then slay them: such is the requital for unbelievers. But if they desist, God is forgiving and kind.

Fight them until sedition comes to an end, and the Law of God [prevails]. If they desist, then cease to be hostile, except against those who oppress. (Qur'an 2:190–193)

Those who believe fight in the way of God; and those who do not, fight only for the powers of evil; so you should fight the allies of Satan. (Qur'an 4:74–76)

A Reader on Classical Islam, *F. E. Peters (Princeton: Princeton University Press, 1994), p. 155.*

La Mezquita, *the Great Mosque at Cordoba, Spain was begun in 786. The city was reconquered in 1236, and the mosque became a place of Christian worship, but its Islamic character remains clear. [Robert Frerck/Woodfin Camp & Associates]*

they felt with the Byzantine Greeks may have been offset by hatred of the Byzantine Greek army of occupation. The Christian community was in any case badly divided. Heraclius's efforts to impose Greek "orthodox" beliefs on the Monophysitic churches of Egypt and Syria only increased the enmity between Greek and Semitic Christians. As a result, many Egyptian and Syrian Christians, hoping for deliverance from Byzantine oppression, may have welcomed the Islamic conquerors.

Although Islam gained converts from among the Christians in North Africa and Spain, its efforts to invade the heart of Christendom were in the end successfully rebuffed. In the West the ruler of the Franks, Charles Martel, defeated a raiding party of Arabs on the western frontier of Europe at Poitiers (today in central France) in 732. This victory ended any possible Arab effort to expand into western Europe by way of Spain. Beginning with Emperor Leo III (r. 717–740), the Isaurian dynasty of Byzantine rulers successfully defended Asia Minor from Islamic aggression. So effective were they that the subsequent Macedonian dynasty of Byzantine rulers (867–1057) expanded militarily and commercially into Arab lands. Muslim disunity after the tenth century greatly aided Byzantine success. The Byzantine Empire would ultimately fall to the Ottoman Turks, who would continue to strike terror in Christian hearts well into the sixteenth century, but after the Seljuk Turks took the Islamic capital of Baghdad in 1055 and the Christian Crusaders captured Jerusalem in 1099, the Muslims never again posed a serious threat to Western Christendom.

The Western Debt to Islamic Culture

Despite the hostility of the Christian West to the Islamic world, there was nonetheless much creative interchange between these two very different cultures, and the West greatly profited from it. The more advanced Arab civilization, which was enjoying its golden age during the West's early Middle Ages, taught Western farmers how to irrigate fields and Western artisans how to tan leather and refine silk. The West also gained from its contacts with Islamic scholars. Thanks to Arabic translators, major Greek works in astronomy, mathematics, and medicine became available in Latin to scholars in much of the West for the first time. And down to the sixteenth century, after the works of the famous ancient physicians Hippocrates and Galen, the basic gynecological and child-care manuals followed by Western midwives and physicians were compilations by the famed Baghdad physician Al-Razi (Rhazes), the philosopher and physician ibn-Sina (Avicenna) (980–1037), and Averröes (1126–1198), Islam's greatest authority on Aristotle. Jewish scholars also thrived amid the intellectual culture Islamic scholars created. The famed Spanish Jewish scholar, Moses Maimonides (1135–1204), wrote in Arabic as well as in Hebrew.

Western Society and the Developing Christian Church

Facing barbarian invasions from the north and east and a strong Islamic presence in the Mediterranean, the West found itself in decline during the fifth and sixth centuries. As trade waned, cities rapidly fell on hard times, depriving the West of centers for the exchange of goods and ideas that would enable it to look and live beyond itself.

In the seventh century, the Byzantine emperors, their hands full with the Islamic threat in the East, were unable to assert themselves in the West, leaving most of the region in the control of the Franks and the Lombards (a Germanic tribe that invaded Italy in the sixth century and settled in the Po Valley). Islamic dominance of the Mediterranean likewise closed the West to much trade or cultural influence from the East. As a result, western Europeans were forced to rely on their own resources and develop their Germanic and Greco-Roman heritage into their own distinctive culture.

As Western shipping declined in the Mediterranean, populations that would otherwise have been engaged in trade-related work in the cities moved in great numbers into interior regions. There they found the employment and protection they sought on the farms of the great landholders. The landholders, for their part, needed laborers and welcomed the new emigrants.

Peasants made up 90 percent of the population. Those who owned their own land were "free peasants." Some peasants became "serfs" by surrendering their land to a more powerful landholder in exchange for assistance in time of dire need, like prolonged crop failure or foreign invasion. Basically serfdom was a status of servitude to an economically and politically stronger person. Powerful landholders, after seizing all the agricultural land they could control, essentially reallocated it to the people who supplied labor and goods, offering them protection in return.

As the demand for agricultural products diminished in the great urban centers and as traffic between town and country declined, the farming belts became regionally insular and self-contained. Production and travel adjusted to local needs. There was little incentive for bold experimentation and exploration. The domains of the great landholders became the basic social and political units of society, and local barter economies sprang up within them. In these developments were sown the seeds of what would later come to be known as manorial and feudal society (which we will discuss in more detail). Manorial society involved a division of land and labor among lords, serfs, and other peasants for the profit of the lords and the protection of all. Feudal society involved the emergence of a special class of aristocratic warrior knights as guarantors of order.

While all of this was going on, one institution remained firmly entrenched within the cities: the Christian Church. The church had long modeled its own structure on that of the imperial Roman administration. Like the imperial government, church government was centralized and hierarchical. Strategically placed "generals" (bishops) in European cities looked for spiritual direction to their leader, the bishop of Rome. As the western empire crumbled, Roman governors withdrew, and populations emigrated to the countryside, the resulting vacuum of authority was filled by local bishops and cathedral chapters. The local cathedral became the center of urban life and the local bishop the highest authority for those who remained in the cities. In Rome, on a larger and more fateful scale, the pope took control of the city as the Western emperors gradually departed and died out. Left to its own devices, western Europe soon discovered that the Christian Church was its best repository of Roman administrative skills and classical culture.

The Christian Church had been graced with special privileges, great lands, and wealth by Emperor Constantine and his successors. In the first half of the fourth century, Christians gained legal standing and a favored status within the empire. In 391 Emperor Theodosius I (r. ca. 379–395) raised Christianity to the official religion of the empire. Both Theodosius and his predecessors acted as much for political effect as out of religious conviction. In 313 Christians made up about one-fifth of the population of the empire and Christianity was unquestionably the strongest of the competing religions. Its main rivals were Mithraism, the religion popular among army officers and restricted to males, and the Egyptian cults of Isis and Serapis.

Challenged by Rome's decline to become a major political force, the Christian Church survived the period of Germanic and Islamic invasions a somewhat spiritually weakened and compromised institution. Yet it remained a potent civilizing and unifying force. It had a religious message of providential purpose and individual worth that could give solace and meaning to life at its worst. It had a ritual of baptism and a creedal confession that united people beyond the traditional barriers of social class, education, and gender. And alone in the West, the church retained an effective hierarchical administration, scattered throughout the old empire, staffed by the best-educated minds in Europe, and centered in emperorless Rome.

Writing after the fall of Rome but before the emergence of Islam, Augustine (354–430) eloquently elaborated the Christian message and the force of its appeal in his chaotic times. In his *City of God*, he defended Christianity against those who held it responsible for the collapse of Roman civilization because it allegedly rejected the Roman gods and its message of love and forgiveness fostered weakness. He pointed out the empire's internal weaknesses and the constructive nature of Christian teaching, which he deemed superior to the ancient philosophies. He stressed in particular the discipline of the church and the power of its sacraments to heal and unite humankind in a new spiritual empire. The book became a favorite of the Frankish king Charlemagne nearly 400 years later.

Monastic Culture

The church enjoyed the services of growing numbers of monks, who were not only loyal to its mission but also objects of great popular respect. Monastic culture proved again and again to be the peculiar strength of the church during the Middle Ages.

The first monks were hermits who had withdrawn from society to pursue a more perfect way of life. They were inspired by the Christian ideal of a life of complete self-denial in imitation of Christ. The popularity of monasticism began to grow as

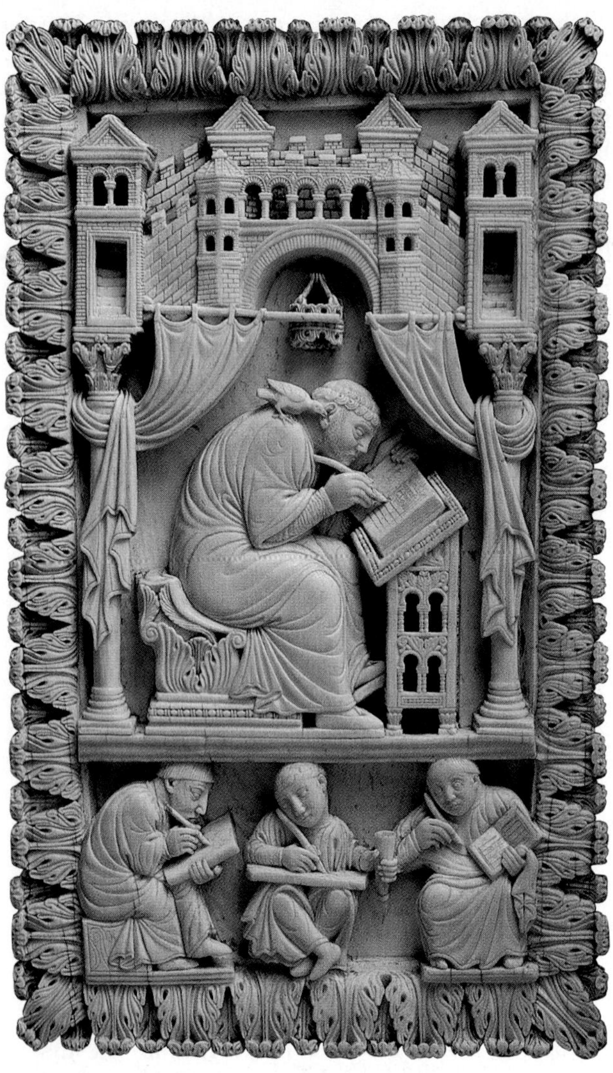

Saint Gregory the Great, shown in a monastic scriptorium, *or study, receiving the divine word from a dove perched on his shoulder. Below him three monks are writing. The middle monk holds an inkwell in his left hand. [Kunsthistorisches Museum, Vienna]*

Roman persecution of Christians waned and Christianity became the favored religion of the empire during the fourth century. Monasticism replaced martyrdom as the most perfect way to imitate Christ and to confess one's faith.

Christians came to view monastic life—embracing, as it did, the biblical "counsels of perfection" (chastity, poverty, and obedience)—as the purest form of religious practice, going beyond the baptism and creedal confession that identified ordinary believers. This view evolved during the Middle Ages into a belief in the general superiority of the clergy and in the church's mission over the laity and the state. This belief served the papacy in later confrontations with secular rulers.

Anthony of Egypt (ca. 251–356), the father of hermit monasticism, was inspired by Jesus' command to the rich young ruler: "If you will be perfect, sell all that you have, give it to the poor, and follow me" (Matthew 19:21). Anthony went into the desert to pray and work, setting an example followed by hundreds in Egypt, Syria, and Palestine in the fourth and fifth centuries.

This hermit monasticism was soon joined by the development of communal monasticism. In the first quarter of the fourth century, Pachomius (ca. 286–346) organized monks in southern Egypt into a highly regimented community in which hundreds shared a life of labor, order, and discipline enforced by a strict penal code. Such monastic communities grew to contain a thousand or more inhabitants. They were little "cities of God," trying to separate themselves from the collapsing Roman and the nominal Christian world. Basil the Great (329–379) popularized communal monasticism throughout the East, providing a rule that lessened the asceticism of Pachomius and directed monks beyond their segregated enclaves of perfection into such social worldly services as caring for orphans, widows, and the infirm in surrounding communities.

Athanasius (ca. 293–373) and Martin of Tours (ca. 315–399) introduced monasticism to the West. The teachings of John Cassian (ca. 360–435) and Jerome (ca. 340–420) then helped shape the basic values and practices of Western monasticism. The great organizer of Western monasticism, however, was Benedict of Nursia (ca. 480–547). In 529 he established a monastery at Monte Cassino, in Italy, founding the form of monasticism—Benedictine—that bears his name and that quickly came to dominate in the West. It eventually replaced an Irish, non-Benedictine monasticism that was common until the 600s in the British Isles and Gaul.

Benedict wrote *Rule for Monasteries*, a sophisticated and comprehensive plan for every activity of the monks, even detailing the manner in which they were to sleep. His *Rule* opposed the severities of earlier monasticism that tortured the body and anguished the mind. Benedict insisted on good food and even some wine, adequate clothing, and proper amounts of sleep and relaxation. Periods of devotion (about four hours each day) were set aside for the "work of God." That is, regular prayers, liturgical activities, and study alternated with manual labor (farming). This program permitted not a moment's idleness and carefully nurtured the religious, intellectual, and physical well-being of the cloistered monks. The monastery was directed by an abbot, whose command had to be obeyed unquestioningly.

Individual Benedictine monasteries remained autonomous until the later Middle Ages, when the Benedictines became a unified order of the church. During the early Middle Ages Benedictine missionaries Christianized both England and Germany. Their disciplined organization and devotion to hard work made the Benedictines an economic and political power as well as a spiritual force wherever they settled.

The Doctrine of Papal Primacy

Constantine and his successors, especially the Eastern emperors, ruled religious life with an iron hand and consistently looked on the church as little more

The Benedictine Order Sets Its Requirements for Entrance

Much was demanded of the new monk, both during and after his probationary period, described herein. Benedict tried to improve the quality of cloistered life. His Rule *is a balanced blend of religious, physical, and intellectual activities within a secure and well-structured community.*

✦ *Why did the religious life have such a great appeal at this time in history? Were there materialistic as well as spiritual reasons for entering a cloister? What are Benedict's reasons for not allowing a monk to change his mind and leave the cloister once vows have been taken?*

When anyone is newly come for the reformation of his life, let him not be granted an easy entrance; but, as the Apostle says, "Test the spirits to see whether they are from God." If the newcomer, therefore, perseveres in his knocking, and if it is seen after four or five days that he bears patiently the harsh treatment offered him and the difficulty of admission, and that he persists in his petition, then let entrance be granted him, and let him stay in the guest house for a few days.

After that let him live in the novitiate, where the novices study, eat, and sleep. A senior shall be assigned to them who is skilled in winning souls, to watch over them with the utmost care. Let him examine whether the novice is truly seeking God, and whether he is zealous for the Work of God, for obedience and for humiliations. Let the novice be told all the hard and rugged ways by which the journey to God is made.

If he promises stability and perseverance, then at the end of two months let this Rule be read through to him, and let him be addressed thus: "Here is the law under which you wish to fight. If you can observe it, enter; if you cannot, you are free to depart." If he still stands firm, let him be taken to the above-mentioned novitiate and again tested in all patience. And after the lapse of six months let the Rule be read to him, that he may know on what he is entering. And if he still remains firm, after four months let the same Rule be read to him again.

Then, having deliberated with himself, if he promises to keep it in its entirety and to observe everything that is commanded him, let him be received into the community. But let him understand that, according to the law of the Rule, from that day forward he may not leave the monastery nor withdraw his neck from under the yoke of the Rule which he was free to refuse or to accept during that prolonged deliberation.

St. Benedict's Rule for Monasteries, *trans. by Leonard J. Doyle (Collegeville, Minn.: Liturgical Press, 1948), pp. 79–80.*

than a department of the state. Such political assumption of spiritual power involved the emperor directly in the church's affairs, even to the point of playing the theologian and imposing conciliar solutions on its doctrinal quarrels. State control of religion was the original church–state relation in the West. The bishops of Rome, however, never accepted such intervention and opposed it in every way they could. In the fifth and sixth centuries, taking advantage of imperial weakness and distraction, they developed for their own defense the weaponry of the doctrine of papal primacy. This doctrine raised the Roman pontiff to an unassailable supremacy within the church when it came to defining all other church doctrine. It also put him in a position to make important secular claims, leading to repeated conflicts between church and state, pope and emperor, throughout the Middle Ages.

Papal primacy was first asserted as a response to the decline of imperial Rome that accompanied the shift of the imperial residence in the West to Milan and, later, Ravenna. It was also a response to the concurrent claims of the patriarchs of the Eastern Church, who, after imperial power was transferred to Constantinople, looked on the bishop of Rome as a peer, not as a superior. In 381 the ecumenical Council of Constantinople declared the bishop of Constantinople to be of first rank after the bishop of Rome "because Constantinople is the new Rome." In 451 the ecumenical Council of Chalcedon recognized Constantinople as having the same religious primacy in the East as Rome had traditionally possessed in the West. By the mid-sixth century the bishop of Constantinople regularly described himself in correspondence as a "universal" patriarch.

Roman pontiffs, understandably jealous of such claims and resentful of the ecclesiastical interference of Eastern emperors, launched a counteroffensive. Pope Damasus I (r. 366–384)[3] took the first of several major steps in the rise of the Roman church when he declared a Roman "apostolic" primacy. Pointing to Jesus' words to Peter in the Gospel of Matthew (16:18) ("Thou art Peter, and upon this rock I will build my church"), he claimed himself and all other popes to be Peter's direct successors as the unique "rock" on which the Christian Church was built. Pope Leo I (r. 440–461) took still another fateful step by assuming the title *pontifex maximus*, or "supreme priest." He further proclaimed himself to be endowed with a "plentitude of power," thereby establishing the supremacy of the bishop of Rome over all other bishops in the church. During Leo's reign an imperial decree recognized his exclusive jurisdiction over the Western church. At the end of the fifth century, Pope Gelasius I (r. 492–496) proclaimed the authority of the clergy to be "more weighty" than the power of kings because priests had charge of divine affairs and the means of salvation.

Events as well as ideology favored the papacy. The Germanic and Islamic invasions, just as they had isolated the West by diverting the attention of the eastern empire, also prevented either emperors or eastern patriarchs from interfering in the affairs of the Western church. Islam may even be said to have "saved" the Western church from Eastern domination. At the same time, the emergent Lombards and Franks provided the church with new political allies. Eastern episcopal competition with Rome ended as bishopric after bishopric fell to Islamic armies in the East. The power of the exarch of Ravenna—the Byzantine emperor's viceroy in the West—was eclipsed by invading Lombards, who, thanks to Frankish prodding, became Nicene Christians loyal to Rome and increasingly a counterweight to Eastern power and influence in the West. In an unprecedented act, Pope Gregory I, "the Great" (r. 590–604), negotiated an independent peace treaty with the Lombards, completely ignoring the Eastern emperor and the imperial authorities in Ravenna, who were too weak to resist.

The Division of Christendom

As the events just discussed suggest, the division of Christendom into Eastern (Byzantine) and Western (Roman Catholic) churches has its roots in the early Middle Ages. The division was due in part to linguistic and cultural differences between the Greek East and the Roman, Latin-speaking West. A novel combination of Greek, Roman, and Asian elements shaped Byzantine culture, giving Eastern Christianity more of a mystical orientation than Western Christianity. Compared with their Western counterparts, Eastern Christians seemed to attribute less importance to life in this world and to be more concerned about questions affecting their eternal destiny. This strong mystical orientation toward the next world may also have permitted the Eastern patriarchs to submit more passively than

[3] *Dates after popes' names are the years of each reign.*

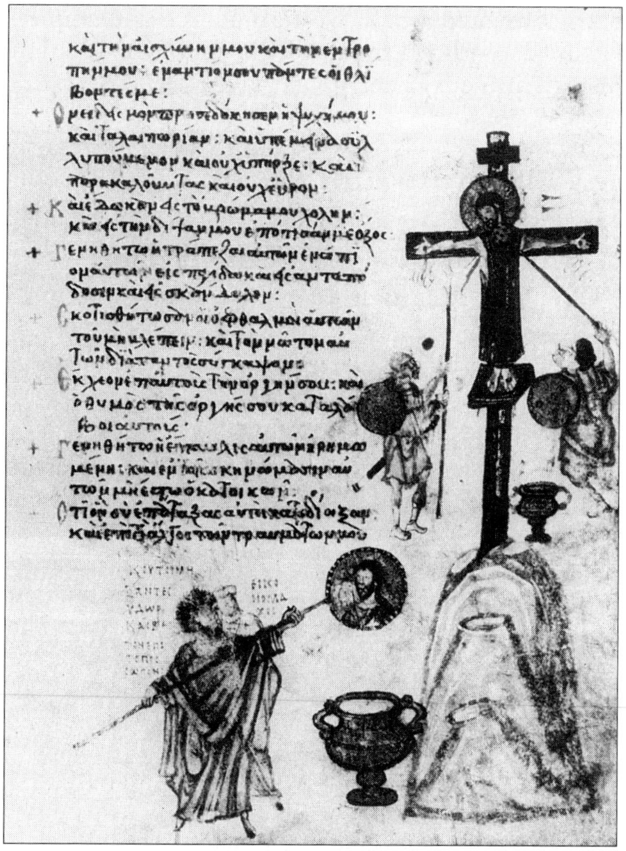

A ninth-century Byzantine manuscript shows an iconoclast whiting out an image of Christ. The Iconoclastic Controversy was an important factor in the division of Christendom into separate Latin and Greek branches. [State Historical Museum, Moscow]

Western popes could ever do to royal intervention in church affairs.

As in the West, Eastern Church organization closely followed that of the secular state. A patriarch ruled over metropolitans and archbishops in the cities and provinces; and they, in turn, ruled over bishops, who stood as authorities over the local clergy. Except for the patriarch Michael Cerularius, who tried unsuccessfully in the eleventh century to free the church from its traditional tight state control, the patriarchs were normally carefully regulated by the emperor.

Contrary to the evolving Western tradition of universal clerical celibacy (which Western monastic culture encouraged), the Eastern Church permitted the marriage of parish priests (but not monks), while strictly forbidding bishops to marry. The Eastern Church also used leavened bread in the Eucharist, contrary to the Western custom of using unleavened bread, and rejected the Western doctrine of purgatory. Unlike the Roman Church, the Eastern Church accommodated the laity by recognizing divorce and by using vernacular liturgies. The Roman Church also objected to the tendency of the Eastern Church to compromise doctrinally with the politically powerful Arian and Monophysite Christians. Finally, in the background, the Eastern and Western churches both laid claim to jurisdiction over the newly converted areas in the North Balkans.

Beyond these issues, three major factors lay behind the religious break between East and West. The first revolved around questions of doctrinal authority. The Eastern Church put more stress on the authority of the Bible and the ecumenical councils of the church in the definition of Christian doctrine than on the counsel and decrees of the bishop of Rome. The claims of Roman popes to a special primacy of authority on the basis of the apostle Peter's commission from Jesus in the Gospel of Matthew were unacceptable to the East. In the East the independence and autonomy of national churches held sway. As Steven Runciman summarized, "The Byzantine ideal was a series of autocephalous state churches, linked by intercommunion and the faith of seven councils."[4] This basic issue of authority in matters of faith lay behind the mutual excommunication of Pope Nicholas I and Patriarch Photius in the ninth century and that of Pope Leo IX (through his ambassador to Constantinople, Cardinal Humbert) and Patriarch Michael Cerularius in 1054.

A second major factor in the separation of the two churches was the Western addition of the *filioque* clause to the Nicene-Constantinopolitan Creed. According to this anti-Arian clause, the Holy Spirit proceeds "also from the Son" (*filioque*) as well as from the Father. This addition made clear the Western belief that Christ was "fully substantial with God the Father" and not a lesser being.

The third factor dividing the Eastern and Western churches was the iconoclastic controversy of the first half of the eighth century. As noted in the discussion of the Byzantine Empire, after 725 the Eastern emperor, Leo III, banned the use of images in Eastern churches and attempted to enforce the ban in the West also. Images were greatly cherished in the West, and his actions met fierce official and

[4]*Steven Runciman,* Byzantine Civilization *(London: A. and C. Black, 1933), p. 128.*

Major Political and Religious Developments of the Early Middle Ages

313	Emperor Constantine issues the Edict of Milan
325	Council of Nicaea defines Christian doctrine
410	Rome invaded by Visigoths under Alaric
413–426	Saint Augustine writes *The City of God*
451	Council of Chalcedon further defines Christian doctrine
451–453	Europe invaded by the Huns under Attila
476	Barbarian Odovacer deposes Western emperor and rules as king of the Romans
489–493	Theodoric establishes kingdom of Ostrogoths in Italy
529	Saint Benedict founds monastery at Monte Cassino
533	Justinian codifies Roman law
622	Muhammad's flight from Mecca (Hegira)
732	Charles Martel defeats Muslims at Poitiers
754	Pope Stephen II and Pepin III ally

popular resistance there. To punish the West for this disobedience, Leo confiscated papal lands in Sicily and Calabria (in southern Italy) and placed them under the jurisdiction of the subservient patriarch of Constantinople. Because these territories provided essential papal revenues, the Western church could not but view the emperor's action as a declaration of war. (Later Empress Irene made peace with the Roman Catholic Church on this issue and restored the use of images at the ecumenical Council of Nicaea in 787.)

Emperor Leo's direct challenge of the pope coincided with a renewed threat to Rome and the Western church from the Lombards of northern Italy. Assailed on two fronts, the Roman papacy seemed surely doomed. There has not, however, been a more resilient and enterprising institution in Western history than the papacy. Since Gregory the Great, who 150 years earlier had negotiated a treaty with the Lombards, popes had recognized the Franks of northern Gaul as Europe's ascendant power and had seen in them their surest protectors. In 754, Pope Stephen II (r. 752–757), initiating the most fruitful political alliance of the Middle Ages, enlisted the Franks and their ruler, Pepin III, to defend the church against the Lombards and as a Western counterweight to the Eastern emperor. This marriage of religion and politics created a new Western church and empire; it also determined much of the course of Western history into our time.

The Kingdom of the Franks

Merovingians and Carolingians: From Clovis to Charlemagne

A warrior chieftain, Clovis (ca. 466–511), who converted to orthodox Christianity around 496, founded the first Frankish dynasty, the Merovingians, named for Merovich, an early leader of one branch of the Franks. Clovis and his successors united the Salian and Ripuarian Franks, subdued the Arian Burgundians and Visigoths, and established the kingdom of the Franks within ancient Gaul, making the Franks and the Merovingian kings a significant force in western Europe. The Franks themselves occupied a broad belt of territory that extended throughout modern France, Belgium, the Netherlands, and western Germany, and their loyalties remained strictly tribal and local.

Governing the Franks In attempting to govern this sprawling kingdom, the Merovingians encountered what proved to be the most persistent problem of medieval political history—the competing claims of the "one" and the "many." On the one hand, the king struggled for a centralized government and transregional loyalty, and on the other, powerful local magnates strove to preserve their regional autonomy and traditions.

The Merovingian kings addressed this problem by making pacts with the landed nobility and by creating the royal office of *count*. The counts were men without possessions to whom the king gave great lands in the expectation that they would be, as the landed aristocrats often were not, loyal officers of the kingdom. But like local aristocrats, the Merovingian counts also let their immediate self-interest gain the upper hand. Once established in office for a period of time, they too became territorial rulers in their own right, so that the Frankish kingdom progressively fragmented into independent regions and tiny principalities. This centrifugal tendency was further aided by the Frankish custom of dividing the kingdom equally among the king's legitimate male heirs.

Rather than purchasing allegiance and unity within the kingdom, the Merovingian largess

Clovis Converts to Christianity

One of the attractions of Christianity in the late ancient and early medieval world was its belief in a God providentially active in history who assisted those loyal to him against their enemies. In the following account of Clovis's conversion, provided by the Christian Church historian Gregory of Tours, the Frankish king is said to have turned Christian because he believed that the Christian God had given him a military victory over a rival German tribe, the Alemanni.

✦ *Does Clovis's conversion to Christianity under duress suggest that his newfound faith was insincere and only opportunistic? What does his subsequent religious life suggest? What were the political implications of his conversion? Why did he receive further instruction in Christianity "secretly"?*

Clovis took to wife Clotilde, daughter of the king of the Burgundians and a Christian. The queen unceasingly urged the king to acknowledge the true God, and forsake idols. But he could not in any wise be brought to believe until a war broke out with the Alemanni. . . . The two armies were in battle and there was great slaughter. Clovis' army was near to utter destruction. He saw the danger . . . and raised his eyes to heaven, saying: Jesus Christ, whom Clotilde declares to be the son of the living God, who it is said givest aid to the oppressed and victory to those who put their hope in thee, I beseech thy . . . aid. If thou shalt grant me victory over these enemies . . . I will believe in thee and be baptized in thy name. For I have called upon my gods, but . . . they are far removed from my aid. So I believe that they have no power, for they do not succor those who serve them. Now I call upon thee, and I long to believe in thee. . . . When he had said these things, the Alemanni turned their backs and began to flee. When they saw that their king was killed, they submitted to the sway of Clovis, saying . . . Now we are thine.

After Clovis had forbidden further war and praised his soldiers, he told the queen how he had won the victory by calling on the name of Christ. Then the queen sent for the blessed Remigius, bishop of the city of Rheims, praying him to bring the gospel of salvation to the king. The priest, little by little and secretly, led him to believe in the true God . . . and to forsake idols, which could not help him nor anybody else.

James Harvey Robinson, ed., Readings in European History, *vol. 1 (Boston: Athenaeum, 1904), pp. 52–54.*

simply occasioned the rise of competing magnates and petty tyrants, who became laws unto themselves within their regions. By the seventh century the Frankish king was king in title only and had no effective executive power. Real power came to be concentrated in the office of the *mayor of the palace*, spokesperson at the king's court for the great landowners of the three regions into which the Frankish kingdom was divided: Neustria, Austrasia, and Burgundy. Through this office the Carolingian dynasty rose to power.

The Carolingians controlled the office of the mayor of the palace from the ascent to that post of Pepin I of Austrasia (d. 639) until 751, when, with the enterprising connivance of the pope, they simply expropriated the Frankish crown. Pepin II (d. 714) ruled in fact if not in title over the Frankish kingdom. His illegitimate son, Charles Martel ("the Hammer," d. 741), created a great cavalry by bestowing lands known as *benefices*, or *fiefs*, on powerful noblemen. In return, they agreed to be ready to serve as the king's army. It was such an army that checked the Islamic probings on the western front at Poitiers in 732—an important battle that helped to secure the borders of western Europe.

The fiefs so generously bestowed by Charles Martel to create his army came in large part from landed property that he usurped from the church. His alliance with the landed aristocracy in this grand manner permitted the Carolingians to have some measure of political success where the Merovingians had failed. The Carolingians created counts almost entirely out of the landed nobility from which the Carolingians themselves had risen. The Merovingians, in contrast, had tried to compete directly with these great aristocrats by raising landless men to power. By playing to strength rather than challenging it, the Carolingians strengthened themselves, at least for the short term. The church, by this time dependent on the protection of the Franks against the Eastern emperor and the Lombards, could only suffer in silence the usurpation of lands to which it held claim. Later, although they never returned them, the Franks partially compensated the church for these lands.

A bejeweled tenth-century reliquary. From the Church of Saint Foy, Conques, France. [Giraudon/Art Resource, N.Y.]

THE FRANKISH CHURCH The church came to play a large and enterprising role in the Frankish government. By Carolingian times monasteries were a dominant force. Their intellectual achievements made them respected centers of culture. Their religious teaching and example imposed order on surrounding populations. Their relics and rituals made them magical shrines to which pilgrims came in great numbers. And, thanks to their many gifts and internal discipline and industry, many had become very profitable farms and landed estates, their abbots rich and powerful magnates. Already in Merovingian times the higher clergy were employed in tandem with counts as royal agents.

It was the policy of the Carolingians, perfected by Charles Martel and his successor, Pepin III ("the Short," d. 768), to use the church to pacify conquered neighboring tribes—Frisians, Thüringians, Bavarians, and especially the Franks' archenemies, the Saxons. Conversion to Nicene Christianity became an integral part of the successful annexation of conquered lands and people. The cavalry broke their bodies, while the clergy won their hearts and minds. The Anglo-Saxon missionary Saint Boniface (born Wynfrith; 680?–754) was the most important cleric to serve Carolingian kings in this way. Christian bishops in missionary districts and elsewhere became lords, appointed by and subject to the king. In this ominous integration of secular and religious policy lay the seeds of the later Investiture Controversy of the eleventh and twelfth centuries. (See Chapter 7.)

The church served more than Carolingian territorial expansion. Pope Zacharias (r. 741–752) also sanctioned Pepin the Short's termination of the vestigial Merovingian dynasty and supported the Carolingian accession to outright kingship of the Franks. With the pope's public blessing, Pepin was proclaimed king by the nobility in council in 751, while the last of the Merovingians, the puppet king Childeric III, was hustled off to a monastery and dynastic oblivion. According to legend, Saint Boniface first anointed Pepin, thereby investing Frankish rule from the very start with a certain sacral character.

Zacharias's successor, Pope Stephen II (r. 752–757), did not let Pepin forget the favor of his predecessor. In 753, when the Lombards besieged Rome, Pope Stephen crossed the Alps and appealed directly to Pepin to cast out the invaders and to guarantee papal claims to central Italy, largely dominated at this time by the Eastern emperor. As already noted, in 754 the Franks and the church formed an alliance against the Lombards and the Eastern emperor. Carolingian kings became the protectors of the Catholic Church and thereby "kings by the grace of God." Pepin gained the title *patricius Romanorum*, "patrician of the Romans," a title first borne by the ruling families of Rome and heretofore applied to the representative of the Eastern emperor. In 755 the Franks defeated the Lombards and gave the pope the lands surrounding Rome, creating what came to be known as the *Papal States*.

In this period a fraudulent document appeared—the *Donation of Constantine* (written between 750 and 800)—that was enterprisingly designed to remind the Franks of the church's importance as the heir of Rome. Many believed it to be genuine until it was definitely exposed as a forgery in the fifteenth century by the humanist Lorenzo Valla.

The papacy had looked to the Franks for an ally strong enough to protect it from the Eastern emperors. It is an irony of history that the church found in the Carolingian dynasty a Western imperial government that drew almost as slight a boundary between state and church, secular and religious policy, as did eastern emperors. Although Carolingian patronage was eminently preferable to Eastern domination for the popes, it proved in its own way to be no less constraining.

The Reign of Charlemagne (768–814)

Charlemagne, the son of Pepin the Short, continued the role of his father as papal protector in Italy and his policy of territorial conquest in the north. After decisively defeating King Desiderius and the Lombards of northern Italy in 774, Charlemagne took upon himself the title "King of the Lombards" in Pavia. He widened the frontiers of his kingdom further by subjugating surrounding pagan tribes, foremost among them the Saxons, whom the Franks brutally Christianized and dispersed in small groups throughout Frankish lands. The Muslims were chased beyond the Pyrenees, and the Avars (a tribe related to the Huns) were practically annihilated, bringing the Danubian plains into the Frankish orbit. The defeat of the Avars was so complete that the expression "vanished like the Avars" came to be applied to anything that was irretrievably lost.

By the time of his death on January 28, 814, Charlemagne's kingdom embraced modern France, Belgium, Holland, Switzerland, almost the whole of western Germany, much of Italy, a portion of Spain, and the island of Corsica—an area about equal to that of the modern European Common Market. (See Map 6–4.)

THE NEW EMPIRE Encouraged by his ambitious advisers, Charlemagne came to harbor imperial designs. He desired to be not only king of all the Franks but a universal emperor as well. He had his sacred palace city, Aachen (in French, Aix-la-Chapelle), constructed in conscious imitation of the courts of the ancient Roman and contemporary Eastern emperors. Although he permitted the church its independence, he looked after it with a paternalism almost as great as that of any Eastern emperor. He used the church, above all, to promote social stability and hierarchical order throughout the kingdom—as an aid in the creation of a great Frankish Christian Empire. Frankish Christians were ceremoniously baptized, professed the Nicene Creed (with the *filioque* clause), and learned in church to revere Charlemagne.

The formation of a distinctive Carolingian Christendom was made clear in the 790s when Charlemagne issued the so-called *Libri Carolini*. These documents attacked the ecumenical Council of Nicaea, which, in what was actually a friendly gesture to the West, had met in 787 to formulate a new, more accommodating position for the Eastern Church on the use of images.

Charlemagne fulfilled his imperial pretensions on Christmas Day, 800, when Pope Leo III (r. 795–816) crowned him emperor. This event began what would come to be known as the Holy Roman Empire, a revival of the old Roman Empire in the West, based after 870 in Germany.

In 799, Pope Leo III had been imprisoned by the Roman aristocracy but escaped to the protection of Charlemagne, who restored him as pope. The fate-

MAP 6–4 THE EMPIRE OF CHARLEMAGNE TO 814 *Building on the successes of his predecessors, Charlemagne greatly increased the Frankish domains. Such traditional enemies as the Saxons and the Lombards fell under his sway.*

ful coronation of Charlemagne was thus in part an effort by the pope to enhance the church's stature and to gain some leverage over this powerful king. It was, however, no papal coup d'etat; Charlemagne's control over the church remained as strong after as before the event. If the coronation benefitted the church, as it certainly did, it also served Charlemagne's purposes.

Before his coronation, Charlemagne had been a minor Western potentate in the eyes of Eastern emperors. After the coronation, Eastern emperors reluctantly recognized his new imperial dignity; and Charlemagne even found it necessary to disclaim ambitions to rule as emperor over the East.

THE NEW EMPEROR Charlemagne stood a majestic six feet three and one half inches tall—a fact confirmed when his tomb was opened and exact measurements of his remains were taken in 1861. He was restless, ever ready for a hunt. Informal and gregarious, he insisted on the presence of friends even when he bathed. He was widely known for his practical jokes, lusty good humor, and warm hospitality. Aachen was a festive palace city to which people and gifts came from all over the world. In 802 Charlemagne even received from the caliph of Baghdad, Harun-al-Rashid, a white elephant, the transport of which across the Alps was as great a wonder as the creature itself.

Charlemagne had five official wives in succession, many mistresses and concubines, and he sired numerous children. This connubial variety created special problems. His oldest son by his first marriage, Pepin, jealous of the attention shown by his father to the sons of his second wife and fearing the loss of paternal favor, joined with noble enemies in a conspiracy against his father. He spent the rest of his life in confinement in a monastery after the plot was exposed.

PROBLEMS OF GOVERNMENT Charlemagne governed his kingdom through counts, of whom there were perhaps as many as 250. They were strategically located within the administrative districts into which the kingdom was divided. In Carolingian practice the count tended to be a local magnate, one who already possessed the armed might and the self-interest to enforce the will of a generous king. He had three main duties: to maintain a local army loyal to the king, to collect tribute and dues, and to administer justice throughout his district.

This last responsibility he undertook through a district law court known as the *mallus*. The *mallus* received testimony from witnesses familiar with the parties involved in a dispute or criminal case, much as a modern court does. Through such testimony it sought to discover the character and believability of each side. On occasion, in very difficult cases where such testimony was insufficient to determine guilt or innocence, recourse would be taken to judicial duels or to a variety of "divine" tests or ordeals. Among these was the length of time it took a defendant's hand to heal after immersion in boiling water. In another, the ordeal by water, a defendant was thrown with his hands and feet bound into a river or pond that a priest had blessed. If he floated, he was pronounced guilty, because the pure water had obviously rejected him; if, however, the water received him and he sank, he was deemed innocent.

In such ordeals God was believed to render a verdict. Once guilt had been made clear to the *mallus*, either by testimony or by ordeal, it assessed a monetary compensation to be paid to the injured party. This most popular way of settling grievances usually ended hostilities between individuals and families.

As in Merovingian times, many counts used their official position and new judicial powers to their own advantage and became little despots

An equestrian figure of Charlemagne (or possibly one of his sons) from the early ninth century. [Giraudon/Art Resource, N.Y.]

within their districts. As the strong became stronger, they also became more independent. They began to look on the land grants with which they were paid as hereditary possessions rather than generous royal donations—a development that began to fragment Charlemagne's kingdom. Charlemagne tried to oversee his overseers and improve local justice by creating special royal envoys known as *missi dominici*. These were lay and clerical agents (counts and archbishops and bishops) who made annual visits to districts other than their own. But their impact was marginal. Permanent provincial governors, bearing the title of prefect, duke, or margrave, were created in what was still another attempt to supervise the counts and organize the outlying regions of the kingdom. But as these governors became established in their areas, they proved no less corruptible than the others.

Charlemagne never solved the problem of creating a loyal bureaucracy. Ecclesiastical agents proved no better than secular ones in this regard. Landowning bishops had not only the same responsibilities but also the same secular lifestyles and aspirations as the royal counts. Save for their attendance to the liturgy and to church prayers, they were largely indistinguishable from the lay nobility. Capitularies, or royal decrees, discouraged the more outrageous behavior of the clergy. But Charlemagne also sensed, rightly, as the Gregorian reform of the eleventh century would prove, that the emergence of a distinctive, reform-minded class of ecclesiastical landowners would be a danger to royal government. He purposefully treated his bishops as he treated his counts, that is, as vassals who served at the king's pleasure.

To be a Christian in this period was more a matter of ritual and doctrine (being baptized and reciting the creed) than of following a prescription for ethical behavior and social service. Both clergy and laity were more concerned with contests over the most basic kinds of social protections than with more elevated ethical issues. An important legislative achievement of Charlemagne's reign, for example, was to give a free vassal the right to break his oath of loyalty to his lord if the lord tried to kill him, to reduce him to an unfree serf, to withhold promised protection in time of need, or to seduce his wife.

Alcuin and the Carolingian Renaissance

Charlemagne accumulated a great deal of wealth in the form of loot and land from conquered tribes. He used a substantial part of this booty to attract Europe's best scholars to Aachen, where they developed court culture and education. By making scholarship materially as well as intellectually rewarding, Charlemagne attracted such scholars as Theodulf of Orleans, Angilbert, his own biographer Einhard, and the renowned Anglo-Saxon master Alcuin of York (735–804). In 782, at almost fifty years of age, Alcuin became director of the king's palace school. He brought classical and Christian learning to Aachen in schools run by the monasteries. Alcuin was handsomely rewarded for his efforts with several monastic estates, including that of Saint Martin of Tours, the wealthiest in the kingdom.

Although Charlemagne also appreciated learning for its own sake, his grand palace school was not created simply for the love of antiquity. Charlemagne intended it to upgrade the administrative skills of the clerics and officials who staffed the royal bureaucracy. By preparing the sons of the nobility to run the religious and secular offices of the realm, court scholarship served kingdom building. The school provided basic instruction in the seven liberal arts, with special concentration on grammar, logic, rhetoric, and the basic mathematical arts. It therefore provided training in reading, writing, speaking, sound reasoning, and counting—the basic tools of bureaucracy.

Among the results of this intellectual activity was the appearance of a more accurate Latin in official documents and the development of a clear style of handwriting known as Carolingian minuscule, which was far more legible than Merovingian script. By making reading both easier and more pleasurable, Carolingian minuscule helped lay the foundations of subsequent Latin scholarship. It also increased lay literacy.

A modest renaissance of antiquity occurred in the palace school as scholars collected and preserved ancient manuscripts for a more curious posterity. Alcuin worked on a correct text of the Bible and made editions of the works of Gregory the Great and the monastic *Rule* of Saint Benedict. These scholarly activities aimed at concrete reforms and served official efforts to bring uniformity to church law and liturgy, to educate the clergy, and to improve moral life within the monasteries. Through personal correspondence and visitations, Alcuin created a genuine, if limited, community of scholars and clerics at court. He did much to infuse the highest administrative levels with a sense of comradeship and common purpose.

THE CAROLINGIAN MANOR The agrarian economy of the early Middle Ages was organized and controlled through village farms known as manors. On these, peasants labored as tenants for a lord, that is, a more powerful landowner who allotted them land and tenements in exchange for their services and a portion of their crops. The part of the land tended for the lord was the *demesne*, on average about one-quarter to one-third of the arable land. All crops grown there were harvested for the lord. The manor also included common meadows for grazing animals, and forests reserved exclusively for the lord to hunt in.

Peasants were treated according to their personal status and the size of their tenements. A *freeman*, that is, a peasant with his own modest allodial, or hereditary, property (property free from the claims of an overlord), became a serf by surrendering his property to a greater landowner—a lord—in exchange for protection and assistance. The freeman received his land back from the lord with a clear definition of his economic and legal rights. Although the land was no longer his property, he had full possession and use of it and the number of services and amount of goods he was to supply to the lord were carefully spelled out.

Peasants who entered the service of a lord with little real property (perhaps only a few farm implements and animals) ended up as *unfree serfs*. Such serfs were much more vulnerable to the lord's demands, often spending up to three days a week working the lord's fields. Truly impoverished peasants, those who had nothing to offer a lord except their hands, had the lowest status and were the least protected from excessive demands on their labor.

All classes of serfs were subject to various dues in kind: firewood for cutting the lord's wood, sheep for being allowed to graze their sheep on the lord's land, and the like. Thus the lord, who, for his part, furnished shacks and small plots of land from his vast domain, had at his disposal an army of servants of varying status who provided him with everything from eggs to boots. Weak serfs often fled to monasteries rather than continue their servitude. That many serfs were discontented is reflected in the high number of recorded escapes. An astrological calendar from the period even marks the days most favorable for escaping. Escaped serfs roamed the land as beggars and vagabonds, searching for new and better masters.

By the time of Charlemagne, the moldboard plow and the three-field system of land cultivation were coming into use. These developments greatly improved agricultural productivity. The older "scratch" plow had crisscrossed the field with only slight penetration and required light, well-drained soils. The moldboard plow, by contrast, cut deep

In this eleventh-century manuscript, peasants harvest vines and plough fields behind yoked oxen. [Ardos Studio]

into the soil and turned it to form a ridge, providing a natural drainage system and permitting the deep planting of seeds. This new type of plow made cultivation possible in the regions north of the Mediterranean, where soils were dense and waterlogged from heavy precipitation.

Unlike the earlier two-field system of crop rotation, which simply alternated fallow with planted fields each year, the three-field system increased the amount of cultivated land by leaving only one third fallow in a given year. Indeed, the third field might be reclaimed from previously passed over heavier soils now made workable by the moldboard plow, thus increasing the amount of land under cultivation in a dramatic fashion. It also better adjusted crops to seasons. In fall one field was planted with winter crops of wheat or rye and harvested in early summer. In late spring a second field was planted with summer crops of oats, barley, lentils, and legumes, which were harvested in August or September. The third field was left fallow, to be planted in its turn with winter and summer crops. The new summer crops, especially legumes, restored nitrogen to the soil and helped increase yields.

Religion and the Clergy The lower clergy lived among and were drawn from peasant ranks. They fared hardly better than peasants in Carolingian times. As owners of the churches on their lands, the lords had the right to raise chosen serfs to the post of parish priest, placing them in charge of the churches on the lords' estates. Church law directed a lord to set a serf free before he entered the clergy. Lords, however, were reluctant to do this and risk thereby a possible later challenge to their jurisdiction over the ecclesiastical property with which the serf, as priest, was invested. Lords preferred a "serf priest," one who not only said the mass on Sundays and holidays but who also continued to serve his lord during the week, waiting on the lord's table and tending his steeds. Like Charlemagne with his bishops, Frankish lords cultivated a docile parish clergy.

The ordinary people looked to religion for comfort and consolation. They especially associated religion with the major Christian holidays and festivals, like Christmas and Easter. They baptized their children, attended mass, tried to learn the Lord's Prayer and the Apostles' Creed, and received the last rites from the priest as death approached. This was all probably done with more awe and simple faith than understanding. Because local priests on the manors were no better educated than their congregations, religious instruction in the meaning of Christian doctrine and practice remained at a bare minimum. The church sponsored street dramas in accordance with the church calendar. These were designed to impart the highlights of the Bible and church history and to instill basic Christian moral values.

People understandably became particularly attached in this period to the more tangible veneration of saints and relics. The Virgin Mary was also widely revered, although a true cult of Mary would not develop until the eleventh and twelfth centuries. Religious devotion to saints has been compared to subjection to powerful lords in the secular world. Both the saint and the lord were protectors whose honor the serfs were bound to defend and whose favor and help in time of need they hoped to receive. Veneration of saints also had strong points of contact with old tribal customs, from which the commonfolk were hardly detached. (Indeed, Charlemagne enforced laws against witchcraft, sorcery, and the ritual sacrifice of animals by monks.)

But religion also had an intrinsic appeal and special meaning to those masses of medieval men and women who found themselves burdened, fearful, and with little hope of material betterment on this side of eternity. Charlemagne shared many of the religious beliefs of his ordinary subjects. He collected and venerated relics, made pilgrimages to Rome, and frequented the Church of Saint Mary in Aachen several times a day. In his last will and testament he directed that all but a fraction of his great treasure be spent to endow masses and prayers for his departed soul.

Breakup of the Carolingian Kingdom

In the last years of his life, an ailing Charlemagne knew that his empire was ungovernable. The seeds of dissolution lay in regionalism, that is, the determination of each region, no matter how small, to look first—and often only—to its own self-interest. Despite his considerable skill and resolve, Charlemagne's realm became too fragmented among powerful regional magnates. Although they were his vassals, these same men were also landholders and lords in their own right. They knew that their sovereignty lessened as Charlemagne's increased and accordingly became reluctant royal servants. In feudal society a direct relationship existed between physical proximity to authority and loyalty to authority. Local people obeyed local lords more readily than they obeyed a glorious but distant king.

Charlemagne had been forced to recognize and even to enhance the power of regional magnates to win needed financial and military support. But as in the Merovingian kingdom, the tail came increasingly to wag the dog. Charlemagne's major attempt to enforce transregional discipline and the subordination of local interests to royal dictates was to create the institution of the *missi dominici*—royal overseers of the king's law and justice. But these new officials themselves fell prey to narrow, regional self-interest, and this effort also proved ultimately unsuccessful.

LOUIS THE PIOUS The Carolingian kings did not give up easily, however. Charlemagne's only surviving son and successor was Louis the Pious (r. 814–840), so-called because of his close alliance with the church and his promotion of puritanical reforms. Before his death, Charlemagne secured the imperial succession for Louis by raising him to "co-emperor" in a grand public ceremony. After Charlemagne's death, Louis no longer referred to himself as king of the Franks. He bore instead the single title of emperor. The assumption of this title reflected not only Carolingian pretense to an imperial dynasty, but also Louis's determination to unify his kingdom and raise its people above mere regional and tribal loyalties.

Unfortunately Louis's own fertility joined with Salic, or Frankish, law and Frankish custom to prevent the attainment of this high goal. Louis had three sons by his first wife. According to Salic law, a ruler partitioned his kingdom equally among his surviving sons. (Salic law forbade women to inherit the throne.) Louis, who saw himself as an emperor and no mere king, recognized that a tripartite kingdom would hardly be an empire and acted early in his reign, in the year 817, to break this legal tradition. This he did by making his eldest son, Lothar (d. 855), co-regent and sole imperial heir. To Lothar's brothers he gave important but much lesser appanages, or assigned hereditary lands; Pepin

MAP 6–5 THE TREATY OF VERDUN, 843, AND THE TREATY OF MERSEN, 870 *The Treaty of Verdun divided the kingdom of Louis the Pious among his three feuding children, Charles the Bald, Lothar, and Louis the German. After Lothar's death in 855, his lands and titles were divided among his three sons, Louis, Charles, and Lothar II. When Lothar II, who had received his father's northern kingdom, died in 870, Charles the Bald and Louis the German claimed the middle kingdom and divided it between themselves in the Treaty of Mersen.*

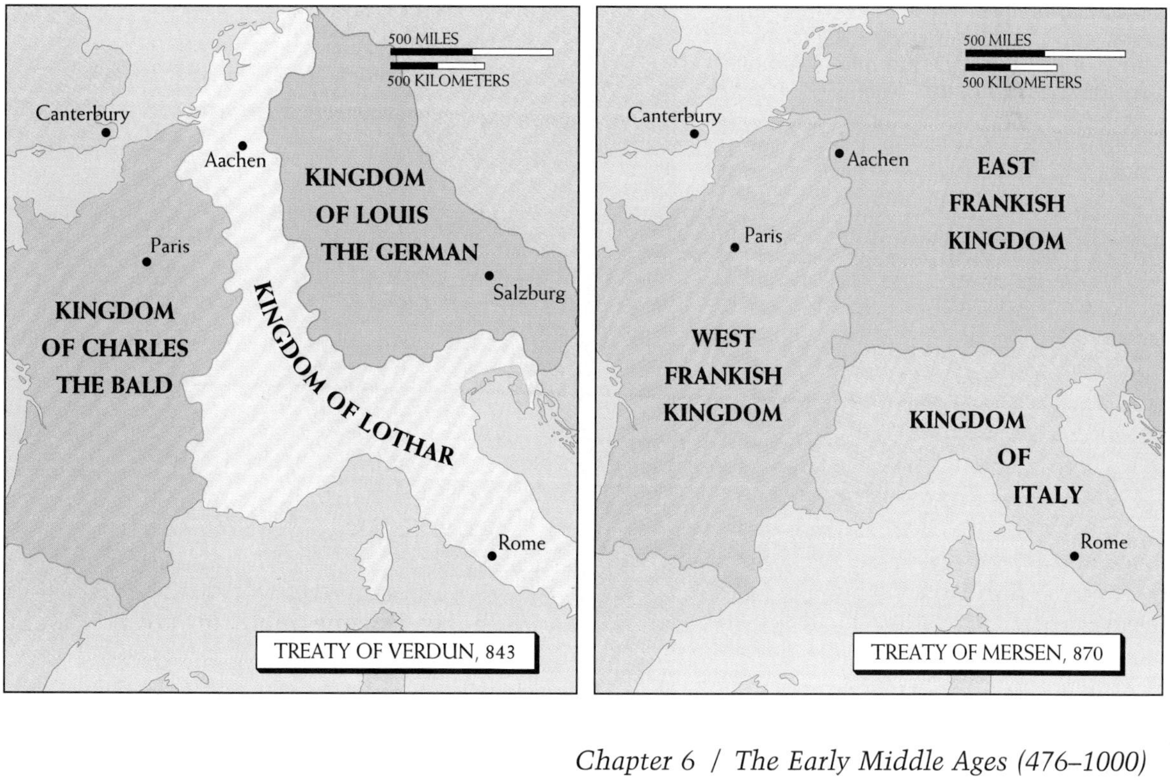

(d. 838) became king of Aquitaine, and Louis "the German" (d. 876) became king of Bavaria, over the eastern Franks.

In 823 Louis's second wife, Judith of Bavaria, bore him a fourth son, Charles, later called "the Bald" (d. 877). Mindful of Frankish law and custom and determined that her son should receive more than just a nominal inheritance, the queen incited the brothers Pepin and Louis against Lothar, who fled for refuge to the pope. More important, Judith was instrumental in persuading Louis to adhere to tradition and divide the kingdom equally among his four living sons. As their stepmother and the young Charles rose in their father's favor, the three brothers, fearing still further reversals, decided to act against their father. Supported by the pope, they joined forces and defeated their father in a battle near Colmar in 833.

As the bestower of crowns on emperors, the pope had an important stake in the preservation of the revived western empire and the imperial title. Louis's belated agreement to an equal partition of his kingdom threatened to weaken the pope as well as the royal family. Therefore, the pope condemned Louis and restored Lothar to his original inheritance. But Lothar's regained imperial dignity only stirred anew the resentments of his brothers, including his stepbrother, Charles, who joined in renewed warfare against him.

THE TREATY OF VERDUN AND ITS AFTERMATH In 843, with the Treaty of Verdun, peace finally came to the surviving heirs of Louis the Pious (Pepin had died in 838). But this agreement also brought about the disaster that Louis had originally feared. The great Carolingian Empire was partitioned into three equal parts. Lothar received a middle section, known as Lotharingia, which embraced roughly modern Holland, Belgium, Switzerland, Alsace-Lorraine, and Italy. Charles the Bald acquired the western part of the kingdom, or roughly modern France. And Louis the German took the eastern part, or roughly modern Germany. (See Map 6–5.)

Although Lothar retained the imperial title, the universal empire of Charlemagne and Louis the Pious ceased to exist after Verdun. Not until the sixteenth century, with the election in 1519 of Charles I of Spain as Holy Roman Emperor Charles V (see Chapter 11), would the Western world again see a kingdom so vast as Charlemagne's.

The tenth-century crown of the Holy Roman Emperor (the title applied to rulers who succeeded to the remains of Charlemagne's empire) reveals the close alliance between church and throne. The crown is surmounted by a cross, and it includes panels depicting the great kings of the Bible, David and Solomon. [Kunsthistorisches Museum, Vienna]

The Treaty of Verdun proved to be only the beginning of Carolingian fragmentation. When Lothar died in 855, his middle kingdom was divided equally among his three surviving sons, the eldest of whom, Louis II, retained Italy and the imperial title. This partition of the partition sealed the dissolution of the great empire of Charlemagne. Henceforth, western Europe saw an eastern and a western Frankish kingdom—roughly Germany and France—at war over the fractionalized middle kingdom, a contest that has continued into modern times.

In Italy the demise of the Carolingian emperors enhanced for the moment the power of the popes, who had become adept at filling vacuums. The popes were now strong enough to excommunicate weak emperors and override their wishes. In a major church crackdown on the polygyny of the Germans, Pope Nicholas I (r. 858–867) excommunicated Lothar II for divorcing his wife. After the death of the childless emperor Louis II in 875, Pope John VIII (r. 872–882) installed Charles the Bald as emperor against the express last wishes of Louis II.

When Charles the Bald died in 877, both the papal and the imperial thrones suffered defeat. They became pawns in the hands of powerful Italian and German magnates, respectively. Neither pope nor emperor knew dignity and power again until a new western imperial dynasty—the Saxons—attained dominance during the reign of Otto I (r. 962–973).

It is especially at this juncture in European history—the last quarter of the ninth and the first half of the tenth century—that one may speak with some justification of a "dark age." The internal political breakdown of the empire and the papacy coincided with new barbarian attacks, set off probably by overpopulation and famine in northern Europe. The late ninth and tenth centuries saw suc-

MAP 6–6 VIKING, ISLAMIC, AND MAGYAR INVASIONS TO THE ELEVENTH CENTURY *Western Europe was sorely beset by new waves of outsiders from the ninth to the eleventh century. From north, east, and south a stream of invading Vikings, Magyars, and Muslims brought the West at times to near collapse and of course gravely affected institutions within Europe.*

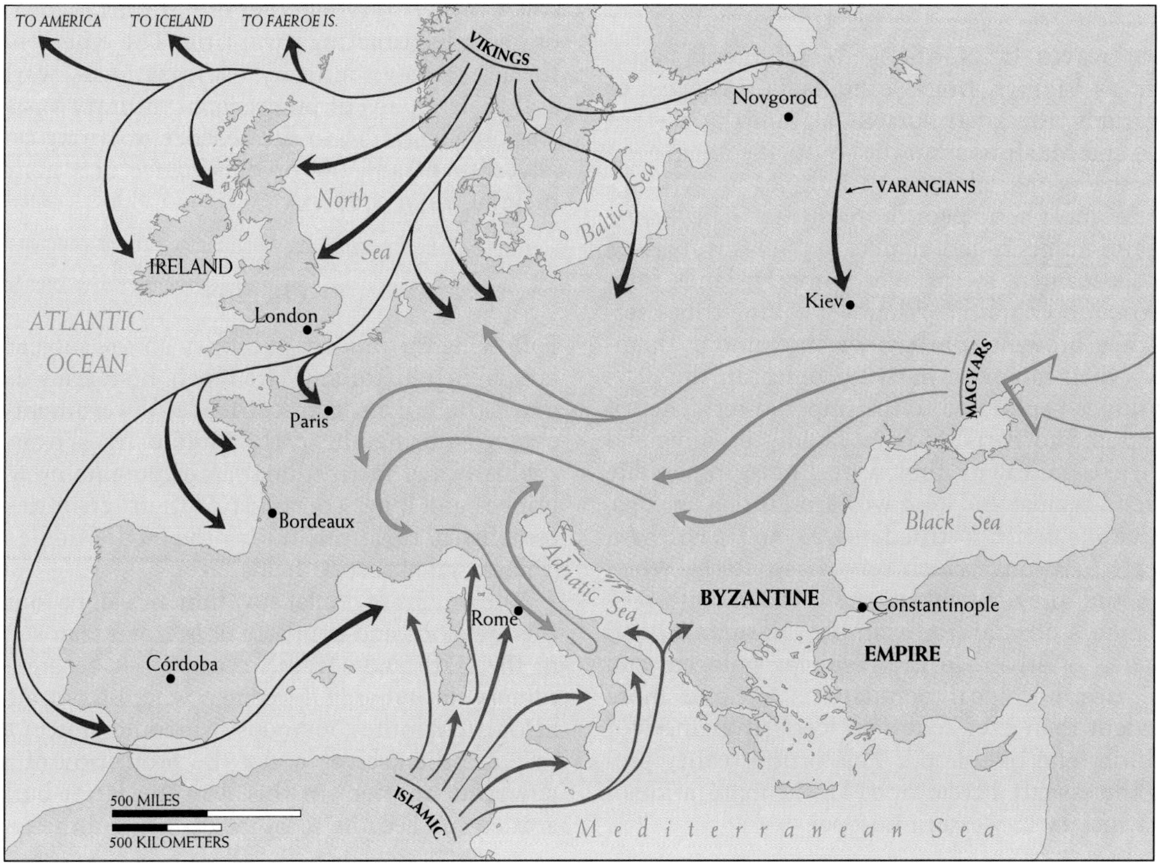

The Carolingian Dynasty (751–987)

750–800	*Donation of Constantine* protests Frankish domination of church
751	Pepin II "the Short" becomes king of the Franks
755	Franks protect church against Lombards and create the Papal States
768–814	Charlemagne rules as king of the Franks
774	Charlemagne defeats Lombards in northern Italy
800	Pope Leo III crowns Charlemagne emperor
814–840	Louis the Pious succeeds Charlemagne as emperor
843	Treaty of Verdun partitions the Carolingian Empire
870	Treaty of Mersen allows eastern and western Frankish kingdoms to absorb the fragmented middle lands
962	Saxons under Otto I firmly established as successors to Carolingians in Germany
987	Capetian dynasty succeeds Carolingian in France

cessive waves of Normans (North-men), better known as Vikings, from Scandinavia; Magyars, or Hungarians, the great horsemen from the eastern plains; and Muslims from the south. (See Map 6–6.)

For the people of western Europe, the Vikings were the most serious of these threats. They came in greater numbers and, thanks to their unsurpassed skills as seamen, swept over European lands from Novgorod to Gibraltar. Wherever Viking tribes settled, they brought conflict, warring among themselves when not with native peoples. In the 880s the Vikings penetrated to the imperial residence of Aachen and to Paris. Moving rapidly in ships and raiding coastal towns, they were almost impossible to defend against and kept western Europe on edge. The Franks built fortified towns and castles in strategic locations, which served as refuges. When they could, they bought off the invaders with outright grants of land (for example, Normandy) and payments of silver. In the resulting political and social turmoil, local populations became more dependent than ever before on local strongmen for life, limb, and livelihood. This brutal reality provided the essential conditions for the maturation of feudal society in western Europe.

Feudal Society

The Middle Ages were characterized by a chronic absence of effective central government and the constant threat of famine, disease, and foreign invasion. In this state of affairs the weaker sought the protection of the stronger, and the true lords and masters became those who could guarantee immediate security from rapine and starvation. The term *feudal society* refers to the social, political, military, and economic system that emerged from these conditions.

The feudal society of the Middle Ages was a society dominated by warlords. What people needed most was the firm assurance that others could be depended on in time of dire need. Lesser men pledged themselves to powerful individuals—warlords or princes—recognizing them as personal superiors and promising them faithful service. Large warrior groups of vassals sprang up, and these developed into a prominent professional military class with its own code of knightly conduct. The result was a network of relationships based on mutual loyalty that enabled warlords to acquire armies and to rule over territory whether or not they owned land or had a legitimating royal title. The emergence of these extensive military organizations—warlords and their groups of professional military vassals—was an adaptation to the absence of strong central government and the predominance of a noncommercial, rural economy.

Origins

Following the modern authority on the subject, the late French historian Marc Bloch, historians distinguish the cruder forms of feudal government that evolved during the early Middle Ages from the sophisticated institutional arrangements by which princes and kings consolidated their territories and established royal rule during the High Middle Ages (the so-called second feudal age).

The origins of feudal government can be found in the divisions and conflicts of Merovingian society. In the sixth and seventh centuries it became customary for individual freemen who did not already belong to families or groups that could protect them to place themselves under the protection of more powerful freemen. In this way the latter built up armies and became local magnates, and the former

Bishop Fulbert Describes the Obligations of Vassal and Lord

Trust held the lord and vassal together. Their duties in this regard were carefully defined. Here are six general rules for vassal and lord, laid down by Bishop Fulbert of Chartres in a letter to William, Duke of Aquitaine, in 1020.

✦ *What are the respective obligations of vassal and lord? Do they seem fair for each side? Why might a vassal have more responsibilities and a lord fewer?*

He who swears fealty to his lord ought always to have these six things in memory: what is harmless, safe, honorable, useful, easy, practicable. *Harmless*, that is to say, that he should not injure his lord in his body; *safe*, that he should not injure him by betraying his secrets or the defenses upon which he relies for his safety; *honorable*, that he should not injure him in his possessions; *easy* and *practicable*, that that good which his lord is able to do easily he make not difficult, nor that which is practicable he make not impossible to him.

That the faithful vassal should avoid these injuries is certainly proper, but not for this alone does he deserve his holding; for it is not sufficient to abstain from evil, unless what is good is done also. It remains, therefore, that in the same six things mentioned above he should faithfully counsel and aid his lord, if he wishes to be looked upon as worthy of his benefice and to be safe concerning the fealty which he has sworn.

The lord also ought to act toward his faithful vassal reciprocally in all these things. And if he does not do this, he will be justly considered guilty of bad faith, just as the former, if he should be detected in avoiding or consenting to the avoidance of his duties, would be perfidious and perjured.

James Harvey Robinson, ed., Readings in European History, *vol. 1 (Boston: Athenacum, 1904), p. 184.*

solved the problem of simple survival. Freemen who so entrusted themselves to others were known as *ingenui in obsequio*, or "freemen in a contractual relation of dependence." Those who gave themselves to the king in this way were called *antrustiones*. All men of this type came to be described collectively as *vassi* or "those who serve," from which evolved the term *vassalage*, meaning the placement of oneself in the personal service of another who promises protection in return.

Landed nobles, like kings, tried to acquire as many such vassals as they could, because military strength in the early Middle Ages lay in numbers. Because it proved impossible to maintain these growing armies within the lord's own household (as was the original custom) or to support them by special monetary payments, the practice evolved of simply granting them land as a "tenement." Vassals were expected to dwell on these *benefices*, or fiefs, and maintain horses and other accouterments of war in good order. Originally vassals, therefore, were little more than gangs-in-waiting.

Vassalage and the Fief

Vassalage involved "fealty" to the lord. To swear fealty was to promise to refrain from any action that might in any way threaten the lord's well-being and to perform personal services for him on his request. Chief among the expected services was military duty as a mounted knight. This could involve a variety of activities: a short or long military expedition, escort duty, standing castle guard, or the placement of one's own fortress at the lord's disposal, if the vassal was of such stature as to have one. Continuous bargaining and bickering occurred over the terms of service. Limitations were placed on the number of days a lord could require services from a vassal. In France in the eleventh century, about forty days of service a year were considered sufficient. It also became possible for vassals to buy their way out of military service by a monetary payment, known as *scutage*. The lord, in turn, applied this payment to the hiring of mercenaries, who often proved more efficient than contract-conscious vassals.

Beyond his military duty, the vassal was also expected to give the lord advice when he requested it and to sit as a member of his court when the latter was in session. The vassal also owed his lord financial assistance when his lord was in obvious need or distress, for example, when he had been captured by his enemies and needed to be ransomed, or when he was outfitting himself for a crusade or a major military campaign. And gifts of money might also be expected when the lord's daughters married and his sons became knights.

Beginning with the reign of Louis the Pious (r. 814–840), bishops and abbots swore fealty to the king and received their offices from him as a *benefice*. The king formally "invested" these clerics in their offices during a special ceremony in which he presented them with a ring and a staff, the symbols of high spiritual office. Louis's predecessors had earlier confiscated church lands with only modest and belated compensation to the church in the form of a tithe required of all Frankish inhabitants. Long a sore point with the church, the presumptuous practice of the lay investiture of the clergy provoked a serious confrontation of church and state in the late tenth and eleventh centuries. At that time reform-minded clergy rebelled against what they then believed to be a kind of involuntary clerical vassalage. Even reform-minded clerics, however, welcomed the king's grants of land and power to the clergy.

The lord's obligations to his vassals were very specific. First, he was obligated to protect the vassal from physical harm and to stand as his advocate in public court. After fealty was sworn and homage paid, the lord provided for the vassal's physical maintenance by the bestowal of a *benefice*, or fief. The fief was simply the physical or material wherewithal to meet the vassal's military and other obligations. It could take the form of liquid wealth as well as the more common grant of real property. There were so-called money fiefs, which empowered a vassal to receive regular payments from the lord's treasury. Such fiefs created potential conflicts because they made it possible for a nobleman in one land to acquire vassals among the nobility in another. Normally the fief consisted of a landed estate of anywhere from a few to several thousand acres. But it could also take the form of a castle.

In Carolingian times a *benefice*, or fief, varied in size from one or more small villas to several *mansi*, agricultural holdings of twenty-five to forty-eight acres. The king's vassals are known to have received *benefices* of at least 30 and as many as 200 such *mansi*, truly a vast estate. Royal vassalage with a *benefice* understandably came to be widely sought by the highest classes of Carolingian society. As a royal policy, however, it ultimately proved deadly to the king. Although Carolingian kings jealously guarded their rights over property granted in *benefice* to vassals, resident vassals were still free to dispose of their *benefices* as they pleased. Vassals of the king, strengthened by his donations, in turn created their own vassals. These, in turn, created still further vassals of their own—vassals of vassals of vassals—in a pyramiding effect that had fragmented land and authority from the highest to the lowest levels by the late ninth century.

Fragmentation and Divided Loyalty

In addition to the fragmentation brought about by the multiplication of vassalage, effective occupation of land led gradually to claims of hereditary possession. Hereditary possession became a legally recognized principle in the ninth century and laid the basis for claims to real ownership. Fiefs given as royal donations became hereditary possessions and, with the passage of time, sometimes even the real property of the possessor.

Further, vassal engagements came to be multiplied in still another way as enterprising freemen sought to accumulate as much land as possible. One man could become a vassal to several different lords. This development led in the ninth century to the "liege lord"—that one master whom the vassal must obey even to the detriment of his other masters, should a direct conflict arise among them.

The problem of loyalty was reflected not only in the literature of the period, with its praise of the virtues of honor and fidelity, but also in the ceremonial development of the very act of "commendation" by which a freeman became a vassal. In the mid-eighth century an "oath of fealty" highlighted the ceremony. A vassal reinforced his promise of fidelity to the lord by swearing a special oath with his hand on a sacred relic or the Bible. In the tenth and eleventh centuries paying homage to the lord involved not only the swearing of such an oath but also the placement of the vassal's hands between the lord's and the sealing of the ceremony with a kiss.

As the centuries passed, personal loyalty and service became quite secondary to the acquisition of property. In developments that signaled the waning of feudal society in the tenth century, the fief came to overshadow fealty, the *benefice* became more important than vassalage, and freemen proved themselves prepared to swear allegiance to the highest bidder.

Feudal arrangements nonetheless provided stability throughout the early Middle Ages and aided the difficult process of political centralization during the High Middle Ages. The genius of feudal government lay in its adaptability. Contracts of different kinds could be made with almost anybody, as circumstances required. The process embraced a wide spectrum of people, from the king at the top to the lowliest vassal in the remotest part of the kingdom. The foundations of the modern nation-state would emerge in France and England from the fine tuning of essentially feudal arrangements as kings sought to adapt their goal of centralized government to the reality of local power and control.

✦

The centuries between 476 and 1000 saw both the decline of classical civilization and the birth of a new European civilization in the regions of what had been the western Roman Empire. Beginning in the fifth century, barbarian invasions separated western Europe culturally from much of its classical past. Although some important works and concepts survived from antiquity and the Christian Church preserved major features of Roman government, the West would be recovering its classical heritage for centuries in "renaissances" that stretched into the sixteenth century. Out of the mixture of barbarian and surviving (or recovered) classical culture, a distinct Western culture was born. Aided and abetted by the Christian Church, the Franks created a new imperial tradition and shaped basic Western political and social institutions for centuries to come.

The early Middle Ages also saw the emergence of a rift in Christendom between the Eastern and Western branches of the church. Evolving from the initial division of the Roman Empire into eastern and western parts, this rift widened, resulting in bitter conflict between popes and patriarchs.

During this period, the capital of the Byzantine Empire, Constantinople, far exceeded in population and culture any city of the West. Serving as both a buffer against Persian, Arab, and Turkish invasions of the West, and as a major repository of classical learning and science for western scholars, the Byzantine Empire did much to make possible the development of western Europe as a distinctive political and cultural entity. Another cultural and religious rival of the West, Islam, also saw its golden age during these same centuries. Like the Byzantine world, the Muslim world also preserved ancient scholarship, and, especially through Muslim Spain, provided a conduit for retransmitting it to the West. But despite examples of coexistence and even friendship, the cultures of the Western and Muslim worlds were too different and their people too estranged and suspicious of one another for them to become good neighbors.

The early Middle Ages were not centuries of great ambition in the West. It was a time when modest foundations were being laid. Despite a certain common religious culture, Western society remained primitive and fragmented, probably more so than anywhere else in the contemporary world. Two distinctive social institutions developed in response to these conditions: manorialism and feudalism. Manorialism ensured that all would be fed and cared for; feudalism provided protection from outside predators. Western people were concerned primarily to satisfy basic needs; great cultural ambition would come later.

Review Questions

1. Trace the history of Christianity to the coronation of the emperor Charlemagne in 800. What distinctive features characterized the early church? What role did the church play in the world after the fall of the western Roman Empire?
2. Discuss the growth of the Frankish kingdom, including its relationship with the church, through the reign of Charlemagne. What were the characteristics of Charlemagne's rule? Why did Charlemagne encourage learning at his court? How could the Carolingian renaissance

have been dangerous to Charlemagne's rule? Why did his empire break apart?

3. How and why was the history of the eastern half of the Roman empire so different from that of the western half? How would you assess the rule of Justinian over the Byzantine empire? How would you compare Justinian to Charlemagne?
4. What were the tenets of Islam and how were the Muslims suddenly able to build an empire? Assess the importance of the Muslim invasions for the development of western Europe.
5. How and why did feudal society begin? What were the essential ingredients of feudalism? How easy do you think it would be for modern society to "slip back" into a feudal pattern?

Suggested Readings

G. Barraclough, *The Crucible of Europe: The Ninth and Tenth Centuries* (1976). Sweeping survey of political history.

R. Bartlett, *Trial by Fire and Water: The Medieval Judicial Ordeal* (1986). Makes sense of these seemingly bizarre ways of letting God decide guilt or innocence.

M. Bloch, *Feudal Society*, vols. 1 and 2, trans. by L. A. Manyon (1971). A classic on the topic and as an example of historical study.

P. Brown, *Augustine of Hippo: A Biography* (1967). Late antiquity seen through the biography of its greatest Christian thinker.

H. Chadwick, *The Early Church* (1967). Among the best treatments of early Christianity.

R. H. C. Davis, *A History of Medieval Europe: From Constantine to St. Louis* (1972). Unsurpassed in clarity.

K. F. Drew (Ed.), *The Barbarian Invasions: Catalyst of a New Order* (1970). Collection of essays that focuses the issues.

G. Duby, *The Early Growth of the European Economy: Warriors and Peasants from the Seventh to the Twelfth Century* (1974). Readable, authoritative account of rural society.

H. Fichtenau, *The Carolingian Empire: The Age of Charlemagne*, trans. by Peter Munz (1964). Strongest on political history of the era.

J. V. A. Fine, *The Early Medieval Balkans: Sixth–Twelfth Centuries* (1983). Insight into the ethnic divisions that form the background to modern conflict in the region.

F. L. Ganshof, *Feudalism*, trans. by Philip Grierson (1964). The most profound brief analysis of the subject.

D. J. Geanakoplos, *Byzantine East and Latin West: Two Worlds of Christendom in the Middle Ages and Renaissance* (1966). Essays by the authority on eastern influence on the West.

A. F. Havighurst (Ed.), *The Pirenne Thesis: Analysis, Criticism, and Revision* (1958). Excerpts from the scholarly debate over the extent of western trade in the East during the early Middle Ages.

R. Hodges and D. Whitehouse, *Mohammed, Charlemagne and the Origins of Europe* (1982). For the social and economic history of early medieval Europe.

A. Hourani, *A History of the Arab Peoples* (1991). A comprehensive text that includes an excellent overview of the origins and early history of Islam.

D. Knowles, *Christian Monasticism* (1969). Sweeping survey with helpful photographs.

M. L. W. Laistner, *Thought and Letters in Western Europe, 500 to 900* (1957). Among the best surveys of early medieval intellectual history.

J. Leclercq, *The Love of Learning and the Desire for God: A Study of Monastic Culture*, trans. by Catherine Misrahi (1962). Lucid, delightful, absorbing account of the ideals of monks.

J. Leclercq, F. Vandenbroucke, and L. Bouyer, *The Spirituality of the Middle Ages* (1968). Perhaps the best survey of medieval Christianity, east and west, to the eve of the Protestant Reformation.

B. Lewis, *The Muslim Discovery of Europe* (1982). Authoritative account from the Muslim perspective.

C. Mango, *Byzantium: The Empire of New Rome* (1980). Perhaps the most readable account.

M. McCormick, "Byzantium and the West, A.D. 700–900," in *The New Cambridge Medieval History*, vol. 2: *The Early Medieval West 700–900* (1993). Up-to-date framing of events and political developments.

R. McKitterick, *The Frankish Kingdoms Under the Carolingians*, 751–987 (1983). The fate of Carolingian government.

P. Munz, *The Age of Charlemagne* (1971). Penetrating social history of the period.

H. Pirenne, *A History of Europe, I: From the End of the Roman World in the West to the Beginnings of the Western States*, trans. by Bernhard Maill (1958). Comprehensive survey, with now-controversial views on the demise of western trade and cities in the early Middle Ages.

S. Runciman, *Byzantine Civilization* (1970). Succinct, comprehensive account by a master.

P. Sawyer, *The Age of the Vikings* (1962). Among the best accounts.

R. W. Southern, *The Making of the Middle Ages* (1973). Originally published in 1953, but still a fresh account by an imaginative historian.

C. Stephenson, *Medieval Feudalism* (1969). Excellent short summary and introduction.

A. A. Vasiliev, *History of the Byzantine Empire* 324–1453 (1952). The most comprehensive treatment in English.

W. Walther, *Woman in Islam* (1981). One hour spent with this book teaches more about the social import of Islam than days spent with others.

S. Wemple, *Women in Frankish Society: Marriage and the Cloister 500–900* (1981). What marriage and the cloister meant to women in these early centuries.

L. White, Jr., *Medieval Technology and Social Change* (1962). Often fascinating account of the way primitive technology changed life.

CHAPTER

7

The crusaders capture the city of Antioch in 1098 during the First Crusade. From Le Miroir Historial *(fifteenth century) by Vincent de Beauvais. [Musee Conde Chantilly. E.T. Archive, London]*

The High Middle Ages (1000–1300): The Ascendancy of the Church and the Rise of States

KEY TOPICS

- The revival of the Holy Roman Empire by a new German dynasty, the Saxons
- The emergence of a great reform movement in the church and the church's successful challenge to political domination by kings and emperors
- The development of strong, national monarchies in England and France
- The fragmentation of Germany in the wake of a centuries-long struggle between the emperors of the Hohenstaufen dynasty and the papacy

The High Middle Ages mark a period of political expansion and consolidation and of intellectual flowering and synthesis. The noted medievalist Joseph Strayer called it the age that saw "the full development of all the potentialities of medieval civilization."[1] *Some even argue that as far as the development of Western institutions is concerned, this was a more creative period than the later Italian Renaissance and the German Reformation.*

The High Middle Ages saw the borders of western Europe largely secured against foreign invaders. Although intermittent Muslim aggression continued well into the sixteenth century, fear of assault from without diminished. On the contrary, a striking change occurred during the late eleventh century and the twelfth century. Western Europe, which had for so long been the prey of foreign powers, became, through the Crusades and foreign trade, the feared hunter within both the eastern Byzantine world and the Muslim world.

[1]*Western History in the Middle Ages—A Short History* (New York: Appleton-Century-Crofts, 1955), pp. 9, 127.

During the High Middle Ages "national" monarchies emerged. Rulers in England and France successfully adapted feudal principles of government to create newly centralized political realms. At the same time, parliaments and popular assemblies emerged to secure the rights and customs of the privileged many—the nobility, the clergy, and propertied townspeople—against the desires of kings. In the process the foundations of modern European states were laid. The Holy Roman Empire, however, proved the great exception to this centralizing trend. Despite a revival of the empire under the Ottonians (Otto I, the most powerful member of the Saxon imperial dynasty, and his immediate successors, Otto II and Otto III), the events of these centuries left it weak and fragmented until modern times.

The High Middle Ages also saw the Latin, or Western, church establish itself in concept and law as a spiritual authority independent of monarchical secular government, thus sowing the seeds of the distinctive Western separation of church and state. During the Investiture Controversy, the confrontation between popes and emperors that began in the late eleventh century and lasted through the twelfth, a reformed papacy overcame its long subservience to the Carolingian and Ottonian kings. In this struggle over the authority of rulers to designate bishops and other high clergy and to invest them with their symbols of authority, the papacy, under Gregory II and his immediate successors, won out. It did so, however, by becoming itself a monarchy among the world's emerging monarchies, preparing the way for still more dangerous confrontations between popes and emperors in the later Middle Ages. Some religious reformers later saw in the Gregorian papacy of the High Middle Ages the fall of the church from its spiritual mission as well as a declaration of its independence from secular power.

Otto I and the Revival of the Empire

The fortunes of both the old empire and the papacy began to revive after the dark period of the late ninth century and the early tenth century. In 918 the Saxon Henry I ("the Fowler," d. 936), the strongest of the German dukes, became the first non-Frankish king of Germany.

Unifying Germany

Henry rebuilt royal power by forcibly combining the duchies of Swabia, Bavaria, Saxony, Franconia, and Lotharingia. He secured imperial borders by checking the invasions of the Hungarians and the Danes. Although much smaller than Charlemagne's empire, the German kingdom Henry created placed his son and successor Otto I (r. 936–973) in a strong territorial position.

The very able Otto maneuvered his own kin into positions of power in Bavaria, Swabia, and Franconia. He refused to recognize each duchy as an independent hereditary entity, as the nobility increasingly expected, dealing with each instead as a subordinate member of a unified kingdom. In a truly imperial gesture in 951, he invaded Italy and proclaimed himself its king. In 955 he won his most magnificent victory when he defeated the Hungarians at Lechfeld. This victory secured German borders against new barbarian attack, further unified the German duchies, and earned Otto the well-deserved title "the Great." In defining the boundaries of the western Europe, Otto's conquest was comparable with Charles Martel's earlier triumph over the Saracens at Poitiers in 732.

Embracing the Church

As part of a careful rebuilding program, Otto, following the example of his predecessors, enlisted the church. Bishops and abbots—men who possessed a sense of universal empire, yet because they did not marry, could not found competitive dynasties—were made royal princes and agents of the king. Because these clergy, as royal bureaucrats, received great land holdings and immunity from local counts and dukes, they also found such vassalage to the king very attractive. The medieval church did not become a great territorial power reluctantly. It appreciated the blessings of receiving, while teaching the blessedness of giving.

In 961 Otto, who had long aspired to the imperial crown, responded to a call for help from Pope John XII (955–964), who was then being bullied by an Italian enemy of the German king, Berengar of Friuli. In recompense for this rescue, Pope John crowned Otto emperor on February 2, 962. Otto, for his part, recognized the existence of the Papal States and proclaimed himself their special protector. The church was now more than ever under royal control. Its bishops and abbots were Otto's appointees

Otto I presents the Magdeburg Cathedral to Christ, as the pope (holding the keys to the kingdom of heaven) watches, a testimony to Otto's guardianship of the church. [Metropolitan Museum of Art, bequest of George Blumenthal, 1941]

and bureaucrats, and the pope reigned in Rome only by the power of the emperor's sword.

Pope John, belatedly recognizing the royal web in which the church had become entangled, joined in Italian opposition to the new emperor. This turnabout brought Otto's swift revenge. An ecclesiastical synod over which Otto presided deposed Pope John and proclaimed that henceforth no pope could take office without first swearing an oath of allegiance to the emperor. Under Otto I popes ruled at the emperor's pleasure.

As these events reflect, Otto had shifted the royal focus from Germany to Italy. His successors—Otto II (r. 973–983) and Otto III (r. 983–1002)—became so preoccupied with running the affairs of Italy that their German base began to disintegrate, sacrificed to imperial dreams. They might have learned a lesson from the contemporary Capetian kings, the successor dynasty to the Carolingians in France. These kings, perhaps more by circumstance than by design, pursued a very different course than the Ottonians. They mended local fences and concentrated their limited resources to secure a tight grip on their immediate royal domain, never neglecting it for the sake of foreign adventure.

The Ottonians, in contrast, reached far beyond their grasp when they tried to subdue Italy. As the briefly revived empire began to crumble in the first quarter of the eleventh century, the church, long unhappy with Carolingian and Ottonian domination, prepared to declare its independence and exact its own vengeance.

The Reviving Catholic Church

During the late ninth and early tenth centuries the clergy had become tools of kings and magnates and the papacy a toy of Italian nobles. The Ottonians made bishops their servile princes and likewise dominated the papacy. The church was about to gain renewed respect and authority, however, thanks not only to the failing fortunes of the overextended empire but also to a new, determined force for reform within the church itself.

The Cluny Reform Movement

The great monastery in Cluny in east-central France gave birth to a monastic reform movement that progressively won the support of secular lords and German kings. In doing so, this movement enabled the church to challenge its domination by royal authority at both the episcopal and papal levels.

The reformers of Cluny were aided by widespread popular respect for the church that found expression in lay religious fervor and generous baronial patronage of religious houses. One reason so many people admired clerics and monks was that the church was medieval society's most democratic institution as far as lay participation was concerned. In the Middle Ages any man could theoretically rise to the position of pope, who was supposed to be elected by "the people and the clergy." All people were candidates for the church's grace and salvation. The church promised a better life to come to the great mass of ordinary people, who found the present one brutish and without hope.

Since the fall of the Roman Empire, popular support for the church had been especially inspired by the example set by monks. Monasteries provided an important alternative way of life for the religiously earnest in an age when most people had

Benedictine monks at choir. The reform movement that began at the Benedictine monastery at Cluny in northern France in the tenth century spread throughout the church and was ultimately responsible for the reassertion of papal authority. [Courtesy of the Trustees of the British Library]

very few options. Monks remained the least secularized and most spiritual of the church's clergy. Their cultural achievements were widely admired, their relics and rituals were considered magical, and their high religious ideals and sacrifices were imitated by the laity.

The tenth and eleventh centuries saw an unprecedented boom in the construction of monasteries. William the Pious, duke of Aquitaine, founded Cluny in 910. It was a Benedictine monastery devoted to the strictest observance of Saint Benedict's *Rule for Monasteries*, with a special emphasis on liturgical purity. Although the reformers who emerged at Cluny were loosely organized and their demands not always consistent, they shared a determination to maintain a spiritual church. They absolutely rejected the subservience of the clergy, especially that of the German bishops, to royal authority. They taught that the pope in Rome was sole ruler over all the clergy.

No local secular ruler, the Cluniacs asserted, could have any control over their monasteries. They further denounced the transgression of ascetic piety by "secular" parish clergy, who maintained concubines in a relationship akin to marriage. (Later a distinction would be formalized between the *secular* clergy who lived and ministered in the world [*saeculum*] and the *regular* clergy, monks and nuns withdrawn from the world and living according to a special rule [*regula*].)

The Cluny reformers resolved to free the clergy from both kings and "wives," to create an independent and chaste clergy. The church alone was to be the clergy's lord and spouse. Thus, the distinctive Western separation of church and state and the celibacy of the Catholic clergy, both of which continue today, had their definitive origins in the Cluny reform movement.

Cluny rapidly became a center from which reformers were dispatched to other monasteries throughout France and Italy. Under its aggressive abbots, especially Saint Odo (r. 926–946), it grew to embrace almost 1,500 dependent cloisters, each devoted to monastic and church reform. In the latter half of the eleventh century, the Cluny reformers reached the summit of their influence when the papacy itself embraced their reform program.

The proclamation of a series of church decrees called the Peace of God in the late ninth and early tenth centuries reflected the influence of the Cluny movement. Emerging from a cooperative venture between the clergy and the higher nobility, these decrees tried to lessen the endemic warfare of medieval society by threatening excommunication for all who, at any time, harmed members of such vulnerable groups as women, peasants, merchants, and the clergy. The Peace of God was subsequently reinforced by the Truce of God, a church order proclaiming that all men must abstain from every form of violence and warfare during a certain part of each week (eventually from Wednesday night to Monday morning) and in all holy seasons.

Popes devoted to reforms like those urged by Cluny came to power during the reign of Emperor

Henry III (r. 1039–1056). Pope Leo IX (r. 1049–1054) promoted regional synods to oppose simony (the selling of spiritual things, especially as church offices) and clerical marriage (celibacy was not strictly enforced among the secular clergy until after the eleventh century). He also placed Cluniacs in key administrative posts in Rome. Imperial influence over the papacy, however, was still strong during Henry III's reign, and provided a counterweight to the great aristocratic families that manipulated the elections of popes for their own gain. Before Leo IX's papacy, Henry had deposed three such popes, each a pawn of a Roman noble faction, and had installed a German bishop of his own choosing who ruled as Pope Clement II (r. 1046–1047).

Such highhanded practices ended soon after Henry III's death. During the turbulent minority of his successor, Henry IV (r. 1056–1106), reform popes began to assert themselves more openly. Pope Stephen IX (1057–1058) reigned without imperial ratification, contrary to the earlier declaration of Otto I. To prevent local factional control of papal elections, Pope Nicholas II (1059–1061) decreed in 1059 that a body of high church officials and advisers known as the College of Cardinals would henceforth choose the pope, establishing the procedures for papal succession that the Catholic Church still follows. With this action the papacy declared its full independence from both local Italian and distant royal interference. Rulers continued nevertheless to have considerable indirect influence on the election of popes.

Pope Nicholas II also embraced Cluny's strictures against simony and clerical concubinage and even struck his own political alliances with the Normans in Sicily and with France and Tuscany. His successor, Pope Alexander II (r. 1061–1073), was elected solely by the College of Cardinals, although not without a struggle.

The Investiture Struggle: Gregory VII and Henry IV

Alexander's successor was Pope Gregory VII (r. 1073–1085), a fierce advocate of Cluny's reforms who had entered the papal bureaucracy a quarter century earlier during the pontificate of Leo IX. It was he who put the church's declaration of independence to the test. Cluniacs had repeatedly inveighed against simony. Cardinal Humbert, a prominent reformer, argued that lay investiture of the clergy—that is, the appointment of bishops and other church officials by secular officials and rulers—was the worst form of this evil practice. In 1075 Pope Gregory embraced these arguments and condemned under penalty of excommunication lay investiture of clergy at any level. He had primarily in mind the emperor's well-established custom of installing bishops by presenting them with the ring and staff that symbolized episcopal office.

After Gregory's ruling, emperors were no more able to install bishops than they were to install popes. As popes were elected by the College of Cardinals and were not raised up by kings or nobles, so bishops would henceforth be installed in their offices by high ecclesiastical authority empowered by the pope. The spiritual origins and allegiance of episcopal office would thereby be made clear.

Gregory's prohibition came as a jolt to royal authority. Since the days of Charlemagne, emperors had routinely passed out bishoprics to favored clergy. Bishops, who received royal estates, were the emperors' appointees and servants of the state. Henry IV's Carolingian and Ottonian predecessors had carefully nurtured the theocratic character of the empire in both concept and administrative bureaucracy. The church and religion had become integral parts of government.

Now the emperor, Henry IV, suddenly found himself ordered to secularize the empire by drawing a distinct line between the spheres of temporal and spiritual—royal and ecclesiastical—authority and jurisdiction. But if his key administrators were no longer to be his own carefully chosen and sworn servants, then was not his kingdom in jeopardy? Henry considered Gregory's action a direct challenge to his authority. The territorial princes, on the other hand, ever tending away from the center and eager to see the emperor weakened, were quick to see the advantages of Gregory's ruling. If a weak emperor could not gain a bishop's ear, then a strong prince might, thus bringing the offices of the church into his orbit of power. In the hope of gaining an advantage over both the emperor and the clergy in their territory, the princes fully supported Gregory's edict.

The lines of battle were quickly drawn. Henry assembled his loyal German bishops at Worms in January 1076 and had them proclaim their independence from Gregory. Gregory promptly responded with the church's heavy artillery: he excommunicated Henry and absolved all Henry's subjects from loyalty to him. This turn of events

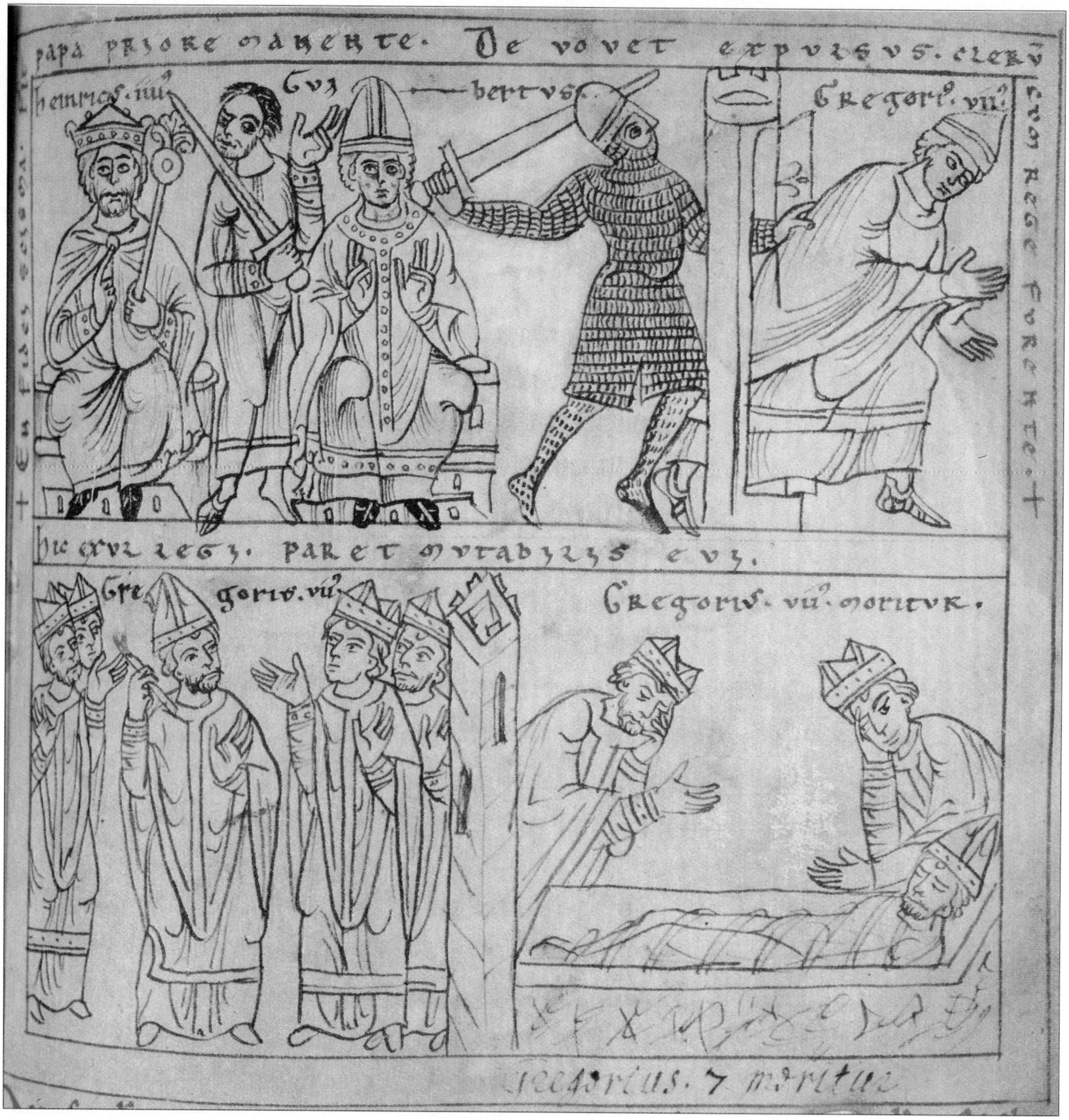

A twelfth-century German manuscript portrays the struggle between Emperor Henry IV and Pope Gregory VII. In the top panel, Henry installs the puppet pope Clement III and drives Gregory from Rome. Below, Gregory dies in exile. The artist was a monk; his sympathies were with Gregory, not Henry. [Thuringer Universitäts- und Landesbibliothek, Jena]

delighted the German princes, and Henry found himself facing a general revolt led by the duchy of Saxony. He had no recourse but to come to terms with Gregory. In a famous scene Henry prostrated himself outside Gregory's castle retreat at Canossa on January 25, 1077. There he reportedly stood barefoot in the snow off and on for three days before the pope agreed to absolve him.

Papal power had at this moment reached a pinnacle (it would attain even greater heights during the papacy of Innocent III [r. 1198–1216], who also had rulers at his mercy). But such peaks must also be descended. Gregory's power, as he must have known when he restored Henry to power, was soon to be challenged.

Henry regrouped his forces, regained much of his power within the empire, and soon acted as if the humiliation at Canossa had never occurred. In March 1080 Gregory excommunicated Henry once again, but this time the action was ineffectual. (Historically, repeated excommunications of the same individual have proved to have diminishing returns.) In 1084 Henry, absolutely dominant, installed his own antipope, Clement III, and forced Gregory into exile, where he died the following year. It appeared as if the old practice of kings controlling popes had been restored, and with a vengeance. Clement, however, was never recognized within the church, and Gregory's followers, who retained wide popular support, regained power during the pontificates of Victor III (r. 1086–1087) and Urban II (r. 1088–1099).

The settlement of the investiture controversy came in 1122 with the Concordat of Worms. Emperor Henry V (r. 1106–1125), having early abandoned his predecessors' practice of nominating

Pope Gregory Describes in a Letter Henry IV's Penance at Canossa

Had Henry IV not succeeded in having the papal ban revoked, his powerful vassals in the empire were prepared to remove him from office. Both sides were aware of the high stakes; hence, Henry's extreme penance to win absolution and the pope's long delay in granting it.

✦ *Would it have been possible for Pope Gregory not to have pardoned Henry IV? Since doing so appears not to have been in the pope's interest, why did he do so?*

Gregory . . . to all archbishops, bishops, dukes, counts, and other princes of the realm . . .

Inasmuch as for love of justice you assumed common cause and danger with us in the struggle [with Henry] . . . we have taken care to inform you . . . how the king, humbled to penance, obtained the pardon of absolution . . . .

Before entering Italy, he sent to us . . . offering in all things to render satisfaction . . . . And he renewed his promise that, besides amending his way of living, he would observe all obedience, if only he might deserve to obtain from us the favor of absolution and the apostolic benediction. When, after long postponing a decision, we . . . severely [took] him to task . . . he came at length of his own accord, with a few followers, showing nothing of hostility or boldness, to the town of Canossa where we were tarrying. And there, having laid aside all the belongings of royalty, wretchedly with bare feel and clad in wool, he continued for three days to stand before the gate of the castle. Nor did he desist from imploring with many tears the aid and consolation of the apostolic mercy until he had moved all . . . present . . . to such pity and depth of compassion that, interceding for him with many prayers and tears, all wondered at the unaccustomed hardness of our heart, while some actually cried out that we were exercising, not the dignity of apostolic severity, but the cruelty . . . of a tyrannical madness.

Finally, won by the persistence of his suit . . . we loosed the chain of anathema and . . . received him into the favor of communion and into the lap of the Holy Mother Church.

Frederic Austen Ogg, ed., A Source Book of Mediaeval History: Documents Illustrative of European Life and Institutions from the German Invasions to the Renaissance *(New York: American Book Company, 1908), pp. 275–276.*

popes and raising up antipopes, formally renounced his power to invest bishops with ring and staff. In exchange, Pope Calixtus II (r. 1119–1124) recognized the emperor's right to be present and to invest bishops with fiefs before and after their investment with ring and staff by the church. The old church–state "back scratching" in this way continued, but now on very different terms. The clergy received their offices and attendant religious powers solely from ecclesiastical authority and no longer from kings and emperors. Rulers continued to bestow lands and worldly goods on high clergy in the hope of influencing them. The Concordat of Worms thus made the clergy more independent but not necessarily less worldly.

The Gregorian party may have won the independence of the clergy, but the price it paid was to encourage division among the feudal forces within the empire. The pope made himself strong by making imperial authority weak. In the end those who profited most from the investiture controversy were the German princes.

The new Gregorian fence between temporal and spiritual power did not prevent kings and popes from being good neighbors if each was willing. Succeeding centuries, however, proved that the aspirations of kings were too often in conflict with those of popes for peaceful coexistence to endure. The most bitter clash between church and state was still to come. It would occur during the late thirteenth century and early fourteenth century in the confrontation between Pope Boniface VIII and King Philip IV of France. (See Chapter 9.)

The First Crusades

If an index of popular piety and support for the pope in the High Middle Ages is needed, the Crusades amply provide it. What the Cluny reform was to the clergy, the first Crusades to the Holy Land were to the laity: an outlet for the heightened religious zeal of the late eleventh and twelfth centuries, Europe's most religious period before the Protestant Reformation.

Late in the eleventh century, the Byzantine Empire was under severe pressure from the Seljuk Turks, and the eastern emperor, Alexius I Comnenus, appealed for Western aid. At the Council of Clermont in 1095, Pope Urban II responded positively to this appeal, setting the First Crusade in motion. This event has puzzled some historians, because the First Crusade was a risky venture. But the pope, the nobility, and western society at large had much to gain by removing large numbers of nobility temporarily from Europe. Too many idle, restless noble youths were spending a great part of their lives feuding with each other and raiding other people's land. The pope recognized that peace and tranquility might be gained at home by sending factious aristocrats abroad with their accouterments of war (100,000 went with the First Crusade). And the nobility recognized there were fortunes to be made in foreign wars. This was especially true of the younger sons of noblemen, who, in an age of growing population and shrinking landed wealth, saw the Crusades as an opportunity to become landowners. Pope Urban may also have envisioned the Crusade leading to a reconciliation and possible reunion with the Eastern Church.

Religion was not the only motive inspiring the Crusaders; hot blood and greed were equally influential. But unlike the later Crusades, undertaken for patently mercenary reasons, the early Crusades were to a very high degree inspired by genuine religious piety and were carefully orchestrated by the revived papacy. Popes promised participants in the First Crusade a plenary indulgence should they die in battle, that is, a complete remission of any outstanding temporal punishment for their unrepented mortal sins and hence release from suffering for them in purgatory. In addition to this direct spiritual reward, the Crusaders were also impelled by their enthusiasm for a Holy War against the hated infidel and the romance of a holy pilgrimage to the Holy Land. All these elements combined to make the First Crusade a rousing success (at least from the Christian point of view). Crusading zeal also sparked anti-Jewish riots and massacres in Europe, an expression of intolerance to Jews that would prove to be an enduring feature of militant Christianity.

THE FIRST VICTORY The eastern emperor welcomed any aid against advancing Islamic armies. The Crusaders did not, however, assemble to defend Europe's borders against aggression. They freely took the offensive to rescue the holy city of Jerusalem, which had been in non-Christian hands since the seventh century, from the Seljuk Turks. To this end three great armies—tens of thousands of Crusaders—gathered in France, Germany, and Italy. Following different routes, they reassembled in Constantinople in 1097. (See Map 7–1.)

Pope Urban II (r. 1088–1099) Preaches the First Crusade

When Pope Urban II summoned the First Crusade in a sermon at the Council of Clermont on November 26, 1095, he painted a most savage picture of the Muslims who controlled Jerusalem. Urban also promised the Crusaders, who responded by the tens of thousands, remission of their unrepented sins and assurance of heaven. Robert the Monk is one of four witnesses who has left us a summary of the sermon.

✦ *Is the pope engaging in a propaganda and smear campaign? What are the images he creates of the enemy and how accurate and fair are they? Did the Christian Church have a greater claim to Jerusalem than the people then living there? Does a religious connection with the past entitle one group to confiscate the land of another?*

From the confines of Jerusalem and the city of Constantinople a horrible tale has gone forth and very frequently has been brought to our ears, namely, that a race from the kingdom of the Persians [that is, the Seljuk Turks], an accursed race, a race utterly alienated from God, a generation forsooth which has not directed its heart and has not entrusted its spirit to God, has invaded the lands of those Christians and has depopulated them by the sword, pillage and fire; it has led away a part of the captives into its own country, and a part it has destroyed by cruel tortures; it has either entirely destroyed the churches of God or appropriated them for the rites of its own religion. They destroy the altars, after having defiled them with their uncleanness. They circumcise the Christians, and the blood of the circumcision they either spread upon the altars or pour into the vases of the baptismal font. When they wish to torture people by a base death, they perforate their navels, and dragging forth the extremity of the intestines, bind it to a stake; then with flogging they lead the victim around until the viscera having gushed forth the victim falls prostrate upon the ground. Others they bind to a post and pierce with arrows. Others they compel to extend their necks and then, attacking them with naked swords, attempt to cut through the neck with a single blow. What shall I say of the abominable rape of the women? The kingdom of the Greeks is now dismembered by them and deprived of territory so vast in extent that it can not be traversed in a march of two months. On whom therefore is the labor of avenging these wrongs and of recovering this territory incumbent, if not upon you? . . .

Jerusalem is the navel of the world; the land is fruitful above others, like another paradise of delights. This the Redeemer of the human race has made illustrious by His advent, has beautified by residence, has consecrated by suffering, has redeemed by death, has glorified by burial. This royal city, therefore, situated at the centre of the world, is now held captive by His enemies, and is in subjection to those who do not know God, to the worship of the heathens. She seeks therefore and desires to be liberated, and does not cease to implore you to come to her aid. From you especially she asks succor, because, as we have already said, God has conferred upon you above all nations great glory in arms. Accordingly undertake this journey for the remission of your sins, with the assurance of the imperishable glory of the kingdom of heaven.

Translations and Reprints from the Original Sources of European History, *vol. 1 (Philadelphia: Department of History, University of Pennsylvania, 1910), pp. 5–7.*

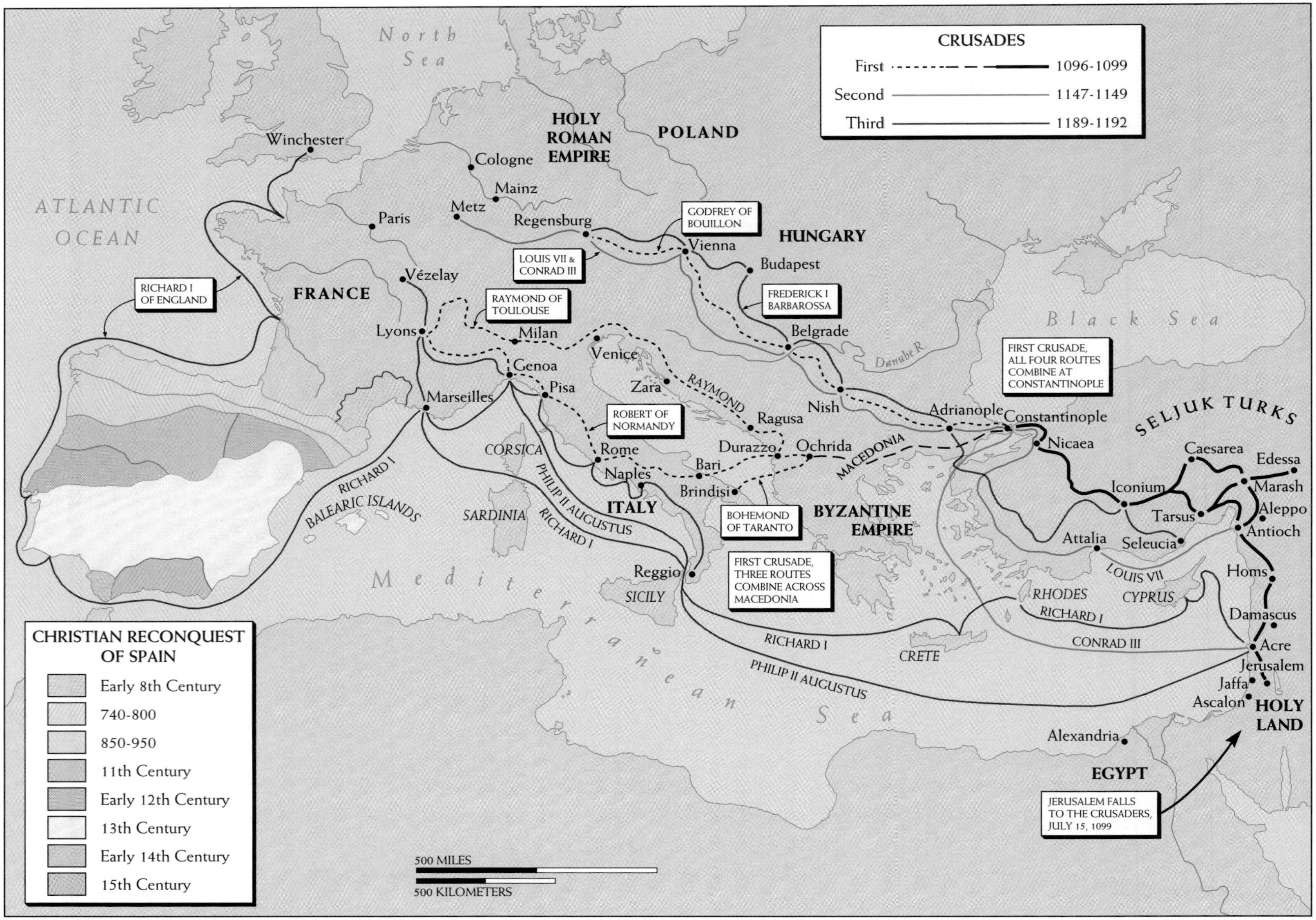

MAP 7–1 THE EARLY CRUSADES *Routes and several leaders of the Crusades during the first century of the movement are shown. The names on this map do not exhaust the list of great nobles who went on the First Crusade. The even showier array of monarchs of the Second and Third Crusades still left the Crusades, on balance, ineffective in achieving their goals.*

The convergence of these spirited soldiers on the eastern capital was a cultural shock that only deepened antipathy toward the West. The eastern emperor suspected their true motives, and the common people, whom they pillaged and suppressed, hardly considered them Christian brothers in a common cause. Nonetheless these fanatical Crusaders accomplished what no eastern army had been able to do. They soundly defeated one Seljuk army after another in a steady advance toward Jerusalem, which fell to them on July 15, 1099. The Crusaders' success resulted from their superior military discipline and weaponry. It also helped that they had descended upon a politically divided and factious Islamic world that initially lacked the unity to organize an effective resistance.

The victorious Crusaders divided the conquered territory into the feudal states of Jerusalem, Edessa, and Antioch, which they held as alleged fiefs from the pope. Godfrey of Bouillon, leader of the French–German army (and after him his brother Baldwin), ruled over the kingdom of Jerusalem. The Crusaders, however, remained only small islands within a great sea of Muslims, who looked on the Western invaders as hardly more than savages. And once settled in the Holy Land, the Crusaders found themselves increasingly on the defensive. Now an occupying rather than a conquering army, they became obsessed with fortifying their position. They built castles throughout the Holy Land, the ruins of many of which are still visible today.

Once secure within their castle enclaves, the Crusaders ceased to live off the land, as they had done since leaving Europe, and relied more and more on imports from home. The once fierce warriors became international businesspeople as they developed the economic resources of their new possessions. The Knights Templars, originally a military–religious order, became castle stewards and escorts of Western pilgrims to and from the Holy Land, in the process accumulating great wealth and becoming important bankers and moneylenders.

THE SECOND CRUSADE Native resistence finally broke the Crusaders around mid-century, and the forty-odd-year Latin presence in the East began to crumble. Edessa fell to Islamic armies in 1144. A Second Crusade, preached by the eminent Bernard of Clairvaux (1091–1153), Christendom's most powerful monastic leader, attempted a rescue, but it met with dismal failure. In October 1187, Saladin (r. 1138–1193), king of Egypt and Syria, reconquered Jerusalem itself. Save for a brief interlude in the thirteenth century, it remained thereafter in Islamic hands until modern times.

THE THIRD CRUSADE A Third Crusade in the twelfth century (1189–1192) attempted yet another rescue, enlisting as its leaders the most powerful western rulers: Emperor Frederick Barbarossa; Richard the Lion-Hearted, king of England; and Philip Augustus, king of France. But the Third Crusade proved a tragicomic commentary on the passing of the original crusading spirit. Frederick Barbarossa accidentally drowned while fording the Saleph River, a small stream, near the end of his journey across Asia Minor. Richard the Lion-Hearted and Philip Augustus reached the outskirts of Jerusalem, but their intense personal rivalry shattered the Crusaders' unity and chances of victory. Philip Augustus returned to France and made war on Richard's continental territories. Richard fell captive to the Emperor Henry VI as he was returning to England. (Henry VI suspected Richard of plotting against him with Henry's mortal enemy, Henry the Lion, the duke of Saxony, who happened also to be Richard's brother-in-law.)

The English paid a handsome ransom for their adventurous king's release. Popular resentment of taxes levied for this ransom became part of the background of the revolt against the English monarchy that led to the royal recognition of Magna Carta in 1215 (discussed later in the chapter).

The long-term results of the first three Crusades had little to do with their original purpose. Politically and religiously they were a failure, and the Holy Land reverted as firmly as ever to Muslim hands. The Crusades did, however, act for centuries as a safety valve for violence-prone Europe. More importantly, they stimulated Western trade with the East. The merchants of Venice, Pisa, and Genoa followed the Crusaders across to lucrative new markets. The need to resupply the new Christian settlements in the Near East reopened old trade routes that had long been closed by Islamic domination of the Mediterranean and established important new ones as well.

It is a commentary on both the degeneration of the original crusading ideal and the Crusaders' true historical importance that the Fourth Crusade turned into a large commercial venture manipulated by the Venetians. And wherever new trading centers sprang up along the Crusader routes, cultural as well as economic commerce occurred.

*The Castle of the Knights (*Krak-des-Chevaliers*), the most magnificent of the many Crusader castles built in the Holy Land in the twelfth and thirteenth centuries, the ruins of which remain in modern Syria, Lebanon, and Jordan. This castle is situated in northern Syria a few miles from the Lebanese border. Its defense consisted of two massive walls, one overhanging the other, divided by a great moat. The Muslims of the same period used very similar military architecture. [Arab Information Center, New York]*

Western Christians learned firsthand about Islamic culture and Muslims about the Christian West.

The Pontificate of Innocent III (r. 1198–1216)

Pope Innocent III was a papal monarch in the Gregorian tradition of papal independence from secular domination. He proclaimed and practiced as none before him the doctrine of the plenitude of papal power. In a famous statement, he likened the relationship of the pope to the emperor—or the church to the state—to that of the sun to the moon. As the moon received its light from the sun, so the emperor received his brilliance (that is, his crown) from the hand of the pope—an allusion to the famous precedent set on Christmas Day, 800, when Pope Leo III crowned Charlemagne.

Although this pretentious theory greatly exceeded Innocent's ability to practice it, he and his successors did not hesitate to act on the ambitions it reflected. When Philip II, the king of France, tried unlawfully to annul his marriage, Innocent placed France under interdict, suspending all church services save baptism and the last rites. The same punishment befell England with even greater force when King John refused to accept Innocent's nominee for archbishop of Canterbury. And as we will see later in the chapter, Innocent intervened frequently and forcefully in the affairs of the Holy Roman Empire.

THE NEW PAPAL MONARCHY Innocent made the papacy a great secular power, with financial resources and a bureaucracy equal to those of contemporary monarchs. During his reign the papacy transformed itself, in effect, into an efficient ecclesio-commercial complex, which would be attacked by reformers throughout the later Middle Ages. Innocent consolidated and expanded ecclesiastical taxes on the laity, the chief of which was "Peter's pence." In England, that tax, long a levy on all but the poorest houses, became a lump-sum payment by the English crown during Innocent's reign. Innocent also imposed an income tax of 2.5 percent on the clergy. Annates (the payment of a portion or all of the first year's income received by the holder of a new *benefice)* and fees for the *pallium* (an archbishop's symbol of office) became especially favored revenue-gathering devices.

Innocent also reserved to the pope the absolution of many sins and religious crimes, forcing those desirous of pardons or exemptions to bargain directly with Rome. It was a measure of the degree to which the papacy had embraced the new money economy that it employed Lombard merchants and bankers to collect the growing papal revenues.

CRUSADES IN FRANCE AND THE EAST Innocent's predilection for power politics also expressed itself in his use of the Crusade, the traditional weapon of the church against Islam, to suppress internal dissent and heresy. Heresy had grown under the influence of native religious reform movements that tried, often naïvely, to disassociate the church from the growing materialism of the age and to keep it pure of political scheming. A good deal of heresy also stemmed from anticlericalism fed by real abuses of the clergy witnessed directly by the laity, such as immorality, greed, and poor pastoral service.

The idealism of these movements was too extreme for the papacy. In 1209 Innocent launched a Crusade against the Albigensians, also known as Cathars, or "pure ones." These advocates of an ascetic, dualist religion were concentrated in the area of Albi in Languedoc in southern France, but Catharism also had adherents among the laity in Italy and Spain. The Albigensians generally sought a pure and simple religious life, following the model of the apostles of Jesus in the New Testament. They opposed Christian teaching on several points. They denied the Old Testament and its God of wrath, as well as the Christian belief in God's incarnation in Jesus Christ. They conceived of the church as an invisible, spiritual force, and resisted it as a legal, financial, and dogmatic institution.

The more radical Cathars opposed human procreation because to reproduce corporeal bodies was to prolong the imprisonment of immortal souls in dying matter. They avoided it either through extreme sexual asceticism or the use of contraceptives (sponges and acidic ointments) and even abortion. On the other hand, the Cathars' strong dualism justified latitude in sexual behavior on the part of ordinary believers, this in the belief that the flesh and the spirit were so fundamentally different that it mattered little what the former did. It was in opposition to such beliefs that the church developed its social teachings condemning contraception and abortion.

The Crusades against the Albigensians were carried out by powerful noblemen from northern France. These great magnates, led by Simon de Montfort, were as much attracted by the great wealth of the area of Languedoc as they were moved by Christian conscience to stamp out heresy. The Crusades also allowed the northerners to extend their political power into the south. They resulted in a succession of massacres and ended with a special Crusade led by King Louis VIII of France from 1225 to 1226, which destroyed the Albigensians as a political entity. Pope Gregory IX (r. 1227–1241) introduced the Inquisition into the region to complete the work of the Crusaders. This institution, a formal tribunal for the detection and punishment of heresy, had been in use by the church since the mid-twelfth century as a way for bishops to maintain diocesan discipline. During Innocent's pontificate it became centralized in the papacy. Papal legates were dispatched to chosen regions to conduct interrogations and the subsequent trials and executions.

THE FOURTH CRUSADE It was also during Innocent's pontificate that the Fourth Crusade to the Holy Land was launched. In 1202, some 30,000 Crusaders arrived in Venice to set sail for Egypt. When they were unable to pay the price of transport, the Venetians negotiated an alternative to payment: conquest of Zara, a rival Christian port city on the Adriatic. To the shock of Pope Innocent III, the Crusaders obliged. This digression of the Crusaders from their original goal proved to be only their first. They soon besieged Constantinople itself, which was completely in Western hands by 1204.

This stunning event brought Venice new lands and maritime rights that assured its domination of the eastern Mediterranean. Constantinople now became the center for Western trade throughout the Near East. Although its capture had been an embarrassment to the pope, the papacy soon adjusted to this unforeseen turn of events and shared in the spoils. The Western church had a unique opportunity to extend its presence into the East. A confidant of Innocent's became patriarch of Constantinople and launched a mission to win the Greeks and the Slavs to the Roman Church. Western control of Constantinople continued until 1261, when the Eastern emperor Michael Paleologus, helped by the Genoese, who envied Venetian prosperity in the East, finally recaptured the city. The more than fifty-year occupation of Constantinople did nothing to heal the political and religious divisions between East and West. When Constantinople returned to eastern hands, East–West relations were at a new low.

THE FOURTH LATERAN COUNCIL Under Innocent's direction, the Fourth Lateran Council met in 1215 to formalize church discipline throughout the hierarchy, from pope to parish priest. Many important landmarks in ecclesiastical legislation issued from this council. It gave full dogmatic sanction to the controversial doctrine of transubstantiation, according to which the bread and wine of the Lord's Supper become the true body and blood of Christ when consecrated by a priest in the sacrament of the Eucharist. This doctrine has been part of Catholic teaching ever since. It reflects the influence of the Cluniac monks and those of a new order, the Cistercians. During the twelfth century, these orders made the adoration of the Virgin Mary (the patron saint of the Cistercians) and the worship of Christ in the Eucharist the centerpieces of

Saint Francis of Assisi Sets Out His Religious Ideals

Saint Francis of Assisi (1182–1226) was the founder of the Franciscan order of friars. The religious principles by which he required his followers to live were stated in the Rule of the Order, *which Pope Honorius III approved in 1223. The chief principle was to lead a life of poverty. The ideal of poverty caused conflict between the order and the pope, who feared some Franciscans carried it too far.*

✦ *Can ideals be so high that they threaten the well-being of an institution? What would have happened to the church if all clergy, including the pope, had lived a life of poverty, begging, and working with their hands, as the* Rule of Saint Francis *instructs? What provisions are there in the* Rule *to assure the pope of the order's loyalty?*

This is the rule and way of living of the Minorite brothers, namely, to observe the holy Gospel of our Lord Jesus Christ, living in obedience, without personal possessions, and in chastity. Brother Francis promises obedience and reverence to our lord Pope Honorius, and to his successors who canonically enter upon their office, and to the Roman Church. And the other brothers shall be bound to obey Brother Francis and his successors.

I firmly command all the brothers by no means to receive coin or money, of themselves or through an intervening person. But for the needs of the sick and for clothing the other brothers, the ministers alone and the guardians shall provide through spiritual friends, as it may seem to them that necessity demands, according to time, place, and the coldness of the temperature. This one thing being always borne in mind, that, as has been said, they receive neither coin nor money.

Those brothers to whom God has given the ability to labor shall do so faithfully and devoutly, but in such manner that idleness, the enemy of the soul, being averted, they may not extinguish the spirit of holy prayer and devotion, to which other temporal things should be subservient. As a reward, moreover, for their labor, they may receive for themselves and their brothers the necessities of life, but not coin or money; and this humbly, as becomes the servants of God and the followers of most holy poverty.

The brothers shall appropriate nothing to themselves, neither a house, nor a place, nor anything; but as pilgrims and strangers in this world, in poverty and humility serving God, they shall confidently go seeking for alms. Nor need they be ashamed, for the Lord made Himself poor for us in this world.

Frederic Austin Ogg, ed., A Source Book of Mediaeval History: Documents Illustrative of European Life and Institutions from the German Invasions to the Renaissance *(New York: Telegraph Books, 1908), pp. 375–376.*

a reformed, christocentric piety. The doctrine of transubstantiation is an expression of the popularity of this piety. It also enhanced the power and authority of the clergy, because it specified that only they could perform the miracle of the Eucharist.

The council also made annual confession and Easter communion mandatory for every adult Christian. This legislation formalized the sacrament of penance as the church's key instrument of religious education and discipline in the later Middle Ages.

FRANCISCANS AND DOMINICANS During his reign, Pope Innocent gave official sanction to two new monastic orders: the Franciscans and the Dominicans. No other action of the pope had more of an effect on spiritual life. Unlike other regular clergy, the members of these mendicant orders, known as friars, did not confine themselves to the cloister.

They went out into the world to preach the church's mission and to combat heresy, begging or working to support themselves (hence the term *mendicant*).

Lay interest in spiritual devotion, especially among urban women, was particularly intense at the turn of the twelfth century. In addition to the heretical Albigensians, there were movements of Waldensians, Beguines, and Beghards, each of which stressed biblical simplicity in religion and a life of poverty in imitation of Christ. Such movements were especially active in Italy and France. Their heterodox teachings—teachings that, although not necessarily heretical, nonetheless challenged church orthodoxy—and the critical frame of mind they promoted caused the pope deep concern. Innocent feared they would inspire lay piety to turn militantly against the church. The Franciscan and Dominican orders, however, emerged from the same background of intense religiosity. By sanctioning them and thus keeping their followers within the confines of church organization, the pope provided a response to heterodox piety as well as an answer to lay criticism of the worldliness of the papal monarchy.

The Franciscan order was founded by Saint Francis of Assisi (1182–1226), the son of a rich Italian cloth merchant, who became disaffected with wealth and urged his followers to live a life of extreme poverty. Pope Innocent recognized the order in 1210, and its official rule was approved in 1223. The Dominican order, the Order of Preachers, was founded by Saint Dominic (1170–1221), a well-educated Spanish cleric, and was sanctioned in 1216. Both orders received special privileges from the pope and were solely under his jurisdiction. This special relationship with Rome gave the friars an independence from local clerical authority that bred resentment among some secular clergy.

Pope Gregory IX (r. 1227–1241) canonized Saint Francis only two years after Francis's death—a fitting honor for Francis and a stroke of genius on the part of the pope. By bringing the age's most popular religious figure, one who had even miraculously received the stigmata (bleeding wounds like those of the crucified Jesus), so emphatically within the confines of the church, he enhanced papal authority over lay piety.

Two years after the canonization, however, Gregory canceled Saint Francis's own *Testament* as an authoritative rule for the Franciscan order. He did so because he found it to be an impractical guide for the order and because the unconventional nomadic life of strict poverty it advocated conflicted with

Dominicans (left), and Franciscans (right). Unlike the other religious orders, the Dominicans and Franciscans did not live in cloisters, but wandered about preaching and combating heresy. They depended for support on their own labor and the kindness of the laity. [Bibliothèque Nationale, Paris]

papal plans to enlist the order as an arm of church policy. Most Franciscans themselves, under the leadership of moderates like Saint Bonaventure, general of the order between 1257 and 1274, also came to doubt the wisdom of extreme asceticism. During the thirteenth century the main branch of the order progressively complied with papal wishes. In the fourteenth century the pope condemned a radical branch, the Spiritual Franciscans, extreme followers of Saint Francis who considered him almost a new Messiah. In his condemnation, the pope declared absolute poverty a fictitious ideal that not even Christ endorsed.

The Dominicans, a less factious order, combated doctrinal error through visitations and preaching. They conformed convents of Beguines to the church's teaching, led the church's campaign against heretics in southern France, and staffed the offices of the Inquisition after its centralization by Pope Gregory IX in 1223. The great Dominican theologian, Thomas Aquinas (d. 1274), was canonized in 1322. His efforts to synthesize faith and reason resulted in a definitive and enduring statement of Catholic belief. (See Chapter 8.)

The Dominicans and the Franciscans strengthened the church among the laity. Through the institution of so-called Third orders, they provided ordinary men and women the opportunity to affiliate with the monastic life and pursue the high religious ideals of poverty, obedience, and chastity, while remaining laypeople. Laity who joined such orders were known as *tertiaries*. Such organizations helped keep lay piety orthodox and within the church during a period of heightened religiosity.

England and France: Hastings (1066) to Bouvines (1214)

In 1066 the death of the childless Anglo-Saxon ruler Edward the Confessor (so-named because of his reputation for piety) occasioned the most important change in English political life. Edward's mother was a Norman, giving the duke of Normandy a hereditary claim to the English throne. Before his death, Edward, who was not a strong ruler, acknowledged the duke's claim and even directed that his throne be given to William, the reigning duke of Normandy (d. 1087). But the Anglo-Saxon assembly, which customarily bestowed the royal power, had a mind of its own and vetoed Edward's last wishes, choosing instead Harold Godwinsson. This defiant action triggered the swift conquest of England by the powerful Normans. William's forces defeated Harold's army at Hastings on October 14, 1066. Within weeks of the invasion William was crowned king of England in Westminster Abbey, both by right of heredity and by right of conquest.

William the Conqueror

Thereafter, William embarked on a twenty-year conquest that eventually made all of England his domain. Every landholder, whether large or small, was henceforth his vassal, holding land legally as a fief from the king. William organized his new English nation shrewdly. He established a strong monarchy whose power was not fragmented by independent territorial princes. He kept the Anglo-Saxon tax system and the practice of court writs

William the Conqueror on horseback urging his troops into combat with the English at the Battle of Hastings (October 14, 1066). From the Bayeux Tapestry, about 1073–1083. [Giraudon/Art Resource, N.Y.]

The Growing Power and Influence of the Church

910	Cluny founded by William the Pious
1059	Pope Nicholas II establishes College of Cardinals
1075	Pope Gregory VII condemns lay investiture of clergy under penalty of excommunication
1076	Emperor Henry IV excommunicated by Pope Gregory VII for defying ban on lay investiture
1077	Henry IV begs for and receives papal absolution in Canossa
1084	Henry IV installs an antipope and forces Gregory VII into exile
1095	Pope Urban II preaches the First Crusade at the Council of Clermont
1099	Jerusalem falls to the Crusaders; forty-five years of Western rule in the Holy Land begins
1122	Concordat of Worms between Emperor Henry V and Pope Calixtus II ends Investiture Controversy
1144	Islamic armies reconquer Edessa
1187	Jerusalem reconquered by Saladin, King of Egypt and Syria
1189–1192	Third Crusade fails to recover the Holy Land from Islamic armies
1202	Fourth Crusade launched; captures Constantinople instead of going to Holy Land
1209	Pope Innocent III launches Albigensian Crusade in southern France; excommunicates King John of England
1210	Pope Innocent III recognizes the Franciscan order
1215	Fourth Lateran Council sanctions doctrine of transubstantiation and mandates annual confession by all adult Christians
1216	Pope Innocent III recognizes the Dominican order

(legal warnings) as a flexible form of central control over localities. And he took care not to destroy the Anglo-Saxon quasi democratic tradition of frequent "parleying"—that is, the holding of conferences between the king and lesser powers who had vested interests in royal decisions.

The practice of parleying had been initially nurtured by Alfred the Great (r. 871–899). A strong and willful king who had forcibly unified England, Alfred cherished the advice of his councilors in the making of laws. His example was respected and emulated by Canute (r. 1016–1035), the Dane who restored order and brought unity to England after the civil wars that engulfed the land during the reign of the incompetent Ethelred II (r. 978–1016). The new Norman king, William, although he thoroughly subjugated his noble vassals to the crown, maintained the tradition of parleying by consulting with them regularly about decisions of state. The result was a unique blending of the "one" and the "many," a balance between monarchical and parliamentary elements that has ever since been a feature of English government—although the English Parliament as we know it today did not formally develop as an institution until the late thirteenth century.

For administration and taxation purposes William commissioned a county-by-county survey of his new realm, a detailed accounting known as the *Domesday Book* (1080–1086). The title of the book may reflect the thoroughness and finality of the survey. As none would escape the doomsday judgment of God, so none was overlooked by William's assessors.

Henry II

William's son, Henry I (r. 1100–1135), died without a male heir, throwing England into virtual anarchy until the accession of Henry II (r. 1154–1189). Son of the duke of Anjou and Matilda, daughter of Henry I, Henry mounted the throne as head of the new Plantagenet dynasty, the family name of the Angevin (or Anjouan) line of kings who ruled England until the death of Richard III in 1485. Henry tried to recapture the efficiency and stability of his grandfather's regime, but in the process he steered the English monarchy rapidly toward an oppressive rule. Partly by inheritance from his father (Anjou) and partly by his marriage to Eleanor of Aquitaine (ca. 1122–1204), Henry brought to the throne greatly expanded French holdings, virtually the entire west coast of France.

The union with Eleanor created the so-called Angevin, or English–French Empire. Eleanor married Henry while he was still the count of Anjou and not yet king of England. The marriage occurred only eight weeks after the annulment of Eleanor's fifteen-year marriage to the ascetic French king Louis VII in March 1152. Although the annulment was granted on grounds of consanguinity (blood relationship), the true reason for the dissolution of the marriage was Louis's suspicion of infidelity (according to rumor, Eleanor had been intimate with a cousin). The annulment was very costly to Louis, who lost Aquitaine together with his wife. Eleanor and Henry had eight children, five of them sons, among them the future kings Richard the Lion-Hearted and John.

In addition to gaining control of most of the coast of France, Henry also conquered a part of Ireland and made the king of Scotland his vassal. Louis VII saw a mortal threat to France in this English expansion. He responded by adopting what came to be a permanent French policy of containment and expulsion of the English from their continental holdings in France. This policy was not finally successful until the mid-fifteenth century, when English power on the continent collapsed after the Hundred Years' War.

Eleanor of Aquitaine and Court Culture

Eleanor of Aquitaine was a powerful influence on both politics and culture in twelfth-century France and England. She had accompanied her first husband, King Louis VII, on the Second Crusade, becoming an example for women of lesser stature, who were also then venturing in increasing numbers into war and business and other areas previously considered the province of men. After marrying Henry, she settled in Angers, the chief town of Anjou, where she sponsored troubadours and poets at her lively court. There the troubadour Bernart de Ventadorn composed in Eleanor's honor many of the most popular love songs of high medieval aristocratic society. Eleanor spent the years 1154 to 1170 as Henry's queen in England. She separated from Henry in 1170, partly because of his public philandering and cruel treatment, and took revenge on him by joining Louis VII in provoking Henry's three surviving sons, who were unhappy with the terms of their inheritance, into unsuccessful rebellion against their father in 1173. From 1179 until his death in 1189, Henry kept Eleanor under mild house arrest to prevent any further such mischief from her.

After her separation from Henry in 1170 and until Henry confined her in England, Eleanor lived in Poitiers with her daughter Marie, the countess of Champagne; the two made the court of Poitiers a famous center for the literature of courtly love. This genre, with its thinly veiled eroticism, has been viewed as an attack on medieval ascetic values. Be that as it may, it was certainly a commentary on contemporary domestic life within the aristocracy. The troubadours hardly promoted promiscuity at court—the code of chivalry that guided relations between lords and their vassals condemned the seduction of the wife of one's lord as the most heinous of offenses, punishable, in some places, by castration and/or execution. Rather the troubadours presented in a frank and entertaining way stories that satirized carnal love or depicted it with tragic irony while glorifying the ennobling power of friendly, or "courteous," love. The most famous courtly literature was that of Chrétien de Troyes, whose stories of King Arthur and the Knights of the Round Table contained the tragic story of Sir Lancelot's secret and illicit love for Arthur's wife, Guinevere.

Popular Rebellion and Magna Carta

As Henry II acquired new lands abroad, he became more autocratic at home. He forced his will on the

An effigy of Eleanor of Aquitaine, queen by marriage of both France and England. [Giraudon/Art Resource, N.Y.]

A depiction of the murder of Saint Thomas à Becket in Canterbury cathedral. From the Playfair Book of Hours. *[Victoria and Albert Museum/Art Resource, N.Y., Ms. L 475–1918]*

clergy in the Constitutions of Clarendon (1164). These measures placed limitations on judicial appeals to Rome, subjected the clergy to the civil courts, and gave the king control over the election of bishops. The result was strong political resistance from both the nobility and the clergy. The archbishop of Canterbury, Thomas à Becket (1118?–1170), once Henry's compliant chancellor, broke openly with the king and fled to Louis VII. Becket's subsequent assassination in 1170 and his canonization by Pope Alexander III in 1172 helped focus popular resentment against the king's heavy-handed tactics. (Two hundred years later, Geoffrey Chaucer, writing in an age made cynical by the Black Death and the Hundred Years' War, had the pilgrims of his *Canterbury Tales* journey to the shrine of Thomas à Becket.)

Under Henry's successors, the brothers Richard the Lion-Hearted (r. 1189–1199) and John (r. 1199–1216), burdensome taxation in support of unnecessary foreign Crusades and a failing war with France turned resistance into outright rebellion. Richard had to be ransomed at a high price from the Holy Roman emperor Henry VI, who had taken him prisoner during his return from the ill-fated Third Crusade. In 1209 Pope Innocent III, in a dispute with King John over the pope's choice for archbishop of Canterbury, excommunicated the king and placed England under interdict. To extricate himself and keep his throne, John had to make humiliating concessions, even declaring his country a fief of the pope. The last straw for the English, however, was the defeat of the king's forces by the French at Bouvines in 1214. With the full support of the clergy and the townspeople, English barons revolted against John. The popular rebellion ended with the king's grudging recognition of Magna Carta, or "Great Charter" in 1215.

The Magna Carta put limits on autocratic behavior of the kind exhibited by Norman kings and their successors, the Angevin or Plantagenet kings. It also secured the rights of the many, at least the privileged many, against the monarchy. In Magna Carta the privileged preserved their right to be represented at the highest levels of government in important matters like taxation. But the monarchy was also preserved and left strong. Some argue that just such a balancing of the one and the many, the stronger and the comparatively weaker—preserving both sides and giving real power to each—was precisely the goal of feudal government.

Political accident clearly had more to do with Magna Carta than political genius. Nevertheless, the English did manage to avoid both a dissolution of the monarchy by the nobility and the abridgment of the rights of the nobility by the monarchy. Although King John continued to resist the Magna Carta in every way, and succeeding kings ignored it, Magna Carta nonetheless became a cornerstone of modern English law.

Philip II Augustus

The English struggle in the High Middle Ages was to secure the rights of the many, not the authority of the king. The French, on the other hand, faced the opposite problem. In 987, noblemen chose Hugh Capet to succeed the last Carolingian ruler, replacing the Carolingian dynasty with the Capetian

The English Nobility Imposes Restraints on King John

The gradual building of a sound English constitutional monarchy in the Middle Ages required the king's willingness to share power. He had to be very strong but could not act as a despot or rule by fiat. The danger of despotism became acute in England under the rule of King John. In 1215 the English nobility forced him to recognize Magna Carta, which reaffirmed traditional rights and personal liberties that are still enshrined in English law.

✦ *Does the Magna Carta protect basic rights or special privileges? Does this suggest there was a sense of "fairness" in the past? Does the granting of such protections in any way weaken the king?*

A free man shall not be fined for a small offense, except in proportion to the gravity of the offense; and for a great offense he shall be fined in proportion to the magnitude of the offense, saving his freehold [property]; and a merchant in the same way, saving his merchandise; and the villein [a free serf, bound only to his lord] shall be fined in the same way, saving his wainage [wagon], if he shall be at [the king's] mercy. And none of the above fines shall be imposed except by the oaths of honest men of the neighborhood . . . .

No constable or other bailiff of [the king] shall take anyone's grain or other chattels without immediately paying for them in money, unless he is able to obtain a postponement at the good will of the seller.

No constable shall require any knight to give money in place of his ward of a castle [i.e., standing guard], if he is willing to furnish that ward in his own person, or through another honest man, if he himself is not able to do it for a reasonable cause; and if we shall lead or send him into the army, he shall be free from ward in proportion to the amount of time which he has been in the army through us.

No sheriff or bailiff of [the king], or any one else, shall take horses or wagons of any free man, for carrying purposes, except on the permission of that free man.

Neither we nor our bailiffs will take the wood of another man for castles, or for anything else which we are doing, except by the permission of him to whom the wood belongs . . . .

No free man shall be taken, or imprisoned, or dispossessed, or outlawed, or banished, or in any way injured, nor will we go upon him, nor send upon him, except by the legal judgment of his peers, or by the law of the land.

To no one will we sell, to no one will we deny or delay, right or justice.

James Harvey Robinson, ed., Readings in European History, *vol. 1 (Boston: Athenaeum, 1904), pp. 236–237.*

dynasty. For two centuries thereafter, until the reign of Philip II Augustus (r. 1180–1223), powerful feudal princes dominated France.

During this period, after a rash initial attempt to challenge the more powerful French nobility before they had enough strength to do so, the Capetian kings concentrated their limited resources on securing the royal domain, their uncontested territory around Paris and the Île-de-France to the northeast. Aggressively exercising their feudal rights, French kings, especially after 1100, gained near absolute obedience from the noblemen in this area, and in the process established a solid base of power. By the reign of Philip II, Paris had become the center of French government and culture and the Capetian dynasty a secure hereditary monarchy. Thereafter, the kings of France could impose their will on the French nobles, who were always in law, if not in political fact, the king's sworn vassals.

In an indirect way the Norman conquest of England helped stir France to unity and made it possible for the Capetian kings to establish a truly national monarchy. The duke of Normandy, who after 1066 was master of the whole of England, was also among the vassals of the French king in Paris. Capetian kings understandably watched with alarm as the power of their Norman vassal grew. Other powerful vassals of the king also watched with alarm. King Louis VI, the Fat (r. 1108–1137), entered an alliance with Flanders, traditionally a Norman enemy. King Louis VII (r. 1137–1180), assisted by a brilliant minister, Suger, the abbot of St. Denis and famous for his patronage of Gothic architecture, found allies in the great northern French cities and used their wealth to build a royal army.

When he succeeded Louis VII as king, Philip II Augustus inherited financial resources and a skilled bureaucracy that put him in a strong position. He was able to resist the competition of the French nobility and the clergy and to focus on the contest with the English king. Confronted at the same time with an internal and an international struggle, he proved successful in both. His armies occupied all the English king's territories on the French coast except for Aquitaine. As a showdown with the English neared on the continent, however, Holy Roman Emperor Otto IV (r. 1198–1215) entered the fray on the side of the English, and the French found themselves assailed from both east and west. But when the international armies finally clashed at Bouvines in Flanders on July 27, 1214, in what history records as the first great European battle, the French won handily over the opposing Anglo–Flemish–German army. This victory unified France politically around the monarchy and thereby laid the foundation for French ascendancy in the later Middle Ages. The defeat so weakened Otto IV that he fell from power in Germany. (It also, as we have seen, sparked the rebellion in England that forced King John to accept Magna Carta.)

France in the Thirteenth Century: The Reign of Louis IX

If Innocent III realized the fondest ambitions of medieval popes, Louis IX (r. 1226–1270), the grandson of Philip Augustus, embodied the medieval view of the perfect ruler. Coming to power in the wake of the French victory at Bouvines (1214), Louis inherited a unified and secure kingdom.

King Louis IX (1226–1270) teaching lessons to his son Philip. Louis, who was canonized in 1297, was the medieval ideal of a perfect ruler. [Musee Conde, Chantilly, France. Giraudon/Art Resource]

Although he was endowed with a moral character that far exceeded that of his royal and papal contemporaries, he was also at times prey to naïveté. Not beset by the problems of sheer survival, and a reformer at heart, Louis found himself free to concentrate on what medieval people believed to be the business of civilization.

Generosity Abroad

Magnanimity in politics is not always a sign of strength, and Louis could be very magnanimous. Although in a strong position during negotiations for the Treaty of Paris (1259), which momentarily settled the dispute between France and England, he refused to take advantage of it to drive the English from their French possessions. Had he done so and ruthlessly confiscated English territories on the French coast, he might have lessened, if not averted altogether, the conflict underlying the Hundred Years' War, which began in the fourteenth century. Instead he surrendered disputed territory on the borders of Gascony to the English king, Henry III, and confirmed Henry's possession of the duchy of Aquitaine.

Although he occasionally chastised popes for their crude political ambitions, Louis remained neutral during the long struggle between the German Hohenstaufen emperor Frederick II and the papacy (discussed later in the chapter); and his neutrality redounded very much to the pope's advantage. Louis also remained neutral when his brother, Charles of Anjou, intervened in Italy and Sicily against the Hohenstaufens, again to the pope's advantage. Urged on by the pope and his noble supporters, Charles was crowned king of Sicily in Rome, and his subsequent defeat of the son and grandson of Frederick II ended the Hohenstaufen dynasty. For such service to the church, both by action and by inaction, the Capetian kings of the thirteenth century became the objects of many papal favors.

Order and Excellence at Home

Louis's greatest achievements lay at home. The efficient French bureaucracy, which his predecessors had used to exploit their subjects, became under Louis an instrument of order and fair play in local government. He sent forth royal commissioners (*enquêteurs*), reminiscent of Charlemagne's far less successful *missi dominici*. Their mission was to monitor the royal officials responsible for local governmental administration (especially the *baillis* and *prévôts*, whose offices had been created by his predecessor, Philip Augustus) and to ensure that justice would truly be meted out to all. These royal ambassadors were received as genuine tribunes of the people. Louis further abolished private wars and serfdom within his royal domain. He gave his subjects the judicial right of appeal from local to higher courts, and made the tax system, by medieval standards, more equitable. The French people came to associate their king with justice; consequently, national feeling, the glue of nationhood, grew very strong during his reign.

Respected by the kings of Europe and possessed of far greater moral authority than the pope, Louis became an arbiter among the world's powers. During his reign French society and culture became an example to all of Europe, a pattern that would continue into the modern period. Northern France became the showcase of monastic reform, chivalry, and Gothic art and architecture. Louis's reign also coincided with the golden age of Scholasticism, which saw the convergence of Europe's greatest thinkers on Paris, among them Saint Thomas Aquinas and Saint Bonaventure. (See Chapter 8.)

Louis's perfection remained, however, that of a medieval king. Like his father, Louis VIII (r. 1223–1226), who had taken part in the Albigensian Crusade, Louis was something of a religious fanatic. He sponsored the French Inquisition. He led two French Crusades against the Muslims, which, although inspired by the purest religious motives, proved to be personal disasters. During the first (1248–1254), Louis was captured and had to be ransomed out of Egypt. He died of a fever during the second in 1270. It was especially for this selfless, but also useless, service on behalf of the church that Louis later received the rare honor of sainthood. Probably not coincidentally, the church bestowed this honor when it was under pressure from a more powerful and less than "most Christian" French king, the ruthless Philip IV, "the Fair" (r. 1285–1314). (See Chapter 9.)

The Hohenstaufen Empire (1152–1272)

During the twelfth and thirteenth centuries, stable governments developed in both England and France. In England Magna Carta balanced the rights of the nobility against the authority of the kings, and in France the reign of Philip II Augustus secured the authority of the king over the competitive claims of the nobility. During the reign of Louis IX, the French exercised international influence over politics and culture. The story within the Holy Roman Empire, which embraced Germany, Burgundy, and northern Italy by the mid-thirteenth century, was very different. (See Map 7–2.) There, primarily because of the efforts of the Hohenstaufen dynasty to extend imperial power into southern Italy, disunity and blood feuding remained the order of the day for two centuries. It left as a legacy the fragmentation of Germany until modern times.

Frederick I Barbarossa

The investiture struggle had earlier weakened imperial authority. After the Concordat of Worms, the German princes held the dominant lay influence over episcopal appointments and within the rich ecclesiastical territories.

MAP 7–2 GERMANY AND ITALY IN THE MIDDLE AGES *Medieval Germany and Italy were divided lands. The Holy Roman Empire (Germany) embraced hundreds of independent territories that the emperor ruled only in name. The papacy controlled the Rome area and tried to enforce its will on Romagna. Under the Hohenstaufens (mid-twelfth to mid-thirteenth century), internal German divisions and papal conflict reached new heights; German rulers sought to extend their power to southern Italy and Sicily.*

Frederick I Barbarossa, wearing the imperial crown, leads the Third Crusade to Jerusalem. He drowned in the Saleph River while en route. [Bürgerbibliothek, Bern]

Imperial power seemed to recuperate, however, with the accession to the throne of Frederick I Barbarossa (r. 1152–1190) of the new Hohenstaufen dynasty, the most powerful line of emperors yet to succeed the Ottonians. The Hohenstaufens not only reestablished imperial authority but also started a new phase in the contest between popes and emperors, one that was to prove even deadlier than the investiture struggle had been. Never have kings and popes despised and persecuted one another more than during the Hohenstaufen dynasty.

As Frederick I surveyed his empire, he saw powerful feudal princes in Germany and Lombardy and a pope in Rome who believed that the emperor was his creature. Disaffection was widespread, however, with the incessant feudal strife of the princes and the turmoil caused by the theocratic pretensions of the papacy. Thus popular opinion was on the emperor's side, giving Frederick a foundation on which to rebuild imperial authority, and he was shrewd enough to take advantage of it. In Bologna at the time, Roman law (the law of the Roman Empire, particularly the Justinian *Code*) was undergoing a revival under the scholar Irnerius (d. 1125), and Frederick championed its application within his empire. Roman law served Frederick on both of his fronts. On one hand, it enhanced centralized authority against the nobility; on the other, it stressed the *secular* foundation of imperial power against the tradition of Roman election of the emperor, and especially against the tradition of papal coronation of the emperor, thereby keeping papal influence at a minimum.

Switzerland became Frederick's base of operation. From there he tried to hold the empire together by invoking feudal bonds. He was relatively successful in Germany, thanks largely to the fall from power in 1180 and the exile to Normandy of his strongest German rival, Henry the Lion (d. 1195), the duke of Saxony. Although realistically acknowledging the power of the German duchies, Frederick never missed an opportunity to apprise each of its prescribed duties as a fief of the king. If Frederick was not everywhere ruler in fact, he was clearly so in law, and he permitted no one to forget it. The same tactic had been successfully employed by the Capetian kings of France when they faced superior noble forces.

Italy proved to be the great obstacle to imperial plans. In 1155 Frederick restored Pope Adrian IV (r. 1154–1159) to power in Rome after a religious revolutionary, Arnold of Brescia (d. 1155), had gained control of the city. For his efforts Frederick won a coveted papal coronation—and strictly on his terms, not on those of the pope. The door to Italy thereby opened and an imperial diet, or general assembly, gave official sanction to his Italian claims. But there was fierce resistance to him in Italy, led by Milan.

As this challenge to royal authority was occurring, one of Europe's most skilled lawyers, Cardinal Roland, was elected Pope Alexander III (r. 1159–1181). While a cardinal, he had negotiated an alliance between the papacy and the Norman kingdom of Sicily in a clever effort to strengthen the papacy against imperial influence. Perceiving him to be a very capable foe, Frederick had opposed his election as pope and had even backed a schismatic pope against him in a futile effort to undo Alexander's election. Frederick now found himself at war with the pope, Milan, and Sicily. In 1167 the combined forces of the north Italian communes drove him back into Germany. The final blow to imperial plans in Italy came a decade later, in 1176, when Italian forces soundly defeated Frederick at Legnano. In the final Peace of Constance in 1183, Frederick recognized the claims of the Lombard cities to full rights of self-rule.

Henry VI and the Sicilian Connection

Frederick's reign ended with stalemate in Germany and defeat in Italy. At his death in 1190 he was not, as a ruler, equal in stature to the kings of England and France. After the Peace of Constance in 1183 he seems himself to have conceded as much, accepting the reality of the empire's indefinite division among the feudal princes of Germany. In the last years of his reign, however, he had an opportunity both to solve his problem with Sicily, still a papal ally, and to form a new territorial base of power for future emperors. The Norman ruler of the kingdom of Sicily, William II (r. 1166–1189), sought an alliance with Frederick that would free him to pursue a scheme to conquer Constantinople. In 1186 a most fateful marriage between Frederick's son, the future Henry VI (r. 1190–1197), and Constance, heiress to the kingdom of Sicily, sealed the alliance.

This alliance proved, however, to be only another well-laid political plan that went astray. The Sicilian connection became a fatal distraction for the succeeding Hohenstaufen kings. It led them in the end to sacrifice their traditional territorial base in northern Europe to the temptations of imperialism. Equally ominous, this union of the empire with Sicily left Rome encircled, thereby ensuring the undying hostility of a papacy already thoroughly distrustful of the emperor. The marriage alliance with Sicily proved to be the first step in what soon became a fight to the death between pope and emperor.

When Henry VI came to rule in 1190, he faced a multitude of enemies: a hostile papacy, still smarting from the refusal of his father to recognize territorial claims within the Papal States; supremely independent German princes, led by the archbishop of Cologne; and an England whose adventurous king, Richard the Lion-Hearted, was encouraged to plot against Henry by the exiled duke of Saxony, Henry the Lion.

Into this divided kingdom a son, the future Frederick II, was born in 1194. Heretofore the German princes had not recognized birth alone as entitling the offspring of emperors to the imperial throne, although it did give them an inside track. To stabilize his monarchy, Henry campaigned vigorously for the recognition of the principle of hereditary succession. He won many German princes to this point of view by granting them full hereditary rights to their own fiefs—an appropriate exchange. But the encircled papacy was not disposed to secure Hohenstaufen power by supporting a hereditary right to the imperial throne. The pope wanted, rather, to return to the period before 1152, when imperial power had been diffused among many princes and future emperors could be more easily created from among the pope's allies. He accordingly joined dissident German princes against Henry.

Otto IV and the Welf Interregnum

When Henry died in September 1197, leaving his son Frederick a ward of the pope, chaos was his immediate heir. Henry's brother, Philip of Swabia, succeeded him as German king, but the Welf family, rivals of the Hohenstaufens, put forth a rival claimant, Otto of Brunswick. The English supported Otto; the French, beginning a series of interventions in German affairs, supported the Hohenstaufens; and the papacy supported first one side and then the other as each in turn threatened to encircle Rome. Germany was thrown into anarchy and civil war.

Otto, crowned Otto IV by his supporters in Aachen in 1198, outlasted his rival, and later won general recognition in Germany. Hohenstaufen support remained alive, however, and Otto reigned over a very divided kingdom. Then, in October 1209, Pope Innocent III (r. 1198–1216) crowned him emperor, enhancing his authority. Innocent, however, was a shrewd pope who was determined to curb imperial power in Italy and restore papal power there, and he was willing to play one German dynasty against the other to do so. When, after his coronation, Otto proceeded to attack Sicily, pursuing an imperial policy that once again threatened to encircle Rome, the pope quickly moved from benefactor to mortal enemy; four months after crowning Otto emperor, the pope excommunicated him.

Frederick II

Pope Innocent, casting about for a counterweight to the treacherous Otto, joined the French, who had remained loyal to the Hohenstaufens against the English–Welf alliance. His new ally, the French king Philip Augustus, impressed on Innocent that a solution to their problems with Otto IV lay near at hand in the person of Innocent's ward, Frederick of Sicily, the son of the late Hohenstaufen Emperor Henry VI, who was now of age. Unlike Otto, Frederick had an immediate hereditary claim to the imperial throne. In December 1212, the young Frederick, with papal, French, and German support, was crowned king of the Romans in Mainz. Within a year and a half, Philip Augustus ended the reign of Otto IV on the battlefield of Bouvines. In 1215 Frederick, now Frederick II, was crowned emperor again, this time in the imperial city of Aachen.

During his reign, Frederick effectively turned dreams of a unified Germany into a nightmare of disunity, and he may be credited with assuring German fragmentation until modern times. Frederick was Sicilian and dreaded travel beyond the Alps. He spent only nine of his thirty-eight years as emperor in Germany, and six of those were before 1218. Although he pursued his royal interests in Germany, he did so mostly through representatives. He seemed to desire only the imperial title for himself and his sons, and, to secure it, he was willing to give the German princes what they wanted. His eager compliance with their demands laid the foundation for six centuries of German division. In 1220 he recognized the jurisdictional claims of the ecclesiastical princes of Germany. In 1232 he extended the same recognition to the secular princes. Their power greatly enhanced, the German princes were thereafter undisputed lords over their territories.

Frederick's concessions were tantamount to an abdication of imperial responsibility in Germany. They have been characterized as a German equivalent to Magna Carta in the sense that they secured the rights of the German nobility. But unlike the king of England who signed Magna Carta, Frederick did little to secure the rights of monarchy in Germany. Whereas Magna Carta may be said to have had the long-term consequence of promoting a balance of authority between king and parliament, Frederick simply made the German princes little emperors within their realms. Centuries of petty absolutism, not parliamentary government, were the result.

Frederick's relations with the pope were equally disastrous. He was excommunicated no fewer than four times, the first in 1227 for refusing to carry through a crusade he had begun at the pope's request. The papacy came to view Frederick as the Antichrist, the biblical beast of the Apocalypse, whose persecution of the faithful signaled the end of the world. The basis of the conflict lay once again in imperial policies that threatened to encircle Rome. Although Frederick abandoned Germany, he was determined to control Lombardy. His efforts to establish a dominant Lombardy-Sicily axis in Italy brought his excommunication in 1238.

The papacy finally won the long struggle that ensued, although its victory proved in time to be a Pyrrhic one. During this contest, Pope Innocent IV (r. 1243–1254) launched the church into European politics on a massive scale. This wholesale secularization made the church highly vulnerable to criticism from religious reformers and royal apologists. Innocent organized and led the German princes

Major Political Events of High Middle Ages

955	Otto I defeats Hungarians at Lechfeld, securing Europe's eastern border
1066	Normans win the Battle of Hastings and assume English rule
1152	Frederick I Barbarossa becomes first Hohenstaufen emperor; reestablishes imperial authority
1154	Henry II assumes the English throne as the first Plantagenet or Angevin king
1164	Henry II forces the Constitutions of Clarendon on the English clergy
1170	Henry II's defiant archbishop, Thomas à Becket, assassinated
1176	Papal and other Italian armies defeat Frederick I at Legnano
1194	Birth of future Hohenstaufen ruler Frederick II, who becomes a ward of the pope
1198	Welf interregnum in the empire begins under Otto IV
1212	Frederick II crowned emperor in Mainz with papal, French, and German support
1214	French armies under Philip II Augustus defeat combined English and German forces at Bouvines in the first major European battle
1215	English barons revolt against King John and force the king's recognition of Magna Carta
1227	Frederick II excommunicated for the first of four times by the pope; conflict between Hohenstaufen dynasty and papacy begins
1250	Frederick II dies, having been defeated by the German princes with papal support
1257	German princes establish their own electoral college to elect future emperors
1270	French king Louis IX, having unified and reformed France, dies a Crusader in the Holy Land

against Frederick, who—thanks to Frederick's grand concessions to them—had become a superior force and were in full control of Germany by the 1240s. German and Italian resistance kept Frederick completely on the defensive throughout his last years.

When Frederick died in 1250, the German monarchy died with him. The princes established their own informal electoral college in 1257, which thereafter controlled the succession. Through this institution, which the emperor formally recognized in 1356, the "king of the Romans" became a puppet, and one with firmly attached strings. The princes elected him directly; his offspring had no hereditary right to succeed him.

Between 1250 and 1272 the Hohenstaufen dynasty slowly faded into oblivion. Its legacy was to make permanent the divisions within the empire. Independent princes now controlled Germany. Italy fell to local magnates. The connection between Germany and Sicily, established by Frederick I, was permanently broken. And the papal monarchy emerged as one of Europe's most formidable powers, soon to enter its most costly conflict with the French and the English.

Medieval Russia

In the late tenth century, Prince Vladimir of Kiev (972–1015), at that time Russia's dominant city, received delegations of Muslims, Roman Catholics, Jews, and Greek Orthodox Christians, each of which hoped to see Russians embrace their religion. Vladimir chose Greek Orthodoxy, which became the religion of Russia, adding strong cultural bonds to the close commercial ties that had long linked Russia to the Byzantine Empire.

Politics and Society

Vladimir's successor, Yaroslav the Wise (1016–1054), developed Kiev into a magnificent political and cultural center, with architecture rivaling that of Constantinople. He also sought contacts with the West in an unsuccessful effort to counter the political influence of the Byzantine emperors. After his death, rivalry among their princes slowly divided Russians into three cultural groups: the Great Russians, the White Russians, and the Little Russians (Ukrainians). Autonomous principalities also challenged Kiev's dominance, and it became just one of several national centers.

Government in the principalities combined monarchy (the prince), aristocracy (the prince's council of noblemen), and democracy (a popular assembly of all adult males). The broadest social division was between freemen and slaves. Freemen included the clergy, army officers, boyars (wealthy landowners), townspeople, and peasants. Slaves were mostly prisoners of war. Debtors working off their debts made up a large, semifree, intermediate group.

Mongol Rule (1243–1480)

In the thirteenth century, Mongol, or Tatar, armies swept over China, much of the Islamic world, and Russia. Ghengis Khan (1155–1227) invaded Russia in 1223, and Kiev fell to Batu Khan in 1240. Russian cities became dependent, tribute-paying principalities of the segment of the Mongol Empire called the *Golden Horde* (a phrase derived from the Tatar words for the color of Batu Khan's tent), which included the steppe region of what is now southern Russia and had its capital at Sarai, on the Lower Volga. The Golden Horde stationed officials in all the principal Russian towns to oversee taxation and the conscription of soldiers into Tatar armies.

Mongol rule created further cultural divisions between Russia and the West. The Mongols intermarried with the Russians and also created harems filled with Russian women. Russians who resisted were sold into slavery in foreign lands. Russian women—under the influence of Islam, which had become the religion of the Golden Horde—began to wear veils and to lead more secluded lives. The Mongols, however, left Russian political and religious institutions largely intact and, thanks to their far-flung trade, brought most Russians greater peace and prosperity than they had enjoyed before.

Russian Liberation

The princes of Moscow cooperated with their overlords in the collection of tribute and grew wealthy under the Mongols. As Mongol rule weakened, the princes took control of the territory surrounding the city. In a process that has come to be known as "the gathering of the Russian Land," they then gradually expanded the principality of Moscow through land purchases, colonization, and conquest.

In 1380, Grand Duke Dimitri of Moscow (1350–1389) defeated Tatar forces at Kulikov Meadow in a victory that marks the beginning of the decline

The Cathedral of Saint Basil in Moscow. Built between 1544 and 1560 during the reign of Ivan the Terrible, it reflects the enduring Byzantine influence on Russian architecture. [Sovfoto]

of Mongol hegemony. Another century would pass before Ivan III, called Ivan the Great (d. 1505), would bring all of northern Russia under Moscow's control and end Mongol rule (1480). By the last quarter of the fourteenth century, however, Moscow had become the political and religious center of Russia, replacing Kiev. In Russian eyes it was destined to become the "third Rome" after the fall of Constantinople to the Turks in 1453.

✦

With its borders finally secured, western Europe was free to develop its political institutions and cultural forms during the High Middle Ages. The map of Europe as we know it today began to take shape. England and France can be seen forming into modern nation-states, but within Germany and the Holy Roman Empire the story was different. There, imperial rule first revived (under the Ottonians) and then collapsed totally (under the Hohenstaufen dynasty). The consequences for Germany were ominous; thereafter, it became Europe's most fractured land. On a local level, however, an effective organization of society from noble to serf emerged throughout western Europe.

The major disruption of the period was an unprecedented conflict between church and state, former allies. During the Investiture Struggle and the period of the Crusades, the church became a powerful monarchy in its own right. For the first time it competed with secular states on the latter's own terms, dethroning emperors, kings, and princes by excommunication and interdict. In doing so, it inadvertently laid the foundation for the Western doctrine of the separation of church and state.

Having succeeded so brilliantly in defending its spiritual authority against rulers, popes ventured boldly into the realm of secular politics as well, especially during the pontificates of Innocent III and Innocent IV. As the sad story of the Hohenstaufen dynasty attests, the popes had remarkable, if short-lived, success there also. But the Church was to pay dearly for its successes, both spiritually and politically. Secularization of the papacy during the High Middle Ages left it vulnerable to the attacks of a new breed of unforgiving religious reformers, and the powerful monarchs of the later Middle Ages were to subject it to bold and vengeful bullying.

Review Questions

1. Discuss the rise of the German Empire and the accomplishments of the Saxon king, Otto I. How was he able to consolidate political rule over the various German duchies and use the church to his advantage? Does he deserve the title "the Great"?
2. What were the main reasons for the Cluny reform movement? How do you account for its success? How important was the impact of this reform movement on the subsequent history of the medieval church?
3. Discuss the conflict between Pope Gregory VII and King Henry IV over the issue of lay investiture. What were the causes of the controversy, the actions of the contending parties, and the outcome of the struggle? What was at stake for each of the disputants and what were the ramifications of the struggle?
4. The eighteenth-century French intellectual Voltaire said the Holy Roman Empire was neither holy, nor Roman. What did he mean? Do you agree with him?

5. What major development in western and eastern Europe encouraged the emergence of the Crusades? Why were the Crusaders unsuccessful in establishing lasting political and religious control over the Holy Land? What were the political, religious, and economic results of the Crusades? Which do you consider most important and why?
6. Hohenstaufen rule proved disastrous for Germany's development as a nation. What were some of the factors preventing German consolidation during that era? Why did Germany remain in feudal chaos while France and England eventually coalesced into reasonably strong states?

Suggested Readings

M. W. Baldwin (Ed.), *History of the Crusades, I: The First Hundred Years* (1955). Basic historical narrative.

J. W. Baldwin, *The Government of Philip Augustus* (1986). An important scholarly work.

G. Barraclough, *The Origins of Modern Germany* (1946). Dated but penetrating political narrative setting modern Germany in the perspective of the Middle Ages.

G. Barraclough, *The Medieval Papacy* (1968). Brief survey with pictures.

A. Capellanus, *The Art of Courtly Love,* trans. by J. J. Parry (1941). Documents from the court of Marie de Champagne.

M. Clagett, G. Post, and R. Reynolds (Eds.), *Twelfth-Century Europe and the Foundations of Modern Society* (1966). A demanding but stimulating collection of essays.

H. E. J. Cowdrey, *Popes, Monks, and Crusaders* (1984). Re-creation of the atmosphere that gave birth to the Crusades.

R. H. C. Davis, *A History of Medieval Europe: From Constantine to St. Louis* (1972), Part 2. Succinct, lucid survey.

E. M. Hallam, *Capetian France 987–1328* (1980). Very good on politics and heretics.

J. C. Holt, *Magna Carta,* 2nd ed. (1992). The famous document and its interpretation by succeeding generations.

E. H. Kantorowicz, *The King's Two Bodies* (1957). Controversial analysis of political concepts in the High Middle Ages.

H. Leyser, *Hermits and the New Monasticism: A Study of Religious Communities in Western Europe, 1000–1150* (1984). The new power and influence of reformed monasticism.

K. Leyser, *Rule and Conflict in Early Medieval Society: Ottonian Saxony* (1979). Basic and authoritative.

K. Leyser, *Medieval Germany and Its Neighbors, 900–1250* (1982). Basic and authoritative.

P. Mandonnet, *St. Dominic and His Work* (1944). On the origins of the Dominican order.

H. E. Mayer, *The Crusades,* trans. by John Gilligham (1972). Extremely detailed; the best one-volume account.

J. Moorman, *A History of the Franciscan Order* (1968). The best survey.

J. B. Morrall, *Political Thought in Medieval Times* (1962). Readable and illuminating account.

C. Petit-Dutaillis, *The Feudal Monarchy in France and England from the Tenth to the Thirteenth Century,* trans. by E. D. Hunt (1964). Political narrative in great detail.

S. Reynolds, *Kingdoms and Communities in Western Europe 900–1300* (1984). For the medieval origins of Western political and cultural traditions.

T. Reuter (Ed.), *The Medieval Nobility* (1979). Collection of scholarly essays.

J. Riley-Smith, *The Crusades: A Short History* (1987). Up-to-date, lucid, and readable.

I. Spector, *Russia: A New History* (1935). Admirable simplicity.

B. Tierney, *The Crisis of Church and State* (1964). Extremely useful collection of key documents.

G. Vernadsky, *A History of Russia, I–IV* (1946–1963). A graspable magisterial survey.

W. L. Wakefield and A. P. Evans (Eds.), *Heresies of the High Middle Ages* (1969). A major document collection.

S. Williams (Ed.), *The Gregorian Epoch: Reformation, Revolution, Reaction* (1964). Scholarly debate over Gregory's reign.

R. L. Wolff and H. W. Hazard (Eds.), *History of the Crusades, II: The Later Crusades 1189–1311* (1962).

CHAPTER 8

A lover (Lord Rubin) sends his love a message by (one hopes, well-aimed) crossbow. From a German manuscript (Manesse Codex, 1305–40), University Library, Heidelberg. [E.T. Archive, London]

The High Middle Ages (1000–1300): People, Towns, and Universities

KEY TOPICS

- The major groups composing medieval society
- The rise of towns and a new merchant class
- The founding of universities and educational curriculum
- How women and children fared in the Middle Ages

Between the tenth and twelfth centuries, European agricultural production steadily improved, due to a warming climate and improved technology. With increased food supplies came something of a population explosion by the eleventh century. The recovery of the countryside in turn stimulated new migration into and trade with the long-dormant towns. A revival of old towns and the creation of new ones resulted. A rich and complex fabric of life developed, closely integrating town and countryside and allowing civilization to flourish in the twelfth and thirteenth centuries as it had not done in the West since the Roman Empire. Beginning with the Crusades, trade also revived with distant towns and foreign lands. With the rise of towns a new merchant class, the ancestors of modern capitalists, came into being. Enormous numbers of skilled artisans and day workers, especially in the cloth-making industries, were the foundation of the new urban wealth.

Urban culture and education also flourished. The revival of trade with the East and contacts with Muslim intellectuals, particularly in Spain, made possible the recovery of ancient scholarship and science. Unlike the comparative dabbling in antiquity during Carolingian times, the twelfth century enjoyed a true renaissance of classical learning. Schools and curricula also broadened beyond the clergy during the twelfth century to educate laity, thereby greatly increasing lay literacy and the role of the laity in government and culture.

In the mid-twelfth century in France, Gothic architecture began to replace the plain and ponderous Romanesque preferred by fortress Europe during the early Middle Ages. Its new grace and beauty—soaring arches, bold flying buttresses, dazzling light, and stained glass—were a testament to the vitality of humankind as well as to the glory of God in this unique period of human achievement.

The Traditional Order of Life

In the art and literature of the Middle Ages, three basic social groups were represented: those who fought as mounted knights (the landed nobility), those who prayed (the clergy), and those who labored in fields and shops (the peasantry and village artisans). After the revival of towns in the eleventh century, there emerged a fourth social group: the long-distance traders and merchants. Like the peasantry, they also labored, but in ways strange to the traditional groups. They were freemen who often possessed great wealth, yet unlike the nobility and the clergy, they owned no land, and unlike the peasantry, they did not toil in fields and shops. Their rise to power caused an important crack in the old social order, for they drew behind them the leadership of the urban artisan groups created by the new urban industries that grew up in the wake of the revival of trade. During the late Middle Ages these new "middling classes" firmly established themselves and their numbers have been enlarging ever since.

Nobles

As a distinctive social group, not all nobles were originally great men with large hereditary lands. Many rose from the ranks of feudal vassals or warrior knights. The successful vassal attained a special social and legal status based on his landed wealth (accumulated fiefs), his exercise of authority over others, and his distinctive social customs—all of which set him apart from others in medieval society. By the late Middle Ages there had evolved a distinguishable higher and lower nobility living in both town and country. The higher were the great landowners and territorial magnates, long the dominant powers in their regions; the lower were petty landlords, the descendants of minor knights, newly rich merchants who could buy country estates, or wealthy farmers patiently risen from ancestral serfdom.

It was a special mark of the nobility that they lived off the labor of others. Basically lords of manors, the nobility of the early and High Middle Ages neither tilled the soil like the peasantry nor engaged in the commerce of merchants—activities considered beneath their dignity. The nobleman resided in a country mansion or, if he were particularly wealthy, a castle. Personal preference drew him to the countryside as much as that his fiefs were usually rural manors.

WARRIORS Arms were the nobleman's profession; his sole occupation and reason for living were to wage war. In the eighth century the adoption of stirrups made mounted warriors, or cavalry, the key ingredient of a successful army. (Stirrups had the advantage of permitting the rider to strike a blow without falling to the ground.) Good horses (and a warrior needed several) and the accompanying armor and weaponry of horse warfare were expensive. Only those with means could pursue the life of a cavalryman. The nobleman's fief provided the means to acquire the expensive military equipment that his rank required. He maintained his enviable position as he had gained it, by fighting for his chief.

The nobility accordingly celebrated the physical strength, courage, and constant activity of warfare. Warring gave them both new riches and an opportunity to gain honor and glory. Knights were paid a share in the plunder of victory, and in time of war everything became fair game. Special war wagons, designed for the collection and transport of booty, followed them into battle. Sadness greeted periods of peace, as they meant economic stagnation and boredom. Whereas the peasants and the townspeople counted peace the condition of their occupational success, the nobility despised it as unnatural to their profession.

They looked down on the peasantry as cowards who ran and hid in time of war. Urban merchants, who amassed wealth by business methods strange to feudal society, were held in equal contempt, which increased as the affluence and political power of the townspeople grew. The nobility possessed as strong a sense of superiority over these "unwarlike" people as the clergy did over the general run of laity.

KNIGHTHOOD The nobleman nurtured his sense of distinctiveness within medieval society by the chivalric ritual of dubbing to knighthood. This ceremonial entrance into the noble class became almost a religious sacrament. The ceremony was preceded by a bath of purification, confession, communion, and a prayer vigil. Thereafter, the priest blessed the knight's standard, lance, and sword. As prayers were chanted, the priest girded the knight with his sword and presented him his shield, enlisting him as much in the defense of the church as in the service of his lord. Dubbing raised the nobleman to a state as sacred in his sphere as clerical ordination made the priest in his. The comparison is legitimate. The clergy and the nobility were medieval society's privileged estates. The appointment of noblemen to high ecclesiastical office and their eager participation in the church's Crusades had strong ideological and social underpinnings as well as economic and political motives.

In the twelfth century, knighthood was legally restricted to men of high birth. This circumscription of noble ranks came in reaction to the growing wealth, political power, and successful social climbing of newly rich townspeople (mostly merchants), who formed a new urban patriciate that was increasingly competitive with the lower nobility. Kings remained free, however, to raise up knights at will and did not shrink from increasing royal revenues by selling noble titles to wealthy merchants. But the law was building fences—fortunately not without gates—between town and countryside in the High Middle Ages.

Noblewomen watch a tournament. These mock battles were designed to provide the excitement of war without its mayhem. However, they tended to get out of hand, resulting in bloodshed and even death. [University of Heidelberg]

SPORTSMEN In peacetime the nobility had two favorite amusements: hunting and tournaments. Where they could, noblemen progressively monopolized the rights to game, forbidding the commoners from hunting in "lords'" forests. This practice built resentment among common people to the level of revolt. Free game, fishing, and access to wood were basic demands in the petitions of grievance and the revolts of the peasantry throughout the High and later Middle Ages.

The pastime of tournaments also sowed seeds of social disruption, but more within the ranks of the nobility itself. Tournaments were designed not only to keep men fit for war, but also to provide the excitement of war without the useless maiming and killing of prized vassals. But as regions competed fiercely with one another for victory and glory, even mock battles with blunted weapons proved to be deadly. Often, tournaments got out of hand, ending with bloodshed and animosity among the combatants. (The intense emotions and occasional violence that accompany interregional soccer in Europe today may be seen as a survival of this kind of rivalry.) The church came to oppose tournaments as occasions of pagan revelry and senseless violence. Kings and princes also turned against them as sources of division within their realms. Henry II of England proscribed them in the twelfth century. They did not end in France until the mid-sixteenth century, after Henry II of France was mortally wounded by a shaft through his visor during a tournament celebrating his daughter's marriage.

COURTLY LOVE From the repeated assemblies in the courts of barons and kings, set codes of social conduct, or "courtesy," developed in noble circles. With the French leading the way, mannered behavior and court etiquette became almost as important as battlefield expertise. Knights became literate gentlemen, and lyric poets sang and moralized at court. The cultivation of a code of behavior and a special literature to eulogize it was not unrelated to problems within the social life of the nobility. Noblemen were notorious philanderers; their illegitimate children mingled openly with their legitimate offspring in their houses. The advent of courtesy was in part an effort to reform this situation.

A lady and her knight going hunting. [Bildarchiv Preussischer Kulturbesitz]

Although the poetry of courtly love was sprinkled with frank eroticism and the beloved in these epics were married women pursued by those to whom they were not married, the love recommended by the poet was usually love at a distance, unconsummated by sexual intercourse. It was love without touching, a kind of sex without physical contact, and only as such was it considered ennobling. Court poets depicted those who succumbed to illicit carnal love as reaping at least as much suffering as joy from it.

Social Divisions No medieval social group was absolutely uniform—not the nobility, the clergy, the townspeople, not even the peasantry. Not only was the nobility a class apart, it also had strong social divisions within its own ranks. Noblemen formed a broad spectrum—from minor vassals without subordinate vassals to mighty barons, the principal vassals of a king or prince, who had many vassals of their own. Dignity and status within the nobility were directly related to the exercise of authority over others; a chief with many vassals obviously far excelled the small country nobleman who served another and was lord over none but himself.

Even among the domestic servants of the nobility, a social hierarchy developed according to assigned manorial duties. Although they were peasants in the eyes of the law, the chief stewards—charged to oversee the operation of the lord's manor and entrusted with the care and education of the noble children—became powerful "lords" within their "domains." Some freemen found the status of the steward enviable enough to surrender their own freedom and become domestic servants in the hope of attaining it. In time the social superiority of the higher ranks of domestic servants won legal recognition as medieval law adjusted to acknowledge the privileges of wealth and power at whatever level they appeared.

By the late Middle Ages, several factors forced the landed nobility into a steep economic and political decline from which it never recovered. Climatic changes and agricultural failures created large famines, while the great plague (see Chapter 9) brought about unprecedented population losses. Changing military tactics occasioned by the use of infantry and heavy artillery during the Hundred Years' War made the noble cavalry nearly obsolete. And the alliance of wealthy towns with the king weakened the nobility within their very own domains. One can speak of a waning of the landed nobility after the fourteenth century. Thereafter, the effective possession of land and wealth counted far more than parentage and lineage as qualifications for entrance into the highest social class.

Clergy

Unlike the nobility and the peasantry, the clergy was an open estate. Although the clerical hierarchy reflected the social classes from which the clergy came, one was still a cleric by religious training and ordination, not by the circumstances of birth or military prowess.

Regular and Secular Clerics There were two basic types of clerical vocation: the regular clergy and the secular clergy. The regular clergy was made up of the orders of monks who lived according to a special ascetic rule (*regula*) in cloisters separated from the world. They were the spiritual elite among the clergy, and theirs was not a way of life lightly entered. Canon law required that one be at least twenty-one years of age before making a final profession of the monastic vows of poverty, chastity, and obedience. The monks' personal sacrifices and high religious ideals made them much respected in high medieval society. This popularity was a major factor in the success of the Cluny reform movement and of the Crusades of the eleventh and twelfth centuries. The Crusades provided laypeople with a way to participate in the admired life of asceticism and prayer; in these holy pilgrimages they had the opportunity to imitate the suffering and perhaps even the death of Jesus, as the monks imitated his suffering and death by retreat from the world and severe self-denial.

Many monks (and also nuns, who increasingly embraced the vows of poverty, obedience, and chastity without a clerical rank) secluded themselves altogether. The regular clergy, however, were never completely cut off from the secular world. They maintained frequent contact with the laity through such charitable activities as feeding the destitute and tending the sick, through liberal arts instruction in monastic schools, through special pastoral commissions from the pope, and as supplemental preachers and confessors in parish churches during Lent and other peak religious seasons. It became the mark of the Dominican and Franciscan friars to live a common life according to a special rule, and still to be active in a worldly ministry. Some monks, because of their learning and rhetorical skills, even rose to prominence as secretaries and private confessors to kings and queens.

The secular clergy, those who lived and worked directly among the laity in the world (*saeculum*), formed a vast hierarchy. At the top were the high prelates—the wealthy cardinals, archbishops, and bishops, who were drawn almost exclusively from the nobility—and below them the urban priests, the cathedral canons, and the court clerks. Finally, there was the great mass of poor parish priests, who were neither financially nor intellectually very far above the common people they served (the basic educational requirement was an ability to say the mass). Until the Gregorian reform in the eleventh century, parish priests lived with women in a relationship akin to marriage, and their concubines and children were accepted within the communities they served. Because of their relative poverty, it was not unusual for priests to "moonlight" as teachers, artisans, or farmers. Their parishioners also accepted and even admired this practice.

Monks singing from a choir book (fifteenth century). [Pierpont Morgan Library, 1994, M.685.f.lr.]

New Orders One of the results of the Gregorian reform was the creation of new religious orders aspiring to a life of poverty and self-sacrifice in imitation of Christ and the first apostles. The more important were the Canons Regular (founded 1050–1100), the Carthusians (founded 1084), the Cistercians (founded 1098), and the Praemonstratensians (founded 1121). Carthusians, Cistercians, and Praemonstratensians practiced extreme austerity in their quest to recapture the pure religious life of the early Church.

Strictest of them all were the Carthusians. Members lived in isolation and fasted three days a week. They also devoted themselves to long periods of silence and even self-flagellation in their quest for perfect self-denial and conformity to Christ.

The Cistercians (from Cîteaux in Burgundy) were a reform wing of the Benedictine order and were known as the "white monks," a reference to their all-white attire, symbolic of apostolic purity. (The

Praemonstratensians also wore white.) They hoped to avoid the materialistic influences of urban society and maintain uncorrupted the original Rule of Saint Benedict, which their leaders believed Cluny was compromising. The Cistercians accordingly stressed anew the inner life and spiritual goals of monasticism. They located their houses in remote areas and denied themselves worldly comforts and distractions. Remarkably successful, the order could count 300 chapter houses within a century of its founding, and many others imitated its more austere spirituality.

The Canons Regular were independent groups of secular clergy (and also earnest laity) who, in addition to serving laity in the world, also adopted the *Rule* of Saint Augustine (a monastic guide dating from around the year 500) and practiced the ascetic virtues of regular clerics. There were monks who renounced exclusive withdrawal from the world. There were also priests who renounced exclusive involvement in it. By merging the life of the cloister with traditional clerical duties, the Canons Regular foreshadowed the mendicant friars of the thirteenth century—the Dominicans and the Franciscans, who combined the ascetic ideals of the cloister with a very active ministry in the world.

The monasteries and nunneries of the established orders recruited candidates from among the wealthiest social groups. Crowding in the convents and the absence of patronage gave rise in the thirteenth century to lay satellite convents known as Beguine houses. These convents housed religiously earnest unmarried women from the upper and middle social strata. Cologne established 100 such houses between 1250 and 1350, each containing eight to twelve women. Several of these convents, in Cologne and elsewhere, became heterodox in religious doctrine and practice, falling prey to heresy. Among the responsibilities of the new religious orders of Dominicans and Franciscans was the "regularization" of such convents.

PROMINENCE OF THE CLERGY The clergy constituted a far greater proportion of medieval society than modern society. Estimates suggest that 1.5 percent of fourteenth-century Europe was in clerical garb. The clergy were concentrated in urban areas, especially in towns with universities and cathedrals, where in addition to their studies they found work in a wide variety of religious services. In late-fourteenth-century England there was one cleric for every seventy laypeople, and in counties with a cathedral or a university the proportion rose to one cleric for every fifty laypeople.[1] In large university towns the clergy could exceed 10 percent of the population.

Despite the moonlighting of poorer parish priests, the clergy as a whole, like the nobility, lived on the labor of others. Their income came from the regular collection of tithes and church taxes according to an elaborate system that evolved in the High and later Middle Ages. The church was, of course, a major landowner and regularly collected rents and fees. Monastic communities and high prelates amassed great fortunes; there was a popular saying that the granaries were always full in the monasteries. The immense secular power attached to high clerical posts can be seen in the intensity of the investiture struggle. The loss of the right to present chosen clergy with the ring and staff of episcopal office was a direct threat to the emperor's control of his realm. The bishops had become royal agents and were endowed to that purpose with royal lands that the emperor could ill afford to have slip from his control.

During the greater part of the Middle Ages, the clergy were the "first estate," and theology was the queen of the sciences. How did the clergy come into such prominence? A lot of it was self-proclaimed. However, there was also popular respect and reverence for the clergy's role as mediator between God and humanity. The priest brought the very Son of God down to earth when he celebrated the sacrament of the Eucharist; his absolution released penitents from punishment for mortal sin. It was declared improper for mere laypeople to sit in judgment on such a priest.

Theologians elaborated the distinction between the clergy and the laity very much to the clergy's benefit. The belief in the superior status of the clergy underlay the evolution of clerical privileges and immunities in both person and property. As holy persons, the clergy were not supposed to be taxed by secular rulers without special permission from the proper ecclesiastical authorities. Clerical crimes were under the jurisdiction of special ecclesiastical courts, not the secular courts. Because churches and monasteries were deemed holy places, they, too, were free from secular taxation and legal jurisdiction. Hunted criminals, lay and clerical, regularly sought asylum within them, disrupting the normal processes of law and order. When city offi-

[1]Denys Hay, *Europe in the Fourteenth and Fifteenth Centuries*, 2nd ed. (New York: Holt, Rinehart, 1966), pp. 58–59.

cials violated this privilege of asylum, ecclesiastical authorities threatened excommunication and interdict. People feared this suspension of the church's sacraments, including Christian burial, almost as much as they feared the criminals to whom the church gave asylum.

By the late Middle Ages, townspeople came increasingly to resent the special immunities of the clergy. They complained that it was not proper for the clergy to have greater privileges yet far fewer responsibilities than all others who lived within the town walls. An early-sixteenth-century lampoon reflected what had by then become a widespread sentiment:

Priests, monks, and nuns
Are but a burden to the earth.
They have decided
That they will not become citizens.
That's why they're so greedy—
They stand firm against our city
And will swear no allegiance to it.
And we hear their fine excuses:
"It would cause us much toil and trouble
Should we pledge our troth as burghers."[2]

The separation of church and state and the distinction between the clergy and the laity have persisted into modern times. After the fifteenth century, however, the clergy ceased to be the superior class they had been for so much of the Middle Ages. In both Protestant and Catholic lands governments progressively subjected them to the basic responsibilities of citizenship.

Peasants

The largest and lowest social group in medieval society was the one on whose labor the welfare of all the others depended: the agrarian peasantry. Many peasants lived on and worked the manors of the nobility, the primitive cells of rural social life. All were to one degree or another dependent on their lords and were considered their property. The manor in Frankish times was a plot of land within a village, ranging from twelve to seventy-five acres in size, assigned to a certain member by a settled tribe or clan. This member and his family became lords of the land, and those who came to dwell there formed a smaller, self-sufficient community within a larger village community. In the early Middle Ages such manors consisted of the dwellings of the lord and his family, the cottages of the peasant workers, agricultural sheds, and fields.

THE DUTIES OF TENANCY The landowner or lord of the manor required a certain amount of produce (grain, eggs, and the like) and a certain number of services from the peasant families that came to dwell on and farm his land. The tenants were free to divide the labor as they wished; and what goods remained after the lord's levies were met were their own. A powerful lord might own many such manors. Kings later based their military and tax assessments on the number of manors owned by a vassal landlord. No set rules governed the size of manors. There were manors of a hundred acres or less and some of several thousand or more.

There were both servile and free manors. The tenants of the latter had originally been freemen known as *coloni*. Original inhabitants and petty landowners, they swapped their small possessions for a guarantee of security from a more powerful lord, who came in this way to possess their land. Unlike the pure serfdom of the servile manors, whose tenants had no original claim to a part of the land, the tenancy obligations on free manors tended to be limited and the tenants' rights more carefully defined. It was a milder serfdom. Tenants of servile manors were by comparison far more vulnerable to the whims of their landlords. These two types of manor tended, however, to merge. The most common situation was the manor on which tenants of greater and lesser degrees of servitude dwelt together, their services to the lord defined by their personal status and local custom. In many regions free, self-governing peasant communities existed without any overlords and tenancy obligations.

The lord held both judicial and police powers. He owned and operated the machines that processed crops into food and drink. Marc Bloch, the modern authority on manorial society, has vividly depicted the duties of tenancy:

On certain days the tenant brings the lord's steward perhaps a few small silver coins or, more often, sheaves of grain harvested on his fields, chickens from his farmyard, cakes of wax from his beehives or from the swarms of the neighboring forest. At other times he works on the arable or the meadows of the demesne [the lord's plot of land in the manorial fields, between one-third and one-half of that available]. Or else we find him carting casks of wine or sacks of grain on behalf of the master to distant residences. His is the labour which repairs the walls or moats

[2]Cited by S. Ozment, *The Reformation in the Cities* (New Haven, Conn.: Yale University Press, 1975), p. 36.

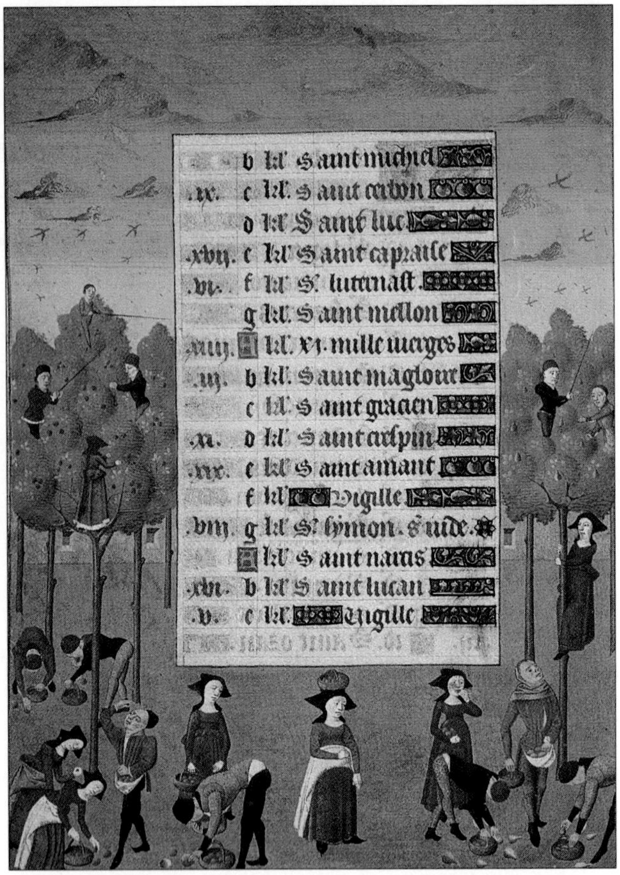

Men and women harvesting pears. From a Book of Hours *(fifteenth century). [Lauros-Giraudon/Art Resource, N.Y.]*

> of the castle. If the master has guests the peasant strips his own bed to provide the necessary extra bed-clothes. When the hunting season comes round he feeds the pack. If war breaks out he does duty as a footsoldier or orderly, under the leadership of the reeve of the village.[3]

The lord also had the right to subject his tenants to exactions known as banalities. He could, for example, force them to breed their cows with his bull, and to pay for the privilege; to grind their bread grains in his mill; to bake their bread in his oven; to make their wine in his wine press; to buy their beer from his brewery; and even to surrender to him the tongues or other choice parts of all animals slaughtered on his lands. The lord also collected as an inheritance tax a serf's best animal. Without the lord's permission, serfs could neither travel nor marry outside the manor in which they served.

[3]Marc Bloch, *Feudal Society*, trans. by L. A. Manyon (Chicago: University of Chicago Press, 1968), p. 250.

THE LIFE OF A SERF Exploited as the serfs may appear to have been from a modern point of view, their status was far from chattel slavery. It was to the lord's advantage to keep his serfs healthy and happy; his welfare, like theirs, depended on a successful harvest. Serfs had their own dwellings and modest strips of land and lived by the produce of their own labor and organization. They were permitted to market for their own profit what surpluses might remain after the harvest. They were free to choose their spouses within the local village, although the lord's permission was required if a wife or husband was sought from another village. And serfs could pass their property (their dwellings and field strips) and worldly goods on to their children.

Peasants lived in timber-framed huts. Except for the higher domestic servants, they seldom ventured far beyond their own villages. The local priest often was their window on the world, and church festivals were their major communal entertainment. Their religiosity was based in large part on the church being the only show in town, although their religious beliefs were by no means unambiguously Christian.

Despite the social distinctions between free and servile serfs—and, within these groups, between those who owned ploughs and oxen and those who possessed only hoes—the common dependence on the soil forced close cooperation. The ratio of seed to grain yield was consistently poor; about two bushels of seed were required to produce six to ten bushels of grain in good times. There was rarely an abundance of bread and ale, the staple peasant foods. Two important American crops, potatoes and corn (maize), were unknown in Europe until the sixteenth century. Pork was the major source of protein, and every peasant household had its pigs. At slaughter time a family might also receive a little tough beef. But basically everyone depended on the grain crops. When they failed or fell short, the peasantry simply went hungry unless the lord had surplus stores that he was willing to share.

CHANGES IN THE MANOR Two basic changes occurred in the evolution of the manor from the early to the later Middle Ages. The first was the fragmentation of the manor and the rise to dominance of the single-family holding. This development was aided by such technological advances as the collar harness (ca. 800), the horseshoe (ca. 900), and the three-field system of crop rotation, which made it easier for smaller familial units to support themselves. As the lords parceled out their land to new tenants, their own plots became progressively smaller. The increase in tenants and the decrease in the lord's fields brought about a corresponding reduction in the labor services exacted from the tenants. Also, the bringing of new fields into production increased individual holdings and modified labor services. In France, by the reign of Louis IX (r. 1226–1270), only a few days a year were required, whereas in the time of Charlemagne peasants had worked the lords' fields several days a week.

As the single-family unit replaced the clan as the basic nuclear group, assessments of goods and services fell on individual fields and households, no longer on manors as a whole. Family farms replaced manorial units. The peasants' carefully nurtured communal life made possible a family's retention of its land and dwelling after the death of the head of the household. In this way, land and property remained in the possession of a single family from generation to generation.

The second change in the evolution of the manor was the conversion of the serf's dues into money payments, a change made possible by the revival of trade and the rise of the towns. This development, completed by the thirteenth century, permitted serfs to hold their land as rent-paying tenants and to overcome their servile status. Although tenants thereby gained greater freedom, they were not necessarily better off materially. Whereas servile workers could have counted on the benevolent assistance of their landlords in hard times, rent-paying workers were left, by and large, to their own devices. Their independence caused some landlords to treat them with indifference and even resentment.

Lands and properties that had been occupied by generations of peasants and were recognized as their own were always under the threat of the lord's claim to a prior right of inheritance and even outright usurpation. As their demesnes declined, the lords were increasingly tempted to encroach on such traditionally common lands. The peasantry fiercely resisted such efforts, instinctively clinging to the little they had. In many regions they successfully organized to gain a voice in the choice of petty rural officials.

By the mid-fourteenth century a declining nobility in England and France, faced with the ravages of the great plague and the Hundred Years' War, tried to turn back the historical clock by increasing taxes on the peasantry and passing laws to restrict their migration into the cities. The peasantry responded with armed revolts in the countryside. These revolts became the rural equivalents of the organization of medieval cities in sworn communes to protect their self-interests against powerful territorial rulers. The revolts of the agrarian peasantry, like those of the urban proletariat, were brutally crushed. They stand out at the end of the Middle Ages as violent testimony to the breakup of medieval society. As growing national sentiment would break its political unity and heretical movements end its nominal religious unity, the peasantry's revolts revealed the absence of medieval social unity.

Towns and Townspeople

In the eleventh and twelfth centuries, towns held only about 5 percent of western Europe's population. By modern comparison they were not very large. Of Germany's 3,000 towns, for example, 2,800 had populations under 1,000. Only fifteen German towns exceeded 10,000. The largest, Cologne, had 30,000. In England only London had

Many medieval towns, especially in northern Europe, were entirely enclosed by walls for protection. Here is the mid-fifteenth century walled city of Lüneburg in northern Germany. [Foto Makovec]

more than 10,000. Paris was larger than London, but not by much. The largest European towns were in Italy; Florence approached 100,000 and Milan was not far behind. Despite their comparatively small size, towns then, as now, were where the action was. One could find there the whole of medieval society and its most creative segments.

The Chartering of Towns

Towns were originally dominated by feudal lords, both lay and clerical. The lords created the towns by granting charters to those who would agree to live and work within them. The charters guaranteed their safety and gave inhabitants a degree of independence unknown on the land. The purpose was originally to concentrate skilled laborers who could manufacture the finished goods desired by lords and bishops. In this way, manorial society may be seen actually creating its urban challenger and weakening itself. Because they longed for finished goods and for the luxuries that came from faraway places, noblemen had urged their serfs to become skilled at making such things. The new skills required to do this in turn gave serfs a new importance and power. By the eleventh century skilled serfs began to pay their manorial dues in manufactured goods, rather than in field labor, eggs, chickens, and beans, as they had earlier. In return for a fixed rent and proper subservience, serfs were also encouraged to settle and work in towns. There they gained special rights and privileges by way of the charters.

The Rue du Matelas, a French street in Rouen, Normandy, was preserved intact from the Middle Ages to World War II. Note the narrowness of the street and the open sewer running down its center. The houses were built of rough cast stone, mud, and timber. [H. Roger Viollet]

As towns grew and beckoned, many serfs fled the countryside with their skills and went directly to the new urban centers. There they found the freedom and profits that could lift an industrious craftsperson into higher social ranks. As this migration of serfs to the towns accelerated, the lords in the countryside offered them more favorable terms of tenure to keep them on the land. In this way the growth of towns improved the lot of serfs generally. But serfs could not easily be kept down on the farms after they had discovered the opportunities of town life.

The Rise of Merchants

Rural society not only gave the towns their craftspeople and day laborers, but the first merchants themselves may also have been enterprising serfs. Certainly, some of the long-distance traders were men who had nothing to lose and everything to gain by the enormous risks of foreign trade. They traveled together in armed caravans and convoys, buying goods and products as cheaply as possible at the source, and selling them for all they could get in Western ports. (See Map 8-1.) More than anything else, it was the greed and daring of these rough-hewn men that created Western urban life as we know it today. (See The West and the World, page 300.)

At first the merchants were not liked by the traditional social groups of nobility, clergy, and peasantry, who considered them an oddity. As late as the fifteenth century, we find the landed nobility still snubbing the urban patriciate. Such snobbery probably never died out among the older landed nobility, who looked down on the traders as men

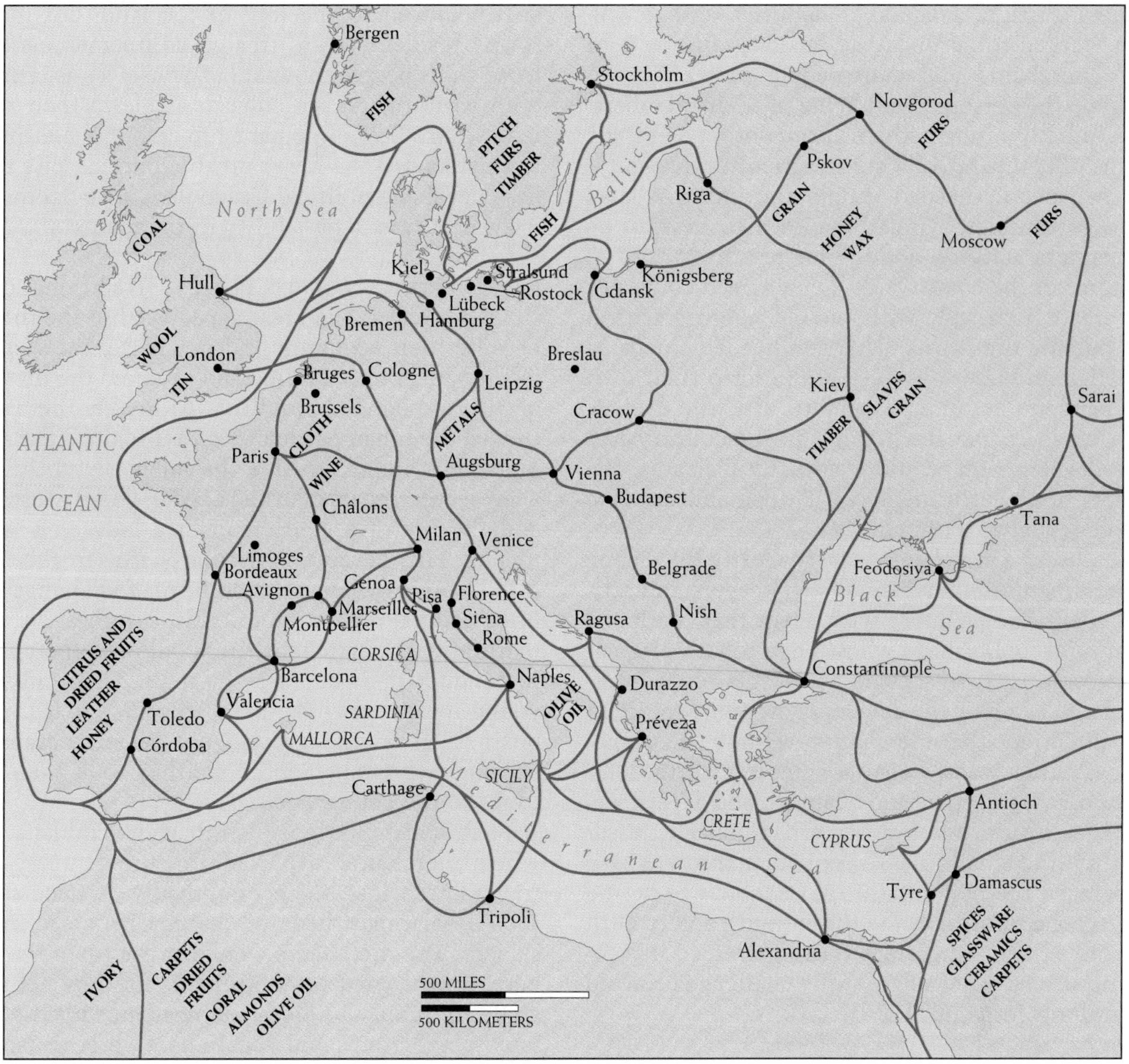

MAP 8–1 SOME MEDIEVAL TRADE ROUTES AND REGIONAL PRODUCTS *The map shows some of the channels that came to be used in interregional commerce and what was traded in a particular region. For a comparison with trans-Saharan trade, see The West and the World essay on Mali, page 300.*

with poor breeding, little character, and money they did not properly earn or deserve. Over time, however, the powerful grew to respect the merchants, and the weak always tried to imitate them, because wherever the merchants went, they left a trail of wealth behind.

Challenging the Old Lords

As the traders established themselves in towns, they grew in wealth and numbers, formed their own protective associations, and soon found themselves able to challenge traditional seigneurial authority. Merchants especially wanted to end the arbitrary tolls and tariffs imposed by regional magnates over the surrounding countryside. Such regulations hampered the flow of commerce on which both merchant and craftsperson in the growing urban export industries depended. Wherever merchants settled in large numbers they opposed the tolls, tariffs, and other petty restrictions that discouraged the flow of trade. Merchant guilds or protective associations sprang up in the eleventh century, followed in the twelfth by guilds of craftspeople (drapers, haberdashers, furriers, hosiers, goldsmiths, and so on), who worked to advance the business interests of both merchants and craftspeople as well as to enhance the personal well-being of their members. This quickly brought them into conflict with the norms of comparatively static agricultural society.

Townspeople needed simple and uniform laws and a government sympathetic to their new forms of business activity, not the fortress mentality of the lords of the countryside. Such a need could not but create a struggle with the old nobility within and outside the towns. This conflict led towns in the High and later Middle Ages to form their own independent communes and to ally themselves with kings against the nobility in the countryside. This development would eventually rearrange the centers of power in medieval Europe and dissolve classic feudal government.

Because the merchants were so clearly the engine of the urban economy, small shopkeepers and artisans identified far more with them than with the aloof lords and bishops who were a town's original masters. Most townspeople found their own interests best served by the development of urban life in the direction the merchants wanted it to go. Namely, they wanted greater commercial freedom, fewer barriers to trade and business, and a freer secular life; in sum, a less closed urban life. The lesser nobility (the small knights) outside the towns also recognized the new mercantile economy to be the wave of the future. During the eleventh and twelfth centuries the burgher upper class increased its economic strength and successfully challenged the old urban lords for control of the towns.

New Models of Government

With urban autonomy came new models of self-government. Around 1100 the old urban nobility and the new burgher upper class merged. It was a marriage between those wealthy by birth (inherited property) and those who made their fortunes in long-distance trade. From this new ruling class was born the aristocratic town council, which henceforth came to govern towns.

Enriching and complicating the situation even more, small artisans and craftspeople also slowly developed their own protective associations or guilds and began to gain a voice in government. The towns' ability to provide opportunities for the "little person" had created the slogan, "Town air brings freedom." In the countryside the air one breathed still belonged to the lord of the land; but in the towns residents were treated as freemen. Within town walls people thought of themselves as citizens with basic rights, not subjects liable to their masters' whim. Economic hardship certainly continued to exist among the lower urban groups despite their basic legal and political freedoms. But social mobility was at least a possibility in the towns.

Keeping People in Their Places Traditional measures of success had great appeal within the towns. Despite their economic independence, the wealthiest urban groups admired and imitated the lifestyle of the old landed nobility. Although the latter treated the urban patriciate with disdain, successful merchants longed to live the noble, knightly life. They wanted coats of arms, castles, country estates, and the life of a gentleman or a lady on a great manor. This became particularly true in the later Middle Ages, when reliable bills of exchange and international regulation of trade, together with the maturation of merchant firms, allowed merchants to conduct their business by mail. Then only the young apprentices did a lot of traveling, to learn the business from the ground up. When merchants became rich enough to do so, they took their fortunes to the countryside.

Such social-climbing disturbed city councils, and when merchants departed for the countryside, towns often lost out economically. A need to be socially distinguished and distinct pervaded urban society. The merchants were just the tip of the iceberg. Towns tried to control this need by defining grades of luxury in dress and residence for the various social groups and vocations. Overly conspicuous consumption was a kind of indecent exposure punishable by law. Such sumptuary laws restricted the types and amount of clothing one might wear (the length and width of fur pieces, for example) and how one might decorate one's dwelling architecturally. In this way, people were forced to dress and live according to their station in life. The intention of such laws was positive: to maintain social order and dampen social conflict by keeping everyone clearly and peacefully in their place.

Social Conflict and Protective Associations (Guilds) Despite unified resistance to external domination, medieval towns were not internally harmonious social units. They were a collection of many selfish and competitive communities, each seeking to advance its own business and family

The Laws and Customs of Chester

The following laws and customs appear in the Domesday Book *(1080–1086). They were included there because the English town of Chester was among the forty or so towns in which the king had a financial interest. The town paid a portion of the fines it collected for criminal behavior to the king's representative.*

✦ *In terms of fine and financial loss, what were the most serious crimes? Was simple negligence punished? Did religion play a role in the setting of any of these fines? Do the fines suggest vigilance or pettiness?*

If any free man of the king broke the peace which had been granted and killed a man in his house, all his land and money came to the king, and he himself became an outlaw.

He who shed blood between Monday morning and the ninth hour of Saturday compounded for it with [i.e., paid a fine of] ten shillings. From the ninth hour of Saturday to Monday morning bloodshed was compounded for with twenty shillings. Similarly any one paid twenty shillings who shed blood in the twelve days after Christmas, on the day of the Purification of the Blessed Mary, on the first day after Easter, the first day of Pentecost, Ascension day, on the Assumption or Nativity of the Blessed Mary, and on the day of All Saints. . . .

He who committed theft or robbery, or exercised violence upon a woman in a house, compounded for each of these with forty shillings. . . .

If fire burned the city, he from whose house it started compounded for it with three oras [about two shillings worth] of pennies, and gave to his next neighbor two shillings. Of all these forfeitures, two parts belonged to the king and the third to the earl.

A man or a woman making false measure in the city, and being arrested, compounded for it with four shillings. Similarly a person making bad ale was either placed in the ducking stool or gave four shillings to the reeve [the bailiff]. This forfeiture the officer of the king and of the earl received in the city, in whosesoever land it has been done, either of the bishop or of another man. Similarly also, if any one held the toll back beyond three nights, he compounded for it with forty shillings.

James Harvey Robinson, ed., Readings in European History, *vol. 1 (Boston: Athenaeum, 1904), pp. 406–407.*

interests. Conflict between "haves" and "have-nots" was inevitable, especially because medieval towns had little concept of social and economic equality. Theoretically, poor artisans could work their way up from lower social and vocational levels, and some lucky ones did. But so long as they had not done so, they were excluded from the city council. Only families of long standing in the town who owned property had full rights of citizenship and a direct say in the town's government at the highest levels. Government, in other words, was inbred and aristocratic.

Conflict also existed between the poorest workers in the export trades (usually the weavers and woolcombers) and the economically better off and socially ascending independent workers and small shopkeepers. The better-off workers also had their differences with the merchants, whose export trade often brought competitive foreign goods into the city. So independent workers and small shopkeepers organized to restrict foreign trade to a minimum and corner the local market in certain items.

Over time, the formation of artisan guilds gave workers in the trades a direct voice in government. Ironically, a long-term effect of this gain was to limit the social mobility of the poorest artisans. The guilds gained representation on city councils, where, to discourage imports, they used their power

Skilled workers were an integral component of the commerce of medieval towns. This scene shows the manufacture of cannons in a foundry in Florence. [Scala/Art Resource, N.Y.]

to enforce quality standards and fair prices on local businesses. These actions created tight restrictions on guild membership, squeezing out poorer artisans and trades. As a result, lesser merchants and artisans found their opportunities progressively limited. So rigid and exclusive did the dominant guilds become that they often stifled their own creativity and inflamed the journeymen whom they excluded from their ranks. Unrepresented artisans and craftspeople constituted a true urban proletariat prevented by law from forming their own guilds or entering existing ones. The efforts by guild-dominated governments to protect local craftspeople and industries tended to narrow trade and depress the economy for all.

Towns and Kings

By providing kings with the resources they needed to curb factious noblemen, towns became a major force in the transition from feudal societies to national governments. In many places kings and towns formally allied against the traditional lords of the land. A notable exception to this general development is England, where the towns joined with the barons against the oppressive monarchy of King John (r. 1199–1216), becoming part of the parliamentary opposition to the crown. But by the fifteenth century, kings and towns had also joined forces in England, so much so that by century's end Henry Tudor (r. 1485–1509) was known as the "burgher king."

Towns attracted kings and emperors for obvious reasons. Towns were a ready source of educated bureaucrats and lawyers who knew Roman law, the tool for running kingdoms and empires. Money was also to be found in the towns in great quantity, enabling kings to hire their own armies and free themselves from dependence on the nobility. Towns had the human, financial, and technological resources to empower kings. By such alliances, towns won royal political recognition and had their constitutions guaranteed. This proved somewhat easier to do in the stronger coastal areas than in interior areas, where urban life remained less vigorous and territorial government was on the rise. In France, towns became integrated early into royal government. In Germany, they fell under ever tighter control by the princes. In Italy, uniquely, towns expanded to dominate the surrounding countryside, becoming genuine city-states during the Renaissance.

It was also in the towns' interest to have a strong monarch as their protector against despotic local lords and princes, who were always eager to integrate or engulf the towns within their expanding territories. Unlike a local magnate, a king tended to remain at a distance, allowing towns to exercise their precious autonomy. A king was thus the more desirable overlord. It was also an advantage to a town to have its long-distance trade conducted in the name of a known powerful monarch. This gave predators pause and improved official cooperation along the way. Both sides—kings and towns—gained from such alliances.

Between the eleventh and fourteenth centuries, towns had considerable freedom and autonomy. As in Roman times, they again became the flourishing centers of Western civilization. But after the fourteenth century, and even earlier in France and England, the towns, like the church before them, were steadily bent to the political will of kings and princes in most places. By the seventeenth century few would be truly autonomous, the vast majority integrated thoroughly into the larger purposes of the "state."

Jews in Christian Society

Towns also attracted large numbers of Jews. It was within the major urban centers, particularly in France and Germany, that Jews gathered between the late twelfth and thirteenth centuries. They did so both by choice and for safety in the increasingly hostile Christian world. Mutually wary of one another, Christians and Jews sought to limit their contacts with each other to exchanges between merchants and scholars. The church expressly forbade Jews from hiring Christians in their businesses and from holding any public authority over them. In the cities, Jews plied trades in their own small businesses, and many became wealthy bankers to kings and popes, as well as having private business clients among both Christians and Jews. Jewish intellectual and religious culture had always been very elaborate and sophisticated, both dazzling and threatening to Christians who viewed it from outside. These various factors—the separateness of Jews, their economic power, and their cultural strength—encouraged suspicion and distrust among Christians, whose religious teaching held Jews responsible for the death of Christ.

Between the late twelfth and early fourteenth centuries, Jews were exiled from France and persecuted elsewhere as well. Two factors were behind this unprecedented surge in anti-Jewish sentiment. The first was a desire on the part of kings to confiscate Jewish wealth and property and eliminate the Jews as economic competitors with the monarchy. (French kings acted similarly in the fourteenth century against a wealthy Christian military order known as the Knights Templars; see chapters 7 and 9.) The other factor behind the surge in anti-Jewish sentiment was the church's increasing political vulnerability to the new dynastic monarchies. Faced with the loss of its political power, the church became more determined than ever to maintain its spiritual hegemony. With the beginning of the Crusades and the creation of new mendicant orders, the church powerfully reasserted claims to spiritual sovereignty over Europe and beyond, instigating major campaigns against dissenters, heretics, witches, and Jews at home as well as against the infidel abroad.

Schools and Universities

In the twelfth century, Byzantine and Spanish Islamic scholars made it possible for the works in logic of Aristotle, the writings of Euclid and Ptolemy, the basic works of Greek physicians and Arab mathematicians, and the larger texts of Roman law to circulate among Western scholars. Islamic scholars especially preserved these works. They also wrote extensive, thought-provoking commentaries on Greek texts, which were translated into Latin and made available to Western scholars and students. The result of this renaissance of ancient knowledge was an intellectual ferment that gave rise to Western universities.

University of Bologna

The first important Western university was in Bologna, established by Emperor Frederick Barbarossa in 1158. There we find the first formal organizations of students and masters and the first degree programs—the institutional foundations of the modern university. Originally the term *university* meant simply a corporation of individuals (students and masters) who joined for their mutual protection from overarching episcopal authority (the local bishop oversaw the university) and from the local townspeople. Because townspeople then looked on students as foreigners without civil rights, such protective unions were necessary. They followed the model of an urban trade guild.

Bolognese students also "unionized" to guarantee fair rents and prices from their often reluctant hosts. And students demanded regular, high-quality teaching from their masters. In Italy, students

Philip II Augustus Orders Jews Out of France

Long the objects of Christian polemic, hated as moneylenders by ordinary people, and feared by the clergy as successful competitors with Christianity, Jews became easy scapegoats for rulers who wished to exploit fear and prejudice. In 1182, Philip II Augustus, eyeing the wealthy Jews of Paris, ordered all nonconverting Jews out of France and confiscated their property and possessions.

✦ *What is the king's argument for exiling Jews? Did Jewish moneylenders threaten the well-being of Christians? Are economic and political motives apparent in the king's actions? Why was religious pluralism and toleration so difficult for people then?*

[When Philip became king] a great multitude of Jews had been dwelling in France for a long time. . . . [In Paris] they grew so rich that they claimed as their own almost half of the whole city, and they had Christians in their houses as menservants and maidservants, who were backsliders from the faith of Jesus Christ and judaized with the Jews. . . .

And whereas the Lord had said . . . in Deuteronomy (23:19–20): "Thou shall not lend upon usury to thy brother, but to the stranger," the Jews . . . understood by "stranger" every Christian, and they took from the Christians their money at usury. And so heavily burdened in this wise were citizens and soldiers and peasants . . . that many of them were constrained to part with their possessions. Others were bound under oath in houses of the Jews in Paris, held as if captives in prison.

The most Christian King Philip hearing of these things . . . released all Christians of his kingdom from their debts to the Jews, and kept a fifth part of the whole amount for himself. . . . [Then in] 1182, in the month of April . . . an edict went forth from . . . the king . . . that all the Jews of his kingdom should be prepared to go forth by the coming feast of St. John the Baptist. And the king gave them leave to sell each his movable goods before the time fixed.

When faithless Jews heard this edict some of them . . . converted to the Lord [Jesus Christ, and] to them the king, out of regard for the Christian religion, restored all their possessions . . . and gave them perpetual liberty. Others were blinded by their ancient error and persisted in their perfidy. . . . The infidel Jews . . . astonished and stupefied by the strength of mind of Philip the king and his constancy in the Lord . . . prepared to sell all their household goods. The time was now at hand when the king ordered them to leave France. . . . Then did the Jews sell all their movable possessions in great haste, while their landed property reverted to the crown. Thus the Jews, having sold their goods and taken the price for the expenses of their journey, departed with their wives and children and all their households in the . . . year of the Lord 1182.

James Harvey Robinson, ed., Readings in European History, *vol. 2 (Boston: Atheneaum, 1906), pp. 426–428.*

actually hired their own teachers, set pay scales, and drew up desired lecture topics. Masters who did not keep their promises or live up to student expectations were boycotted. Price gouging by townspeople was met with the threat to move the university to another town. This could rather easily be done because the university was not yet tied to a fixed physical plant. Students and masters moved freely from town to town as they chose. Such mobility gave them a unique independence from their surroundings.

Masters also formed their own protective associations and established procedures and standards for certification to teach within their ranks. The first academic degree was a certificate that licensed one to teach, a *licentia docendi*. It granted gradu-

The University of Bologna in central Italy was distinguished as the center for the revival of Roman law. This carving on the tomb of a Bologna professor of law shows students attending one of his lectures. [Scala/Art Resource, N.Y.]

ates in the liberal arts program, the program basic to all higher learning, as well as those in the higher professional sciences of medicine, theology, and law, "the right to teach anywhere" (*ius ibique docendi*).

Bologna was famous for the revival of Roman law. During the Frankish era and later, from the seventh to the eleventh centuries, only the most rudimentary manuals of Roman law had survived. With the growth of trade and towns in the late eleventh century, Western scholars had come into contact with the larger and more important parts of the *Corpus juris civilis* of Justinian, which had been lost during the intervening centuries. The study and dissemination of this recovered material was now undertaken in Bologna under the direction of a learned man named Irnerius, who flourished in the early twelfth century. He and his students made authoritative commentaries, or glosses, on existing laws based on their newly broadened knowledge of the *Corpus juris civilis*. They thereby expanded legal knowledge. Around 1140, a monk named Gratian, also resident in Bologna, created the standard legal text in church, or canon, law, the *Concordance of Discordant Canons*, known simply as Gratian's *Decretum*.

As Bologna was the model for southern European universities (that is, those of Spain, Italy, and southern France) and the study of law, so Paris became the model for northern European universities and the study of theology. Oxford, Cambridge, and (much later) Heidelberg were among its imitators. All these universities required a foundation in the liberal arts for advanced study in the higher sciences of medicine, theology, and law. The arts program consisted of the *trivium* (grammar, rhetoric, and logic) and the *quadrivium* (arithmetic, geometry, astronomy, and music) or, more simply, the language arts and the mathematical arts.

Cathedral Schools

Before the emergence of universities, the liberal arts had been taught in cathedral and monastery schools. The purpose of these schools was to train the clergy, and their curricula tended understandably to be narrowly restricted to this goal. But by the late eleventh and twelfth centuries, cathedral schools also began to provide lectures for nonclerical students and they broadened their curricula to include some training for purely secular vocations. In 1179, a papal decree obliged cathedrals to provide teachers gratis for laity who wanted to learn.

After 1200, increasing numbers of future notaries and merchants who had no particular interest in

The architecture of the early Middle Ages is known as Romanesque *because it is closely related to the style of the late Roman Empire. It is characterized by thick stone walls and rounded arches that support the roof. The few windows are often very small, mere slits, giving Romanesque buildings a fortresslike appearance. Shown here is the Abbey of Germigny-des-Prés in northern France. [Giraudon/Art Resource, N.Y.]*

Beginning in the mid-twelfth century, the Gothic style evolved from Romanesque architecture. The word gothic *at first meant "barbaric," and was applied to the new style by its critics. Gothic architecture's most distinctive visible features are its ribbed, criss-crossing vaulting, its pointed rather than rounded arches, and its prominent exterior "flying" buttresses. The vaulting, the exterior flying buttresses, and the increased height they made possible give prominence to the strong vertical aspect of Gothic buildings. The buttresses, by shifting much of the structural weight of the buildings off the walls, also made possible wide expanses of windows—hence the extensive use of stained glass and the characteristic colored light that often floods Gothic cathedrals. Use of the windows to show stories from the Bible, saints' lives, and local events was similar to earlier use of mosaics. Shown here is an example of French Gothic, Rheims Cathedral, where the kings of France were crowned. [Scala/Art Resource, N.Y.]*

becoming priests, but who needed Latin and related intellectual disciplines to fill their secular positions, studied side by side with aspiring priests in cathedral and monastery schools. By the thirteenth century, the demand for secretaries and notaries in the growing urban and territorial governments and for literate personnel in the expanding merchant firms gave rise to special schools for strictly secular vocational preparation. With the appearance of these schools, the church began for the first time to lose some of its monopoly on higher education.

The most famous of the cathedral schools were those of Rheims and Chartres. Chartres won fame under the direction of such distinguished teachers as Fulbert, Saint Ivo, and Saint Bernard of Chartres (not to be confused with the more famous Saint Bernard of Clairvaux). Gerbert, who later became Pope Sylvester II (r. 999–1003), guided Rheims to greatness in the last quarter of the tenth century. Gerbert was filled with enthusiasm for knowledge and promoted both logical and rhetorical studies. He did much to raise the study of logic to preeminence within the liberal arts, despite his personal belief in the greater relevance of rhetoric to the promotion of Christianity.

University of Paris

The University of Paris grew institutionally out of the cathedral school of Notre Dame, among others. King Philip Augustus and Pope Innocent III gave the new university its charter in 1200. At Paris the college, or house system, originated. At first, a college was just a hospice providing room and board for poor students who could not afford to rent rooms in town. But the educational life of the university quickly expanded into fixed structures and began to thrive on their sure endowments. University-run colleges made the overseeing and protection of students easier and gave the university a new prominence as a permanent urban institution.

In Paris, the most famous college was the Sorbonne, founded around 1257 by Robert de Sorbon, chaplain to the king, for the housing of theology students. In Oxford and Cambridge, the colleges became the basic unit of student life and were indistinguishable from the university proper. By the end of the Middle Ages such colleges had tied universities to physical plants and fixed foundations. Their mobility was forevermore restricted, as was, compared with earlier times, their autonomy and freedom.

As a group, students at Paris had power and prestige. They enjoyed royal protections and privileges denied ordinary citizens. Many Parisian students were well-to-do, and not a few were spoiled and petulant. They did not endear themselves to the townspeople, whom they considered to be inferior. That townspeople sometimes let their resentments of such students lead to violence against them is made clear from the city's ordinances, which were highly protective of students. For example, city law forbade the beating of students. Only those students who had clearly committed serious crimes could be imprisoned. Only in self-defense might a citizen strike a student. All citizens were obligated to testify against anyone seen abusing a student. University laws also required all teachers to be carefully examined before being licensed to teach Parisian students. The law thus recognized students as both a valuable and a vulnerable resource.

The Curriculum

Before the so-called renaissance of the twelfth century, when many Greek and Arabic texts became available to Western scholars and students in Latin translations, the education available within the cathedral and monastery schools had been quite limited. Students learned grammar, rhetoric, and some elementary geometry and astronomy. They had the classical Latin grammars of Donatus and Priscian, Saint Augustine's treatise, *On Christian Doctrine*, and Cassiodorus's treatise, *On Divine and Secular Learning*. The writings of Boethius provided instruction in arithmetic and music and preserved the small body of Aristotle's works on logic then known in the West. After the textual finds of the early twelfth century, Western scholars recovered the whole of Aristotle's logic, the astronomy of Ptolemy, the writings of Euclid, and many Latin classics. By the mid-thirteenth century, almost all of Aristotle's works circulated in the West.

In the High Middle Ages the learning process remained very basic. The assumption was that truth already existed; it was not something that one had to go out and find. It was there, requiring only to be properly organized, elucidated, and defended. Such conviction made logic and dialectic the focus of education. Students wrote commentaries on authoritative texts, especially those of Aristotle and the Church Fathers. Teachers did not encourage students to strive independently for undiscovered truth. Students rather learned to organize and har-

A Renaissance allegory of the Liberal Arts, beginning at the bottom with Grammar (represented by Priscian or Donatus) and proceeding to geometry, each stage represented by a classical authority. By Biagio d'Antonio da Firenze (c.1445–c.1510). [Musee Conde, Chantilly, France. PE 14024 Allegory of the Liberal Arts. The Bridgeman Art Library]

monize the accepted truths of tradition, which were drilled into them.

This method of study, based on logic and dialectic, was known as *Scholasticism*. It reigned supreme in all the faculties, in law and medicine as well as in philosophy and theology. Students read the traditional authorities in their field, formed short summaries of their teaching, disputed them with their peers by elaborating traditional arguments pro and con, and then drew conclusions. Logic and dialectic dominated arts training because they were the tools that could discipline knowledge and thought. DIALECTIC IS A negative logical inquiry, the art of discovering a truth by finding the contradictions in arguments against it. Astonishingly, medical students did no practical work; they studied and debated the authoritative texts just as the law and theology students did.

Few books existed for students and, because printing with movable type did not yet exist, those available were expensive hand-copied works. So students could not leisurely master a subject in the quiet of their studies. They had rather to learn it in discussion, lecture, and debate. There was a lot of memorizing and the ability to think on one's feet was stressed. Rhetoric, or persuasive argument, was the ultimate goal, that is, the ability to make an eloquent defense of the knowledge one had clarified by logic and dialectic. Successful students became virtual walking encyclopedias; their education both filled their heads with knowledge and gave them the ability to recite it impressively.

The Summa The twelfth century saw the rise of the *summa*, an authoritative summary of allegedly all that was known about a particular subject. The summa's main purpose was to conciliate traditional authorities and heap up clarified truth. In canon law there was Gratian's *Concordance of Discordant Canons* (around 1142), whose very title embodies the scholastic method. In theology, there was Peter Lombard's *Four Books of Sentences* (1155–1157). Embracing traditional teaching on God, the Creation, Christ, and the sacraments, it was destined to become the standard theological textbook until the Protestant reformers declared it unbiblical. It had evolved from Peter Abelard's *Sic et Non* (around 1122), a much smaller work that juxtaposed seemingly contradictory statements on the same subject by revered authorities. Out of this same tradition came Saint *Thomas Aquinas's magnificent* Summa *Theologiae* (begun in 1265), to many the last word on theology, which the medieval summa was always intended to be.

University study normally began between the ages of twelve and fifteen. Students coming to university were expected to bring with them a good knowledge of Latin gained in local schools or from a private tutor. Once there, students spent four years perfecting their Latin (particularly in the study of the *trivium*) before attaining the bachelor of arts degree. A master's degree thereafter might take three or four years, during which time students

Student Life at the University of Paris

As the following account by Jacques de Vitry makes clear, not all students at the University of Paris in the thirteenth century were there to gain knowledge. Students fought constantly and subjected each other to ethnic insults and slurs.

✦ *Why were students from different lands so prejudiced against one another? Does the rivalry of faculty members appear to have been as intense as that among students? What are the student criticisms of the faculty? Do they sound credible?*

Almost all the students at Paris, foreigners and natives, did absolutely nothing except learn or hear something new. Some studied merely to acquire knowledge, which is curiosity; others to acquire fame, which is vanity; others still for the sake of gain, which is cupidity and the vice of simony. Very few studied for their own edification, or that of others. They wrangled and disputed not merely about the various sects or about some discussions; but the differences between the countries also caused dissensions, hatreds and virulent animosities among them, and they impudently uttered all kinds of affronts and insults against one another.

They affirmed that the English were drunkards and had tails; the sons of France proud, effeminate and carefully adorned like women. They said that the Germans were furious and obscene at their feasts; the Normans, vain and boastful; the Poitevins, traitors and always adventurers. The Burgundians they considered vulgar and stupid. The Bretons were reputed to be fickle and changeable, and were often reproached for the death of Arthur. The Lombards were called avaricious, vicious and cowardly; the Romans, seditious, turbulent and slanderous; the Sicilians, tyrannical and cruel; the inhabitants of Brabant, men of blood, incendiaries, brigands and ravishers; the Flemish, fickle, prodigal, gluttonous, yielding as butter, and slothful. After such insults from words they often came to blows.

I will not speak of those logicians [professors of logic and dialectic] before whose eyes flitted constantly "the lice of Egypt," that is to say, all the sophistical subtleties, so that no one could comprehend their eloquent discourses in which, as says Isaiah, "there is no wisdom." As to the doctors of theology, "seated in Moses' seat," they were swollen with learning, but their charity was not edifying. Teaching and not practicing, they have "become as sounding brass or a tinkling cymbal," or like a canal of stone, always dry, which ought to carry water to "the bed of spices." They not only hated one another, but by their flatteries they enticed away the students of others; each one seeking his own glory, but caring not a whit about the welfare of souls.

Translations and Reprints from the Original Sources of European History, *vol. 2 (Philadelphia: Department of History, University of Pennsylvania, 1902), pp. 19–20.*

studied mathematics, natural science, and philosophy by way of classical texts. A degree in theology at Paris might take more than twenty years of study from beginning to end.

Critics of Scholasticism Even in the heyday of Scholasticism, this kind of education had its strong critics. Prominent among them were John of Salisbury (ca. 1120–1180) and Saint Bernard of Clairvaux (1090–1153), who thought the scholastic method was a heartless and presumptuous way to train minds and a threat to the church.

There were critics also within the ordinary faculty ranks, the so-called *dictatores*. These professional grammarians and rhetoricians, the forerunners of later humanists, gave students practical

Thomas Aquinas Proves the Existence of God

People in the Middle Ages saw continuity between Earth and heaven, the world of the living and the world of the dead. For intellectuals, reason and revelation, while different, were also believed to be connected, so that reasoned argument could prove some of what the Bible revealed to faith. Thomas Aquinas, perhaps the greatest medieval theologian, here states his famous five arguments for the existence of God, which he believed any rational person would agree with.

✦ *Are these arguments persuasive? Which is the most persuasive, which the least? Are they basically the same argument?*

Is there a God?

REPLY: There are five ways in which one can prove that there is a God.

The FIRST . . . is based on change. Some things . . . are certainly in process of change: this we plainly see. Now anything in the process of change is being changed by something else. . . . Hence one is bound to arrive at some first cause of change not itself being changed by anything, and this is what everybody understands by God.

The SECOND way is based on the nature of causation. In the observable world causes are found to be ordered in series. . . . Such a series must however stop somewhere. . . . One is therefore forced to suppose some first cause, to which everyone gives the name "God."

The THIRD way is based on what need not be and on what must be. . . . Some . . . things . . . can be, but need not be for we find them springing up and dying away. . . . Now everything cannot be like this [for then we must conclude that] once upon a time there was nothing. But if that were true there would be nothing even now, because some thing that does not exist can only be brought into being by something already existing. . . . One is forced therefore to suppose something which must be . . . [and] is itself the cause that other things must be.

The FOURTH way is based on the gradation observed in things. Some things are found to be more good, more true, more noble . . . and other things less [so]. But such comparative terms describe varying degrees of approximation to a superlative . . . [something that is] the truest and best and most noble of things. . . . There is something, therefore, which causes in all other things their being, their goodness, and whatever other perfection they have. And this we call "God."

The FIFTH way is based on the guidedness of nature. An orderedness of actions to an end is observed in all bodies obeying natural laws . . . ; they truly tend to a goal and do not merely hit it by accident. . . . Everything in nature, therefore, is directed to its goal by someone with intelligence, and this we call "God."

Thomas Aquinas, Summa Theologiae, I, *ed. by Thomas Gilby (Image Books, New York: 1969), pp. 67–70.*

instruction in the composition of letters and documents. They taught good writing and speaking and, in contrast to the highly abstract logic and dialectic of scholastic education, they stressed practice over theory. (The difference might be compared with that between a modern expository writing program, where execution is the focus, and a modern English department, where theory is the focus.) Later humanists, establishing an approach still favored in modern liberal arts education, would urge scholars to go directly to sources in their original languages and draw their own conclusions.

Philosophy and Theology

Scholastics quarreled over the proper relationship between philosophy (which, for them, meant almost exclusively the writings of Aristotle) and

A Bishop Complains About the New Scholastic Learning

Scholasticism involved an intellectual, learned approach to religion and its doctrines rather than simple, uncritical piety. Many clergy saw in Scholasticism a threat to the Church Fathers and to the study of the Bible, because Scholasticism rationally dissected doctrines the clergy believed should be simply accepted and revered. Here Stephen, Bishop of Tournai, in a letter to the pope written between 1192 and 1203, sets forth some of the objections of clerics to Scholastism.

✦ *Are there indications of a generation gap in the bishop's criticism? What do you make of his classical allusions? Is he guilty of the same "intellectualism" he criticizes? Are there parallels in the modern university?*

The studies of sacred letters among us are fallen into the workshop of confusion, while both disciples applaud novelties alone and masters watch out for glory rather than learning. They everywhere compose new and recent *summulae* [little summaries] and commentaries, by which they attract, detain, and deceive their hearers, as if the works of the holy fathers were not still sufficient, who, we read, expounded Holy Scripture in the same spirit in which we believe the apostles and prophets composed it in. They prepare strange and exotic courses for their banquet, when at the nuptials of the son of the king of Taurus his own flesh and blood are killed and all prepared, and the wedding guests have only to take and eat what is set before them. Contrary to the sacred canons there is public disputation over the incomprehensible deity; [when discussing] the Incarnation of the Word, verbose flesh and blood irreverently litigate, the indivisible Trinity is cut up and wrangled over . . . so that now there are as many errors as doctors, as many scandals as classrooms, as many blasphemies as squares. . . .

Faculties called liberal having lost their pristine liberty are sunk in such servitude that adolescents with long hair impudently usurp their professorships, and beardless youths sit in the seat of their seniors, and those who don't yet know how to be disciples strive to be named masters. And they write their *summulae* moistened with drool and dribble but unseasoned with the salt of philosophers. Omitting the rules of the arts and discarding the authentic books of the artificers, they seize the flies of empty words in their sophisms like the claws of spiders. Philosophy cries out that her garments are torn and disordered and, modestly concealing her nudity by a few specific tatters, neither is consulted nor consoles as of old. All these things, father, call for the hand of apostolic correction. . . .

Lynn Thorndike, University Records and Life in the Middle Ages *(New York: Octagon Books, 1971), pp. 22–24.*

theology (which they believed to be a special "science" based on divine revelation). The problem between philosophy and theology arose because, in Christian eyes, there was a lot of heresy in Aristotle's writings, especially as his teaching was interpreted by certain Islamic commentators. These commentators did not treat his work as a handmaiden to Christianity. For example, Aristotle believed in the eternality of the world (that the world had always been). This plainly called into question the Judeo-Christian teaching that the world had been created in time, as stressed in the book of Genesis. Aristotle also taught that intellect, or mind, was ultimately one, a seeming denial of individuality and hence of Christian teaching about individual responsibility and personal immortality.

When theologians took the logic and metaphysics of Aristotle over into their theologies, some critics believed it posed a threat to biblical teaching and traditional church authority. Berengar of Tours (d. 1088), for example, was a Scholastic who applied logic to the sacrament of the Eucharist; and before long he found himself questioning the church's teaching on transubstantiation (which was not yet official dogma). Peter Abelard (1079–1142) tried to subject the Trinity to logical examination. He found that, by Aristotle's logic, three could not be one nor one three, in contrast to the church's teachings about the unity of God the Father, Son, and Holy Ghost.

The boldness of these new logicians shocked conservatives. Monastic leaders especially wondered whether the liberal arts course of study, dominated by Aristotle's writings, was more foe than ally of theological study. The love of learning had clearly gotten in the way of the love of God as far as the critics of Scholasticism were concerned.

A century of such suspicion and criticism of Aristotle's alleged undermining of Christian theology culminated in 1277 when the bishop of Paris condemned 219 philosophical propositions. The condemnation was directed against scholars who seemed to the authorities to be more interested in secular philosophy than in Christian truth. It chilled the relationship between learning and religion. Reason and revelation thereafter became two very different spheres of knowledge, much as church and state were then also being forced apart in the world of secular politics. William of Ockham (d. 1349) represented conservative opinion on the issue and signaled its future direction when he denied that essential matters of theology could be addressed as if they were empirical. To know God's mind, Christians must content themselves with biblical revelation; reason could not know God directly.

Women in Medieval Society

The image and the reality of medieval women are two very different things. The image, both for contemporaries and for us today, was strongly influenced by the views of male Christian clergy, whose ideal was the celibate life of chastity, poverty, and obedience. Drawing on classical medical, philosophical, and legal traditions that predated Christianity, as well as on ancient biblical theology, Christian theologians depicted women as physically, mentally, and morally weaker than men.

On the basis of such assumptions, medieval church and society sanctioned the coercive treatment of women, including corrective wife beating in extreme cases. Christian clergy generally considered marriage a debased state by comparison with the religious life, and in their writings they praised virgins and celibate widows over wives. Women, as the Bible clearly taught, were the "weaker vessel." In marriage their role was to be subject and obedient to their husbands, who, as the stronger, had a duty to protect and discipline them.

This image of the medieval woman suggests that she had two basic options in life: to become either a subjugated housewife or a confined nun. In reality, the vast majority of medieval women were neither.

Image and Status Both within and outside Christianity this image of women—not yet to speak of the reality of their lives—was contradicted. In chivalric romances and courtly love literature of the twelfth and thirteenth centuries, as in the contemporaneous cult of the Virgin Mary, women were presented as objects of service and devotion to be praised and admired, even put on pedestals and treated as superior to men. If the church shared traditional misogynist sentiments, it also condemned them, as in the case of the *Romance of the Rose* (late thirteenth century) and other popular "bawdy" literature.

The learned churchman Peter Lombard (1100–1169) sanctioned an image of women that didactic Christian literature often invoked. Why, he asked, was Eve created from Adam's rib and not instead taken from his head or his feet? The answer was clear. God took Eve from Adam's side because he wanted woman neither to rule over nor to be enslaved by man, but to stand squarely at his side, as his companion and partner in mutual aid and trust. By so insisting on the spiritual equality of men and women and their shared responsibility to one another within marriage, the church also helped to raise the dignity of women.

Germanic law treated women better than Roman law had done. Women had basic rights under law that prevented their being treated as chattels. And there was far greater equality between the sexes. Unlike Roman women, who as teens married men much older than themselves, German women married as adults and their husbands were of similar age. Another practice unknown to the Romans was the groom's conveyance of a marriage portion, or dowry, to his bride to have and to hold as her own in the event of widowhood. All the major Germanic law codes recognized the economic freedom of women, that is, their right to inherit, administer, dispose of, and confer on their children family property and wealth. They could also press charges in court against men for bodily injury and rape. Depending on the country in question, punishments for rape ranged from fines, flogging, and banishment to blinding, castration, and death.

LIFE CHOICES The nunnery was an option for only a very few unmarried women from the higher social classes. Entrance required a dowry (*dos*) and could be almost as expensive as a wedding, although usually it was less. Within the nunnery, a woman could rise to a position of leadership as abbess or mother superior and could exercise an organizational and administrative authority denied her in much of secular life. The nunneries of the established religious orders were also under male supervision, however, so that even abbesses had finally to answer to higher male authority.

Nunneries also provided women an escape from the debilitating effects of multiple pregnancies. In the ninth century, under the influence of Christianity, the Carolingians made monogamous marriage their official policy. Heretofore they had practiced polygyny and concubinage and had permitted divorce. The result was both a boon and a burden to women. On one hand, the selection of a wife now became a very special event, and wives gained greater dignity and legal security. On the other hand, a woman's labor as household manager and bearer of children greatly increased.

The aristocratic wife not only ran a large household but was also the agent of her husband during his absence. In addition to these responsibilities, one wife now had sole responsibility for the propagation of heirs. The Carolingian wife also became the sole object of her husband's wrath and displeasure. Such demands clearly took their toll. The

A fifteenth-century rendering of an eleventh- or twelfth-century marketplace. Medieval women were active in all trades, but especially in the food and clothing industries. [Scala/Art Resource, N.Y.]

mortality rates of Frankish women increased and their longevity decreased after the ninth century.

Under such conditions the cloister could serve as a welcome refuge to women. The number of women in cloisters was never very great, however. In late medieval England, for example, there are estimated to have been no more than 3,500 women.

The vast majority of medieval women were neither aristocratic housewives nor nuns, but working women. Much evidence suggests that they were respected and loved by their husbands, perhaps because they worked shoulder by shoulder and hour by hour with them. Between the ages of ten and fifteen, girls were apprenticed in a trade much as were boys, and they learned to be skilled workers. If they married, they might continue their particular trade, operating their bakeshops or dress shops next to their husbands' business, or become assistants and partners in the shops of their husbands. Women appeared in virtually every "blue-collar" trade, from butcher to goldsmith, although they were especially prominent in the food and clothing industries. Women belonged to guilds, just like men, and they became craftmasters. In the later Middle Ages, townswomen increasingly had the opportunity to go to school and to gain vernacular literacy.

It is also true that women did not have as wide a range of vocations as men, although the vocational destinies of the vast majority of men were as fixed as those of women. Women were excluded from the learned professions of scholarship, medicine, and law. They often found their freedom of movement within a profession more carefully regulated than a man's. Usually, women performed the same work as men for a wage 25 percent lower. And, as is still true today, women filled the ranks of domestic servants in urban households in disproportionate numbers. Still, women remained as prominent and as creative a part of workaday medieval society as men.

The Lives of Children

The image of medieval children and the reality of their lives seem also to have been two very different things. Until recently historians were inclined to believe that parents were emotionally distant from their children during the Middle Ages. Evidence of low esteem for children comes from a variety of sources.

CHILDREN AS "LITTLE ADULTS" Some historians maintain that children are rarely portrayed as different from adults in medieval art and sculpture. If pictorially children and adults look alike, were people in the Middle Ages aware of childhood as a separate period of life requiring special care and treatment? There was also high infant and child mortality, which, it seems, could only have discouraged parents from making a high emotional investment in their children. How could a parent dare to have a deep emotional attachment to a child who had a 30–50 percent chance of dying before age five?

During the Middle Ages, children assumed adult responsibilities early in life. The children of peasants labored in the fields alongside their parents as soon as they could physically manage the work. Urban artisans and burghers sent their children out of their homes into apprenticeships in various crafts and trades between the ages of eight and twelve. Can such early removal of children from their homes be taken for anything but low affection for children? That children were expected to grow up fast is attested by the canonical ages for marriage, twelve for girls and fourteen for boys (although few married at these ages).

The practice of infanticide is an even more striking suggestion of low esteem for children in ancient and early medieval times. According to Tacitus, the Romans exposed unwanted children, especially girls, at birth. In this way they regulated family size. The surviving children appear to have been given plenty of attention and affection. The Germanic tribes of medieval Europe, by contrast, had large families, but tended to neglect their children in comparison with the Romans. Infanticide, particularly of girls, continued to be practiced in the early Middle Ages, as shown by its condemnation in penance books and by church synods. Parents were forbidden to sleep with infants and small children to prevent them from being suffocated, either by accident or by design.

Among the German tribes, one paid a much lower *wergild*, or compensatory fine, for injury to a child than for injury to an adult. The *wergild* for injuring a child was only one-fifth that for injuring an adult. That paid for injury to a female child under fifteen was one-half that for injury to a male child—a strong indication that female children were the least esteemed members of German tribal society. Mothers appear also to have nursed boys longer than they did girls, which favored boys' health and survival. A woman's *wergild*, however, increased a full eightfold between infancy and her childbearing years, at which time she had obviously become highly prized.[4]

CHILDHOOD AS A SPECIAL STAGE Despite such varied evidence of parental distance and neglect, there is another side to the story. Since the early Middle Ages, physicians and theologians, at least, have clearly understood childhood to be a distinct and special stage of life. Isidore (560–636), the metropolitan of Seville and a leading intellectual authority throughout the Middle Ages, carefully distinguished six ages of life, the first four of which were infancy (between one and seven years of age), childhood (seven to fourteen), adolescence, and youth.

According to the medical authorities, infancy proper extended from birth to anywhere between six months and two years (depending on the authority) and covered the period of speechlessness and suckling. The period thereafter, until age seven, was considered a higher level of infancy, marked by the beginning of a child's ability to speak and his or her weaning. At age seven, when a child could think and act decisively and speak clearly, childhood proper began. After this point, a child could be reasoned with, could profit from regular discipline, and could begin to train for a lifelong vocation. At seven a child was ready for schooling, private tutoring, or apprenticeship in a chosen craft or trade. Until physical growth was completed, however—and that could extend to twenty-one years of age—a child or youth was legally under the guardianship of parents or a surrogate authority.

There is evidence that high infant and child mortality, rather than distancing parents from children, actually made parents look on children as all the more precious. The medical authorities respected during the Middle Ages—Hippocrates, Galen, and Soranus of Ephesus—dealt at length with postnatal care and childhood diseases. Both in learned and popular medicine, sensible as well as fanciful cures can be found for the leading killers of children (diarrhea, worms, pneumonia, and fever). When infants and children died, medieval parents grieved as pitiably as modern parents do. In the art and literature of the Middle Ages, we find mothers baptizing dead infants and children or carrying them to pilgrim shrines in the hope of reviving them. There are also examples of mental illness and suicide brought on by the death of a child.[5]

Clear evidence of special attention being paid to children is also found in the great variety of children's toys, and even devices like walkers and potty chairs, which existed in the Middle Ages. The medieval authorities on child rearing widely condemned child abuse and urged moderation in the disciplining of children. In church art and drama, parents were urged to love their children as Mary loved Jesus. And early apprenticeships may also be interpreted as an expression of parental love and concern rather than indifference and low esteem. For in the Middle Ages, no parental responsibility was thought greater than that of equipping a child for useful and gainful work. Certainly by the High Middle Ages, if not earlier, children were widely viewed as special creatures with their own needs and rights.

✦

During the High Middle Ages, the growth of Mediterranean trade revived old cities and caused the creation of new ones. The Crusades aided and abetted this development. Italian cities especially flourished during the late eleventh and twelfth centuries. Venice dominated Mediterranean trade and extended its political and economic influence throughout the Near East. It had its own safe ports as far away as Syria. As cities grew in population and became rich with successful trade, a new social group, the long-distance traders, rose to prominence. By marriage and political organization, these merchant families organized themselves into an unstoppable force. They successfully challenged the old nobility in and around the cities. A new elite of merchants gained control of city governments almost everywhere. They brought with them a policy of open trade and the blessings and problems of nascent capitalism. Artisans and small shopkeepers at the lower end of the economic spectrum aspired to follow their example, as new opportunities opened for all. The seeds of social conflict and of urban class struggle had been sown.

[4]David Herlihy, "Medieval Children," in *Essays on Medieval Civilization*, ed. by B. K. Lackner and K. R. Phelp (University of Texas Press, 1978), pp. 109–131.

[5]Klaus Arnold, *Kind und Gesellschaft im Mittelalter und Renaissance* (Paderborn: 1980), pp. 31, 37.

One very positive result of the new wealth of towns was the patronage of education and culture. These matters were given an emphasis not experienced since Roman times. Western Europe's first universities appeared in the eleventh century and universities steadily expanded over the next four centuries. There were twenty by 1300. Not only did Scholasticism flourish, but a new literature, art, and architecture developed as well, reflecting both a new human vitality and the reshaping of society and politics. For all of this, western Europeans had no one to thank so much as the new class of merchants, whose greed, daring, and ambition made it all possible.

Review Questions

1. How did the responsibilities of the nobility differ from those of the clergy and the peasantry during the High Middle Ages? In what ways did each social class contribute to the stability of society?
2. What led to the revival of trade and the growth of towns in the twelfth century? What political and social conditions were essential for a revival of trade? How did towns change medieval society?
3. From your understanding of the functions of the medieval university, assess the strengths and weaknesses of higher education in that period. Comment especially on the curriculum.
4. How would you define Scholasticism? What was the Scholastic program and method of study? Who were the main critics of Scholasticism and what were their complaints?
5. How would you assess the position of women in Germanic law and Roman law? What were the options and responsibilities for women in each social class? What are the differing theories regarding the image of children in the Middle Ages?

Suggested Readings

E. AMT (ED.), *Women's Lives in Medieval Europe: A Sourcebook* (1993). Outstanding collection of sources.

P. ARIÈS, *Centuries of Childhood: A Social History of Family Life* (1962). Pioneer effort on the subject.

J. W. BALDWIN, *The Scholastic Culture of the Middle Ages: 1000–1300* (1971). Best brief synthesis available.

R. L. BENSON AND G. CONSTABLE (EDS.), *Renaissance and Renewal in the Twelfth Century* (1982). The world of twelfth-century education documented in great detail.

M. BLOCH, *French Rural History*, trans. by J. Sondheimer (1966). A classic by a great modern historian.

G. DUBY, *The Three Orders: Feudal Society Imagined*, trans. by A. Goldhammer (1981). Large, comprehensive, authoritative.

E. GILSON, *Heloise and Abelard* (1968). Analysis and defense of medieval scholarly and gender values.

B. A. HANAWALT, *The Ties That Bound: Peasant Families in Medieval England* (1986). Illuminating demographic and economic study of rural life.

C. H. HASKINS, *The Renaissance of the Twelfth Century* (1927). Still the standard account.

C. H. HASKINS, *The Rise of Universities* (1972). A short, minor classic.

D. HERLIHY, *Medieval Households* (1985). Bread-and-butter account of household structure in antiquity and the Middle Ages.

G. KÜNSTLER, *Romanesque Art in Europe* (1973). Standard survey.

G. LEFF, *Paris and Oxford Universities in the Thirteenth and Fourteenth Centuries: An Institutional and Intellectual History* (1968). Very good on Scholastic debates.

R. S. LOOMIS (ED.), *The Development of Arthurian Romance* (1963). Essays debating its meaning and significance.

R. LOPEZ, *The Commercial Revolution of the Middle Ages 900–1350* (1971). A master's brief survey.

E. MÂLE, *The Gothic Image: Religious Art in France in the Thirteenth Century* (1913). An enduring classic.

L. DE MAUSE (ED.), *The History of Childhood* (1974). Very substantive and provocative essays with an interest in the inner as well as the material lives of children.

K. MERTES, *The English Noble Household 1250–1600* (1988). Good background for the debate over the structure and quality of English family life.

R. I. MOORE, *The Formation of a Persecuting Society: Power and Deviance in Western Europe, 950–1250* (1987). A sympathetic look at heresy and dissent.

A. MURRAY, *Reason and Society in the Middle Ages* (1978). A view of the Middle Ages as an age of reason as well as of faith.

J. T. NOONAN, *Contraception: A History of Its Treatment by the Catholic Theologians and Canonists* (1967). Fascinating account of medieval theological attitudes toward sexuality and sex-related problems.

E. PANOFSKY, *Gothic Architecture and Scholasticism* (1951). A controversial classic.

H. PIRENNE, *Medieval Cities: Their Origins and the Revival of Trade*, trans. by F. D. Halsey (1970). A minor classic.

H. RASHDALL, *The Universities of Europe in the Middle Ages*, vols. 1–3 (1936). Dated but still extremely useful for documents of the period.

S. REYNOLDS, *Kingdoms and Communities in Western Europe, 900–1300* (1984). A study of the shaping of Europe.

I. S. ROBINSON, *The Papacy 1073–1198: Continuity and Innovation* (1990). A fresh look at the papacy in this period of its reform and independence.

F. RÖRIG, *The Medieval Town*, trans. by D. J. A. Matthew (1972). Excellent study of the towns of northern Europe.

S. SHAHAR, *The Fourth Estate: A History of Women in the Middle Ages* (1983). A comprehensive survey, making clear the great variety of women's work.

R. W. SOUTHERN, *Medieval Humanism and Other Studies* (1970). Provocative and far-ranging essays on topics in intellectual history.

B. STOCK, *The Implications of Literacy* (1983). How the ability to read changed medieval society.

L. THORNDIKE, *University Records and Life in the Middle Ages* (1975). Rich primary sources for both curricular and extracurricular life.

The West & the World

SOCIAL LIFE IN MALI (1200–1400)

The Mali Empire encompassed a vast territory that was nearly as large as medieval Western Europe. Formed by the Malinke people, the enormous state of Mali embraced much of western Africa south of the Sahara Desert and controlled the highly profitable trans-Saharan trade. As the first king, or "Mansa," Sundiata and his ruling clan laid the foundation for the power and prosperity that characterized Mali for nearly two centuries. The wealth and the longevity of the empire, however, was not simply a function of a great leader. Instead, the viability of such a vast state depended upon two other important factors. First, the trans-Saharan trade gave rise to a series of large towns throughout Mali. These urban centers, much like those of medieval Europe, were exciting locations that attracted diverse groups of people and allowed for exchanges of both goods and ideas. In addition, the quality of Mali's social and political organizations, the introduction of Islam, and the character of its people were extremely important. The day-to-day life of the Africans in Mali had common elements that created a sense of social cohesiveness and identity.

The Growth of Urban Centers and the Introduction of Islam. The introduction of Islam into Mali provided the most important unifying element. The trans-Saharan trade and the emergence of flourishing urban centers made possible the triumph of Islam. Muslim traders from North Africa traveled across the Sahara to exchange goods with the merchants of Mali. Most of the empire's major towns were established on the southern fringe of the Sahara Desert in a region called the *Sahel* (the Arabic word for *shore).* On the backs of their camels—which could number as many as 20,000—the north African traders brought salt from the Sahara Desert's mines and luxury goods from the Mediterranean basin and the Middle East. In exchange, they received seemingly endless supplies of gold and slaves from the Mali traders. It is in this trading region of the *Sahel* that urban centers such as Timbuktu, Walata, and Gao emerged. These towns were both commercial centers and centers of Muslim culture and social organization. The adoption of Islam provided the empire with a code of law, called the *shari'a*, which helped to regulate commerce and political activity. In addition, the Koran provided an important guide to social organization and family relations in the newly emerging towns.

The Social Order. The order of social life in Mali was both similar to and different from that of medieval Europe. At the top of the social order were the ruling elite. As in Europe, men comprised this group, but in Mali, the ruling elite were neither landed nobles, nor feudal vassals nor warrior knights. Instead, those who wielded political power and high social position within the Mansa's court were those men who had amassed wealth and status through the trans-Saharan trade. While the noble class in Europe was closed and based upon landed wealth, Mali's was open to anyone who had the ambition to enter the trading occupation. However, social divisions still existed within the group of traders. Certain extended fam-

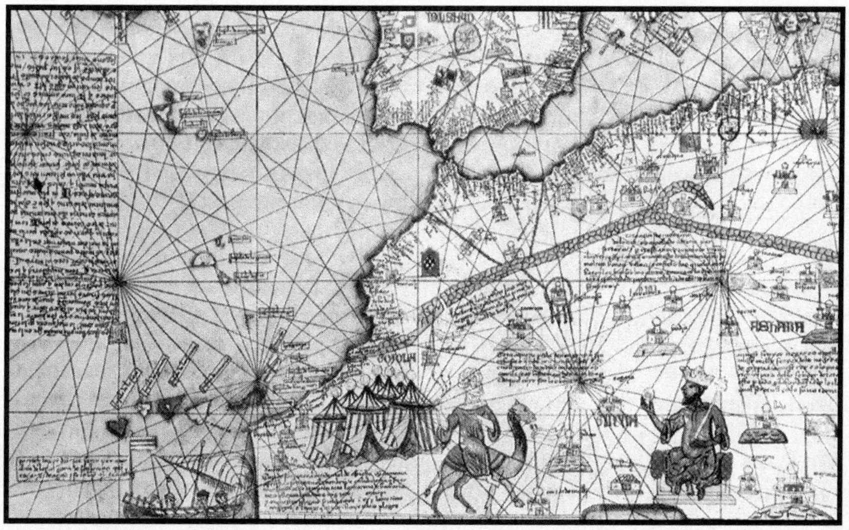

Crossing the Sahara on their camels, North African traders came to the urban centers of Mali to exchange salt and luxury goods for gold and slaves. This map, drawn in 1375, shows a Muslim coming to trade with Mali's ruler. The writing on the lower right says, "This Negro Lord is called Musa Mali, lord of the Negroes of Guinea. So Abundant is the gold which is found in his land that he is the richest and most noble king in all the land." [The Granger Collection]

ilies became dominant as they were able to control many of the lucrative, long-distance trading routes. Other short-distance traders and small-scale urban traders rounded out the social group. Together, the traders were primarily responsible for expanding the empire of Mali and were thus highly respected.

Traders were not the only people who lived in Mali. The other basic social groups were the *`ulama*, or Muslim clerics and holy men; freemen who worked in the towns as artisans and shopkeepers, or in rural areas as peasants and herdsmen; and slaves. The *`ulama* shared many of the same distinctions as their European counterparts in the church. Most Muslim holy men lived in urban areas where they were dedicated to the study of the Koran, the shari'a, and other important Islamic texts. Also, membership in the *`ulama* was not predicated on birth, but rather on strict religious training. In effect, the *`ulama* were the most pious and observant believers of Islam in the Mali Empire.

The next social group, the laborers, performed the same types of work as the laborers of medieval Europe. Farmers dominated in rural areas, while blacksmiths, carpenters, and shopkeepers were concentrated in urban areas. Unlike the European serfs, however, the rural peasants in Mali generally did not labor for a wealthy landowner. Instead, they worked with a larger social network of relatives who grew crops and raised animals together. While rural society did have status divisions, with elders dominating decision making, it did not have manors and authoritarian feudal lords. At the same time, however, the nuclear family unit did not emerge as it did in medieval Europe. In the rural areas, the extended family unit, or clan, dominated production.

Mali society also had slaves in both rural and urban areas. Slaves were often closely integrated into the domestic lives of their masters. Many female slaves labored within their masters' households and performed such tasks as cooking and cleaning, wet nursing, and mid-wifing. Slaves often helped to expand the size of a family, thus increasing the number of laborers.

Urban Versus Rural Society. Much like Europe in the Middle Ages, rural and urban society in the Mali Empire were quite different. In the rural areas, the basic social group was the clan. This large, extended family dominated social and cultural life, but the clan's influence was particularly strong in the realm of religion. Unlike the urban areas of Mali, the rural areas were relatively untouched by the force of Islam. African indigenous religions dominated the hinterlands where men and women worshiped not only a creator God and many lower deities, but also their ancestors. Ancestral veneration, or the reverence for family members who lived before one, was an integral component of the religious life for the men and women in rural Mali.

Urban Mali was a completely different world. Towns like Timbuktu were bustling centers of activity. Islam, which had little impact on rural communities, gained strong ground in the urban centers, in the trading communities, and among the ruling elite. Indeed, trade and Islam dominated town life—and together, they permeated social activities and family relations.

The concept of a European-type state, an organization independent from social and religious life, did not exist in urban Mali. According to Islamic ideology, a Muslim town seeks to attain the status of an *`umma*, or religiously shaped community. Within an ideal *`umma*, the townspeople of Mali sought to build many aspects of their lives on the foundation of Islam. The basis of Mali urban life rested on the five pillars of Islam—acknowledging that there was no other God but Allah, observing ritual prayer five times a day, fasting during the month of *Ramadan,* giving alms to the poor, and making a pilgrimage, or *hajj*, to the Sacred Mosque at Mecca at least once in one's life.

The formation of a Muslim community, however, went far beyond upholding the five pillars of Islam. In an ideal *`umma*, all members had to follow the rules of social behavior and relations as laid down in the Islamic texts. In urban Mali, the Islamic texts and the Muslim clerics who interpreted them helped to regulate religious, social, and ethical dealings in the community. Wine, gambling, usury, and pork were all forbidden. The Muslim holy men strongly discouraged the worship of indigenous gods and the making of images or representations. Penalties for certain crimes like stealing, fraud, and murder were clearly laid down, as were rituals for marking life-cycle events, like marriage, puberty, child rearing, and inheritance.

The existence of an *`umma* meant that the people who lived in urban Mali, like those who lived in Christian Europe, had a type of quasi-"national" consciousness. There was a sense of sharing an idealized way of life and belonging to something larger than a single family or village. The peoples of an *`umma* in Mali also felt a loyalty to a much larger, global community of Muslims.

Family Relationships. Although the urban peoples of Mali did have allegiances and identities that stretched beyond their towns, relatives by blood and marriage were central to their day-to-day lives. The Koran ordered that the adherents of Islam had to trace their descent through the patrilineal lines. Therefore, membership in a patrilineage, a group that traced its history through untold male generations, was very important. As a result, much like the later Middle Ages in Europe, matrilineal affiliations became suppressed and descent through the father's side of the family gained importance. Within an extended patrilineal family, the basic unit of social organization was the family. The family in urban Mali, however, differed greatly from the "nuclear family" or child–parent unit in Europe. Strictly regulated by Islamic codes, an ideal family in urban Mali lived in a compound, which could be either a single large home or a series of smaller huts. According to the Koran, a man could have up to four wives and an unlimited number of concubines. A concubine was a slave who took on the role of a wife, though she was not legally recognized as one. Together, the husband, wife or wives, concubines, and all of their children lived together and formed one family. A man's first wife, the *senior wife*, held special status. She often directed the other wives and concubines in decision making over domestic and household matters. In addition, male and female slaves circulated within the household and were often considered part of the family.

Polygamous families—or those with more than one wife—tended to reflect the husband's wealth. Islam stresses a husband's duty to support his wife, thus women were often relieved of any domestic work, particularly those who were wives of the ruling elite. Large families, dependent upon the wealth and prestige of a husband, were a luxury as well as a mark of being a good Muslim.

Arranged Marriage. As in Europe, the fathers in urban Mali found husbands for their daughters. According to the Koran, a Muslim woman had to marry a Muslim, and fathers usually respected this rule. They also considered men within their own family as suitable husbands for their daughters. While some cultures consider marriage between first cousins incestuous, Islamic communities, supported by the Koran, encouraged such unions. Cousin marriages helped to keep property within the same family and reinforced the importance of the extended family. Regardless of whether a future husband came from within or outside the family, the future bride and groom had little to say about whom they married. While the emotional compatibility of a couple was becoming an important condition for marriage in medieval Europe, marriages in Mali were often arranged by the fathers and male members of the extended family to form beneficial family alliances.

Once a spouse had been chosen, the male relations of both families assembled at the bride's house and participated in a contract ceremony. The fathers were each represented by a *wali*, or close male relative who conveyed the family's wishes. The *walis* negotiated over the transaction. An *`ulama* was present and he announced the acceptance of the settlement and the transference of the bride to the groom. He then presided over a series of traditional Islamic prayers. In addition to the contract ceremony, other traditional marriage rites marked the transference of the bride to the bridegroom's house. These included the bathing of the bride, followed by the henna ceremony, where the bride's skin was decorated with red henna. Veiling followed, and after the bride was taken to her husband's home, a traditional marriage feast ended the marriage rites.

Married Life. A married woman's freedom depended on her husband's economic circumstances and how strictly they observed Islam at home. According to Muslim law, married women were to be sequestered in their homes, and even there, socializing with men was sharply limited to their husbands and male family members. In practice, however, this law was difficult to follow. Married women did walk about the streets of Timbuktu, but not if they were in the privileged classes. Indeed, wife seclusion was a status symbol, reflecting reflecting a husband's ability to hire servants who could perform domestic chores outside of the home. A married woman did have specific rights: A husband had to provide each wife with a separate room or house within his compound, and he was responsible for the physical and spiritual well-being of their children. If these and other rights were not upheld, Islamic law allowed a wife to seek a divorce.

The goal of a family in urban Mali was to raise children who obeyed to their parents, who respected the members of their extended family, and were infused with the spirituality of the Muslim faith. Urban parents sought to inculcate the "Muslim way of life," as distinct from the "pagan way of life" of the rural areas.

Education in Mali. As in Europe, child rearing became stricter by age six or seven, when formal schooling began. Koranic schools were considered very important. As in Europe, the urban areas of Mali were great cultural and learning centers that attracted some of the finest Islamic scholars throughout the Muslim world. Parents wanted their children to learn from these great scholars, but for all children, memorizing parts of the Koran was at the heart of early education. Both boys and girls were instructed in the Koran and other formal duties of Islam, but only boys could receive advanced learning.

In contrast to the emerging universities in medieval Europe, the system of higher education in Mali was designed and directed by the learned, Islamic scholars, not by their students. The scholars were highly revered, and families would present them with untold numbers of gifts to educate their sons. The Muslim scholars would train their students in advanced Islamic learning, including in-depth study of the Koran, mastery of written Arabic, and a full understanding of the Islamic legal code, or shari'a. A child was assured a stronger link to the Muslim community (the *`umma*) if he was steeped in Islamic learning and spirituality. However, formal Islamic education was much more than just religious training. There was a very close association between commerce and Islamic scholarship, so understanding the laws and customs that governed the trans-Saharan trade was very important in amassing future wealth and status. The parents in Mali thought worldly success would bring honor not only to the greater Muslim community, but also to the individual family. Indeed, family honor was an important value shared by the parents of Mali and Europe.

✦ *How did the rise of towns and the formation of an urban culture differ in Mali and Western Europe between 1000 and 1300? Compare and contrast rural and urban life in both lands. Compare the lives of Mali and Western Europe women between 1000 and 1300. Why are Western societies in these centuries considered to be more secular than those of Africa? Were African societies in fact more religious? How does one explain the existence of slavery in Western Europe and Africa? Was it more widespread in one area than in the other?*

Edward William Bovill, *The Golden Trade of the Moors: West African Kingdoms in the Fourteenth Century* (Princeton: Markus Wiener Publishers, 1958); Said Hamdun and Noel King, *Ibn Battuta in Black Africa* (Princeton: Markus Wiener Publishers, 1975), Nehemia Levtzion, *Ancient Ghana and Mali* (London: Methuen & Co., Ltd., 1973); and J. Spencer Trimingham, *Islam in West Africa* (Oxford: Clarendon Press, 1959).

Europe in Transition, 1300–1750

Between the early fourteenth and the mid-eighteenth centuries, Europe underwent many far-reaching changes. These were years of massive physical suffering brought on by disease and war and of new political and cultural construction made possible by better government and growing wealth.

The era began with one of the greatest disasters in European history: a bubonic plague, known as the *Black Death,* that had killed an estimated two-fifths of the population by the mid-fourteenth century. A hundred years of sharp conflicts between popes and secular rulers preceded this demographic crisis and a hundred years of warfare between England and France followed it. The emergence of strong, ruthless monarchs accompanied the decline in papal power during the later Middle Ages. Commanding greater economic and military resources, these new rulers gained control over the church in their lands. By the fourteenth century, the nation-states of Europe were warring with one another, no longer with the armies of the pope.

The fourteenth century also saw the beginning of the great cultural resurgence in Europe known as the *Renaissance.* This rebirth of education and culture was closely associated with the rediscovery of forgotten classical Greek and Latin writings and the rapid growth of colleges and universities throughout western Europe.

The past was not the only previously uncharted region Europeans set out to explore. In the late fifteenth century, they began voyages to America, around Africa, and across the Indian Ocean to Asia that introduced them to exotic cultures and non-Western values. Beginning with Copernicus and culminating with Sir Isaac Newton, scientists charted a new view of the universe. Between them the voyages of discovery and the Scientific Revolution gave Europeans both new confidence in the power of the human mind and a new perspective on their society.

In the sixteenth century, a religious revolt divided Europe spiritually and led to a major restructuring of Western Christendom. The Protestant Reformation began in 1517 when an obscure German professor named Martin Luther challenged the religious teaching and authority of the papacy. Within a quarter century, Europe was permanently divided among a growing variety of Protestant churches and the Roman Catholic Church. For a century and a half, these new religious differences also fueled political conflict. Religious warfare devastated France in the second half of the sixteenth century and wreaked havoc on Germany in the first half of the seventeenth century.

By the middle of the seventeenth century, most religious warfare had ended. The religious turmoil had strengthened the hand of the secular state. For many rulers and their subjects, political stability came to have a higher value than religious allegiance. By the early eighteenth century, Europe's rulers (with the notable exception of the English monarchs, who had the will but not the ability) imitated the French king Louis XIV. Through efficient taxation, a loyal administration, and a powerful standing army, Louis bent France to his will, making it the model of the new absolute state to which rulers everywhere aspired. By the second half of the seventeenth century, the balance of power shifted away from Spain, which had dominated Europe during the sixteenth century. France, Austria, and Prussia joined the new parliamentary monarchy of Great Britain as Europe's new masters. And, for the first time, Russia emerged as a major European power.

With the end of religious conflict, energies turned toward economic expansion. New and more efficient farming methods appeared, and nations took the first steps toward industrialization. In the New World, the colonies grew and were consolidated. By the eighteenth century, competition over trade had replaced religion as the cause of war. The demand for political independence, most notably by the English colonies in America, replaced the earlier demands for religious independence. A new age had dawned, one still believing in the power of God, but increasingly fascinated by human political power. ✦

1300–1750 C.E.

	POLITICS AND GOVERNMENT	SOCIETY AND ECONOMY	RELIGION AND CULTURE
1300–1400	1309–1377 Pope resides in Avignon 1337–1453 Hundred Years' War 1356 *Golden Bull* creates German electoral college	1315–1317 Greatest famine of the Middle Ages 1347–1350 Black Death peaks 1358 *Jacquerie* shakes France 1378 Ciompi Revolt in Florence 1381 English peasants' revolt	1300–1325 Dante Alighieri writes *Divine Comedy* 1302 Boniface VIII issues bull *Unam Sanctam* 1350 Boccaccio, *Decameron* 1375–1527 The Renaissance in Italy 1378–1417 The Great Schism 1380–1395 Chaucer writes *Canterbury Tales* 1390–1430 Christine de Pisan writes in defense of women
1400–1500	1415–1433 Hussite revolt in Bohemia 1428–1519 Aztecs expand in central Mexico 1429 Joan of Arc leads French to victory in Orleans 1434 Medici rule begins in Florence 1453–1471 Wars of the Roses in England 1469 Marriage of Ferdinand and Isabella 1487 Henry Tudor creates Court of Star Chamber	1450 Johann Gutenberg invents printing with movable type 1492 Christopher Columbus encounters the Americas 1498 Vasco da Gama reaches India	1414–1417 The Council of Constance 1425–1450 Lorenzo Valla exposes the *Donation of Constantine* 1450 Thomas à Kempis, *Imitation of Christ* 1492 Expulsion of Jews from Spain
1500–1600	1519 Charles V crowned Holy Roman emperor 1530 *Augsburg Confession* defines Lutheranism 1547 Ivan the Terrible becomes tsar of Russia 1555 *Peace of Augsburg* recognizes the legal principle, *cuius regio, eius religio* 1568–1603 Reign of Elizabeth I of England 1572 Saint Bartholomew's Day Massacre 1588 English defeat of Spanish Armada 1598 Edict of Nantes gives Huguenots religious and civil rights	1519 Hernan Cortes lands in Mexico 1519–1522 Ferdinand Magellan circumnavigates the Earth 1525 German Peasants' Revolt 1531–1533 Francisco Pizarro conquers the Incas 1540 Spanish open silver mines in Peru, Bolivia, and Mexico 1550–1600 The great witch panics	1513 Niccolo Machiavelli, *The Prince* 1516 Erasmus compiles a Greek New Testament 1516 Thomas More, *Utopia* 1517 Martin Luther's Ninety-five theses 1534 Henry VIII declared head of English Church 1540 Jesuit order founded 1541 John Calvin becomes Geneva's reformer 1543 Copernicus, *On the Revolutions* 1545–1563 Council of Trent 1549 English *Book of Common Prayer*

Elizabeth I, The Armada Portrait

	POLITICS AND GOVERNMENT	SOCIETY AND ECONOMY	RELIGION AND CULTURE
1600–1700	1624–1642 **Era of Richelieu in France** 1629–1640 **Charles I's years of personal rule** 1640 **Long Parliament convenes** 1642 **Outbreak of civil war in England** 1643–1661 **Cardinal Mazarin regent for Louis XIV** 1648 **Peace of Westphalia** 1649–1652 **The *Fronde* in France** 1649 **Charles I executed** 1660 **Charles II restored to the English throne** 1661–1715 **Louis XIV's years of personal rule** 1682–1725 **Reign of Peter the Great** 1685 **James II becomes king of England** **Louis XIV revokes Edict of Nantes** 1688 **"Glorious Revolution" in Britain**	1600–1700 **Period of greatest Dutch economic prosperity** 1600–early 1700s **Spain maintains commercial monopoly in Latin America** 1607 **English settle Jamestown, Virginia** 1608 **French settle Quebec** 1618–1648 **Thirty Years' War devastates German economy** 1619 **African slaves first bought at Jamestown, Virginia** 1650s–1670s **Commercial rivalry between Dutch and English** 1661–1683 **Colbert seeks to stimulate French economic growth** 1690 **Paris Foundling Hospital established**	1605 **Bacon, *The Advancement of Learning*; Shakespeare, *King Lear*, Cervantes, *Don Quixote*** 1609 **Kepler, *On the Motion of Mars*** 1611 **King James Version of the English Bible** 1632 **Galileo, *Dialogues on the Two Chief Systems of the World*** 1637 **Descartes, *Discourse on Method*** 1651 **Hobbes, *Leviathan*** 1687 **Newton, *Principia Mathematica*** 1689 **English Toleration Act** 1690 **Locke, *Essay Concerning Human Understanding***
1700–1789	1700–1721 **Great Northern War between Sweden and Russia** 1702–1714 **War of Spanish Succession** 1713 **Peace of Utrecht** 1720–1740 **Age of Walpole in England and Fleury in France** 1740 **Maria Theresa succeeds to the Habsburg throne** 1740–1748 **War of the Austrian Succession** 1756–1763 **Seven Years' War** 1767 **Legislative Commission in Russia** 1772 **First Partition of Poland** 1776 **American Declaration of Independence** 1778 **France aids the American colonies**	1715–1763 **Era of major colonial rivalry in the Caribbean** 1719 **Mississippi Bubble in France** 1733 **James Kay's flying shuttle** 1750s **Agricultural Revolution in Britain** 1750–1840 **Growth of new cities** 1763 **Britain becomes dominant in India** 1763–1789 **Enlightened absolutist rulers seek to spur economic growth** 1765 **James Hargreaves's spinning jenny** 1769 **Richard Arkwright's waterframe** 1771–1775 **Pugachev's Rebellion**	1739 **Wesley begins field preaching** 1748 **Montesquieu, *Spirit of the Laws*** 1750 **Rousseau, *Discourse on the Moral Effects of the Arts and Sciences*** 1751 **First volume Diderot's *Encyclopedia*** 1762 **Rousseau, *Social Contract* and *Émile*** 1763 **Voltaire, Treatise on Toleration** 1774 **Goethe, *Sorrow of Young Werther*** 1775 **Smith, *Wealth of Nations*** 1781 **Kant, *Critique of Pure Reason*** **Joseph II adopts policy of toleration in Austria**

Declaration of Independence

CHAPTER 9

The apparition of the Knight of Death, an allegory of the plague approaching a city, whose defenses against it are all too unsure. From the Tres Riches Heures du Duc de Berry *(1284), [Limbourg Brothers. Ms. 65/1284, fol. 90v. Musee Conde, Chantilly, France. Giraudon/Art Resource, N.Y.]*

The Late Middle Ages (1300–1527): Centuries of Crisis

KEY TOPICS

- The Hundred Years' War between England and France
- The effects of the bubonic plague on population and society
- The growing power of secular rulers over the papacy
- Schism, heresy, and reform of the church

The late Middle Ages saw almost unprecedented political, social, and ecclesiastical calamity. France and England grappled with each other in a bitter conflict known as the Hundred Years' War (1337–1453), an exercise in seemingly willful self-destruction that was made even more terrible in its later stages by the introduction of gunpowder and the invention of heavy artillery. Bubonic plague, known to contemporaries as the "Black Death," swept over almost all of Europe, killing as much as one-third of the population in many regions between 1348 and 1350 and transforming many pious Christians into believers in the omnipotence of death. A schism emerged within the church, which lasted thirty-nine years (1378–1417) and led, by 1409, to the election of no fewer than three competing popes and colleges of cardinals. In 1453 the Turks marched seemingly invincibly through Constantinople and toward the West. As their political and religious institutions buckled, as disease, bandits, and wolves attacked their cities in the wake of war, and as Islamic armies gathered at their borders, Europeans beheld what seemed to be the imminent total collapse of Western civilization.

It was in this period that such scholars as Marsilius of Padua, William of Ockham, and Lorenzo Valla produced lasting criticisms of medieval assumptions about the nature of God, humankind, and society. Kings worked through parliaments and clergy through councils to place lasting limits on the pope's temporal power. The notion, derived from Roman law, that a secular ruler is accountable to the body of which he or she is head had already found expression in documents like Magna Carta. It came increasingly to carry the force of accepted principle and conciliarists (advocates of the judicial superiority of a church council over a pope) sought to extend it to establish papal accountability to the church.

But viewed for their three great calamities—war, plague, and schism—the fourteenth and fifteenth centuries were years in which politics resisted wisdom, nature strained mercy, and the church was less than faithful to its mandate.

Political and Social Breakdown

The Hundred Years' War and the Rise of National Sentiment

Medieval governments were by no means all-powerful and secure. The rivalry of petty lords kept localities in turmoil and dynastic rivalries could plunge entire lands into war, especially when power was being transferred to a new ruler, and woe to the ruling dynasty that failed to produce a male heir.

To field the armies and collect the revenues that made their existence possible, late medieval rulers depended on carefully negotiated alliances among a wide range of lesser powers. Like kings and queens in earlier centuries, they too practiced the art of feudal government, but on a grander scale and with greater sophistication. To maintain the order they required, the Norman kings of England and the Capetian kings of France fine-tuned traditional feudal relationships, stressing the duties of lesser to higher power and the unquestioning loyalty noble vassals owed the king. The result was a degree of centralized royal power unseen before in these lands and a nascent "national" consciousness that equipped both France and England for international warfare.

THE CAUSES OF THE WAR The conflict that came to be known as the Hundred Years' War began in May 1337 and lasted until October 1453. The English king Edward III (r. 1327–1377), the grandson of Philip the Fair of France (r. 1285–1314), may be said to have started the war by asserting a claim to the French throne when the French king Charles IV (r. 1322–1328), the last of Philip the Fair's surviving sons, died without a male heir. The French barons had no intention of placing the then fifteen-year-old Edward on the French throne, choosing instead the first cousin of Charles IV, Philip VI of Valois (r. 1328–1350), the first of a new French dynasty that ruled into the sixteenth century.

But there was more to the war than just an English king's assertion of a claim to the French throne. England and France were then emergent territorial powers in too close proximity to one another. Edward was actually a vassal of Philip's, holding several sizable French territories as fiefs from the king of France, a relationship that went back to the days of the Norman conquest. English possession of any French land was repugnant to the French because it threatened the royal policy of centralization. England and France also quarreled over control of Flanders, which, although a French fief, was subject to political influence from England because its principal industry, the manufacture of cloth, depended on supplies of imported English wool. Compounding these frictions was a long history of prejudice and animosity between the French and English people, who constantly confronted one another on the high seas and in port towns. Taken together, these various factors made the Hundred Years' War a struggle for national identity as well as for control of territory.

Edward III pays homage to his feudal lord Philip VI of France. Legally, Edward was a vassal of the king of France. [Archives Snark International/Art Resource, N.Y.]

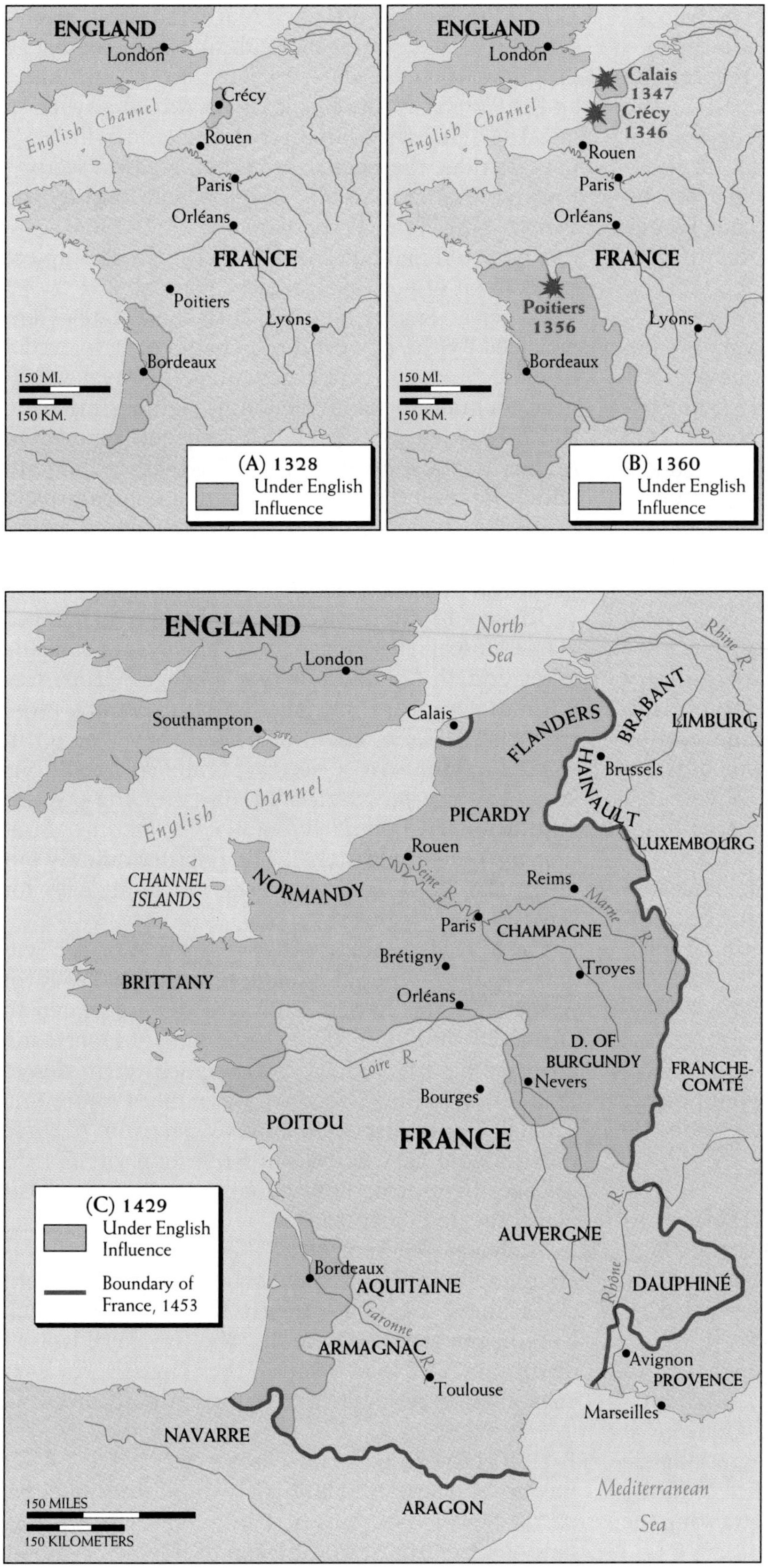

MAP 9–1 THE HUNDRED YEARS' WAR *The Hundred Years' War went on intermittently from the late 1330s until 1453. These maps show the remarkable English territorial gains up to the sudden and decisive turning of the tide of battle in favor of the French by the forces of Joan of Arc in 1429.*

French Weakness France had three times the population of England, was far the wealthier of the two countries, and fought on its own soil. Yet, for the greater part of the conflict, until after 1415, the major battles ended in often stunning English victories. (See Map 9-1.) The primary reason for these French failures was internal disunity caused by endemic social conflicts. Unlike England, France was still struggling in the fourteenth century to make the transition from a fragmented feudal society to a centralized "modern" state.

Desperate to raise money for the war, French kings resorted to such financial policies as depreciating the currency and borrowing heavily from Italian bankers, which aggravated internal conflicts. In 1355, in a bid to secure funds, the king convened a representative council of townspeople and nobles that came to be known as the Estates General. Although it levied taxes at the king's request, its members also used the king's plight to enhance their own regional rights and privileges, thereby deepening territorial divisions.

France's defeats also reflected English military superiority. The English infantry was more disciplined than the French, and English archers carried a formidable weapon, the longbow, capable of firing six arrows a minute with enough force to pierce an inch of wood or the armor of a knight at two hundred yards.

Finally, French weakness during the Hundred Years' War was due in no small degree to the comparative mediocrity of its royal leadership. English kings were far the shrewder.

Progress of the War

The war had three major stages of development, each ending with a seemingly decisive victory by one or the other side.

The Conflict During the Reign of Edward III In the first stage of the war, Edward embargoed English wool to Flanders, sparking urban rebellions by merchants and the trade guilds. Inspired by a rich merchant, Jacob van Artevelde, the Flemish cities, led by Ghent, revolted against the French and in 1340 these same cities signed an alliance with England acknowledging Edward as king of France. On June 23 of that same year, in the first great battle of the war, Edward defeated the French fleet in the Bay of Sluys, but his subsequent effort to invade France by way of Flanders failed.

In 1346 Edward attacked Normandy and, after a series of easy victories that culminated at the Battle of Crécy, seized Calais. Exhaustion of both sides and the onset of the Black Death forced a truce in late 1347, and the war entered a brief lull. In 1356, near Poitiers, the English won their greatest victory, routing France's noble cavalry and taking the French king, John II the Good (r. 1350–1364), captive back to England. The defeat brought a complete breakdown of political order to France.

Power in France now lay with the Estates General. Led by the powerful merchants of Paris under Étienne Marcel, it took advantage of royal weakness, demanding and receiving rights similar to those granted the English privileged classes in Magna Carta. But unlike the English Parliament, which represented the interests of a comparatively unified English nobility, the French Estates General was too divided to be an instrument for effective government.

To secure their rights, the French privileged classes forced the peasantry to pay ever-increasing taxes and to repair their war-damaged properties without compensation. This bullying became more than the peasants could bear, and they rose up in several regions in a series of bloody rebellions known as the *Jacquerie* in 1358 (after the peasant revolutionary popularly known as *Jacques Bonhomme* or "simple Jack"). The nobility quickly put down the revolt, matching the rebels atrocity for atrocity.

On May 9, 1360, another milestone of the war was reached when England forced the Peace of Brétigny on the French. This agreement declared an end to Edward's vassalage to the king of France and affirmed his sovereignty over English territories in France (including Gascony, Guyenne, Poitou, and Calais). France also agreed to pay a ransom of three million gold crowns to win King John the Good's release. In return, Edward simply renounced his claim to the French throne.

Such a partition of French territorial control was completely unrealistic, and sober observers on both sides knew it could not last long. France struck back in the late 1360s and by the time of Edward's death in 1377 had beaten the English back to coastal enclaves and the territory of Bordeaux.

French Defeat and the Treaty of Troyes After Edward's death the English war effort lessened, partly because of domestic problems within England. During the reign of Richard II (r. 1377–1399),

This miniature illustrates two scenes from the English peasant revolt of 1381. On the left, Wat Tyler, one of the leaders of the revolt, is executed in the presence of King Richard II. On the right, King Richard urges armed peasants to end their rebellion. [The Bridgeman Art Library/Art Resource, N.Y.]

England had its own version of the *Jacquerie*. In June 1381 long-oppressed peasants and artisans joined in a great revolt of the unprivileged classes under the leadership of John Ball, a secular priest, and Wat Tyler, a journeyman. As in France, the revolt was brutally crushed within the year. But it left the country divided for decades.

The war intensified under Henry V (r. 1413–1422), who took advantage of internal French turmoil created by the rise to power of the duchy of Burgundy. With France deeply divided, Henry V struck hard in Normandy. Happy to see the rest of France besieged, the Burgundians foolishly watched from the sidelines while Henry's army routed the opposition led by the count of Armagnac, who had picked up the royal banner at Agincourt on October 25, 1415. In the years thereafter, belatedly recognizing that the defeat of France would leave them easy prey for the English, the Burgundians closed ranks with French royal forces. This renewed French unity, loose as it was, promised to bring eventual victory over the English, but it was shattered in September 1419 when the duke of Burgundy was assassinated. In the aftermath of this shocking event the duke's son and heir, determined to avenge his father's death, joined forces with the English.

France now became Henry V's for the taking—at least in the short run. The Treaty of Troyes in 1420 disinherited the legitimate heir to the French throne and proclaimed Henry V the successor to the French king, Charles VI. When Henry and Charles died within months of one another in 1422, the infant Henry VI of England was proclaimed in Paris to be king of both France and England. The dream of Edward III that had set the war in motion—to make the ruler of England the ruler also of France—had been realized, at least for the moment.

The son of Charles VI went into retreat in Bourges, where, on the death of his father, he became Charles VII to most of the French people, who ignored the Treaty of Troyes. Displaying unprecedented national feeling inspired by the remarkable Joan of Arc, they soon rallied to his cause and came together in an ultimately victorious coalition.

JOAN OF ARC AND THE WAR'S CONCLUSION Joan of Arc (1412–1431), a peasant from Domrémy, presented herself to Charles VII in March 1429, declaring that the King of Heaven had called her to deliver besieged Orléans from the English. The king was understandably skeptical, but being in retreat from what seemed to be a hopeless war, he was willing to try anything to reverse French fortunes. And the deliverance of Orléans, a city strategic to the control of the territory south of the Loire, would be a godsend. Charles's desperation overcame his skepticism, and he gave Joan his leave.

Circumstances worked perfectly to her advantage. The English force was already exhausted by a six-month siege of Orléans and at the point of withdrawal when Joan arrived with fresh French troops. After repulsing the English from Orléans, the French enjoyed a succession of victories they popularly attributed to Joan. She deserved much of this credit, but not because she was a military genius. She provided the French with something military experts could not: inspiration and a sense of national identity and self-confidence. Within a few months of the liberation of Orléans, Charles VII received his crown in Rheims and ended the nine-year "disinheritance" prescribed by the Treaty of Troyes.

Charles forgot his liberator as quickly as he had embraced her. When the Burgundians captured Joan in May 1430, he was in a position to secure her release but did little for her. The Burgundians and the English wanted her publicly discredited, believing this would also discredit Charles VII and demoralize French resistance. She was turned over to the Inquisition in English-held Rouen. The inquisitors broke the courageous "Maid of Orléans" after ten weeks of interrogation, and she was executed as a relapsed heretic on May 30, 1431. Twenty-five years

Joan of Arc Refuses to Recant Her Beliefs

Joan of Arc, threatened with torture, refused to recent her beliefs and instead defended the instructions she had received from the voices that spoke to her.

✦ *In the following excerpt from her self-defense, do you get the impression that the judges have made up their minds about Joan in advance? How does this judicial process, which was based on intensive interrogation of the accused, differ from a trial today? Why was Joan deemed heretical and not insane when she acknowledged hearing voices?*

On Wednesday, May 9th of the same year [1431], Joan was brought into the great tower of the castle of Rouen before us the said judges. And [she] was required and admonished to speak the truth on many different points contained in her trial which she had denied or to which she had given false replies, whereas we possessed certain information, proofs, and vehement presumptions upon them. Many of the points were read and explained to her, and she was told that if she did not confess them truthfully she would be put to the torture, the instruments of which were shown to her all ready in the tower. There were also present by our instruction men ready to put her to the torture in order to restore her to the way and knowledge of truth, and by this means to procure the salvation of her body and soul which by her lying inventions she exposed to such grave perils.

To which the said Joan answered in this manner: "Truly if you were to tear me limb from limb and separate my soul from my body, I would not tell you anything more: and if I did say anything, I should afterwards declare that you had compelled me to say it by force." Then she said that on Holy Cross Day last she received comfort from St. Gabriel; she firmly believes it was St. Gabriel. She knew by her voices whether she should submit to the Church, since the clergy were pressing her hard to submit. Her voices told her that if she desired Our Lord to aid her she must wait upon Him in all her doings. She said that Our Lord has always been the master of her doings, and the Enemy never had power over them. She asked her voices if she would be burned and they answered that she must wait upon God, and He would aid her.

The Trial of Jeanne D'Arc, trans. by W. P. Barrett (New York: Gotham House, 1932), pp. 303–304.

A contemporary portrait of Joan of Arc (1412–1431) in the National Archives in Paris. [Giraudon/Art Resource, N.Y.]

later (1456) Charles reopened her trial, and she was declared innocent of all the charges. In 1920 the church declared her a saint.

In 1435 the duke of Burgundy made peace with Charles. France, now unified and at peace with Burgundy, continued progressively to force the English back. By 1453, the date of the war's end, the English held only their coastal enclave of Calais.

The Hundred Years' War, with sixty-eight years of at least nominal peace and forty-four of hot war, had lasting political and social consequences. It devastated France, but it also awakened French nationalism and hastened the transition there from a feudal monarchy to a centralized state. It saw Burgundy become a major European political power. And it encouraged the English, in response to the seesawing allegiance of the Netherlands throughout the conflict, to develop their own clothing industry and foreign markets. In both France and England the burden of the on-again, off-again war fell most heavily on the peasantry, who were forced to support it with taxes and services.

The Hundred Years' War (1337–1443)

1340	English victory at Bay of Sluys
1346	English victory at Crécy and seizure of Calais
1347	Black Death strikes
1356	English victory at Poitiers
1358	*Jacquerie* disrupts France
1360	Peace of Brétigny recognizes English holdings in France
1381	English peasants revolt
1415	English victory at Agincourt
1422	Treaty of Troyes proclaims Henry VI ruler of both England and France
1429	Joan of Arc leads French to victory at Orléans
1431	Joan of Arc executed as a heretic
1453	War ends; English retain only coastal town of Calais

The Black Death

Preconditions and Causes

In the late Middle Ages, nine-tenths of the population worked the land. The three-field system, in use in most areas since well before the fourteenth century, had increased the amount of arable land and thereby the food supply. The growth of cities and trade had also stimulated agricultural science and productivity. But as the food supply grew, so also did the population. It is estimated that Europe's population doubled between the years 1000 and 1300 and by 1300 had begun to outstrip food production. There were now more people than there was food available to feed them or jobs to employ them, and the average European faced the probability of extreme hunger at least once during his or her expected thirty-five-year life span.

Between 1315 and 1317 crop failures produced the greatest famine of the Middle Ages. Densely populated urban areas like the industrial towns of the Netherlands experienced great suffering. Decades of overpopulation, economic depression, famine, and bad health progressively weakened Europe's population and made it highly vulnerable to a virulent bubonic plague that struck with full force in 1348.

This "Black Death," so called by contemporaries because of the way it discolored the body, was probably introduced by sea-borne rats from Black Sea areas, and followed the trade routes from Asia into

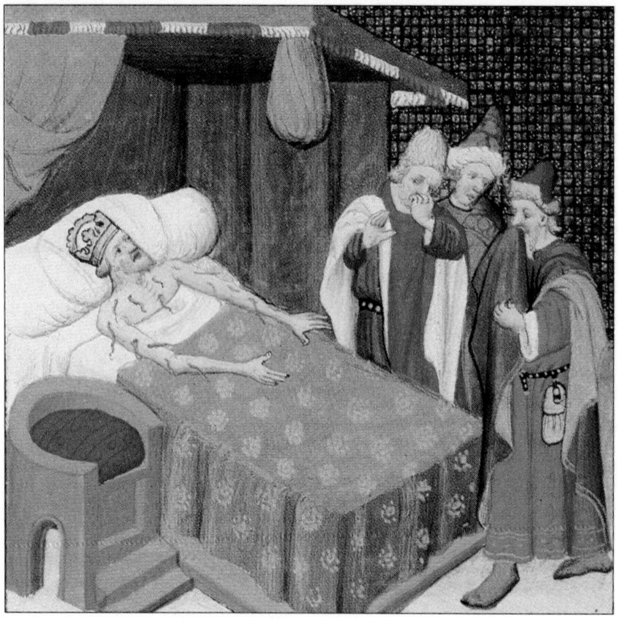

In this scene from an illustrated manuscript of Boccaccio's Decameron, *physicians apply leeches to an emperor. The text says he suffered from a disease that caused a terrible stench, which is why the physicians are holding their noses. Bleeding was the agreed-upon best way to prevent and cure illness and was practiced as late as the nineteenth century. Its popularity was rooted in the belief that a build-up of foul matter in the body caused illness by disrupting the body's four humors (blood, phlegm, yellow bile, and black bile). Bleeding released the foul matter and restored equilibrium among the humors, thus preserving good health by strengthening resistance to disease. [Jean-Loup Charmet/Science Photo Library]*

Europe. Appearing in Sicily in late 1347, it entered Europe through the port cities of Venice, Genoa, and Pisa in 1348, and from there it swept rapidly through Spain and southern France and into northern Europe. Areas that lay outside the major trade routes, like Bohemia, appear to have remained virtually unaffected.

Bubonic plague made numerous reappearances in succeeding decades. By the early fifteenth century, it is estimated that western Europe as a whole had lost as much as two-fifths of its population. There was not a full recovery until the sixteenth century. (See Map 9-2.)

Popular Remedies

The plague, transmitted by rat- or human-borne fleas, often reached a victim's lungs during the course of the disease. From the lungs it could be spread from person to person by the victim's sneezing and wheezing. Contemporary physicians had no understanding of these processes, and so even the most rudimentary prophylaxis against the disease was lacking. To the people of the time the Black Death was a catastrophe with no apparent explanation and against which there was no known defense. Throughout much of western Europe it inspired an obsession with death and dying and a deep pessimism that endured for decades after the plague years.

Popular wisdom held that a corruption in the atmosphere caused the disease. Some blamed poisonous fumes released by earthquakes. Many adopted aromatic amulets as a remedy. According to the contemporary observations of Boccaccio, who recorded the varied reactions to the plague in the *Decameron* (1353), some sought a remedy in moderation and a temperate life; others gave themselves over entirely to their passions (sexual promiscuity within the stricken areas apparently ran high); and still others, "the most sound, perhaps, in judgment," chose flight and seclusion as the best medicine.

Among the most extreme social reactions were processions of flagellants. These religious fanatics beat themselves in ritual penance until they bled, believing that such action would bring divine intervention. The terror created by the flagellants (whose dirty bodies may have actually served to transport the disease) became so socially disruptive and threatening even to established authority that the church finally outlawed such processions.

Jews were cast as scapegoats for the plague. Centuries of Christian propaganda had bred hatred toward them, as had their willing role as society's moneylenders. Pogroms occurred in several cities, sometimes incited by the arrival of flagellants.

Social and Economic Consequences

Whole villages vanished in the wake of the plague. Among the social and economic consequences of this depopulation were a shrunken labor supply and a decline in the value of the estates of the nobility.

FARMS DECLINE As the number of farm laborers decreased, their wages increased and those of skilled artisans soared. Many serfs now chose to commute their labor services by money payments or to abandon the farm altogether and pursue more interesting and rewarding jobs in skilled craft industries in the cities. Agricultural prices fell because of low-

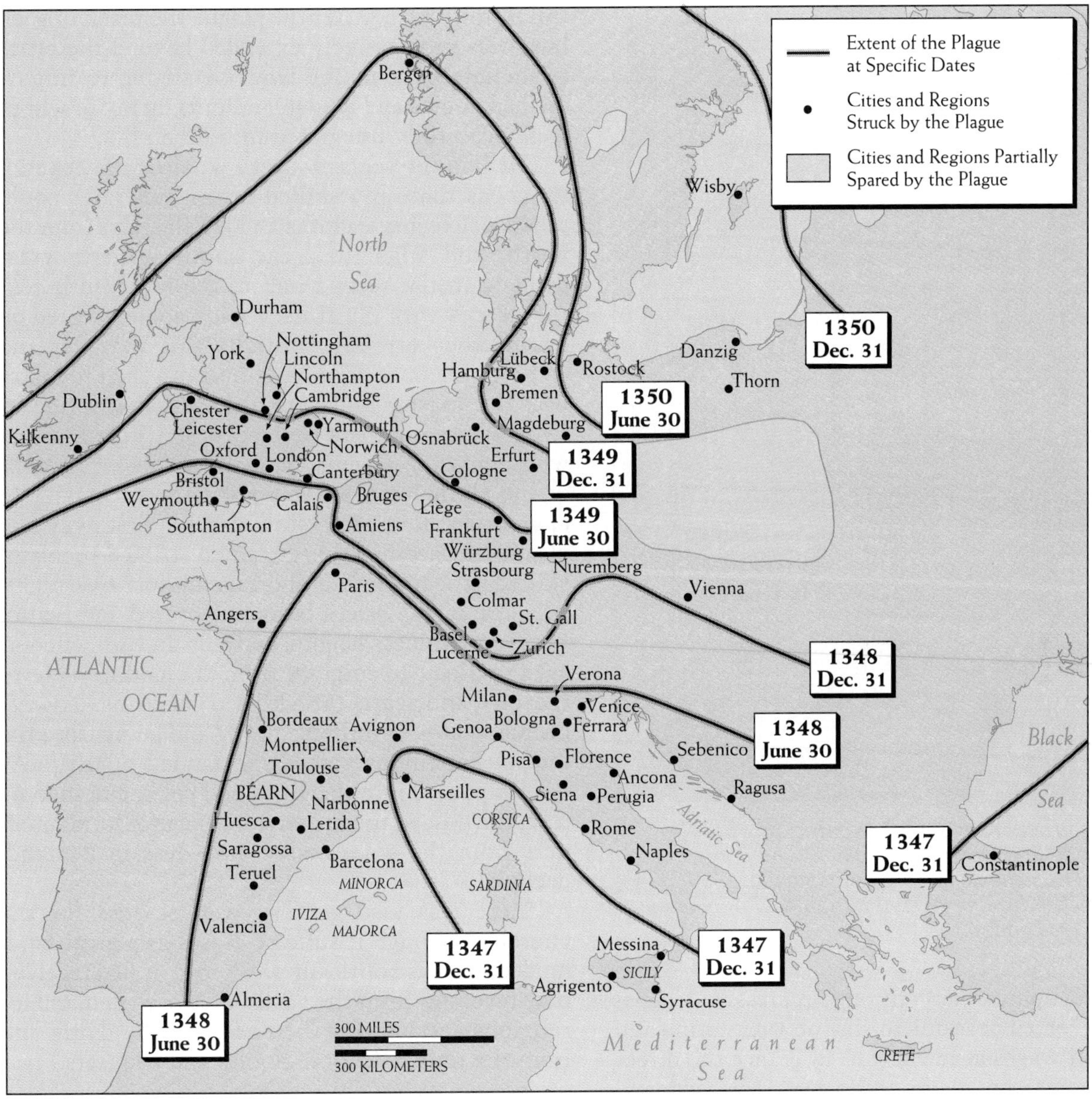

MAP 9–2 SPREAD OF THE BLACK DEATH *Apparently introduced by sea-borne rats from Black Sea areas where plague-infested rodents have long been known, the Black Death brought huge human, social, and economic consequences. One of the lower estimates of Europeans dying is 25,000,000. The map charts the plague's spread in the mid-fourteenth century. Generally following trade routes, the plague reached Scandinavia by 1350, and some believe it then went on to Iceland and even Greenland. Areas off the main trade routes were largely spared.*

ered demand, and the price of luxury and manufactured goods—the work of skilled artisans—rose. The noble landholders suffered the greatest decline in power from this new state of affairs. They were forced to pay more for finished products and for farm labor but received a smaller return on their agricultural produce. Everywhere their rents were in steady decline after the plague.

PEASANTS REVOLT To recoup their losses, some landowners converted arable land to sheep pasture, substituting more profitable wool production for labor-intensive grain crops. Others abandoned the effort to farm their land and simply leased it to the highest bidder. Landowners also sought simply to reverse their misfortune—to close off the new economic opportunities opened for the peasantry by

A Renaissance portrayal of the sixth century (590) procession of St. Gregory to St. Peter's, an effort to end a plague. From the Soane Book of Hours *(c. 1500). [Sir John Soane's Museum. AD590 for removal of placque. E.T. Archive, London.]*

the demographic crisis—through repressive legislation that forced peasants to stay on their farms and froze their wages at low levels. In France the direct tax on the peasantry, the *taille*, was increased, and opposition to it was prominent among the grievances behind the *Jacquerie*. In 1351, the English Parliament passed a Statute of Laborers, which limited wages to preplague levels and restricted the ability of peasants to leave the land of their traditional masters. Opposition to such legislation was also a prominent factor in the English peasants' revolt in 1381.

CITIES REBOUND Although the plague hit urban populations especially hard, the cities and their skilled industries came, in time, to prosper from its effects. Cities had always been careful to protect their interests; as they grew, they passed legislation to regulate competition from rural areas and to control immigration. After the plague the reach of such laws was progressively extended beyond the cities to include surrounding lands belonging to impoverished nobles and feudal landlords, many of whom were peacefully integrated into urban life.

The omnipresence of death whetted the appetite for goods that only skilled urban industries could produce. Expensive cloths and jewelry, furs from the north, and silks from the south were in great demand in the second half of the fourteenth century. Faced with life at its worst, people insisted on having the very best. Initially this new demand could not be met. The basic unit of urban industry was the master and apprentices (usually one or two), whose numbers were purposely kept low and whose privileges were jealously guarded. The craft of the skilled artisan was passed from master to apprentice only very slowly. The first wave of plague transformed this already restricted supply of skilled artisans into a shortage almost overnight. As a result, the prices of manufactured and luxury items rose to new heights and this, in turn, encouraged workers to migrate from the countryside to the city and learn the skills of artisans. Townspeople in effect profited coming and going from the forces that impoverished the landed nobility. As wealth poured into the cities and per capita income rose, the cost to urban dwellers of agricultural products from the countryside, now less in demand, declined.

There was also gain as well as loss for the church. Although it suffered losses as a great landholder and was politically weakened, it had received new revenues from the vastly increased demand for religious services for the dead and the dying and from the multiplication of gifts and bequests.

New Conflicts and Opportunities

By increasing the importance of skilled artisans, the plague contributed to new conflicts within the cities. The economic and political power of local artisans and trade guilds grew steadily in the late Middle Ages along with the demand for their goods and services. The merchant and patrician classes found it increasingly difficult to maintain their traditional dominance and grudgingly gave guild masters a voice in city government. As the guilds won political power, they encouraged restrictive legislation to protect local industries. These restrictions, in turn, brought confrontations between master artisans, who wanted to keep their numbers low and expand their industries at a snail's pace, and the many journeymen, who were eager to rise to the rank of master. To the long-existing conflict between the guilds and the urban patriciate was now added a conflict within the guilds themselves.

After 1350 the two traditional "containers" of monarchy—the landed nobility and the church—were politically on the defensive, and to no small degree as a consequence of the plague. Kings took full advantage of the new situation, drawing on growing national sentiment to centralize their governments and economies. As already noted, the plague reduced the economic power of the landed nobility. In the same period the battles of the Hundred Years' War demonstrated the military superiority of paid professional armies over the traditional noble cavalry, thus bringing into question the traditional role of the nobility. The plague also killed many members of the clergy—perhaps one-third of the German clergy fell victim to it as they

Boccaccio Describes the Ravages of the Black Death in Florence

The Black Death provided an excuse to the poet, humanist, and storyteller Giovanni Boccaccio (1313–1375) to assemble his great collection of tales, the Decameron. *Ten congenial men and women flee Florence to escape the plague and while away the time telling stories. In one of the stories, Boccaccio embeds a fine clinical description of plague symptoms as seen in Florence in 1348 and of the powerlessness of physicians and the lack of remedies.*

✦ *What did people do to escape the plague? Was any of it sound medical practice? What does the study of calamities like the Black Death tell us about the people of the past?*

In Florence, despite all that human wisdom and forethought could devise to avert it, even as the cleansing of the city from many impurities by officials appointed for the purpose, the refusal of entrance to all sick folk, and the adoption of many precautions for the preservation of health; despite also humble supplications addressed to God, and often repeated both in public procession and otherwise, by the devout; towards the beginning of the spring of the said year [1348] the doleful effects of the pestilence began to be horribly apparent by symptoms that [appeared] as if miraculous.

Not such were these symptoms as in the East, where an issue of blood from the nose was a manifest sign of inevitable death; but in men and women alike it first betrayed itself by the emergence of certain tumours in the groin or the armpits, some of which grew as large as a common apple, others as an egg, some more, some less, which the common folk called gavoccioli. From the two said parts of the body this deadly gavoccioli soon began to propagate and spread itself in all directions indifferently; after which the form of the malady began to change, spots black or livid making their appearance in many cases on the arm or the thigh or elsewhere, now few and large, now minute and numerous. And as the gavoccioli had been and still were an infallible token of approaching death, such also were these spots on whomsoever they shewed themselves. Which maladies seemed to set entirely at naught both the art of the physician and the virtues of physic; indeed, whether it was that the disorder was of a nature to defy such treatment, or that the physicians were at fault . . . and, being in ignorance of its source, failed to apply the proper remedies; in either case, not merely were those that recovered few, but almost all died within three days of the appearance of the said symptoms . . . and in most cases without any fever or other attendant malady.

The Decameron of Giovanni Boccaccio, *trans. by J. M. Rigg (London: J. M. Dent & Sons, 1930), p. 5.*

A caricature of physicians (early sixteenth century). In the Middle Ages and later, people recognized the shortcomings of physicians and surgeons and visited them only as a last resort. Here a physician carries a uroscope (for collecting and examining urine); cloudy or discolored urine signaled an immediate need for bleeding. The physician/surgeon wears surgical shoes and his assistant carries a flail—a comment on the risks of medical services. [Hacker Art Books]

dutifully ministered to the sick and dying. The reduction in clerical ranks occurred in the same century in which the residence of the pope in Avignon (1309–1377) and the Great Schism (1378–1415) were undermining much of the church's popular support.

Ecclesiastical Breakdown and Revival: The Late Medieval Church

At first glance the popes may appear to have been in a very favorable position in the latter half of the thirteenth century. Frederick II had been vanquished and imperial pressure on Rome had been removed. The French king, Louis IX, was an enthusiastic supporter of the church, as evidenced by his two disastrous Crusades, which won him sainthood. Although it lasted only seven years, a reunion of the Eastern church with Rome was proclaimed by the Council of Lyons in 1274, when the Western church took advantage of Emperor Michael Palaeologus's request for aid against the Turks. But despite these positive events, the church was not really in as favorable a position as it appeared.

The Thirteenth-Century Papacy

As early as the reign of Pope Innocent III (r. 1198–1216), when papal power reached its height, there were ominous developments. Innocent had elaborated the doctrine of papal plenitude of power and on that authority had declared saints, disposed of *benefices*, and created a centralized papal monarchy with a clearly political mission. Innocent's transformation of the papacy into a great secular power weakened the church spiritually even as it strengthened it politically. Thereafter the church as a papal monarchy and the church as the "body of the faithful" came increasingly to be differentiated. It was against the "papal church" and in the name of the "true Christian Church" that both reformers and heretics raised their voices in protest until the Protestant Reformation.

What Innocent began, his successors perfected. Under Urban IV (r. 1261–1264) the papacy established its own law court, the *Rota Romana*, which tightened and centralized the church's legal proceedings. The latter half of the thirteenth century saw an elaboration of the system of clerical taxation; what had begun in the twelfth century as an emergency measure to raise funds for the Crusades became a fixed institution. In the same period, papal power to determine appointments to many major and minor church offices—the "reservation of *benefices*"—was greatly broadened. The thirteenth-century papacy became a powerful political institution governed by its own law and courts, serviced by an efficient international bureaucracy, and preoccupied with secular goals.

Papal centralization of the church undermined both diocesan authority and popular support. Rome's interests, not local needs, came to control church appointments, policies, and discipline. Discontented lower clergy appealed to the higher authority of Rome against the disciplinary measures of local bishops. In the second half of the thirteenth century, bishops and abbots protested such undercutting of their power. To its critics, the church in Rome was hardly more than a legalized, fiscalized, bureaucratic institution. As early as the late twelfth century, heretical movements of Cathars and Waldensians had appealed to the biblical ideal of simplicity and separation from the world. Other reformers unquestionably loyal to the church, such as Saint Francis of Assisi, would also protest a perceived materialism in official religion.

Political Fragmentation The church of the thirteenth century was being undermined by more than internal religious disunity. The demise of imperial power meant that the papacy in Rome was no longer the leader of anti-imperial (Guelf, or propapal) sentiment in Italy. Instead of being the center of Italian resistance to the emperor, popes now found themselves on the defensive against their old allies. That was the ironic price paid by the papacy to vanquish the Hohenstaufens.

Rulers with a stake in Italian politics now directed the intrigue formerly aimed at the emperor toward the College of Cardinals. For example, Charles of Anjou, king of Sicily, managed to create a French–Sicilian faction within the college. Such efforts to control the decisions of the college led Pope Gregory X (r. 1271–1276) to establish the practice of sequestering the cardinals immediately on the death of the pope. The purpose of this so-called conclave of cardinals was to minimize extraneous political influence on the election of new popes, but the college had become so politicized that it proved to be of little avail.

In 1294 such a conclave, in frustration after a deadlock of more than two years, chose a saintly but inept Calabrian hermit as Pope Celestine V. Celestine abdicated under suspicious circumstances after only a few weeks in office. He also died under suspicious circumstances; his successor's critics later argued that he had been murdered for political reasons by the powers behind the papal throne to ensure the survival of the papal office. His tragicomic reign shocked a majority of the College of Cardinals into unified action. He was quickly replaced by his very opposite, Pope Boniface VIII (r. 1294–1303), a nobleman and a skilled politician. His pontificate, however, would augur the beginning of the end of papal pretensions to great power status.

Pope Boniface VIII (r. 1294–1303), depicted here, opposed the taxation of the clergy by the kings of France and England and issued one of the strongest declarations of papal authority over rulers, the bull Unam Sanctam. *This statue is in the Museo Civico, Bologna, Italy. [Scala/Art Resource, N.Y.]*

Boniface VIII and Philip the Fair

Boniface came to rule when England and France were maturing as nation-states. In England a long

Boniface VIII Reasserts the Church's Claim to Temporal Power

Defied by the French and the English, Pope Boniface VIII (r. 1294–1303) boldly reasserted the temporal power of the church in the bull Unam Sanctam *(November 1302). This document claimed that both spiritual and temporal power on earth were under the pope's jurisdiction, because in the hierarchy of the universe spiritual power both preceded and sat in judgment on temporal power.*

✦ *On what does the pope base his claims to supremacy? Is his argument logical, or does he beg the question? On what basis did secular rulers attack his arguments?*

We are taught by the words of the Gospel that in this church and in her power there are two swords, a spiritual one and a temporal one. . . . Certainly anyone who denies that the temporal sword is in the power of Peter has not paid heed to the words of the Lord when he said, "Put up thy sword into its sheath" (Matthew 26:52). Both then are in the power of the church, the material sword and the spiritual. But the one is exercised for the church, the other by the church, the one by the hand of the priest, the other by the hand of kings and soldiers, though at the will and suffrance of the authority subject to the spiritual power. . . . For, according to the blessed Dionysius, it is the law of divinity for the lowest to be led to the highest through intermediaries. In the order of the universe all things are not kept in order in the same fashion and immediately but the lowest are ordered by the intermediate and inferiors by superiors. But that the spiritual power excels any earthly one in dignity and nobility we ought the more openly to confess in proportion as spiritual things excel temporal ones. Moreover we clearly perceive this from the giving of tithes, from benediction and sanctification, from the acceptance of this power and from the very government of things. For, the truth bearing witness, the spiritual power has to institute the earthly power and to judge it if it has not been good. So it is verified the prophecy of Jeremiah (1:10) concerning the church and the power of the church, "Lo, I have set thee this day over the nations and over kingdoms."

As quoted in Brian Tierney, The Crisis of Church and State 1050–1300 *(Englewood Cliffs, N.J.: Prentice-Hall, 1964), pp. 188–189. Used by permission of the publisher.*

tradition of consultation between the king and powerful members of English society evolved into formal "parliaments" during the reigns of Henry III (r. 1216–1272) and Edward I (r. 1272–1307), and these meetings helped to create a unified kingdom. The reign of the French king Philip IV the Fair (1285–1314) saw France become an efficient, centralized monarchy. Philip was no Saint Louis, but a ruthless politician. He was determined to end England's continental holdings, control wealthy Flanders, and establish French hegemony within the Holy Roman Empire.

Boniface had the further misfortune of bringing to the papal throne memories of the way earlier popes had brought kings and emperors to their knees. Very painfully he was to discover that the papal monarchy of the early thirteenth century was no match for the new political powers of the late thirteenth century.

The Royal Challenge to Papal Authority

France and England were on the brink of all-out war when Boniface became pope in 1294. Only Edward I's preoccupation with rebellion in Scotland, which the French encouraged, prevented him from invading France and starting the Hundred Years' War a half century earlier than it did start. As both countries mobilized for war, they used the pretext of preparing for a Crusade to tax the clergy heavily. In 1215 Pope Innocent III had decreed that the clergy were to pay no taxes to rulers without prior papal consent. Viewing English and French taxation of the clergy as an assault on traditional clerical rights, Boniface took a strong stand against it. On February 5, 1296, he issued a bull, *Clericis laicos*, which forbade lay taxation of the clergy without prior papal approval and took back all previous papal dispensations in this regard.

In England Edward I retaliated by denying the clergy the right to be heard in royal court, in effect removing from them the protection of the king. But it was Philip the Fair who struck back with a vengeance. In August 1296 he forbade the exportation of money from France to Rome, thereby denying the papacy revenues it needed to operate. Boniface had no choice but to come quickly to terms with Philip. He conceded Philip the right to tax the French clergy "during an emergency," and, not coincidentally, he canonized Louis IX in the same year.

Boniface was then also under siege by powerful Italian enemies, whom Philip did not fail to patronize. A noble family (the Colonnas), rivals of Boniface's family (the Gaetani) and radical followers of Saint Francis of Assisi (the Spiritual Franciscans), were at this time seeking to invalidate Boniface's election as pope on the grounds that Celestine V had resigned the office under coercion. Charges of heresy, simony, and even the murder of Celestine were hurled against Boniface.

Boniface's fortunes appeared to revive in 1300, a "Jubilee year." During such a year, all Catholics who visited Rome and fulfilled certain conditions had the penalties for their unrepented sins remitted. Tens of thousands of pilgrims flocked to Rome in that year, and Boniface, heady with this display of popular religiosity, reinserted himself into international politics. He championed Scottish resistance to England, for which he received a firm rebuke from an outraged Edward I and from Parliament.

But once again a confrontation with the king of France proved the more costly. Philip seemed to be eager for another fight with the pope. He arrested Boniface's Parisian legate, Bernard Saisset, the bishop of Pamiers and also a powerful secular lord, whose independence Philip had opposed. Accused of heresy and treason, Saisset was tried and convicted in the king's court. Thereafter, Philip demanded that Boniface recognize the process against Saisset, something that Boniface could do only if he was prepared to surrender his jurisdiction over the French episcopate. This challenge could not be sidestepped, and Boniface acted swiftly to champion Saisset as a defender of clerical political independence within France. He demanded Saisset's unconditional release, revoked all previous agreements with Philip in the matter of clerical taxation, and ordered the French bishops to convene in Rome within a year. A bull, *Ausculta fili* or "listen, My Son," was sent to Philip in December 1301, pointedly informing him that "God has set popes over kings and kingdoms."

Unam Sanctam (1302) Philip unleashed a ruthless antipapal campaign. Two royal apologists, Pierre Dubois and John of Paris, refuted papal claims to the right to intervene in temporal matters. Increasingly placed on the defensive, Boniface made a last-ditch stand against state control of national churches. On November 18, 1302, he issued the bull *Unam Sanctam*. This famous statement of papal power declared that temporal authority was "subject" to the spiritual power of the church. On its face a bold assertion, *Unam Sanctam* was in truth the desperate act of a besieged papacy.

After *Unam Sanctam* the French and the Colonnas moved against Boniface with force. Guillaume de Nogaret, Philip's chief minister, denounced Boniface to the French clergy as a common heretic and criminal. An army, led by Nogaret and Sciarra Colonna, surprised the pope in mid-August 1303 at his retreat in Anagni. Boniface was badly beaten and almost executed before an aroused populace liberated and returned him safely to Rome. But the ordeal proved too much for him and he died a few months later, in October 1303.

Boniface's immediate successor, Benedict XI (r. 1303–1304), excommunicated Nogaret for his deed, but there was to be no lasting papal retaliation. Benedict's successor, Clement V (r. 1305–1314), was forced into French subservience. A former archbishop of Bordeaux, Clement declared that *Unam Sanctam* should not be understood as in any way diminishing French royal authority. He released Nogaret from excommunication and pliantly condemned the Knights Templars, whose treasure Philip thereafter forcibly expropriated.

In 1309 Clement moved the papal court to Avignon, an imperial city on the southeastern border of France. Situated on land that belonged to the pope, the city maintained its independence from the king. In 1311 Clement made it his permanent residence, to escape both a Rome ridden with strife after the confrontation between Boniface and Philip and further pressure from Philip. There the papacy was to remain until 1377.

After Boniface's humiliation, popes never again seriously threatened kings and emperors, despite continuing papal excommunications and political intrigue. In the future the relation between church and state would tilt in favor of the state and the control of religion by powerful monarchies. Ecclesiastical authority would become subordinate to larger secular political purposes.

The Avignon Papacy (1309–1377)

The Avignon papacy was in appearance, although not always in fact, under strong French influence. During Clement V's pontificate the French came to dominate the College of Cardinals, testing the papacy's agility both politically and economically. Finding itself cut off from its Roman estates, the papacy had to innovate to get needed funds. Clement expanded papal taxes, especially the practice of collecting *annates*, the first year's revenue of a church office or *benefice* bestowed by the pope. Clement VI (r. 1342–1352) began the practice of selling indulgences, or pardons for unrepented sins. To make the purchase of indulgences more compelling, church doctrine on purgatory—a place of punishment where souls would atone for venial sins—also developed during this period. By the fifteenth century the church had extended indulgences to cover the souls of people already dead, allowing the living to buy a reduced sentence in purgatory for their deceased loved ones. Such practices contributed to the Avignon papacy's reputation for materialism and political scheming and gave reformers new ammunition.

POPE JOHN XXII Pope John XXII (r. 1316–1334), the most powerful Avignon pope, tried to restore papal independence and to return to Italy. This goal led him into war with the Visconti, the most powerful ruling family of Milan, and a costly contest with Emperor Louis IV. John had challenged Louis's election as emperor in 1314 in favor of the rival Habsburg candidate. The result was a minor replay of the confrontation between Philip the Fair and Boniface VIII. When John obstinately and without legal justification refused to recognize Louis's election, the emperor retaliated by declaring John deposed and putting in his place an antipope. As Philip the Fair had also done, Louis enlisted the support of the Spiritual Franciscans, whose views on absolute poverty had been condemned by John as heretical. Two outstanding pamphleteers wrote lasting tracts for the royal cause: William of Ockham, whom John excommunicated in 1328, and Marsilius of Padua (ca. 1290–1342), whose teaching John declared heretical in 1327.

In his *Defender of Peace* (1324), Marsilius of Padua stressed the independent origins and autonomy of secular government. Clergy were subjected to the strictest apostolic ideals and confined to purely spiritual functions, and all power of coercive judgment was denied the pope. Marsilius argued that spiritual crimes must await an eternal punishment. Transgressions of divine law, over which the pope had jurisdiction, were to be punished in the next life, not in the present one, *unless* the secular ruler declared a divine law also a secular law. This assertion was a direct challenge of the power of the pope to excommunicate rulers and place countries under interdict. The *Defender of Peace* depicted the pope as a subordinate member of a society over which the emperor ruled supreme and in which temporal peace was the highest good.

John XXII made the papacy a sophisticated international agency and adroitly adjusted it to the growing European money economy. The more the *Curia*, or papal court, mastered the latter, however, the more vulnerable it became to criticism. Under John's successor, Benedict XII (r. 1334–1342), the papacy became entrenched in Avignon. Seemingly forgetting Rome altogether, Benedict began construction of the great Palace of the Popes and attempted to reform both papal government and the religious life. His high-living French successor, Clement VI, placed papal policy in lockstep with the French. In this period the cardinals became barely more than lobbyists for policies favorable to their secular patrons.

NATIONAL OPPOSITION TO THE AVIGNON PAPACY As Avignon's fiscal tentacles probed new areas, monarchies took strong action to protect their interests. The latter half of the fourteenth century saw legislation restricting papal jurisdiction and taxation in France, England, and Germany. In England, where the Avignon papacy was identified with the French enemy after the outbreak of the Hundred Years' War, statutes that restricted payments and appeals to Rome and the pope's power to make high ecclesiastical appointments were several times passed by Parliament between 1351 and 1393.

The Palace of the Popes in Avignon, France. In 1311, Pope Clement V made the city his permanent residence, and the popes remained there until 1377. [Fritz Henle/Photo Researchers, Inc.]

In France ecclesiastical appointments and taxation were regulated by the so-called Gallican liberties. These national rights over religion had long been exercised in fact and were legally acknowledged by the church in the *Pragmatic Sanction of Bourges*, published by Charles VII (r. 1422–1461) in 1438. This agreement recognized the right of the French church to elect its own clergy without papal interference, prohibited the payment of annates to Rome, and limited the right of appeals from French courts to the *Curia* in Rome. In German and Swiss cities in the fourteenth and fifteenth centuries, local governments also took the initiative to limit and even to overturn traditional clerical privileges and immunities.

JOHN WYCLIFFE AND JOHN HUSS The popular lay religious movements that most successfully assailed the late medieval church were the Lollards in England and the Hussites in Bohemia. The Lollards looked to the writings of John Wycliffe (d. 1384) to justify their demands, and both moderate and extreme Hussites to the writings of John Huss (d. 1415), although both Wycliffe and Huss would have disclaimed the extremists who revolted in their names.

Wycliffe was an Oxford theologian and a philosopher of high standing. His work initially served the anticlerical policies of the English government. He became within England what William of Ockham and Marsilius of Padua had been at the Bavarian court of Emperor Louis IV: a major intellectual spokesman for the rights of royalty against the secular pretensions of popes. After 1350 English kings greatly reduced the power of the Avignon papacy to make ecclesiastical appointments and collect taxes within England, a position that Wycliffe strongly supported. His views on clerical poverty followed original Franciscan ideals and, more by accident than by design, gave justification to government restriction and even confiscation of church properties within England. Wycliffe argued that the clergy "ought to be content with food and clothing."

Wycliffe also maintained that personal merit, not rank and office, was the only basis of religious authority. This was a dangerous teaching because it raised allegedly pious laypeople above allegedly corrupt ecclesiastics, regardless of the latter's offi-

Marsilius of Padua Denies Coercive Power to the Clergy

According to Marsilius, the Bible gave the pope no right to pronounce and execute sentences on any person. The clergy held a strictly moral and spiritual rule, their judgments to be executed only in the afterlife, not in the present one. Here, on earth, they should be obedient to secular authority. Marsilius argued this point by appealing to the example of Jesus.

✦ *How do Marsilius's arguments compare with those of Pope Boniface in the preceding document? Does Marsilius's argument, if accepted, destroy the worldly authority of the church? Why was his teaching condemned as heretical?*

We now wish . . . to adduce the truths of the holy Scripture . . . which explicitly command or counsel that neither the Roman bishop called pope, nor any other bishop or priest, or deacon, has or ought to have any rulership or coercive judgment or jurisdiction over any priest or nonpriest, ruler, community, group, or individual of whatever condition. . . . Christ himself came into the world not to dominate men, nor to judge them [coercively] . . . not to wield temporal rule, but rather to be subject as regards the . . . present life; and moreover, he wanted to and did exclude himself, his apostles and disciples, and their successors, the bishops or priests, from all coercive authority or worldly rule, both by his example and by his word of counsel or command. . . . When he was brought before Pontius Pilate . . . and accused of having called himself king of the Jews, and [Pilate] asked him whether he had said this . . . [his] reply included these words . . . "My kingdom is not of this world," that is, I have not come to reign by temporal rule or dominion, in the way . . . worldly kings reign. . . . This, then, is the kingdom concerning which he came to teach and order, a kingdom which consists in the acts whereby the eternal kingdom is attained, that is, the acts of faith and the other theological virtues; not however, by coercing anyone thereto.

Marsilius of Padua: The Defender of Peace: The Defensor Pacis, *trans. by Alan Gewirth (New York: Harper, 1967), pp. 113–116.*

cial stature. There was a threat in such teaching to secular as well as to ecclesiastical dominion and jurisdiction. At his posthumous condemnation by the pope, Wycliffe was accused of the ancient heresy of Donatism—the teaching that the efficacy of the church's sacraments did not lie in their true performance but also depended on the moral character of the clergy who administered them. Wycliffe also anticipated certain Protestant criticisms of the medieval church by challenging papal infallibility, the sale of indulgences, the authority of scripture, and the dogma of transubstantiation.

The Lollards, English advocates of Wycliffe's teaching, like the Waldensians, preached in the vernacular, disseminated translations of Holy Scripture, and championed clerical poverty. At first, they came from every social class. Lollards were especially prominent among the groups that had something tangible to gain from the confiscation of clerical properties (the nobility and the gentry) or that had suffered most under the current church system (the lower clergy and the poor people). After the English 1381 peasants' revolt in 1381, an uprising filled with egalitarian notions that could find support in Wycliffe's teaching, Lollardy was officially viewed as subversive. Opposed by an alliance of church and crown, it became a capital offense in England by 1401.

Heresy was not so easily brought to heel in Bohemia, where it coalesced with a strong national movement. The University of Prague, founded in 1348, became the center for both Czech nationalism

Petrarch Describes the Papal Residence at Avignon

Petrarch, the "father of humanism," lived in Avignon and personally observed the papacy there over a long period of time. In this letter written between 1340 and 1353, he describes with deep, pious outrage the ostentation and greed of the Avignon popes.

✦ *Is this criticism realistic? Was it possible for the papacy at this time in its history to live as Petrarch proposes? Can a religious institution survive without real power and its trappings?*

I am now living in [Avignon], in the Babylon of the West. . . . Here reign the successors of the poor fishermen of Galilee [who] have strangely forgotten their origin. I am astounded, as I recall their predecessors, to see these men loaded with gold and clad in purple, boasting of the spoils of princes and nations; to see luxurious palaces and heights crowned with fortifications, instead of a boat turned downwards for [their] shelter. We no longer find the simple nets which were once used to gain a frugal living from the lake of Galilee. . . . One is stupefied nowadays to hear the lying tongues, and to see worthless parchments turned by a leaden seal [i.e., official bulls of the pope] into nets which are used, in Christ's name, but by the arts of Belial [i.e., the devil], to catch hordes of unwary Christians. These fish, too, are dressed and laid on the burning coals of anxiety before they fill the insatiable maw of their captors.

Instead of holy solitude we find a criminal host and crowds . . .; instead of sobriety, licentious banquets . . .; instead of pious pilgrimages . . . foul sloth; instead of the bare feet of the apostles . . . horses decked in gold . . . . In short, we seem to be among the kings of the Persians or Parthians, before whom we must fall down and worship, and who cannot be approached except presents be offered.

James Harvey Robinson, ed., Readings in European History, *vol. 1 (Boston:Athenaeum, 1904).*

and a native religious reform movement. The latter began within the bounds of orthodoxy. It was led by local intellectuals and preachers, the most famous of whom was John Huss, the rector of the university after 1403.

The Czech reformers supported vernacular translations of the Bible and were critical of traditional ceremonies and allegedly superstitious practices, particularly those relating to the sacrament of the Eucharist. They advocated lay communion with cup as well as bread, which was traditionally reserved only for the clergy as a sign of the clergy's spiritual superiority over the laity. Hussites taught that bread and wine remained bread and wine after priestly consecration, and questioned the validity of sacraments performed by priests in mortal sin.

Wycliffe's teaching appears to have influenced the movement very early. Regular traffic between England and Bohemia had existed for decades, ever since the marriage in 1381 of Anne of Bohemia to King Richard II. Czech students studied at Oxford, and many returned with copies of Wycliffe's writings.

Huss became the leader of the pro-Wycliffe faction at the University of Prague. In 1410 his activities brought about his excommunication and the placement of Prague under papal interdict. In 1414 Huss won an audience with the newly assembled Council of Constance. He journeyed to the council eagerly, armed with a safe-conduct pass from Emperor Sigismund, naïvely believing that he would convince his strongest critics of the truth of his teaching. Within weeks of his arrival in early November 1414, he was formally accused of heresy and imprisoned. He died at the stake on July 6, 1415, and was followed there less than a year later by his colleague Jerome of Prague.

A portrayal of Jan Huss as he was led to the stake at Constance. After his execution, his bones and ashes were scattered in the Rhine River to prevent his followers from claiming them as relics. This pen-and-ink drawing is from Ulrich von Richenthal's Chronicle of the Council of Constance *(ca. 1450). [The Bettman Archive]*

The reaction in Bohemia to the execution of these national heroes was fierce revolt. Militant Hussites, the Taborites, set out to transform Bohemia by force into a religious and social paradise under the military leadership of John Ziska. After a decade of belligerent protest, the Hussites won significant religious reforms and control over the Bohemian church from the Council of Basel.

The Great Schism (1378–1417) and the Conciliar Movement to 1449

Pope Gregory XI (r. 1370–1378) reestablished the papacy in Rome in January 1377, ending what had come to be known as the "Babylonian Captivity" of the church in Avignon, a reference to the biblical bondage of the Israelites. The return to Rome proved to be short-lived, however.

URBAN VI AND CLEMENT VII On Gregory's death the cardinals, in Rome, elected an Italian archbishop as Pope Urban VI (r. 1378–1389), who immediately announced his intention to reform the *Curia.* This was an unexpected challenge to the cardinals, most of whom were French, and they responded by calling for the return of the papacy to Avignon. The French king, Charles V, wanting to keep the papacy within the sphere of French influence, lent his support to a schism, which came to be known as the "Great Schism."

On September 20, 1378, five months after Urban's election, thirteen cardinals, all but one of whom was French, formed their own conclave and elected Pope Clement VII (r. 1378–1397), a cousin of the French king. They insisted that they had voted for Urban in fear of their lives, surrounded by a Roman mob demanding the election of an Italian pope. Be that as it may, the papacy now became a "two-headed thing" and a scandal to Christendom. Allegiance to the two papal courts divided along political lines. England and its allies (the Holy Roman Empire, Hungary, Bohemia, and Poland) acknowledged Urban VI, whereas France and those in its orbit (Naples, Scotland, Castile, and Aragon) supported Clement VII. The Roman line of popes has, however, been recognized de facto in subsequent church history.

Two approaches were initially taken to end the schism. One tried to win the mutual cession of both popes, thereby clearing the way for the election of a new pope. The other sought to secure the resignation of the one in favor of the other. Both approaches proved completely fruitless. Each pope considered himself fully legitimate, and too much was at stake for a magnanimous concession on the part of either. One way remained : the forced deposition of both popes by a special council of the church.

CONCILIAR THEORY OF CHURCH GOVERNMENT Legally a church council could be convened only by a pope, but the competing popes were not inclined to summon a council they knew would depose them. Also, the deposition of a legitimate pope against his will by a council of the church was as serious a matter then as the forced deposition of a monarch by a representative assembly.

The correctness of a conciliar deposition of a pope was thus debated a full thirty years before any direct action was taken. Advocates sought to fashion a church in which a representative council could effectively regulate the actions of the pope. The conciliarists defined the church as the whole body of the faithful, of which the elected head, the pope, was only one part. And the pope's sole purpose was to maintain the unity and well-being of the church—something that the schismatic popes were far from doing. The conciliarists further argued that a council of the church acted with greater authority than the pope alone. In the eyes of the pope(s) such a concept of the church threatened both its political and its religious unity.

THE COUNCIL OF PISA (1409–1410) On the basis of the arguments of the conciliarists, cardinals representing both popes convened a council on their own authority in Pisa in 1409, deposed both the Roman and the Avignon popes, and elected a new pope, Alexander V. To the council's consternation, neither pope accepted its action, and Christendom suddenly faced the spectacle of three contending popes. Although the vast majority of Latin Christendom accepted Alexander and his Pisan successor John XXIII (r. 1410–1415), the popes of Rome and Avignon refused to step down.

THE COUNCIL OF CONSTANCE (1414–1417) This intolerable situation ended when Emperor Sigismund prevailed on John XXIII to summon a new council in Constance in 1414, which the Roman pope Gregory XII also recognized. In a famous declaration entitled *Sacrosancta*, the council asserted their supremacy and proceeded to elect a new pope, Martin V (r. 1417–1431), after the three contending popes had either resigned or been deposed. The council then made provisions for regular meetings of church councils, within five, then seven, and thereafter every ten years.

Despite its role in ending the Great Schism, in the official eyes of the church, Constance was not a legitimate council. Nor have the schismatic popes of Avignon and Pisa been recognized as legitimate (for this reason, another pope could take the name John XXIII in 1958).

THE COUNCIL OF BASEL (R. 1431–1449) Conciliar government of the church peaked at the Council of Basel, when the council negotiated church doctrine with heretics. In 1432 the Hussites of Bohemia presented the *Four Articles of Prague* to the council as a basis for the negotiations. This document contained requests for (1) giving the laity the Eucharist with cup as well as bread; (2) free, itinerant preaching; (3) the exclusion of the clergy from holding secular offices and owning property; and (4) just punishment of clergy who commit mortal sins.

In November 1433 an agreement was reached between the emperor, the council, and the Hussites, giving the Bohemians jurisdiction over their church similar to that held by the French and the English. Three of the four Prague articles were conceded: communion with cup, free preaching by ordained clergy, and like punishment of clergy and laity for mortal sins.

The end of the Hussite wars and the reform legislation curtailing the papal power of appointment and taxation were the high points of the Council of Basel. The exercise of such power by a council did not please the pope, and in 1438 he gained the opportunity to upstage the Council of Basel by negotiating reunion with the Eastern Church. The agreement, signed in Florence in 1439, was short-lived, but it restored papal prestige and signaled the demise of the Conciliar Movement. The Council of Basel collapsed in 1449. A decade later Pope Pius II (r. 1458–1464) issued the papal bull *Execrabilis* (1460) condemning appeals to councils as "erroneous and abominable" and "completely null and void."

Although many who had worked for reform now despaired of ever attaining it, the Conciliar Movement was not a total failure. It planted deep within the conscience of all Western peoples the conviction that the role of a leader of an institution is to provide for the well-being of its members, not just for that of the leader.

A second consequence of the Conciliar Movement was the devolving of religious responsibility onto the laity and secular government. Without papal leadership, secular control of national or territorial churches increased. Kings asserted power over the church in England and France. In German, Swiss, and Italian cities magistrates and city councils reformed and regulated religious life. This development could not be reversed by the powerful popes of the High Renaissance. On the contrary, as the papacy became a limited territorial regime, national control of the church ran apace. Perceived as just one among several Italian states, the Papal States could now be opposed as much on the grounds of "national" policy as for religious reasons.

✦

War, plague, and schism convulsed much of late medieval Europe throughout the fourteenth and into the fifteenth century. Two-fifths of the popu-

lation, particularly along the major trade routes, died from plague in the fourteenth century. War and famine continued to take untold numbers after the plague had passed. The introduction of gunpowder and heavy artillery during the long years of warfare between England and France resulted in new forms of human destruction. Periodic revolts erupted in town and countryside as ordinary people attempted to defend their traditional communal rights and privileges against the new autocratic territorial regimes. Even God's house seemed to be in shambles in 1409, when no fewer than three popes came to rule simultaneously.

There is, however, another side to the late Middle Ages. By the end of the fifteenth century the population losses were rapidly being made up. Between 1300 and 1500, education had become far more accessible, especially to laypeople. The number of universities increased 250 percent, from twenty to seventy, and the rise in the number of residential colleges was even more impressive, especially in France, where sixty-three were built. The fourteenth century saw the birth of Humanism and the fifteenth century gave us the printing press. Most impressive were the artistic and cultural achievements of the Italian Renaissance during the fifteenth century. The later Middle Ages were thus a period of growth and creativity as well as one of waning and decline.

Review Questions

1. What were the underlying and precipitating causes of the Hundred Years' War? What advantages did each side have? Why were the French finally able to drive the English almost entirely out of France?
2. What were the causes of the Black Death and why did it spread so quickly throughout western Europe? Where was it most virulent? What were its effects on European society? How important do you think disease is in changing the course of history?
3. Discuss the struggle between Pope Boniface VIII and King Philip the Fair. Why was Boniface so impotent in the conflict? How had political conditions changed since the reign of Pope Innocent III in the late twelfth century, and what did that mean for the papacy?
4. Briefly trace the history of the church from 1200 to 1450. How did it respond to political threats from the growing power of monarchs? How great an influence did the church have on secular events?
5. What was the Avignon Papacy, and why did it occur? What effect did it have on the state of the papacy? What relation does it have to the Great Schism? How did the church become divided and how was it reunited? Why was the Conciliar Movement a setback for the papacy?
6. Why were kings in the late thirteenth and early fourteenth centuries able to control the church more than the church could control the kings? How did kings attack the church during this period? Contrast these events with earlier ones in which the pope dominated rulers.

Suggested Readings

C. Allmand, *The Hundred Years' War: England and France at War, c. 1300–c. 1450* (1988). Good overview of the war's development and consequences.

P. Ariès, *The Hour of Our Death* (1983). People's familiarity with and philosophy of death in the Middle Ages.

R. Barber (Ed.), *The Pastons: Letters of a Family in the War of the Roses* (1984). Revelations of English family life in an age of crisis.

J. le Goff, *The Birth of Purgatory*, trans. by A. Goldhammer (1984). Cultural impact of the idea.

D. Hay, *Europe in the Fourteenth and Fifteenth Centuries* (1966). Many-sided treatment of political history.

J. Huizinga, *The Waning of the Middle Ages: A Study of the Forms of Life, Thought, and Art in France and the Netherlands in the Dawn of the Renaissance* (1924). A classic study of "mentality" at the end of the Middle Ages; exaggerated, but engrossing.

G. Leff, *Heresy in the Later Middle Ages, I–II* (1967). Magisterial survey of all the major heretical movements.

W. H. McNeill, *Plagues and Peoples* (1976). The Black Death in a broader context.

F. Oakley, *The Western Church in the Later Middle Ages* (1979). Eloquent, sympathetic survey.

S. Ozment, *The Age of Reform, 1250–1550* (1980). Highlights of late medieval intellectual and religious history.

E. Perroy, *The Hundred Years' War*, trans. by W. B. Wells (1965). Still the most comprehensive one-volume account.

C. Platt, *The Castle in Medieval England and Wales* (1982). Has an illustrated chapter on English coastal castles built during the Hundred Years' War.

Y. RENOVARD, *The Avignon Papacy 1305–1403*, trans. by D. Bethell (1970). The standard narrative account.

M. SPINKA, *John Huss's Concept of the Church* (1966). Lucid and authoritative account of Hussite theology.

B. TIERNEY, *Foundations of the Conciliar Theory* (1955). Important study showing the origins of Conciliar theory in canon law.

B. TIERNEY, *The Crisis of Church and State 1050–1300* (1964). Part IV provides the major documents in the clash between Boniface VIII and Philip the Fair.

W. ULLMANN, *Origins of the Great Schism* (1948). A basic study by a controversial interpreter of medieval political thought.

C. T. WOOD, *Philip the Fair and Boniface VIII* (1967). Excerpts from the scholarly debate over the significance of this confrontation.

H. B. WORKMAN, *John Wyclif*, vols. 1 and 2 (1926). Dated but still standard.

P. ZIEGLER, *The Black Death* (1969). Highly readable account.

CHAPTER 10

Commissioned in 1501, when the artist was 26, Michelangelo's David *became the symbol of the Florentine republic and was displayed in front of the Palazzo Vecchio. The detail shown here highlights the restrained emotion and dignity for which the statue is famous. [Michelangelo (1475–1564) David-p. (testa di profilo.) Scala/Art Resource]*

Renaissance and Discovery

KEY TOPICS

- The politics, culture, and art of the Italian Renaissance
- Political struggle and foreign intervention in Italy
- The powerful new monarchies of northern Europe
- The thought and culture of the northern Renaissance

*If the late Middle Ages saw unprecedented chaos, it also witnessed a rebirth that would continue into the seventeenth century. Two modern Dutch scholars have employed the same word (*Herfsttij*, or "harvesttide") with different connotations to describe the period. Johan Huizinga has used the word to mean a "waning," or "decline," and Heiko Oberman has used it to mean "harvest." If something was dying away, some ripe fruit was being gathered and seed grain was sown. The late Middle Ages was a time of creative fragmentation.*

By the late fifteenth century, Europe was recovering well from two of the three crises of the late Middle Ages: the demographic and the political. The great losses in population were being recaptured, and increasingly able monarchs and rulers were imposing a new political order. A solution to the religious crisis, however, would have to await the Reformation and Counter-Reformation of the sixteenth century.

Although the opposite would be true in the sixteenth and seventeenth centuries, the city-states of Italy survived the century and a half between 1300 and 1450 better than the territorial states of northern Europe. This was due to Italy's strategic location between East and West and its lucrative Eurasian trade. Great wealth gave rulers and merchants the ability to work their will on both society and culture. They became patrons of government, education, and the arts, always as much for self-aggrandizement as out of benevolence, for whether a patron was a family, a firm, a government, or the church, their endowments enhanced their reputation and power. The result of such patronage was a cultural Renaissance in Italian cities unmatched elsewhere.

With the fall of Constantinople to the Turks in 1453, the shrinkage of Italy's once unlimited trading empire began. City-state soon turned against city-state, and by the 1490s the armies of France invaded Italy. Within a quarter century, Italy's great Renaissance had peaked.

The fifteenth century also saw an unprecedented scholarly renaissance. Italian and northern humanists made a full recovery of classical knowledge and languages and set in motion educational reforms and cultural changes that would spread throughout Europe in the fifteenth and sixteenth centuries. In the process the Italian humanists invented, for all practical purposes, critical historical scholarship and exploited a new fifteenth-century invention, the "divine art" of printing with movable type.

In this period the vernacular—the local language—began to take its place alongside Latin, the international language, as a widely used literary and political language. And European lands progressively superseded the universal Church as the community of highest allegiance, as patriotism and incipient nationalism seized hearts and minds as strongly as religion. Nations henceforth "transcended" themselves not by journeys to Rome but by competitive voyages to the Far East and the Americas, as the age of global exploration opened.

For Europe the late fifteenth and sixteenth centuries were a period of unprecedented territorial expansion and ideological experimentation. Permanent colonies were established within the Americas, and the exploitation of the New World's human and mineral resources was begun. Imported American gold and silver spurred scientific invention and a new weapons industry and touched off an inflationary spiral that produced an escalation in prices by the century's end. The new bullion also helped create an international traffic in African slaves as rival African tribes sold their captives to the Portuguese. These slaves were brought in ever-increasing numbers to work the mines and the plantations of the New World as replacements for faltering American natives. These centuries also saw social engineering and political planning on a large scale. Newly centralized governments began to put long-range economic policies into practice, a development that came to be known as mercantilism.

The Renaissance in Italy (1375–1527)

A Renaissance historian has described the Renaissance as the "prototype of the modern world." In his *Civilization of the Renaissance in Italy* (1860), Jacob Burckhardt argues that in fourteenth- and fifteenth-century Italy, through the revival of ancient learning, new secular and scientific values began to supplant traditional religious beliefs. This was the period in which people began to adopt a rational, objective, and statistical approach to reality and to rediscover the importance of the individual and his or her artistic creativity. The result, in Burckhardt's words, was a release of the "full, whole nature of man."

Other scholars have found Burckhardt's description far too modernizing an interpretation of the Renaissance and have accused him of overlooking the continuity between the Middle Ages and the Renaissance. His critics especially stress the still strongly Christian character of Renaissance humanism. They point out that earlier "renaissances," especially that of the twelfth century, also saw the revival of the ancient classics, interest in Latin language and Greek science, and appreciation of the worth and creativity of individuals.

Despite the exaggeration and bias of Burckhardt's portrayal of the Renaissance, most scholars agree that the Renaissance was a time of transition from the medieval to the modern world. Medieval Europe, especially before the twelfth century, had been a fragmented feudal society with an agricultural economy, and its thought and culture were largely dominated by the church. Renaissance Europe, especially after the fourteenth century, was characterized by growing national consciousness and political centralization, an urban economy based on organized commerce and capitalism, and ever greater lay and secular control of thought and culture, including religion.

The distinctive features and achievements of the Renaissance are most strikingly revealed in Italy from roughly 1375 to 1527, the year of the infamous sack of Rome by imperial soldiers. What was achieved in Italy during the late fourteenth to the early sixteenth centuries also deeply influenced northern Europe.

The Italian City-State

Renaissance society was no simple cultural transformation. It first took distinctive shape within the cities of late medieval Italy. Italy had always had a cultural advantage over the rest of Europe because its geography made it the natural gateway between East and West. Venice, Genoa, and Pisa traded uninterruptedly with the Near East throughout the Middle Ages and maintained vibrant urban societies. When commerce revived on a large scale in the eleventh century, Italian merchants quickly mastered the business skills of organization, bookkeeping, scouting new markets, and securing monopolies. During the thirteenth and fourteenth centuries, trade-rich cities expanded to become powerful city-states, dominating the political and economic life of the surrounding countryside. By the fifteenth century, the great Italian cities had become the bankers of much of Europe.

Growth of City-States The growth of Italian cities and urban culture was assisted by the endemic warfare between the emperor and the pope and the Guelf (propapal) and Ghibelline (pro-imperial) factions that this warfare had created. Either of these might have successfully challenged the cities had they permitted each other to concentrate on it. They chose instead to weaken one another and thus strengthened the merchant oligarchies of the cities. Unlike those of northern Europe, which tended to be dominated by kings and territorial princes, the great Italian cities were left free to expand. They became independent states, absorbing the surrounding countryside and assimilating the area's nobility in a unique urban meld of old and new rich. There were five such major, competitive states in Italy: the duchy of Milan; the republics of Florence and Venice; the Papal States; and the kingdom of Naples. (See Map 10–1.)

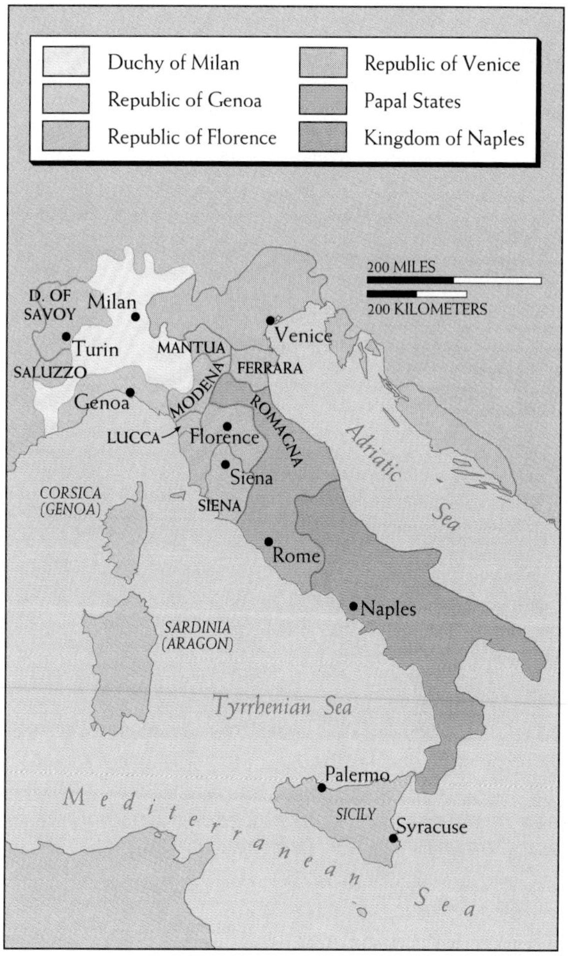

Map 10–1 Renaissance Italy *The city-states of Renaissance Italy were self-contained principalities whose internal strife was monitored by their despots and whose external aggression was long successfully controlled by treaty.*

Social strife and competition for political power were so intense within the cities that most had evolved into despotisms by the fifteenth century—just to survive. Venice was a notable exception. It was ruled by a successful merchant oligarchy with power located in a patrician senate of 300 members and a ruthless judicial body, the Council of Ten, which anticipated and suppressed rival groups. Elsewhere, the new social classes and divisions within society produced by rapid urban growth fueled chronic, near-anarchic conflict.

Social Class and Conflict Florence was the most striking example. There were four distinguishable social groups within the city. The first was the old rich, or *grandi*, the nobles and merchants who traditionally ruled the city. The second group was the emergent new-rich merchant class, capitalists and bankers known as the *popolo grosso*, or "fat people." They began to challenge the old rich for political power in the late thirteenth and early fourteenth centuries. Then there were the middle-burgher ranks of guildmasters, shopowners, and professionals, those smaller businesspeople who, in Florence as elsewhere, tended to take the side of the new rich against the conservative policies of the old rich. Finally, there was the *popolo minuto*, or the "little people," the lower economic classes. In 1457 one-third of the population of Florence, about 30,000 people, were officially listed as paupers, that is, having no wealth at all.

Cosimo de' Medici (1389–1464), Florentine banker and statesman, in his lifetime the city's wealthiest man and most successful politician. This portrait is by Pontormo. [Erich Lessing, Art Resource, N.Y.]

These social divisions produced conflict at every level of society, to which was added the ever-present fear of foreign intrigue. In 1378 there was a great revolt of the poor known as the Ciompi Revolt. It resulted from a combination of three factors that made life unbearable for those at the bottom of society: the feuding between the old and the new rich; the social anarchy that had resulted from the Black Death, which cut the city's population almost in half; and the collapse of the banking houses of Bardi and Peruzzi, which left the poor more economically vulnerable than ever. The successful revolt established a chaotic four-year reign of power by the lower Florentine classes. True stability did not return to Florence until the ascent to power of Cosimo de' Medici (1389–1464) in 1434.

DESPOTISM AND DIPLOMACY The wealthiest Florentine, Cosimo de' Medici, was an astute statesman. He controlled the city internally from behind the scenes, skillfully manipulating the constitution and influencing elections. Florence was governed by a council, first of six and later of eight members, known as the *Signoria*. These men were chosen from the most powerful guilds—those representing the major clothing industries (cloth, wool, fur, and silk) and such other groups as bankers, judges, and doctors. Through his informal, cordial relations with the electoral committee, Cosimo was able to keep councillors loyal to him in the *Signoria*. As head of the Office of Public Debt, he was able to favor congenial factions. His grandson Lorenzo the Magnificent (1449–1492, r. 1478–1492) ruled Florence in almost totalitarian fashion during the last quarter of the fifteenth century. The assassination of his brother in 1478 by a rival family, the Pazzi, who plotted with the pope against Medici rule, made Lorenzo a cautious and determined ruler.

Despotism was less subtle elsewhere. To prevent internal social conflict and foreign intrigue from paralyzing their cities, the dominant groups cooperated to install a hired strongman. Known as a *podestà*, his purpose was to maintain law and order. He was given executive, military, and judicial authority. His mandate was direct and simple: to permit, by whatever means required, the normal flow of business activity without which not the old rich, the new rich, nor the poor of a city could long survive. Because these despots could not depend on the divided populace, they operated through mercenary armies, which they obtained through military brokers known as *condottieri*.

It was a hazardous job. Despots were not only subject to dismissal by the oligarchies that hired them, but they were also popular objects of assassination attempts. The spoils of success, however, were very great. In Milan, it was as despots that the Visconti family came to power in 1278 and the Sforza family in 1450. Both ruled without constitutional restraints or serious political competition. The latter produced one of Machiavelli's heroes, Ludovico il Moro.

Political turbulence and warfare gave birth to diplomacy. Consequently, the various city-states could stay abreast of foreign military developments and, if shrewd enough, gain power and advantage short of actually going to war. Most city-states established resident embassies in the fifteenth century. Their ambassadors not only represented them in ceremonies and as negotiators but also became their watchful eyes and ears at rival courts.

Whether within the comparatively tranquil republic of Venice, the strong-arm democracy of Florence, or the undisguised despotism of Milan, the disciplined Italian city proved a most congenial

Florentine women doing needlework, spinning, and weaving. These activities took up much of a woman's time and contributed to the elegance of dress for which Florentine men and women were famed. [Alinari/Art Resource]

climate for an unprecedented flowering of thought and culture. Italian Renaissance culture was promoted as vigorously by despots as by republicans and by secularized popes as enthusiastically as by the more spiritually minded. Such widespread support occurred because the main requirement for patronage of the arts and letters was the one thing that Italian cities of the High Renaissance had in abundance: great wealth.

Humanism

There are several schools of thought on the meaning of "humanism." There are those who see the Italian Renaissance as the birth of modernity, characterized by an un-Christian philosophy that stressed the dignity of humankind and championed individualism and secular values (these are the followers of the nineteenth-century historian Jacob Burckhardt). Others argue that humanists were the very champions of authentic Catholic Christianity, who opposed the pagan teaching of Aristotle and the ineloquent Scholasticism that his writings nurtured. Still others see humanism as a form of scholarship consciously designed to promote a sense of civic responsibility and political liberty.

An authoritative modern commentator on humanism, Paul O. Kristeller, has accused all these views of dealing more with the secondary effects than with the essence of humanism. Humanism, he believes, was no particular philosophy or value system but simply an educational program that concentrated on rhetoric and sound scholarship for their own sake.

There is truth in each of these definitions. Humanism was the scholarly study of the Latin and Greek classics and of the ancient Church Fathers both for its own sake and in the hope of a rebirth of ancient norms and values. Humanists advocated the *studia humanitatis*, a liberal arts program of study that embraced grammar, rhetoric, poetry, history, politics, and moral philosophy. Not only were these subjects considered a joy in themselves, they were also seen as celebrating the dignity of humankind and preparing people for a life of virtuous action. The Florentine, Leonardo Bruni (ca. 1370–1444), first gave the name *humanitas* or "humanity," to the learning that resulted from such scholarly pursuits. Bruni was a student of Manuel Chrysoloras, a Byzantine scholar who opened the world of Greek scholarship to a generation of young Italian humanists when he taught at Florence between 1397 and 1403.

The first humanists were orators and poets. They wrote original literature, in both the classical and the vernacular languages, inspired by and modeled on the newly discovered works of the ancients. They also taught rhetoric within the universities. When humanists were not employed as teachers of rhetoric, their talents were sought as secretaries, speech writers, and diplomats in princely and papal courts.

The study of classical and Christian antiquity existed before the Italian Renaissance. There were recoveries of ancient civilization during the Carolingian renaissance of the ninth century, within the cathedral school of Chartres in the twelfth century, during the great Aristotelian revival in Paris in the thirteenth century, and among the Augustinians in the early fourteenth century. These precedents, however, only partially compare with the grand achievements of the Italian Renaissance of the late Middle Ages. The latter was far more secular and lay-dominated, had much broader interests, was blessed with far more recovered manuscripts, and possessed far superior technical skills than had been the case in the earlier "rebirths" of antiquity.

Unlike their Scholastic rivals, humanists were less bound to recent tradition; they did not focus all their attention on summarizing and comparing the views of recognized authorities on a text or question, but went directly to the original sources themselves. And their most respected sources were classical and biblical, not the medieval philosophers and theologians. Avidly searching out manuscript collections, Italian humanists made the full sources of Greek and Latin antiquity available to scholars during the fourteenth and fifteenth centuries. Mastery of Latin and Greek was the surgeon's tool of the humanist. There is a kernel of truth—but only a kernel—in the humanists' arrogant assertion that the period between themselves and classical civilization was a "dark middle age."

PETRARCH, DANTE, AND BOCCACCIO Francesco Petrarch (1304–1374) was the "father of humanism." He left the legal profession to pursue letters and poetry. Most of his life was spent in and around Avignon. He was involved in Cola di Rienzo's popular revolt and two-year reign (1347–1349) in Rome as "tribune" of the Roman people. Petrarch also served the Visconti family in Milan in his later years.

Petrarch celebrated ancient Rome in his *Letters to the Ancient Dead*, fancied personal letters to Cicero, Livy, Vergil, and Horace. He also wrote a Latin epic poem (*Africa*, a poetic historical tribute to the Roman general Scipio Africanus), and a set of biographies of famous Roman men (*Lives of Illustrious Men*). Petrarch's most famous contemporary work was a collection of highly introspective love sonnets to a certain Laura, a married woman whom he romantically admired from a safe distance.

His critical textual studies, elitism, and contempt for the allegedly useless learning of the Scholastics were features that many later humanists also shared. Classical and Christian values coexist, not always harmoniously, in his work, an uneasy coexistence that is seen in many later humanists. Medieval Christian values can be seen in Petrarch's imagined dialogues with Saint Augustine and in tracts written to defend the personal immortality of the soul against the Aristotelians.

Petrarch was, however, far more secular in orientation than his famous near-contemporary Dante Alighieri (1265–1321), whose *Vita Nuova* and *Divine Comedy* form, with Petrarch's sonnets, the cornerstones of Italian vernacular literature. Petrarch's student and friend Giovanni Boccaccio (1313–1375) was also a pioneer of humanist studies. His *Decameron*—100 often bawdy tales told by three men and seven women in a country retreat from the plague that ravaged Florence in 1348—is both a stinging social commentary (especially in its exposé of sexual and economic misconduct) and a sympathetic look at human behavior. An avid collector of manuscripts, Boccaccio also assembled an encyclopedia of Greek and Roman mythology.

Dante Alighieri (1265–1321) portrayed with scenes of hell, purgatory, and paradise from the Divine Comedy, *his classic epic poem. [Scala/Art Resource, N.Y.]*

Petrarch's Letter to Posterity

In old age Petrarch wrote a highly personal letter to posterity in which he summarized the lessons he had learned during his lifetime. The letter also summarizes the original values of Renaissance humanists: their suspicion of purely materialistic pleasure, the importance they attached to friendship, and their utter devotion to and love of antiquity.

✦ *Does Petrarch's letter give equal weight to classical and Christian values? Why would he have preferred to live in another age?*

I have always possessed extreme contempt for wealth; not that riches are not desirable in themselves, but because I hate the anxiety and care which are invariably associated with them . . . . I have, on the contrary, led a happier existence with plain living and ordinary fare . . . .

The pleasure of dining with one's friends is so great that nothing has ever given me more delight than their unexpected arrival, nor have I ever willingly sat down to table without a companion . . . .

The greatest kings of this age have loved and courted me . . . . I have fled, however, from many . . . to whom I was greatly attached; and such was my innate longing for liberty that I studiously avoided those whose very name seemed incompatible with the freedom I loved.

I possess a well-balanced rather than a keen intellect—one prone to all kinds of good and wholesome study, but especially to moral philosophy and the art of poetry. The latter I neglected as time went on, and took delight in sacred literature . . . . Among the many subjects that interested me, I dwelt especially upon antiquity, for our own age has always repelled me, so that, had it not been for the love of those dear to me, I should have preferred to have been born in any other period than our own. In order to forget my own time, I have constantly striven to place myself in spirit in other ages, and consequently I delighted in history . . . .

If only I have lived well, it matters little to me how I have talked. Mere elegance of language can produce at best but an empty fame.

Frederic Austen Ogg, ed., A Source Book of Mediaeval History: Documents Illustrative of European Life and Institutions from the German Invasions to the Renaissance *(New York: American Book Company, 1908), pp. 470–473.*

Educational Reforms and Goals Humanists were not bashful scholars. They delighted in going directly to primary sources and refused to be slaves to tradition. Such an attitude not only made them innovative educators, it also kept them constantly in search of new sources of information. Magnificent manuscript collections were assembled with great care, as if they were potent medicines for the ills of contemporary society.

The goal of humanist studies was to be wise and to speak eloquently, to know what is good, and to practice virtue. Learning was not to remain abstract and unpracticed. "It is better to will the good than to know the truth," Petrarch had taught, and this became a motto of many later humanists, who, like Petrarch, believed that learning ennobled people. Pietro Paolo Vergerio (1349–1420), the author of the most influential Renaissance tract on education, *On the Morals That Befit a Free Man*, left a classic summary of the humanist concept of a liberal education:

> We call those studies liberal which are worthy of a free man; those studies by which we attain and practice virtue and wisdom; that education which calls forth, trains, and develops those highest gifts of body and mind which ennoble men and which are rightly judged to rank next in dignity to virtue only, for to a vulgar temper, gain and pleasure are the one aim of existence, to a lofty nature, moral worth and fame.[1]

[1]Cited by De Lamar Jensen, *Renaissance Europe: Age of Recovery and Reconciliation* (Lexington, Mass.: D. C. Health, 1981), p. 111.

The ideal of a useful education and well-rounded people inspired far-reaching reforms in traditional education. Quintilian's *Education of the Orator*, the complete text of which was discovered in 1416, became the basic classical guide for the humanist revision of the traditional curriculum. Vittorino da Feltre (d. 1446) exemplified the ideals of humanist teaching. He not only had his students read the difficult works of Pliny, Ptolemy, Terence, Plautus, Livy, and Plutarch, he also subjected them to vigorous physical exercise and games. Another famous educator, Guarino da Verona (d. 1460), rector of the new University of Ferrara and a student of the age's most renowned Greek scholar, Manuel Chrysoloras, streamlined the study of classical languages and gave it systematic form.

Humanist learning was not confined to the classroom, as Baldassare Castiglione's (1478–1529) famous *Book of the Courtier* illustrates. Written as a practical guide for the nobility at the court of Urbino, it embodies the highest ideals of Italian humanism. It depicts the successful courtier as one who knew how to integrate knowledge of ancient languages and history with athletic, military, and musical skills, while practicing good manners and exhibiting moral character.

Noblewomen also played a role at court in education and culture, and among them none more so than Christine de Pisan (1363?–1434). The Italian-born daughter of the physician and astrologer of the French king Charles V, she received at the French court as fine an education as anyone could have. She became expert in classical, French, and Italian languages and literature. Married at fifteen and the widowed mother of three at twenty-seven, she turned to writing lyric poetry to support herself. She soon became a well-known woman of letters much read throughout the courts of Europe. Her most famous work, *The City of Ladies*, is a chronicle of the accomplishments of the great women of history.

THE FLORENTINE "ACADEMY" AND THE REVIVAL OF PLATONISM Of all the important recoveries of the past made during the Italian Renaissance, none stands out more than the revival of Greek studies, especially the works of Plato, in fifteenth-century Florence. Many factors combined to bring this revival about. An important foundation was laid in 1397 when the city invited Manuel Chrysoloras to come from Constantinople and promote Greek learning. A half century later (1439), the ecumenical Council of Ferrara–Florence, having convened to negotiate the reunion of the Eastern and Western churches, opened the door for many Greek scholars and manuscripts to enter the West. After the fall of Constantinople to the Turks in 1453, Greek scholars fled to Florence for refuge. This was the background against which the Florentine Platonic Academy evolved under the patronage of Cosimo de' Medici and the supervision of Marsilio Ficino (1433–1499) and Pico della Mirandola (1463–1494).

The thinkers of the Renaissance were interested in every variety of ancient wisdom. They were especially attracted, however, to the Platonic tradition and to those Church Fathers who tried to synthesize Platonic philosophy and Christian teaching. The "Florentine Academy" was actually not a formal school, but an informal gathering of influential Florentine humanists devoted to the revival of the works of Plato and the Neoplatonists: Plotinus, Proclus, Porphyry, and Dionysius the Areopagite. To this end, Ficino edited and published the complete works of Plato.

The appeal of Platonism lay in its flattering view of human nature. It distinguished between an eternal sphere of being and the perishable world in which humans actually lived. Human reason was believed to belong to the former, indeed, to have preexisted in this pristine world and to continue to commune with it, as the present knowledge of mathematical and moral truth bore witness.

Strong Platonic influence can be seen in Pico's *Oration on the Dignity of Man*, perhaps the most famous Renaissance statement on the nature of humankind. Pico wrote the *Oration* as an introduction to a pretentious collection of 900 theses. Published in Rome in December 1486, the theses were intended to serve as the basis for a public debate on all of life's important topics. The *Oration* drew on Platonic teaching to depict humans as the only creatures in the world who possessed the freedom to be whatever they chose, able at will to rise to the height of angels or to descend to the level of pigs.

CRITICAL WORK OF THE HUMANISTS: LORENZO VALLA Because they were guided by a scholarly ideal of philological accuracy and historical truthfulness, the humanists could become critics of tradition even when that was not their intention. Dispassionate critical scholarship shook long-standing foundations, not the least of which were those of the medieval church.

The work of Lorenzo Valla (1406–1457), author of the standard Renaissance text on Latin philology, the *Elegances of the Latin Language* (1444), reveals the explosive character of the new learning. Although a good Catholic, Valla became a hero to later Protestants. His popularity among Protestants stemmed from his defense of predestination against the advocates of free will, and especially from his exposé of the *Donation of Constantine* (see Chapter 6).

The fraudulent *Donation*, written in the eighth century, purported to be a grant of vast territories made by the fourth-century Roman emperor Constantine to the pope. Valla did not intend the exposé of the *Donation* to have the devastating force that Protestants later attributed to it. He only proved in a careful, scholarly way what others had long suspected. Using the most rudimentary textual analysis and historical logic, Valla proved that the document was filled with such anachronistic terms as *fief* and that it contained material that could not be in a genuine fourth-century document. In the same dispassionate way Valla also pointed out errors in

Christine de Pisan Instructs Women on How to Handle Their Husbands

Renowned Renaissance noblewoman Christine de Pisan has the modern reputation of being perhaps the first feminist, and her book, The Treasure of the City of Ladies *(also known as* The Book of Three Virtues*) has been described as the Renaissance woman's survival manual. Here she gives advice to the wives of artisans.*

✦ *How does Christine de Pisan's image of husband and wife compare with other medieval views? Would the church take issue with her advice in any way? As a noblewoman commenting on the married life of artisans, does her high social standing influence her advice? Would she give similar advice to women of her own social class?*

All wives of artisans should be very painstaking and diligent if they wish to have the necessities of life. They should encourage their husbands or their workmen to get to work early in the morning and work until late . . . . [And] the wife herself should [also] be involved in the work to the extent that she knows all about it, so that she may know how to oversee his workers if her husband is absent, and to reprove them if they do not do well . . . . And when customers come to her husband and try to drive a hard bargain, she ought to warn him solicitously to take care that he does not make a bad deal. She should advise him to be chary of giving too much credit if he does not know precisely where and to whom it is going, for in this way many come to poverty . . . .

In addition, she ought to keep her husband's love as much as she can, to this end: that he will stay at home more willingly and that he may not have any reason to join the foolish crowds of other young men in taverns and indulge in unnecessary and extravagant expense, as many tradesmen do, especially in Paris. By treating him kindly she should protect him as well as she can from this. It is said that three things drive a man from his home: a quarrelsome wife, a smoking fireplace, and a leaking roof. She too ought to stay at home gladly and not go off every day traipsing hither and yon gossiping with the neighbours and visiting her chums to find out what everyone is doing. That is done by slovenly housewives roaming about the town in groups. Nor should she go off on these pilgrimages got up for no good reason and involving a lot of needless expense.

Christine de Pisan, The Treasure of the City of Ladies or The Book of the Three Virtues, *trans. by Sarah Lawson (Penguin Books: New York, 1985), pp. 167–168.*

the Latin Vulgate, still the authorized version of the Bible for the Western church.

Such discoveries did not make Valla any less loyal to the church, nor did they prevent his faithful fulfillment of the office of apostolic secretary in Rome under Pope Nicholas V. Nonetheless, historical criticism of this type served those less loyal to the medieval church. It was no accident that young humanists formed the first identifiable group of Martin Luther's supporters.

Civic Humanism Italian humanists were exponents of applied knowledge; their basic criticism of traditional education was that much of it was useless. Education, they believed, should promote individual virtue and public service. This ideal inspired what has been called civic humanism, by which is meant examples of humanist leadership of the political and cultural life. The most striking instance is to be found in Florence. There three humanists served as chancellors: Colluccio Salutati (1331–1406), Leonardo Bruni (ca. 1370–1444), and Poggio Bracciolini (1380–1459). Each used his rhetorical skills to rally the Florentines against the aggression of Naples and Milan. Bruni and Poggio also wrote adulatory histories of the city. Another accomplished humanist scholar, Leon Battista Alberti (1402–1472), was a noted architect and builder in the city. Whether it was humanism that accounted for such civic activity or just a desire to exercise great power remains a debated issue.

On the other hand, many humanists became cliquish and snobbish, an intellectual elite concerned only with pursuing narrow, antiquarian interests and writing pure, classical Latin in the quiet of their studies. It was in reaction against this elitist trend that the humanist historians Niccolò Machiavelli (1469–1527) and Francesco Guicciardini (1483–1540) adopted the vernacular and made contemporary history their primary source and subject matter.

Renaissance Art

In Renaissance Italy, as in Reformation Europe, the values and interests of the laity were no longer subordinated to those of the clergy. In education, culture, and religion the laity assumed a leading role and established models for the clergy to imitate. This was a development due in part to the church's loss of international power during the great crises of the late Middle Ages. It was also encouraged by the rise of national sentiment, the creation of competent national bureaucracies staffed by the laity rather than by clerics, and the rapid growth of lay education during the fourteenth and fifteenth centuries. Medieval Christian values were adjusting to a more this-worldly spirit. Men and women began again to appreciate and even glorify the secular world, secular learning, and purely human pursuits as ends in themselves.

This new perspective on life is prominent in the painting and sculpture of the High Renaissance—the late fifteenth and early sixteenth centuries, when Renaissance art reached its full maturity. Whereas medieval art tended to be abstract and formulaic, Renaissance art was emphatically concerned with the observation of the natural world and the communication of human emotions. Renaissance artists also tried to give their works a greater rational (chiefly mathematical) order, a symmetry and proportionality that reflected pictorially their deeply held belief in the harmony of the universe. The interest of Renaissance artists in ancient Roman art was closely allied to an independent interest in humanity and nature.

Renaissance artists had the advantage of new technical skills developed during the fifteenth century. In addition to the availability of oil paints, two special techniques were perfected: that of using shading to enhance naturalness (*chiaroscuro*) and that of adjusting the size of figures to give the viewer a feeling of continuity with the painting (linear perspective). These techniques permitted the artist to "rationalize" space and paint a more natural world. The result was that, when compared with their flat Byzantine and Gothic counterparts, Renaissance paintings were filled with energy and life and stood out from the canvas in three dimensions.

The new direction was signaled by Giotto (1266–1336), the father of Renaissance painting. An admirer of Saint Francis of Assisi, whose love of nature he shared, Giotto painted a more natural world than his Byzantine and Gothic predecessors. Though still filled with religious seriousness, his work was no longer so abstract and unnatural a depiction of the world. The painter Masaccio (1401–1428) and the sculptor Donatello (1386–1466) continued to portray the world around them more literally and naturally. The heights were reached by the great masters of the High Renaissance: Leonardo da Vinci (1452–1519), Raphael (1483–1520), and Michelangelo Buonarroti (1475–1564).

Giotto's portrayal of the funeral of Saint Francis of Assisi. The saint is surrounded by his admiring brothers and a knight of Assisi (first on the right). Giotto's (1266–1336) work signals the evolution toward Renaissance art. The damaged areas on this fresco resulted from the removal of nineteenth-century restorations. [Scala/Art Resource, N.Y.]

LEONARDO DA VINCI More than any other person in the period, Leonardo exhibited the Renaissance ideal of the universal person. He was a true master of many skills. One of the greatest painters of all time, he was also a military engineer for Ludovico il Moro in Milan, Cesare Borgia in Romagna, and the French king Francis I. Leonardo advocated scientific experimentation, dissected corpses to learn anatomy, and was an accomplished, self-taught botanist. His inventive mind foresaw such modern machines as airplanes and submarines. Indeed, the variety of his interests was so great that it could shorten his attention span, so that he was constantly moving from one activity to another. His great skill in conveying inner moods through complex facial features can be seen in the most famous of his paintings, the Mona Lisa, as well as in his self-portrait.

RAPHAEL Raphael, a man of great sensitivity and kindness, was apparently loved by contemporaries as much for his person as for his work. His premature death at thirty-seven cut short his artistic career. He is famous for his tender madonnas, the best known of which graced the monastery of San Sisto in Piacenza and is now in Dresden. Art historians praise his fresco *The School of Athens*, a grandly conceived portrayal of the great masters of Western philosophy, as a virtually perfect example of Renaissance technique. It depicts Plato and Aristotle surrounded by the great philosophers and scientists of antiquity, who are portrayed with features of Raphael's famous contemporaries, including Leonardo and Michelangelo.

MICHELANGELO The melancholy genius Michelangelo also excelled in a variety of arts and crafts. His eighteen-foot godlike sculpture David, which long stood majestically in the great square of Florence, is a perfect example of the Renaissance artist's devotion to harmony, symmetry, and proportion, as well as the extreme glorification of the human form. Four different popes commissioned works by Michelangelo. The most famous are the frescoes for the Sistine Chapel, painted during the pontificate of Pope Julius II (r. 1503–1513), who also set Michelangelo to work on the pope's own magnificent tomb. The Sistine frescoes originally covered 10,000 square feet and involved 343 figures, over half of which exceeded 10 feet in height. But it is their originality and perfection as works of art that impress most. This labor of love and piety took four years to complete. A person of incredible energy and endurance who lived to be almost ninety, Michelangelo insisted on doing almost everything himself and permitted his assistants only a few of the many chores involved in his work. (For an example of Michelangelo's work, see the photo on page 332.)

His later works are more complex and suggest deep personal changes. They mark, artistically and philosophically, the passing of High Renaissance painting and the advent of a new style known as mannerism, which reached its peak in the late sixteenth and early seventeenth centuries. A reaction

These two works by Donatello, sculpted fifteen years apart, reveal the psychological complexity of Renaissance artists and their work. On the left is a youthful, sexy David, standing awkwardly and seemingly puzzled on the head of the slain Goliath. Created in 1440, it is the earliest free-standing nude made in the West since Roman times. [Art Resource, N.Y.] On the right, sculpted in 1454–1455 from poplar wood, is Mary Magdalen returned from her desert retreat; she is a frightful, toothless old woman, shorn of all dignity. [Scala/Art Resource, N.Y.]

against the simplicity and symmetry of High Renaissance art (which also found expression in music and literature), mannerism made room for the strange and even the abnormal and gave freer reign to the subjectivity of the artist. Mannerism acquired its name because the artist was permitted to express his or her own individual perceptions and feelings, to paint, compose, or write in a "mannered," or "affected," way. Tintoretto (d. 1594) and especially El Greco (d. 1614) became mannerism's supreme representatives.

Slavery in the Renaissance

Throughout Renaissance Italy, slavery flourished as extravagantly as art and culture. A thriving western slave market existed as early as the twelfth century, when the Spanish sold Muslim slaves captured in raids and war to wealthy Italians and other interested buyers. Contemporaries looked on such slavery as a merciful act, since these captives would otherwise have been killed. In addition to widespread household or domestic slavery, collective plantation slavery, following East Asian models, also developed during the High Middle Ages in the eastern Mediterranean. In the savannas of Sudan and on Venetian estates on the islands of Cyprus and Crete, gangs of slaves worked sugar cane plantations, the model for later western Mediterranean and New World slavery.

After the Black Death (1348–1350) had reduced the supply of laborers everywhere in western Europe, the demand for slaves soared. Slaves now began to be imported from Africa, the Balkans, Constantinople, Cyprus, Crete, and the lands surrounding the Black Sea. Because slaves were taken randomly from conquered people, they consisted of many races: Tatars, Circassians, Greeks, Russians, Georgians, and Iranians as well as Asians and Africans. According to one source, "By the end of the fourteenth century, there was hardly a well-to-do household in Tuscany without at least one slave: brides brought them [to their marriages] as

Michelangelo and Pope Julius II

Vasari here describes how Pope Julius, the most fearsome and worldly of the Renaissance popes, forced Michelangelo to complete the Sistine Chapel before Michelangelo was ready to do so.

✦ *Did Michelangelo hold his own with the pope? What does this interchange suggest about the relationship of patrons and artists in the Renaissance? Were great artists like Michelangelo so revered that they could do virtually as they pleased?*

[The pope was very anxious to see the decoration of the Sistine Chapel completed, and constantly inquired when it would be finished.] On one occasion, therefore, Michelangelo replied, "It will be finished when I shall have done all that I believe is required to satisfy Art." "And we command," rejoined the pontiff, "that you satisfy our wish to have it done quickly," adding that if it were not at once completed, he would have Michelangelo thrown headlong from the scaffolding. Hearing this, our artist, who feared the fury of the pope, and with good cause, without taking time to add what was wanting, took down the remainder of the scaffolding to the great satisfaction of the whole city on All Saints' day, when Pope Julius went into that chapel to sing mass. But Michelangelo had much desired to retouch some portions of the work a secco [that is, after the damp plaster upon which the paint had been originally laid al fresco had dried], as had been done by the older masters who had painted the stories on the walls. He would also have gladly added a little ultramarine to the draperies and gilded other parts, to the end that the whole might have a richer and more striking effect.

The pope, too, hearing that these things were still wanting, and finding that all who beheld the chapel praised it highly, would now fain have had the additions made. But as Michelangelo thought reconstructing the scaffold too long an affair, the pictures remained as they were, although the pope, who often saw Michelangelo, would sometimes say, "Let the chapel be enriched with bright colors and gold; it looks poor." When Michelangelo would reply familiarly, "Holy Father, the men of those days did not adorn themselves with gold; those who are painted here less than any, for they were none too rich; besides which they were holy men, and must have despised riches and ornaments."

James Harvey Robinson, ed., Readings in European History, *vol. 1 (Boston: Athenaeum, 1904), pp. 538–539.*

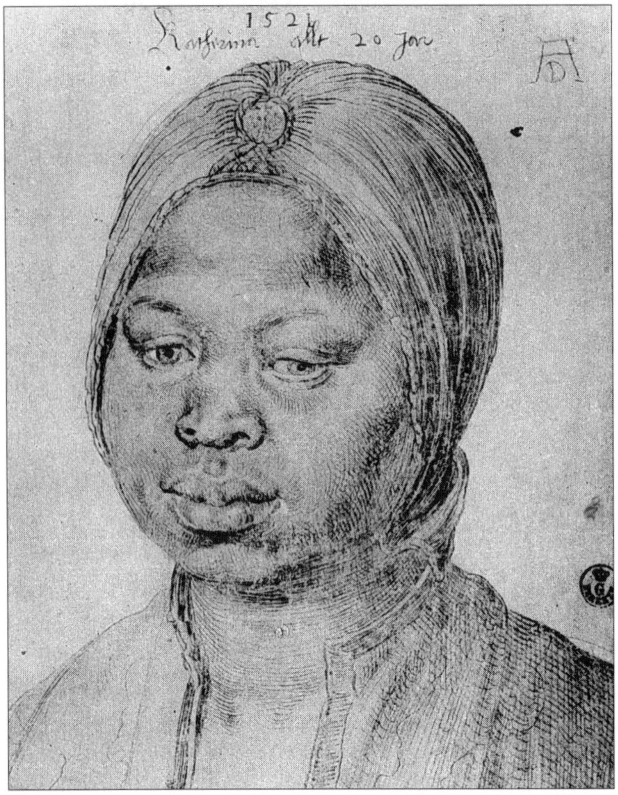

This portrait of Katharina, by Albrecht Dürer, provides evidence of African slavery in Europe during the sixteenth century. Katharina was in the service of one João Bradao, a Portuguese economic minister living in Antwerp, then the financial center of Europe. Dürer became friends with Bradao during his stay in the Low Countries in the winter of 1520–1521. [Bildarchiv Foto Marburg/Art Resource, N.Y.]

part of their dowry, doctors accepted them from their patients in lieu of fees—and it was not unusual to find them even in the service of a priest."[2]

Owners had complete dominion over their slaves; in Italian law, this meant the "[power] to have, hold, sell, alienate, exchange, enjoy, rent or unrent, dispose of in [their] will[s], judge soul and body, and do with in perpetuity whatsoever may please [them] and [their] heirs and no man may gainsay [them]."[3] A strong, young, healthy slave cost the equivalent of the wages paid a free servant over several years. Considering the lifetime of free service thereafter, slaves could be well worth the cost.

The Tatars and Africans appear to have been the worst treated. But as in ancient Greece and Rome, slaves at this time were generally accepted as family members and were integrated into households. Not a few women slaves became mothers of their masters' children. Quite a few children of such unions were adopted and raised as legitimate heirs of their fathers. It was clearly in the interest of their owners to keep slaves healthy and happy; otherwise they were of little use and could even become a threat. Still, slaves remained a foreign and suspected presence in Italian society; they were, as all knew, uprooted and resentful people.

Italy's Political Decline: The French Invasions (1494–1527)

The Treaty of Lodi

As a land of autonomous city-states, Italy's peace and safety from foreign invasion, especially from invasion by the Turks, had always depended on internal cooperation. Such cooperation had been maintained during the latter half of the fifteenth century, thanks to a carefully constructed political alliance known as the Treaty of Lodi (1454–1455). The terms of the treaty brought Milan and Naples, long traditional enemies, into alliance with Florence. These three stood together for decades against Venice, which was frequently joined by the Papal States, to create an internal balance of power. When a foreign enemy threatened Italy, however, the five formed a united front.

Around 1490, following the rise to power of the Milanese despot Ludovico il Moro, hostilities between Milan and Naples resumed. The peace made possible by the Treaty of Lodi ended in 1494 when Naples, supported by Florence and the Borgia Pope Alexander VI (r. 1492–1503), prepared to attack Milan. Ludovico made what proved to be a fatal response in these new political alignments; he appealed for aid to the French. French kings had ruled Naples from 1266 to 1435, before they were driven out by Duke Alfonso of Sicily. Breaking a wise Italian rule, Ludovico invited the French to reenter Italy and revive their dynastic claim to Naples. In his haste to check his rival Naples, Ludovico did not recognize sufficiently that France also had dynastic claims to Milan. Nor did he foresee how insatiable the French appetite for Italian territory would become once French armies had crossed the Alps.

[2]Iris Origo, *The Merchant of Prato: Francesco di Marco Datini 1335–1410* (New York: David Godine, 1986), pp. 90–91.

[3]Ibid., p. 209.

Charles VIII's March Through Italy

The French king Louis XI had resisted the temptation to invade Italy, while nonetheless keeping French dynastic claims in Italy alive. His successor, Charles VIII (r. 1483–1498), an eager youth in his twenties, responded to Ludovico's call with lightning speed. Within five months he had crossed the Alps (August 1495) and raced as conqueror through Florence and the Papal States into Naples. As Charles approached Florence, the Florentine ruler, Piero dé Medici, who had allied with Naples against Milan, tried to placate the French king by handing over Pisa and other Florentine possessions. Such appeasement only brought about Piero's forced exile by a population that was revolutionized then by the radical Dominican preacher Girolamo Savonarola (1452–1498). Savonarola convinced most of the fearful Florentines that the French king's arrival was a long-delayed and fully justified divine vengeance on their immorality.

Charles entered Florence without resistance. Thanks to Savonarola's flattery and the payment of a large ransom, the city was spared a threatened destruction. Savonarola continued to exercise virtual rule over Florence for four years after Charles's departure. The Florentines proved, however, not to be the stuff theocracies are made of. Savonarola's moral rigor and antipapal policies made it impossible for him to survive indefinitely. This became especially true after the Italian cities reunited and the ouster of the French invader, whom Savonarola had praised as a godsend, became national policy. Savonarola was imprisoned and executed in May 1498.

Charles's lightning march through Italy also struck terror in non-Italian hearts. Ferdinand of Aragon, who hoped to expand his own possessions in Italy from his kingdom of Sicily, now found himself vulnerable to a French–Italian axis. He took the initiative to create a counteralliance—the League of Venice, formed in March 1495—in which he joined with Venice, the Papal States, and Emperor Maximilian I against the French. The alliance set the stage for a conflict between France and Spain that would not end until 1559.

Ludovico il Moro meanwhile recognized that he had sown the wind; having desired a French invasion only so long as it weakened his enemies, he now saw Milan threatened by the whirlwind of events that he had himself created. In reaction he joined the League of Venice, and this alliance was able to send Charles into retreat by May. Charles remained thereafter on the defensive until his death in April 1498.

Pope Alexander VI and the Borgia Family

The French returned to Italy under Charles's successor, Louis XII (r. 1498–1515). This time they were assisted by a new Italian ally, the Borgia pope, Alexander VI. Alexander was probably the most corrupt pope who ever sat on the papal throne. He openly promoted the political careers of Cesare and Lucrezia Borgia, the children he had had before he became pope, and he placed papal policy in tandem with the efforts of his powerful family to secure a political base in Romagna.

In Romagna several principalities had fallen away from the church during the Avignon papacy. And Venice, the pope's ally within the League of Venice, continued to contest the Papal States for their loyalty. Seeing that a French alliance could give him the opportunity to reestablish control over the region, Alexander took steps to secure French favor. He annulled Louis XII's marriage to Charles VIII's sister so Louis could marry Charles's widow, Anne of Brittany—a popular political move designed to keep Brittany French. The pope also bestowed a cardinal's hat on the archbishop of Rouen, Louis's favorite cleric. Most important, Alexander agreed to abandon the League of Venice; this withdrawal of support made the league too weak to resist a French reconquest of Milan. In exchange, Cesare Borgia received the sister of the king of Navarre, Charlotte d'Albret, in marriage, a union that greatly enhanced Borgia military strength. Cesare also received land grants from Louis XII and the promise of French military aid in Romagna.

All in all it was a scandalous trade-off, but one that made it possible for both the French king and the pope to realize their ambitions within Italy. Louis successfully invaded Milan in August 1499. Ludovico il Moro, who had originally opened the Pandora's box of French invasion, spent his last years languishing in a French prison. In 1500 Louis and Ferdinand of Aragon divided Naples between them, while the pope and Cesare Borgia conquered the cities of Romagna without opposition. Alexander awarded his victorious son the title "duke of Romagna."

Pope Julius II

Cardinal Giuliano della Rovere, a strong opponent of the Borgia family, succeeded Alexander VI as Pope Julius II (r. 1503–1513). He suppressed the Borgias and placed their newly conquered lands in Romagna under papal jurisdiction. Julius came to be known as the "warrior pope" because he brought the Renaissance papacy to a peak of military prowess and diplomatic intrigue. Shocked, as were other contemporaries, by this thoroughly secular papacy, the humanist Erasmus (1466?–1536), who had witnessed in disbelief a bullfight in the papal palace during a visit to Rome, wrote a popular anonymous satire entitled *Julius Excluded from Heaven*. This humorous account purported to describe the pope's unsuccessful efforts to convince Saint Peter that he was worthy of admission to heaven.

Assisted by his powerful allies, Pope Julius succeeded in driving the Venetians out of Romagna in 1509. Thus he ended Venetian claims in the region and fully secured the Papal States. Having realized this long-sought papal goal, Julius turned to the second major undertaking of his pontificate: ridding Italy of his former ally, the French invader. Julius, Ferdinand of Aragon, and Venice formed a second Holy League in October 1511, and within a short period Emperor Maximilian I and the Swiss joined them. By 1512 the league had the French in full retreat, and they were soundly defeated by the Swiss in 1513 at Novara.

The French were nothing if not persistent. They invaded Italy a third time under Louis's successor, Francis I (r. 1515–1547). French armies massacred Swiss soldiers of the Holy League at Marignano in September 1515, revenging the earlier defeat at Novara. The victory won from the pope the Concordat of Bologna in August 1516. This agreement gave the French king control over the French clergy in exchange for French recognition of the pope's superiority over church councils and his right to collect annates in France. This was an important compromise that helped keep France Catholic after the outbreak of the Protestant Reformation. But the new French entry into Italy also led to the first of four major wars with Spain in the first half of the sixteenth century: the Habsburg–Valois wars, none of which France won.

Niccolò Machiavelli

The period of foreign invasions made a shambles of Italy. The same period that saw Italy's cultural peak in the work of Leonardo, Raphael, and Michelangelo also witnessed Italy's political tragedy. One who watched as French, Spanish, and German armies wreaked havoc on this country was Niccolò Machiavelli (1469–1527). The more he saw, the more convinced he became that Italian political unity and independence were ends that justified any means.

A humanist and a careful student of ancient Rome, Machiavelli was impressed by the way Roman rulers and citizens had then defended their homeland. They possessed *Virtù*, the ability to act decisively and heroically for the good of their country. Stories of ancient Roman patriotism and self-sacrifice were Machiavelli's favorites, and he lamented the absence of such traits among his compatriots. Such romanticizing of the Roman past caused some exaggeration of both ancient virtue and contemporary failings. His Florentine contemporary, Francesco Guicciardini, a more sober historian less given to idealizing antiquity, wrote truer chronicles of Florentine and Italian history.

Machiavelli also held deep republican ideals, which he did not want to see vanish from Italy. He believed that a strong and determined people could struggle successfully with fortune. He scolded the

Major Political Events of the Italian Renaissance (1375–1527)

1378–1382	The Ciompi Revolt in Florence
1434	Medici rule in Florence established by Cosimo de' Medici
1454–1455	Treaty of Lodi allies Milan, Naples, and Florence (in effect until 1494)
1494	Charles VIII of France invades Italy
1494–1498	Savonarola controls Florence
1495	League of Venice unites Venice, Milan, the Papal States, the Holy Roman Empire, and Spain against France
1499	Louis XII invades Milan (the second French invasion of Italy)
1500	The Borgias conquer Romagna
1512–1513	The Holy League (Pope Julius II, Ferdinand of Aragon, Emperor Maximilian, and Venice) defeats the French
1513	Machiavelli writes *The Prince*
1515	Francis I leads the third French invasion of Italy
1516	Concordat of Bologna between France and the papacy
1527	Sack of Rome by imperial soldiers

Machiavelli Discusses the Most Important Trait for a Ruler

Machiavelli believed that the most important personality trait of a successful ruler was the ability to instill fear in his subjects.

✦ *Why did Machiavelli maintain that rulers must be feared? Do American politicians of today appear to embrace Machiavelli's theory?*

Here the question arises; whether it is better to be loved than feared or feared than loved. The answer is that it would be desirable to be both but, since that is difficult, it is much safer to be feared than to be loved, if one must choose. For on men in general this observation may be made: they are ungrateful, fickle, and deceitful, eager to avoid dangers, and avid for gain, and while you are useful to them they are all with you, offering you their blood, their property, their lives, and their sons so long as danger is remote, as we noted above, but when it approaches they turn on you. Any prince, trusting only in their words and having no other preparations made, will fall to his ruin, for friendships that are bought at a price and not by greatness and nobility of soul are paid for indeed, but they are not owned and cannot be called upon in time of need. Men have less hesitation in offending a man who is loved than one who is feared, for love is held by a bond of obligation which, as men are wicked, is broken whenever personal advantage suggests it, but fear is accompanied by the dread of punishment which never relaxes.

Niccolò Machiavelli, The Prince *(1513), trans. and ed. by Thomas G. Bergin (New York: Appleton-Century-Crofts, 1947), p. 48.*

Italian people for the self-destruction their own internal feuding was causing. He wanted an end to that behavior above all, so that a reunited Italy could drive all foreign armies out.

But were his fellow citizens up to such a challenge? The juxtaposition of what Machiavelli believed the ancient Romans had been with the failure of his contemporaries to attain such high ideals made him the famous cynic whose name—in the epithet *Machiavellian*—has become synonymous with ruthless political expediency. Only a strongman, he concluded in the end, could impose order on so divided and selfish a people; the salvation of Italy required, for the present, a cunning dictator.

It has been argued that Machiavelli wrote *The Prince* in 1513 as a cynical satire on the way rulers actually did behave and not as a serious recommendation of unprincipled despotic rule. To take his advocacy of tyranny literally, it is argued, contradicts both his earlier works and his own strong family tradition of republican service. But Machiavelli seems to have been in earnest when he advised rulers to discover the advantages of fraud and brutality, at least as a temporary means to the higher end of a unified Italy. He apparently hoped to see a strong ruler emerge from the Medici family, which had captured the papacy in 1513 with the pontificate of Leo X (r. 1513–1521). At the same time, the Medici family retained control over the powerful territorial state of Florence. The situation was similar to that of Machiavelli's hero Cesare Borgia and his father Pope Alexander VI, who had earlier brought factious Romagna to heel by placing secular family goals and religious policy in tandem. *The Prince* was pointedly dedicated to Lorenzo de' Medici, duke of Urbino and grandson of Lorenzo the Magnificent.

Whatever Machiavelli's hopes may have been, the Medicis were not destined to be Italy's deliverers. The second Medici pope, Clement VII (r. 1523–1534), watched helplessly as Rome was sacked by the army of Emperor Charles V in 1527, also the year of Machiavelli's death.

Revival of Monarchy in Northern Europe

After 1450 there was a progressive shift from divided feudal to unified national monarchies as "sovereign" rulers emerged. This is not to say that the dynastic and chivalric ideals of feudal monarchy vanished. Territorial princes did not pass from the scene; representative bodies persisted and in some areas even grew in influence. But in the late fifteenth and early sixteenth centuries, the old problem of the one and the many was decided in favor of the interests of monarchy.

The feudal monarchy of the High Middle Ages was characterized by the division of the basic powers of government between the king and his semiautonomous vassals. The nobility and the towns had acted with varying degrees of unity and success through evolving representative assemblies such as the English Parliament, the French Estates General, and the Spanish *Cortes* to thwart the centralization of royal power. Because of the Hundred Years' War and the Great Schism in the church, the nobility and the clergy were in decline by the late Middle Ages and less able to contain expanding monarchies.

The increasingly important towns began to ally with the king. Loyal, business-wise townspeople, not the nobility and the clergy, increasingly staffed the royal offices and became the king's lawyers, bookkeepers, military tacticians, and foreign diplomats. This new alliance between king and town broke the bonds of feudal society and made possible the rise of sovereign states.

In a sovereign state, the powers of taxation, war making, and law enforcement no longer belong to semiautonomous vassals but are concentrated in the monarch and are exercised by his or her chosen agents. Taxes, wars, and laws become national rather than merely regional matters. Only as monarchs became able to act independently of the nobility and representative assemblies could they overcome the decentralization that had been the basic obstacle to nation building. Ferdinand and Isabella of Spain rarely called the *Cortes* into session. The French Estates General did not meet at all from 1484 to 1560. Henry VII (r. 1485–1509) of England managed to raise revenues without going begging to Parliament after Parliament voted him customs revenues for life in 1485. Monarchs were also assisted by brilliant theorists, from Marsilius of Padua in the fourteenth century to Machiavelli to Jean Bodin in the sixteenth, who eloquently argued the sovereign rights of monarchy.

The many were, of course, never totally subjugated to the one. But in the last half of the fifteenth century, rulers demonstrated that the law was their creature. They appointed civil servants whose vision was no longer merely local or regional. In Castile, they were the *corregidores,* in England, the justices of the peace, and in France, bailiffs operating through well-drilled lieutenants. These royal ministers and agents could become closely attached to the localities they administered in the ruler's name. And regions were able to secure congenial royal appointments. Throughout England, for example, local magnates served as representatives of the Tudors. Nonetheless these new executives remained royal executives, bureaucrats whose outlook was "national" and whose loyalty was to the "state."

Monarchies also began to create standing national armies in the fifteenth century. The noble cavalry receded as the infantry and the artillery became the backbone of royal armies. Mercenary soldiers were recruited from Switzerland and Germany to form the major part of the "king's army." Professional soldiers who fought for pay and booty proved far more efficient than feudal vassals who fought simply for honor's sake. Monarchs who failed to meet their payrolls, however, faced a new danger of mutiny and banditry on the part of foreign troops.

The growing cost of warfare in the fifteenth and sixteenth centuries increased the need of monarchs for new national sources of income, but their efforts to expand royal revenues were hampered by the stubborn belief among the highest classes that they were immune from government taxation. The nobility guarded their properties and traditional rights and despised taxation as an insult and a humiliation. Royal revenues accordingly grew at the expense of those least able to resist, and least able to pay.

The monarchs had several options when it came to raising money. As feudal lords they could collect rents from their royal domain. They could also levy national taxes on basic food and clothing, such as the *gabelle,* or "salt tax," in France and the *alcabala,* or 10 percent sales tax on commercial transactions, in Spain. The rulers could also levy direct taxes on the peasantry. This they did through agreeable representative assemblies of the privileged classes in which the peasantry did not sit. The *taille,* which the French kings independently determined from year to year after the Estates General was suspended in 1484, was such a tax. Innovative fund-raising devices in the fifteenth century included the sale of public offices and the issuance of high-interest government bonds. But rulers did not levy taxes on the powerful nobility. Rather, they borrowed from rich nobles and the great bankers of Italy and Germany. In money matters, the privileged classes remained as much the kings' creditors and competitors as their subjects.

France

Charles VII (r. 1422–1461) was a king made great by those who served him. His ministers created a permanent professional army, which—thanks initially to the inspiration of Joan of Arc—drove the English out of France. And largely because of the enterprise of an independent merchant banker named Jacques Coeur, the French also developed a strong economy, diplomatic corps, and national administration during Charles's reign. These were the sturdy tools with which Charles's son and successor, the ruthless Louis XI (r. 1461–1483), made France a great power.

There were two cornerstones of French nation building in the fifteenth century. The first was the collapse of the English Empire in France following the Hundred Years' War. The second was the defeat of Charles the Bold and his duchy of Burgundy. Perhaps Europe's strongest political power in the mid-fifteenth century, Burgundy aspired to dwarf both France and the Holy Roman Empire as the leader of a dominant middle kingdom. It might have done so had not the continental powers joined in opposition.

When Charles the Bold died in defeat in a battle at Nancy in 1477, the dream of Burgundian Empire died with him. Louis XI and Habsburg emperor Maximilian I divided the conquered Burgundian lands between them, with the treaty-wise Habsburgs getting the better part. The dissolution of Burgundy ended its constant intrigue against the French king and left Louis XI free to secure the monarchy. The newly acquired Burgundian lands and his own Angevin inheritance permitted the king to end his reign with a kingdom almost twice the size of that with which he had started. Louis successfully harnessed the nobility, expanded the trade and industry so carefully nurtured by Jacques Coeur, created a national postal system, and even established a lucrative silk industry at Lyons (later transferred to Tours).

A strong nation is a two-edged sword. Because Louis's successors inherited a secure and efficient government, they felt free to pursue what proved ultimately to be a debilitating foreign policy. Conquests in Italy in the 1490s and a long series of losing wars with the Habsburgs in the first half of the sixteenth century left France by the mid-sixteenth century again a defeated nation almost as divided internally as during the Hundred Years' War.

Spain

Spain, too, became a strong country in the late fifteenth century. Both Castile and Aragon had been poorly ruled and divided kingdoms in the mid-fifteenth century. The union of Isabella of Castile (r. 1474–1504) and Ferdinand of Aragon (r. 1479–1516) changed that situation. The two future sovereigns married in 1469, despite strong protests from neighboring Portugal and France, both of whom foresaw the formidable European power the marriage would create. Castile was by far the richer and more populous of the two, having an estimated five million inhabitants to Aragon's population of under one million. Castile was also distinguished by its lucrative sheep-farming industry, run by a government-backed organization called the Mesta, another example of developing centralized economic planning. Although the marriage of Ferdinand and Isabella dynastically united the two kingdoms, they remained constitutionally separated. Each retained its respective government agencies—separate laws, armies, coinage, and taxation—and cultural traditions.

Ferdinand and Isabella could do together what neither was able to accomplish alone: subdue their realms, secure their borders, venture abroad militarily, and Christianize the whole of Spain. Between 1482 and 1492 they conquered the Moors in Granada. Naples became a Spanish possession in 1504. By 1512 Ferdinand had secured his northern borders by conquering the kingdom of Navarre. Internally, Ferdinand and Isabella won the allegiance of the *Hermandad*, a powerful league of cities and towns, which served them against stubborn landowners. Townspeople allied themselves with the crown and progressively replaced the nobility within the royal administration. The crown also extended its authority over the wealthy chivalric orders, a further circumscription of the power of the nobility.

Spain had long been remarkable among European lands as a place where three religions—Islam, Judaism, and Christianity—co-existed with a certain degree of toleration. This toleration was to end dramatically under Ferdinand and Isabella, who made Spain the prime exemplar of state-controlled religion.

Ferdinand and Isabella exercised almost total control over the Spanish church as they placed religion in the service of national unity. They appointed the higher clergy and the officers of the Inquisition. The Inquisition, run by Tomás de Torquemada (d. 1498), Isabella's confessor, was a key national agency established in 1479 to monitor the activity of converted Jews (*conversos*) and Muslims (*Moriscos*) in Spain. In 1492 the Jews were exiled and their properties were confiscated. In 1502 non-converting Moors in Granada were driven into exile by Cardinal Francisco Jiménez de Cisneros (1437–1517), under whom Spanish spiritual life remained largely uniform and successfully controlled. This was a major reason Spain remained a loyal Catholic country throughout the sixteenth century and provided a base of operation for the European Counter-Reformation.

Despite a certain internal narrowness, Ferdinand and Isabella were rulers with wide horizons. They contracted anti-French marriage alliances that came to determine a large part of European history in the sixteenth century. In 1496 their eldest daughter, Joanna, later known as "the Mad," married Archduke Philip, the son of Emperor Maximilian I. The fruit of this union, Charles I of Spain, was the first ruler over a united Spain; by his inheritance and election as emperor in 1519, he came to rule over a European kingdom almost equal in size to that of Charlemagne. A second daughter, Catherine of Aragon, wed Arthur, the son of the English king Henry VII. After Arthur's premature death, she was betrothed to his brother, the future King Henry VIII (r. 1509–1547), whom she married eight years later in 1509. The failure of this marriage became the key factor in the emergence of the Anglican church and the English Reformation.

The new power of Spain was also revealed in Ferdinand and Isabella's promotion of overseas exploration. They sponsored the Genoese adventurer Christopher Columbus (1451–1506), who arrived at the islands of the Caribbean while sailing west in search of a shorter route to the spice markets of the Far East. This patronage led to the creation of the Spanish Empire in Mexico and Peru, whose gold and silver mines helped to make Spain Europe's dominant power in the sixteenth century.

England

The latter half of the fifteenth century was a period of especially difficult political trial for the English. Following the Hundred Years' War, a defeated England was subjected to internal warfare between two rival branches of the royal family, the House of York and the House of Lancaster. This conflict, known to us today as the Wars of the Roses (because York's symbol, according to legend, was a white rose, and Lancaster's a red rose), kept England in turmoil from 1455 to 1485.

The Lancastrian monarchy of Henry VI (r. 1422–1461) was consistently challenged by the duke of York and his supporters in the prosperous southern towns. In 1461 Edward IV (r. 1461–1483), son of the duke of York, successfully seized power and instituted a strong-arm rule that lasted more than twenty years; it was only briefly interrupted in 1470–1471 by Henry VI's short-lived restoration. Assisted by loyal and able ministers, Edward effectively increased the power and finances of the monarchy.

His brother, Richard III (r. 1483–1485), usurped the throne from Edward's son, and after Richard's death, the new Tudor dynasty portrayed him as an unprincipled villain who had also murdered Edward's sons in the Tower of London to secure his hold on the throne. The best-known version of this characterization—unjust according to some—is found in Shakespeare's *Richard III*. Be that as it may, Richard's reign saw the growth of support for the exiled Lancastrian Henry Tudor, who returned to England to defeat Richard on Bosworth Field in August 1485.

Henry Tudor ruled as Henry VII (r. 1485–1509), the first of the new Tudor dynasty that would dominate England throughout the sixteenth century. To bring the rival royal families together and to make the hereditary claim of his offspring to the throne uncontestable, Henry married Edward IV's daughter, Elizabeth of York. He succeeded in disciplining the English nobility through a special instrument of the royal will known as the *Court of Star Chamber*. Created with the sanction of Parliament in 1487, the court was intended to end the perversion of English justice by "over-mighty subjects," that is, powerful nobles who used intimidation and bribery to win favorable verdicts in court cases. In the Court of Star Chamber, the king's councillors sat as judges and were not swayed by such tactics. The result was a more equitable court system.

It was also a court more amenable to the royal will. Henry shrewdly construed legal precedents to the advantage of the crown, using English law to further the ends of monarchy. He managed to confiscate noble lands and fortunes with such success that he was able to govern without dependence on Parliament for royal funds, always a cornerstone of strong monarchy. In these ways, Henry began to shape a monarchy that would develop into one of early modern Europe's most exemplary governments during the reign of his granddaughter, Elizabeth I.

The Holy Roman Empire

Germany and Italy were the striking exceptions to the steady development of politically centralized lands in the last half of the fifteenth century. Unlike England, France, and Spain, the Holy Roman Empire saw the many thoroughly repulse the one. In Germany territorial rulers and cities resisted every effort at national consolidation and unity. As in Carolingian times, rulers continued to partition their kingdoms, however small, among their sons. By the late fifteenth century, Germany was hopelessly divided into some 300 autonomous political entities.

The princes and the cities did work together to create the machinery of law and order, if not of union, within the divided empire. The emperor and the major German territorial rulers reached an agreement in 1356, the *Golden Bull*. It established a seven-member electoral college consisting of the archbishops of Mainz, Trier, and Cologne; the duke of Saxony; the margrave of Brandenburg; the count Palatine; and the king of Bohemia. This group also functioned as an administrative body. They elected the emperor and, in cooperation with him, provided what transregional unity and administration existed.

The figure of the emperor gave the empire a single ruler in law, if not in fact. The conditions of his rule and the extent of his powers over his subjects, especially the seven electors, were renegotiated with every imperial election. Therefore, the rights of the many (the princes) were always balanced against the power of the one (the emperor).

In the fifteenth century an effort was made to control incessant feuding by the creation of an imperial diet (*Reichstag*). This was a national assembly of the seven electors, the nonelectoral princes, and the sixty-five imperial free cities. The cities were the weakest of the three bodies represented in the diet. During such an assembly in Worms in 1495, the members won from Emperor Maximilian I (r. 1493–1519) an imperial ban on private warfare and the creation of a Supreme Court of Justice to enforce internal peace, and an imperial Council of Regency to coordinate imperial and internal German policy. The latter was very grudgingly conceded by the emperor because it gave the princes a share in executive power.

Although important, these reforms were still a poor substitute for true national unity. In the sixteenth and seventeenth centuries, the territorial princes became virtually sovereign rulers in their various domains. Such disunity aided religious dissent and conflict. It was in the cities and territories of still-feudal, fractionalized, backward Germany that the Protestant Reformation broke out in the sixteenth century.

The Northern Renaissance

The scholarly works of northern humanists created a climate favorable to religious and educational reforms on the eve of the Reformation. Northern humanism was initially stimulated by the importation of Italian learning through such varied intermediaries as students who had studied in Italy, merchants who traded there, and the Brothers of the Common Life. This last was an influential lay religious movement that began in the Netherlands and permitted men and women to live a shared religious life without making formal vows of poverty, chastity, and obedience.

The northern humanists, however, developed their own distinctive culture. They tended to come from more diverse social backgrounds and to be more devoted to religious reforms than their Italian counterparts. They were also more willing to write for lay audiences as well as for a narrow intelligentsia. Thanks to the invention of printing with movable type, it became possible for humanists to convey their educational ideals to laypeople and clerics alike. Printing gave new power and influence to elites in both church and state, who now could popularize their viewpoints freely and widely.

The Printing Press

A variety of forces converged in the fourteenth and fifteenth centuries to give rise to the invention of the printing press. Since the days of Charlemagne,

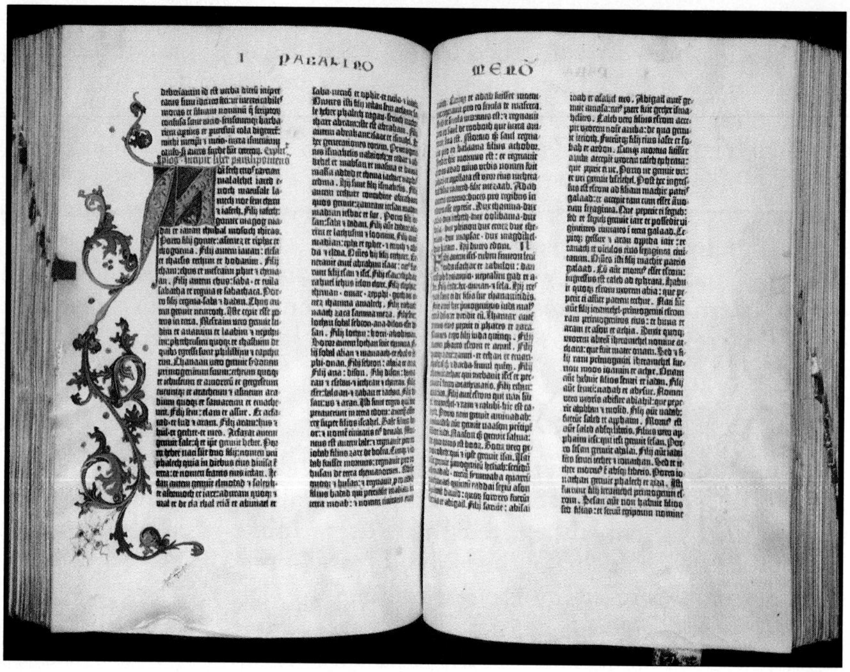

The printing press made possible the diffusion of Renaissance learning. But no book stimulated thought more at this time than did the Bible. With Gutenberg's publication of a printed Bible in 1454, scholars gained access to a dependable, standardized text, so that Scripture could be discussed and debated as never before. [Huntington Library]

kings and princes had encouraged schools and literacy to help provide educated bureaucrats to staff the offices of their kingdoms. Without people who could read, think critically, and write reliable reports, no kingdom, large or small, could be properly governed. By the fifteenth century, a new literate lay public had been created, thanks to the enormous expansion of schools and universities during the late Middle Ages (the number of universities more than tripled between 1300 and 1500, growing from twenty to seventy).

The invention of a process of cheap paper manufacture also helped to make books economical and to broaden their content. Manuscript books had been inscribed on vellum, a cumbersome and expensive medium. (It required 170 calfskins or 300 sheepskins to make a single vellum Bible.) Single-sheet woodcuts had long been printed. This involved carving a block of wood and inking it, then stamping out as many copies as one could make before the wood deteriorated. The end product was much like a modern poster.

In response to the demand for books created by the expansion of lay literacy, Johann Gutenberg (d. 1468) invented printing with movable type in the mid-fifteenth century in the German city of Mainz, the center of printing for the whole of western Europe. Thereafter, books were rapidly and handsomely produced on topics both profound and practical, and intended for ordinary lay readers, scholars, and clerics alike. Especially popular in the early decades of print were books of piety and religion, calendars and almanacs, and "how-to" books (for example, on child rearing, making brandies and liquors, curing animals, and farming successfully).

The new technology proved enormously profitable to printers, whose numbers exploded. By 1500, within a scant fifty years of Gutenberg's press, printing presses operated in at least sixty German cities and in more than 200 cities throughout Europe. The printing press was a boon to the careers of humanists, who now gained international audiences.

Literacy deeply affected people everywhere, nurturing self-esteem and a critical frame of mind. By standardizing texts, the print revolution made anyone who could read an instant authority. Rulers in church and state now had to deal with a less credulous and docile laity. Print was also a powerful tool for political and religious propaganda as well. Kings could now indoctrinate people as never before, and the clergy found themselves able to mass produce both indulgences and pamphlets.

Erasmus

The far-reaching influence of Desiderius Erasmus (1466?–1536), the most famous of the northern humanists and the "prince of the humanists," illustrates the impact of the printing press. Erasmus gained fame both as an educational and as a religious reformer. His life and work make clear that many loyal Catholics wanted major reforms long before the Reformation made them a reality.

Erasmus earned his living by tutoring when patrons were scarce. He prepared short Latin dialogues for his students that were intended to teach them how to speak and live well, inculcating good manners and language by encouraging them to imitate what they read.

These dialogues were published under the title *Colloquies*; they grew in number and length in consecutive editions, coming also to embrace anticlerical dialogues and satires on popular religious superstition. Erasmus collected ancient and contemporary proverbs as well, which he published under the title *Adages*. Beginning with about 800 examples, he increased his collection to more than 5,000 in the final edition of the work. Among the sayings that the *Adages* popularized are such common modern expressions as "to leave no stone unturned" and "where there is smoke, there is fire."

Erasmus aspired to unite the classical ideals of humanity and civic virtue with the Christian ideals of love and piety. He believed that disciplined study of the classics and the Bible, if begun early enough, was the best way to reform both individuals and society. He summarized his own beliefs with the phrase *philosophia Christi*, a simple, ethical piety in imitation of Christ. He set this ideal in starkest contrast to what he believed to be the dogmatic, ceremonial, and factious religious practice of the later Middle Ages. What most offended him about the Scholastics, both those of the late Middle Ages and, increasingly, the new Lutheran ones, was their letting doctrine and disputation overshadow humble piety and Christian practice.

To promote his own religious beliefs, Erasmus labored to make the ancient Christian sources available in their original versions. He believed that only as people drank from the pure, unadulterated sources could moral and religious health result. He edited the works of the Church fathers and produced a Greek edition of the New Testament (1516), which became the basis for his new, more accurate Latin translation (1519).

These various enterprises did not please church authorities. They were unhappy with both Erasmus's "improvements" on the Vulgate, Christendom's Bible for over a thousand years, and his popular anticlerical satires. At one point in the mid-sixteenth century, all of Erasmus's works were placed on the *Index of Forbidden Books*. Erasmus also received Luther's unqualified condemnation for his views on the freedom of human will. Still, Erasmus's works became basic tools of reform in the hands of both Protestant and Catholic reformers.

Humanism and Reform

In France, Spain, England, and Germany, humanism stirred both educational and religious reform.

GERMANY Rudolf Agricola (1443–1485), the "father of German humanism," spent ten years in Italy and he introduced Italian learning to Germany when he returned. Conrad Celtis (d. 1508), the first German poet laureate, and Ulrich von Hutten (1488–1523), a fiery knight, gave German humanism a nationalist coloring hostile to non-German cultures, especially Roman. Von Hutten especially illustrates the union of humanism, German nationalism, and Luther's religious reform. A poet who admired Erasmus, he attacked indulgences and published an edition of Valla's exposé of the Donation of Constantine (see the earlier section on Valla). He died in 1523 the victim of a hopeless knights' revolt against the princes.

The *cause célèbre* that brought von Hutten onto the historical stage and unified reform-minded German humanists was the Reuchlin affair. Johann Reuchlin (1455–1522) was Europe's foremost Christian authority on Hebrew and Jewish learning. He wrote the first reliable Hebrew grammar by a Christian scholar and was personally attracted to Jewish mysticism. Around 1506 a Christian who had converted from Judaism, supported by the Dominican order in Cologne, began a movement to suppress Jewish writings. When this man, whose name was Pfefferkorn, attacked Reuchlin, many German humanists, in the name of academic freedom and good scholarship and not for any pro-Jewish sentiment, rushed to Reuchlin's defense. The controversy lasted several years and produced one of the great satires of the period, the *Letters of Obscure Men* (1515), a merciless satire of monks and Scholastics to which von Hutten contributed. When Martin Luther came under attack in 1517 for his famous ninety-five theses against indulgences, many German humanists saw a repetition of the Scholastic attack on Reuchlin and rushed to his side.

Thomas More (1478–1535), painted by Hans Holbein the Younger in 1527. The English statesman and author was beheaded by Henry VIII for his refusal to recognize the king's sovereignty over the English church. [The Frick Collection]

ENGLAND Italian learning came to England by way of English scholars and merchants and visiting Italian prelates. Lectures by William Grocyn (d. 1519) and Thomas Linacre (d. 1524) at Oxford and those of Erasmus at Cambridge marked the scholarly maturation of English humanism. John Colet (1467–1519), dean of Saint Paul's Cathedral, patronized humanist studies for the young and promoted religious reform as well.

Thomas More (1478–1535), a close friend of Erasmus, is the best known English humanist. His *Utopia* (1516), a conservative criticism of contemporary society, rivals the plays of Shakespeare as the most-read sixteenth-century English work. Utopia depicted an imaginary society based on reason and tolerance that overcame social and political injustice by holding all property and goods in common and requiring everyone to earn their bread by their own work.

More became one of Henry VIII's most trusted diplomats. But his repudiation of the Act of Supremacy (1534), which made the king of England head of the English church in place of the pope (see Chapter 11), and his refusal to recognize the king's marriage to Anne Boleyn led to his execution in July 1535. Although More remained Catholic, humanism in England, as also in Germany, played an important role in preparing the way for the English Reformation.

FRANCE The French invasions of Italy made it possible for Italian learning to penetrate France, stirring both educational and religious reform. Guillaume Budé (1468–1540), an accomplished Greek scholar, and Jacques Lefèvre d'Étaples (1454–1536), a biblical authority, were the leaders of French humanism. Lefèvre's scholarly works exemplified the new critical scholarship and influenced Martin Luther. Guillaume Briçonnet (1470–1533), the bishop of Meaux, and Marguerite d'Angoulême (1492–1549), sister of King Francis I, the future queen of Navarre, and a successful spiritual writer in her own right, cultivated a generation of young reform-minded humanists. The future Protestant reformer John Calvin was a product of this native reform circle.

SPAIN Whereas in England, France, and Germany, humanism prepared the way for Protestant reforms, in Spain it entered the service of the Catholic Church. Here the key figure was Francisco Jiménez de Cisneros (1437–1517), a confessor to Queen Isabella, and after 1508 the "Grand Inquisitor"—a position that allowed him to enforce the strictest religious orthodoxy. Jiménez founded the University of Alcalá near Madrid in 1509, printed a Greek edition of the New Testament, and translated many religious tracts designed to reform clerical life and better direct lay piety. His great achievement, taking fifteen years to complete, was the *Complutensian Polyglot Bible*, a six-volume work that placed the Hebrew, Greek, and Latin versions of the Bible in parallel columns. Such scholarly projects and internal church reforms joined with the repressive measures of Ferdinand and Isabella to keep Spain strictly Catholic throughout the Age of Reformation.

Voyages of Discovery and the New Empire in the West

On the eve of the Reformation, the geographical as well as the intellectual horizons of Western people were changing. The fifteenth century saw the beginning of western Europe's global expansion and the transference of commercial supremacy from the Mediterranean and the Baltic to the Atlantic seaboard.

Gold and Spices

Mercenary motives, reinforced by traditional missionary ideals, inspired the Portuguese prince Henry the Navigator (1394–1460) to sponsor the Portuguese exploration of the African coast. His main object was the gold trade, which for centuries Muslims had monopolized. By the last decades of the fifteenth century, gold from Guinea was entering Europe by way of Portuguese ships calling at the port cities of Lisbon and Antwerp, rather than by the traditional Arab land routes. Antwerp became the financial center of Europe, a commercial crossroads where the enterprise and derring-do of the Portuguese, the Spanish, and especially the Flemish met the capital funds of the German banking houses of Fugger and Welser.

The rush for gold quickly expanded into a rush for the spice markets of India. In the fifteenth century the diet of most Europeans was a dull combination of bread and gruel, cabbage, turnips, peas, lentils, and onions, together with what meat became available during seasonal periods of slaughter. Spices, especially pepper and cloves, were in great demand both to preserve and to enhance the taste of food.

Bartholomew Dias (d. 1500) opened the Portuguese Empire in the East when he rounded the Cape of Good Hope at the tip of Africa in 1487. A decade later, in 1498, Vasco da Gama (d. 1524) reached the coast of India. When he returned to Portugal, he brought with him a cargo worth sixty times the cost of the voyage. Later, the Portuguese established themselves firmly on the Malabar Coast with colonies in Goa and Calcutta and successfully challenged the Arabs and the Venetians for control of the European spice trade. (See Political Transformations, pp. 360.)

While the Portuguese concentrated on the Indian Ocean, the Spanish set sail across the Atlantic. They did so in the hope of establishing a shorter route to the rich spice markets of the East Indies. But rather than beating the Portuguese at their own game, Christopher Columbus (1451–1506) came upon the Americas instead.

Amerigo Vespucci (1451–1512) and Ferdinand Magellan (1480–1521) showed that these new lands were not the outermost territory of the Far East, as Columbus died believing. Their travels proved the lands to be an entirely new continent that opened on the still greater Pacific Ocean. Magellan, in search of a westward route to the East Indies, died in the Philippines.

The Spanish Empire in the New World

Columbus's voyage of 1492 marked, unknowingly to those who undertook and financed it, the beginning of more than three centuries of Spanish conquest, exploitation, and administration of a vast American empire. That imperial venture produced important results for the cultures of both the European and the American continents. The gold and silver extracted from its American possessions financed Spain's major role in the religious and political conflicts of the age and contributed to European inflation of the sixteenth century.

In large expanses of both South and North America, Spanish government set an imprint of Roman Catholicism, economic dependence, and hierarchical social structure that has endured to the present day. Such influence was already clear with Columbus. On October 12, 1492, after a thirty-three day voyage from the Canary Islands, Columbus landed in San Salvador (Watlings Island) in the eastern Bahamas. He thought that he was on an outer island of Japan (or what he called Cipangu); he had undertaken his journey in the mistaken notion that the island of Japan would be the first land mass he would reach as he sailed west. This belief was based on Marco Polo's accounts of his years in China in the thirteenth century and the first globe map of the world, by Martin Behaim. That map, published in 1492, showed only ocean between the west coast of Europe and the east coast of Asia. Not until his third voyage to the Caribbean did Columbus realize that the island of Cuba was not Japan and that the South American continent beyond it was not China.

When Columbus landed in San Salvador, his three ships were met on the beach by naked and extremely friendly natives. Like all the natives Columbus met on his first voyage, they were Taino Indians, who spoke a variant of a language known as Arawak. From the start, the natives' generosity amazed Columbus. They freely gave his men all the corn and yams they desired and many sexual favors as well. "They never say no," Columbus marveled. At the same time Columbus observed how very easily they could be enslaved.

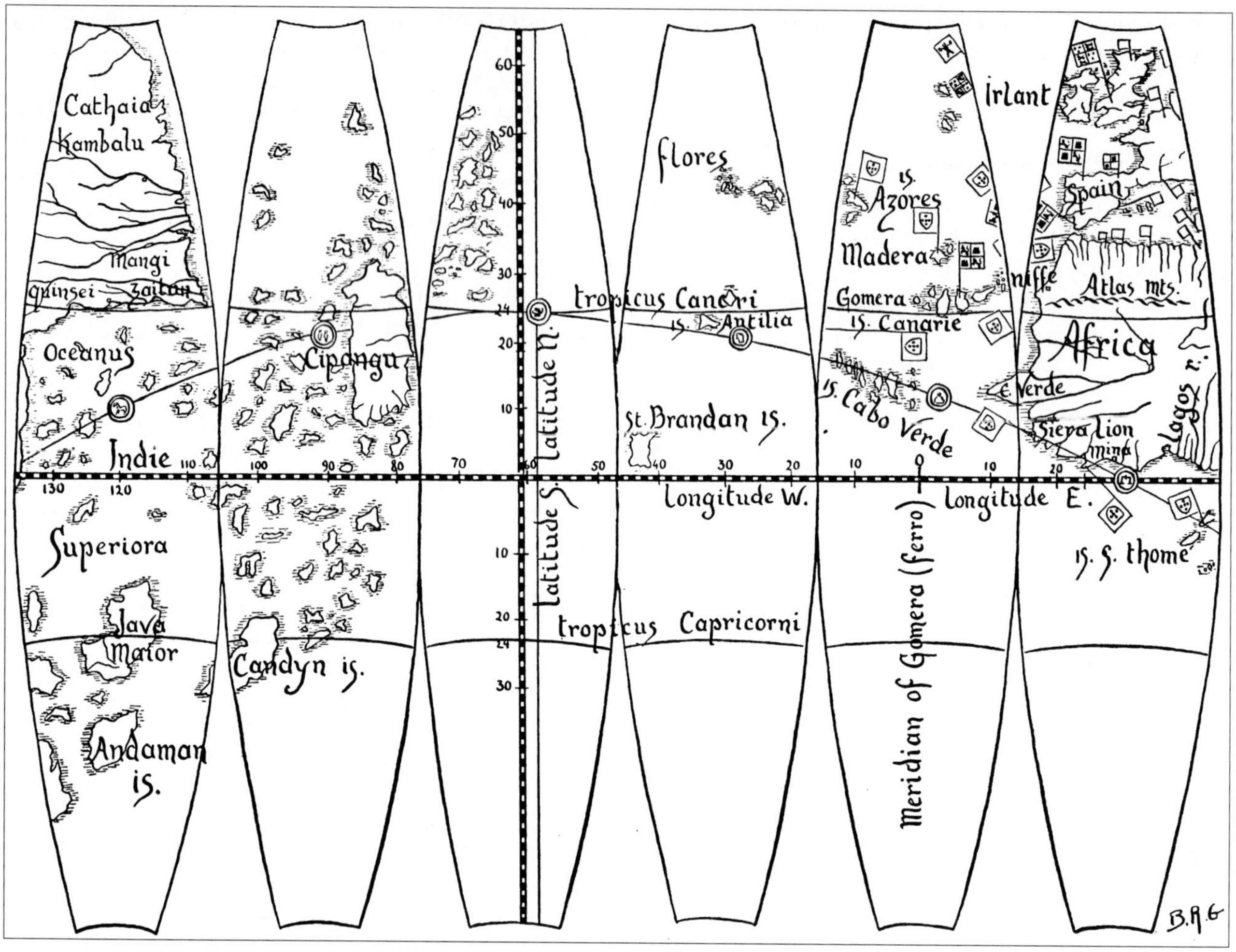

What Columbus knew of the world in 1492 was contained in this map by the Nuremberg geographer Martin Behaim, creator of the first spherical globe of the Earth. The ocean section of Behaim's globe is reproduced here. Departing the Canary Islands (in the second section from the right), Columbus expected his first major landfall to be Japan (Cipangu, in the second section from the left). When he landed at San Salvador, he thought he was on the outer island of Japan. And when he arrived in Cuba, he thought he was in Japan. [Reprinted from Samuel Eliot Morison, Admiral of the Ocean Sea. *Little, Brown and Company, Boston. 1942]*

A Conquered World

Mistaking the islands where he landed for the East Indies, Columbus called the native peoples whom he encountered "Indians." That name persisted even after it had become clear that this was new continent and not the East Indies. These native peoples had migrated across the Bering Straits from Asia onto the American landmass many thousands of years before the European voyages of discovery, creating communities all the way from Alaska to South America. The islands that Columbus mistakenly believed to be the East Indies came to be known as the West Indies.

Native Americans had established advanced civilizations going back to as early as the first millennium B.C.E. in two parts of what is today known as Latin America: Mesoamerica, which stretches from central Mexico into the Yucatan and Guatemala, and the Andean region of South America, primarily modern-day Peru and Bolivia. The earliest civilization in Mesoamerica, that of the Olmec, dates to about 1200 B.C.E. By the early centuries of the first millennium C.E. much of the region was dominated by the powerful city of Teotihuacán, which at the time was one of the largest urban centers in the world. The first millennium C.E. saw the flowering of the remarkable civilization of the Mayas in the

Yucatan region. The Mayans built large cities with immense pyramids and achieved considerable skills in mathematics and astronomy.

The first great interregional civilization in Andean South America, that of Chavín, emerged during the first millennium B.C.E. Regional cultures of the succeeding Early Intermediate Period (100–600 C.E.) included the Nazca on the south coast of Peru and the Moche on the north coast. The Huari-Tiahuanco culture again imposed interregional conformity during the Middle Horizon (600–1000). In the Late Intermediate Period, the Chimu Empire (800–1400) dominated the valleys of the Peruvian north coast. These early Andean societies built major ceremonial centers throughout the Andes, constructed elaborate irrigation systems, canals, and highways, and created exquisite pottery, textiles, and metalwork.

At the time of the arrival of the first Spanish explorers, the Aztec Empire dominated Mesoamerica and the Inca Empire dominated Andean South America. (See Map 10–3.) Both were very rich, and their conquest promised the Spanish the possibility of acquiring large quantities of gold.

THE AZTECS IN MEXICO The forebears of the Aztecs had arrived in the Valley of Mexico early in the twelfth century, where they lived as a subservient people. In 1428, under the leadership of Chief Itzcoatl, they rebelled against their rulers. That rebellion opened a period of Aztec conquest that reached its climax just after 1500. Their capital, Tenochtitlán (modern-day Mexico City), was located on an island in the center of a lake. By the time the Spanish conquerors arrived, the Aztecs governed many smaller tribes harshly, forcing labor and tribute from them. Believing that the gods must literally be fed with human bodies to guarantee continuing sunshine and soil fertility, the Aztecs also demanded and received thousands of captives each year to be sacrificed to their gods. Such policies left the Aztecs surrounded by terrorized tribes that felt no loyalty to them and longed for a liberator.

In 1519, Hernán Cortés landed on the coast of Mexico with a force of about 600 men. He opened communication with tribes nearby and then with Montezuma, the Aztec ruler. Montezuma initially believed Cortés to be a god. Aztec religion contained the legend of a priest named Quetzalcoatl who had been driven away four centuries earlier and had promised to return in the very year in which Cortés arrived. Montezuma initially attempted to appease Cortés with gifts of gold. The Indians had recently been ravaged by epidemic diseases of European origin, principally smallpox, and were in no position to oppose him. After several weeks of negotiations and the forging of alliances with subject tribes, Cortés's forces marched on Tenochtitlán, conquered it, and imprisoned Montezuma, who later died under unexplained circumstances. The Aztecs tried to drive the Spanish out, but by late 1521 they were defeated after great loss of life. Cortés proclaimed the former Aztec Empire to be New Spain.

THE INCAS IN PERU The second great Native American civilization conquered by the Spanish was that of the Incas, located in the highlands of Peru. Like the Aztecs, they had conquered many neighboring states and tribes and by the early sixteenth century ruled harshly over several million subject people, whom they compelled to build their roads and cities, farm their lands, and fight their wars.

In 1531, largely inspired by Cortés's example in Mexico, Francisco Pizarro sailed from Panama and landed on the western coast of South America to undertake a campaign against the Inca Empire. His force included perhaps 200 men armed with guns and swords and equipped with horses, the military power of which the Incas did not fathom.

In late 1531, Pizarro lured the Inca chief Atahualpa into a conference, where he captured him and killed many of his followers. Atahualpa attempted to ransom himself by having a vast horde of gold transported from all over Peru to Pizarro. Discovering that he could not turn Atahualpa into a puppet ruler, Pizarro executed him in 1533. Division within the ranks of the Spanish conquerors prevented effective royal control of the sprawling Inca civilization until the late 1560s.

The conquests of Mexico and Peru stand among the most brutal episodes in modern Western history. One civilization armed with advanced weaponry subdued, in a remarkably brief time, two powerful peoples. Beyond the drama and bloodshed, these conquests made it very difficult for these Native American cultures to have a major impact on Western civilization. Some scholars believe, however, that the Iroquois tribes of North America set examples of freedom of speech, assembly, and religion that may have influenced the framers of the American Constitution.

The Spanish and the Native Americans made some accommodations to each other, but in the end

POLITICAL TRANSFORMATIONS

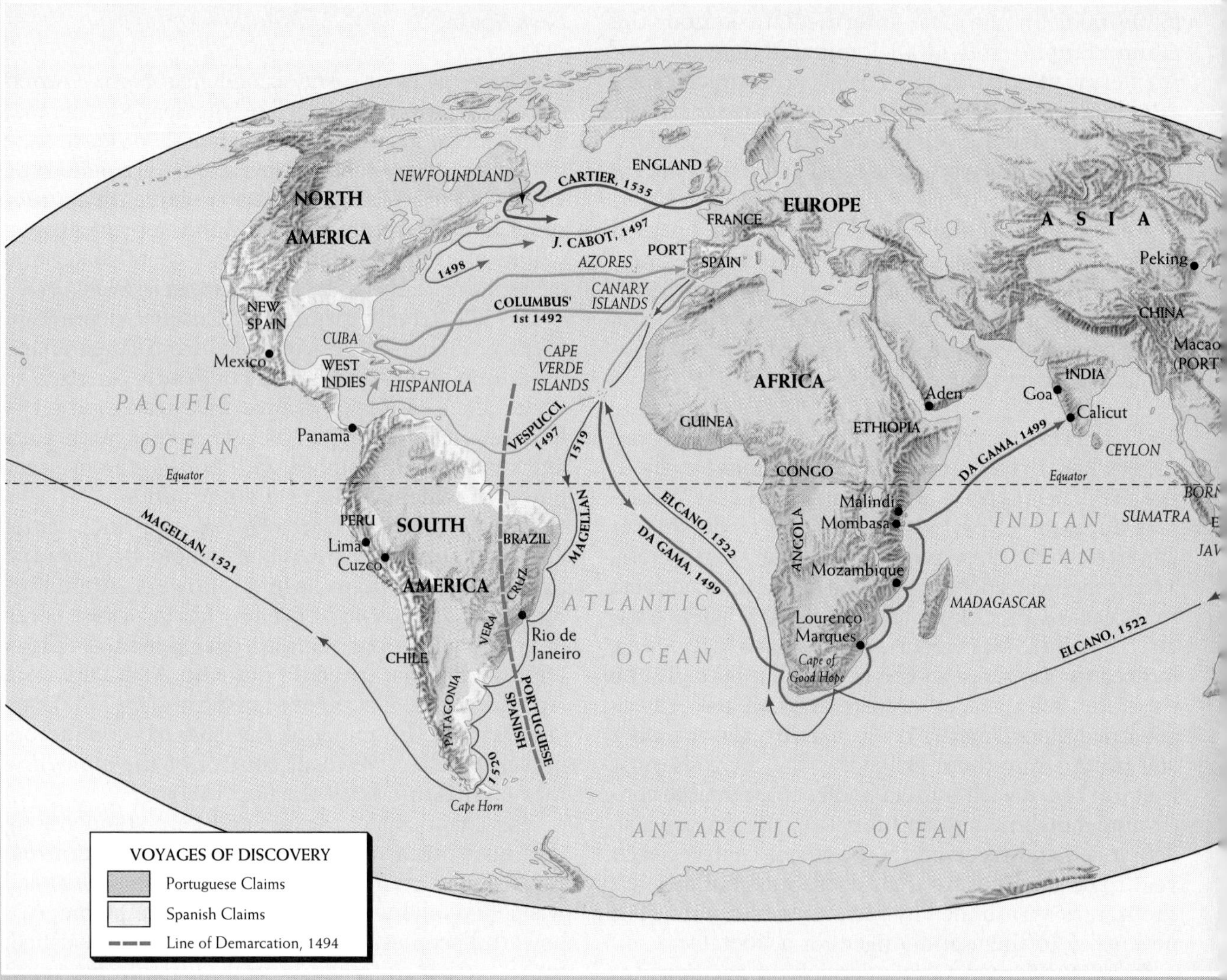

MAP 10–2

Voyages of Discovery and the Colonial Claims of Spain and Portugal

In 1487, Bartholew Diaz began a voyage around the Cape of Good Hope. His mission was benign—to map the geography of the African coast and assess the political stability of the people there with an eye to the possibilities for Western trade. Later voyages east and west would become increasingly less exploratory and benign. That was especially true of the voyages to the West Indies, Central America, and Mexico, where European settlement of the coastal regions drove native populations inland and established an aggressive Western rule and culture. By the late sixteenth and seventeenth centuries, European diseases greatly reduced native populations, causing planters and developers to import Europeans as indentured servants to replace native workers on the plantations of the new colonies. When the Europeans proved inadequate to the job, African slaves were brought across the ocean by the tens of thousands.

The transition from reconnaissance to settlement and exploitation of the world beyond Europe began with Vasco da Gama's voyage east in 1497. Focused strictly on commerce and carrying well-armed troops with an eye to establishing a Western trading empire, da Gama made the first passage across the southern Atlantic, arriving in Calcutta in 1498. En route, he had both peaceful and hostile confrontations with natives. Arriving at the Bay of São Braz (also called Mossel Bay and the site of Seal Island) while rounding the Cape of Good Hope in early December, 1497, he encountered the natives of South Africa for the first time. The journal that describes this encounter and the rest of the voyage was not written by da Gama, but by an unidentified sailor. The account portrays the good intentions of the Portuguese visitors and the friendliness of most of the natives, while also making clear the suspicion of both sides and European condescension and exploitation.

On Saturday [December 2] about two hundred negroes came, both young and old. They brought with them about a dozen oxen and cows and four or five sheep. As soon as we saw them we went ashore. They forthwith began to play on four or five flutes [known as "goras"], some producing high notes and others low ones, thus making a pretty harmony for negroes who are not expected to be musicians; and they danced in the style of negroes. The captain-major [da Gama] then ordered the trumpets to be sounded, and we, in the boats, danced, and the captain-major did so likewise when he rejoined us. This festivity ended, we landed . . . and bought a black ox for three bracelets. This ox we dined off on Sunday. We found him very fat, and his meat as toothsome as the beef of Portugal.

A Journal of the First Voyage of Vasco da Gama, 1497–1499, *translated and edited by E.G. Ravenstein (London, Hakluyt Society, 1898), p. 11.*

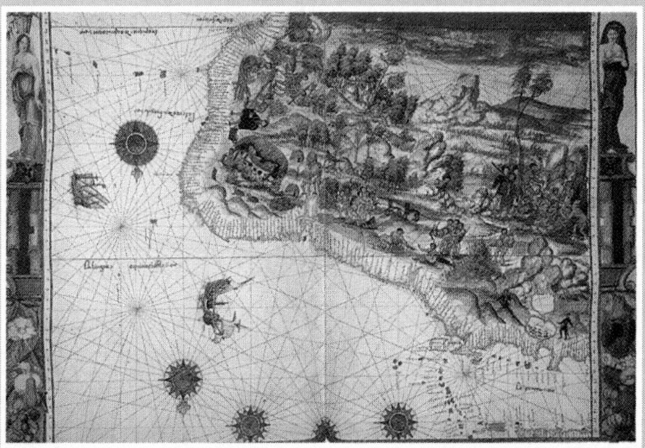

This map of Brazil, c1547, was drawn "upside-down," as if viewed from North America. Note Spanish cruelties to Indians, as well as scenes from daily life. [The Granger Collection, N.Y.]

European values, religion, economic goals, and language dominated. No group that retained indigenous religion, language, or values could become part of the new dominant culture or of the political power elite. In that sense, the Spanish conquests of the early sixteenth century marked the beginning of the process whereby South America was transformed into Latin America.

A sixteenth-century Aztec drawing depicts the Spanish conquest of Mexico. [The Bettmann Archive]

The Economy of Exploitation

From the beginning, the native peoples of America and their lands were drawn into the Atlantic economy and the world of competitive European commercialism. For the Indians of Latin America and somewhat later the blacks of Africa, that drive for gain meant various arrangements of forced labor.

There were three major components in the colonial economy of Latin America: mining, agriculture, and shipping. Each of them involved either labor or servitude or a relationship of dependence of the New World economy on that of Spain.

Mining The early *conquistadores*, or "conquerors," were primarily interested in gold, but by the middle of the sixteenth century, silver mining provided the chief source of metallic wealth. The great mining centers were Potosí in Peru and somewhat smaller sites in northern Mexico. The Spanish crown was particularly interested in mining because it received one-fifth (the *quinto*) of all mining revenues. For this reason, the crown maintained a monopoly over the production and sale of mercury, required in the silver-mining process. Exploring for silver never lost predominance during the colonial era. Its production by forced labor for the benefit of Spaniards and the Spanish crown epitomized the wholly extractive economy that stood at the foundation of colonial life.

Agriculture The major rural and agricultural institution of the Spanish colonies was the *hacienda*. This was a large landed estate owned by persons originally born in Spain (*peninsulares*) or persons of Spanish descent born in America (*creoles*). Laborers on the hacienda usually stood in some relation of formal servitude to the owner and were rarely free to move from the services of one landowner to another.

The *hacienda* economy produced two major products: foodstuffs for mining areas and urban centers and leather goods used in mining machinery. Both farming and ranching were subordinate to the mine economy.

In the West Indies, the basic agricultural unit was the plantation. In Cuba, Hispaniola, Puerto Rico, and other islands, the labor of black slaves from Africa produced sugar to supply an almost insatiable demand for the product in Europe.

A final major area of economic activity in the Spanish colonies was urban service occupations. These included government offices, the legal profession, and shipping. Their practitioners were either *peninsulares* or *creoles*, with the former dominating more often than not.

Labor Servitude All of this extractive and exploitive economic activity required labor, and the Spanish in the New World decided very early that the native population would supply that labor. A series of social devices was used to draw them into the new economic life imposed by the Spanish.

The first of these was the *encomienda*. This was a formal grant of the right to the labor of a specific number of Indians, usually a few hundred, but sometimes thousands, for a particular period of time. The institution stood in decline by the middle of the sixteenth century because the Spanish monarchs feared that the holders of *encomienda* might become a powerful independent nobility in the New World. They were also persuaded on humani-

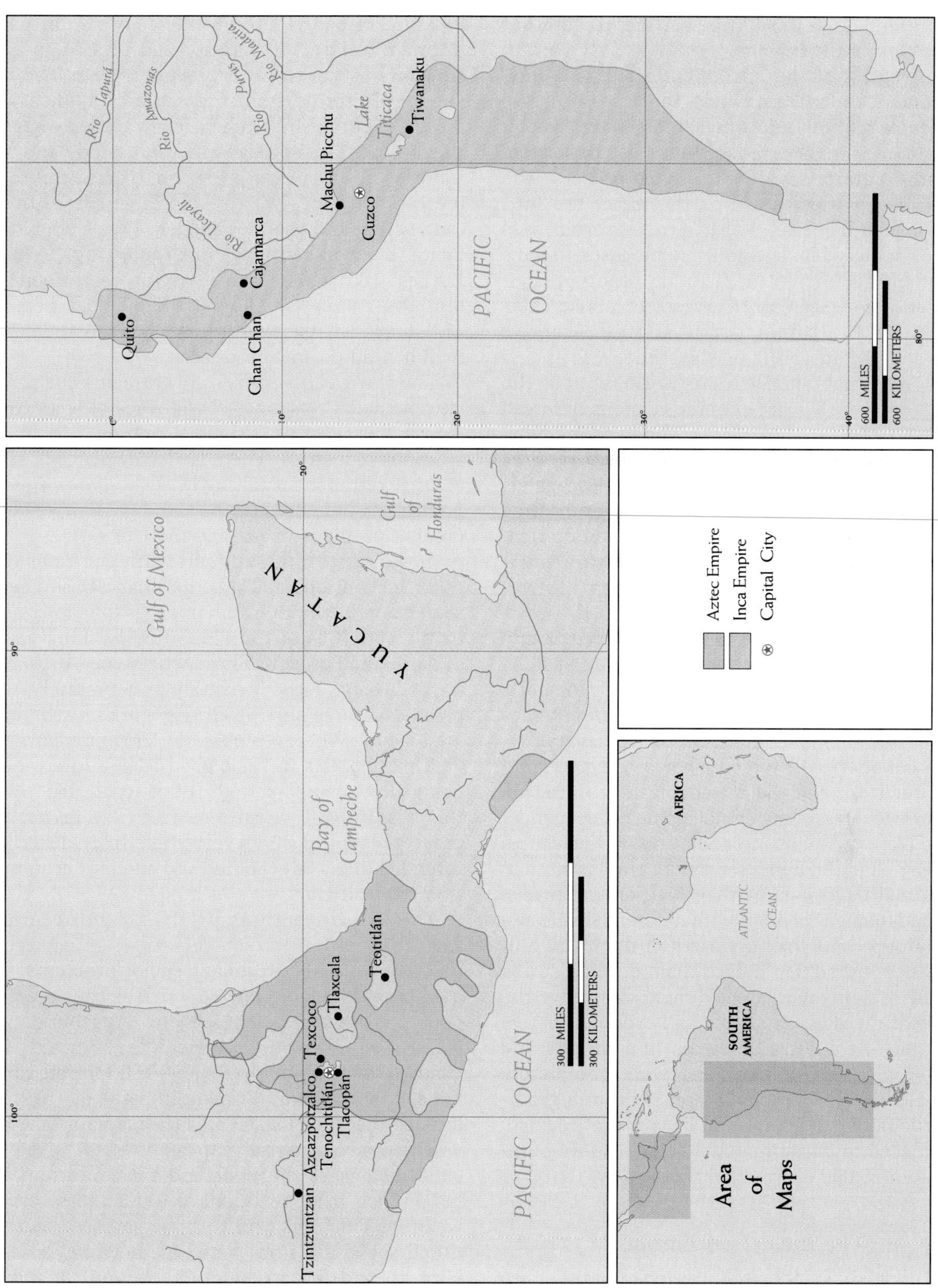

Map 10–3 The Aztec and Inca Empires on the Eve of the Spanish Conquest

tarian grounds against this particular kind of exploitation of the Indians.

The passing of the *encomienda* led to a new arrangement of labor servitude, the *repartimiento*. This device required adult male Indians to devote a certain number of days of labor annually to Spanish economic enterprises. In the mines of Peru, the *repartimiento* was known as the *mita*, the Inca term for their labor tax. *Repartimiento* service was often extremely harsh, and in some cases Indians did not survive their stint. The limitation of labor time led some Spanish managers to abuse their workers on the assumption that fresh workers would soon be appearing on the scene.

The eventual shortage of workers and the crown's pressure against extreme versions of forced labor led to the use of free labor. The freedom, however, was more in appearance than reality. Free Indian laborers were required to purchase goods from the land or mine owner, to whom they became forever indebted. This form of exploitation, known as *debt peonage*, continued in Latin America long after the nineteenth-century wars of liberation.

Black slavery was the final mode of forced or subservient labor in the New World. Both the Spanish and the Portuguese had earlier used African slaves in Europe. The sugar plantations of the West Indies now became the major center of black slavery.

The conquest, the forced labor of the economy of exploitation, and the introduction of European diseases had devastating demographic consequences for the Native American population. For centuries Europeans had lived in a far more complex human and animal environment than Native Americans. They had frequent contact with different ethnic and racial groups and with a variety of domestic animals. Such interaction helped them develop strong immune systems that enabled them to survive the ravages of measles, smallpox, and typhoid. Native Americans, by contrast, grew up in a simpler and more sterile environment and were completely defenseless against these diseases. Within a generation the native population of New Spain (Mexico) was reduced to an estimated 8 percent of its numbers, from 25,000,000 to 2,000,000.

The Impact on Europe

The influx of spices and precious metals into Europe from the new Spanish Empire was a mixed blessing. It contributed to a steady rise in prices during the sixteenth century that created an inflation rate estimated at 2 percent a year. The new supply of bullion from the Americas joined with enlarged European production to increase greatly the amount of coinage in circulation, and this increase in turn fed inflation. Fortunately, the increase in prices was by and large spread over a long period and was not sudden. Prices doubled in Spain by mid-century, quadrupled by 1600. In Luther's Wittenberg, the cost of basic food and clothing increased almost 100 percent between 1519 and 1540. Generally wages and rents remained well behind the rise in prices.

The new wealth enabled governments and private entrepreneurs to sponsor basic research and expansion in the printing, shipping, mining, textile, and weapons industries. There is also evidence of large-scale government planning in such ventures as the French silk industry and the Habsburg–Fugger development of mines in Austria and Hungary.

In the thirteenth and fourteenth centuries capitalist institutions and practices had already begun to develop in the rich Italian cities (one may point to the activities of the Florentine banking houses of Bardi and Peruzzi). Those who owned the means of production, either privately or corporately, were clearly distinguished from the workers who operated them. Wherever possible, entrepreneurs created monopolies in basic goods. High interest was charged on loans—actual, if not legal, usury. And the "capitalist" virtues of thrift, industry, and orderly planning were everywhere in evidence—all intended to permit the free and efficient accumulation of wealth.

The late fifteenth and the sixteenth centuries saw the maturation of this type of capitalism together with its attendant social problems. The Medicis of Florence grew very rich as bankers of the pope, as did the Fuggers of Augsburg, who bankrolled Habsburg rulers. The Fuggers lent Charles I of Spain more than 500,000 florins to buy his election as Holy Roman Emperor in 1519, and boasted that they had created the emperor. The new wealth and industrial expansion also raised the expectations of the poor and the ambitious and heightened the reactionary tendencies of the wealthy. This effect, in turn, aggravated the traditional social divisions between the clergy and the laity, the urban patriciate and the guilds, and the landed nobility and the agrarian peasantry.

Montaigne on "Cannibals" in Foreign Lands

The French philosopher Michel de Montaigne (1533–1592) had seen a Brazilian native in Rouen in 1562, an alleged cannibal brought to France by the explorer Villegagnon. The experience gave rise to an essay on the subject of what constitutes a "savage." Montaigne concluded that no people on earth were more barbarous than Europeans who take natives of other lands captive.

✦ *Is Montaigne romanticizing New World natives? Is he being too hard on Europeans? Had the Aztecs or Incas had the ability to discover and occupy Europe, would they have enslaved and exploited Europeans?*

Now, to return to my subject, I think there is nothing barbarous and savage in that nation [Brazil], from what I have been told . . . . Each man calls barbarism whatever is not his own practice; for indeed it seems we have no other test of truth and reason than the example and pattern of the opinions and customs of the country we live in. There [we] always [find] the perfect religion, the perfect government, the perfect and accomplished manners in all things. Those [foreign] people are wild, just as we call wild the fruits that Nature has produced by herself and in her normal course; where really it is those that we have changed artificially and led astray from the common order that we should rather call wild. The former retain alive and vigorous their genuine virtues and properties, which we have debased in the latter by adapting them to gratify our corrupted taste. And yet for all that, the savor and delicacy of some uncultivated fruits of those countries is quite as excellent, even to our taste, as that of our own. It is not reasonable that [our human] art should win the place of honor over our great and powerful mother Nature. We have so overloaded the beauty and richness of her works by our inventions that we have quite smothered her. Yet wherever her purity shines forth, she wonderfully puts to shame our vain and frivolous attempts: "Ivy comes readier without our care;/In lonely caves the arbutus grows more fair;/No art with artless bird song can compare."[1] All our efforts cannot even succeed in reproducing the nest of the tiniest little bird, its contexture, its beauty and convenience; or even the web of the puny spider. All things, says Plato,[2] are produced by nature, by fortune, or by art; the greatest and most beautiful by one or the other of the first two, the least and most imperfect by the last.

These nations, then, seem to me "barbarous" in this sense, that they have been fashioned very little by the human mind, and are still very close to their original naturalness. The laws of nature still rule them, very little corrupted by ours; and they are in such a state of purity that I am sometimes vexed that they were unknown earlier, in the days when there were men able to judge them better than we.

[1]*Propertius*, 1.11.10
[2]*Laws*, 10

The Complete Essays of Montaigne, *trans. by Donald M. Frame (Stanford: Stanford University Press, 1958), pp. 153–154.*

These divisions may indirectly have prepared the way for the Reformation as well by making many people critical of traditional institutions and open to new ideas—especially those that seemed to promise greater freedom and a chance at a better life.

✦

As it recovered from national wars during the late Middle Ages, Europe saw the establishment of permanent centralized states and regional governments. The foundations of modern France, Spain,

England, Germany, and Italy were laid at this time. As rulers imposed their will on regions outside their immediate domains, the "one" progressively took control of the "many," and previously divided lands came together as nations.

Thanks to the work of Byzantine and Islamic scholars, ancient Greek science and scholarship found their way into the West in these centuries. Europeans had been separated from their classical cultural heritage for almost eight centuries. No other world civilization had experienced such a disjunction from its cultural past. The discovery of classical civilization occasioned a rebirth of intellectual and artistic activity in both southern and northern Europe. One result was the splendor of the Italian Renaissance, whose scholarship, painting, and sculpture remain among western Europe's most impressive achievements.

Ancient learning was not the only discovery of the era. New political unity spurred both royal greed and national ambition. By the late fifteenth century, Europeans were in a position to venture far away to the shores of Africa, the southern and eastern coasts of Asia, and to the New World of the Americas. European discovery was not the only outcome of these voyages; the exploitation of the peoples and lands of the New World revealed a dark side of Western civilization. Some penalties were paid even then. The influx of New World gold and silver created new human and economic problems on the European mainland. In some circles Europeans even began to question their civilization's traditional values.

Review Questions

1. Discuss Jacob Burkhardt's interpretation of the Renaissance. What criticisms have been leveled against it? How would you define the term *Renaissance* in the context of fifteenth- and sixteenth-century Italy?
2. How would you define *Renaissance humanism*? In what ways was the Renaissance a break with the Middle Ages, and in what ways did it owe its existence to medieval civilization?
3. Who were some of the famous literary and artistic figures of the Italian Renaissance? What did they have in common that might be described as "the spirit of the Renaissance"?
4. Why did the French invade Italy in 1494? How did this event trigger Italy's political decline? How do the actions of Pope Julius II and the ideas of Niccolò Machiavelli signify a new era in Italian civilization?
5. A common assumption is that creative work proceeds best in periods of calm and peace. Given the combination of political instability and cultural productivity in Renaissance Italy, do you think this assumption is valid?
6. How did the Renaissance in the north differ from the Italian Renaissance? In what ways was Erasmus the embodiment of the northern Renaissance?
7. What factors led to the voyages of discovery? How did the Spanish establish their empire in the Americas? Why was the conquest so violent? What was the experience of native peoples during and after the conquest?

Suggested Readings

L. B. ALBERTI, *The Family in Renaissance Florence,* trans. by R. N. Watkins (1962). A contemporary humanist, who never married, explains how a family should behave.

M. ASTON, *The Fifteenth Century: The Prospect of Europe* (1968). Crisp social history, with pictures.

R. H. BAINTON, *Erasmus of Christendom* (1960). Charming presentation.

H. BARON, *The Crisis of the Early Italian Renaissance,* vols. 1 and 2 (1966). A major work, setting forth the civic dimension of Italian humanism.

B. BERENSON, *Italian Painters of the Renaissance* (1957). Eloquent and authoritative.

C. BOXER, *Four Centuries of Portuguese Expansion, 1415–1825* (1961). Comprehensive survey by the leading authority.

G. A. BRUCKER, *Renaissance Florence* (1969). Comprehensive survey of all facets of Florentine life.

G. A. BRUCKER, *Giovanni and Lusanna: Love and Marriage in Renaissance Florence* (1986). Love in the Renaissance shown to be more Bergman than Fellini.

J. BURCKHARDT, *The Civilization of the Renaissance in Italy* (1867). The old classic that still has as many defenders as detractors.

R. E. CONRAD, *Children of God's Fire: A Documentary History of Black Slavery in Brazil* (1983). Not for the squeamish.

A. W. CROSBY, *The Columbian Exchange: Biological and Cultural Consequences of 1492* (1973). A study of the epidemiological disaster that Columbus visited upon Native Americans.

E. L. EISENSTEIN, *The Printing Press As an Agent of Change: Communications and Cultural Transformations in Early Modern Europe,* 2 vols. (1979). Bold, stimulating account of the centrality of printing to all progress in the period.

W. K. Ferguson, *Europe in Transition, 1300–1520* (1962). A major survey that deals with the transition from medieval society to Renaissance society.

C. Gibson, *Spain in America* (1956). A splendidly clear and balanced narrative.

C. Gibson, *The Aztecs Under Spanish Rule: A History of the Indians of the Valley of Mexico* (1964). Exceedingly interesting book.

F. Gilbert, *Machiavelli and Guicciardini* (1984). The two great Renaissance historians lucidly compared.

M. Gilmore, *The World of Humanism, 1453–1517* (1952). A comprehensive survey, especially strong in intellectual and cultural history.

W. L. Gundersheimer (ed.), *French Humanism, 1470–1600* (1969). Essays summarizing research and provoking further study.

J. R. Hale, *Renaissance Europe: The Individual and Society, 1480–1520* (1971). A galloping social history.

L. Hanke, *Bartholome de Las Casas: An Interpretation of His Life and Writings* (1951). Biography of the great Dominican critic of Spanish exploitation of Native Americans.

J. Hankins, *Plato in the Renaissance* (1992). A majesterial study of how Plato was read and interpreted by Renaissance scholars.

D. Herlihy, *The Family in Renaissance Italy* (1974). Excellent on family structure and general features.

D. Herlihy and C. Klapisch-Zuber, *Tuscans and Their Families* (1985). Important work based on unique demographic data that gives the reader a new appreciation of quantitative history.

D. L. Jensen, *Renaissance Europe: Age of Recovery and Reconciliation* (1981). Up-to-date and comprehensive survey.

F. Katz, *The Ancient American Civilizations* (1972). An excellent introduction.

B. Keen and M. Wasserman, *A Short History of Latin America* (1984). A good survey with very helpful bibliographical guides.

R. Kelso, *Doctrine of the Lady of the Renaissance* (1978). Noblewomen in the Renaissance.

C. Klapisch-Zuber, *Women, Family, and Ritual in Renaissance Italy* (1985). Provocative, wide-ranging essays documenting Renaissance Italy as very much a man's world.

P. O. Kristeller, *Renaissance Thought: The Classic, Scholastic, and Humanist Strains* (1961). A master shows the many sides of Renaissance thought.

I. Maclean, *The Renaissance Notion of Women* (1980). An account of the views of Renaissance intellectuals and their sources in antiquity.

R. Marius, *Thomas More: A Biography* (1984). Eloquent analysis of the man as well as of the saint.

L. Martines, *Power and Imagination: City States in Renaissance Italy* (1980). Stimulating account of cultural and political history.

H. A. Miskimin, *The Economy of Early Renaissance Europe, 1300–1460* (1975). Shows interaction of social, political, economic, and cultural change.

S. E. Morrison, *Admiral of the Ocean Sea: A Life of Christopher Columbus* (1946). Still the authoritative biography.

E. Panofsky, *Meaning in the Visual Arts* (1955). Eloquent treatment of Renaissance art.

J. H. Parry, *The Age of Reconnaissance* (1964). A comprehensive account of exploration in the years 1450–1650.

P. Partner, *Renaissance Rome, 1500–1559: A Portrait of a Society* (1976). A description of the city from an insider's perspective.

M. M. Phillips, *Erasmus and the Northern Renaissance* (1956). A learned, rewarding account of the man and the movement.

J. B. A. Pocock, *The Machiavellian Moment in Florentine Political Thought and the Atlantic Republican Tradition* (1975). Traces the influence of Florentine political thought in early modern Europe.

I. A. Richter (ed.), *The Notebooks of Leonardo da Vinci* (1985). The master in his own words.

Q. Skinner, *The Foundations of Modern Political Thought I: The Renaissance* (1978). Broad survey, including absolutely every known political theorist, major and minor.

CHAPTER 11

Luther and the Wittenberg reformers with Elector John Frederick of Saxony (1532–1547), painted about 1543. Luther is on the far left, Philip Melanchthon in the front on the far right. [Lucas Cranach the Younger, German, 1515–1586, "Martin Luther and the Wittenberg Reformers," (1926.55), oil on panel, $27^{5}/_{8}$ x $15^{5}/_{8}$ in. The Toledo Museum of Art, Toledo, Ohio; Purchased with funds from the Libbey Endowment, Gift of Edward Drummond Libbey.]

The Age of Reformation

KEY TOPICS

- The social and religious background to the Reformation
- Martin Luther's challenge to the church and the course of the Reformation in Germany
- The Reformation in Switzerland, France, and England
- Transitions in family life between medieval and modern times

In the second decade of the sixteenth century, a powerful religious movement began in Saxony in Germany and rapidly spread throughout northern Europe, deeply affecting society and politics as well as the spiritual lives of men and women. Attacking what they believed to be burdensome superstitions that robbed people of both their money and their peace of mind, Protestant reformers led a broad revolt against the medieval church. In a short span of time, hundreds of thousands of people from all social classes set aside the beliefs of centuries and adopted a more simplified religious practice.

The Protestant Reformation challenged aspects of the Renaissance, especially its tendency to follow classical sources in glorifying human nature and its loyalty to traditional religion. Protestants were more impressed by the human potential for evil than by the inclination to do good; they encouraged parents, teachers, and magistrates to be firm disciplinarians. On the other hand, Protestants also embraced many Renaissance values, especially in the sphere of educational reform and particularly with regard to training in ancient languages. Like the Italian humanists, the Protestant reformers prized the tools that allowed them to go directly to the original sources. For them this meant the study of the Hebrew and Greek scriptures, enabling them to root their consequent challenges to traditional institutions in biblical authority.

Society and Religion

The Protestant Reformation occurred at a time of sharp conflict between the emerging nation-states of Europe, bent on conformity and centralization within their realms, and the self-governing small towns and regions, long accustomed to running their own affairs. Since the fourteenth century, the king's law and custom had progressively overridden local law and custom almost everywhere. Many towns and territories were keenly sensitive to the loss of traditional rights and freedoms. Many townspeople and village folk perceived in the religious revolt an ally in their struggle to remain politically free and independent. The Reformation came to be closely identified in the minds of its supporters with what we today might call states' rights or local control.

Social and Political Conflict

The Reformation broke out first in the free imperial cities of Germany and Switzerland. There were about sixty-five such cities, and each was in a certain sense a little kingdom unto itself. The great majority had Protestant movements, but with mixed success and duration. Some quickly turned Protestant and remained so. Some were Protestant only for a short time. Others developed mixed confessions, frowning on sectarianism and aggressive proselytizing, and letting Catholics and Protestants live side by side with appropriate barriers.

What seemed a life-and-death struggle with higher princely or royal authority was not the only conflict cities were experiencing. They also suffered deep internal social and political divisions. Certain groups favored the Reformation more than others. In many places, guilds whose members were economically prospering and socially rising were in the forefront of the Reformation. The printers' guild is a prominent example. Its members were literate, sophisticated about the world, in a rapidly growing industry, and economically very ambitious. They also had an economic stake in fanning religious conflict with Protestant propaganda, which many of course also sincerely believed. Guilds with a history of opposition to reigning governmental authority also stand out among early Protestant supporters, regardless of whether their members were literate.

There is, in brief, evidence to suggest that people who felt pushed around and bullied by either local or distant authority—a guild by an autocratic local government, an entire city or region by a powerful prince or king—often perceived in the Protestant movement an ally, at least initially.

The Reformation broke out against a background of deep social and political divisions that bred resentment against authority. This early sixteenth-century woodcut by Georg Pencz presents a warning against tyranny. It shows a world turned upside down, with the hunted becoming the hunters. The rabbits capture the hunters and their dogs and subject them to the same brutal treatment—skinning, butchering, and cooking—that the hunters and dogs routinely inflict on rabbits. The message: tyranny eventually begets rebellion. [Hacker Art Books]

Injustice. This woodcut by an unknown artist compares the law, represented by the court scene in the center, to a spider's web, shown in the window on the right. Just as the web traps small, weak insects, the law ensnares the poor, seen hanging on the gallows and the wheel through the window on the left. And just as the large bee flies easily through the web, the rich and powerful escape punishment for their crimes. [Hacker Art Books]

Social and political experience thus coalesced with the larger religious issues in both town and countryside. A Protestant sermon or pamphlet seemed directly relevant, for example, to the townspeople of German and Swiss cities who faced incorporation into the territory of a powerful local prince, who looked on them as obedient subjects rather than as free citizens. When Martin Luther and his comrades wrote, preached, and sang about a priesthood of all believers, scorned the authority of ecclesiastical landlords, and ridiculed papal laws as arbitrary human inventions, they touched political as well as religious nerves. And this was as true in the villages as in the towns. Like city dwellers, the peasants on the land also heard in the Protestant sermon and pamphlet a promise of political liberation and even a degree of social betterment. More than the townspeople, the peasants found their traditional liberties—from fishing and hunting rights to representation at local diets—progressively being chipped away by the great secular and ecclesiastical landlords who ruled over them.

Popular Religious Movements and Criticism of the Church

The Protestant Reformation could also not have occurred without the monumental crises of the medieval church during the "exile" in Avignon, the Great Schism, the Conciliar period, and the Renaissance papacy. For increasing numbers of people, the medieval church had ceased to provide a viable foundation for religious piety. Many intellectuals and laypeople felt a sense of crisis about the traditional teaching and spiritual practice of the church. Between the secular pretensions of the papacy and the dry teaching of Scholastic theologians, laity and clerics alike began to seek a more heartfelt, idealistic, and—often, in the eyes of the pope—increasingly heretical religious piety. The late Middle Ages were marked by independent lay and clerical efforts to reform local religious practice and by widespread experimentation with new religious forms.

A variety of factors contributed to the growth of lay criticism of the church. The laity in the cities were becoming increasingly knowledgeable about the world and those who controlled their lives. They traveled widely—as soldiers, pilgrims, explorers, and traders. New postal systems and the printing press increased the information at their disposal. The new age of books and libraries raised literacy and heightened curiosity. Laypeople were increasingly able to take the initiative in shaping the cultural life of their communities.

From the Albigensians, Waldensians, Beguines, and Beghards in the thirteenth century to the Lollards and Hussites in the fifteenth, lay religious movements shared a common goal of religious simplicity in imitation of Jesus. Almost without exception they were inspired by an ideal of apostolic poverty in religion; that is, all wanted a religion of true self-sacrifice like that of Jesus and the first disciples. The laity sought a more egalitarian church, one that gave the members as well as the head of the church a voice, and a more spiritual church, one that lived manifestly according to its New Testament model.

THE MODERN DEVOTION One of the most constructive lay religious movements in northern Europe on the eve of the Reformation was that of the Brothers of the Common Life, or what came to be known as the Modern Devotion. The brothers

This sculpture illustrates the new piety of feeling that emerged in the fifteenth century in reaction to the cold, ritualized religious practice that had become predominant. Here the Virgin Mary is caught as she swoons over the crucifixion of her Son. During the sixteenth century, both Protestants and Catholics tried to accommodate the desire for personal involvement in religion. [Bebenhausen, Württembergisches Landesmuseum]

fostered religious life outside formal ecclesiastical offices and apart from formal religious vows. Established by Gerard Groote (1340–1384), the Modern Devotion was centered at Zwolle and Deventer in the Netherlands. The brother and (less numerous) sister houses of the Modern Devotion, however, spread rapidly throughout northern Europe and influenced parts of southern Europe as well. In these houses clerics and laity came together to share a common life, stressing individual piety and practical religion. Lay members were not expected to take special religious vows or to wear special religious dress, nor did they abandon their ordinary secular vocations.

The brothers were also active in education. They worked as copyists, sponsored many religious and a few classical publications, ran hospices for poor students, and conducted schools for the young, especially for boys preparing for the priesthood or a monastic vocation. As youths, Nicholas of Cusa, Johann Reuchlin, and Desiderius Erasmus were looked after by the brothers. Thomas à Kempis (d. 1471) summarized the philosophy of the brothers in what became the most popular religious book of the period, the *Imitation of Christ*. This semimystical guide to the inner life was intended primarily for monks and nuns, but was widely appropriated by laity who also wanted to pursue the ascetic life.

The Modern Devotion has been seen as the source of humanist, Protestant, and Catholic reform movements in the sixteenth century. Some scholars, however, believe that it represented an individualistic approach to religion, indifferent and even harmful to the sacramental piety of the church. It was actually a very conservative movement. The brothers retained the old clerical doctrines and values, while placing them within the new framework of an active common life. Their practices clearly met a need for a more personal piety and a better-informed religious life. Their movement appeared at a time when the laity were demanding good preaching in the vernacular and were even taking the initiative to endow special preacherships to ensure it. The Modern Devotion permitted laypeople to practice a full religious life without surrendering their life in the world.

LAY CONTROL OVER RELIGIOUS LIFE On the eve of the Reformation, Rome's international network of church offices, which had unified Europe religiously during the Middle Ages, began to fall apart in many areas. This collapse was hurried along by a growing sense of regional identity—incipient nationalism—and local secular administrative competence. The long-entrenched *benefice* system of the medieval church had permitted important ecclesiastical posts to be sold to the highest bidders and had left residency requirements in parishes unenforced. Such a system did not result in a vibrant local religious life. The substitutes hired by nonresident holders of *benefices* lived elsewhere, mostly in Rome. They milked the revenues of their offices, often performed their chores mechanically, and had neither firsthand knowledge of nor much sympathy with local needs and problems. Rare was the late medieval German town that did not have complaints about the maladministration, concubinage, or fiscalism of their clergy, especially the higher clergy (bishops, abbots, and prelates).

Communities had protested loudly the financial abuses of the medieval church long before Luther published his famous summary of economic grievances in 1520 in the *Address to the Christian Nobility of the German Nation*. The sale of indulgences in particular had been repeatedly attacked before Luther came on the scene. On the eve of the Reformation, this practice had expanded to permit people to buy release from time in purgatory for both themselves and their deceased loved ones. Rulers and magistrates had little objection to their sale, and might even encourage it so long as a generous portion of the income they generated remained in the local coffers. But when an indulgence was offered primarily for the benefit of distant interests, as with the Saint Peter's indulgence protested by Luther, resistance arose for strictly financial reasons, because their sale drained away local revenues.

The sale of indulgences would not end until rulers found new ways to profit from religion, and the laity found a more effective popular remedy for religious anxiety. The Reformation provided the former by sanctioning the secular dissolution of monasteries and the confiscation of ecclesiastical properties. It held out the latter in its new theology of justification by faith.

City governments also undertook to improve local religious life on the eve of the Reformation by endowing preacherships. These positions, supported by *benefices*, provided for well-trained and dedicated pastors who could provide regular preaching and pastoral care that went beyond the routine performance of the mass and traditional religious functions. In many instances these preacherships became platforms for Protestant preachers.

Magistrates also carefully restricted the growth of ecclesiastical properties and clerical privileges. During the Middle Ages, canon and civil law had come to recognize special clerical rights in both property and person. Because they were holy places, churches and monasteries had been exempted from the taxes and laws that affected others. They were treated as special places of "sacral peace" and asylum. It was considered inappropriate for holy persons (clergy) to be burdened with such "dirty jobs" as military service, compulsory labor, standing watch at city gates, and other obligations of citizenship. Nor was it thought right that the laity, of whatever rank, should sit in judgment on those who were their shepherds and intermediaries with God. The clergy, accordingly, came to enjoy an immunity of place (which exempted ecclesiastical properties from taxes and recognized their right of asylum) and an immunity of person (which exempted the clergy from the jurisdiction of civil courts).

On the eve of the Reformation measures were passed to restrict these privileges and to end their abuses. Among them we find efforts to regulate ecclesiastical acquisition of new property, to circumvent the right of asylum in churches and monasteries (a practice that posed a threat to the normal administration of justice), and to bring the clergy under the local tax code. Governments had understandably tired of ecclesiastical interference in what to them were strictly political spheres of competence and authority.

Martin Luther and German Reformation to 1525

Unlike France and England, late medieval Germany lacked the political unity to enforce "national" religious reforms during the late Middle Ages. There were no lasting Statutes of Provisors and *Praemunire*, as in England, nor a Pragmatic Sanction of Bourges, as in France, limiting papal jurisdiction and taxation on a national scale. What happened on a unified national level in England and France occurred only locally and piecemeal within German territories and towns. As popular resentment of clerical immunities and ecclesiastical abuses, especially over the selling of indulgences, spread among German cities and towns, an unorganized "national" opposition to Rome formed. German humanists had long given voice to such criticism, and by 1517 it was pervasive enough to provide a solid foundation for Martin Luther's reform.

Luther (1483–1546) was the son of a successful Thüringian miner. He was educated in Mansfeld, Magdeburg (where the Brothers of the Common Life were his teachers), and Eisenach. Between 1501 and 1505 he attended the University of Erfurt, where the nominalist teachings of William of Ockham and Gabriel Biel (d. 1495) prevailed. After receiving his master of arts degree in 1505, Luther registered with the Law Faculty following his parents' wishes. But he never began the study of law. To the disappointment of his family, he instead entered the Order of the Hermits of Saint Augustine in Erfurt on July 17, 1505. This decision had apparently been building for some time and was resolved during a lightning storm in which Luther, terrified, crying out to Saint Anne for assistance (Saint Anne was the patron saint of travelers in distress), promised to enter a monastery if he escaped death.

Ordained in 1507, Luther pursued a traditional course of study. In 1510 he journeyed to Rome on the business of his order, finding there justification for the many criticisms of the church he had heard in Germany. In 1511 he moved to the Augustinian monastery in Wittenberg, where he earned his doctorate in theology in 1512. Thereafter, he became a leader within the monastery, the new university, and the spiritual life of the city.

Justification by Faith Alone

Reformation theology grew out of a problem then common to many of the clergy and the laity: the failure of traditional medieval religion to provide either full personal or intellectual satisfaction. Luther was especially plagued by the disproportion between his own sense of sinfulness and the perfect righteousness that medieval theology taught that God required for salvation. Traditional church teaching and the sacrament of penance proved to be of no consolation. Luther wrote that he came to despise the phrase "righteousness of God," for it seemed to demand of him a perfection he knew neither he nor any other human being could ever achieve. His insight into the meaning of "justification by faith alone" was a gradual process that extended between 1513 and 1518. The righteousness that God demands, he concluded, did not result from many religious works and ceremonies but was given in full measure to those who believe and trust in Jesus Christ, who alone is the perfect righteousness satisfying to God. To believe in Christ meant to stand before God clothed in Christ's sure righteousness.

The Attack on Indulgences

An indulgence was a remission of the temporal penalty imposed by priests on penitents as a "work of satisfaction" for their mortal sins. According to medieval theology, after the priest absolved a penitent of guilt for the sins, the penitent remained under an eternal penalty, a punishment God justly imposed for sin. After absolution, however, this eternal penalty was said to be transformed into a temporal penalty, a manageable "work of satisfaction" that the penitent might perform here and now (for example, prayers, fasting, almsgiving, retreats, and pilgrimages). Penitents who defaulted on such prescribed works of satisfaction could expect to suffer for them in purgatory.

At this point, indulgences, which had earlier been given to Crusaders who did not complete their penances because they had fallen in battle, became

Lutherans made Jesus' blessing of infants and small children (Mark 10:13) a new theme in art and a forceful polemic both against Catholics, who believed good works to be a condition of salvation, and Anabaptists, who rejected infant baptism. Lucas Cranach the Elder painted over twenty versions of this scene. Here he portrays Jesus directly accessible to those with simple childlike faith, who do no special good works and have nothing to recommend them except God's grace. [Elke Walford, Hamburger Kunsthalle]

an aid to laity, made genuinely anxious by their belief in a future suffering in purgatory for neglected penances or unrepented sins. In 1343 Pope Clement VI (r. 1342–1352) had proclaimed the existence of a "treasury of merit," an infinite reservoir of good works in the church's possession that could be dispensed at the pope's discretion. On the basis of this declared treasury the church sold "letters of indulgence," which covered the works of satisfaction owed by penitents. In 1476 Pope Sixtus IV (r. 1471–1484) extended indulgences also to purgatory.

Originally, indulgences had been given only for the true self-sacrifice of going on a Crusade to the Holy Land. By Luther's time, they were regularly dispensed for small cash payments (very modest sums that were regarded as a good work of almsgiving). They were presented to the laity as remitting not only their own future punishments, but also those of their dead relatives presumed to be suffering in purgatory.

In 1517 a Jubilee indulgence was proclaimed during the pontificate of Pope Julius II (r. 1503–1513) to raise funds for the rebuilding of Saint Peter's in Rome. It was preached on the borders of Saxony in the territories of Archbishop Albrecht of Mainz. Albrecht was much in need of revenues because of the large debts he had incurred in order to hold, contrary to church law, three ecclesiastical appointments. The selling of the indulgence was a joint venture by Albrecht, the Augsburg banking-house of Fugger, and Pope Leo X, half the proceeds going to the pope and half to Albrecht and his cred-

A contemporary caricature depicts John Tetzel, the famous indulgence preacher. The last lines of the jingle read: "As soon as gold in the basin rings, right then the soul to Heaven springs." It was Tetzel's preaching that spurred Luther to publish his ninety-five theses. [Staatliche Lutherhalle, Wittenberg]

itors. The famous indulgence preacher John Tetzel (d. 1519) was enlisted to preach the indulgence in Albrecht's territories because he was a seasoned professional who knew how to stir ordinary people to action. As he exhorted on one occasion:

> Don't you hear the voices of your dead parents and other relatives crying out, "Have mercy on us, for we suffer great punishment and pain. From this you could release us with a few alms. . . . We have created you, fed you, cared for you, and left you our temporal goods. Why do you treat us so cruelly and leave us to suffer in the flames, when it takes only a little to save us?"[1]

When on October 31, 1517, Luther, according to tradition, posted his ninety-five theses against indulgences on the door of Castle Church in Wittenberg, he protested especially against the impression created by Tetzel that indulgences actually remitted sins and released the dead from punishment in purgatory. Luther believed these claims went far beyond the traditional practice and seemed to make salvation something that could be bought and sold.

Election of Charles V

The ninety-five theses were embraced by humanists and other proponents of reform. The theses made Luther famous overnight and prompted official proceedings against him. In October he was called before the general of the Dominican order in Augsburg. But as sanctions were being prepared against Luther, Emperor Maximilian I died (January 12, 1519), and this event, fortunate for the Reformation, turned attention away from heresy in Saxony to the contest for a new emperor.

The pope backed the French king, Francis I. However, Charles I of Spain, a youth of nineteen, succeeded his grandfather and became Emperor Charles V. (See Map 11–1.) Charles was assisted by both a long tradition of Habsburg imperial rule and a massive Fugger campaign chest, which secured the votes of the seven electors. The electors, who

[1]*Die Reformation in Augenzeugen berichten*, ed. by Helmar Junghaus (Düsseldorf: Karl Rauch Verlag, 1967), p. 44.

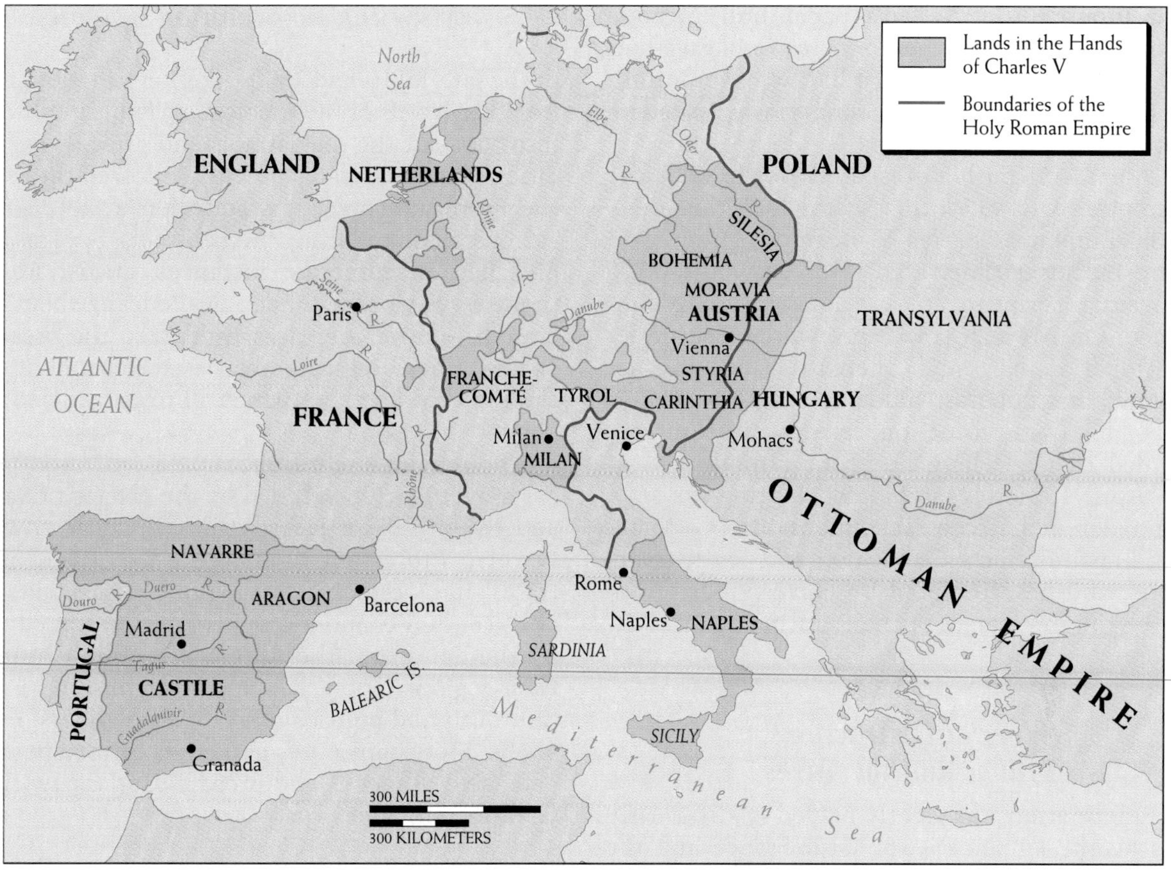

MAP 11–1 THE EMPIRE OF CHARLES V *Dynastic marriages and simple chance concentrated into Charles's hands rule over the lands shown here, plus Spain's overseas possessions. Crowns and titles rained down on him; election in 1519 as emperor gave him new distractions and responsibilities.*

traditionally enhanced their power at every opportunity, wrung new concessions from Charles for their votes. The emperor agreed to a revival of the Imperial Supreme Court and the Council of Regency and promised to consult with a diet of the empire on all major domestic and foreign affairs that affected the empire. These measures also helped the development of the Reformation by preventing unilateral imperial action against the Germans, something Luther could be thankful for in the early years of the Reformation.

Luther's Excommunication and the Diet of Worms

In the same month in which Charles was elected emperor, Luther entered a debate in Leipzig (June 27, 1519) with the Ingolstadt professor John Eck. During this contest, Luther challenged the infallibility of the pope and the inerrancy of church councils, appealing, for the first time, to the sovereign authority of Scripture alone. He burned all his bridges to the old church when he further defended certain teachings of John Huss that had been condemned by the Council of Constance.

In 1520 Luther signaled his new direction with three famous pamphlets. The *Address to the Christian Nobility of the German Nation* urged the German princes to force reforms on the Roman church, especially to curtail its political and economic power in Germany. The *Babylonian Captivity of the Church* attacked the traditional seven sacraments, arguing that only two, Baptism and the Eucharist, were biblical, and exalted the authority of Scripture, church councils, and secular princes over that of the pope. The eloquent *Freedom of a Christian* summarized the new teaching of salvation by faith alone.

On June 15, 1520, Leo's papal bull *Exsurge Domine* condemned Luther for heresy and gave him sixty days to retract. The final bull of excommunication, *Decet Pontificem Romanum*, was issued on January 3, 1521.

In April 1521 Luther presented his views before the empire's Diet of Worms, over which the newly elected Emperor Charles V presided. Ordered to recant, Luther declared that to do so would be to act against Scripture, reason, and his own conscience. On May 26, 1521, he was placed under the imperial ban and thereafter became an "outlaw" to secular as well as to religious authority. For his own protection, friends hid him in a secluded castle, where he spent almost a year, from April 1521 to March 1522. During his stay, he translated the New Testament into German, using Erasmus's new Greek text and Latin translation , and he attempted by correspondence to oversee the first stages of the Reformation in Wittenberg.

Imperial Distractions: France and the Turks

The Reformation was greatly helped in these early years by the emperor's war with France and the advance of the Ottoman Turks into eastern Europe. Against both adversaries Charles V, who also remained a Spanish king with dynastic responsibilities outside the empire, needed German troops, and to that end he promoted friendly relations with the German princes. Between 1521 and 1559 Spain (the Habsburg dynasty) and France (the Valois dynasty) fought four major wars over disputed territories in Italy and along their borders. In 1526 the Turks overran Hungary at the Battle of Mohacs, while in western Europe the French-led League of Cognac formed against Charles for the second Habsburg–Valois war.

Thus preoccupied, the emperor agreed through his representatives at the German Diet of Speyer in 1526 that each German territory was free to enforce the Edict of Worms (1521) against Luther "so as to be able to answer in good conscience to God and the emperor." That concession, in effect, gave the German princes territorial sovereignty in religious matters and the Reformation time to put down deep roots. Later (in 1555) the Peace of Augsburg would enshrine such local princely control over religion in imperial law.

How the Reformation Spread

In the late 1520s and 1530s, the Reformation passed from the hands of the theologians and pamphleteers into those of the magistrates and princes. In many cities, the magistrates quickly followed the lead of the Protestant preachers and their sizable congregations in mandating the religious reforms they preached. In numerous instances, magistrates had themselves worked for decades to bring about basic church reforms and thus welcomed the preachers as new allies. Reform now ceased to be merely slogans and became laws which all townspeople had to obey.

The religious reform became a territorial political movement as well, led by the elector of Saxony and the prince of Hesse, the two most powerful German Protestant rulers. Like the urban magistrates, the German princes quickly recognized the political and economic opportunities offered them by the demise of the Roman Catholic Church in their regions. Soon they too were pushing Protestant faith and politics onto their neighbors. By the 1530s, Protestant cities and lands formed powerful defensive alliances and prepared for war with the Catholic emperor.

The Peasants' Revolt

In its first decade the Protestant movement suffered more from internal division than from imperial interference. By 1525 Luther had become as much an object of protest within Germany as was the pope. Original allies, sympathizers, and fellow travelers declared their independence from him.

Like the German humanists, the German peasantry also had at first believed Luther to be an ally. The peasantry had been organized since the late fifteenth century against efforts by territorial princes to override their traditional laws and customs and to subject them to new regulations and taxes. Peasant leaders, several of whom were convinced Lutherans, saw in Luther's teaching about Christian freedom and his criticism of monastic landowners a point of view close to their own. They openly solicited Luther's support of their political and economic rights, including their revolutionary request for release from serfdom.

Luther and his followers sympathized with the peasants. Indeed, for several years Lutheran pamphleteers made Karsthans, the burly, honest peasant

The peasant revolt of 1524–1525 frightened both Protestant and Catholic rulers, who united to suppress it. Many peasants died in the revolt, but in its early stages the peasant armies inflicted substantial casualties and committed atrocities of their own. Here Albrecht Dürer (1471–1528) portrays three armed peasants conversing. [Sachsische Landesbibliothek, Abteilung Deutsche Fotothek]

who earned his bread by the sweat of his brow and sacrificed his own comfort and well-being for others, a symbol of the simple life that God desired all people to live. The Lutherans, however, were not social revolutionaries. When the peasants revolted against their masters in 1524–1525, Luther, not surprisingly, condemned them in the strongest possible terms as "un-Christian" and urged the princes to crush their revolt without mercy. Tens of thousands of peasants (estimates run between 70,000 and 100,000) died by the time the revolt was put down.

For Luther, the freedom of the Christian was to be found in an inner release from guilt and anxiety, not in a right to restructure society by violent revolution. Had Luther supported the peasants' revolt, he would not only have contradicted his own teaching, but would probably also have ended any chance of the survival of his reform beyond the 1520s. Still, many believe that his decision

German Peasants Protest Rising Feudal Exactions

In the late fifteenth and early sixteenth centuries, German feudal lords, both secular and ecclesiastical, tried to increase the earnings from their lands by raising demands on their peasant tenants. As the personal freedoms of peasants were restricted, their properties confiscated, and their traditional laws and customs overridden, massive revolts occurred in southern Germany in 1525. Some historians see this uprising and the social and economic conditions that gave rise to it as the major historical force in early modern history. The following is the most representative and well-known statement of peasant grievances.

✦ *Are the peasants' demands reasonable given the circumstances of the sixteenth century? Are the peasants more interested in material than in spiritual freedom? Which of the demands are the most revolutionary?*

1. It is our humble petition and desire . . . that in the future . . . each community should choose and appoint a pastor, and that we should have the right to depose him should he conduct himself improperly. . . .

2. We are ready and willing to pay the fair tithe of grain. . . . The small tithes [of cattle], whether [to] ecclesiastical or lay lords, we will not pay at all, for the Lord God created cattle for the free use of man. . . .

3. We . . . take it for granted that you will release us from serfdom as true Christians, unless it should be shown us from the Gospel that we are serfs.

4. It has been the custom heretofore that no poor man should be allowed to catch venison or wildfowl or fish in flowing water, which seems to us quite unseemly and unbrotherly as well as selfish and not agreeable to the Word of God. . . .

5. We are aggrieved in the matter of woodcutting, for the noblemen have appropriated all the woods to themselves. . . .

6. In regard to the excessive services demanded of us which are increased from day to day, we ask that this matter be properly looked into so that we shall not continue to be oppressed in this way. . . .

7. We will not hereafter allow ourselves to be further oppressed by our lords, but will let them demand only what is just and proper according to the word of the agreement between the lord and the peasant. The lord should no longer try to force more services or other dues from the peasant without payment. . . .

8. We are greatly burdened because our holdings cannot support the rent exacted from them. . . . We ask that the lords may appoint persons of honor to inspect these holdings and fix a rent in accordance with justice. . . .

9. We are burdened with a great evil in the constant making of new laws. . . . In our opinion we should be judged according to the old written law. . . .

10. We are aggrieved by the appropriation . . . of meadows and fields which at one time belonged to a community as a whole. These we will take again into our own hands. . . .

11. We will entirely abolish the due called Todfall [that is, heriot or death tax, by which the lord received the best horse, cow, or garment of a family upon the death of a serf] and will no longer endure it, nor allow widows and orphans to be thus shamefully robbed against God's will, and in violation of justice and right. . . .

12. It is our conclusion and final resolution, that if any one or more of the articles here set forth should not be in agreement with the Word of God, as we think they are, such article we will willingly retract.

Translations and Reprints from the Original Sources of European History, *vol. 2 (Philadelphia: Department of History, University of Pennsylvania, 1897).*

ended the promise of the Reformation as a social revolution.

The Reformation Elsewhere

Although Luther's was the first, Switzerland and France had their own independent church reform movements almost simultaneously with Germany's. From them developed new churches as prominent and lasting as the Lutheran.

Zwingli and the Swiss Reformation

Switzerland was a loose confederacy of thirteen autonomous cantons, or states, and allied areas. (See MAP 11–2.) SOME cantons became Protestant, some remained Catholic, and a few other cantons and regions managed to effect a compromise. There were two main preconditions of the Swiss Reformation. First was the growth of national sentiment occasioned by popular opposition to foreign mercenary service (providing mercenaries for Europe's warring nations was a major source of Switzerland's livelihood). Second was a desire for church reform that had persisted in Switzerland since the councils of Constance (1414–1417) and Basel (1431–1449).

THE REFORMATION IN ZURICH Ulrich Zwingli (1484–1531), the leader of the Swiss Reformation, had been humanistically educated in Bern, Vienna, and Basel. He was strongly influenced by Erasmus, whom he credited with having set him on the path to reform. He served as a chaplain with Swiss mercenaries during the disastrous Battle of Marignano in Italy in 1515 and thereafter became an eloquent critic of mercenary service. Zwingli believed that this service threatened both the political sovereignty and the moral well-being of the Swiss confederacy. By 1518 Zwingli was also widely known for opposition to the sale of indulgences and to religious superstition.

In 1519 he entered the competition for the post of people's priest in the main church of Zurich. His candidacy was contested because of his acknowledged fornication with a barber's daughter, an affair he successfully minimized in a forcefully written self-defense. Actually, his conduct was less scandalous to his contemporaries, who sympathized with the plight of the celibate clergy, than it may be to the modern reader. One of Zwingli's first acts as a reformer was to petition for an end to clerical celibacy and for the right of all clergy to marry, a practice that quickly became accepted in all Protestant lands.

From his new position as people's priest in Zurich, Zwingli engineered the Swiss Reformation. In March 1522 he was party to the breaking of the Lenten fast—an act of protest analogous to burning one's national flag today. Zwingli's reform guideline was very simple and very effective. Whatever lacked literal support in Scripture was to be neither believed nor practiced. As had also happened with Luther, that test soon raised questions about such honored traditional teachings and practices as fasting, transubstantiation, the worship of saints, pilgrimages, purgatory, clerical celibacy, and certain sacraments. A disputation held on January 29, 1523, concluded with the city government granting its sanction to Zwingli's Scripture test. Thereafter Zurich became to all intents the center of the Swiss Reformation. The new regime imposed a harsh discipline that made the city one of the first examples of puritanical Protestantism.

THE MARBURG COLLOQUY Landgrave Philip of Hesse (1504–1567) sought to unite Swiss and German Protestants in a mutual defense pact, a potentially significant political alliance. His efforts were spoiled, however, by theological disagreements between Luther and Zwingli over the nature of Christ's presence in the Eucharist. Zwingli maintained a symbolic interpretation of Christ's words, "This is my body"; Christ, he argued, was only spiritually, not bodily, present in the bread and wine of the Eucharist. Luther, to the contrary, insisted that Christ's human nature could share the properties of his divine nature; hence, where Christ was spiritually present, he could also be bodily present, for his was a special nature. Luther wanted no part of an abstract, spiritualized Christ. Zwingli, on the other hand, feared that Luther had not broken sufficiently with medieval sacramental theology.

Philip of Hesse brought the two Protestant leaders together in his castle in Marburg in early October 1529, but they were unable to work out their differences on this issue. Luther left thinking Zwingli a dangerous fanatic. Although cooperation between the two sides did not cease, the disagreement splintered the Protestant movement theologically and politically. Separate defense leagues formed, and semi-Zwinglian theological views came to be embodied in the *Tetrapolitan Confession*. This confession of faith was prepared by the

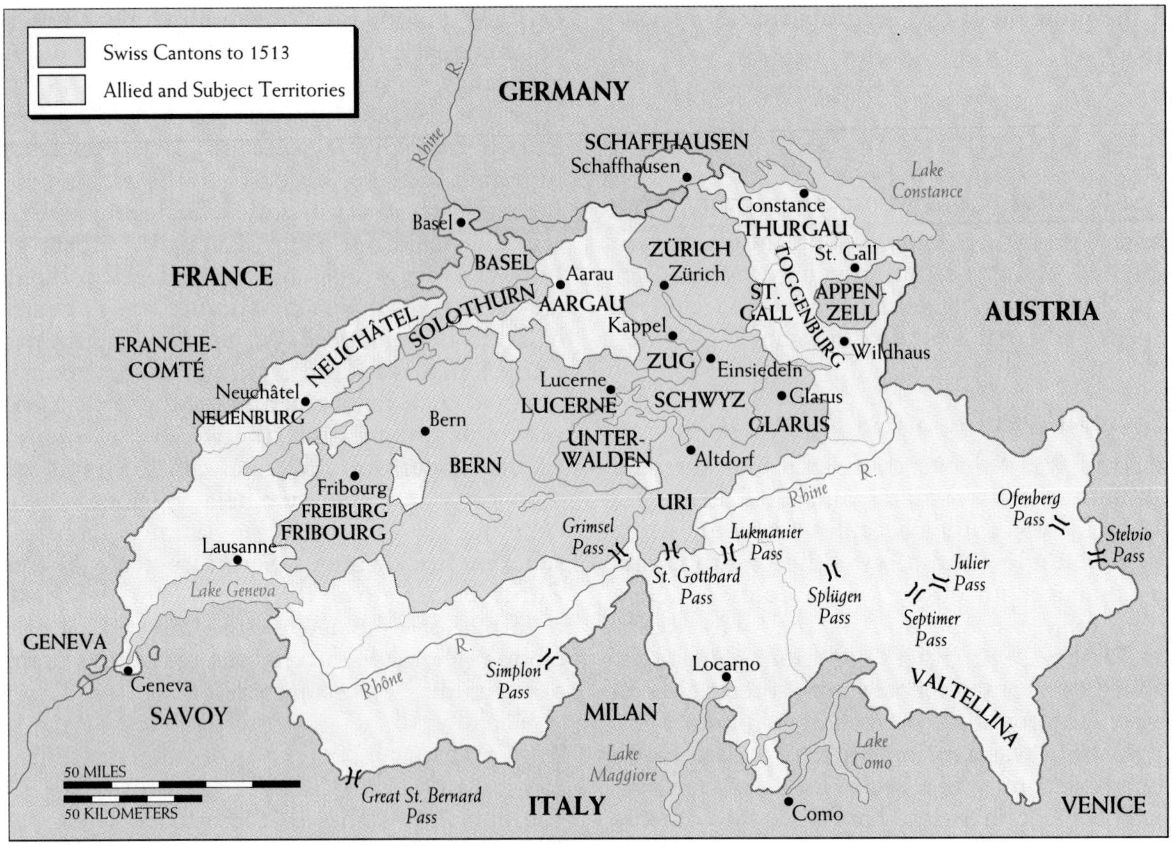

MAP 11–2 THE SWISS CONFEDERATION *While nominally still a part of the Holy Roman Empire, Switzerland grew from a loose defensive union of the central "forest cantons" in the thirteenth century into a fiercely independent association of regions with different languages, histories, and, finally, religions.*

Strasbourg reformers Martin Bucer and Caspar Hedio for presentation to the Diet of Augsburg (1530) as an alternative to the Lutheran *Augsburg Confession.*

SWISS CIVIL WARS As the Swiss cantons divided between Protestantism and Catholicism, civil wars began. There were two major battles, both at Kappel, one in June 1529 and a second in October 1531. The first ended in a Protestant victory, which forced the Catholic cantons to break their foreign alliances and to recognize the rights of Swiss Protestants. During the second battle Zwingli was found wounded on the battlefield and was unceremoniously executed, his remains scattered to the four winds so his followers would have no relics to console and inspire them. The subsequent treaty confirmed the right of each canton to determine its own religion. Heinrich Bullinger (1504–1575), who was Zwingli's protégé and later married his daughter, became the new leader of the Swiss Reformation and guided its development into an established religion.

Anabaptists and Radical Protestants

The moderate pace and seemingly low ethical results of the Lutheran and Zwinglian reformations discontented many people, among them some of the original followers of Luther and Zwingli. They desired a more rapid and thorough implementation of apostolic Christianity—that is, a more visible moral transformation—and accused the major reformers of going only halfway. The most important of these radical groups were the Anabaptists, the sixteenth-century ancestors of the modern Mennonites and Amish. The Anabaptists were especially distinguished by their rejection of infant baptism and their insistence on only adult baptism (Anabaptism derives from the Greek word meaning "to rebaptize"). They believed that baptism performed on a consenting adult conformed to Scripture and was more respectful of human freedom.

CONRAD GREBEL AND THE SWISS BRETHREN Conrad Grebel (1498–1526), with whom Anabaptism originated, performed the first adult rebaptism in Zurich in January 1525. Initially a co-worker with Zwingli and an even greater biblical literalist, Grebel broke openly with Zwingli. In a religious disputation in October 1523, Zwingli supported the city government's plea for a very gradual removal of traditional religious practices.

The alternative of the Swiss Brethren, as Grebel's group came to be called, was embodied in the *Schleitheim Confession* of 1527. This document distinguished Anabaptists not only by their practice of adult baptism but also by their refusal to go to war, to swear oaths, and to participate in the offices of secular government. Anabaptists physically separated from society to form a more perfect community in imitation of what they believed to be the example of the first Christians. Because of the close connection between religious and civic life in this period, the political authorities viewed such separatism as a threat to basic social bonds.

THE ANABAPTIST REIGN IN MÜNSTER At first, Anabaptism drew its adherents from all social classes. But as Lutherans and Zwinglians joined with Catholics in opposition to the Anabaptists and persecuted them within the cities, a more rural, agrarian class came to make up the great majority. In 1529, rebaptism became a capital offense throughout the Holy Roman Empire. Estimates are that between 1525 and 1618 at least 1,000 and perhaps as many as 5,000 men and women were executed for rebaptizing themselves as adults. Brutal measures were universally applied against nonconformists after Anabaptist extremists came to power in the German city of Münster in 1534–1535.

Led by two Dutch emigrants, a baker, Jan Matthys of Haarlem, and a tailor, Jan Beukelsz of Leiden, the Anabaptist majority in this city forced Lutherans and Catholics either to convert or to emigrate. The Lutherans and Catholics left and the city was blockaded by besieging armies. Münster transformed itself into an Old Testament theocracy, replete with charismatic leaders and the practice of polygamy. The latter was undertaken as a measure of social control because there were so many more women, recently widowed or deserted, than men in the city. Many women revolted against the practice and were allowed to leave the resented polygynous marriages.

The outside world was deeply shocked by such developments in Münster. Protestant and Catholic armies united to crush the radicals. The skeletons of their leaders long hung in public view as a warning to all who would so offend traditional Christian sensitivities. After this episode, moderate, pacifistic Anabaptism became the norm among most nonconformists. The moderate Anabaptist leader Menno Simons (1496–1561), the founder of the Mennonites, set the example for the future.

SPIRITUALISTS Another radical movement, that of the Spiritualists, was made up mostly of isolated individuals distinguished by their disdain of all traditions and institutions. They believed that the only religious authority was God's spirit, which spoke here and now to every individual. Among them were several former Lutherans. Thomas Müntzer (d. 1525), who had close contacts with Anabaptist leaders in Germany and Switzerland, died as a leader of a peasants' revolt. Sebastian Franck (d. 1541), a freelance critic of all dogmatic religion, proclaimed the religious autonomy of every individual soul. Caspar Schwenckfeld (d. 1561) was a prolific writer and wanderer after whom the Schwenckfeldian Church is named.

ANTITRINITARIANS A final group of radical Protestants was the Antitrinitarians, exponents of a commonsense, rational, and ethical religion. Chief among this group were the Spaniard Michael Servetus (1511–1553), executed in 1553 in Geneva for "blasphemies against the Holy Trinity," and the Italians Lelio (d. 1562) and Faustus Sozzini (d. 1604), the founders of Socinianism. These thinkers were the strongest opponents of Calvinism, especially its belief in original sin and predestination, and have a deserved reputation as defenders of religious toleration.

John Calvin and the Genevan Reformation

In the second half of the sixteenth century, Calvinism replaced Lutheranism as the dominant Protestant force in Europe. Calvinism was the religious ideology that inspired or accompanied massive political resistance in France, the Netherlands, and

A portrait of the young John Calvin. [Bibliothèque Publique et Universitaire, Geneva]

Scotland. It established itself within the geographical region of the Palatinate during the reign of Elector Frederick III (r. 1559–1576). Calvinists believed strongly in both divine predestination and the individual's responsibility to reorder society according to God's plan. They became zealous reformers determined to transform and order society so that men and women would act externally as they believed, or should believe, internally and were presumably destined to live eternally.

In his famous study, *The Protestant Ethic and the Spirit of Capitalism* (1904), the German sociologist Max Weber argues that this peculiar combination of religious confidence and self-disciplined activism produced an ethic that stimulated and reinforced the spirit of emergent capitalism. According to this argument, there was thus a close association between Calvinism and other later forms of Puritanism and the development of modern capitalist societies.

The founder of Calvinism, John Calvin (1509–1564), was born into a well-to-do family, the son of the secretary to the bishop of Noyon in Picardy. He received church *benefices* at age twelve, which financed the best possible education at Parisian colleges and a law degree at Orléans. In the 1520s, he associated with the indigenous French reform party. Although he would finally reject this group as ineffectual, its members contributed to his preparation as a religious reformer.

It was probably in the spring of 1534 that Calvin experienced that conversion to Protestantism by which he said his "long stubborn heart" was "made teachable" by God. His own experience became a personal model of reform that he would later apply to the recalcitrant citizenry of Geneva. His mature theology stressed the sovereignty of God over all creation and the necessity of humankind's conformity to his will. In May 1534 he dramatically surrendered the *benefices* he had held for so long and at such profit and joined the Reformation.

Political Revolt and Religious Reform in Geneva

Whereas in Saxony religious reform paved the way for a political revolution against the emperor, in Geneva a political revolution against the local prince-bishop laid the foundation for the religious change. Genevans successfully revolted against their resident prince-bishop in the late 1520s, and the city council assumed his legal and political powers in 1527.

In late 1533 the Protestant city of Bern dispatched two reformers to Geneva: Guillaume Farel (1489–1565) and Antoine Froment (1508–1581). In the summer of 1535, after much internal turmoil, the Protestants triumphed, and the traditional mass and other religious practices were removed. On May 21, 1536, the city voted officially to adopt the Reformation: "to live according to the Gospel and the Word of God . . . without . . . any more masses, statues, idols, or other papal abuses."

Calvin arrived in Geneva after these events, in July 1536. He was actually en route to a scholarly refuge in Strasbourg, in flight from the persecution of Protestants in France, when warring between France and Spain forced him to turn sharply south to Geneva. Farel successfully pleaded with him to stay in the city and assist the Reformation, threatening Calvin with divine vengeance if he turned away from this task.

Before a year had passed, Calvin had drawn up articles for the governance of the new church as well as a catechism to guide and discipline the people. Both were presented for approval to the city councils in early 1537. Because of the strong measures they proposed to govern Geneva's moral life, many suspected the reformers were intent upon creating a "new papacy." Opponents attacked Calvin and Farel, fearing that they were going too far too fast. Geneva's powerful Protestant ally, Bern, which had adopted a more moderate Protestant reform, pressured Geneva's magistrates to restore traditional religious ceremonies and holidays that Calvin and Farel had abolished. When the reformers opposed these actions, they were exiled from the city.

Calvin went to Strasbourg, a model Protestant city, where he became pastor to French exiles and wrote biblical commentaries. He also produced a second edition of his masterful *Institutes of the Christian Religion*, which many consider the definitive theological statement of the Protestant faith. Most important, he learned from the Strasbourg reformer Martin Bucer how to implement his goals successfully.

A caricature of drunkenness by Hans Weidt, The Winebag and His Wheelbarrow *addressed the very serious problem of alcoholism that plagued the sixteenth century. Both Catholic and Protestant clergy railed against it. [Hacker Art Books]*

CALVIN'S GENEVA In 1540 Geneva elected syndics who were both favorable to Calvin and determined to establish full Genevan political and religious independence from Bern. They knew Calvin would be a valuable ally in this project and invited him to return. This he did in September 1540, never to leave the city again. Within months of his return, the city implemented new ecclesiastical ordinances that provided for cooperation between the magistrates and the clergy in matters of internal discipline.

Following the Strasbourg model, the Genevan Church was organized into four offices: (1) pastors, of whom there were five; (2) teachers or doctors to instruct the populace in and to defend true doctrine; (3) elders, a group of twelve laypeople chosen by and from the Genevan councils and empowered to "oversee the life of everybody"; and (4) deacons to dispense church goods and services to the poor and the sick.

Calvin and his followers were motivated above all by a desire to transform society morally. Faith, Calvin taught, did not sit idly in the mind but conformed one's every action to God's law. The "elect" should live in a manifestly God-pleasing way, if they were truly God's "elect." In the attempted realization of this goal, Calvin spared no effort. The *consistory*, or regulatory court, became his instrument of power. This body was composed of the elders and the pastors and was presided over by one of the four syndics. It enforced the strictest moral discipline.

Among the many personal conflicts in Geneva that gave Calvin his reputation as a stern moralist, none proved more damaging than his active role in the capture and execution of the Spanish physician and amateur theologian Michael Servetus in 1553. Servetus had earlier been condemned by the Inquisition. He died at the stake in Protestant Geneva for denying the doctrine of the Trinity, a subject on which he had written a scandalous book.

After 1555, the city's syndics were all devout Calvinists, greatly strengthening Calvin's position and Geneva became home to thousands of exiled Protestants who had been driven out of France, England, and Scotland. Refugees (more than 5,000), most of them utterly loyal to Calvin, eventually made up more than one-third of the population of Geneva.

To the thousands of persecuted Protestants who flocked to Geneva in mid-century, the city was a beacon and a refuge, Europe's only free city. During Calvin's lifetime Geneva also gained the reputation of being a "woman's paradise" because the laws there severely punished men who beat their wives.

Theodore Beza Describes John Calvin's Final Days

Calvin's ceaseless labor to make Geneva a bulwark of Protestantism left him an ill and worn-out man at age fifty-five. He remained nonetheless a model of discipline to the end. The following description comes from an admiring biography by Calvin's successor, Theodore Beza.

✦ *Is Calvin's self-denial reminiscent of the fasting and mortification of the flesh practiced by earlier Christian mystics and fanatics? Compare the extreme discipline Calvin imposed on himself to that which he and his followers imposed upon the citizens of Geneva. Does his suffering indicate that he was "elect"?*

On the 6th of February, 1564, . . . he delivered his last sermon. . . . From this period he taught no more in public, except that he was carried at different times, until the last day of March, to the meeting of the congregation, and addressed them in a few words. His diseases, contracted by incredible labours of mind and body, were various and complicated. . . . He was naturally of a spare and feeble frame, tending to consumption. During sleep he seemed almost awake, and spent a great part of the year in preaching, teaching, and dictating. For at least ten years, the only food he [had taken] was at supper, so that it is astonishing how he could so long escape consumption. He frequently suffered from migraine, which he cured only by fasting, so as occasionally to refrain from food for thirty-six hours. But by overstraining his voice and . . . by an immoderate use of aloes, he suffered from hemorrhoids, which degenerated into ulcers, and five years before his death he was occasionally attacked by a spitting of blood. [He also suffered from] gout in the right leg, frequently returning pains of colic, and stone, which he had only felt a few months before his death. . . . The physicians neglected no remedies, and he observed the directions of his medical attendants with a strictness which none could surpass. . . . Though tormented by so many diseases, no one ever heard him utter a word unbecoming a man of bravery, much less a Christian. Only lifting up his eyes to heaven, he used to say, "How long, O Lord!" for even in health he often had this sentence on his lips, when he spoke of the calamities of his brethren, with whose sufferings he was both day and night more afflicted than with any of his own. When admonished and entreated by us to forbear, at least in his sickness, from the labour of dictating, or at least of writing, "What, then," he said, "would you have my Lord find me idle when he cometh?"

Theodore Beza, The Life of John Calvin, *trans. by Francis Gibson (Philadelphia: Westminster, 1836), pp. 78–79.*

Political Consolidation of the Lutheran Reformation

By 1530, the Reformation was in Europe to stay. It would, however, take several decades and major attempts to eradicate it, before all would recognize this fact. With the political triumph of Lutheranism in the empire by the 1550s, Protestant movements elsewhere gained a new lease on life.

The Diet of Augsburg

Emperor Charles V, who spent most of his time on politics and military maneuvers outside the empire, especially in Spain and Italy, returned to the empire in 1530 to direct the Diet of Augsburg. This meeting of Protestant and Catholic representatives assembled to impose a settlement of the religious divisions. With its terms dictated by the Catholic emperor, the diet adjourned with a blunt order to all Lutherans to revert to Catholicism.

The Reformation was by this time too firmly established for that to occur. In February 1531 the Lutherans responded with the formation of their own defensive alliance, the Schmalkaldic League. The league took as its banner the *Augsburg Confession*, a moderate statement of Protestant beliefs that had been spurned by the emperor at the Diet of Augsburg. In 1538 Luther drew up a more strongly worded Protestant confession known as the *Schmalkaldic Articles*. Under the leadership of Landgrave Philip of Hesse and Elector John Frederick of Saxony, the league achieved a stalemate with the emperor, who was again distracted by renewed war with France and the ever-resilient Turks.

The Expansion of the Reformation

In the 1530s German Lutherans formed regional consistories, judicial bodies composed of theologians and lawyers, which oversaw and administered the new Protestant churches. These consistories replaced the old Catholic episcopates. Philip Melanchthon, the "praeceptor of Germany," oversaw the enactment of educational reforms that provided for compulsory primary education, schools for girls, a humanist revision of the traditional curriculum, and catechetical instruction of the laity in the new religion.

The Reformation also entrenched itself elsewhere. Introduced into Denmark by Christian II (r. 1513–1523), Lutheranism thrived there under Frederick I (r. 1523–1533), who joined the Schmalkaldic League. Under Christian III (r. 1536–1559), Lutheranism became the official state religion.

In Sweden, King Gustavus Vasa (r. 1523–1560), supported by a Swedish nobility greedy for church lands, embraced Lutheranism, confiscated church property, and subjected the clergy to royal authority at the Diet of Vesteras (1527).

In politically splintered Poland, Lutherans, Anabaptists, Calvinists, and even Antitrinitarians found room to practice their beliefs. Poland, primarily because of the absence of a central political authority, became a model of religious pluralism and toleration in the second half of the sixteenth century.

Reaction Against Protestants: The Interim

Charles V made abortive efforts in 1540–1541 to enforce a compromise agreement between Protestants and Catholics. As these and other conciliar efforts failed, he turned to a military solution. In 1547 imperial armies crushed the Protestant Schmalkaldic League, defeating John Frederick of Saxony in April and taking Philip of Hesse captive shortly thereafter.

The emperor established puppet rulers in Saxony and Hesse and issued as imperial law the Augsburg Interim, a new order that Protestants everywhere must readopt old Catholic beliefs and practices. Protestants were granted a few cosmetic concessions, for example, clerical marriage (with papal approval of individual cases) and communion in both kinds (that is, bread and wine). Although the Interim met only surface acceptance within Germany, it forced many Protestant leaders into exile. The Strasbourg reformer Martin Bucer, for example, departed to England, where he would play an important role in drafting the religious documents of the English Reformation during the reign of Edward VI. In Germany, the city of Magdeburg became a refuge for persecuted Protestants and the center of Lutheran resistance.

The Peace of Augsburg

The Reformation was too entrenched by 1547 to be ended even by brute force. Maurice of Saxony, handpicked by Charles V to rule Saxony, recognized the inevitable and shifted his allegiance to the Protes-

Rules Governing Genevan Moral Behavior

During Calvin's lifetime, Geneva gained the reputation of being a model evangelical city. Persecuted Protestants in the outside world considered it Europe's freest and most godly city. Strict moral enforcement conformed faith and practice. It also gave the city and the new church the order they needed to survive against their enemies. The following selections are from ordinances governing the village churches around Geneva.

✦ *Are Calvin's rules designed primarily to protect the Reformation? What do these rules suggest that he fears most? Are the penalties heavy or slaps on the wrist? Is it a sign of the failure of his reform that the Genevan people never stopped doing these things?*

Concerning the Time of Assembling at Church

That the temples be closed for the rest of the time [when religious services are not being held] in order that no one shall enter therein out of hours, impelled thereto by superstition; and if any one be found engaged in any special act of devotion therein or near by he shall be admonished for it: if it be found to be of a superstitious nature for which simple correction is inadequate, then he shall be chastised.

Blasphemy

Whoever shall have blasphemed, swearing by the body or by the blood of our Lord, or in similar manner, he shall be made to kiss the earth for the first offence; for the second to pay 5 sous, and for the third 6 sous, and for the last offence be put in the pillory for one hour.

Drunkenness

1. That no one shall invite another to drink under penalty of 3 sous.
2. That taverns shall be closed during the sermon, under penalty that the tavern-keeper shall pay 3 sous, and whoever may be found therein shall pay the same amount.
3. If any one be found intoxicated he shall pay for the first offence 3 sous and shall be remanded tot he consistory; for the second offence he shall be held to pay the sum of 6 sous, and for the third 10 sous and be put in prison.
4. That no one shall make *roiaumes* [great feasts] under penalty of 10 sous.

Songs and Dances

If any one sing immoral, dissolute or outrageous songs, or dance the *virollet* or other dance, he shall be put in prison for three days and then sent to the Consistory.

Usury

That no one shall take upon interest or profit more than five per cent upon penalty of confiscation of the principal and of being condemned to make restitution as the case may demand.

Games

That no one shall play at any dissolute game or at any game whatsoever it may be, neither for gold nor silver nor for any excessive stake, upon penalty of 5 sous and forfeiture of stake played for.

Translations and Reprints from the Original Sources of European History, Vol. 3 (Philadelphia Department of History, University of Pennsylvania, 1909), pp. 10–11.

tants. Confronted by fierce resistance and weary from three decades of war, the emperor was forced to relent. After suffering a defeat by Protestant armies in 1552, Charles reinstated the Protestant leaders and guaranteed Lutheran religious freedoms in the Peace of Passau (August 1552). With this declaration he effectively surrendered his lifelong quest for European religious unity.

The Peace of Augsburg in September 1555 made the division of Christendom permanent. This agreement recognized in law what had already been well established in practice: *cuius regio, eius religio*, meaning that the ruler of a land would determine the religion of the land. Lutherans were permitted to retain all church lands forcibly seized before 1552. An "ecclesiastical reservation" was added, however, that was intended to prevent high Catholic prelates who converted to Protestantism from taking their lands, titles, and privileges with them. Those discontented with the religion of their region were permitted to migrate to another.

The Peace of Augsburg did not extend official recognition to Calvinism and Anabaptism as legal forms of Christian belief and practice. Anabaptists had long adjusted to such exclusion by forming their own separatist communities. Calvinists, however, were not separatists and could not choose that route. They remained determined not only to secure the right to worship publicly as they pleased but also to shape society according to their own religious convictions. While Anabaptists retreated and Lutherans enjoyed the security of an established religion, Calvinists organized to lead national revolutions throughout northern Europe in the second half of the sixteenth century.

Progress of Protestant Reformation on the Continent

1513–1517	Fifth Lateran Council fails to bring about reform in the church
1517	Luther posts ninety-five theses against indulgences
1519	Charles I of Spain elected Holy Roman Emperor (as Charles V)
1519	Luther challenges authority of pope and inerrancy of church councils at Leipzig Debate
1521	Papal bull excommunicates Luther for heresy
1521	Diet of Worms condemns Luther
1521–1522	Luther translates the New Testament into German
1524–1525	Peasants' revolt in Germany
1527	The *Schleitheim Confession* of the Anabaptists
1529	Marburg Colloquy between Luther and Zwingli
1530	Diet of Augsburg fails to settle religious differences
1531	Formation of Protestant Schmalkaldic League
1534–1535	Anabaptists assume political power in city of Münster
1536	Calvin arrives in Geneva
1540	Jesuits, founded by Ignatius of Loyola, recognized as order by pope
1546	Luther dies
1547	Armies of Charles V crush Schmalkaldic League
1548	Augsburg Interim outlaws Protestant practices
1555	Peace of Augsburg recognizes rights of Lutherans to worship as they please
1545–1563	Council of Trent institutes reforms and responds to the Reformation

The English Reformation to 1533

Late medieval England had a well-earned reputation for maintaining the rights of the crown against the pope. Edward I (r. 1272–1307) had rejected efforts by Pope Boniface VIII to prevent secular taxation of the clergy. Parliament passed the first Statutes of Provisors and *Praemunire* in the mid-fourteenth century curtailing payments and judicial appeals to Rome as well as papal appointments in England. Lollardy, humanism, and widespread anticlerical sentiment prepared the way religiously and intellectually for Protestant ideas, which entered England in the early sixteenth century.

The Preconditions of Reform

In the early 1520s future English reformers met at the White Horse Inn in Cambridge to discuss Lutheran writings smuggled into England by merchants and scholars. One of these future reformers was William Tyndale (ca. 1492–1536), who translated the New Testament into English in 1524–1525, while in Germany. Printed in Cologne and Worms, Tyndale's New Testament began to circulate in England in 1526.

Cardinal Thomas Wolsey (ca. 1475–1530), the chief minister of King Henry VIII (r. 1509–1547), and Sir Thomas More (1478–1535), Wolsey's successor, guided royal opposition to incipient English Protestantism. The king himself defended the seven sacraments against Luther, receiving as a reward the title "Defender of the Faith" from Pope Leo X. Following Luther's intemperate reply to Henry's amateur theological attack, More wrote a lengthy *Response to Luther* in 1523.

The King's Affair

While Lollardy and humanism may be said to have provided the native seeds for religious reform, it was Henry's unhappy marriage that broke the soil and allowed the seeds to take root. In 1509 Henry had married Catherine of Aragon (d. 1536), daughter of Ferdinand and Isabella of Spain, and the aunt of Emperor Charles V. By 1527 the union had produced no male heir to the throne and only one surviving child, a daughter, Mary. Henry was justifiably concerned about the political consequences of leaving only a female heir. In this period, people believed it unnatural for women to rule over men. At best, a woman ruler meant a contested reign; at worst, turmoil and revolution.

Henry even came to believe that his union with Catherine, who had many miscarriages and stillbirths, had been cursed by God, because Catherine had first been the wife of his brother, Arthur. Henry's father, King Henry VII, had betrothed Catherine to Henry after Arthur's untimely death to keep the English alliance with Spain intact. They were officially married in 1509, a few days before Henry VIII received his crown. Because marriage to the wife of one's brother was prohibited by both canon and biblical law (see Leviticus 18:16, 20:21), the marriage had required a special dispensation from Pope Julius II.

By 1527 Henry was thoroughly enamored of Anne Boleyn, one of Catherine's ladies in waiting. He determined to put Catherine aside and take Anne as his wife. This he could not do in Catholic England, however, without papal annulment of the marriage to Catherine. And therein lay a special problem. The year 1527 was also the year when soldiers of the Holy Roman Empire mutinied and sacked Rome. The reigning pope, Clement VII, was at the time a prisoner of Charles V, who happened also to be Catherine's nephew. Even if this had not been the case, it would have been virtually impossible for the pope to grant an annulment of a marriage that not only had survived for eighteen years but had been made possible in the first place by a special papal dispensation.

Cardinal Wolsey, who aspired to become pope, was placed in charge of securing the royal annulment. Lord Chancellor since 1515 and papal legate-at-large since 1518, Wolsey had long been Henry's "heavy" and the object of much popular resentment. When he failed to secure the annulment through no fault of his own, he was dismissed in disgrace in 1529. Thomas Cranmer (1489–1556) and Thomas Cromwell (1485–1540), both of whom harbored Lutheran sympathies, thereafter became the king's closest advisers. Finding the way to a papal annulment closed, Henry's new advisers struck a different course. Why not simply declare the king supreme in English spiritual affairs as he was in English temporal affairs? Then the king could settle the king's affair himself.

The "Reformation Parliament"

In 1529 Parliament convened for what would be a seven-year session that earned it the title the "Reformation Parliament." During this period, it passed a flood of legislation that harassed and finally placed royal reins on the clergy. In doing so, it established a precedent that would remain a feature of English government: whenever fundamental changes are made in religion, the monarch must consult with and work through Parliament. In January 1531 the clergy in Convocation (a legislative assembly representing the English clergy) publicly recognized Henry as head of the church in England "as far as the law of Christ allows." In 1532 Parliament published official grievances against the church, ranging from alleged indifference to the needs of the laity to an excessive number of religious holidays. In the same year Parliament passed the Submission of the Clergy, which effectively placed canon law under royal control and thereby the clergy under royal jurisdiction.

In January 1533 Henry wed the pregnant Anne Boleyn, with Thomas Cranmer officiating. In February 1533 Parliament made the king the highest court of appeal for all English subjects. In March 1533 Cranmer became archbishop of Canterbury and led the Convocation in invalidating the king's marriage to Catherine. In 1534 Parliament ended all payments by the English clergy and laity to Rome and gave Henry sole jurisdiction over high ecclesiastical appointments. The Act of Succession in the same year made Anne Boleyn's children legitimate heirs to the throne, and the Act of Supremacy declared Henry "the only supreme head in earth of the Church of England."

When Thomas More and John Fisher, bishop of Rochester, refused to recognize the Act of Succession and the Act of Supremacy, Henry had them

The Execution of Fisher and More

In 1535 Bishop John Fisher, a long-time pamphleteer for Queen Catherine's cause, and Sir Thomas More, famed humanist and former lord chancellor, were beheaded for refusing to recognize the king's supremacy. They were the most distinguished of Henry VIII's adversaries and victims. As reported by Hall's Chronicle, More managed to find humor in the proceedings.

✦ *How could More die so boldly? What does the author mean by asking whether he was a foolish wise man or a wise foolish man? Is the description propaganda? What impact did More's execution have on Henry's reign?*

The twenty-second day of the same month John Fisher, bishop of Rochester, was beheaded, and his head set upon London Bridge. This bishop was of very many men lamented; for he was reported to be a man of great learning, and a man of very good life, but therein wonderfully deceived, for he maintained the pope to be supreme head of the Church, and very maliciously refused the king's title of supreme head. . . .

Also the sixth day of July was Sir Thomas More beheaded for the like treason before rehearsed, which, as you have heard, was for the denying of the king's Majesty's supremacy. This man was also counted learned, and, as you have heard before, he was lord chancellor of England, and in that time a great persecutor of such as detested the supremacy of the bishop of Rome, which he himself so highly favored that he stood to it until he was brought to the scaffold on the Tower Hill, where on a block his head was stricken from his shoulders and had no more harm.

I cannot tell whether I should call him a foolish wise man or a wise foolish man, for undoubtedly he, beside his learning, had a great wit, but it was so mingled with taunting and mocking, that it seemed to them that best knew him that he thought nothing to be well spoken except he had ministered some mock in the communication, insomuch as at his coming to the Tower one of the officers demanded his upper garment for his fee, meaning his gown, and he answered he should have it and took him his cap, saying that it was the uppermost garment that he had. . . .

Also the hangman kneeled down to him asking him forgiveness of his death (as the manner is), to whom he said, "I forgive thee, but I promise thee that thou shalt never have honesty of the striking of my head, my neck is so short." Also even when he should lay down his head on the bock he, having a great gray beard, struck out his beard, and said to the hangman, "I pray you let me lay my beard over the block lest ye should cut it." Thus with a mock he ended his life.

James Harvey Robinson, ed., Readings in European History, Vol. 2 (Boston, Athenaeum: 1906), pp. 142–143.

executed, making clear his determination to have his way regardless of the cost. In 1536 and 1538 Parliament dissolved England's monasteries and nunneries.

Wives of Henry VIII

Henry's domestic life proved to lack the consistency of his political life. In 1536 Anne Boleyn was executed for alleged treason and adultery, and her daughter, Elizabeth, was declared illegitimate. Henry had four further marriages. His third wife, Jane Seymour, died in 1537 shortly after giving birth to the future Edward VI. Henry wed Anne of Cleves sight unseen on the advice of Cromwell, the purpose being to create by the marriage an alliance with the Protestant princes. Neither the alliance nor the marriage proved worth the trouble; the marriage was annulled by Parliament, and Cromwell was dismissed and eventually executed. Catherine

An allegorical depiction of the Tudor succession by the painter Lucas de Heere (1534–1584). On Henry VIII's right stands his Catholic daughter Mary (1533–1558) and her husband Philip II of Spain. They are accompanied by Mars, the god of war. Henry's son, Edward VI (r. 1547–1553), kneels at the king's left. Elizabeth I (1558–1603) is shown standing in the foreground attended by Peace and Plenty, allegorical figures of what her reign brought to England. [Sudeley Castle]

Howard, Henry's fifth wife, was beheaded for adultery in 1542. His last wife, Catherine Parr, a patron of humanists and reformers, for whom Henry was the third husband, survived him to marry still a fourth time—obviously she was a match for the English king.

The King's Religious Conservatism

Henry's boldness in politics and his domestic affairs did not extend to religion. True, because of Henry's actions the pope had ceased to be head of the English Church and English Bibles were placed in English churches, but despite the break with Rome, Henry remained decidedly conservative in his religious beliefs. With the Ten Articles of 1536, he made only mild concessions to Protestant tenets, otherwise maintaining Catholic doctrine in a country filled with Protestant sentiment. Despite his many wives and amorous adventures, Henry absolutely forbade the English clergy to marry and threatened any clergy who were twice caught in concubinage with execution.

Angered by the growing popularity of Protestant views, even among his chief advisers, Henry struck directly at them in the Six Articles of 1539. These reaffirmed transubstantiation, denied the Eucharistic cup to the laity, declared celibate vows inviolable, provided for private masses, and ordered the continuation of auricular confession. (Protestants referred to the articles as the "whip with six stings.") Although William Tyndale's English New Testament grew into the Coverdale Bible (1535) and the Great Bible (1539), and the latter was mandated for every English parish, England had to await Henry's death before it could become a genuinely Protestant country.

The Protestant Reformation Under Edward VI

When Henry died, his son and successor, Edward VI (r. 1547–1553), was only ten years old. Edward reigned under the successive regencies of Edward Seymour, who became the duke of Somerset (1547–1550), and the earl of Warwick, who became known as the duke of Northumberland (1550–1553). During this time England fully enacted the Protestant Reformation. The new king and Somerset corresponded directly with John Calvin. During Somerset's regency, Henry's Six Articles and laws against heresy were repealed, and clerical marriage and communion with cup were sanctioned.

In 1547 the chantries, places where endowed masses had traditionally been said for the dead, were dissolved. In 1549 the Act of Uniformity imposed Thomas Cranmer's *Book of Common Prayer* on all English churches. Images and altars were removed from the churches in 1550. After Charles V's victory over the German princes in 1547, German Protestant leaders had fled to England for refuge. Several of these refugees now directly assisted the completion of the English Reformation, Martin Bucer prominent among them.

The Second Act of Uniformity, passed in 1552, imposed a revised edition of the *Book of Common Prayer* on all English churches. A forty-two-article confession of faith, also written by Thomas Cranmer, was adopted, setting forth a moderate Protestant doctrine. It taught justification by faith and the supremacy of Holy Scripture, denied transubstantiation (although not real presence), and recognized only two sacraments.

All these changes were short-lived, however. In 1553 Catherine of Aragon's daughter succeeded Edward (who had died in his teens) to the English throne as Mary I (r. 1553–1558) and proceeded to restore Catholic doctrine and practice with a singlemindedness that rivaled that of her father. It was not until the reign of Anne Boleyn's daughter, Elizabeth I (r. 1558–1603), that a lasting religious settlement was worked out in England.

Catholic Reform and Counter-Reformation

The Protestant Reformation did not take the medieval church completely by surprise. There were many internal criticisms and efforts at reform before there was a Counter-Reformation in reaction to Protestant successes.

Sources of Catholic Reform

Before the Reformation began, ambitious proposals had been made for church reform. But sixteenth-century popes, ever mindful of how the councils of Constance and Basel had stripped the pope of his traditional powers, quickly squelched such efforts to bring about basic changes in the laws and institutions of the church. They preferred the charge

Main Events of the English Reformation

1529	Reformation Parliament convenes
1532	Parliament passes the Submission of the Clergy
1533	Henry VIII weds Anne Boleyn; Convocation proclaims marriage to Catherine of Aragon invalid
1534	Act of Succession makes Anne Boleyn's children legitimate heirs to the English throne
1534	Act of Supremacy declares Henry VIII "the only supreme head of the Church of England"
1535	Thomas More executed for opposition to Acts of Succession and Supremacy
1535	Publication of Coverdale Bible
1539	Henry VIII imposes the Six Articles
1547	Edward VI succeeds to the throne under protectorships of Somerset and Northumberland
1549	First Act of Uniformity imposes *Book of Common Prayer* on English churches
1553–1558	Mary Tudor restores Catholic doctrine
1558–1603	Elizabeth I fashions an Anglican religious settlement

given to the Fifth Lateran Council (1513–1517) in the key-note address by the superior general of the Hermits of Saint Augustine: "Men are to be changed by, not to change, religion."

Despite such papal foot-dragging, the church was not without its reformers. Many new religious orders also sprang up in the sixteenth century to lead a broad revival of piety within the church. The first of these orders was the Theatines, founded in 1524 to groom devout and reform-minded leaders at the higher levels of the church hierarchy. One of the co-founders was Bishop Gian Pietro Carafa, who would be Pope Paul IV. Another new order, whose mission pointed in the opposite direction, was the Capuchins. Recognized by the pope in 1528, they sought to return to the original ascetic and charitable ideals of Saint Francis and became very popular among the ordinary people to whom they directed their ministry. The Somaschi, who became active in the mid-1520s, and the Barnabites, founded in 1530, directed their efforts at repairing the moral, spiritual, and physical damage done to people in war-torn areas of Italy.

For women, there was the new order of Ursulines, founded in 1535. It established convents in Italy and France for the religious education of girls from all social classes and became very influential. Another new religious order, the Oratorians, officially recognized in 1575, was an elite group of secular clerics who devoted themselves to the promotion of religious literature and church music. Among their members was the great Catholic hymnist and musician Giovanni Perluigi da Palestrina (1526–1594).

In addition to these lay and clerical movements the Spanish mystics Saint Teresa of Avila (1515–1582) and Saint John of the Cross (1542–1591) revived and popularized the mystical piety of medieval monasticism.

The Ecstasy of Saint Teresa of Avila, *by Gianlorenzo Bernini (1598–1680). Mystics like Saint Teresa and Saint John of the Cross helped revive the traditional piety of medieval monasticism. [Scala/Art Resource, N.Y.]*

Ignatius of Loyola and the Jesuits

Of the various reform groups, none was more instrumental in the success of the Counter-Reformation than the Society of Jesus, the new order of Jesuits. Organized by Ignatius of Loyola in the 1530s, it was officially recognized by the church in 1540. The society grew within the space of a century from its original 10 members to more than 15,000 members scattered throughout the world, with thriving missions in India, Japan, and the Americas.

The founder of the Jesuits, Ignatius of Loyola (1491–1556), was a heroic figure. A dashing courtier and *caballero* in his youth, he began his spiritual pilgrimage in 1521 after he had been seriously wounded in the legs during a battle with the French. During a lengthy and painful convalescence, he passed the time by reading Christian classics. So impressed was he with the heroic self-sacrifice of the church's saints and their methods of overcoming mental anguish and pain that he underwent a profound religious conversion. Henceforth, he, too, would serve the church as a soldier of Christ.

After recuperating, Ignatius applied the lessons he had learned during his convalescence to a program of religious and moral self-discipline that came to be embodied in the *Spiritual Exercises*. This psychologically perceptive devotional guide contained mental and emotional exercises designed to teach one absolute spiritual self-mastery over

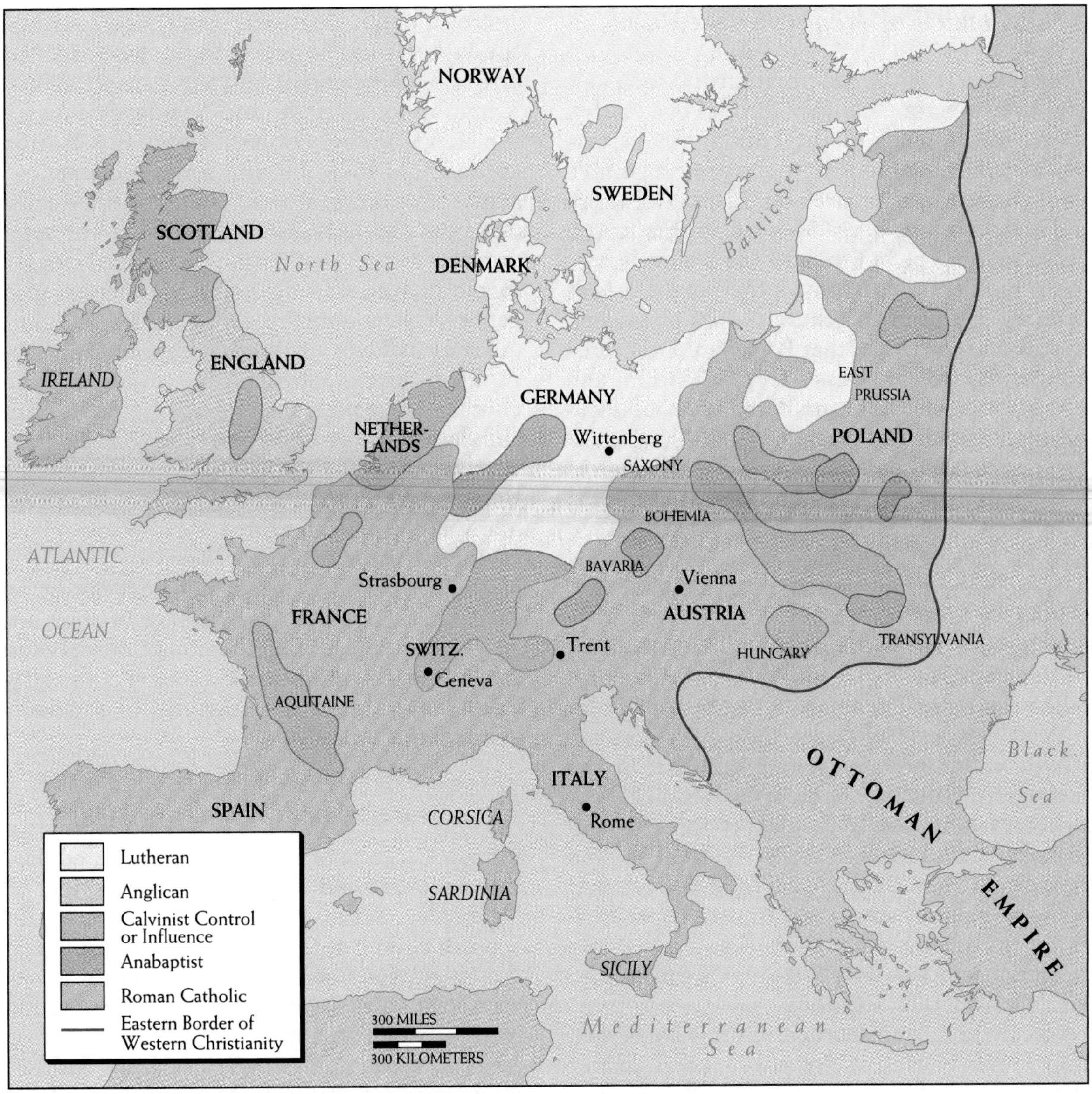

MAP 11–3 THE RELIGIOUS SITUATION ABOUT 1560 *By 1560 Luther, Zwingli, and Loyola were dead, Calvin near the end of his life, the English break from Rome fully accomplished, and the last session of the Council of Trent about to assemble. Here is the religious geography of western Europe then.*

one's feelings. It taught that a person could shape his or her own behavior, even create a new religious self, through disciplined study and regular practice.

Whereas in Jesuit eyes Protestants had distinguished themselves by disobedience to church authority and religious innovation, the exercises of Ignatius were intended to teach good Catholics to deny themselves and submit without question to higher church authority and spiritual direction. Perfect discipline and self-control were the essential conditions of such obedience. To these were added the enthusiasm of traditional spirituality and mysticism and uncompromising loyalty to the church's cause above all else. This was a potent combination that helped counter the Reformation and win many Protestants back to the Catholic fold, especially in Austria and Bavaria and along the Rhine.

The Council of Trent (1545–1563)

The broad success of the Reformation and the insistence of the Emperor Charles V forced Pope Paul to call a general council of the church to reassert church doctrine. In anticipation, the pope appointed a reform commission, chaired by Caspar Contarini (1483–1542), a leading liberal theologian. His report, presented to the pope in February 1537, bluntly criticized the fiscality and simony of the papal *Curia* as the primary source of the church's loss of esteem. The report was so critical that Pope Paul attempted unsuccessfully to suppress its publication and Protestants reprinted and circulated it as justification of their criticism.

The long-delayed council of the church met in 1545 in the imperial city of Trent in northern Italy. There were three sessions, spread over eighteen years, with long interruptions due to war, plague, and imperial and papal politics. The council met from 1545 to 1547, from 1551 to 1552, and from 1562 to 1563, a period that spanned the careers of four different popes.

Unlike the general councils of the fifteenth century, Trent was strictly under the pope's control, with high Italian prelates very prominent in the proceedings. Initially four of the five attending archbishops and twenty-one of the twenty-three attending bishops were Italians. Even at its final session in 1562, more than three-quarters of the council fathers were Italians. Voting was limited to the high levels of the clergy; university theologians, the lower clergy, and the laity were not permitted to share in the council's decisions.

The council's most important reforms concerned internal church discipline. Steps were taken to curtail the selling of church offices and other religious goods. Many bishops who resided in Rome rather than within their dioceses were forced to move to their appointed seats of authority. Trent strengthened the authority of local bishops so they could effectively discipline popular religious practice. The bishops were also subjected to new rules that required them not only to reside in their dioceses, but also to be highly visible by preaching regularly and conducting annual visitations. Trent also sought to give the parish priest a brighter image by requiring him to be neatly dressed, better educated, strictly celibate, and active among his parishioners. To this end, Trent also called for the construction of a seminary in every diocese.

Not a single doctrinal concession was made to the Protestants, however. In the face of Protestant criticism the Council of Trent gave a ringing reaffirmation to the traditional Scholastic education of the clergy; the role of good works in salvation; the authority of tradition; the seven sacraments; transubstantiation; the withholding of the Eucharistic cup from the laity; clerical celibacy; the reality of purgatory; the veneration of saints, relics, and sacred images; and the granting of letters of indulgence. The council resolved medieval Scholastic quarrels in favor of the theology of Saint Thomas Aquinas, further enhancing his authority within the church. Thereafter, the church offered its strongest resistance to groups like the Jansenists, who strongly endorsed the medieval Augustinian tradition, a source of alternative Catholic as well as many Protestant doctrines.

Rulers initially resisted Trent's reform decrees, fearing a revival of papal political power within their lands. But with the passage of time and the pope's assurances that religious reforms were his sole intent, the new legislation took hold and parish life revived under the guidance of a devout and better-trained clergy.

The Church in Spanish America

Roman Catholic priests had accompanied the earliest explorers and the conquerors of the Native Americans. Because of internal reforms within the Spanish church at the turn of the sixteenth century, these first clergy tended to be imbued with many of the social and religious ideals of Christian humanism. They believed that they could foster Erasmus's concept of the "philosophy of Christ" in the New World. Consequently these missionary priests were filled with zeal not only to convert the inhabitants to Christianity but also to bring to them learning and civilization of a European kind.

A very real tension existed between the early Spanish conquerors and the mendicant friars who sought to minister to the Indians. Without conquest, the church could not convert the Indians, but the priests often deplored the harsh labor conditions imposed on them. During the first three-quarters of a century of Spanish domination, priests were among the most eloquent and persuasive defenders of the rights of native peoples in the New World.

Bartolomé de Las Casas, a Dominican, contended that conquest was not necessary for con-

A Defense of American Natives

Bartolomé de Las Casas (1474–1566), a Dominican missionary to the New World, describes the native people of the islands of the Caribbean and their systematic slaughter by the Spanish.

✦ *Is Las Casas romanticizing the American natives? Does he truly respect their native culture and beliefs?*

This infinite multitude of people was so created by God that they were without fraud . . . subtilty or malice. . . . Toward the Spaniards whom they serve, patient, meek, and peaceful, [they] lay aside all contentious and tumultuous thoughts, and live without any hatred or desire of revenge. The people are most delicate and tender, enjoying such a feeble constitution of body as does not permit them to endure labour. . . . The[ir] nation [the West Indies] is very poor and indigent, possessing little, and by reason that they gape not after temporal goods, [being] neither proud nor ambitious. Their diet is such that the most holy hermit cannot feed more sparingly in the wildernesse. They go naked . . . and a poor shag mantle . . . is their greatest and their warmest covering. They lie upon mats; only those who have larger fortunes lie upon a kind of net which is tied at the four corners and so fasten'd to the roof, which the Indians in their natural language call Hamecks [hammocks]. They are of a very apprehensive and docile wit, and capable of all good learning, and very apt to receive our Religion, which when they have but once tasted [it], they are carried [off] with a very ardent and zealous desire to make further progress in it; so that I have heard divers Spaniards confess that they had nothing else to hinder them from enjoying heaven, but the ignorance of the true God.

To these quiet Lambs, endued with such blessed qualities, came the Spaniards like most cruel Tygres, Wolves, and Lions . . . for these forty years, minding nothing else but the slaughter of these unfortunate wretches . . . [whom] they have so cruelly and inhumanely butchered, [so] that of three millions of people which Hispaniola [modern Haiti and Dominican Republic] itself did contain, there are left remaining alive scarce three hundred persons. And the island of Cuba . . . lies wholly desert, untilled and ruined. The islands of St. John and Jamaica lie waste and desolate. The Lycayan islands neighboring to the north upon Cuba and Hispaniola . . . are now totally unpeopled and destroyed; the inhabitants thereof amounting to above 500,000 souls, partly killed, and partly forced away to work in other places. . . . Other islands there were near the island of St. John more than thirty in number, which were totally made desert. All which islands . . . lie now altogether solitary without any people or inhabitant.

Bartolomé de Las Casas, The Tears of the Indians, *trans. by John Phillips (1656), from reprint of original edition (Academic Reprints, Stanford, Calif., n.d.), pp. 2–4.*

Bartolomé de Las Casas (1474–1566) was the most outspoken and effective defender of the Native Americans against Spanish exploitation. [Bildarchiv Preussischer Kulturbesitz]

version. One result of his campaign was new royal regulation of conquest after 1550. Another result was the "Black Legend," which portrayed all Spanish treatment of Indians as unprincipled and inhumane. Those who held this point of view drew heavily on Las Casas's writings. Although largely true, the "Black Legend" nonetheless exaggerated the case against Spain and has been exploited by Spanish critics. Many of the Indian rulers had also been exceedingly cruel, as witnessed by the Aztec demands for human sacrifice, and both the Aztecs and the Incas enslaved other peoples. Had the Aztecs discovered Spain and held the upper hand there, the persecution of native Europeans would likely have been as great as that of native Americans at the hands of the Spanish.

By the end of the sixteenth century, the church in Spanish America had become largely an institution upholding the colonial status quo. On many occasions, individual priests did defend the communal rights of Indian tribes, but the colonial church also prospered as the Spanish elite prospered. The church became a great landowner through crown grants and through bequests from Catholics who died in the New World. The monasteries took on an economic as well as a spiritual life of their own. Whatever its concern for the spiritual welfare of the Indians, the church remained one of the indications that Spanish America was a conquered world. And those who spoke for the church did not challenge Spanish domination or any but the most extreme modes of Spanish economic exploitation. By the end of the colonial era in the late eighteenth century, the Roman Catholic Church had become one of the most conservative forces in Latin America.

The Social Significance of the Reformation in Western Europe

It was a common trait of the Lutheran, Zwinglian, and Calvinist reformers to work within the framework of reigning political power. Luther, Zwingli, and Calvin saw themselves and their followers as subject to definite civic responsibilities and obligations. Their conservatism in this regard has led scholars to characterize them as "magisterial reformers," meaning not only that they were the leaders of the major Protestant movements but also that they succeeded by the force of the magistrate's sword. Some have argued that this willingness to resort to coercion led the reformers to compromise their principles. They themselves, however, never contemplated reform outside or against the societies of which they were members. They wanted it to take shape within the laws and institutions of the sixteenth century. To that end, they remained highly sensitive to what was politically and socially possible in their age. Some scholars believe that the reformers were too conscious of the historically possible, that their reforms went forward with such caution that they changed late medieval society very little and actually encouraged acceptance of the sociopolitical status quo.

The Revolution in Religious Practices and Institutions

The Reformation may have been politically conservative, but by the end of the sixteenth century it had brought about radical changes in traditional religious practices and institutions in those lands where it succeeded.

RELIGION IN FIFTEENTH-CENTURY LIFE In the fifteenth century, on the streets of the great cities of central Europe that later turned Protestant (for example, Zurich, Strasbourg, Nuremberg, or Geneva), the clergy and the religious were everywhere. They made up 6 to 8 percent of the total urban population, and they exercised considerable political as well as spiritual power. They legislated and taxed; they tried cases in special church courts; and they enforced their laws with threats of excommunication.

The church calendar regulated daily life. About one-third of the year was given over to some kind of religious observance or celebration. There were frequent periods of fasting. On almost a hundred days out of the year a pious Christian could not, without special dispensation, eat eggs, butter, fat, or meat.

Monasteries and especially nunneries were prominent and influential institutions. The children of society's most powerful citizens resided there. Local aristocrats were closely identified with particular churches and chapels, whose walls recorded their lineage and proclaimed their generosity. On the streets, friars from near and far begged alms from passersby. In the churches the mass and liturgy were read entirely in Latin. Images of saints were regularly displayed, and on certain holidays their relics were paraded about and venerated.

There was a booming business at local religious shrines. Pilgrims gathered there by the hundreds, even thousands, many sick and dying, all in search of a cure or a miracle, but also for diversion and entertainment. Several times during the year special preachers arrived in the city to sell letters of indulgence.

Many clergy walked the streets with concubines and children, although they were sworn to celibacy and forbidden marriage. The church tolerated such relationships upon payment of penitential fines.

People everywhere could be heard complaining about the clergy's exemption from taxation and, in many instances, also from the civil criminal code. People also grumbled about having to support church offices whose occupants actually lived and worked elsewhere. Townspeople also expressed concern that the church had too much influence over education and culture.

RELIGION IN SIXTEENTH-CENTURY LIFE In these same cities after the Reformation had firmly established itself, few changes in politics and society were evident. The same aristocratic families governed as before, and the rich generally got richer and the poor poorer. But overall numbers of clergy fell by two-thirds and religious holidays shrunk by one-third. Cloisters were nearly gone, and many that remained were transformed into hospices for the sick and poor or into educational institutions, their endowments also turned over to these new purposes. A few cloisters remained for very devout old monks and nuns, who could not be pensioned off or who lacked families and friends to care for them. But these remaining cloisters died out with their inhabitants.

In the churches, which had also been reduced in number by at least one-third, worship was conducted almost completely in the vernacular. In some, particularly those in Zwinglian cities, the walls were stripped bare and whitewashed to make sure the congregation meditated only on God's word. The laity observed no obligatory fasts. Indulgence preachers no longer appeared. Local shrines were closed down, and anyone found openly venerating saints, relics, and images was subject to fine and punishment.

Copies of Luther's translation of the New Testament or, more often, excerpts from it could be found in private homes, and meditation on them was encouraged by the new clergy. The clergy could marry, and most did. They paid taxes and were punished for their crimes in civil courts. Domestic moral life was regulated by committees composed of roughly equal numbers of laity and clergy, over whose decisions secular magistrates had the last word.

The Instructions of a Father to His Youngest Son

At age fourteen, in the year 1539, Christoph Ravensburg departed Augsburg, Germany, for an apprenticeship in Lyons, France, bearing with him these words of advice from his father.

✦ *What are the father's overriding concerns as his son leaves home for the first time? What does his father consider to be the traits of a "true man"? On what is Christoph to rely in time of temptation and danger?*

Dear son Christoph, . . . If you heed the instructions that follow, you will become a true man.

Love God and be mindful of Him, and see to the keeping of His commandments. Attend the traditional religious service in the land where you will be, as other devout and honorable people there do. And argue neither little nor much over any matter of faith, for that will put you at a disadvantage and even threaten your life.

Sebastian Weyer and his brother [the father's business associates in Lyons] will try to place you with a proper master. . . . They will also look after your basic needs, be it clothing or something else. Therefore, try your best to do what they tell you. And when you are with your master, do what he and his wife tell you, and do it with the utmost diligence, always willingly and obediently.

Above all else, take care that you do not lie and steal. Should you have the merchants' money in your hand or see their many wares lying before you, take none of it for yourself. For it often happens that money or something else is purposefully placed before one such as you as a test. So as dear to you as your life and my favor are, for the sake of life and limb, be false to no one about anything.

Avoid bad company, and when you sometimes hear it said, or actually see other Germans acting improperly and wanting to be Junkers [wealthy noblemen indulging themselves], let it be an example and a warning to you that you not do so.

Do not let your master's other servants or maids with whom you will be living teach you to steal anything in the house, be it food, drink, or anything else that it is wrong to take, for this may bring you great misfortune. They will tempt one such as you to see if he lets himself be led astray.

When bathing or swimming, avoid the great threatening waters of the Saone and the Rhone [which meet in Lyons]. Do not enter them; if you are tempted to do so, resist, as I have told you many times before. Use other waters for your needs, so that you do not drown. . . .

Avoid strong drink by mixing a lot of water in with the wine. Resolve not to get drunk

Not all Protestant clergy remained enthusiastic about this new lay authority in religion. And the laity themselves were also ambivalent about certain aspects of the Reformation. Over half of the original converts returned to the Catholic fold before the end of the sixteenth century. Whereas one-half of Europe could be counted in the Protestant camp in the mid-sixteenth century, only one-fifth would be there by the mid-seventeenth century.[2]

[2]Geoffrey Parker, *Europe in Crisis, 1598–1648* (Ithaca, N.Y.: Cornell University Press, 1979), p. 50.

The Reformation and Education

Another important cultural achievement of the Reformation was its implementation of many of the educational reforms of humanism in the new Protestant schools and universities. Many Protestant reformers in Germany, France, and England were humanists. Even when their views on Church doctrine and humankind separated them from the humanist movement, the Protestant reformers continued to share with the humanists a common opposition to Scholasticism and a belief in the unity

either during your journey or upon your arrival. When you are thirsty, drink only water or well-watered wine, because your natural disposition is to eat and drink a lot. Take care of yourself in this way so that you become all the less susceptible to illness.

Avoid gambling, whoring, partying, cursing, and other bad associations and vices. Place yourself in the company of honest people, whom you know to be good and accomplished, and from whom you can learn something good yourself. And when you can find the time, be sure to practice your writing and arithmetic so that you do not forget them . . . .

Keep yourself and your clothes clean, and take good care of your clothes. Be always ready and willing, not argumentative. And do not give up too soon when someone reproaches you for something, for they do it for your own good.

Concentrate on your needs and be frugal and sparing. Don't spend money needlessly, because when you are larger and older, you will want and need it. Do not take comfort in [any expected] wealth [from me]; resolve to learn how to earn [your own] money and to spend it wisely.

As you well know, great expenditures are now being made on your behalf and they will also be made on behalf of your brothers and sisters, so that after my death, you will discover all the less [money for yourself]. Therefore, look to your own needs; plan well now to support yourself and also to be in a position to help the children of your brothers and sisters as well.

Take care that in your innocence you not let yourself be talked into entering a marriage on your own or become entangled [with some woman]. Stay away from dishonest women so that you do not get the pox [syphilis] and other maladies that flow from them.

Keep your feet warm and dry, for the world is an unholy bath; this will make you less vulnerable to foot ailments.

Do not go about the streets at night unless your master sends you out. He will instruct you and arrange things so that you may go safely. Many corrupt youth hang out on the bridge over the Saone and villainy often occurs there.

. . .

Write often to me and your mother, and let me know what kind of master you have there, what his name is and what he does, also how many servants he has and how he treats you.

Finally, as I said at the beginning and as has long been your custom, above all else be god-fearing with your reading, prayer, etc. and act as other devout people there do. Buy yourself a Latin prayerbook like the others there have so that almighty God may help you and you suffer no want. May the Lord God care for you.

Written by your father in Augsburg,
26 March, 1539.
Leo Ravenspurg

Friedrich Beyschlag, ed., "Ein Vater an seinen Sohn (1539)," Archiv für Kulturgeschichte 4 (1906): 296–302, trans. by S. Ozment.

of wisdom, eloquence, and action. The humanist program of studies, which provided the language skills to deal authoritatively with original sources, proved to be a more appropriate tool for the elaboration of Protestant doctrine than did scholastic dialectic, which remained ascendant in the Counter-Reformation.

The Catholic counterreformers recognized the close connections between humanism and the Reformation. Ignatius of Loyola observed the way in which the new learning had been embraced by and served the Protestant cause. In his *Spiritual Exercises*, he insisted that when the Bible and the Church Fathers were read directly, they be read under the guidance of the authoritative scholastic theologians: Peter Lombard, Bonaventure, and Thomas Aquinas. The latter, Ignatius argued, being "of more recent date," had the clearer understanding of what Scripture and the Fathers meant and therefore should guide the study of the past.

When in August 1518 Philip Melanchthon (1497–1560), a young humanist and professor of Greek, arrived at the University of Wittenberg, his first act was to implement curricular reforms on the

A village wedding as portrayed by Pieter Bruegel the Younger (1564–1638). [Scala/Art Resource, N.Y.]

humanist model. In his inaugural address, entitled *On Improving the Studies of the Young*, Melanchthon presented himself as a defender of good letters and classical studies against "barbarians who practice barbarous arts." By the latter he meant the scholastic theologians of the later Middle Ages, whose methods of juxtaposing the views of conflicting authorities and seeking to reconcile them by disputation had, he believed, undermined both good letters and sound biblical doctrine. Scholastic dominance in the universities was seen by Melanchthon as having bred contempt for the Greek language and learning and as having encouraged neglect of the study of mathematics, sacred studies, and the art of oratory. Melanchthon urged the careful study of history, poetry, and other humanist disciplines.

Together Luther and Melanchthon restructured the University of Wittenberg's curriculum. Commentaries on Lombard's Sentences were dropped, as was canon law. Straightforward historical study replaced old Scholastic lectures on Aristotle. Students read primary sources directly, not by way of accepted Scholastic commentators. Candidates for theological degrees defended the new doctrine on the basis of their own exegesis of the Bible. New chairs of Greek and Hebrew were created. Luther and Melanchthon also pressed for universal compulsory education so both boys and girls could reach vernacular literacy in the Bible.

In Geneva, John Calvin and his successor, Theodore Beza, founded the Genevan Academy, which later evolved into the University of Geneva. That institution, created primarily for training Calvinist ministers, pursued ideals similar to those set forth by Luther and Melanchthon. Calvinist refugees trained in the academy carried Protestant educational reforms to France, Scotland, England, and the New World. Through such efforts a working knowledge of Greek and Hebrew became commonplace in educated circles in the sixteenth and seventeenth centuries.

Some contemporaries decried what they saw as a narrowing of the original humanist program as Protestants took it over. Erasmus, for example, came to fear the Reformation as a threat to the liberal arts and good learning. Sebastian Franck pointed to parallels between Luther's and Zwingli's debates over Christ's presence in the Eucharist and such old scholastic disputations as that over the Immaculate Conception of the Virgin.

Humanist culture and learning nonetheless remained indebted to the Reformation. The Protestant endorsement of the humanist program of studies remained as significant for the humanist movement as the latter had been for the Reformation. Protestant schools and universities consolidated and preserved for the modern world many of the basic pedagogical achievements of humanism. There the *studia humanitatis*, although often as little more than a handmaiden to theological doctrine, found a permanent home, one that remained hospitable even in the heyday of Conservative Protestantism.

Albrecht Dürer's portrait of a young girl (1515). The Protestant movement encouraged girls to be literate in their native languages. [Kupferstichkabinett Staatliche Museen, Preussischer Kulturbesitz, Berlin]

The Reformation and the Changing Role of Women

The Protestant reformers took a positive stand on clerical marriage and strongly opposed monasticism and the celibate life. From this position they challenged the medieval tendency alternately to degrade women as temptresses (following the model of Eve) and to exalt them as virgins (following the model of Mary). Protestants opposed the popular antiwoman and antimarriage literature of the Middle Ages. They praised woman in her own right, but especially in her biblical vocation as mother and housewife. Although from a modern perspective, women remained subject to men, new marriage laws gave them greater security and protection.

Relief of sexual frustration and a remedy of fornication were prominent in Protestant arguments for marriage. But the reformers also viewed their wives as indispensable companions in their work, and this not solely because they took domestic cares off their husbands' minds. Luther, who married in 1525 at the age of forty-two, wrote of women:

> Imagine what it would be like without women. The home, cities, economic life, and government would virtually disappear. Men cannot do without women. Even if it were possible for men to beget and bear children, they still could not do without women.[3]

John Calvin wrote at the death of his wife:

> I have been bereaved of the best companion of my life, of one who, had it been so ordered, would not only have been the willing sharer of my indigence, but even of my death. During her life she was the faithful helper of my ministry.[4]

Such tributes were intended in part to overcome Catholic criticism that marriage distracted the cleric from his ministry. They were primarily the

[3] *Luther's Works, Vol. 54: Table Talk*, ed. and trans. by Theodore G. Tappert (Philadelphia: Fortress Press, 1967), p. 161.

[4] *Letters of John Calvin*, Vol. 2, trans. by J. Bonnet (Edinburgh: T. Constable, 1858), p. 216.

The family of Hans Holbein the Younger (1497–1534), as painted by the artist himself. [Via Foto Hans Hinz, Basel]

expression of a new value placed on the estate of marriage and family life. In opposition to the celibate ideal of the Middle Ages, Protestants stressed as no religious movement before them the sacredness of home and family. This attitude contributed to a more respectful and sharing relationship between husbands and wives and between parents and children.

The ideal of the companionate marriage—that is, of husband and wife as co-workers in a special God-ordained community of the family, sharing authority equally within the household—led to an important expansion of the grounds for divorce in Protestant cities as early as the 1520s. Women now had an equal right with men to divorce and remarry in good conscience—unlike in Catholicism, where only a separation from bed and table, not divorce and remarriage, was permitted a couple in a failed marriage. The reformers were actually more willing to permit divorce and remarriage on grounds of adultery and abandonment than were secular magistrates, who feared liberal divorce laws would lead to social upheaval.

Protestant doctrines were as attractive to women as they were to men. Renegade nuns wrote exposés of the nunnery in the name of Christian freedom and justification by faith, declaring that the nunnery was no special woman's place at all and that supervisory male clergy (who alone could hear the nuns' confessions and administer sacraments to them) made their lives as unpleasant and burdensome as any abusive husband. Women in the higher classes, who enjoyed new social and political freedoms during the Renaissance, found in Protestant theology a religious complement to their greater independence in other walks of life. Some cloistered noblewomen, however, protested the closing of nunneries. They believed the cloister provided them a more interesting and independent way of life than they would have known in the secular world.

Because they wanted women to become pious housewives, Protestants encouraged the educatino of girls to literacy in the vernacular, with the expectation that they would thereafter model their lives on the Bible. During their studies, however, women found biblical passages that suggested they were equal to men in the presence of God. Education also gave some women a role as independent authors in the Reformation. From a modern perspective, these may seem like small advances, but they were significant, if indirect, steps in the direction of the emancipation of women.

Changes in the timing and duration of marriage, in family size, and in infant and child care suggest that family life was under a variety of social and economic pressures in the sixteenth and seventeenth centuries. The Reformation was a factor in these changes, but not the only or even the major one. [For a comparison of the family in western Europe and China, see The West & the World essay on p. 408.]

✦

During the early Middle Ages, Christendom had been divided into Western and Eastern churches with irreconcilable theological differences. When, in 1517, Martin Luther posted ninety-five theses questioning the selling of indulgences and the traditional sacrament of penance that lay behind them, he created a division within Western Christendom itself—an internal division between Protestants and Catholics.

The Lutheran protest came at a time of political and social discontent with the church. Not only princes and magistrates, but many ordinary people as well resented traditional clerical rights and privileges. In many instances the clergy were exempted from secular laws and taxes, while remaining powerful landowners whose personal lifestyles were not all that different from those of the laity. Spiritual and secular protest combined to make the Protestant Reformation a successful assault on the old church. In town after town and region after region within Protestant lands, the major institutions and practices of traditional piety were significantly transformed.

It soon became clear, however, that the division would not stop with the Lutherans. Making Scripture the only arbiter in religion had opened a Pandora's box. People proved to have very different ideas about what Scripture taught. Indeed, there seemed to be as many points of view as there were readers. Rapidly the Reformation created Lutheran, Zwinglian, Anabaptist, Spiritualist, Calvinist, and Anglican versions of biblical religion—a splintering of Protestantism that still endures.

Catholics had been pursuing reform before the Reformation broke out in Germany, although without papal enthusiasm, and certainly not along clear Protestant lines. When major reforms finally came in the Catholic Church around the mid-sixteenth century, they were doctrinally reactionary but administratively and spiritually flexible. The church enforced strict obedience and conformity to its teaching, but it also provided the laity with a better educated and disciplined clergy. For laity who wanted a deeper and more individual piety, experimentation with proven spiritual practices was now permitted. By century's end, such measures had successfully countered and in some areas even spectacularly reversed Protestant gains.

After the Reformation, pluralism steadily became a fact of Western religious life. It did so at first only by sheer force, since no one religious body was then prepared to concede the validity of alternative Christian beliefs and practices. During the sixteenth and seventeenth centuries, only those groups that fought doggedly for their faith gained the right to practice it freely. Despite these struggles, religious pluralism endured. Never again would there be only a Catholic Christian Church in Europe.

Review Questions

1. What were the main problems of the church that contributed to the Protestant Reformation? Why was the church unable to suppress dissent as it had earlier?
2. What were the basic similarities and differences between the ideas of Luther and Zwingli? Between Luther and Calvin? Did the differences

tend to split the Protestant ranks and thereby lessen the effectiveness of the movement?

3. Why did the Reformation begin in Germany? What political factors contributed to the success of the Reformation there as opposed to France or Italy?
4. What was the Catholic reformation and what principal decisions and changes were instituted by the Council of Trent? Was the Protestant Reformation a healthy movement for the Catholic Church?
5. Why did Henry VIII finally break with the Catholic Church? Was the "new" religion he established really Protestant? What problems did his successors face as a result of Henry's move?
6. What impact did the Reformation have on women in the sixteenth and seventeenth centuries? What new factors and pressures affected relations between men and women, family size, and child care during this period?

Suggested Readings

W. BOUWSMA, *John Calvin: A Sixteenth Century Portrait* (1988). Interpretation of Calvin against background of Renaissance intellectual history.

J. DELUMEAU, *Catholicism Between Luther and Voltaire: A New View of the Counter Reformation* (1977). Programmatic essay for a social history of the Counter-Reformation.

A. G. DICKENS, *The Counter Reformation* (1969). Brief narrative with pictures.

A. G. DICKENS, *The English Reformation* (1974). The best one-volume account.

A. G. DICKENS AND JOHN M. TONKIN, *The Reformation in Historical Thought* (1985). The standard critical guide to the main developments in Reformation studies.

G. DONALDSON, *The Scottish Reformation* (1960). Dependable, comprehensive narrative.

G. ELTON, *Reform and Reformation: England, 1509–1558* (1977). Standard political narrative.

H. O. EVENNETT, *The Spirit of the Counter Reformation* (1968). Essay on the continuity of Catholic reform and its independence from the Protestant Reformation.

J. FLANDRIN, *Families in Former Times* (1979). Family life in France.

B. GOTTLIEB, *The Family in the Western World* (1992). Accessible overview with up-to-date annotated bibliographies.

R. HOULBROOKE, *English Family Life, 1450–1716. An Anthology from Diaries* (1988). A rich collection of documents illustrating family relationships.

R. P. HSIA (ED.), *The German People and the Reformation* (1988). Substantial excerpts from the latest research.

J. L. IRWIN (ED.), *Womanhood in Radical Protestantism, 1525–1675* (1979). Sources illustrating images of women in sectarian Protestant thought.

H. JEDIN, *A History of the Council of Trent*, vols. 1 and 2 (1957–1961). Comprehensive, detailed, authoritative.

D. L. JENSEN, *Reformation Europe, Age of Reform and Revolution* (1981). Excellent, up-to-date survey.

W. K. JORDAN, *Edward VI: The Young King* (1968). The basic biography.

R. M. KINGDON (ED.), *Transition and Revolution: Problems and Issues of European Renaissance and Reformation History* (1974). Covers politics, printing, theology, and witchcraft.

A. MACFARLANE, *The Family Life of Ralph Josselin: A Seventeenth Century Clergyman* (1970). A model study of Puritan family life!

J. F. MCNEILL, *The History and Character of Calvinism* (1954). The most comprehensive account and very readable.

E. W. MONTER, *Calvin's Geneva* (1967). Dependable sketch derived from authoritative studies.

H. A. OBERMAN, *Luther: Man Between God and the Devil* (1989). Perhaps the best account of Luther's life, by a Dutch master.

J. O'MALLEY, *The First Jesuits* (1993). Extremely detailed account of the creation of the Society of Jesus and its original purposes.

S. OZMENT, *The Age of Reform 1250–1550: An Intellectual and Religious History of Late Medieval and Reformation Europe* (1980). A broad survey of major religious ideas and beliefs.

S. OZMENT, *When Fathers Ruled: Family Life in Reformation Europe* (1983). A survey of sixteenth-century attitudes toward marriage and parenthood.

S. OZMENT, *Three Behaim Boys: Growing Up in Early Modern Germany* (1990). The lives of three boys in their late teens and early adulthood told in their own words.

S. OZMENT, *Protestants: The Birth of a Revolution* (1992). The Reformation in Germany as a religious and cultural movement.

R. R. POST, *The Modern Devotion* (1968). Currently the authoritative interpretation.

E. F. RICE, JR., *The Foundations of Early Modern Europe 1460–1559* (1970). Broad, succinct narrative.

J. G. RIDLEY, *Thomas Cranmer* (1962). The basic biography.

J. J. SCARISBRICK, *The Reformation and the English People* (1990). Eloquent argument that the Reformation changed little religiously, and that it was a political, not a spiritual, triumph.

Q. SKINNER, *The Foundations of Modern Political Thought II: The Age of Reformation* (1978). A comprehensive survey that treats every political thinker and tract.

L. W. Spitz, *The Protestant Reformation 1517–1559* (1985). Sweeping survey with rich bibliographies.

D. Starkey, *The Reign of Henry VIII* (1985). Portrayal of the king as in control of neither his life nor his court.

J. Stayer, *Anabaptists and the Sword* (1972). The political philosophies of sectarians.

L. Stone, *The Family, Sex and Marriage in England 1500–1800* (1977). Controversial but in many respects still reigning view of English family history.

G. Strauss (ed. and Trans.), *Manifestations of Discontent in Germany on the Eve of the Reformation* (1971). Rich collection of sources for both rural and urban scenes.

G. Strauss, *Luther's House of Learning: The Indoctrination of the Young in the German Reformation* (1978). Account of Protestant efforts to rear children in the new faith, stressing the negative side.

R. H. Tawney, *Religion and the Rise of Capitalism* (1947). Advances beyond Max Weber's arguments relating Protestantism and capitalist economic behavior.

E. Troeltsch, *The Social Teaching of the Christian Churches*, vols. 1 and 2, trans. by O. Wyon (1960). Old, liberal account of the Reformation and its critics with fondness for the latter.

M. Weber, *The Protestant Ethic and the Spirit of Capitalism*, trans. by T. Parsons (1958). First appeared in 1904–1905 and has continued to stimulate debate over the relationship between religion and society.

F. Wendel, Calvin: *The Origins and Development of His Religious Thought*, trans. by P. Mairet (1963). The best treatment of Calvin's theology.

G. H. Williams, *The Radical Reformation* (1962). Broad survey of the varieties of dissent within Protestantism.

The West & the World

THE FAMILY IN EUROPE AND CHINA (1400–1800)

A family has a certain internal force and logic of its own. Time, place, and culture, however, are also important in making it what it is. A person raised in a twelfth-century household is different from one raised in a twentieth-century household, and growing up in Europe is not the same as growing up in Asia. The differences do not, however, lie in the ability of husbands and wives to love one another, or of parents to love their children. Rather, they result from the different ways in which a society or a culture infuses its larger communal values, shaped by politics, economics, and religious beliefs, into family life.

THE WESTERN EUROPEAN FAMILY

Later Marriages. Between 1500 and 1800, men and women in western Europe and England married at later ages than they had in previous centuries. Men tended to be in their mid- to late twenties rather than in their late teens and early twenties, and women in their early to mid-twenties rather than in their teens. The canonical, or church-sanctioned, age for marriage remained fourteen for men and twelve for women, and engagements might occur at these young ages, especially among royalty and nobility. As it had done throughout the high and later Middle Ages, the church also recognized as valid the free, private exchange of vows between a man and a woman at these minimal ages. However, after the Reformation, which condemned such clandestine unions, the church increasingly required both parental agreement and public vows in church before a marriage could be recognized as fully licit—procedures it had always actually preferred.

Late marriage in the West reflected the difficulty couples had supporting themselves independently. The difficulty arose because of the population growth that occurred during the late fifteenth and early sixteenth centuries, when western Europe recovered much of the population loss incurred during the plague. Larger families meant more heirs and hence a grater division of resources. In Germanic and Scandinavian countries, the custom of a fair sharing of inheritance among all male children worked to delay marriages, for divided inheritances often meant small incomes for the recipients. It simply took the average couple a longer time than previously to prepare themselves materially for marriage. In the sixteenth century, one in five women never married, and these, combined with the estimated 15 percent who were unmarried widows, constituted a sizable unmarried female population.

A later marriage meant a marriage of shorter duration because couples who married in their thirties would not spend as much time together as couples who married in their twenties. Such marriages also contributed to more frequent remarriage for men because women who bore children for the first time at advanced ages had higher mortality rates than younger mothers. Moreover, as growing church condemnation and the rapid growth of orphanages and foundling homes between 1600 and 1800 confirm, delayed marriage

A sixteenth century French tribute to the happiness of a peaceful, productive marriage and loving children. "La Famille de Berchem," by Frans Floris (ca. 1516–1570). [Corbis-Bettmann]

increased premarital sex and raised the number of illegitimate children.

Arranged Marriages. Marriage tended to be "arranged" in the sense that the parents customarily met and discussed the terms of the marriage. By the fifteenth century, the wealth and social standing of the bride and the bridegroom were not the only things considered when parents arranged a marriage. The two involved people may have known each other in advance and even to have had some prior relationship. Also, emotional feeling for one another was increasingly respected by parents. Parents did not force total strangers to live together, and children had a legal right to resist an unwanted marriage. A forced marriage was by definition invalid, and parents understood that unwanted marriages could fail. The best marriage was one desired by both the couple and their families.

Family Size. The western European family was conjugal, or nuclear; that is, it consisted of a father and a mother and two to four children who survived into adulthood. This nuclear family lived within a larger household, consisting of in-laws, servants, laborers, and boarders. The average husband and wife had seven or eight children, a birth about every two years. Of these, however, an estimated one-third died by age five, and one-half by their teens. Rare is the family, at any social level, that did not experience infant mortality and child death.

Birth Control. Artificial birth control has existed since antiquity. The ancient Egyptians used alligator dung and other acidic sperm killers, and sponges were also popular. In the West, the church's condemnation of *coitus interruptus* (male withdrawal before ejaculation) during the thirteenth and fourteenth centuries suggests that a contraceptive mentality—that is, a conscious and regular effort at birth control—may have been developing at this time. But early birth control measures, when applied, were not very effective,

A young couple in love (ca. 1480) by an anonymous artist. [Bildarchiv Preussischer Kulturbesitz]

Wet nurses were women who had recently had a baby or were suckling a child of their own, and who, for a fee, agreed also to suckle another child. The practice appears to have increased the risk of infant mortality, exposing infants to a strange and shared milk supply from women who were usually not as healthy as the infants' own mothers and who often lived under less sanitary conditions. But nursing an infant was a chore some upper-class women found distasteful, and their husbands also preferred that they not do it. Among women, vanity and convenience appear to have been motives for turning to wet nurses. For husbands, more was at stake in the practice. Because the church forbade sexual intercourse while a woman was lactating, and sexual intercourse was also believed to spoil a lactating woman's milk (pregnancy, of course, eventually ended her milk supply), a nursing wife was often a reluctant lover. In addition, nursing had a contraceptive effect (about 75 percent effective). Some women prolonged nursing their children precisely to delay a new pregnancy, and some husbands understood and cooperated in this form of family planning. For other husbands, however, especially noblemen and royalty who desired an abundance of male heirs, nursing seemed to rob them of offspring and to jeopardize the patrimony; hence, their support of wet nursing.

and for both historical and moral reasons the church firmly opposed them. During the eleventh century it suppressed an extreme ascetic sect, the Cathars, whom it accused of practicing birth control. The church also opposed (and still opposes) contraception on moral grounds. According to Saint Thomas Aquinas, a moral act mut always aid and abet, never frustrate, the natural end of the being or thing in question, and he believed that the natural end of sex could be only the birth of children and their godly rearing within the bounds of holy matrimony and the community of the church.

Wet Nursing. The church allied with the physicians of early modern Europe on another intimate family matter: the condemnation of women who hired nurses to suckle their newborn children, sometimes for as long as a year and a half. The practice was popular among upper-class women, who looked on it as a symbol of their high rank.

Loving Families? The traditional western European family had features that may seem cold and unloving. When children were between the ages of eight and thirteen, parents routinely sent them out of their homes into apprenticeships, off to school, or into employment in the homes and businesses of relatives, friends, and even strangers. In addition, the emotional ties between spouses seem to have been as tenuous as those between parents and children. Widowers and widows often married again within a few months of their spouses' deaths, and marriages with extreme disparity in age—between older men and younger women and between older women and younger men—also suggest limited affection.

In response to such modern-day criticism, an early modern parent would surely have asked, "What greater love can parents have for their children than to equip them to make their way vocationally in the world?" An apprenticed child was a self-supporting child, and hence a child with a future. Considering primitive living conditions, contemporaries could also appreciate the purely utilitarian and humane side of marriage and understand when widowers and widows quickly married again. On the other hand, marriages with extreme disparity in age were no more the norm in early modern Europe than the practice of wet nursing, and they received just as much criticism and ridicule.

THE TRADITIONAL CHINESE FAMILY[1]

The Meaning of Family. In Chinese the word for "family" and "home" is the same: all who live together under one roof. For the Chinese, as for the European family, the child–parent unit (the "nuclear family") distinguished itself from its kin by marriage, and both groups separated themselves from servants, boarders, and/or workers, who circulated or lived within the household. And both cultures recognized the family as society's fundamental unit.

In addition to its many relatives by blood and marriage, the Chinese family also thought of itself as part of the ruling regime, or "state," another group identity beyond the immediate family, village, and clan that rulers, attempting to unify their lands, encouraged. They did this primarily by exalting patrilineage, or membership in a group that traced its history over untold generations of males. During the later Middle Ages, patrilineage played a similar role in Europe: With matrilineal lines ignored, the maternal side of a family's history was suppressed. Despite the effects of their rulers, the Chinese never felt as close to the state as they did to their families and kin. In Europe, by contrast, a quasi "national" consciousness—that is, a sense of being "German," "French," or "English" as well as a member of a particular family, village, or clan—was more successful inculcated.

The Chinese family also counted its dead ancestors as intimate family members, their spirits said to roam the earth and scrutinize the conduct of their kin, a belief that encouraged good behavior and achievement. As in Western Christendom, the Chinese believed that the world of the living communed with that of the dead. Children were admonished to act in ways that pleased and honored the spirits of their ancestors, lest the latter bring misfortune upon their families. In Europe, by contrast, the living were thought to be of more help to the dead than the dead to the living. By special prayers and masses, people believed they could help their deceased relatives pass through purgatory and into heaven.

Family Size. The average Chinese family was slightly smaller than the average European family, numbering five or six members instead of seven or eight. Like Western Christianity, Confucianism exalted the authority of the father over the family and stressed the virtues of order and obedience within it. No religious virtue was said to be greater than loyalty to one's family.

Family Relationships. For the family of the bride, a wedding was a costly affair and arranged with the greatest of care. Whereas in Europe, fathers usually took the lead in finding husbands for their daughters, mothers played that role in China. This actually worked to the bride's favor, for a mother better understood what marriage involved for a woman and probably got her daughter the best possible mate. Also unlike in Europe, where by 1500 a couple's emotional compatibility had become almost as important a consideration in the making of a marriage as wealth and social standing, a prospective Chinese bride and bridegroom had both less to say about whom they married and a smaller role in the arrangements.

The life of a new daughter-in-law was not completely enviable. Her new family often looked on her as an unnatural member, an alien artificially incorporated by marriage. A bride's transition into her husband's family was often traumatic. After the wedding, she became the sole legal responsibility of her husband's family, breaking her ties with her own family to a degree unheard of in Europe. No longer able to count on her own family for security and affection, she often found her husband's household stressful, especially during the first years. Confucianism contributed to this state of affairs by stressing family solidarity against foreign influence, including that of daughters-in-law, whom it instructed families to isolate.

[1]The sources for the following are Maurice Freedman, *The Study of Chinese Society: Essays by Maurice Freedman* (Stanford, CA: Stanford University Press, 1979); Martin C. Yang, *A Chinese Village: Taitou, Shantung Province* (New York: Columbia University Press, 1965); and Margery Wolf, "Child Training and the Chinese Family," in Maurice Freedman, ed., *Family and Kinship in Chinese Society* (Stanford, CA: Stanford University Press, 1970), pp. 37–62.

A Chinese Merchant's Family, ca. 1856. In a pose reflecting the gender divisions within the traditional Chinese family, the father sits with his sons on the right, his wife and daughter sit on the left. [Mark Sexton/Courtesy Peabody & Essex Museum, Salem, MA]

Particularly in well-ordered, high-status families, a new wife came immediately under the authority of her mother-in-law, who, with her son's concurrence (Chinese sons did not challenge their mothers), regulated and supervised her every activity within the new household. A daughter-in-law also could not protest this situation because of her dependence on the good will of her mother-in-law. Regardless of the disagreement, a daughter-in-law who found herself at odds with her mother-in-law faced a difficult life. In the end, it often became a simple choice between capitulation or misery. Only with the passage of time and the bearing of children did the bride gain grater respect and freedom within her new household.

A daughter-in-law also faced an up-hill battle with her mother-in-law for the loyalty and affection of her husband. Deeply committed to both, he found himself in a delicate situation, having to treat each in such a way that the other would not be offended.

Child Rearing. The goal of Chinese parents was to raise loyal and obedient children who would support them in their old age. That was also true of European parents in rural society, while the urban upper classes also looked on worldly success and family honor as equally important goals. As in Europe, Chinese parents treated their children differently after they had reached six or seven years of age. Boys especially came under the strict discipline of their fathers, who henceforth dealt with them in a consciously aloof and formal manner, the best way, it was believed, to render children dutiful and loyal. Fear and shame were also employed to discourage behavior that displeased or dishonored parents. As among European, Chinese parents now resisted overly generous displays of affection and indulgence, fearing such treatment might spoil their children and make them unreliable in later life, when the parents' survival and well-being would depend totally on their loyalty and devotion.

Mothers took a different approach to child rearing. Along with the promise of future security, bearing a child gave a woman a greater importance within the family. Whereas fathers sought to retain the loyalty of a child by inculcating fear and shame, mothers attempted a friendlier relationship, often becoming their children's advocate and mediator with the father. Both parents beat disobedient children, but as a child matured, corporal punishment became almost wholly the responsibility of the father, another feature the Chinese family shared with the European. The mother was the parent in whom a child might trustingly confide and with whom a joke might be shared.

On the whole, daughters were treated more affectionately than sons. This was because Chinese parents knew that a daughter would never be theirs again once she had married and joined her husband's household. Not being dependent on their daughters for their future well-being, parents had less need to drill loyalty and obedience into them, and could thus treat a daughter with greater informality and affection than they could a son. The result was a shorter, but comparatively happier relationship between parents and daughters.

✦ *What did Western European and Chinese families consider to be the most important factors in a successful marriage?*

✦ *Why was a new wife more harmoniously integrated into a Western European family than into a Chinese family?*

✦ *Did Western European and Chinese parents have the same goals in child-rearing?*

✦ *Did Western European and Chinese parents express pride in and affection for their children in the same way?*

✦ *In which culture do you think the family had greater independence from outside influences (religion, politics, and mass culture)?*

CHAPTER 12

The massacre of worshiping Protestants at Vassy, France (March 1, 1562), which began the French wars of religion. An engraving by an unidentified seventeenth century artist. [The Granger Collection, N.Y.]

The Age of Religious Wars

KEY TOPICS

- The war between Calvinists and Catholics in France
- The Spanish occupation of the Netherlands
- The struggle for supremacy between England and Spain
- The devastation of central Europe during the Thirty Years' War

The late sixteenth century and the first half of the seventeenth century are described as the "age of religious wars" because of the bloody opposition of Protestants and Catholics across Europe. Both genuine religious conflict and bitter dynastic rivalries fueled the wars. In France, the Netherlands, England, and Scotland in the second half of the sixteenth century, Calvinists fought Catholic rulers for the right to govern their own territories and to practice their chosen religion openly. In the first half of the seventeenth century, Lutherans, Calvinists, and Catholics marched against one another in central and northern Europe during the Thirty Years' War. By the middle of the seventeenth century, English Puritans had successfully revolted against the Stuart monarchy and the Anglican Church.

Renewed Religious Struggle

During the first half of the sixteenth century, religious conflict had been confined to central Europe and was primarily a struggle by Lutherans to secure rights and freedoms for themselves. In the second half of the sixteenth century, the focus shifted to western Europe—to France, the Netherlands, England, and Scotland—and became a struggle by Calvinists for recognition. After the Peace of Augsburg (1555), and with it acceptance of the principle that a region's ruler would determine its religion (*cuius regio, eius religio*), Lutheranism became a legal religion in the Holy Roman Empire. The Peace of Augsburg did not, however, extend recognition to non-Lutheran Protestants. Both Catholics and Lutherans scorned Anabaptists and other sectarians as anarchists, and Calvinists were not yet strong enough to demand legal standing.

Outside the empire the struggle for Protestant religious rights had intensified in most countries by the mid-sixteenth century. After the Council of Trent adjourned in 1563, Catholics began a Jesuit-led international counteroffensive against Protestants. At the time of John Calvin's death in 1564, Geneva had become both a refuge for Europe's persecuted Protestants and an interna-

The religious conflicts of the sixteenth and seventeenth centuries are reflected in the art and architecture of the period. This eighteenth-century cloister-church in Ottobeuren in Bavaria, designed by Johann Michael Fischer, is in the baroque style congenial to the Catholic Counter-Reformation. The interior explodes with energy and is filled with sculptures and paintings and magnificent woodwork that catch the eye. The intent was to inspire and move the worshiper to self-transcendence. [Bildarchiv Preussicscher Kulturbesitz]

tional school for Protestant resistance, producing leaders fully equal to the new Catholic challenge.

Genevan Calvinism and Catholicism as revived by the Council of Trent were two equally dogmatic, aggressive, and irreconcilable church systems. Calvinists may have looked like "new papists" to critics when they dominated cities like Geneva. Yet when, as minorities, they found their civil and religious rights denied, they became true firebrands and revolutionaries. Calvinism adopted a presbyterian organization that magnified regional and local religious authority. Boards of presbyters, or elders, representing the many individual congregations of Calvinists, directly shaped the policy of the church at large.

By contrast, the Counter-Reformation sponsored a centralized episcopal church system, hierarchically arranged from pope to parish priest, that stressed absolute obedience to the person at the top. The high clergy—the pope and his bishops—not the synods of local churches, ruled supreme. Calvinism proved attractive to proponents of political decentralization who opposed totalitarian rulers, whereas Catholicism remained congenial to proponents of absolute monarchy determined to maintain "one king, one church, one law."

The opposition between the two religions can be seen even in the art and architecture that each came to embrace. The Catholic Counter-Reformation found the baroque style congenial. A successor to mannerism, baroque art is a grandiose, three-dimensional display of life and energy. Great baroque artists like Peter Paul Rubens (1571–1640) and Gianlorenzo Bernini (1598–1680) were Catholics. Protestants by contrast opted for a simpler and more restrained art and architecture, as can be seen in the English churches of Christopher Wren (1632–1723) and the gentle, searching portraits of the Dutch Mennonite, Rembrandt van Rijn (1606–1669).

As religious wars engulfed Europe, the intellectuals perceived the wisdom of religious pluralism and toleration more quickly than did the politicians. A new skepticism, relativism, and individualism in religion became respectable in the sixteenth and seventeenth centuries. (See Chapter 14.) Sebastian Castellio's (1515–1563) pithy censure of John Calvin for his role in the execution of the anti-Trinitarian Michael Servetus summarized a growing sentiment: "To kill a man is not to defend a doctrine, but to kill a man."[1] The French essayist Michel de Montaigne (1533–1592) asked in scorn of the dogmatic mind: "What do I know?" And the Lutheran Valentin Weigel (1533–1588), surveying a half century of religious strife in Germany, advised people to look within themselves for religious truth and no longer to churches and creeds.

Such skeptical views gained currency in larger political circles only at the cost of painful experi-

[1] *Contra libellum Calvini* (N.P., 1562), p. E 2 a.

In stark contrast to the baroque style, this seventeenth-century Calvinist church in the Palatinate has no interior decoration to distract the worshiper from the Word of God. The intent was to create an atmosphere of quiet introspection and reflection on one's spiritual life and God's Word. [German National Museum, Nuremburg]

ence. Religious strife and civil war were best held in check where rulers tended to subordinate theological doctrine to political unity, urging tolerance, moderation, and compromise—even indifference—in religious matters. Rulers of this kind came to be known as *politiques,* and the most successful among them was Elizabeth I of England. By contrast, such rulers as Mary I of England, Philip II of Spain, and Oliver Cromwell, who took their religion with the utmost seriousness and refused every compromise, did not in the long run achieve their political goals.

As we shall see, the wars of religion were both internal national conflicts and truly international wars. Catholic and Protestant subjects struggled against one another for control of the crown of France, the Netherlands, and England. The Catholic governments of France and Spain conspired and finally sent armies against Protestant regimes in England and the Netherlands. The outbreak of the Thirty Years' War in 1618 made the international dimension of the religious conflict especially clear; before it ended in 1648, the war drew every major European nation directly or indirectly into its deadly net.

The French Wars of Religion (1562–1598)

Anti-Protestant Measures and the Struggle for Political Power

French Protestants are known as *Huguenots,* a term derived from Besançon Hugues, the leader of Geneva's political revolt against the House of Savoy in the 1520s, a prelude to that city's Calvinist Reformation. Huguenots were under surveillance in France already in the early 1520s, when Lutheran writings and doctrines began to circulate in Paris. The capture of the French king Francis I by the forces of Emperor Charles V at the Battle of Pavia in 1525 provided a motive for the first wave of Protestant persecution in France. The French government hoped thereby to pacify their Habsburg conqueror, a fierce opponent of German Protestants, and to win their king's swift release.

A second major crackdown came a decade later. When Protestants plastered Paris and other cities with anti-Catholic placards on October 18, 1534, mass arrests of suspected Protestants followed. The government retaliation drove John Calvin and other members of the French reform party into exile. In 1540 the Edict of Fontainebleau subjected French Protestants to the Inquisition. Henry II (r. 1547–1559) established new measures against Protestants in the Edict of Chateaubriand in 1551. Save for a few brief interludes, the French monarchy remained a staunch foe of the Protestants until the ascension to the throne of Henry of Navarre in 1589.

The Habsburg–Valois wars (see Chapter 11) had ended with the Treaty of Cateau-Cambrésis in 1559, after which Europe experienced a moment of peace. But the same year marked the beginning of internal French conflict and the shift of the European balance of power away from France to Spain. The shift began with an accident. During a tournament held to celebrate the marriage of his thirteen-year-old daughter to Philip II, the son of Charles V and heir to the Spanish Habsburg lands, the French king, Henry II, was mortally wounded when a lance pierced his visor. This unforeseen event brought to the throne his sickly fifteen-year-old son, Francis II, under the regency of the queen mother, Catherine de Médicis. With the monarchy so weakened by Henry's death, three powerful families saw their chance to control France and began to compete for the young king's ear. They were the Bourbons, whose power lay in the south and west; the Montmorency-Chatillons, who controlled the center of France; and the Guises, who were dominant in eastern France.

The Guises were by far the strongest and had little trouble establishing firm control over the young king. Francis, duke of Guise, had been Henry II's general, and his brothers, Charles and Louis, were cardinals of the church. Mary Stuart, Queen of Scots and wife of Francis II, was their niece. Throughout the latter half of the sixteenth century, the name of Guise remained interchangeable with militant, reactionary Catholicism.

The Bourbon and Montmorency-Chatillon families, in contrast, developed strong Huguenot sympathies, largely for political reasons. The Bourbon Louis I, prince of Condé (d. 1569), and the Montmorency-Chatillon Admiral Gaspard de Coligny (1519–1572) became the political leaders of the French Protestant resistance. They collaborated early in an abortive plot to kidnap Francis II from his Guise advisers in the Conspiracy of Amboise in 1560. This conspiracy was strongly condemned by John Calvin, who considered such tactics a disgrace to the Reformation.

Appeal of Calvinism

Often for quite different reasons ambitious aristocrats and discontented townspeople joined Calvinist churches in opposition to the Guise-dominated French monarchy. In 1561 more than 2,000 Huguenot congregations existed throughout France. Yet Huguenots were a majority of the population in only two regions: Dauphiné and Languedoc. Although they made up only about one fifteenth of the population, Huguenots were in important geographic areas and were heavily represented among the more powerful segments of French society. More than two-fifths of the French aristocracy became Huguenots. Many apparently hoped to establish within France a principle of territorial sovereignty akin to that secured within the Holy Roman Empire by the Peace of Augsburg. In this way, Calvinism indirectly served the forces of political decentralization.

John Calvin and Theodore Beza consciously sought to advance their cause by currying favor with powerful aristocrats. Beza converted Jeanne d'Albert, the mother of the future Henry IV. The prince of Condé was apparently converted in 1558 under the influence of his Calvinist wife. For many aristocrats—Condé probably among them—Calvinist religious convictions were attractive primarily as aids to long-sought political goals.

The military organization of Condé and Coligny progressively merged with the religious organization of the French Huguenot churches, creating a potent combination that benefitted both political and religious dissidents. Calvinism gave political resistance justification and inspiration, and the forces of political resistance made Calvinism a viable religious alternative in Catholic France. Each side had much to gain from the other. The confluence of secular and religious motives, although beneficial to aristocratic resistance and Calvinist religion alike, tended to cast suspicion on the religious appeal of Calvinism. Clearly religious conviction was neither the only nor always the main reason for becoming a Calvinist in France in the second half of the sixteenth century.

Catherine de Médicis (1519–1589) exercised power in France during the reigns of her three sons Francis II (r. 1559–1560), Charles IX (r. 1560–1574), and Henry III (r. 1574–1589). [H. Roger Viollet]

Catherine de Médicis and the Guises

Following Francis II's death in 1560, Catherine de Médicis continued as regent for her minor son, Charles IX (r. 1560–1574). At a colloquy in Poissy, she tried unsuccessfully to reconcile the Protestant and Catholic factions. Fearing the power and guile of the Guises, Catherine, whose first concern was always to preserve the monarchy, sought allies among the Protestants. In 1562, after conversations with Beza and Coligny, she issued the January Edict, a measure that granted Protestants freedom to worship publicly outside towns—although only privately within them—and to hold synods. In March this royal toleration came to an abrupt end when the duke of Guise surprised a Protestant congregation at Vassy in Champagne and proceeded to massacre several score. That event marked the beginning of the French wars of religion (March 1562).

Had Condé and the Huguenot armies rushed immediately to the queen's side after this attack, Protestants might well have secured an alliance with the crown. The queen mother's fear of Guise power was great at this time. But the hesitation of the Protestant leaders, due primarily to indecision on the part of Condé, placed the young king and the queen mother, against their deepest wishes, in firm Guise control. Cooperation with the Guises became the only alternative to capitulation to the Protestants.

THE PEACE OF SAINT-GERMAIN-EN-LAYE During the first French war of religion, fought between April 1562 and March 1563, the duke of Guise was assassinated. It is a measure of the international character of the struggle in France that troops from Hesse and the Palatinate fought alongside the Huguenots. A brief resumption of hostilities in 1567–1568 was followed by the bloodiest of all the conflicts, between September 1568 and August 1570. In this period, Condé was killed and Huguenot leadership passed to Coligny. This was actually a blessing in disguise for the Protestants because Coligny was far the better military strategist. In the Peace of Saint-Germain-en-Laye (1570), which ended the third war, the crown, acknowledging the power of the Protestant nobility, granted the Huguenots religious freedoms within their territories and the right to fortify their cities.

Perpetually caught between fanatical Huguenot and Guise extremes, Queen Catherine had always sought to balance one side against the other. Like the Guises, she wanted a Catholic France; she did not, however, desire a Guise-dominated monarchy. After the Peace of Saint-Germain-en-Laye the crown tilted manifestly toward the Bourbon faction and the Huguenots, and Coligny became Charles IX's most trusted adviser. Unknown to the king, Catherine began to plot with the Guises against the ascendant Protestants. As she had earlier sought Protestant support when Guise power threatened to subdue the monarchy, she now sought Guise support as Protestant influence grew.

There was reason for Catherine to fear Coligny's hold on the king. Louis of Nassau, the leader of Protestant resistance to Philip II in the Netherlands, had gained Coligny's ear. Coligny used his position of influence to win the king of France over to a planned French invasion of the Netherlands in support of the Dutch Protestants. Such a course of action would have placed France squarely on a collision course with mighty Spain. Catherine recognized far better than her son that France stood little chance in such a contest. She and her advisers had been much sobered in this regard by news of the stunning Spanish victory over the Turks at Lepanto in October 1571 (to be discussed later).

The Saint Bartholemew's Day Massacre, as depicted by the contemporary Protestant painter François Dubois. In this notorious event, 3,000 Protestants were slaughtered in Paris and an estimated 20,000 others died throughout France. The massacre transformed the religious struggle in France from a contest for political power into a war for survival between Protestants and Catholics. [Musée Cantonal des Beaux Arts, Palais de Rumine, Lausanne]

THE SAINT BARTHOLOMEW'S DAY MASSACRE When Catherine lent her support to the infamous Saint Bartholomew's Day Massacre of Protestants, she did so out of a far less reasoned judgment. Her decision appears to have been made in a state of near panic. On August 22, 1572, four days after the Huguenot Henry of Navarre had married the king's sister, Marguerite of Valois—still another sign of growing Protestant power—Coligny was struck down, although not killed, by an assassin's bullet. Catherine had apparently been party to this Guise plot to eliminate Coligny. After its failure, she feared both the king's reaction to her complicity with the Guises and the Huguenot response under a recovered Coligny. Catherine convinced Charles that a Huguenot coup was afoot, inspired by Coligny, and that only the swift execution of Protestant leaders could save the crown from a Protestant attack on Paris.

On Saint Bartholomew's Day, August 24, 1572, Coligny and 3,000 fellow Huguenots were butchered in Paris. Within three days an estimated 20,000 Huguenots were executed in coordinated attacks throughout France. It is a date that has ever since lived in infamy for Protestants.

Pope Gregory XIII and Philip II of Spain reportedly greeted the news of the Protestant massacre with special religious celebrations. Philip especially had good reason to rejoice. By throwing France into civil war, the massacre ended for the moment any planned French opposition to his efforts to subdue his rebellious subjects in the Netherlands. But the massacre of thousands of Protestants also gave the discerning Catholic world cause for new alarm. The event changed the nature of the struggle between Protestants and Catholics both within and beyond the borders of France. It was thereafter no longer an internal contest between Guise and Bourbon factions for French political influence, nor was it simply a Huguenot campaign to win basic religious freedoms. Henceforth, in Protestant eyes, it became an international struggle to the death for sheer survival against an adversary whose cruelty now justified any means of resistance.

PROTESTANT RESISTANCE THEORY Only as Protestants faced suppression and sure defeat did they begin to sanction active political resistance. At first, they tried to practice the biblical precept of obedient subjection to worldly authority (Romans 13:1). Luther had only grudgingly approved resistance to the emperor after the Diet of Augsburg in 1530. In 1550 Lutherans in Magdeburg had published a highly influential defense of the right of lower authorities to oppose the emperor's order that all Lutherans return to the Catholic fold.

Calvin, who never faced the specter of total political defeat after his return to Geneva in September 1540, had always condemned willful disobedience and rebellion against lawfully constituted governments as un-Christian. But he also taught that lower magistrates, as part of the lawfully constituted government, had the right and duty to oppose tyrannical higher authority.

The exiled Scottish reformer John Knox, who had seen his cause crushed by Mary of Guise, the Regent of Scotland, and Mary I of England, laid the groundwork for later Calvinist resistance. In his famous *First Blast of the Trumpet Against the Terrible Regiment of Women* (1558), he declared that the removal of a heathen tyrant was not only permissible, but a Christian duty. He had the Catholic queen of England in mind.

After the great massacre of French Protestants on Saint Bartholomew's Day, 1572, Calvinists everywhere came to appreciate the need for an active defense of their religious rights. Classical Huguenot theories of resistance appeared in three major works of the 1570s. The first was the *Franco-Gallia* of François Hotman (1573), a humanist argument that the representative Estates General of France historically held higher authority than the French king. The second was Theodore Beza's *On the Right of Magistrates over Their Subjects* (1574), which, going beyond Calvin's views, justified the correction and even the overthrow of tyrannical rulers by lower authorities. Finally, Philippe du Plessis Mornay's *Defense of Liberty Against Tyrants* (1579) admonished princes, nobles, and magistrates beneath the king, as guardians of the rights of the body politic, to take up arms against tyranny in other lands.

The Rise to Power of Henry of Navarre

Henry III (r. 1574–1589) was the last of Henry II's sons to wear the French crown. He found the monarchy wedged between a radical Catholic League, formed in 1576 by Henry of Guise, and vengeful Huguenots. Neither group would have been reluctant to assassinate a ruler whom they considered heretical and a tyrant. Like the queen mother, Henry sought to steer a middle course. In this effort he received support from a growing body

Theodore Beza Defends the Right to Resist Tyranny

One of the oldest problems in political and social theory has been that of knowing when resistance to repression in matters of conscience is justified. Since Luther's day, Protestant reformers had urged their followers to obey established political authority. After the 1572 Saint Bartholomew's Day Massacre, however, Protestant pamphleteers urged Protestants to resist tyrants and persecutors with armed force. In 1574 Theodore Beza pointed out the obligation of rulers to act in the best interests of their subjects and the latter's right to resist them when they did not.

✦ *When does a ruler go too far according to Beza? To whom may subjects appeal against a tyrant? Does Beza believe that individuals may take the law into their own hands?*

It is apparent that there is a mutual obligation between the king and the officers of a kingdom; that the government of the kingdom is not in the hands of the king in its entirety, but only the sovereign degree; that each of the officers has a share in accord with his degree; and that there are definite conditions on either side. If these conditions are not observed by the inferior officers, it is the part of the sovereign to dismiss and punish them. . . . If the king, hereditary or elective, clearly goes back on the conditions without which he would not have been recognized and acknowledged, can there be any doubt that the lesser magistrates of the kingdom, of the cities, and of the provinces, the administration of which they have received from the sovereignty itself, are free of their oath, at least to the extent that they are entitled to resist flagrant oppression of the realm which they swore to defend and protect according to their office and their particular jurisdiction? . . .

We must now speak of the third class of subjects, which though admittedly subject to the sovereign in a certain respect, is, in another respect, and in cases of necessity the protector of the rights of the sovereignty itself, and is established to hold the sovereign to his duty, and even, if need be, constrain and punish him. . . . The people is prior to all the magistrates, and does not exist for them, but they for it. . . . Whenever law and equity prevailed, nations neither created nor accepted kings except upon definite conditions. From this it follows that when kings flagrantly violate these terms, those who have the power to give them their authority have no less power to deprive them of it.

Constitutionalism and Resistance in the Sixteenth Century: Three Treatises by Hotman, Beza, and Mornay, *trans. and ed. by Julian H. Franklin (New York: Pegasus, 1969), pp. 111–114.*

of neutral Catholics and Huguenots, who put the political survival of France above its religious unity. Such *politiques* were prepared to compromise religious creeds as might be required to save the nation.

The Peace of Beaulieu in May 1576 granted the Huguenots almost complete religious and civil freedom. France, however, was not ready then for such sweeping toleration. Within seven months of the Peace of Beaulieu, the Catholic League forced Henry to return to the illusory quest for absolute religious unity in France. In October 1577 the king truncated the Peace of Beaulieu and once again circumscribed areas of permitted Huguenot worship. Thereafter Huguenot and Catholic factions quickly returned to their accustomed anarchical military solutions. The Protestants were led by Henry of Navarre, now heir to the French throne by virtue of his marriage to Margaret of Valois, Henry III's sister.

In the mid-1580s the Catholic League, supported by the Spanish, became completely dominant in Paris. In what came to be known as the Day of the

Barricades, Henry III attempted to rout the league with a surprise attack in 1588. The effort failed badly, and the king had to flee Paris. Forced by his weakened position into unkingly guerilla tactics, and also emboldened by news of the English victory over the Spanish Armada in 1588, Henry successfully plotted the assassinations of both the duke and the cardinal of Guise. These assassinations sent France reeling once again. Led by still another Guise brother, the Catholic League reacted with a fury that matched the earlier Huguenot response to the Massacre of Saint Bartholomew's Day. The king now had only one course of action. He struck an alliance with the Protestant Henry of Navarre in April 1589.

As the two Henrys prepared to attack the Guise stronghold of Paris, however, a fanatical Jacobin friar stabbed and killed Henry III. Thereupon the Bourbon Huguenot Henry of Navarre succeeded the childless Valois king to the French throne as Henry IV (r. 1589–1610). Pope Sixtus V and Philip II stood aghast at the sudden prospect of a Protestant France. They had always wanted France to be religiously Catholic and politically weak, and they now acted to achieve that end. Spain rushed troops to support the besieged Catholic League. Philip II apparently even harbored hopes of placing his eldest daughter, Isabella, the granddaughter of Henry II and Catherine de Médicis, on the French throne.

Direct Spanish intervention in the affairs of France seemed only to strengthen Henry IV's grasp on the crown. The French people viewed his right to hereditary succession more seriously than his espoused Protestant confession. Henry was also widely liked. Notoriously informal in dress and manner—a factor that made him especially popular with the soldiers—Henry also had the wit and charm to neutralize the strongest enemy in a face-to-face confrontation. He came to the throne as a *politique*, long weary with religious strife and fully prepared to place political peace above absolute religious unity. He believed that a royal policy of tolerant Catholicism would be the best way to achieve such peace. On July 25, 1593, he publicly abjured the Protestant faith and embraced the traditional and majority religion of his country. "Paris is worth a mass," he is reported to have said.

It was, in fact, a decision he had made only after a long period of personal agonizing. The Huguenots were understandably horrified by this turnabout, and Pope Clement VIII remained skeptical of Henry's sincerity. But most of the French church and people, having known internal strife too long, rallied to the king's side. By 1596 the Catholic League was dispersed, its ties with Spain were broken, and the wars of religion in France, to all intents, had ground to a close.

Henry IV of France (r. 1589–1610) on horseback, painted in 1594. [Giraudon/Art Resource, N.Y.]

Henry IV Recognizes Huguenot Religious Freedom

By the Edict of Nantes (April 13, 1598) Henry IV recognized Huguenot religious freedoms and the rights of Protestants to participate in French public institutions. Here are some of its provisions.

✦ *Are Huguenots given equal religious standing with Catholics? Are there limitations on their freedoms?*

We have by this perpetual and irrevocable Edict pronounced, declared, and ordained and we pronounce, declare and ordain:

Art. I. Firstly, that the memory of everything done on both sides from the beginning of the month of March, 1585, until our accession to the Crown and during the other previous troubles, and at the outbreak of them, shall remain extinct and suppressed, as if it were something which had never occurred. . . .

Art. II. We forbid all our subjects, of whatever rank and quality they may be, to renew the memory of these matters, to attack, be hostile to, injure or provoke each other in revenge for the past, whatever may be the reason and pretext . . . but let them restrain themselves and live peaceably together as brothers, friends, and fellow-citizens. . . .

Art. III. We ordain that the Catholic, Apostolic, and Roman religion shall be restored and reestablished in all places and districts of this our kingdom and the countries under our rule, where its practice has been interrupted. . . .

Art. VI. And we permit those of the so-called Reformed religion to live and dwell in all the towns and districts of this our kingdom and the countries under our rule, without being annoyed, disturbed, molested or constrained to do anything against their conscience, or for this cause to be sought out in their houses and districts where they wish to live, provided that they conduct themselves in other respects to the provisions of our present Edict. . . .

Art. XXI. Books dealing with the matters of the aforesaid so-called Reformed religion shall not be printed and sold publicly, except in the towns and districts where the public exercise of the said religion is allowed. . . .

Art. XXII. We ordain that there shall be no difference or distinction, because of the aforesaid religion, in the reception of students to be instructed in Universities, Colleges, and schools, or of the sick and poor into hospitals, infirmaries, and public charitable institutions. . . .

Art. XXVII. In order to reunite more effectively the wills of our subjects, as is our intention, and to remove all future complaints, we declare that all those who profess or shall profess the aforesaid so-called Reformed religion are capable of holding and exercising all public positions, honours, offices, and duties whatsoever . . . in the towns of our kingdom . . . notwithstanding all contrary oaths.

Church and State Through the Centuries: A Collection of Historic Documents, *trans. and ed. by S. Z. Ehler and John B. Morrall (New York: Biblo and Tannen, 1967), pp. 185–187.*

The Edict of Nantes

On April 13, 1598, Henry IV's famous Edict of Nantes proclaimed a formal religious settlement. The following month, on May 2, 1598, the Treaty of Vervins ended hostilities between France and Spain.

In 1591 Henry IV had already assured the Huguenots of at least qualified religious freedoms. The Edict of Nantes made good that promise. It rec-

Main Events of French Wars of Religion	
1559	Treaty of Cateau-Cambrésis ends Habsburg–Valois wars
1559	Francis II succeeds to French throne under regency of his mother, Catherine de Médicis
1560	Conspiracy of Amboise fails
1562	Protestant worshipers massacred at Vassy in Champagne by the duke of Guise
1572	The Saint Bartholomew's Day Massacre leaves thousands of Protestants dead
1589	Assassination of Henry III brings the Huguenot Henry of Navarre to throne as Henry IV
1593	Henry IV embraces Catholicism
1598	Henry IV grants Huguenots religious and civil freedoms in the Edict of Nantes
1610	Henry IV assassinated

ognized and sanctioned minority religious rights within what was to remain an officially Catholic country. This religious truce—and it was never more than that—granted the Huguenots, who by this time numbered well over one million, freedom of public worship, the right of assembly, admission to public offices and universities, and permission to maintain fortified towns. Most of the new freedoms, however, were to be exercised within their own towns and territories. Concession of the right to fortify their towns reveals the continuing distrust between French Protestants and Catholics. As significant as it was, the edict only transformed a long hot war between irreconcilable enemies into a long cold war. To its critics it had only created a state within a state.

A Catholic fanatic assassinated Henry IV in May 1610. Although he is best remembered for the Edict of Nantes, the political and economic policies Henry IV put in place were equally important. They laid the foundations for the transformation of France into the absolute state it would become under Cardinal Richelieu and Louis XIV. Ironically, in pursuit of the political and religious unity that had escaped Henry IV, Louis XIV, calling for "one king, one church, one law," would revoke the Edict of Nantes in 1685 (see Chapter 13). This action would force France and Europe to learn again by bitter experience the hard lessons of the wars of religion. Rare is the politician who learns from the lessons of history rather than repeating its mistakes.

Titian's portrait of Philip II of Spain (r. 1556–1598), the most powerful ruler of his time. [Alinari/Art Resource]

Imperial Spain and the Reign of Philip II (r. 1556–1598)

Pillars of Spanish Power

Until the English defeated the mighty Spanish Armada in 1588, no one person stood larger in the second half of the sixteenth century than Philip II of Spain. Philip was heir to the intensely Catholic and militarily supreme western Habsburg kingdom.

The battle of Lepanto occurred off the coast of Greece on October 7, 1571. In the largest naval engagement of the sixteenth century, the Spanish and their Italian allies under Don John of Austria smashed the Turkish fleet and ended the Ottoman threat in the western Mediterranean. [National Maritime Museum, London]

The eastern Habsburg lands of Austria, Bohemia, and Hungary had been given over by his father, Charles V, to Philip's uncle, the emperor Ferdinand I. These lands, together with the imperial title, remained in the possession of the Austrian branch of the family.

New World Riches Populous and wealthy Castile gave Philip a solid home base. The regular arrival in Seville of bullion from the Spanish colonies in the New World provided additional wealth. In the 1540s great silver mines had been opened in Potosí in present-day Bolivia and in Zacatecas in Mexico. These gave Philip the great sums needed to pay his bankers and mercenaries. He nonetheless never managed to erase the debts left by his father nor to finance his own foreign adventures fully. He later contributed to the bankruptcy of the Fuggers when, at the end of his life, he defaulted on his enormous debts.

Increased Population The new American wealth brought dramatic social change to the peoples of Europe during the second half of the sixteenth century. As Europe became richer, it was also becoming more populous. In the economically and politically active towns of France, England, and the Netherlands, populations had tripled and quadrupled by the early seventeenth century. Europe's population exceeded 70 million by 1600.

The combination of increased wealth and population triggered inflation. A steady 2 percent a year rise in prices in much of Europe had serious cumulative effects by mid-century. There were more people than before and greater coinage in circulation, but less food and fewer jobs; wages stagnated while prices doubled and tripled in much of Europe.

This was especially the case in Spain. Because the new wealth was concentrated in the hands of a few, the traditional gap between the "haves"—the propertied, privileged, and educated classes—and the "have-nots" greatly widened. Nowhere did the unprivileged suffer more than in Spain, where the Castilian peasantry, the backbone of Philip II's great empire, became the most heavily taxed people of Europe. Those whose labor contributed most to making possible Spanish hegemony in Europe in the second half of the sixteenth century prospered least from it.

Efficient Bureaucracy and Military A subjugated peasantry and wealth from the New World were not the only pillars of Spanish strength. Philip II shrewdly organized the lesser nobility into a loyal and efficient national bureaucracy. A reclusive man, he managed his kingdom by pen and paper rather than by personal presence. He was also a learned and pious Catholic, although some popes suspected that he used religion as much for political as for devotional purposes. That he was a generous patron of the arts and culture can be seen in his unique retreat outside Madrid, the Escorial, a combination palace, church, tomb, and monastery. Philip also knew personal sorrows. His mad and treacherous son, Don Carlos, died under suspicious circumstances in 1568—some contemporaries suspected that Philip had him quietly executed—only three months before the death of the queen.

Supremacy in the Mediterranean During the first half of Philip's reign, attention focused almost exclusively on the Mediterranean and the Turkish threat. By history, geography, and choice, Spain had traditionally been Catholic Europe's champion against Islam. During the 1560s the Turks advanced deep into Austria, while their fleets dominated the Mediterranean. Between 1568 and 1570 armies under Philip's half-brother, Don John of Austria, the illegitimate son of Charles V, suppressed and dispersed the Moors in Granada.

In May 1571 a Holy League of Spain, Venice, and the pope, again under Don John's command, formed to check Turkish belligerence in the Mediterranean. In what was the largest naval battle of the sixteenth century, Don John's fleet engaged the Ottoman navy under Ali Pasha off Lepanto in the Gulf of Corinth on October 7, 1571. Before the engagement ended, over one-third of the Turkish fleet had been sunk or captured and 30,000 Turks had died. The Mediterranean for the moment belonged to Spain, and the Europeans were left to fight each other. Philip's armies also succeeded in putting down resistance in neighboring Portugal, which Spain annexed in 1580. The conquest of Portugal not only added to Spanish seapower but also brought the magnificent Portuguese overseas empire in Africa, India, and the Americas into the Spanish orbit.

The Revolt in the Netherlands

The spectacular Spanish military success in southern Europe was not repeated in northern Europe. When Philip attempted to impose his will within the Netherlands and on England and France, he learned the lessons of defeat. The resistance of the Netherlands especially proved the undoing of Spanish dreams of world empire. (See Map 12–1.)

Cardinal Granvelle The Netherlands was not only the richest area of Philip's Habsburg kingdom, but of Europe as well. In 1559 Philip had departed the Netherlands for Spain, never again to return. His half-sister, Margaret of Parma, assisted by a special council of state, became regent in his absence. The council was headed by Philip's hand-picked lieutenant, the extremely able Antoine Perrenot (1517–1586), after 1561 known as Cardinal Granvelle. Granvelle hoped to check Protestant gains by internal church reforms. He planned to break down the traditional local autonomy of the seventeen Netherlands provinces by stages and establish in its place a centralized royal government directed from Madrid. A politically docile and religiously uniform country was the goal.

The merchant towns of the Netherlands were, however, Europe's most independent; many, like magnificent Antwerp, were also Calvinist strongholds. By tradition and habit the people of the Netherlands inclined far more toward variety and toleration than toward obeisant conformity and hierarchical order. Two members of the council of state formed a stubborn opposition to the Spanish overlords, who now sought to reimpose their traditional rule with a vengeance. They were the Count of Egmont (1522–1568) and William of Nassau, the Prince of Orange (1533–1584), known as "the Silent" because of his extremely small circle of confidants.

Like other successful rulers in this period, William of Orange placed the Netherlands' political autonomy and well-being above religious creeds. He personally passed through successive Catholic, Lutheran, and Calvinist stages. In 1561 he married Anne of Saxony, the daughter of the Lutheran elector Maurice and the granddaughter of the late Landgrave Philip of Hesse. He maintained his Catholic practices until 1567, when he turned Lutheran. After the Saint Bartholomew's Day Massacre (1572), Orange (as he was called) became an avowed Calvinist.

In 1561 Cardinal Granvelle proceeded with a planned ecclesiastical reorganization of the Netherlands. It was intended to tighten the control of the Catholic hierarchy over the country and to acceler-

MAP 12–1 THE NETHERLANDS DURING THE REFORMATION *The northern and southern provinces of the Netherlands. The former, the United Provinces, were mostly Protestant in the second half of the sixteenth century, while the southern Spanish Netherlands made peace with Spain and remained largely Catholic.*

ate its consolidation as a Spanish ward. Orange and Egmont, organizing the Dutch nobility in opposition, succeeded in gaining Granvelle's removal from office in 1564. Aristocratic control of the country after Granvelle's departure, however, proved woefully inefficient. Popular unrest continued to grow, especially among urban artisans, who joined the congregations of radical Calvinist preachers in increasing numbers.

THE COMPROMISE The year 1564 also saw the first fusion of political and religious opposition to Regent Margaret's government. This opposition resulted from Philip II's unwise insistence that the decrees of the Council of Trent be enforced throughout the Netherlands. William of Orange's younger brother, Louis of Nassau, who had been raised a Lutheran, led the opposition, and it received support from the Calvinist-inclined lesser nobility and

A view of the Escorial, Philip II's massive palace-monastery-mausoleum northwest of Madrid. Built between 1563 and 1584, it was a monument to the piety and power of the king. Philip vowed to build the complex after the Spanish defeated the French at Saint-Quentin on Saint Lawrence's day in 1577. The floor plan of the Escorial resembles a grill, the symbol of Saint Lawrence (who, according to legend, was martyred by being roasted alive on a grill). [Odyssey Productions]

townspeople. A national covenant was drawn up called the *Compromise,* a solemn pledge to resist the decrees of Trent and the Inquisition. Grievances were loudly and persistently voiced. When Regent Margaret's government spurned the protesters as "beggars" in 1566, Calvinists rioted through the country. Louis called on French Huguenots and German Lutherans to send aid to the Netherlands, and a full-scale rebellion against the Spanish regency appeared imminent.

THE DUKE OF ALBA The rebellion failed to materialize, however, because the Netherlands' higher nobility would not support it. Their shock at Calvinist iconoclasm and anarchy was as great as their resentment of Granvelle's more subtle repression. Philip, determined to make an example of the Protestant rebels, dispatched the duke of Alba to suppress the revolt. His army of 10,000 journeyed northward from Milan in 1567 in a show of combined Spanish and papal might. A special tribunal, known to the Spanish as the Council of Troubles and among the Netherlanders as the Council of Blood, reigned over the land. The counts of Egmont and Horn and several thousand suspected heretics were publicly executed before Alba's reign of terror ended.

The Spanish levied new taxes, forcing the Netherlands to pay for the suppression of its own revolt. One of these taxes, the "tenth penny," a 10 percent sales tax, met such resistance from merchants and artisans that it remained uncollectible in some areas even after a reduction to 3 percent. Combined persecution and taxation sent tens of thousands fleeing from the Netherlands during Alba's cruel six-year rule. Alba came to be more hated than Granvelle or the radical Calvinists had ever been.

RESISTANCE AND UNIFICATION William of Orange was an exile in Germany during these turbulent years. He now emerged as the leader of a broad movement for the Netherlands' independence from Spain. The northern, Calvinist-inclined provinces of Holland, Zeeland, and Utrecht, of which Orange was the *stadholder,* or governor, became his base. As in France, political resistance in the Netherlands

The Milch Cow, *a sixteenth-century satirical painting depicting the Netherlands as a cow in whom all the great powers of Europe have an interest. Elizabeth of England is feeding her (England had longstanding commercial ties with Flanders); Philip II of Spain is attempting to ride her (Spain was trying to reassert its control over the entire area); William of Orange is trying to milk her (he was the leader of the anti-Spanish rebellion); and the king of France holds her tail (France hoped to profit from the rebellion at Spain's expense). [Rijksmuseum, Amsterdam]*

gained both organization and inspiration by merging with Calvinism.

The early victories of the resistance attest to the popular character of the revolt. A case in point is the capture of the port city of Brill by the "Sea Beggars," an international group of anti-Spanish exiles and criminals, among them many Englishmen. William of Orange did not hesitate to enlist their services. Their brazen piracy, however, had forced Queen Elizabeth to disassociate herself from them and to bar their ships from English ports. In 1572 the Beggars captured Brill and other seaports in Zeeland and Holland. Mixing with the native population, they quickly sparked rebellions against Alba in town after town and spread the resistance southward. In 1574 the people of Leiden heroically resisted a long Spanish siege. The Dutch opened the dikes and flooded their country to repulse the hated Spanish. The faltering Alba had by that time ceded power to Don Luis de Requesens, who replaced him as commander of Spanish forces in the Netherlands in November 1573.

THE PACIFICATION OF GHENT The greatest atrocity of the war came after Requesens's death in 1576. Spanish mercenaries, leaderless and unpaid, ran amok in Antwerp on November 4, 1576, leaving 7,000 people dead in the streets. The event came to be known as the Spanish Fury.

These atrocities accomplished in four short days what neither religion nor patriotism had previously been able to do. The ten largely Catholic southern provinces (what is roughly modern Belgium) now came together with the seven largely Protestant northern provinces (what is roughly the modern Netherlands) in unified opposition to Spain. This union, known as the Pacification of Ghent, was accomplished on November 8, 1576. It declared internal regional sovereignty in matters of religion, a key clause that permitted political cooperation among the signatories, who were not agreed over religion. It was a Netherlands version of the territorial settlement of religious differences brought about in the Holy Roman Empire in 1555 by the Peace of Augsburg. Four provinces initially held out, but they soon made the resistance unanimous by joining the all-embracing Union of Brussels in January 1577. For the next two years the Spanish faced a unified and determined Netherlands.

Don John, the victor over the Turks at Lepanto in 1571, had taken command of Spanish land forces in November 1576. He now experienced his first defeat. Confronted by unified Netherlands resistance, he signed the humiliating Perpetual Edict in February 1577. This edict provided for the removal of all Spanish troops from the Netherlands within twenty days. This withdrawal of troops gave the country to William of Orange and effectively ended

Philip II Declares William of Orange an Outlaw (1580)

In the following proclamation the king of Spain accused William of Orange of being the "chief disturber of the public peace" and offered his captors, or assassins, generous rewards.

✦ *Why was William of Orange perceived by Philip II as such a threat? Why was it important that Spain gain control over the Netherlands?*

Philip, by the grace of God king of Castile, etc. to all to whom these presents may come, greeting:

It is well known to all how favorably the late emperor, Charles V, . . . treated William of Nassau. . . . Nevertheless, as everyone knows, we had scarcely turned our back on the Netherlands before the said William . . . (who had become . . . prince of Orange) began . . . by sinister arts, plots, and intrigues . . . to gain [control] over those whom he believed to be malcontents, or haters of justice, or anxious for innovations, and . . . above all, those who were suspected in the matter of religion. . . . With the knowledge, advice, and encouragement of the said Orange, the heretics commenced to destroy the images, altars, and churches. . . . So soon as the said Nassau was received into the government of the provinces, he began, through his agents and satellites, to introduce heretical preaching. . . . Then he introduced liberty of conscience . . . which soon brought it about that the Catholics were openly persecuted and driven out. . . . Moreover he obtained such a hold upon our poor subjects of Holland and Zeeland . . . that nearly all the towns, one after the other, have been besieged. . . .

Therefore, for all these just reasons, for his evil doings as chief disturber of the public peace . . . we outlaw him forever and forbid our subjects to associate with him . . . in public or in secret. We declare him an enemy of the human race, and in order the sooner to remove our people from his tyranny and oppression, we promise, on the word of a king and as God's servant, that if one of our subjects be found so generous of heart and so desirous of doing us a service and advantaging the public that he shall find the means of executing this decree and of ridding us of the said pest, either by delivering him to us dead or alive, or by depriving him at once of life, we will give him and his heirs landed estates or money, as he will, to the amount of twenty-five thousand gold crowns. If he has committed any crime, of any kind whatsoever, we will pardon him. If he be not noble, we will ennoble him for his valor; and should he require other persons to assist him, we will reward them according to the service rendered, pardon their crimes, and ennoble them too.

James Harvey Robinson, ed., Readings in European History, *vol. 2 (Boston: Athenaeum, 1906), pp. 174–177.*

for the time being whatever plans Philip may have had for using the Netherlands as a staging area for an invasion of England.

THE UNION OF ARRAS AND THE UNION OF UTRECHT The Spanish, however, were nothing if not persistent. Don John and Alessandro Farnese of Parma, the regent Margaret's son, revived Spanish power in the southern provinces, where constant fear of Calvinist extremism had moved the leaders to break the Union of Brussels. In January 1579 the southern provinces formed the Union of Arras, and within five months they made peace with Spain. These provinces later served the cause of the Counter-Reformation. The northern provinces responded with the formation of the Union of Utrecht.

NETHERLANDS INDEPENDENCE Seizing what now appeared to be a last opportunity to break the back of Netherlands resistance, Philip II declared William of Orange an outlaw and placed a bounty of 25,000 crowns on his head. The act predictably stiffened the resistance of the northern provinces. In a famous defiant speech to the Estates General of Holland in December 1580, known as the Apology, Orange publicly denounced Philip as a heathen tyrant whom the Netherlands need no longer obey.

On July 22, 1581, the member provinces of the Union of Utrecht met in The Hague and formally declared Philip no longer their ruler. They turned instead to the French duke of Alençon, Catherine de Médici's youngest son. The southern provinces had also earlier looked to him as a possible middle way between Spanish and Calvinist overlordship. All the northern provinces save Holland and Zeeland accepted Alençon as their "sovereign" (Holland and Zeeland distrusted him almost as much as they did Philip II), but with the understanding that he would be only a titular ruler. But Alençon, an ambitious failure, saw this as his one chance at greatness. When he rashly attempted to take actual control of the provinces in 1583, he was deposed and returned to France.

Spanish efforts to reconquer the Netherlands continued into the 1580s. William of Orange, assassinated in July 1584, was succeeded by his seventeen-year-old son, Maurice (1567–1625), who, with the assistance of England and France, continued Dutch resistance. Fortunately for the Netherlands, Philip II began now to meddle directly in French and English affairs. He signed a secret treaty with the Guises (the Treaty of Joinville in December 1584) and sent armies under Farnese into France in 1590. Hostilities with the English, who had openly aided the Dutch rebels, also increased. Gradually they built toward a climax in 1588, when Philip's great Armada was defeated in the English Channel.

These new fronts overextended Spain's resources, strengthening the Netherlands. Spanish preoccupation with France and England permitted the northern provinces to drive out all Spanish soldiers by 1593. In 1596 France and England formally recognized the independence of these provinces. Peace was not, however, concluded with Spain until 1609, when the Twelve Years' Truce gave the northern provinces virtual independence. Full recognition came finally in the Peace of Westphalia in 1648.

England and Spain (1553–1603)

Mary I

Before Edward VI died in 1553, he agreed to a device to make Lady Jane Grey, the teenage daughter of a powerful Protestant nobleman and, more important, the granddaughter on her mother's side of Henry VIII's younger sister Mary, his successor in place of the Catholic Mary Tudor (r. 1553–1558). But popular support for the principle of hereditary monarchy was too strong to deprive Mary of her rightful rule. Popular uprisings in London and elsewhere led to Jane Grey's removal from the throne within days of her crowning, and she was eventually beheaded.

Once enthroned, Mary proceeded to act even beyond the worst fears of the Protestants. In 1554 she entered a highly unpopular political marriage with Prince Philip (later Philip II) of Spain, a symbol

Portrait of Mary I (r. 1553–1558), Queen of England. By Sir Anthony Mor, Prado, Madrid. [The Bridgeman Art Library, London.]

A Description of Mary Tudor

In 1557 the Venetian Ambassador reported to his government on the state of England, including a description of Mary I. At the time he wrote, she was receiving widespread criticism of her rule, particularly of her foreign policy, which the critics felt tied England too closely to the interests of Spain.

✦ *Does the gender of its subject color this description? Would a king be similarly described? What does the ambassador see as Mary's weaknesses and strengths?*

Queen Mary, the daughter of Henry VIII and of his queen Catherine, daughter of Ferdinand the Catholic, king of Aragon, is a princess of great worth. In her youth she was rendered unhappy by the event of her mother's divorce; by the ignominy and threats to which she was exposed after the change of religion in England, she being unwilling to unbend to the new one; and by the dangers to which she was exposed by the duke of Northumberland, and the riots among the people when she ascended the throne.

She is of short stature, well made, thin and delicate, and moderately pretty; her eyes are so lively that she inspires reverence and respect, and even fear, wherever she turns them; nevertheless she is very shortsighted. Her voice is deep, almost like that of a man. She understands five languages—English, Latin, French, Spanish, and Italian, in which last, however, she does not venture to converse. She is also much skilled in ladies' work, such as producing all sorts of embroidery with the needle. She has a knowledge of music, chiefly on the lute, on which she plays exceedingly well. As to the qualities of her mind, it may be said of her that she is rash, disdainful, and parsimonious rather than liberal. She is endowed with great humility and patience, but withal high-spirited, courageous, and resolute, having during the whole course of her adversity not been guilty of the least approach to meanness of deportment; she is, moreover, devout and staunch in the defense of her religion.

Some personal infirmities under which she labors are the causes to her of both public and private affliction; to remedy these recourse is had to frequent bloodletting, and this is the real cause of her paleness and the general weakness of her frame. These have also given rise to the unfounded rumor that the queen is in a state of pregnancy. The cabal she has been exposed to, the evil disposition of the people toward her, the present poverty and the debt of the crown, and her passion for King Philip, from whom she is doomed to live separate, are so many other causes of the grief with which she is overwhelmed. She is, moreover, a prey to the hatred she bears my Lady Elizabeth, and which has its source in the recollection of the wrongs she experienced on account of her mother, and in the fact that all eyes and hearts are turned towards my Lady Elizabeth as successor to the throne. . . .

James Harvey Robinson, ed., Readings in European History, *vol. 2 (Boston: Athenaeum, 1906), pp. 149–150.*

of militant Catholicism to English Protestants. At his direction she pursued a foreign policy that in 1558 cost England its last enclave on the Continent, Calais.

Mary's domestic measures were equally shocking to the English people and even more divisive. During her reign, Parliament repealed the Protestant statutes of Edward and reverted to the Catholic religious practice of her father, Henry VIII. The great Protestant leaders of the Edwardian Age—John Hooper, Hugh Latimer, and Thomas Cranmer—were executed for heresy. Hundreds of Protestants either joined them in martyrdom (282 were burned at the stake during Mary's reign) or took flight to the Continent. These "Marian exiles" settled in Germany and Switzerland, forming especially large communities in Frankfurt, Strasbourg, and Geneva. (John Knox, the future leader of the Reformation in Scotland, was prominent among these exiles.) There they worshiped in their own congregations, wrote tracts justifying armed resistance, and waited for the time when a Protestant counteroffensive could be launched in their homelands. They were also exposed to religious beliefs more radical than any set forth during Edward VI's reign. Many of these exiles later held positions in the Church of England during Elizabeth I's reign.

Elizabeth I

Mary's successor was her half-sister, Elizabeth I (r. 1558–1603), the daughter of Henry VIII and Anne Boleyn. Elizabeth had remarkable and enduring successes in both domestic and foreign policy. Assisted by a shrewd adviser, Sir William Cecil (1520–1598), she built a true kingdom on the ruins of Mary's reign. Between 1559 and 1563, she and Cecil guided a religious settlement through Parliament that prevented England from being torn asunder by religious differences in the sixteenth century, as the Continent was. Another ruler who subordinated religious to political unity, Elizabeth merged a centralized episcopal system, which she firmly controlled, with broadly defined Protestant doctrine and traditional Catholic ritual. In the resulting Anglican Church inflexible religious extremes were not permitted.

Elizabeth I (r. 1558–1603) standing on a map of England in 1592. An astute politician in both foreign and domestic policy, Elizabeth was perhaps the most successful ruler of the sixteenth century. [National Portrait Gallery, London]

In 1559 an Act of Supremacy passed Parliament repealing all the anti-Protestant legislation of Mary Tudor and asserting Elizabeth's right as "supreme governor" over both spiritual and temporal affairs. An Act of Uniformity in the same year mandated a revised version of the second *Book of Common Prayer* (1552) for every English parish. The issuance of the *Thirty-Nine Articles on Religion* in 1563—which were a revision of Thomas Cranmer's original forty-two—made a moderate Protestantism the official religion within the Church of England.

CATHOLIC AND PROTESTANT EXTREMISTS Elizabeth hoped to avoid both Catholic and Protestant extremism at the official level by pursuing a middle way. Her first archbishop of Canterbury, Matthew Parker (d. 1575), represented this ideal. But Elizabeth could not prevent the emergence of subversive Catholic and Protestant zealots. When she ascended the throne, Catholics were in the majority in England. The extremists among them, encouraged by the Jesuits, plotted against her. Catholic radicals were also encouraged and later directly assisted by the Spanish, who were piqued both by Elizabeth's Protestant sympathies and by her refusal to follow the example of her half-sister Mary and take Philip II's hand in marriage. Elizabeth remained unmarried throughout her reign, using the possibility of a marriage alliance very much to her diplomatic advantage.

Catholic extremists hoped eventually to replace Elizabeth with Mary Stuart, Queen of Scots. Unlike Elizabeth, who had been declared illegitimate during the reign of her father, Mary Stuart had an unblemished claim to the throne by way of her grandmother Margaret, the sister of Henry VIII. Elizabeth acted swiftly against Catholic assassination plots and rarely let emotion override her political instincts. Despite proven cases of Catholic treason and even attempted regicide, she executed

An Unknown Contemporary Describes Queen Elizabeth

No sixteenth-century ruler governed more effectively than Elizabeth I of England (r. 1558–1603), who was both loved and feared by her subjects. An unknown contemporary has left the following description, revealing not only her intelligence and political cunning but also something of her immense vanity.

✦ *How does this description compare with that of Mary I? How do their personal qualities and political skills differ?*

I will proceed with the description of the queen's disposition and natural gifts of mind and body, wherein she either matched or exceeded all the princes of her time, as being of a great spirit yet tempered with moderation, in adversity never dejected, in prosperity rather joyful than proud; affable to her subjects, but always with due regard to the greatness of her estate, by reason whereof she was both loved and feared.

In her later time, when she showed herself in public, she was always magnificent in apparel; supposing haply thereby that the eyes of her people (being dazzled by the glittering aspect of her outward ornaments) would not so easily discern the marks of age and decay of natural beauty; and she came abroad the more seldom, to make her presence the more grateful and applauded by the multitude, to whom things rarely seen are in manner as new.

She suffered not, at any time, any suitor to depart discontented from her, and though ofttimes he obtained not that he desired, yet he held himself satisfied with her manner of speech, which gave hope of success in the second attempt. . . .

Latin, French, and Italian she could speak very elegantly, and she was able in all those languages to answer ambassadors on the sudden. . . . Of the Greek tongue she was also not altogether ignorant. She took pleasure in reading of the best and wisest histories, and some part of Tacitus's *Annals* she herself turned into English for her private exercise. She also translated Boethius's *On the Consolation of Philosophy* and a treatise of Plutarch, *On Curiosity*, with divers others. . . .

It is credibly reported that not long before her death, she had a great apprehension of her own age and declination by seeing her face (then lean and full of wrinkles) truly represented to her in a glass, which she a good while very earnestly beheld; perceiving thereby how often she had been abused by flatterers (whom she held in too great estimation) that had informed her the contrary.

James Harvey Robinson, ed., Readings in European History, *vol. 2 (Boston: Athenaeum, 1906), pp. 191–193.*

fewer Catholics during her forty-five years on the throne than Mary Tudor had executed Protestants during her brief five-year reign. She showed little mercy, however, to separatists and others who threatened the unity of her rule.

Elizabeth dealt cautiously with the Puritans, who were Protestants working within the national church to "purify" it of every vestige of "popery" and to make its Protestant doctrine more precise. The Puritans had two special grievances:

(1) the retention of Catholic ceremony and vestments within the Church of England, which made it appear to the casual observer that no Reformation had occurred,

(2) the continuation of the episcopal system of Church governance, which conceived of the English church theologically as the true successor to Rome, while placing it politically under the firm hand of the queen and her compliant archbishop.

Elizabeth I before Parliament. The artist shows the Queen small and in the background, and places Parliament prominently in the foreground, suggesting that England, despite the enormous power of the Queen, is a land where parliamentary government reigns supreme. [Folger Shakespeare Library]

Sixteenth-century Puritans were not separatists. They enjoyed wide popular support and were led by widely respected men like Thomas Cartwright (d. 1603). They worked through Parliament to create an alternative national church of semiautonomous congregations governed by representative presbyteries (hence, "Presbyterians"), following the model of Calvin and Geneva. Elizabeth dealt firmly but subtly with this group, conceding absolutely nothing that lessened the hierarchical unity of the Church of England and her control over it.

The more extreme Puritans wanted every congregation to be autonomous, a law unto itself, with neither higher episcopal nor presbyterian control. They came to be known as Congregationalists. Elizabeth and her second archbishop of Canterbury, John Whitgift (d. 1604), refused to tolerate this group, whose views on independence they found patently subversive. The Conventicle Act of 1593 gave such separatists the option of either conforming to the practices of the Church of England or facing exile or death.

DETERIORATION OF RELATIONS WITH SPAIN A series of events led inexorably to war between England and Spain, despite the sincerest desires on the part of both Philip II and Elizabeth to avoid a confrontation. In 1567 the Spanish duke of Alba marched his mighty army into the Netherlands, which was, from the English point of view, simply a convenient staging area for a Spanish invasion of England. Pope Pius V (r. 1566–1572), who favored a military conquest of Protestant England, "excommunicated" Elizabeth for heresy in 1570. This mischievous act only encouraged both internal resistance and international intrigue against the queen. Two years later, as already noted, the piratical Sea Beggars, many of whom were Englishmen, occupied the port city of Brill in the Netherlands and aroused the surrounding countryside against the Spanish.

Following Don John's demonstration of Spain's awesome seapower at the famous naval battle of Lepanto in 1571, England signed a mutual defense pact with France. Also in the 1570s, Elizabeth's famous seamen, John Hawkins (1532–1595) and Sir Francis Drake (1545?–1596), began to prey regularly on Spanish shipping in the Americas. Drake's circumnavigation of the globe between 1577 and 1580 was one in a series of dramatic demonstrations of English ascendancy on the high seas.

After the Saint Bartholomew's Day Massacre, Elizabeth was the only protector of Protestants in France and the Netherlands. In 1585 she signed the Treaty of Nonsuch, which provided English soldiers and cavalry to the Netherlands. Funds that had previously been funneled covertly to support Henry of Navarre's army in France now flowed openly.

MARY, QUEEN OF SCOTS These events made a tinderbox of English–Spanish relations. The spark that finally touched it off was Elizabeth's execution of Mary, Queen of Scots (1542–1587).

Mary Stuart was the daughter of King James V of Scotland and Mary of Guise and had resided in France from the time she was six years old. This

In 1588 Philip II sent a massive naval armada to invade England. The English, however, with the help of the weather and the Dutch, dispersed and destroyed the Spanish fleet. Spain never fully recovered from this defeat. [Art Resource, N.Y.]

thoroughly French and Catholic queen had returned to Scotland after the death of her husband, the French king Francis II, in 1561. There she found a successful, fervent Protestant Reformation that had won legal sanction the year before in the Treaty of Edinburgh (1560). As hereditary heir to the throne of Scotland, Mary remained queen by divine and human right. She was not intimidated by the Protestants who controlled her realm. She established an international French court culture, the gaiety and sophistication of which impressed many Protestant nobles whose religion often made their lives exceedingly dour.

Mary was closely watched by the ever-vigilant Scottish reformer John Knox. He fumed publicly and always with effect against the queen's private mass and Catholic practices, which Scottish law made a capital offense for everyone else. Knox won support in his role of watchdog from Elizabeth and Cecil. Elizabeth personally despised Knox and never forgave him for writing the *First Blast of the Trumpet Against the Terrible Regiment of Women*, a work aimed at provoking a revolt against Mary Tudor but published in the year of Elizabeth's ascent to the throne. Elizabeth and Cecil tolerated Knox because he served their foreign policy, never permitting Scotland to succumb to the young Mary and her French and Catholic ways.

In 1568 a public scandal forced Mary's abdication and flight to her cousin Elizabeth in England. Mary's reputed lover, the earl of Bothwell, was, with cause, suspected of having killed her legal husband, Lord Darnley. When a packed court acquitted Bothwell, he subsequently married Mary. The outraged reaction from Protestant nobles forced Mary to surrender the throne to her one-year-old son, who became James VI of Scotland (and, later, Elizabeth's successor as King James I of England). Because of Mary's clear claim to the English throne, she remained an international symbol of a possible Catholic England, and she was consumed by the desire to be queen of England. Her presence in England, where she resided under house arrest for nineteen years, was a constant discomfort to Elizabeth.

In 1583 Elizabeth's vigilant secretary, Sir Francis Walsingham, uncovered a plot against Elizabeth involving the Spanish ambassador Bernardino de Mendoza. After Mendoza's deportation in January 1584, popular antipathy toward Spain and support for Protestant resistance in France and the Netherlands became massive throughout England.

In 1586 Walsingham uncovered still another plot against Elizabeth, the so-called Babington plot (after Anthony Babington, who was caught seeking Spanish support for an attempt on the queen's life). This time he had uncontestable proof of Mary's complicity. Elizabeth believed that the execution of a sovereign, even a dethroned sovereign, weakened royalty everywhere. She was also aware of the outcry that Mary's execution would create throughout the Catholic world, and Elizabeth sincerely wanted peace with English Catholics. But she really had no choice in the matter and consented to Mary's execution on February 18, 1587. This event dashed all Catholic hopes for a bloodless reconversion of Protestant England. After the execution of the Catholic queen of Scotland, Pope Sixtus V (r. 1585–1590), who feared Spanish domination almost as much as he abhorred English Protestantism, could no longer withhold public support for a Spanish invasion of England. Philip II ordered his Armada to make ready.

THE ARMADA Spain's war preparations were interrupted in the spring of 1587 by Sir Francis Drake's successful shelling of the port city of Cadiz, an attack that inflicted heavy damage on Spanish ships and stores. After "singeing the beard of Spain's king," Drake raided the coast of Portugal, further incapacitating the Spanish. The success of these strikes forced the Spanish to postpone their planned invasion of England until the spring of 1588.

On May 30 of that year, a mighty fleet of 130 ships bearing 25,000 sailors and soldiers under the command of the duke of Medina-Sidonia set sail for England. In the end, however, the English won a stunning victory. The invasion barges that were to transport Spanish soldiers from the galleons onto English shores were prevented from leaving Calais and Dunkirk. The swifter English and Netherlands ships, helped by what came to be known as an "English wind," dispersed the waiting Spanish fleet, over one-third of which never returned to Spain.

The news of the Armada's defeat gave heart to Protestant resistance everywhere. Although Spain continued to win impressive victories in the 1590s, it never fully recovered from this defeat. Spanish soldiers faced unified and inspired French, English, and Dutch armies. By the time of Philip's death on September 13, 1598, his forces had been successfully rebuffed on all fronts. His seventeenth-century successors were all inferior leaders who never knew responsibilities equal to Philip's. Nor did Spain ever again know such imperial grandeur. The French soon dominated the Continent, while in the New World the Dutch and the English progressively whittled away Spain's once glorious overseas empire.

Elizabeth died on March 23, 1603, leaving behind her a strong nation poised to expand into a global empire.

The Thirty Years' War (1618–1648)

The Thirty Years' War in the Holy Roman Empire was the last and most destructive of the wars of religion. Religious and political differences had long set Catholics against Protestants and Calvinists against Lutherans. What made the Thirty Years' War so devastating was the now-entrenched hatred of the various sides and their seeming determination to sacrifice all for their religious beliefs. As the conflicts multiplied, virtually every major European land, especially Lutheran Denmark and Sweden, became involved either directly or indirectly. When the hostilities ended in 1648, the peace terms shaped much of the map of northern Europe as we know it today.

Preconditions for War

FRAGMENTED GERMANY In the second half of the sixteenth century, Germany was an almost ungovernable land of about 360 autonomous political entities. There were independent secular principalities (duchies, landgraviates, and marches); ecclesiastical principalities (archbishoprics, bishoprics, and abbeys); numerous free cities; and castle regions dominated by knights. The Peace of Augsburg (1555) had given each a significant degree of sovereignty within its own borders. Each levied its own tolls and tariffs and coined its own money, practices that made land travel and trade between the various regions difficult, where not impossible. In addition, many of these little lands were filled with great

The horror of the Thirty Year's War is captured in this painting by Jan Brueghel (1568–1625) and Sebastien Vranx (1573–1647). During the breaks in fighting, marauding armies ravaged the countryside, destroying villages and massacring the rural population. [Kunsthistorisches Museum, Vienna]

power pretensions. Political decentralization and fragmentation characterized Germany as the seventeenth century opened; it was not a unified nation like Spain, England, or even strife-filled France.

Because of its central location, Germany had always been Europe's highway for merchants and traders going north and south and east and west. During the Thirty Years' War it became its stomping ground. Europe's rulers pressed in on Germany both for reasons of trade and because some of them held lands or legal privileges within certain German principalities. German princes, in their turn, looked to import and export markets beyond German borders. They opposed any efforts to consolidate the Holy Roman Empire, lest their territorial rights, confirmed by the Peace of Augsburg, be overturned. German princes were not loath to turn to Catholic France or to the kings of Denmark and Sweden for allies against the Habsburg emperor. The princes perceived the emperor's dynastic connections with Spain, and the policies he generated as a result, to be against their territorial interests. Even the pope found political reasons for supporting Bourbon France against the menacing international kingdom of the Habsburgs.

After the Council of Trent, Protestants in the empire suspected the existence of an imperial and papal conspiracy to recreate the Catholic Europe of pre-Reformation times. The imperial diet, which was controlled by the German princes, demanded strict observance of the constitutional rights of Germans, as set forth in agreements with the emperor since the mid-fourteenth century. Consequently, it effectively countered every move by the emperor to impose his will in the empire. In the late sixteenth century, the emperor ruled only to the degree to which he was prepared to use force of arms against his subjects.

Religious Division Religious conflict accentuated the international and internal political divisions. (See Map 12–2.) During this period the population within the Holy Roman Empire was about equally divided between Catholics and Protestants, the latter having perhaps a slight numerical edge by 1600. The terms of the Peace of Augsburg had attempted to freeze the territorial holdings of the Lutherans and the Catholics. In the intervening years, however, the Lutherans had gained political control in some Catholic areas, as had the Catholics in a few previously Lutheran areas. Such territorial reversals, or the threat of them, only increased the suspicion and antipathy between the two sides.

The Lutherans had been far more successful in securing their rights to worship in Catholic lands than the Catholics had been in securing such rights in Lutheran lands. The Catholic rulers, who were in a weakened position after the Reformation, had no choice but to make concessions to Protestant communities within their territories. These communities remained a sore point. Also, the Catholics wanted strict enforcement of the "Ecclesiastical Reservation" of the Peace of Augsburg, which Protestants had made little effort to recognize. The

Map 12–2 Religious Divisions About 1600 *By 1600 few could seriously expect Christians to return to a uniform religious allegiance. In Spain and southern Italy, Catholicism remained relatively unchallenged, but note the existence elsewhere of large religious minorities, both Catholic and Protestant.*

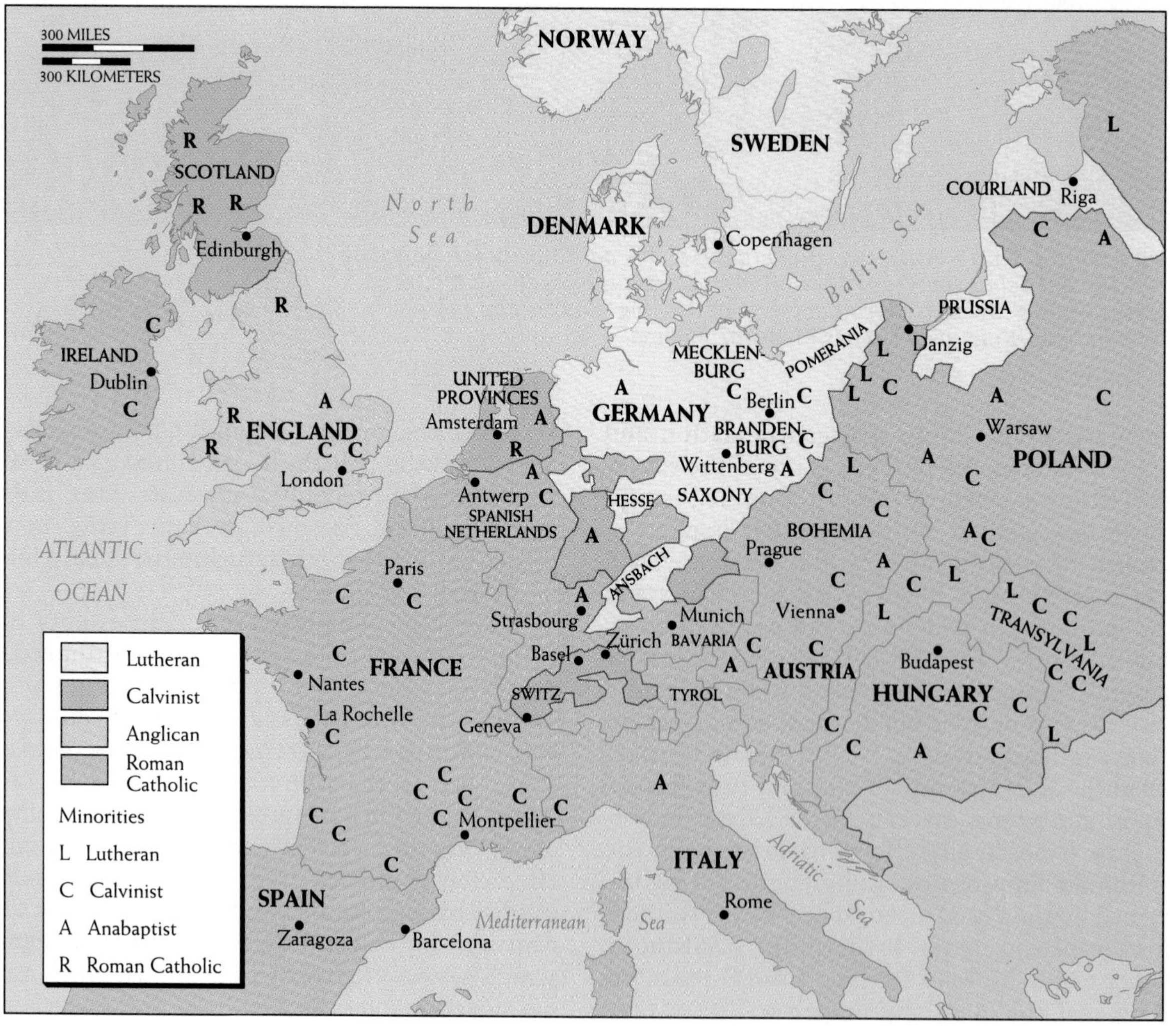

Catholics demanded that all ecclesiastical princes, electors, archbishops, bishops, and abbots who had deserted the Catholic for the Protestant side be immediately deprived of their religious offices and positions and that their ecclesiastical principalities be promptly returned to Catholic control. The Lutherans, and especially the Calvinists in the Palatinate, ignored this stipulation at every opportunity.

There was religious strife in the empire not only between Protestants and Catholics but also between liberal and conservative Lutherans and between Lutherans and the growing numbers of Calvinists. The last half of the sixteenth century was a time of warring Protestant factions within German universities. In addition to the heightened religious strife, the challenge of the new scientific and material culture that was becoming ascendant in intellectual and political circles increased the anxiety of religious people of all persuasions.

CALVINISM AND THE PALATINATE As elsewhere in Europe, Calvinism was the political and religious leaven within the Holy Roman Empire on the eve of the Thirty Years' War. Calvinism was unrecognized as a legal religion by the Peace of Augsburg. It gained a strong foothold within the empire, however, when Frederick III (r. 1559–1576), a devout convert to Calvinism, became elector Palatine (ruler within the Palatinate) and made it the official religion of his domain. Heidelberg became a German Geneva in the 1560s: both a great intellectual center of Calvinism and a staging area for Calvinist penetration into the empire. By 1609 Palatine Calvinists headed a Protestant defensive alliance that received outside support from Spain's sixteenth-century enemies: England, France, and the Netherlands.

The Lutherans came to fear the Calvinists almost as much as they did the Catholics. Palatine Calvinists seemed to the Lutherans directly to threaten the Peace of Augsburg—and hence the legal foundation of the Lutheran states—by their bold missionary forays into the empire. Also, outspoken Calvinist criticism of the doctrine of Christ's real presence in the Eucharist shocked the more religiously conservative Lutherans. The elector Palatine once expressed his disbelief in transubstantiation by publicly shredding the host and mocking it as a "fine God." To Lutherans, such religious disrespect and aggressiveness disgraced the Reformation.

MAXIMILIAN OF BAVARIA AND THE CATHOLIC LEAGUE If the Calvinists were active within the Holy Roman Empire, so also were their Catholic counterparts, the Jesuits. Staunchly Catholic Bavaria, supported by Spain, became militarily and ideologically for the Counter-Reformation what the Palatinate was for Protestantism. From there, the Jesuits launched successful missions throughout the empire, winning such major cities as Strasbourg and Osnabrück back to the Catholic fold by 1600. In 1609 Maximilian, duke of Bavaria, organized a Catholic League to counter a new Protestant alliance that had been formed in the same year under the leadership of the Calvinist Elector Palatine, Frederick IV (r. 1583–1610). When the league fielded a great army under the command of Count Johann von Tilly, the stage was set, both internally and internationally, for the worst of the religious wars, the Thirty Years' War. (See Map 12–3.)

Four Periods of War

The war went through four distinguishable periods. During its course it drew in every major western European nation—at least diplomatically and financially if not by direct military involvement. The four periods were the Bohemian (1618–1625); the Danish (1625–1629); the Swedish (1630–1635); and the Swedish–French (1635–1648).

THE BOHEMIAN PERIOD The war broke out in Bohemia after the ascent to the Bohemian throne in 1618 of the Habsburg Ferdinand, the archduke of Styria, who was also in the line of succession to the imperial throne. Educated by the Jesuits and a fervent Catholic, Ferdinand was determined to restore the traditional faith throughout Austria, Bohemia, and Poland—the eastern Habsburg lands.

No sooner had Ferdinand become king of Bohemia than he revoked the religious freedoms of Bohemian Protestants. In force since 1575, these freedoms had even been recently broadened by Emperor Rudolf II (r. 1576–1612) in his Letter of Majesty in 1609. The Protestant nobility in Prague responded to Ferdinand's act in May 1618 by literally throwing his regents out the window. The event has ever since been known as the "defenestration of Prague." The three officials fell fifty feet into a dry moat that, fortunately, was padded with manure, which cushioned their fall and spared their

MAP 12–3 THE HOLY ROMAN EMPIRE ABOUT 1618 *On the eve of the Thirty Years' War, the Holy Roman Empire was politically and religiously fragmented, as revealed by this somewhat simplified map. Lutherans dominated the north and Catholics the south, while Calvinists controlled the United Provinces and the Palatinate and were important in Switzerland and Brandenburg.*

lives. In the following year Ferdinand became Holy Roman Emperor as Ferdinand II, by the unanimous vote of the seven electors. The Bohemians, however, defiantly deposed him in Prague and declared the Calvinist elector Palatine, Frederick V (r. 1616–1623), their overlord.

What had begun as a revolt of the Protestant nobility against an unpopular king of Bohemia thereafter escalated into an international war. Spain sent troops to Ferdinand, who found more immediate allies in Maximilian of Bavaria and the opportunistic Lutheran elector John George I of Saxony (r. 1611–1656). John George saw a sure route to territorial gain by joining in an easy victory over the weaker elector Palatine. This was not the only time politics and greed would overshadow religion during this long conflict, although Lutheran–Calvinist religious animosity also overrode a common Protestantism.

Ferdinand's army under Tilly routed Frederick V's troops at the Battle of White Mountain in 1620. By 1622 Ferdinand had managed not only to subdue and re-Catholicize Bohemia but to conquer the Palatinate as well. While he and his allies enjoyed the spoils of these victories, the fighting extended into northwestern Germany as the duke of Bavaria pressed the conflict. Laying claim to land as he went, he continued to pursue Ernst von Mansfeld, one of Frederick's surviving mercenary generals, into the north.

THE DANISH PERIOD The emperor's subjugation of Bohemia and the Palatinate and Maximilian's forays into northwestern Germany raised new fears that a reconquest and re-Catholicization of the whole empire now loomed. This was in fact precisely Ferdinand II's design. The Lutheran King Christian IV (r. 1588–1648) of Denmark, who already held territory within the empire as the duke of Holstein, was eager to extend Danish influence over the coastal towns of the North Sea. Encouraged by the English, the French, and the Dutch, he picked up the Protestant banner of resistance, opening the Danish period of the conflict (1625–1629). Christian's forces were not, however, up to the challenge. Entering Germany with his army in 1626, he was quickly humiliated by Maximilian and forced to retreat into Denmark.

As military success made Maximilian stronger and more difficult to control, Ferdinand II sought a more pliant tool for his policies by hiring a powerful, complex mercenary, Albrecht of Wallenstein (1583–1634). Wallenstein was another opportunistic Protestant who had gained a great deal of territory by joining Ferdinand during the conquest of Bohemia. A brilliant and ruthless military strategist, Wallenstein not only completed Maximilian's work by bringing the career of the elusive Ernst von Mansfeld to an end but also penetrated Denmark with an occupying army. By 1628 Wallenstein commanded a crack army of more than 100,000 and became a law unto himself within the empire, completely outside the emperor's control. Pandora's box had now been fully opened.

Wallenstein broke Protestant resistance so successfully that Ferdinand issued the Edict of Restitution in 1629. This proclamation dramatically reasserted the Catholic safeguards of the Peace of Augsburg (1555). It reaffirmed the illegality of Calvinism—a completely unrealistic move in 1629. It also ordered the return of all church lands acquired by the Lutherans since 1552, an equally unrealistic mandate. Compliance would have involved the return of no less than sixteen bishoprics and twenty-eight cities and towns to Catholic allegiance. Although based on legal precedent and certainly within Ferdinand's power to command, the expectations of the edict were not adjusted to the political realities of 1629. It struck panic in the hearts of Protestants and Habsburg opponents everywhere, who now saw clearly the emperor's plan to recreate a Catholic Europe. Resistance quickly reignited.

THE SWEDISH PERIOD Gustavus Adolphus of Sweden (r. 1611–1632), a deeply pious king of a unified Lutheran nation, became the new leader of Protestant forces within the empire, opening the Swedish period of the war (1630–1635). He was handsomely bankrolled by two very interested bystanders: the French minister Cardinal Richelieu, whose foreign policy was to protect French interests by keeping Habsburg armies tied down in Germany, and the Dutch, who had not forgotten Spanish Habsburg domination in the sixteenth century. The Swedish king found ready allies in the electors of Brandenburg and Saxony and soon won a smashing victory at Breitenfeld in 1630. The Protestant victory at Breitenfeld so dramatically reversed the course of the war that it has been regarded as the most decisive, although far from the final, engagement of the long conflict.

One of the reasons for the overwhelming Swedish victory at Breitenfeld was the military genius of Gustavus Adolphus. The Swedish king brought a new mobility to warfare by having both his infantry and his cavalry employ fire and charge tactics. At six deep, his infantry squares were smaller than the traditional ones, and he filled them with equal numbers of musketeers and pikemen. His cavalry also alternated pistol shot with sword charges. His artillery was lighter and more mobile in battle. Each unit of his army—infantry, cavalry, and artillery—had both defensive and offensive capability and could quickly change from one to the other.

Gustavus Adolphus died at the hands of Wallenstein's forces during the Battle of Lützen (November 1632)—a very costly engagement for both sides that created a brief standstill. Ferdinand had long been resentful of Wallenstein's independence,

Map 12–4 Europe in 1648 *At the end of the Thirty Years' War, Spain still had extensive possessions. Austria and Brandenburg–Prussia were prominent, the independence of the United Provinces and Switzerland was recognized, and Sweden held important river mouths in northern Germany.*

although he was the major factor in imperial success. In 1634 Ferdinand had Wallenstein assassinated. By that time, Wallenstein had not only served his purpose for the emperor, but, ever opportunistic, he was even trying openly to strike bargains with the Protestants for his services. The Wallenstein episode is a telling commentary on this war without honor. Despite the deep religious motivations, greed and political gain were the real forces at work in the Thirty Years' War. Even allies that owed one another their success were not above treating each other as mortal enemies.

In the Peace of Prague in 1635 the German Protestant states, led by Saxony, reached a compromise agreement with Ferdinand. The Swedes, however, received continued support from France and the Netherlands. Desiring to maximize their investment in the war, they refused to join the agreement. Their resistance to settlement plunged the war into its fourth and most devastating phase, the Swedish–French period (1635–1648).

THE SWEDISH–FRENCH PERIOD The French openly entered the war in 1635, sending men and munitions as well as financial subsidies. After their entrance the war dragged on for thirteen years, with French, Swedish, and Spanish soldiers looting the length and breadth of Germany—warring, it seemed, simply for the sake of warfare itself. The Germans, long weary of the devastation, were too disunited to repulse the foreign armies; they simply watched and suffered. By the time peace talks began in the Westphalian cities of Münster and Osnabrück in 1644, an estimated one-third of the German population had died as a direct result of the war. It has been called the worst European catastrophe since the Black Death of the fourteenth century.

The Treaty of Westphalia

The Treaty of Westphalia in 1648 brought all hostilities within the Holy Roman Empire to an end. (See Map 12–4.) It rescinded Ferdinand's Edict of Restitution and firmly reasserted the major feature of the religious settlement of the Peace of Augsburg, as the ruler of each land was again permitted to determine the religion of his or her land. The treaty also gave the Calvinists their long-sought legal recognition. The independence of the Swiss Confederacy and the United Provinces of Holland, long recognized in fact, was now proclaimed in law. And the treaty elevated Bavaria to the rank of an elector state. The provisions of the treaty made the German princes supreme over their principalities. Yet, as guarantors of the treaty, Sweden and France found many occasions to meddle in German affairs until the century's end, France to considerable territorial gain. Brandenburg–Prussia emerged as the most powerful northern German state. Because the treaty broadened the legal status of Protestantism, the pope opposed it altogether, but he had no power to prevent it.

France and Spain remained at war outside the empire until 1659, when French victories forced on the Spanish the humiliating Treaty of the Pyrenees. Thereafter France became Europe's dominant power, and the once vast Habsburg kingdom waned.

By confirming the territorial sovereignty of Germany's many political entities, the Treaty of Westphalia perpetuated German division and political weakness into the modern period. Only two German states attained any international significance during the seventeenth century: Austria and Brandenburg–Prussia. The petty regionalism within the empire also reflected on a small scale the drift of larger European politics. In the seventeenth century, distinctive nation-states, each with its own political, cultural, and religious identity, reached maturity and firmly established the competitive nationalism of the modern world.

✦

Both religion and politics played major roles in each of the great conflicts of the Age of Religious Wars—the internal struggle in France, Spain's unsuccessful effort to subdue the Netherlands, England's successful resistance of Spain, and the steady march of virtually every major European power through the hapless empire during the first half of the seventeenth century. Parties and armies of different religious persuasions are visible in each conflict, and in each we also find a life-or-death political struggle.

The wars ended with the recognition of minority religious rights and a guarantee of the traditional boundaries of political sovereignty. In France, the Edict of Nantes (1598) brought peace by granting Huguenots basic religious and civil freedoms and by recognizing their towns and territories. Peace and sovereignty came to the Netherlands with the departure of the Spanish, guaranteed initially by the Twelve Years' Truce

(1609) and secured fully by the Peace of Westphalia (1648). The conflict between England and Spain ended with the removal of the Spanish threat to English sovereignty in politics and religion, which resulted from the execution of Mary, Queen of Scots (1587), and the English victory over the Armada (1588). In the Holy Roman Empire, peace came with the reaffirmation of the political principle of the Peace of Augsburg (1555), as the Peace of Westphalia brought the Thirty Years' War to an end by again recognizing the sovereignty of rulers within their lands and their right to determine the religious beliefs of their subjects. Europe at mid-century had real, if brief, peace.

Review Questions

1. What part did politics play in the religious positions of the French leaders? How did the king (or his regent) decide which side to favor? What led to the infamous Saint Bartholomew's Day Massacre, and what did it achieve?
2. How did Spain achieve a position of dominance in the sixteenth century? What were its strengths and weaknesses as a nation? What were Philip II's goals? Which was he unable to achieve and why?
3. Henry of Navarre (Henry IV of France), Elizabeth I, and William of Orange were all *politiques*. Define the term and explain why it applies to these three rulers.
4. Discuss the background to the establishment of the Anglican church in England. What were the politics of Mary I? What was Elizabeth I's settlement, and how difficult was it to impose on all of England? Who were her detractors and what were their criticisms?
5. Why was the Thirty Years' War fought? To what extent did politics determine the outcome of the war? Discuss the Treaty of Westphalia in 1648. Could matters have been resolved without war?
6. It has been said that the Thirty Years' War is the outstanding example in European history of meaningless conflict. Evaluate this statement and provide specific reasons.

Suggested Readings

F. BRAUDEL, *The Mediterranean and the Mediterranean World in the Age of Philip the Second,* vols. 1 and 2 (1976). Widely acclaimed work of a French master historian.

N. Z. DAVIS, *Society and Culture in Early Modern France* (1975). Essays on popular culture.

R. DUNN, *The Age of Religious Wars 1559–1689* (1979). Excellent brief survey of every major conflict.

J. H. ELLIOTT, *Europe Divided 1559–1598* (1968). Direct, lucid narrative account.

G. R. ELTON, *England Under the Tudors* (1955). Masterly account.

J. H. FRANKLIN (ED. and Trans.), *Constitutionalism and Resistance in the Sixteenth Century: Three Treatises by Hotman, Beza, and Mornay* (1969). Three defenders of the right of people to resist tyranny.

P. GEYL, *The Revolt of the Netherlands, 1555–1609* (1958). The authoritative survey.

J. GUY, *Tudor England* (1990). The standard history and good synthesis of recent scholarship.

C. HAIGH, *Elizabeth I* (1988). Elizabeth portrayed as a magnificent politician and propagandist.

D. LOADES, *Mary Tudor* (1989). Authoritative and good storytelling.

J. LYNCH, *Spain Under the Habsburg I: 1516–1598* (1964). Political narrative.

W. MACCAFFREY, *Queen Elizabeth and the Making of Policy 1572–1588* (1985). Very good on the intricacy of Elizabethan religious policy.

G. MATTINGLY, *The Armada* (1959). A masterpiece and novel-like in style.

J. E. NEALE, *Queen Elizabeth I* (1934). Superb biography.

J. E. NEALE, *The Age of Catherine de Médicis* (1962). Short, concise summary.

G. PARKER, *Philip II* (1978). Readable, admiring account.

G. PARKER, *Europe in Crisis, 1598–1648* (1979). The big picture at a gallop.

T. K. RABB (ED.), *The Thirty Years' War* (1972). Excerpts from the scholarly debate over the war's significance.

J. G. RIDLEY, *John Knox* (1968). Large, detailed biography.

J. H. M. SALMON (ED.), *The French Wars of Religion: How Important Were the Religious Factors?* (1967). Scholarly debate over the relation between politics and religion.

J. H. M. SALMON, *Society in Crisis: France in the Sixteenth Century* (1976). Standard narrative account.

A. SOMAN (ED.), *The Massacre of St. Bartholomew's Day: Reappraisals and Documents* (1974). Results of an international symposium on the anniversary of the massacre.

K. THOMAS, *Religion and the Decline of Magic* (1971). Provocative, much acclaimed work focused on popular culture.

C. V. WEDGWOOD, *The Thirty Years' War* (1939). Extremely detailed account that downplays the war's achievements.

C. V. WEDGWOOD, *William the Silent* (1944). Excellent political biography of William of Orange.

J. WORMALD, *Mary, Queen of Scots: A Study in Failure* (1991). Mary portrayed as a queen who did not understand her country and was out of touch with the times.

CHAPTER 13

Charles I governed England from 1625 to 1649. His attempts to establish an absolutist government in matters of both church and state provoked clashes with the English Parliament and the outbreak of the Civil War in 1642. He was executed in 1649. [Daniel Mytens/The Granger Collection]

Paths to Constitutionalism and Absolutism:

England and France in the Seventeenth Century

KEY TOPICS

- The factors behind the divergent political paths of England and France in the seventeenth century
- The conflict between Parliament and the king over taxation and religion in early Stuart England, the English Civil War, and the abolition of the monarchy
- The Restoration and the development of Parliament's supremacy over the monarchy after the "Glorious Revolution"
- The establishment of an absolutist monarchy in France under Louis XIV
- The wars of Louis XIV

During the seventeenth century England and France moved in two very different political directions. By the close of the century, after decades of fierce civil and religious conflict that pitted Parliament and monarch against each other, England had developed into a parliamentary monarchy with a policy of religious toleration. Parliament, composed of the House of Lords and the House of Commons, shared responsibility for government with the monarch. It met regularly and the Commons, composed primarily of wealthy landed gentry, had to stand for election every three years. By contrast, France developed an absolutist, centralized form of government dominated by a monarchy that shared little power with any other national institutions. Its authority resided rather in a complex set of relationships with local nobility, guilds, and towns and in its ability to support the largest standing army in Europe. In the seventeenth century France also abandoned Henry IV's policy of religious toleration and proscribed all but the Roman Catholic church.

These English and French forms of government became models for other nations. The French model, termed absolutism in the nineteenth century, would be imitated by other monar-

chies across the continent during the eighteenth century. The English model would later inspire the political creed known in the nineteenth century as liberalism. Like all such political labels, these terms, although useful, can conceal considerable complexity. English "parliamentary monarchs" did not share all power with Parliament; they controlled the army, foreign policy, and much patronage. Likewise the "absolute monarchs" of France and their later imitators elsewhere in Europe were not truly absolute; laws, traditions, and many local institutions and customs limited their power.

Two Models of European Political Development

In the second half of the sixteenth century, changes in military organization, weapons, and tactics sharply increased the cost of warfare. Because traditional sources of revenue were inadequate to finance these growing costs—as well as the costs of government—monarchs sought new sources. Only monarchies that succeeded in building a secure financial base that was not deeply dependent on the support of noble estates, diets, or assemblies achieved absolute rule. The French monarchy succeeded in this effort after mid-century, whereas the English monarchy failed. The paths to that success and failure led to the two models of government—absolutism in France and parliamentary monarchy in England—that shaped subsequent political development in Europe.

In their pursuit of adequate income, English monarchs of the seventeenth century threatened the local political interests and economic well-being of the country's nobility and others of great landed and commercial wealth. These politically active groups, invoking traditional English liberties in their defense, effectively resisted the monarchs' attempted intrusions throughout the century.

The experience of Louis XIV, the French king, was different. During the second half of the seventeenth century, he would make the French nobility dependent upon his goodwill and patronage. In turn, he would support their local influence and their place in a firm social hierarchy. But even the French king's dominance of the nobility was not wholly complete. Louis accepted the authority of the noble-dominated *Parlement* of Paris to register royal decrees before they officially became law, and he permitted regional *parlements* to exercise considerable authority over local administration and taxation. Funds from taxes levied by the central monarchy found their way into many local pockets.

Religious factors also affected the political destinies of England and France. A strong Protestant religious movement known as Puritanism arose in England and actively opposed the Stuart monarchy. Puritanism represented a nonpolitical force that sought at first to limit and eventually to overturn the English monarchy. Louis XIV, in contrast, crushed the Protestant communities of France. He was generally supported in these efforts by Roman Catholics, who saw religious uniformity enforced by the monarchy working to their advantage.

There were also major institutional differences between the two countries. In Parliament, England possessed a political institution that had long bargained with the monarch over political issues. In the early seventeenth century, to be sure, Parliament did not meet regularly and was not the strong institution it would become by the close of the century. Nor was there anything certain or inevitable about the transformation it underwent over the course of the century. The institutional basis for it, however, was in place. Parliament was there and expected to be consulted from time to time. Its members—nobility and gentry—had experience organizing and speaking, writing legislation, and criticizing royal policies. Furthermore, the English had a legal and political tradition based on concepts of liberty to which members of Parliament and their supporters throughout the country could and did appeal in their conflict with the monarchy.

For all intents, France lacked a similarly strong tradition of broad liberties, representation, and bargaining between the monarchy and other national institutions. The Estates General had met from time to time to grant certain revenues to the monarch, but it played no role after the early seventeenth century. It met in 1614, but thereafter the monarchy was able to find other sources of income, and the Estates General was not called again until the eve of the French Revolution in 1789. Consequently, whatever political forces might have wished to oppose or limit the monarchy lacked both an institutional base from which to operate and a tradition of meetings during which the necessary political skills might have been developed.

Finally, personalities played an important role. During the first half of the century, France profited from the guidance of two of its most able statesmen, Cardinals Richelieu and Mazarin. Mazarin trained Louis XIV to be a hard-working, if not always wise, monarch. Louis drew strong and capable ministers about himself. The four Stuart monarchs of England, on the other hand, had trouble simply making people trust them. They did not always keep their word. They acted on whim. They often displayed faulty judgment. In a political situation that demanded compromise, they rarely offered any. They offended significant groups of their subjects unnecessarily. In a nation that saw itself as strongly Protestant, they were suspected, sometimes accurately, of Catholic sympathies. Many of Charles's opponents in Parliament, of course, had flaws of their own, but the nature of the situation focused attention and criticism on the king.

In both England and France, the nobility and large landowners stood at the top of the social hierarchy and sought to protect their privileges and local interests. Important segments of the British nobility and landed classes came to distrust the Stuart monarchs, whom they believed sought to undermine their local political control and social standing. Parliamentary government was the result of the efforts of these English landed classes to protect their concerns and limit the power of the monarchy to interfere with life on the local level. The French nobility under Louis XIV, in contrast, eventually concluded that the best way to secure their own interests was to support his monarchy. He provided them with many forms of patronage, and he protected their tax exemptions, their wealth, and their local social standing.

The divergent developments of England and France in the seventeenth century would have surprised most people in 1600. It was not inevitable that the English monarchy would have to govern through Parliament or that the French monarchy would avoid dealing with national political institutions that could significantly limit its authority. The Stuart kings of England certainly aspired to the autocracy Louis XIV achieved, and some English political philosophers eloquently defended the divine right of kings and absolute rule. At the beginning of the seventeenth century, the English monarchy was strong. Queen Elizabeth, after a reign of almost forty-five years, was much revered. Parliament met only when called to provide financial support to the monarch. France, on the other hand, was emerging from the turmoil of its religious wars. The strife of that conflict had torn the society asunder. The monarchy was relatively weak. Henry IV, who had become king in 1589, pursued a policy of religious toleration. The French nobles had significant military forces at their disposal and in the middle of the seventeenth century confronted the king with rebellion. These conditions would change dramatically in both nations by the late seventeenth century.

Constitutional Crisis and Settlement in Stuart England

James I

In 1603 James VI of Scotland (r. 1603–1625), the son of Mary Stuart, Queen of Scots, without opposition or incident succeeded the childless Elizabeth as James I of England. His was a difficult situation. The elderly queen had been very popular and was totally identified with the nation. James was not well known, would never be popular, and, as a Scot, was an outsider. He inherited not only the crown but also a large royal debt and a fiercely divided church—problems that his politically active subjects expected him to address. The new king strongly advocated the divine right of kings, a subject on which he had written a book—*A Trew Law of Free Monarchies*—in 1598. He expected to rule with a minimum of consultation beyond his own royal court.

James quickly managed to anger many of his new subjects, but he did not wholly alienate them. In this period Parliament met only when the monarch summoned it, which James hoped to do rarely. Its chief business was to grant certain sources of income. The real value of these revenues, however, had been falling during the past half century, limiting their importance and thus the importance of Parliament to the king. To meet his needs, James developed other sources of income, largely by levying—solely on the authority of ill-defined privileges claimed to be attached to the office of king—new custom duties known as *impositions*. These were a version of the older customs duties known as *tonnage* and *poundage*. Members of Parliament resented these independent efforts to raise revenues as an affront to their authority over the royal purse, but they did not seek a serious confrontation. Rather, throughout James's reign they wrangled and negotiated behind the scenes.

The religious problem also festered under James. Puritans within the Church of England had hoped

This elegant painting portrays a very quiet London of the mid-1630s. During the next sixty years it would suffer wrenching political turmoil and the devastation of a great fire. [Yale Center for British Art]

that James's experience with the Scottish Presbyterian church and his own Protestant upbringing would incline him to favor their efforts to further the reformation of the English church. Since the days of Elizabeth, they had sought to eliminate elaborate religious ceremonies and replace the hierarchical episcopal system of church governance with a more representative Presbyterian form like that of the Calvinist churches on the Continent.

In January 1604, the Puritans had their first direct dealing with the new king. James responded in that month to a statement of Puritan grievances, the so-called Millenary Petition, at a special religious conference at Hampton Court. The political implications of the demands in this petition concerned him, and their tone offended him. To the dismay of the Puritans, he firmly declared his intention to maintain and even enhance the Anglican episcopacy. "A Scottish presbytery," he snorted, "agreeth as well with monarchy as God and the devil. No bishops, no king." James was not simply being arbitrary. Elizabeth also had not accommodated the Puritan demands. To have done so would have created strife within the Church of England.

Both sides left the conference with their suspicions of one another largely confirmed. The Hampton Court conference did, however, sow one fruitful seed. A commission was appointed to render a new translation of the Bible. That mission was fulfilled in 1611 with the publication of the eloquent Authorized, or King James, Version.

James also offended the Puritans with his opposition to their narrow view of human life and social activities. The Puritans believed that Sunday should be a day taken up largely with religious observances and little leisure or recreation. James believed recreation and sports were innocent activities and good for his people. He also believed Puritan narrowness discouraged Roman Catholics from converting to the Church of England. Consequently, in 1618 he issued the *Book of Sports*, which permitted games on Sunday for people who attended Church of England services. The clergy refused to read his order from the pulpit, and he had to rescind it.

It was during James's reign that some religious dissenters began to leave England. In 1620 Puritan separatists founded Plymouth Colony in Cape Cod Bay in North America, preferring flight from England to Anglican conformity. Later in the 1620s, a larger, better financed group of Puritans left England to found the Massachusetts Bay Colony. In each case, the colonists believed that reformation

King James I Defends Popular Recreation Against the Puritans

The English Puritans believed in strict observance of the Sabbath, disapproving any sports, games, or general social conviviality on Sunday. James I thought these strictures prevented many Roman Catholics from joining the Church of England. In 1618 James ordered the clergy of the Church of England to read the Book of Sports *from their pulpits. In this declaration, he permitted people to engage in certain sports and games after church services. His hope was to allow innocent recreations on Sunday while encouraging people to attend the Church of England. Despite the king's good intentions, the order offended the Puritans. The clergy resisted his order and he had to withdraw it.*

✦ *What motives of state might have led James I to issue this declaration? How does he attempt to make it favorable to the Church of England? Why might so many clergy have refused to read this statement to their congregations?*

With our own ears we heard the general complaint of our people, that they were barred from all lawful recreation and exercise upon the Sunday's afternoon, after the ending of all divine service, which cannot but produce two evils: the one the hindering of the conversion of many [Roman Catholic subjects], whom their priests will take occasion hereby to vex, persuading them that no honest mirth or recreation is lawful or tolerable in our religion, which cannot but breed a great discontentment in our people's hearts, especially as such as are peradventure upon the point of turning [to the Church of England]: the other inconvenience is, that this prohibition barreth the common and meaner sort of people from using such exercises as may make their bodies more able for war, when we or our successors shall have occasion to use them; and in place thereof sets up filthy tipplings and drunkenness, and breeds a number of idle and discontented speeches in their ale-houses. For when shall the common people have leave to exercise, if not upon the Sundays and holy days, seeing they must apply their labor and win their living in all working days? . . .

[A]s for our good people's lawful recreation, our pleasure likewise is, that after the end of divine service our good people be not disturbed, . . . or discouraged from any lawful recreation, such as dancing, either men or women; archery for men, leaping, vaulting, or any other such harmless recreation, or from having of Hay-games, Whitsun-ales, and Morris-dances; and the setting up of May-poles and other sports therewith used; . . . but withal we do here account still as prohibited all unlawful games to be used upon Sundays only, as bear and bull-baitings . . . and at all times in the meaner sort of people by law prohibited, bowling.

And likewise we bar from this benefit and liberty all such known as recusants [Roman Catholics], either men or women, as will abstain from coming to church or divine service, being therefore unworthy of any lawful recreation after the said service, that will not first come to the church and serve God; prohibiting in like sort the said recreations to any that, though [they] conform in religion [i.e., members of the Church of England], are not present in the church at the service of God, before their going to the said recreations.

Henry Bettenson, ed., Documents of the Christian Church, *2nd ed. (London: Oxford University Press, 1963), pp. 400–403.*

had not gone far enough in England and that only in America could they worship freely and organize a truly reformed church.

Although James inherited a difficult situation, he also created special problems for himself. His court became a center of scandal and corruption. He governed by favorites, the most influential of whom was the duke of Buckingham, whom rumor made the king's homosexual lover. Buckingham controlled royal patronage and openly sold peerages and titles to the highest bidders—a practice that angered the nobility because it cheapened their rank. There had always been court favorites, but never before had a single person so controlled access to the monarch.

James's foreign policy also roused opposition. He regarded himself as a peacemaker. Peace reduced pressures on royal revenues and the need for larger debts. The less his demands for money, the less the king had to depend on the goodwill of Parliament. In 1604 he concluded a much-needed peace with Spain, England's chief adversary during the second half of the sixteenth century. His subjects viewed this peace as a sign of pro-Catholic sentiment. James further increased suspicions when he tried unsuccessfully to relax the penal laws against Catholics. The English had not forgotten the brutal reign of Mary Tudor and the acts of treason by Catholics during Elizabeth's reign. In 1618 James hesitated, not unwisely, to rush English troops to the aid of Protestants in Germany at the outbreak of the Thirty Years' War. This hesitation caused some to question his loyalty to the Anglican Church. These suspicions increased when he tried to arrange a marriage between his son Charles and the Spanish *Infanta* (the daughter of the king of Spain). In the king's last years, as his health failed and the reins of government passed increasingly to his son Charles and to Buckingham, parliamentary opposition and Protestant sentiment combined to undo his pro-Spanish foreign policy. In 1624, shortly before James's death, England entered a continental war against Spain largely in response to the pressures of members of Parliament.

Charles I

Parliament had favored the war with Spain but would not adequately finance it because its members distrusted Buckingham. Unable to gain adequate funds from Parliament, Charles I (r. 1625–1649), like his father, resorted to extraparliamentary measures. He levied new tariffs and duties and attempted to collect discontinued taxes. He even subjected the English people to a so-called forced loan (a tax theoretically to be repaid), imprisoning those who refused to pay. The government quartered troops in transit to war zones in private homes. All these actions intruded on life at the local level and challenged the power of the local nobles and landowners to control their districts.

When Parliament met in 1628, its members were furious. Taxes were being illegally collected for a war that was going badly for England and that now, through royal blundering, involved France as well as Spain. Parliament expressed its displeasure by making the king's request for new funds conditional on his recognition of the Petition of Right. This important declaration of constitutional freedom required that henceforth there should be no forced loans or taxation without the consent of Parliament, that no freeman should be imprisoned without due cause, and that troops should not be billeted in private homes. It was thus an expression of resentment and resistance to the intrusion of the monarchy on the local level. Though Charles agreed to the petition, there was little confidence that he would keep his word.

Years of Personal Rule In August 1628, Charles's chief minister, Buckingham, with whom Parliament had been in open dispute since 1626, was assassinated. His death, while sweet to many, did not resolve the hostility between the king and Parliament. In January 1629, Parliament further underscored its resolve to limit royal prerogative. It declared that religious innovations leading to "popery"—by this it meant Charles's high-church policies—and the levying of taxes without parliamentary consent were acts of treason. Perceiving that things were getting out of hand, Charles promptly dissolved Parliament and did not recall it again until 1640, when war with Scotland forced him to do so.

To conserve his limited resources, Charles made peace with France in 1629 and Spain in 1630. This policy again roused fears among some of his subjects that he was too friendly to Roman Catholic powers. The French and Roman Catholic background of Charles's wife furthered these suspicions. Part of her marriage contract permitted her to hear mass daily at the English court. Charles's attitude toward the Church of England also raised suspicions. He supported a group within the church, known as Arminians, who rejected many Puritan

Parliament Presents Charles I with the Petition of Right

After becoming monarch in 1625 Charles I (1625–1649) had imposed unparliamentary taxes, coerced freemen, and quartered troops in transit in private homes. These actions deeply offended Parliament, which in 1628 refused to grant him any funds until he rescinded those practices by recognizing the Petition of Right (June, 1628). The Petition constituted a general catalog of the offenses associated with the exercise of arbitrary royal authority.

✦ *What limits does the Petition attempt to place on royal taxation? How did the Petition criticize arbitrary arrest? Why was the quartering of soldiers in private homes so offensive?*

[The Lords Spirit and Temporal, and commons in Parliament assembled] do humbly pray your Most Excellent Majesty, that no man hereafter be compelled to make or yield any gift, loan, benevolence, tax, or such like charge, without common consent by Act of parliament; and that none be called to make answer, to take such oath, or to give attendance, or be confined, or otherwise molested or disquieted concerning the same, or for refusal thereof; and that no freeman, in any such manner as in before-mentioned, be imprisoned or detained; and that your Majesty will be pleased to remove the said soldiers and mariners [who have been quartered in private homes], and that your people may not be so burdened in time to come; and that the foresaid commissions for proceeding by martial law, may be revoked and annulled; and that hereafter no commissions of like nature may issue forth to any person or persons whatsoever, to be executed as aforesaid, lest by colour of them any of your Majesty's subjects be destroyed or put to death, contrary to the laws and franchise of the land

All which they most humble pray of your Most Excellent Majesty, as their rights and liberties according to the laws and statues of this realm.

The King's Reply: The King willeth that right be done according to the laws and customs of the realm; and that the statues be put in due execution, that his subjects may have no cause to complain of any wrong or oppressions, contrary to their just rights and liberties, to the preservation whereof he holds himself as well obliged as of his prerogative.

Samuel R. Gardiner, ed., The Constitutional Documents of the Puritan Revolution *(Oxford: Clarendon Press, 1889), pp. 4–5.*

doctrines and favored elaborate, high-church practices. The Puritans were convinced these practices would bring a return to Roman Catholicism.

To allow Charles to rule without renegotiating financial arrangements with Parliament, his chief minister, Thomas Wentworth (after 1640, earl of Stafford), instituted a policy known as *thorough.* This policy imposed strict efficiency and administrative centralization in government. Its goal was absolute royal control of England. Its success depended on the king's ability to operate independently of Parliament, which no law required him to summon.

Charles's ministers exploited every legal fundraising device. They enforced previously neglected laws and extended existing taxes into new areas. For example, starting in 1634, they gradually extended inland to the whole of England a tax called *ship money*, normally levied only on coastal areas to pay for naval protection. A great landowner named John Hampden mounted a legal challenge to the extension of this tax. Although the king prevailed in what was a close legal contest, his victory was costly. It deepened the animosity toward him among the powerful landowners, who would elect and sit in Parliament should he need to summon it.

During these years of personal rule, Charles surrounded himself with an elaborate court and patronized some of the greatest artists of the day. Like his father, he sold noble titles and knighthoods, lessening their value and the social exclusiveness conferred on those who already possessed them. Nobles and great landowners feared that the growth of the court, the king's relentless pursuit of revenue, and the inflation of titles and honors would reduce their local influence and social standing. They also feared that the monarch might actually succeed in governing without ever again calling Parliament into session.

Charles might very well have ruled indefinitely without Parliament had not his religious policies provoked war with Scotland. James I had allowed a wide variety of religious observances in England, Scotland, and Ireland. Charles by contrast hoped to impose religious conformity at least within England and Scotland. William Laud (1573–1645), who was first Charles's religious advisor and, after 1633, archbishop of Canterbury, held a high-church view of Anglicanism. He favored powerful bishops, elaborate liturgy, and personal religious observance and devotion rather than the preaching and listening favored by the Puritans. As a member of the Court of High Commission, Laud had already radicalized the English Puritans by denying them the right to publish and preach. In 1637 Charles and Laud, against the opposition of the English Puritans as well as the Scots, tried to impose on Scotland the English episcopal system and a prayerbook almost identical to the Anglican *Book of Common Prayer*.

The Scots rebelled, and Charles, with insufficient resources for a war, was forced to call Parliament. The members of Parliament opposed his policies almost as much as they wanted to crush the rebellion. Led by John Pym (1584–1643), they refused even to consider funds for war until the king agreed to redress a long list of political and religious grievances. The king, in response, immediately dissolved Parliament—hence its name, the Short Parliament (April–May 1640). When the Presbyterian Scots invaded England and defeated an English army at the Battle of Newburn in the summer of 1640, Charles reconvened Parliament, this time on its terms, for a long and most fateful duration.

THE LONG PARLIAMENT The landowners and the merchant classes represented by Parliament had resented the king's financial measures and paternalistic rule for some time. The Puritans in Parliament resented his religious policies and deeply distrusted the influence of the Roman Catholic queen. The Long Parliament (1640–1660) thus acted with widespread support and general unanimity when it convened in November 1640.

The House of Commons impeached both the earl of Stafford and Archbishop Laud. Disgraced and convicted by a parliamentary bill of attainder (a judgment of treason entailing loss of civil rights), Stafford was executed in 1641. Laud was imprisoned and also later executed (1645). Parliament abolished the Court of Star Chamber and the Court of High Commission, royal instruments of political and religious *thorough*, respectively. The levying of new taxes without consent of Parliament and the inland extension of ship money now became illegal. Finally, Parliament resolved that no more than three years should elapse between its meetings and that it could not be dissolved without its own consent. Parliament was determined that neither Charles nor any future English king could again govern without consulting it.

Despite its cohesion on these initial actions, Parliament was divided over the precise direction to take on religious reform. Both moderate Puritans (the Presbyterians) and more extreme Puritans (the Independents) wanted the complete abolition of the episcopal system and the *Book of Common Prayer*. The majority Presbyterians sought to reshape England religiously along Calvinist lines, with local congregations subject to higher representative governing bodies (presbyteries). Independents wanted a much more fully decentralized church with every congregation as its own final authority. Finally, many conservatives in both houses of Parliament were determined to preserve the English church in its current form. Their numbers fell dramatically after 1642, however, when many of them left the House of Commons with the outbreak of civil war.

These divisions further intensified in October 1641, when a rebellion erupted in Ireland and Parliament was asked to raise funds for an army to suppress it. Pym and his followers, loudly reminding the House of Commons of the king's past behavior, argued that Charles could not be trusted with an army and that Parliament should become the commander-in-chief of English armed forces. Parliamentary conservatives, on the other hand, were appalled by such a bold departure from tradition.

ERUPTION OF CIVIL WAR Charles saw the division within Parliament as a chance to reassert his power.

On December 1, 1641, Parliament presented him with the "Grand Remonstrance," a more-than-200-article summary of popular and parliamentary grievances against the crown. In January 1642, he invaded Parliament with his soldiers. He intended to arrest Pym and the other leaders, but they had been forewarned and managed to escape. The king then withdrew from London and began to raise an army. Shocked by his action, a majority of the House of Commons passed the Militia Ordinance, which gave Parliament authority to raise an army of its own. The die was now cast. For the next four years (1642–1646), civil war engulfed England.

Charles assembled his forces at Nottingham, and the war began in August. It was fought over two main issues:

- Would an absolute monarchy or a parliamentary government rule England?
- Would English religion be controlled by the king's bishops and conform to high Anglican practice or adopt a decentralized, Presbyterian system of church governance?

Charles's supporters, known as Cavaliers, were located in the northwestern half of England. The parliamentary opposition, known as Roundheads because of their close-cropped hair, had its stronghold in the southeastern half of the country. Supporters of both sides included nobility, gentry, and townspeople. The chief factor distinguishing them was religion; the Puritans tended to favor Parliament.

Oliver Cromwell's New Model Army defeated the royalists in the English Civil War. After the execution of Charles I in 1649, Cromwell dominated the short-lived English republic, conquered Ireland and Scotland, and ruled as Lord Protector from 1653 until his death in 1658. [Historical Pictures/Stock Montage, Inc.]

Oliver Cromwell and the Puritan Republic

Two factors led finally to Parliament's victory. The first was an alliance with Scotland consummated in 1643 when John Pym persuaded Parliament to accept the terms of the Solemn League and Covenant, an agreement that committed Parliament, with the Scots, to a Presbyterian system of church government. This policy meant for the Scots that they would never again be confronted with an attempt to impose the English prayerbook on their religious services. The second factor was the reorganization of the parliamentary army under Oliver Cromwell (1599–1658), a middle-aged country squire of iron discipline and strong Independent religious sentiment. Cromwell and his "godly men" favored neither the episcopal system of the king nor the pure Presbyterian system of the Solemn League and Covenant. They were willing to tolerate an established majority church, but only if it also permitted Protestant dissenters to worship outside it.

The allies won the Battle of Marston Moor in 1644, the largest engagement of the war. In June 1645, Cromwell's newly reorganized forces, known as the New Model Army, fighting with disciplined fanaticism, won a decisive victory over the king at Naseby. (See Map 13–1.)

Defeated militarily, Charles tried again to take advantage of divisions within Parliament, this time seeking to win the Presbyterians and the Scots over to the royalist side. But Cromwell and his army firmly foiled him. In December 1648, Colonel Thomas Pride physically barred the Presbyterians, who made up a majority of Parliament, from taking

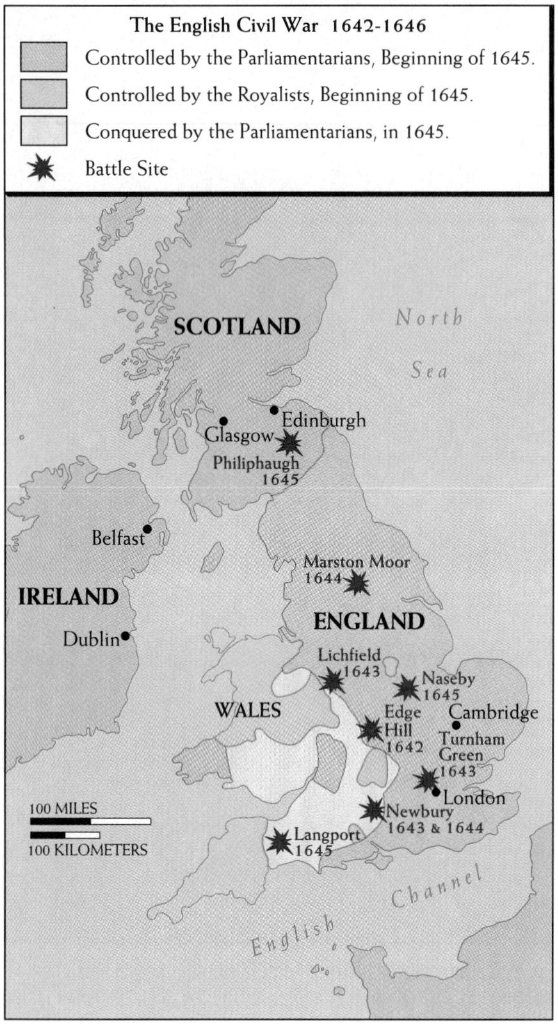

Map 13–1 The English Civil War *This map shows the rapid deterioration of the royalist position in 1645.*

their seats. After "Pride's Purge," only a "rump" of fewer than fifty members remained. Though small in numbers, this Independent Rump Parliament did not hesitate to use its power. On January 30, 1649, after a trial by a special court, the Rump Parliament executed Charles as a public criminal and thereafter abolished the monarchy, the House of Lords, and the Anglican Church. What had begun as a civil war had at this point become a revolution.

From 1649 to 1660, England became officially a Puritan republic, although for much of that time it was dominated by Cromwell. During this period, Cromwell's army conquered Ireland and Scotland, creating the single political entity of Great Britain. Cromwell, however, was a military man and no politician. He was increasingly frustrated by what seemed to him to be pettiness and dawdling on the part of Parliament. When in 1653 the House of Commons entertained a motion to disband his expensive army of 50,000, Cromwell responded by marching in and disbanding Parliament. He ruled thereafter as Lord Protector.

This military dictatorship, however, proved no more effective than Charles's rule had been and became just as harsh and hated. Cromwell's great army and foreign adventures inflated his budget to three times that of Charles. Near chaos reigned in many places, and commerce suffered throughout England. Cromwell was as intolerant of Anglicans as Charles had been of Puritans. People deeply resented his Puritan prohibitions of drunkenness, theatergoing, and dancing. Political liberty vanished in the name of religious liberty.

Cromwell's challenge had been to devise a political structure to replace that of monarch and Parliament. He tried various arrangements, none of which worked. He quarreled with the various Parliaments elected while he was Lord Protector. By the time of his death in 1658, most of the English were ready to end the Puritan religious experiment and the republican political experiment and return to their traditional institutions of government. Negotiations between leaders of the army and the exiled Charles II (r. 1660–1685), son of Charles I, led to the restoration of the Stuart monarchy in 1660.

Charles II and the Restoration of the Monarchy

Charles II returned to England amid great rejoicing. A man of considerable charm and political skill, Charles set a refreshing new tone after eleven years of somber Puritanism. His restoration returned England to the status quo of 1642, with a hereditary monarch once again on the throne, no legal requirement that he summon Parliament regularly, and the Anglican Church, with its bishops and prayerbook, supreme in religion.

The king, however, had secret Catholic sympathies and favored a policy of religious toleration. He wanted to allow all those outside the Church of England, Catholics as well as Puritans, to worship freely so long as they remained loyal to the throne. But in Parliament, even the ultraroyalist Anglicans did not believe patriotism and religion could be separated. Between 1661 and 1665, through a series of laws known as the Clarendon Code, Parliament

The bleeding head of Charles I is exhibited to the crowd after his execution on a cold day in January 1649. The contemporary Dutch artist also professed to see the immediate ascension of Charles's soul to heaven. In fact, many saw the king as a martyr. [DYCK, Sir Anthony van (1599–1641) (after) The Execution of King Charles I of England, *by Weesop (an eyewitness), 1649. Private Collection. The Bridgeman Art Collection.]*

excluded Roman Catholics, Presbyterians, and Independents from the religious and political life of the nation. These laws imposed penalties for attending non-Anglican worship services, required strict adherence to the *Book of Common Prayer* and the *Thirty-Nine Articles*, and demanded oaths of allegiance to the Church of England from all persons serving in local government.

At the time of the Restoration, England adopted Navigation Acts that required all imports to be carried either in English ships or in ships registered to the country from which the cargo originated. Dutch ships carried cargo from many nations, and such laws struck directly at Dutch dominance in the shipping industry. A series of naval wars between England and Holland ensued. Charles also attempted to tighten his grasp on the rich English colonies in North America and the Caribbean, many of which had been settled and developed by separatists who desired independence from English rule.

Although Parliament strongly supported the monarchy, Charles, following the pattern of his predecessors, required greater revenues than Parliament appropriated. These he obtained in part by increased customs duties. Because England and France were both at war with Holland, he also received aid from France. In 1670 England and France formally allied against the Dutch in the Treaty of Dover. In a secret portion of this treaty, Charles pledged to announce his conversion to Catholicism as soon as conditions in England permitted. In return for this announcement (which was never made), Louis XIV of France promised to pay a substantial subsidy to England.

In an attempt to unite the English people behind the war with Holland, and as a sign of good faith to Louis XIV, Charles issued a Declaration of Indulgence in 1672. This document suspended all laws against Roman Catholics and Protestant nonconformists. But again, the conservative Parliament proved less generous than the king and refused to grant money for the war until Charles rescinded the measure. After he did, Parliament passed the Test Act, which required all officials of the crown, civil and military, to swear an oath against the doctrine of transubstantiation—a requirement that no loyal Roman Catholic could honestly meet.

A Portrait of Oliver Cromwell

Oliver Cromwell was one of the most powerful and controversial personalities of seventeenth-century Britain. He became Lord Protector through his command of the army which had first championed the parliamentary cause and later disbanded Parliament. Royalist statesman and historian Edward Hyde, the earl of Clarendon (1609–1674) was an enemy of Cromwell. Yet, his portrait of Cromwell mixed criticism with grudging admiration for the Puritan leader.

✦ *According to the earl of Clarendon, what were the chief features of Cromwell's personality? What was the character of his methods of governing? How did his position at home and abroad depend upon his military standing?*

He was one of those men whom his enemies cannot condemn without at the same time also praising. For he could never have done half that mischief without great parts of courage and industry and judgment. And he must have had a wonderful understanding of the nature and humours of men and a great dexterity in applying them . . . [to] raise himself to such a height. . . .

When he first appeared in the Parliament, he seemed to have a person in no degree gracious, no ornament of discourse, none of those talents which reconcile the affections of the standers-by; yet as he grew into his place and authority, his parts seemed to be renewed, as if he concealed faculties till he had occasion to use them. . . .

After he was confirmed and invested Protector . . . he consulted with very few . . . nor communicated any enterprise he resolved upon with more than those who were to have principal parts in the execution of it; nor to them sooner than was absolutely necessary. What he once resolved . . . he would not be dissuaded from, nor endure any contradiction. . . .

In all other matters which did not concern . . . his jurisdiction, he seemed to have great reverence for the law. . . . and as he proceeded with . . . indignation and haughtiness with those who were refractory and dared to contend with his greatness, so towards those who complied with his good pleasure, and courted his protection, he used a wonderful civility, generosity, and bounty.

To three nations [England, Ireland, and Scotland], which perfectly hated him, to an entire obedience to all his dictates; to awe and govern those nations by an army that was not devoted to him and wished his ruin; this was an instance of a very prodigious address. But his greatness at home was but a shadow of the glory he had abroad. It was hard to discover which feared him most, France, Spain, or the Netherlands. . . . As they did all sacrifice their honour and their interest to his pleasure, so there is nothing he could have demanded that any of them would have denied him.

James Harvey Robinson, ed., Readings in European History, *vol. 2 (Boston: Atheneum, 1906), pp. 248–250.*

Parliament had aimed the Test Act largely at the king's brother, James, duke of York, heir to the throne and a recent, devout convert to Catholicism. In 1678 a notorious liar named Titus Oates swore before a magistrate that Charles's Catholic wife, through her physician, was plotting with Jesuits and Irishmen to kill the king so James could assume the throne. The matter was taken before Parliament, where Oates was believed. In the ensuing hysteria, known as the Popish Plot, several people were tried and executed. Riding the crest of anti-Catholic sentiment and led by the earl of Shaftesbury (1621–1683), opposition members of Parliament, called Whigs, made an impressive but unsuccessful effort to enact a bill excluding James from succession to the throne.

Charles II (r. 1660–1685) was a person of considerable charm and political skill. Here he is portrayed as the founder of the Royal Society. [Robert Harding Picture Library, London]

More suspicious than ever of Parliament, Charles II turned again to increased customs duties and the assistance of Louis XIV for extra income. By these means he was able to rule from 1681 to 1685 without recalling Parliament. In these years, Charles suppressed much of his opposition. He drove the earl of Shaftesbury into exile, executed several Whig leaders for treason, and bullied local corporations into electing members of Parliament submissive to the royal will. When Charles died in 1685 (after a deathbed conversion to Catholicism), he left James the prospect of a Parliament filled with royal friends.

James II and Renewed Fears of a Catholic England

James II (r. 1685–1688) did not know how to make the most of a good thing. He alienated Parliament by insisting on the repeal of the Test Act. When Parliament balked, he dissolved it and proceeded openly to appoint known Catholics to high positions in both his court and the army. In 1687 he issued a Declaration of Indulgence, which suspended all religious tests and permitted free worship. Local candidates for Parliament who opposed the declaration were removed from their offices by the king's soldiers and were replaced by Catholics. In June 1688, James went so far as to imprison seven Anglican bishops who had refused to publicize his suspension of laws against Catholics. Each of these actions represented a direct royal attack on the local power and authority of nobles, landowners, the church, and other corporate bodies whose members believed they possessed particular legal privileges. James was attacking English liberty and challenging all manner of social privileges and influence.

Under the guise of a policy of enlightened toleration, James was actually seeking to subject all English institutions to the power of the monarchy. His goal was absolutism, and even conservative, loyalist Tories, as the royal supporters were called, could not abide this policy. The English feared, with reason, that James planned to imitate the religious intolerance of Louis XIV, who had, in 1685, revoked the Edict of Nantes (which had protected French Protestants for almost a century) and imposed Catholicism on the entire nation, using his dragoons against those who protested or resisted.

James soon faced united opposition. When his Catholic second wife gave birth to a son and Catholic male heir to the throne on June 20, 1688, opposition turned to action. The English had hoped that James would die without a male heir so the throne would pass to Mary, his Protestant eldest daughter. Mary was the wife of William III of Orange, *stadtholder* of the Netherlands, great-grandson of William the Silent, and the leader of European opposition to Louis XIV's imperial designs. Within days of the birth of James's son, Whig and Tory members of Parliament formed a coalition and invited Orange to invade England to preserve "traditional liberties," that is, the Anglican Church and parliamentary government.

The "Glorious Revolution"

William of Orange arrived with his army in November 1688 and was received without opposition by the English people. In the face of sure defeat, James fled to France and the protection of Louis XIV. With James gone, Parliament declared the throne vacant and on its own authority in 1689 proclaimed

William and Mary became the monarchs of England in 1689. Their accession brought England's economic and military resources into the balance against the France of Louis XIV. [Robert Harding Picture Library, London]

England in the Seventeenth Century

1603	James VI of Scotland becomes James I of England
1604	Hampton Court conference
1611	Publication of the Authorized, or King James, Version of the English Bible
1625	Charles I becomes English monarch
1628	Petition of Right
1629	Charles I dissolves Parliament and embarks on eleven years of personal rule
1640	April–May, Short Parliament November, Long Parliament convenes
1641	Grand Remonstrance
1642	Outbreak of the Civil War
1645	Charles I defeated at Naseby
1648	Pride's Purge
1649	Charles I executed
1649–1660	Various attempts at a Puritan Commonwealth
1660	Charles II restored to the English throne
1670	Secret Treaty of Dover between France and England
1672	Parliament passes the Test Act
1678	Popish Plot
1685	James II becomes king of England
1688	"Glorious Revolution"
1689	William and Mary proclaimed English monarchs
1701	Act of Settlement provides for Hanoverian succession
1702–1715	Reign of Queen Anne, the last of the Stuarts

William and Mary the new monarchs, completing the successful bloodless "Glorious Revolution." William and Mary, in turn, recognized a Bill of Rights that limited the powers of the monarchy and guaranteed the civil liberties of the English privileged classes. Henceforth, England's monarchs would be subject to law and would rule by the consent of Parliament, which was to be called into session every three years. The Bill of Rights also pointedly prohibited Roman Catholics from occupying the English throne. The Toleration Act of 1689 permitted worship by all Protestants and outlawed Roman Catholics and anti-Trinitarians (those who denied the Christian doctrine of the Trinity).

The measure closing this century of strife was the Act of Settlement in 1701. This bill provided for the English crown to go to the Protestant House of Hanover in Germany if none of the children of Queen Anne (r. 1702–1714), the second daughter of James II and the last of the Stuart monarchs, was alive at her death. She outlived all of her children, and so in 1714, the elector of Hanover became King George I of England, the third foreign monarch to occupy the English throne in just over a century.

The Glorious Revolution of 1688 established a framework of government by and for the governed that seemed to bear out the arguments of John Locke's *Second Treatise of Government* (1690). In this work, Locke described the relationship of a king and his people as a bilateral contract. If the king broke that contract, the people, by whom Locke meant the privileged and powerful, had the right to depose him. Locke had written the essay before the revolution, but it came to be read as a justification for it. Although neither in fact nor in theory a "popular" revolution such as would occur in America and France a hundred years later, the Glorious Revolution did establish in England a permanent check on monarchical power by the classes represented in Parliament. At the same time, as will be seen in Chapter 15, in its wake the English government had achieved a secure financial base that would allow it to pursue a century of warfare.

Rise of Absolute Monarchy in France

Seventeenth-century France, in contrast to England, saw both discontent among the nobility and religious pluralism smothered by the absolute monarchy and the closed Catholic state of Louis XIV (r. 1643–1715). An aggressive ruler who sought glory (*la gloire*) in foreign wars, Louis XIV subjected his subjects at home to "one king, one law, one faith."

Historians once portrayed Louis XIV's reign as a time when the rising central monarchy exerted far-reaching, direct control of the nation at all levels. A somewhat different picture has now emerged. Louis's predecessors and their chief ministers in the half century before his reign had already tried to impose direct rule, arousing discontent and, at mid-century, a rebellion among the nobility. Louis's genius was to make the monarchy the most important and powerful political institution in France while also assuring the nobles and other wealthy groups of their social standing and political and social influence on the local level. Rather than destroying existing local social and political institutions, Louis largely worked through them. Once nobles understood the king would support their local authority, they supported his central royal authority. In other words, the king and the nobles came to recognize that they needed each other. Nevertheless, Louis made it clear to all concerned that he was the senior partner in the relationship.

Louis's royal predecessors laid the institutional foundations for absolute monarchy and also taught him certain practices to avoid. Just as the emergence of a strong Parliament was not inevitable in England, neither was the emergence of an absolute monarchy in France.

Henry IV and Sully

Coming to the throne after the French wars of religion, Henry IV (r. 1589–1610; see Chapter 12) sought to curtail the privileges of the French nobility. His targets were the provincial governors and the regional *parlements*, especially the powerful *Parlement* of Paris, where a divisive spirit lived on. Here were to be found the old privileged groups, tax-exempt magnates who were largely preoccupied with protecting their self-interests. During the reign of Louis XIII (r. 1610–1643), royal civil servants known as *intendants* subjected these privileged groups to stricter supervision, implementing the king's will with some success in the provinces. An important function of the *intendants* was to prevent abuses from the sale of royal offices that conferred the right to collect revenues, sell licenses, or carry out other remunerative forms of administration. It was usually nobles who acquired these lucrative offices, which was one reason for their ongoing influence.

After decades of religious and civil war, an economy more amenable to governmental regulation emerged during Henry IV's reign. Henry and his finance minister, the duke of Sully (1560–1641), established government monopolies on gunpowder, mines, and salt, preparing the way for the mercantilist policies of Louis XIV and his minister, Colbert. They began a canal system to link the Atlantic and the Mediterranean by joining the Saône, the Loire, the Seine, and the Meuse rivers. They introduced the royal *corvée*, a labor tax that created a national force of drafted workers used to improve roads and the conditions of internal travel. Sully even dreamed of organizing the whole of Europe politically and commercially into a kind of common market.

Louis XIII and Richelieu

Henry IV was assassinated in 1610, and the following year Sully retired. Because Henry's son and successor, Louis XIII, was only nine years old at his father's death, the task of governing fell to the queen mother, Marie de Médicis (d. 1642). Finding herself in a vulnerable position, she sought security abroad by signing a ten-year mutual defense pact with France's archrival Spain in the Treaty of Fontainebleau (1611). This alliance also arranged for the later marriage of Louis XIII to the Spanish *Infanta* as well as for the marriage of the queen's daughter Elizabeth to the heir to the Spanish throne. The queen sought internal security against pressures from the French nobility by promoting the career of Cardinal Richelieu (1585–1642) as the king's chief adviser. Richelieu, loyal and shrewd, aspired to make France a supreme European power. He, more than any other person, was the secret of French success in the first half of the seventeenth century.

An apparently devout Catholic who also believed that the church best served both his own ambition

Cardinal Richelieu laid the foundations for the political ascendancy of the French monarchy. [The National Gallery, London]

and the welfare of France, Richelieu pursued a strongly anti-Habsburg policy. Although he supported the Spanish alliance of the queen and Catholic religious unity within France, he was determined to contain Spanish power and influence, even when that meant aiding and abetting Protestant Europe. It is an indication both of Richelieu's awkward political situation and of his diplomatic agility that he could, in 1631, pledge funds to the Protestant army of Gustavus Adolphus, the king of Sweden, while also insisting that Catholic Bavaria be spared from attack and that Catholics in conquered countries be permitted to practice their religion. One measure of the success of Richelieu's foreign policies can be seen in France's substantial gains in land and political influence when the Treaty of Westphalia (1648) ended hostilities in the Holy Roman Empire (see Chapter 12) and the Treaty of the Pyrenees (1659) sealed peace with Spain.

At home, Richelieu pursued centralizing policies utterly without qualm. Supported by the king, who let his chief minister make most decisions of state, Richelieu stepped up the campaign against separatist provincial governors and parlements. He made it clear that there was only one law, that of the king, and none could stand above it. When disobedient nobles defied his edicts, they were imprisoned and even executed. Such treatment of the nobility won Richelieu much enmity, even from the queen mother, who, unlike Richelieu, was not always willing to place the larger interests of the state above the pleasure of favorite nobles.

Richelieu started the campaign against the Huguenots that would end in 1685 with Louis XIV's revocation of the Edict of Nantes. Royal armies conquered major Huguenot cities in 1629. The subsequent Peace of Alais (1629) truncated the Edict of Nantes by denying Protestants the right to maintain garrisoned cities, separate political organizations, and independent law courts. Only Richelieu's foreign policy, which involved France in ties with Protestant powers, prevented the earlier implementation of the policy of extreme intolerance that marked the reign of Louis XIV. In the same year that Richelieu rescinded the independent political status of the Huguenots in the Peace of Alais, he also entered negotiations to make Gustavus Adolphus his counterweight to the expansion of Habsburg power within the Holy Roman Empire. By 1635 the Catholic soldiers of France were fighting openly with Swedish Lutherans against the emperor's army in the final phase of the Thirty Years' War (see Chapter 12).

Richelieu employed the arts and the printing press to defend his actions and to indoctrinate the French people in the meaning of *raison d'état* ("reason of state"). This also set a precedent for Louis XIV, who made elaborate use of royal propaganda and spectacle to assert and enhance his power.

Young Louis XIV and Mazarin

Although Richelieu helped lay the foundations for a much expanded royal authority, his immediate legacy was strong resentment of the monarchy among the French nobility and wealthy commercial groups. The crown's steady multiplication of royal offices, its replacement of local authorities by "state" agents, and its reduction of local sources of patronage undermined the traditional position of the privileged groups in French society. Among those affected were officers of the crown in the law courts and other royal institutions.

This medallion shows Anne of Austria, the wife of Louis XIII, with her son, Louis XIV. She wisely placed political authority in the hands of Cardinal Mazarin, who prepared Louis to govern France. [Giraudon/Art Resource, N.Y.]

When Louis XIII died in 1643, Louis XIV was only five years old. During his minority, the queen mother, Anne of Austria (d. 1666), placed the reins of government in the hands of Cardinal Mazarin (1602–1661), who continued Richelieu's determined policy of centralization. During Cardinal Mazarin's regency, long-building resentment produced a backlash. Between 1649 and 1652, in a series of widespread rebellions known as the *Fronde* (after the slingshot used by street boys), segments of the nobility and townspeople sought to reverse the drift toward absolute monarchy and to preserve local autonomy.

The *Parlement* of Paris initiated the revolt in 1649, and the nobility at large soon followed. Urging them on were the influential wives of princes whom Mazarin had imprisoned for treason. The many (the nobility) briefly triumphed over the one (the monarchy) when Mazarin released the imprisoned princes in February 1651. He and Louis XIV thereafter entered a short exile (Mazarin leaving France, Louis fleeing Paris). They returned in October 1652 after an interlude of inefficient and nearly anarchic rule by the nobility. The period of the Fronde convinced most French people that the rule of a strong king was preferable to the rule of many regional powers with competing and irreconcilable claims. At the same time, Louis XIV and his later advisors learned that heavy-handed policies like those of Richelieu and Mazarin could endanger the monarchy. Louis would ultimately concentrate unprecedented authority in the monarchy, but his means would be more clever than those of his predecessors.

The Years of Louis's Personal Rule

On the death of Mazarin, Louis XIV assumed personal control of the government. Unlike his royal predecessors, he appointed no single chief minister. One result was to make revolt more difficult. Rebellious nobles would now be challenging the king directly; they could not claim to be resisting only a bad minister.

Mazarin prepared Louis XIV well to rule France. The turbulent events of his youth also made an indelible impression on the king. Louis wrote in his memoirs that the *Fronde* caused him to loathe "kings of straw," and he followed two strategies to assure he would never become one.

First, Louis and his advisors became masters of propaganda and political image creation. Indoctrinated with a strong sense of the grandeur of his crown, Louis never missed an opportunity to impress it on the French people. When the *dauphin* (the heir to the French throne) was born in 1662, for example, Louis appeared for the celebration dressed as a Roman emperor.

Second, Louis made sure the French nobles and other major social groups would benefit from the growth of his own authority. Although he maintained control over foreign affairs and limited the influence of noble institutions on the monarchy, he never tried to abolish those institutions or limit their authority at the local level. The crown, for example, usually conferred informally with regional *parlements* before making rulings that would affect them. Likewise, the crown would rarely enact economic regulations without consulting local opinion. Local *parlements* enjoyed considerable latitude in all regional matters. In an exception to this pattern, Louis did clash with the *Parlement* of Paris, with which he had to register laws, and eventually in 1673 he curtailed much of its power. Many regional *parlements* and other regional authorities, however, had resented the power of that body.

Employing these strategies of propaganda and cooperation, Louis set out to anchor his rule in the principle of the divine right of kings, to domesticate the French nobility by binding them to the court rituals of Versailles, and to crush religious dissent.

King by Divine Right

Reverence for the king and the personification of government in his person had been nurtured in France since Capetian times. It was a maxim of French law and popular opinion that "the king of France is emperor in his realm" and the king's wish the law of the land. Building on this reverence, Louis XIV defended absolute royal authority on the grounds of divine right.

An important source for Louis's concept of royal authority was his devout tutor, the political theorist Bishop Jacques-Bénigne Bossuet (1627–1704).

Bishop Bossuet Defends the Divine Right of Kings

The revolutions of the seventeenth century caused many to fear anarchy far more than tyranny, among them the influential French bishop Jacques-Bénigne Bossuet (1627–1704), the leader of French Catholicism in the second half of the seventeenth century. Louis XIV made him court preacher and tutor to his son, for whom Bossuet wrote a celebrated Universal History. In the following excerpt, Bossuet defends the divine right and absolute power of kings. He depicts kings as embracing in their person the whole body of the state and the will of the people they govern and, as such, as being immune from judgment by any mere mortal.

✦ *Why might Bossuet have wished to make such extravagant claims for absolute royal power? How might these claims be transferred to any form of government? What are the religious bases for Bossuet's argument? How does this argument for absolute royal authority lead also to the need for a single uniform religion in France?*

The royal power is absolute. . . . The prince need render account of his acts to no one. "I counsel thee to keep the king's commandment, and that in regard of the oath of God. Be not hasty to go out of his sight; stand not on an evil thing for he doeth whatsoever pleaseth him. Where the word of a king is, there is power; and who may say unto him, What doest thou? Whoso keepeth the commandment shall feel no evil thing" [Eccles. 8:2–5]. Without this absolute authority the king could neither do good nor repress evil. It is necessary that his power be such that no one can hope to escape him, and finally, the only protection of individuals against the public authority should be their innocence. This confirms the teaching of St. Paul: "Wilt thou then not be afraid of the power? Do that which is good" [Rom. 13:3].

God is infinite, God is all. The prince, as prince, is not regarded as a private person: he is a public personage, all the state is in him; the will of all the people is included in his. As all perfection and all strength are united in God, so all the power of individuals is united in the person of the prince. What grandeur that a single man should embody so much! . . .

Behold an immense people united in a single person; behold this holy power, paternal and absolute; behold the secret cause which governs the whole body of the state, contained in a single head: you see the image of God in the king, and you have the idea of royal majesty. God is holiness itself, goodness itself, and power itself. In these things lies the majesty of God. In the image of these things lies the majesty of the prince.

From Politics Drawn from the Very Words of Holy Scripture, *as quoted in James Harvey Robinson, ed., Readings in European History, vol. 2 (Boston: Athenaeum, 1906), pp. 275–276.*

An ardent champion of the Gallican liberties—the traditional rights of the French king and church in matters of ecclesiastical appointments and taxation—Bossuet defended what he called the "divine right of kings." In support of his claims he cited examples of Old Testament rulers divinely appointed by and answerable only to God. As medieval popes had insisted that only God could judge a pope, so Bossuet argued that none save God could judge the king. Kings may have remained duty-bound to reflect God's will in their rule—in this sense, Bossuet considered them always subject to a higher authority. Yet as God's regents on Earth they could not be bound to the dictates of mere princes and parliaments. Such assumptions lay behind Louis XIV's alleged declaration: *"L'état, c'est moi"* ("I am the state").

Versailles

More than any other monarch of the day, Louis XIV used the physical setting of his royal court to exert political control. The palace court at Versailles on the outskirts of Paris became Louis's permanent residence after 1682. It was a true temple to royalty, architecturally designed and artistically decorated to proclaim the glory of the Sun King, as Louis was known. A spectacular estate with magnificent fountains and acres of orange groves, it became home to thousands of the more important nobles, royal officials, and servants. Although its physical maintenance and new additions, which continued throughout Louis's lifetime, consumed over half his annual revenues, Versailles paid significant political dividends.

Because Louis ruled personally, he was the chief source of favors and patronage in France. To emphasize his prominence, he organized life at court around every aspect of his own daily routine. He encouraged nobles to approach him directly, but required them to do so through elaborate court etiquette. Polite and fawning nobles sought his attention, entering their names on waiting lists to be in attendance at especially favored moments. The king's rising and dressing in particular were times of rare intimacy, when nobles could whisper their special requests in his ear. Fortunate nobles held his night candle as they accompanied him to his bed.

Although only five feet four inches in height, the king had presence and was always engaging in conversation. He turned his own sexuality to political

Louis XIV of France (r. 1643–1715) was the dominant European monarch in the second half of the seventeenth century. The powerful centralized monarchy he created established the prototype for the mode of government later termed absolutism. *[Giraudon/Art Resource, N.Y.]*

ends and encouraged the belief at court that it was an honor to lie with him. Married to the Spanish *Infanta* Marie Thérèse for political reasons in 1660, he kept many mistresses. After Marie's death in 1683, he settled down in a secret marriage to Madame de Maintenon and apparently became much less the philanderer.

Court life was a carefully planned and successfully executed effort to domesticate and trivialize the nobility. Barred by law from high government positions, the ritual and play kept them busy and dependent so they had little time to plot revolt. Dress codes and high-stakes gambling contributed to their indebtedness and dependency on the king. Members of the court spent the afternoons hunting, riding, or strolling about the lush gardens of Versailles. Evenings were given over to planned entertainment in the large salons (plays, concerts, gambling, and the like), followed by supper at 10:00

p.m. Even the king's retirement was part of the day's spectacle.

Moments near the king were important to most court nobles because they were effectively excluded from the real business of government. Louis ruled through powerful councils that controlled foreign affairs, domestic relations, and economic regulations. Each day after morning mass, which Louis always observed, he spent hours with the chief ministers of these councils, whom he chose from families long in royal service or from among people just beginning to rise in the social structure. Unlike the nobles at court, they had no real or potential power bases in the provinces and depended solely on the king for their standing in both government and society.

Some nobles, of course, did not attend Versailles. Some tended to their local estates and cultivated their local influence. Many others were simply too poor to cut a figure at court. All the nobility understood, however, that Louis, unlike Richelieu and Mazarin, would not threaten their local social standing. Louis supported France's traditional social structure and the social privileges of the nobility.

Suppression of the Jansenists

Like Richelieu before him, Louis believed that political unity and stability required religious conformity. His first move in this direction, which came early in his personal reign, was against the Roman Catholic Jansenists.

The French crown and the French church had by long tradition—originating with the so-called Gallican liberties in the fourteenth century—jealously guarded their independence from Rome. A great influx of Catholic religious orders, the Jesuits prominent among them, followed Henry IV's conversion to Catholicism. Because of their leadership at the Council of Trent and their close connections

Versailles, as painted in 1668 by Pierre Patel the Elder (1605–1676). The central building is the hunting lodge built for Louis XII earlier in the century. The wings that appear here were some of Louis XIV's first expansions. [Giraudon/Art Resource, N.Y.]

to Spain, the Jesuits had been banned from France by Catherine de Médicis. Henry IV, however, lifted the ban in 1603, with certain conditions: He required members of the order to swear an oath of allegiance to the king, he limited the number of new colleges they could open, and he required them to have special licenses for public activities.

The Jesuits were not, however, easily harnessed. They rapidly monopolized the education of the upper classes, and their devout students promoted the religious reforms and doctrine of the Council of Trent throughout France. In a measure of their success, Jesuits served as confessors to Henry IV, Louis XIII, and Louis XIV.

Jansenism arose in the 1630s as part of an intra-Catholic opposition to the theology and the political influence of the Jesuits. Jansenists adhered to the Augustinian tradition that had also spawned many Protestant teachings. Serious and uncompromising, they particularly opposed Jesuit teachings about free will. They believed with Saint Augustine that original sin so corrupted humankind that individuals could do nothing good nor secure their own salvation without divine grace. The namesake of the movement, Cornelius Jansen (d. 1638), was a Flemish theologian and the bishop of Ypres. His posthumously published *Augustinus* (1640) assailed Jesuit teaching on grace and salvation.

A prominent Parisian family, the Arnaulds, became Jansenist allies, adding a political element to the Jansenists' theological objections to the Jesuits. Like many other French people, the Arnaulds believed the Jesuits had been behind the assassination of Henry IV in 1610.

The Arnaulds dominated Jansenist communities at Port-Royal and Paris during the 1640s. In 1643 Antoine Arnauld published a work entitled *On Frequent Communion*, in which he criticized the Jesuits for confessional practices that permitted the easy redress of almost any sin. The Jesuits, in turn, condemned the Jansenists as "crypto-Calvinists."

On May 31, 1653, Pope Innocent X declared heretical five Jansenist theological propositions on grace and salvation. In 1656 the pope banned Jansen's *Augustinus* and the Sorbonne censured Antoine Arnauld. In this same year, Antoine's friend, Blaise Pascal (1623–1662), the most famous of Jansen's followers, published the first of his *Provincial Letters* in defense of Jansenism. A deeply religious man, Pascal tried to reconcile the "reasons of the heart" with growing seventeenth-century reverence for the clear and distinct ideas of the mind (see Chapter 14). He objected to Jesuit moral theology not only as being lax and shallow, but also because he felt its rationalism failed to do full justice to the religious experience.

In 1660 Louis permitted the papal bull *Ad Sacram Sedem* (1656) to be enforced in France, thus banning Jansenism. He also closed down the Port-Royal community. Thereafter, Jansenists either retracted their views or went underground. Much later, in 1710, Louis lent his support to a still more thorough purge of Jansenist sentiment.

Jansenism had offered the prospect of a Catholicism broad enough to appeal to France's Protestant Huguenots. By suppressing it, Louis also eliminated the best hope for bringing peaceful religious unity to his country.

Louis's Early Wars

Louis's France was in many ways like much of the rest of contemporary Europe. It had a largely subsistence economy and its cities enjoyed only limited commercial prosperity. It did not, in other words, achieve the economic strength of a modern industrial economy. By the 1660s, however, France was superior to any other European nation in administrative bureaucracy, armed forces, and national unity. Louis had sufficient resources at his disposal to raise and maintain a large and powerful army, and by every external measure he was in a position to dominate Europe. He spent most of the rest of his reign attempting to do so.

GOVERNING FOR WARFARE Three remarkable French ministers established and supported Louis XIV's great war machine: Colbert, Louvois, and Vauban.

Jean-Baptiste Colbert (1619–1683), controller general of finances and Louis's most brilliant minister, created the economic base Louis needed to finance his wars. Colbert worked to centralize the French economy with the same rigor that Louis had worked to centralize the French government. Colbert tried, with modest success, to organize much economic activity under state supervision and, through tariffs, carefully regulated the flow of imports and exports. He sought to create new national industries and organized factories around a tight regimen of work and ideology. He simplified the administrative bureaucracy, abolished unnecessary positions, and reduced the number of tax-exempt nobles. He also increased the *taille*, a direct

The policies of Jean-Baptiste Colbert (1619–1683) transformed France into a major commercial power. [Erich Lessing/Art Resource, N.Y.]

tax on the peasantry and a major source of royal income.

This kind of close government control of the economy came to be known as *mercantilism* (a term invented by later critics of the policy). Its aim was to maximize foreign exports and internal reserves of bullion, the gold and silver necessary for making war. Modern scholars argue that Colbert overcontrolled the French economy and cite his "paternalism" as a major reason for the failure of French colonies in the New World. Be that as it may, his policies unquestionably transformed France into a major commercial power, with foreign bases in Africa, in India, and in the Americas, from Canada to the Caribbean.

Louis's army, about a quarter of a million strong, was the creation of Michel Tellier and his more famous son, the marquis of Louvois (1641–1691). Louis's war minister from 1677 to 1691, Louvois was a superior military tactician.

Before Louvois, the French army had been an amalgam of local recruits and mercenaries, uncoordinated groups whose loyalty could not always be counted on. Without regular pay or a way to supply their everyday needs, troops often lived by pillage. Louvois instituted good salaries and improved discipline, making soldiering a respectable profession. He limited military commissions and introduced a system of promotion by merit, bringing dedicated fighters into the ranks. Enlistment was for four years and was restricted to single men. *Intendants*, the king's ubiquitous civil servants, monitored conduct at all levels.

Because it was well disciplined, this new, large, and powerful standing army had considerable public support. Unlike its undisciplined predecessor, the new army no longer threatened the lives, homes, or well-being of the people it was supposed to protect. It thus provides an excellent example of the kinds of benefits many saw in the growing authority of the central monarchy.

What Louvois was to military organization, Sebastien Vauban (1633–1707) was to military engineering. He perfected the arts of fortifying and besieging towns. He also devised the system of trench warfare and developed the concept of defensive frontiers that remained basic to military tactics through World War I.

THE WAR OF DEVOLUTION Louis's first great foreign adventure was the War of Devolution (1667–1668). It was fought, as would be the later and more devastating War of the Spanish Succession, over Louis's claim to the Spanish Belgian provinces through his wife, Marie Thérèse (1638–1683). According to the terms of the Treaty of the Pyrenees (1659), Marie had renounced her claim to the Spanish succession on condition that a 500,000-crown dowry be paid to Louis within eighteen months of the marriage, a condition that was not met. When Philip IV of Spain died in September 1665, he left all his lands to his sickly four-year-old son by a second marriage, Charles II (r. 1665–1700), and explicitly denied any lands to his daughter. Louis had always harbored the hope of turning the marriage to territorial gain and even before Philip's death had argued that Marie was entitled to a portion of the inheritance.

Louis had a legal argument on his side, which gave the war its name. He maintained that in certain regions of Brabant and Flanders, which were part of the Spanish inheritance, property "devolved" to the children of a first marriage rather than to those of a second. Therefore, Marie had a higher claim than Charles II to these regions. Although

Throughout the age of the splendor at the court of Louis XIV millions of French peasants lived lives of poverty and hardship, as depicted in this 1640 painting, Peasant Family *by Louis LeNain. [Erich Lessing/Art Resource, N.Y.]*

such regional laws could hardly bind the king of Spain, Louis was not deterred from sending his armies, under the viscount of Turenne, into Flanders and the Franche-Comté in 1667. In response to this aggression, England, Sweden, and the United Provinces of Holland formed the Triple Alliance, a force sufficient to compel Louis to agree to peace under the terms in the Treaty of Aix-la-Chapelle (1668). According to the treaty, he gained control of certain towns bordering the Spanish Netherlands. (See Map 13–2.)

INVASION OF THE NETHERLANDS In 1670, with the signing of the Treaty of Dover, England and France became allies against the Dutch. Without the English, the Triple Alliance crumbled. This left Louis in a stronger position to invade the Netherlands for a second time, which he did in 1672. This time he aimed directly at Holland, which had organized the Triple Alliance in 1667, foiling French designs in Flanders. Dutch gloating after the Treaty of Aix-la-Chapelle had mightily offended Louis. Such cartoons as one depicting the sun (Louis was called the "Sun King") eclipsed by a great moon of Dutch cheese distressed him. Without neutralizing Holland, he knew he could never hope to acquire land in the Spanish Netherlands, much less fulfill his dreams of European hegemony.

Louis's successful invasion of the United Provinces in 1672 brought the downfall of Dutch statesmen Jan and Cornelius De Witt. Replacing them was the twenty-seven-year-old Prince of Orange, destined after 1689 to become King William III of England. Orange was the great-grandson of William the Silent, who had repulsed Philip II and dashed Spanish hopes of dominating the Netherlands in the sixteenth century.

Orange, an unpretentious Calvinist, who was in almost every way Louis's opposite, galvanized the seven provinces into a fierce fighting unit. In 1673 he united the Holy Roman Emperor, Spain, Lorraine, and Brandenburg in an alliance against Louis. His enemies now saw the French king as a "Christian Turk," a menace to the whole of western Europe, Catholic and Protestant alike. In the ensuing warfare, both sides experienced gains and losses. Louis lost his ablest generals, Turenne and Condé, in 1675, but a victory by Admiral Duquesne over the Dutch fleet in 1676 gave France control of the Mediterranean. The Peace of Nijmwegen, signed with different parties in successive years (1678, 1679), ended the hostilities of this second war. There were various minor territorial adjustments but no clear victor except the United Netherlands, which retained all of its territory.

Revocation of the Edict of Nantes

In the decade after his invasion of the Netherlands, Louis made his second major move to assure religious conformity. Following the proclamation of the Edict of Nantes in 1598, relations between the great Catholic majority (nine-tenths of the French population) and the Protestant minority remained hostile. There were about 1.75 million Huguenots in France in the 1660s, but their numbers were declin-

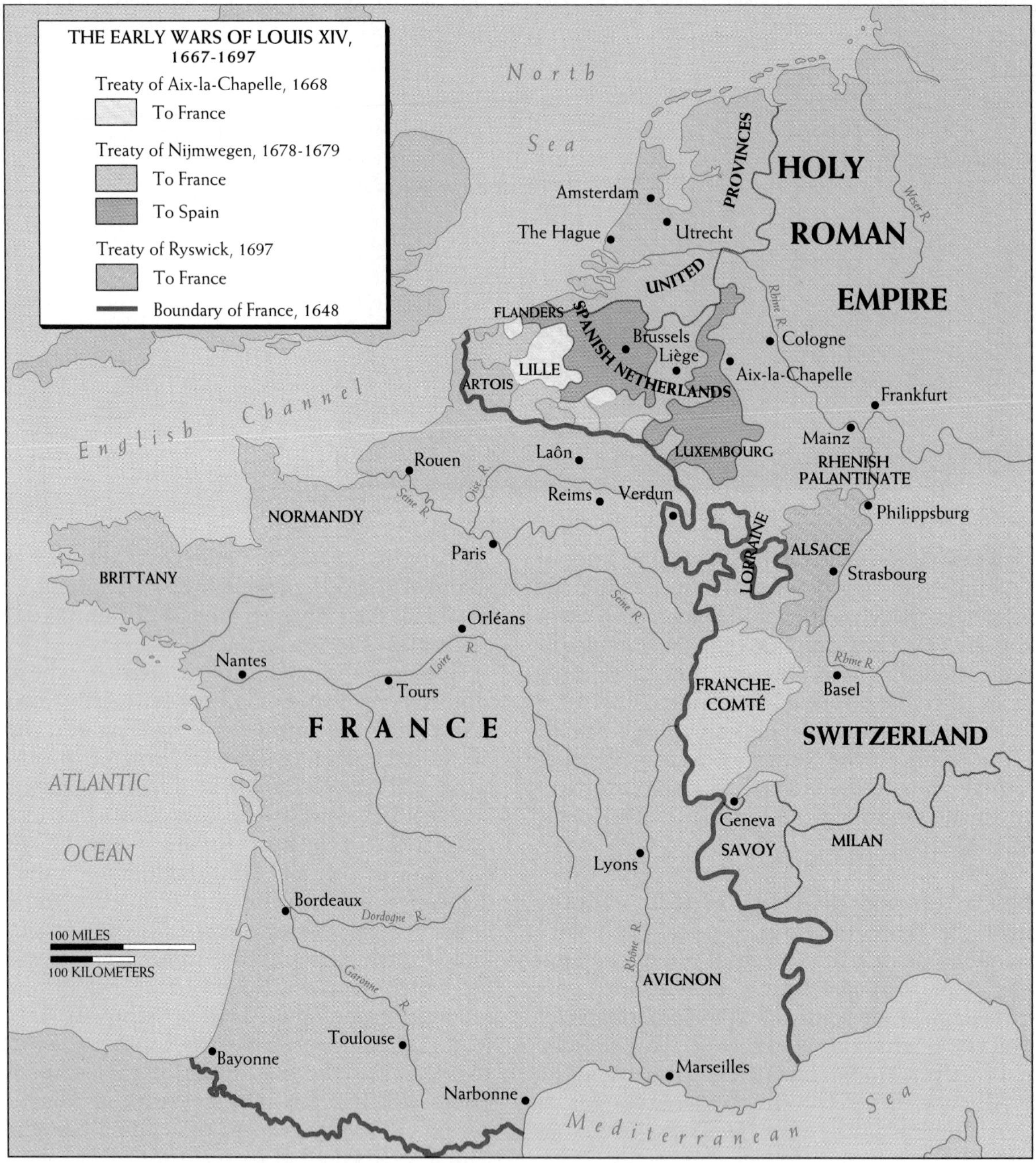

Map 13–2 The Wars of Louis XIV *This map shows the territorial changes resulting from Louis XIV's first three major wars. The War of the Spanish Succession was yet to come.*

ing in the second half of the seventeenth century. The French Catholic Church had long denounced Calvinists as heretical and treasonous and had supported their persecution as both pious and patriotic.

Following the Peace of Nijmwegen in 1678–1679, which halted for the moment his aggression in Europe, Louis launched a methodical government campaign against the French Huguenots in a determined effort to unify France religiously. He hounded the Huguenots out of public life, banning them from government office and excluding them from such professions as printing and medicine. He

Louis XIV Revokes the Edict of Nantes

Believing that a country could not be under one king and one law unless it was also under one religious system, Louis XIV stunned much of Europe in October 1685 by revoking the Edict of Nantes, which had protected the religious freedoms and civil rights of French Protestants since 1598. Compare this document to the one in Chapter 15 in which the elector of Brandenburg welcomes displaced French Protestants into his domains.

✦ *What specific actions does this declaration order against Protestants? Does it offer any incentives for Protestants to convert to Catholicism? How does this declaration compare with the English Test Act?*

Art. 1. Know that we . . . with our certain knowledge, full power and royal authority, have by this present, perpetual and irrevocable edict, suppressed and revoked the edict of the aforesaid king our grandfather, given at Nantes in the month of April, 1598, in all its extent . . . together with all the concessions made by [this] and other edicts, declarations, and decrees, to the people of the so-called Reformed religion, of whatever nature they be . . . and in consequence we desire . . . that all the temples of the people of the aforesaid so-called Reformed religion situated in our kingdom . . . should be demolished forthwith.

Art. 2. We forbid our subjects of the so-called Reformed religion to assemble any more for public worship of the above-mentioned religion. . . .

Art. 3. We likewise forbid all lords, of whatever rank they may be, to carry out heretical services in houses and fiefs . . . the penalty for . . . the said worship being confiscation of their body and possessions.

Art. 4. We order all ministers of the aforesaid so-called Reformed religion who do not wish to be converted and to embrace the Catholic, Apostolic, and Roman religion, to depart from our kingdom and the lands subject to us within fifteen days from the publication of our present edict . . . on pain of the galleys.

Art. 5. We desire that those among the said [Reformed] ministers who shall be converted [to the Catholic religion] shall continue to enjoy during their life, and their wives shall enjoy after their death as long as they remain widows, the same exemptions from taxation and billeting of soldiers, which they enjoyed while they fulfilled the function of ministers. . . .

Art. 8. With regard to children who shall be born to those of the aforesaid so-called Reformed religion, we desire that they be baptized by their parish priests. We command the fathers and mothers to send them to the churches for that purpose, on penalty of a fine of 500 livres or more if they fail to do so; and afterwards, the children shall be brought up in the Catholic, Apostolic, and Roman religion. . . .

Art. 10. All our subjects of the so-called Reformed religion, with their wives and children, are to be strongly and repeatedly prohibited from leaving our aforesaid kingdom . . . or of taking out . . . their possessions and effects. . . .

The members of the so-called Reformed religion, while awaiting God's pleasure to enlighten them like the others, can live in the towns and districts of our kingdom . . . and continue their occupation there, and enjoy their possessions . . . on condition . . . that they do not make public profession of [their religion].

S. Z. Ehler and John B. Morrall, ed. and trans., Church and State Through the Centuries: A Collection of Historic Documents *(New York: Biblo and Tannen, 1967), pp. 209–213.*

used subsidies and selective taxation to encourage Huguenots to convert to Catholicism. And in 1681 he bullied them by quartering his troops in their towns. In the final stage of the persecution, Louis revoked the Edict of Nantes in October 1685. As a result, Protestant churches and schools were closed, Protestant ministers exiled, nonconverting laity forced to be galley slaves, and Protestant children ceremonially baptized by Catholic priests.

The revocation of the Edict of Nantes was a major blunder. Louis was afterwards viewed in Protestant countries as a new Philip II, intent on a Catholic reconquest of the whole of Europe, who must be resisted at all costs. The revocation prompted the voluntary emigration of more than a quarter million French people, who formed new communities and joined the resistance to France in England, Germany, Holland, and the New World. Thousands of French Huguenots served in the army of Louis's archfoe, William of Orange, later King William III of England. Many of those who remained in France became part of an uncompromising guerilla resistance to the king. Despite the many domestic and foreign liabilities it brought him, Louis, to his death, considered the revocation to be his most pious act, one that placed God in his debt.

Louis's Later Wars

THE LEAGUE OF AUGSBURG AND THE NINE YEARS' WAR After the Treaty of Nijmwegen, Louis maintained his army at full strength and restlessly probed beyond his perimeters. In 1681 his forces conquered the free city of Strasbourg, prompting new defensive coalitions to form against him. One of these, the League of Augsburg, created in 1686 to resist French expansion into Germany, had grown by 1689 to include England, Spain, Sweden, the United Provinces, and the electorates of Bavaria, Saxony, and the Palatinate. It also had the support of the Austrian emperor Leopold. Between 1689 and 1697, the league and France battled each other in the Nine Years' War. During the same period, England and France struggled for control of North America in what came to be known as King William's War.

The Nine Years' War ended when stalemate and exhaustion forced both sides to accept an interim settlement. The Peace of Ryswick, signed in September 1697, was a triumph for William of Orange, now William III of England, and Emperor Leopold. It secured Holland's borders and thwarted Louis's expansion into Germany.

WAR OF THE SPANISH SUCCESSION: TREATIES OF UTRECHT AND RASTADT After Ryswick, Louis, who seemed to thrive on partial success, made still a fourth attempt to realize his grand design to dominate Europe. This time an unforeseen turn of events helped him. On November 1, 1700, Charles II of Spain, known as "the Sufferer" because of his genetic deformities and lingering illnesses, died.

Both Louis and the Austrian emperor Leopold had claims to the Spanish inheritance through their grandsons: Louis through his marriage to Marie Thérèse and Leopold through his marriage to her younger sister, Margaret Thérèse. Although Louis's grandson, Philip of Anjou, had the better claim (because Marie Thérèse was Margaret Thérèse's older sister), Marie Thérèse had renounced her right to the Spanish inheritance in the Treaty of the Pyrenees (1659), and the inheritance was expected to go to Leopold's grandson.

Louis nurtured fears that the Habsburgs would dominate Europe should they gain control of Spain as well as the Holy Roman Empire. Most of the nations of Europe, however, feared France more than the Habsburgs and determined to prevent a union of the French and Spanish crowns. As a result, before Charles II's death, negotiations began among the nations involved to partition his inheritance in a way that would preserve the existing balance of power.

Charles II upset these negotiations by leaving his entire inheritance to Philip of Anjou, Louis's grandson. At a stroke, Spain and its possessions had fallen to France. Although Louis had been party to the partition agreements that preceded Charles's death, he now saw God's hand in Charles's will; he chose to enforce its terms over those of the partition agreement. Philip of Anjou moved to Madrid and became Philip V of Spain. Louis, in what was interpreted as naked French aggression, sent his troops again into Flanders, this time to remove Dutch soldiers from Spanish territory in the name of the new French king of Spain. Louis also declared Spanish America open to French ships.

In September 1701, England, Holland, and the Holy Roman Empire formed the Grand Alliance to counter Louis. They sought to preserve the balance of power by once and for all securing Flanders as a neutral barrier between Holland and France and by gaining for the emperor his fair share of the Spanish inheritance. After the formation of the Grand Alliance, Louis increased the stakes of battle by recognizing the claim of James Edward, the son of James II of England, to the English throne.

In 1701 the thirteen-year War of the Spanish Succession (1701–1714) began, and once again total war enveloped western Europe. France, for the first time, went to war with inadequate finances, a poorly equipped army, and mediocre military leadership. The English, in contrast, had advanced weaponry (flintlock rifles, paper cartridges, and ring bayonets) and superior tactics (thin, maneuverable troop columns rather than the traditional deep ones). John Churchill, the duke of Marlborough, who succeeded William of Orange as military leader of the alliance, bested Louis's soldiers in every major engagement. He routed French armies at Blenheim in August 1704 and on the plain of Ramillies in 1706—two decisive battles of the war. In 1708–1709 famine, revolts, and uncollectible taxes tore France apart internally. Despair pervaded the French court. Louis wondered aloud how God could forsake one who had done so much for him.

Though ready to make peace in 1709, Louis could not bring himself to accept the stiff terms of the alliance. These included a demand that he transfer all Spanish possessions to the emperor's grandson Charles and remove Philip V from Madrid. Hostilities continued, and a clash of forces at Malplaquet (September 1709) left carnage on the battlefield unsurpassed until modern times.

France finally signed an armistice with England at Utrecht in July 1713 and concluded hostilities with Holland and the emperor in the Treaty of Rastadt in March 1714. This agreement confirmed Philip V as king of Spain but gave Gibraltar to England, making it a Mediterranean power. (See Map 13–3.) It also won Louis's recognition of the right of the House of Hanover to accede to the English throne.

Politically, the eighteenth century would belong to England as the sixteenth had belonged to Spain and the seventeenth to France. Although France remained intact and strong, the realization of Louis XIV's territorial ambitions had to await the rise of Napoleon Bonaparte. On his deathbed on September 1, 1715, Louis fittingly warned his heir, the *dauphin*, not to imitate his love of buildings and his liking for war.

The Reign of Louis XIV (1643–1715)

1643	Louis ascends the French throne at the age of 5
1643–1661	Cardinal Mazarin directs the French government
1648	Peace of Westphalia
1649–1652	The *Fronde* revolt
1653	The pope declares Jansenism a heresy
1659	Treaty of Pyren´ees between France and Spain
1660	Papal ban on Jansenists enforced in France
1661	Louis commences personal rule
1667–1668	War of Devolution
1670	Secret Treaty of Dover between France and Great Britain
1672–1679	French war against the Netherlands
1685	Louis revokes the Edict of Nantes
1689–1697	War of the League of Augsburg
1701	Outbreak of the War of the Spanish Succession
1713	Treaty of Utrecht between France and Great Britain
1714	Treaty of Rastatt between France and Spain
1715	Death of Louis XIV

Louis XIV's Legacy

Louis XIV left France a mixed legacy. His wars had brought widespread death and destruction, and his armies had shelled civilian populations. Although the monarchy was still strong at his death, it was more feared than admired. Its finances were insecure and dependent on debt. Continued warfare in the eighteenth century would weaken its finances further, leading eventually to the crises that sparked the French Revolution. Louis's policies of centralization would later make it difficult for France to develop effective institutions of representation and self-government. The aristocracy, after its years of domestication at Versailles, would have difficulty providing the nation with effective leaders and ministers.

Yet Louis's reign also had a positive side. He may have loved war too much, but he also built the magnificent palace of Versailles and brought a new majesty to France. He skillfully manipulated the fractious French aristocracy and bourgeoisie, he elevated skilled and trustworthy ministers, councillors, and *intendants,* and he created a new French Empire by expanding trade into Asia and colonizing North America.

Louis's rule was not so absolute as to exert oppressive control over the daily lives of his sub-

MAP 13–3 EUROPE IN 1714 *The War of the Spanish Succession ended in the year before the death of the aged Louis XIV. By then France and Spain, although not united, were both ruled by members of the Bourbon family, and Spain had lost its non-Iberian possessions.*

jects as in the police states of the nineteenth and twentieth centuries. His absolutism functioned primarily in the classic areas of European state action—the making of war and peace, the regulation of religion, and the oversight of economic activity. Even at the height of his power, local institutions, some controlled by townspeople and others by nobles, continued to exert administrative authority at the local level. The king and his ministers supported the high status and tax exemptions of these local elites. But in contrast to the Stuart kings of England, Louis firmly prevented them from capturing or significantly limiting his authority on the national level. Not until the French monarchy was so weakened by financial crisis at the end of the eighteenth century would it succumb to demands for a more representative form of government.

The foreign policy of Louis XIV brought warfare to all of Europe. This eighteenth-century painting by Benjamin West memorializes the British victory over France in the battle of La Hogue in 1692. [National Gallery of Art]

✦

In the seventeenth century, England and France developed divergent forms of government. England became the model for parliamentary monarchy, France for absolute monarchy.

The politically active English elite—the nobility along with the wealthy landowning and commercial classes—struggled throughout the century to limit the authority of rulers—including Oliver Cromwell as well as the Stuart monarchs—over local interests. In the process, they articulated a political philosophy that stressed the need to prevent the central concentration of political power. The Bill of Rights of 1689 and the Toleration Act following the Glorious Revolution of William and Mary seemed to achieve the goals of this philosophy. These acts brought neither democracy nor full religious freedom in a modern sense; the Bill of Rights protected only the privileged, not all the English people, and the Toleration Act outlawed Catholics and Unitarians. Still, they firmly established representative government in England and extended legal recognition, at least in principle, to a variety of religious beliefs. The Bill of Rights required the monarch to call Parliament regularly.

In France, by contrast, the monarchy remained supreme. Although the king had to mollify privileged local elites, by considering the interests of the nobility and the traditional rights of towns and regions, France had no national institution like Parliament through which he had to govern. Louis XIV was able, on his own authority, to fund the largest army in Europe. He could and did crush religious dissent. His own propaganda and the fear of his adversaries may have led to an exaggerated view of Louis's power, but his reign nonetheless provided a model of effective centralized power that later continental rulers tried to follow.

Review Questions

1. By the end of the seventeenth century, England and France had different systems of government with different religious policies. What were the main differences? Similarities? Why did each nation develop as it did? How much did the particular personalities of the rulers of each nation determine the manner in which their political institutions emerged?
2. Why did the English king and Parliament come into conflict in the 1640s? What were the most important issues behind the war between them and who bears more responsibility for it? What role did religion play in the conflict?
3. What was the Glorious Revolution and why did it take place? What were James II's mistakes and what were the issues involved in the events of 1688? What kind of settlement emerged from the revolution? How did England in 1700 differ from England in 1600?
4. Discuss the development of absolutism in France. What policies of Henry IV and Louis XIII were essential in creating the absolute monarchy?
5. What were the chief ways Louis XIV consolidated his monarchy? What limits were there on his authority? What was Louis's religious policy?
6. Assess the success of Louis XIV's foreign policy. What were his aims? Were they realistic? To what extent did he attain them?

Suggested Readings

M. Ashley, *England in the Seventeenth Century* (1980). Readable survey.

Robert Ashton, *Counter-Revolution: The Second Civil War and Its Origins, 1646–1648* (1995). A major examination of the resumption of civil conflict in England that ended with the abolition of the monarchy, House of Lords, and established church.

W. Beik, *Absolutism and Society in Seventeenth-Century France* (1985). An important study that questions the extent of royal power.

J. Bergin, *Cardinal Richelieu: Power and the Pursuit of Wealth* (1985). Considers the role of finance and private wealth in the rise of Richelieu.

R. Bonney, *Political Change in France Under Richelieu and Mazarin, 1624–1661* (1978). A careful examination of how these two cardinals lay the foundation for Louis XIV's absolutism.

R. Briggs, *Early Modern France, 1560–1715* (1977). A useful brief survey.

G. Burgess, *Absolute Monarchy and the Stuart Constitution* (1996). A new study that challenges many of the traditional interpretive categories.

P. Burke, *The Fabrication of Louis XIV* (1992). Examines the manner in which the public image of Louis XIV was forged in art.

P. Collinson, *The Religion of Protestants: The Church in English Society 1559–1625* (1982). The best introduction to Puritanism.

B. Coward, *Cromwell* (1991). A brief biography.

R. S. Dunn, *The Age of Religious Wars, 1559–1715* (1979). Lucid survey setting the conflicting political systems of France and England in larger perspective.

D. Hirst, *Authority and Conflict: England 1603–1658* (1986). Scholarly survey integrating history and historiography.

R. Hutton, *Charles the Second, King of England, Scotland, and Ireland* (1989). Replaces all previous biographies.

P. Lake, *Anglicans and Puritans: Presbyterianism and English Conformist Thought from Whitgift to Hooker* (1988). An important study of religious thought.

R. Lockyer, *Buckingham* (1984). Biography of the English court favorite.

R. Mettam, *Power and Faction in Louis XIV's France* (1988). Examines the political intricacies of the reign and suggests the limits to absolutism.

G. Parker, *Europe in Crisis 1598–1648* (1979). Examines the entire scope of early seventeenth-century Europe.

O. Ranum, *The Fronde: A French Revolution, 1648–1652* (1993). The best recent work on the subject.

D. L. Rubin (Ed.), *The Sun King: The Ascendancy of French Culture During the Reign of Louis XIV* (1992). A collection of useful essays.

C. Russell, *The Fall of the English Monarchies, 1637–1642* (1991). A major revisionist account, which should be read with Stone's book.

K. Sharpe, *The Personal Rule of Charles I* (1992). A major narrative work.

J. Spur, *The Restoration Church of England, 1646–1689* (1992). Now the standard work on this subject.

L. Stone, *The Causes of the English Revolution 1529–1642* (1972). Brief survey stressing social history and ruminating over historians and historical method.

V. Tapié, *France in the Age of Louis XIII and Richelieu* (1984). A narrative account.

G. TREASURE, *Mazarin: The Crisis of Absolutism in France* (1996). An examination not only of Mazarin, but also of the larger national and international background.

N. TYACKE, *Anti-Calvinists: The Rise of English Arminianism c. 1590–1640* (1987). The most important recent study of Archbishop Laud's policies and his predecessors.

D. UNDERDOWN, *Fire from Heaven: Life in an English Town in the Seventeenth Century* (1992). A lively account of the manner in which a single English town experienced the religious and political events of the century.

M. WALZER, *The Revolution of the Saints: A Study in the Origins of Radical Politics* (1965). Effort to relate ideas and politics that depicts Puritans as true revolutionaries.

J. B. WOLF, *Louis XIV* (1968). Very detailed political biography.

CHAPTER 14

Nicolaus Copernicus's revolutionary view of the universe, with the sun in the center, is summarized in this diagram from his De Revolutionibus Orbium Coelestium (On the Revolutions of Heavenly Bodies), *published in 1543. [Library of the Collegium Maius. Collegium Maius, Cracow, Poland. Erich Lessing/Art Resource]*

New Directions in Thought and Culture in the Sixteenth and Seventeenth Centuries

KEY TOPICS

- The astronomical theories of Copernicus, Brahe, Kepler, Galileo, and Newton and the emergence of the scientific worldview
- Witchcraft and witch hunts
- The literary imagination in a changing world
- The philosophical foundations of modern thought

The sixteenth and seventeenth centuries witnessed a sweeping change in the scientific view of the universe. An Earth-centered picture gave way to one in which the Earth was only another planet orbiting about the sun. The sun itself became one of millions of stars. This transformation of humankind's perception of its place in the larger scheme of things led to a profound rethinking of moral and religious matters as well as of scientific theory. Faith and reason needed new modes of reconciliation, as did faith and science. The new ideas and methods of science challenged modes of thought associated with medieval times and Scholasticism. The new outlook on physical nature touched the literary imagination, and religious thinkers had to reconsider many traditional ideas. Philosophers applied rational, scientific thought to the realm of politics. Some supported absolutism; others, parliamentary systems.

The new scientific concepts and the methods of their construction were so impressive that they set the standard for assessing the validity of knowledge in the Western world thereafter. Perhaps no single intellectual development proved to be more significant for the future of European and Western civilization.

Side by side with enlightenment and science, however, came a new wave of superstition and persecution. The changing world of religion and politics also created profound fear and anxiety among both the simple and the learned, resulting in Europe's worst witch hunts.

The Scientific Revolution

The process by which the new view of the universe and of scientific knowledge came to be established is normally termed the *Scientific Revolution.* This metaphor must be used carefully, however. The word *revolution* normally denotes rapid political change involving large numbers of people. The Scientific Revolution was not rapid, nor did it involve more than a few hundred human beings. It was a complex movement with many false starts and many brilliant people with wrong as well as useful ideas. It took place in the studies and the crude laboratories of thinkers in Poland, Italy, Bohemia, France, and Great Britain.

The Scientific Revolution stemmed from two major tendencies. The first, illustrated by Nicolaus Copernicus, was the imposition of important small changes on existing models of thought. The second, embodied by Francis Bacon, was the desire to pose new kinds of questions and to use new methods of investigation. In both cases, scientific thought changed current and traditional opinions in other fields.

Nicolaus Copernicus: Rejection of an Earth-Centered Universe

Nicolaus Copernicus (1473–1543) was a Polish astronomer who enjoyed a high reputation throughout his life. He had been educated in Italy and corresponded with other astronomers throughout Europe. He had not been known, however, for strikingly original or unorthodox thought. In 1543, the year of his death, Copernicus published *On the Revolutions of the Heavenly Spheres*. Because he died near the time of publication, the fortunes of his work are not the story of one person's crusade for progressive science. Copernicus's book was "a revolution-making rather than a revolutionary text."[1] What Copernicus did was to provide an intellectual springboard for a complete criticism of the then-dominant view of the position of the Earth in the universe.

The Ptolemaic System At the time of Copernicus, the standard explanation of the place of the Earth in the heavens was that associated with Ptolemy and his work entitled the *Almagest* (150 C.E.). Commentators on the original work had developed several alternative Ptolemaic systems over the centuries. Most of these assumed that the Earth was the center of the universe. Above the Earth lay a series of crystalline spheres, one of which contained the moon, another the sun, and still others the planets and the stars. This was the astronomy found in such works as Dante's *Divine Comedy*. At the outer regions of these spheres lay the realm of God and the angels. Aristotelian physics provided the intellectual underpinnings of the Ptolemaic systems. The Earth had to be the center because of its heaviness. The stars and the other heavenly bodies had to be enclosed in the crystalline spheres so that they could move. Nothing could move unless something was actually moving it. The state of rest was natural; motion was the condition that required explanation.

Numerous problems were associated with this system, and these had long been recognized. The most important was the observed motions of the planets, which included noncircular patterns around the Earth. At certain times the planets actually appeared to be going backward. The Ptolemaic systems explained these strange motions primarily through epicycles. An epicycle is an orbit upon an orbit, like a spinning jewel on a ring. The planets were said to make a second revolution in an orbit tangent to their primary orbit around the Earth. Other intellectual but nonobservational difficulties related to the immense speed at which the spheres had to move around the Earth. To say the least, the Ptolemaic systems were cluttered. They were effective, however, as long as one assumed Aristotelian physics and the Christian belief that the Earth rested at the center of the created universe.

Copernicus's Universe Copernicus's *On the Revolutions of the Heavenly Spheres* challenged this picture in the most conservative manner possible. It suggested that if the Earth were assumed to move about the sun in a circle, many of the difficulties with the Ptolemaic systems would disappear or become simpler. Although not wholly eliminated, the number of epicycles would be somewhat fewer. The motive behind this shift away from the Earth-

[1]Thomas S. Kuhn, *The Copernican Revolution: Planetary Astronomy in the Development of Western Thought* (New York: Vintage, 1959), p. 135.

centered universe was to find a solution to the problems of planetary motion. By allowing the Earth to move around the sun, Copernicus was able to construct a more mathematically elegant basis for astronomy. He had been discontented with the traditional system because it was mathematically clumsy and inconsistent. The primary appeal of his new system was its mathematical aesthetics. With

Copernicus Ascribes Movement to the Earth

Copernicus published De Revolutionibus Orbium Caelestium *(On the Revolutions of the Heavenly Spheres) in 1543. In his preface, addressed to Pope Paul III, he explained what had led him to think that the Earth moved around the sun and what he thought were some of the scientific consequences of the new theory.*

✦ *How does Copernicus justify his argument to the pope? How important was historical precedent and tradition to the pope? Might Copernicus have thought that the pope would be especially susceptible to such argument, even though what Copernicus proposed (the movement of the Earth) contradicted the Bible?*

I may well presume, most Holy Father, that certain people, as soon as they hear that in this book about the Revolutions of the Spheres of the Universe I ascribe movement to the Earthly globe, will cry out that, holding such views, I should at once be hissed off the stage. . . .

So I should like your Holiness to know that I was induced to think of a method of computing the motions of the spheres by nothing else than the knowledge that the Mathematicians [who had previously considered the problem] are inconsistent in these investigations.

For, first, the mathematicians are so unsure of the movements of the Sun and Moon that they cannot even explain or observe the constant length of the seasonal year. Secondly, in determining the motions of these and of the other five planets, they use neither the same principles and hypotheses nor the same demonstrations of the apparent motions and revolutions. . . . Nor have they been able thereby to discern or deduce the principal thing—namely the shape of the Universe and the unchangeable symmetry of its parts. . . .

I pondered long upon this uncertainty of mathematical tradition in establishing the motions of the system of the spheres. At last I began to chafe that philosophers could by no means agree on any one certain theory of the mechanism of the Universe, wrought for us by a supremely good and orderly Creator. . . . I therefore took pains to read again the works of all the philosophers on whom I could lay hand to seek out whether any of them had ever supposed that the motions of the spheres were other than those demanded by the [Ptolemaic] mathematical schools. I found first in Cicero that Hicetas [of Syracuse, fifth century B.C.] had realized that the Earth moved. Afterwards I found in Plutarch that certain others had held the like opinion. . . .

Thus assuming motions, which in my work I ascribe to the Earth, by long and frequent observations I have at last discovered that, if the motions of the rest of the planets be brought into relation with the circulation of the Earth and be reckoned in proportion to the circles of each planet, not only do their phenomena presently ensue, but the orders and magnitudes of all stars and spheres, nay the heavens themselves, become so bound together that nothing in any part thereof could be moved from its place without producing confusion of all the other parts of the Universe as a whole.

As quoted in Thomas S. Kuhn, The Copernican Revolution: Planetary Astronomy in the Development of Western Thought *(New York: Vintage Books, 1959), pp. 137–139, 141–142.*

the sun at the center of the universe, mathematical astronomy would make more sense. A change in the conception of the position of the Earth meant that the planets were actually moving in circular orbits and only seemed to be doing otherwise because of the position of the observers on Earth.

Except for this modification in the position of the Earth, Copernicus retained Ptolemaic ideas in most of the other parts of his book. The path of the planets remained circular. Genuine epicycles still existed in the heavens. His system was no more accurate than the existing ones for predicting the location of the planets. He had used no new evidence. The major impact of his work was to provide another way of confronting some of the difficulties inherent in Ptolemaic astronomy. It did not immediately replace the old astronomy, but it allowed other people who were also discontented with the Ptolemaic systems to think in new directions.

Copernicus's concern about the relationship between mathematics and the observed behavior of planets is an example of the single most important factor in the developing new science: the fusion of mathematics with empirical data and observation. Mathematics provided the model to which the new scientific thought would conform; new empirical evidence helped persuade the learned public of its validity.

Tycho Brahe in the Uranienburg observatory on the Danish island of Hven (1587). Brahe made the most important observations of the stars since antiquity. Kepler used his data to solve the problem of planetary motion in a way that supported Copernicus's sun-centered view of the universe. Ironically, Brahe himself had opposed Copernicus's view. [Bildarchiv Preussischer Kulturbesitz]

Tycho Brahe and Johannes Kepler: New Scientific Observations

The next major step toward the conception of a sun-centered system was taken by Tycho Brahe (1546–1601). He actually spent most of his life opposing Copernicus and advocating a different kind of Earth-centered system. He suggested that the moon and the sun revolved around the Earth and that the other planets revolved around the sun. In attacking Copernicus, however, he gave the latter's ideas more publicity. More important, this Danish astronomer's major weapon against Copernican astronomy was a series of new naked-eye astronomical observations. Brahe constructed the most accurate tables of observations that had been drawn up for centuries.

When Brahe died, these tables came into the possession of Johannes Kepler (1571–1630), a German astronomer. Kepler was a convinced Copernican, but his reasons for taking that position were not scientific. Kepler was deeply influenced by Renaissance Neoplatonism, which held the sun in special honor. He was determined to find mathematical harmonies in Brahe's numbers that would support a sun-centered universe. After much work Kepler discovered that to keep the sun at the center of things, he must abandon the Copernican concept of circular orbits. The mathematical relationships that emerged from a consideration of Brahe's observations suggested that the orbits of the planets were elliptical. Kepler published his findings in his 1609 book, entitled *On the Motion of Mars*. He had solved the problem of planetary orbits by using Copernicus's sun-centered universe and Brahe's empirical data.

Kepler had also defined a new problem. None of the available theories could explain why the planetary orbits were elliptical. That solution awaited the work of Sir Isaac Newton.

Galileo Galilei: A Universe of Mathematical Laws

From Copernicus to Brahe to Kepler, there had been little new information about the heavens that might not have been known to Ptolemy. In the same year that Kepler published his volume on Mars, however, an Italian scientist named Galileo Galilei (1564–1642) first turned a telescope on the heavens. Through that recently invented instrument he saw stars where none had been known to exist, mountains on the moon, spots moving across the sun, and moons orbiting Jupiter. The heavens were far more complex than anyone had formerly suspected. None of these discoveries proved that the Earth orbited the sun, but they did suggest the complete inadequacy of the Ptolemaic system. It simply could not accommodate itself to all these new phenomena. Some of Galileo's colleagues at the University of Padua were so unnerved that they refused to look through the telescope.

Galileo publicized his findings and arguments for the Copernican system in numerous works, the most famous of which was his *Dialogues on the Two Chief Systems of the World* (1632). This book brought down on him the condemnation of the Roman Catholic Church. He was compelled to recant his opinions. He is reputed, however, to have muttered after the recantation, "*E pur si muove*," or "it [the Earth] still moves."

Galileo's discoveries and his popularization of the Copernican system were of secondary importance in his life work. His most important achievement was to articulate the concept of a universe totally subject to mathematical laws. More than any other writer of the century, he argued that nature in its most minute details displayed mathematical regularity:

> Philosophy is written in that great book which ever lies before our eyes—I mean the universe—but we cannot understand it if we do not first learn the language and grasp the symbols in which it is written. This book is written in the mathematical language, and the symbols are triangles, circles, and other geometrical figures, without whose help it is impossible to comprehend a single word of it; without which one wanders through a dark labyrinth.[2]

The telescope with which Galileo worked after 1609. He observed Earth's moon and the cyclical phases of the planet Venus and discovered the most prominent moons of Jupiter. These observations had revolutionary intellectual and theological implications in the seventeenth century. [Istituto e Museo de Storia della Scienza, Scala/Art Resource, N.Y.]

The universe was rational; however, its rationality was not that of scholastic logic but of mathe-

[2]Quoted in E. A. Burtt, *The Metaphysical Foundations of Modern Physical Science* (Garden City, N.Y.: Anchor-Doubleday, 1954), p. 75.

matics. Copernicus had thought that the heavens conformed to mathematical regularity; Galileo saw this regularity throughout all physical nature. He believed that the smallest atom behaved with the same mathematical precision as the largest heavenly sphere.

A world of quantity was replacing one of qualities. All aspects of the world—including color, beauty, and taste—would increasingly be described in terms of the mathematical relationships among quantities. Mathematical models would eventually be applied even to social relations. Nature was cold, rational, mathematical, and mechanistic. What was real and lasting was what was mathematically measurable. Few intellectual shifts have wrought such momentous changes for Western civilization.

Isaac Newton: The Laws of Gravitation

Englishman Isaac Newton (1642–1727) drew on the work of his predecessors and his own brilliance to solve the major remaining problem of planetary motion and to establish a basis for physics that endured more than two centuries. The question that continued to perplex seventeenth-century scientists who accepted the theories of Copernicus, Kepler, and Galileo was how the planets and other heavenly bodies moved in an orderly fashion. The Ptolemaic and Aristotelian answer had been the crystalline spheres and a universe arranged in the order of the heaviness of its parts. Many unsatisfactory theories had been set forth to deal with the question.

In 1687 Newton published *The Mathematical Principles of Natural Philosophy*, better known by its Latin title of *Principia Mathematica*. Much of the research and thinking for this great work had taken place more than fifteen years earlier. Newton was heavily indebted to the work of Galileo and particularly to the latter's view that inertia applied to bodies both at rest and in motion. Galileo's mathematical bias permeated Newton's thought. Newton reasoned that the planets and all other physical objects in the universe moved through mutual attraction, or gravity. Every object in the universe affected every other object through gravity. The attraction of gravity explained why the planets moved in an orderly rather than a chaotic manner. He had found that "the force of gravity towards the whole planet did arise from and was compounded of the forces of gravity towards all its parts, and towards every one part was in the inverse proportion of the squares of the distances from the part."[3] Newton proved this relationship mathematically. He made no attempt to explain the nature of gravity itself.

Sir Isaac Newton discovered the mathematical and physical laws governing the force of gravity. Newton believed that religion and science were compatible and mutually supportive, and that the study of nature gave one a better understanding of the Creator. This portrait of Newton is by Sir Godfrey Kneller. [Bildarchiv Preussischer Kulturbesitz]

Newton was a great mathematical genius, but he also upheld the importance of empirical data and observation. Like Francis Bacon (see pages 499–501), he believed that one must observe phenomena before attempting to explain them. The final test of any theory or hypothesis for him was whether it described what could actually be observed. He was a great opponent of the rationalism of the French philosopher Descartes (see pages 501–502), which he believed included insufficient guards against error. As Newton's own theory of universal gravi-

[3]Quoted in A. Rupert Hall, *From Galileo to Newton, 1630–1720* (London: Fontana, 1970), p. 300.

Galileo Discusses the Relationship of Science and the Bible

The religious authorities were often critical of the discoveries and theories of sixteenth- and seventeenth-century science. For years before his condemnation by the Roman Catholic Church in 1633, Galileo had contended that scientific theory and religious piety were compatible. In his Letter to the Grand Duchess Christiana *(of Tuscany), written in 1615, he argued that God had revealed truth in both the Bible and physical nature and that the truth of physical nature did not contradict the Bible if the latter were properly understood.*

✦ *Is Galileo's argument based on science or theology? Did the church believe that nature was as much a revelation of God as the Bible? As Galileo describes them, which is the surer revelation of God, nature or the Bible? Why might the pope reject Galileo's argument?*

The reason produced for condemning the opinion that the Earth moves and the sun stands still is that in many places in the Bible one may read that the sun moves and the Earth stands still. . . .

With regard to this argument, I think in the first place that it is very pious to say and prudent to affirm that the holy Bible can never speak untruth—whenever its true meaning is understood. But I believe nobody will deny that it is often very abstruse, and may say things which are quite different from what its bare words signify. . . .

This being granted, I think that in discussions of physical problems we ought to begin not from the authority of scriptural passages, but from sense-experiences and necessary demonstrations; for the holy Bible and the phenomena of nature proceed alike from the divine Word, the former as the dictate of the Holy Ghost and the latter as the observant executrix of God's commands. It is necessary for the Bible, in order to be accommodated to the understanding of every man, to speak many things which appear to differ from the absolute truth so far as the bare meaning of the words is concerned. But Nature, on the other hand, is inexorable and immutable; she never transgresses the laws imposed upon her, or cares a whit whether her abstruse reasons and methods of operation are understandable to men. For that reason it appears that nothing physical which sense-experience sets before our eyes, or which necessary demonstrations prove to us, ought to be called in question (much less condemned) upon the testimony of biblical passages which may have some different meaning beneath their words. For the Bible is not chained in every expression to conditions as strict as those which govern all physical effects; nor is God any less excellently revealed in Nature's actions than in the sacred statements of the Bible. . . .

From this I do not mean to infer that we need not have an extraordinary esteem for the passages of holy Scripture. On the contrary, having arrived at any certainties in physics, we ought to utilize these as the most appropriate aids in the true exposition of the Bible and in the investigation of those meanings which are necessarily contained therein for these must be concordant with demonstrated truths. I should judge the authority of the Bible was designed to persuade men of those articles and propositions which, surpassing all human reasoning, could not be made credible by science, or by any other means than through the very mouth of the Holy Spirit. . . .

But I do not feel obliged to believe that the same God who has endowed us with senses, reason, and intellect has intended to forgo their use and by some other means to give us knowledge which we can attain by them.

Discoveries and Opinions of Galileo, *trans. and ed. by Stillman Drake (Garden City, N.Y.: Doubleday Anchor Books, 1957), pp. 181–183.*

Major Works of the Scientific Revolution

1543	*On the Revolutions of the Heavenly Spheres* (Copernicus)
1605	*The Advancement of Learning* (Bacon)
1609	*On the Motion of Mars* (Kepler)
1620	*Novum Organum* (Bacon)
1632	*Dialogues on the Two Chief Systems of the World* (Galileo)
1637	*Discourse on Method* (Descartes)
1687	*Principia Mathematica* (Newton)

tation became increasingly accepted, so too was Baconian empiricism.

Newton's Reconciliation of Science and Faith

With the work of Newton, the natural universe became a realm of law and regularity. Beliefs in spirits and divinities were no longer necessary to explain its operation. Thus, the Scientific Revolution liberated human beings from the fear of a chaotic or haphazard universe. Most of the scientists were very devout people. They saw in the new picture of physical nature a new picture also of God. The Creator of this rational, lawful nature must also be rational. To study nature was to come to a better understanding of that Creator. Science and religious faith were not only compatible but mutually supporting. As Newton wrote, "The main Business of Natural Philosophy is to argue from Phaenomena without feigning Hypothesis, and to deduce Causes from Effects, till we come to the very first Cause, which certainly is not mechanical."[4]

This reconciliation of faith and science allowed the new physics and astronomy to spread rapidly. At the very time when Europeans were finally tiring of the wars of religion, the new science provided the basis for a view of God that might lead away from irrational disputes and wars over religious doctrine. Faith in a rational God encouraged faith in the rationality of human beings and in their capacity to improve their lot once liberated from the traditions of the past. The Scientific Revolution provided the great model for the desirability of change and of criticism of inherited views. The new science, however, caused some people to feel that the mystery had been driven from the universe and that the rational Creator was less loving and less near to humankind than the God of earlier ages.

[4]Quoted in Franklin Baumer, *Main Currents of Western Thought*, 4th ed. (New Haven: Yale, 1978) p. 323.

Continuing Superstition: Witch Hunts and Panics

The new science by no means swept away all other thought. Traditional beliefs and fears long retained their hold on the culture. During the sixteenth and seventeenth centuries many Europeans remained preoccupied with sin, death, and the Devil. Religious people, including many among the learned and many who were sympathetic to the emerging scientific ideas, continued to believe in the power of magic and the occult. Until the end of the seventeenth century almost all Europeans in one way or another believed in the power of demons.

Nowhere is the dark side of early modern thought and culture better seen than in the witch hunts and panics that erupted in almost every Western land. Between 1400 and 1700, courts sentenced an estimated 70,000–100,000 people to death for harmful magic (*malificium*) and diabolical witchcraft. In addition to inflicting harm on their neighbors, these witches were said to attend mass meetings known as *sabbats*, to which they were believed to fly. They were also accused of indulging in sexual orgies with the Devil, who appeared at such gatherings in animal form, most often as a he-goat. Still other charges against them were cannibalism (they were alleged to be especially fond of small Christian children) and a variety of ritual acts and practices designed to insult every Christian belief and value.

Where did such beliefs come from, and how could seemingly enlightened people believe them? Their roots were in both popular and elite cultures, especially in clerical culture.

Village Origins

In village societies, so-called cunning folk played a positive role in helping people cope with calamity. People turned to them for help when such natural disasters as plague and famine struck or when such physical disabilities as lameness or inability to conceive offspring befell either humans or animals. The cunning folk provided consolation and gave people

Newton Contemplates the Nature of God

Isaac Newton believed there was a close relationship between his scientific theory and the truths of religion. He and many other scientists of his generation were convinced that the investigation of physical nature would lead to proofs of the existence of God. In this passage, taken from comments he added to later editions of the Principia Mathematica, *Newton explains how the character of planetary motion leads one to conclude that God exists.*

✦ *How do Newton's arguments for God's existence compare with those of Thomas Aquinas (see Chapter 8, page 292)? If the pope could accept Aquinas's arguments, why not also those of Galileo and Newton? Why is Newton, like Copernicus and Galileo before him, so convinced that science and religion are in harmony? Are they still "medieval" men, or did the times in which they lived force them to argue this way to justify their work?*

The six primary planets are revolved about the sun in circles concentric with the sun. . . . Ten moons are revolved about the earth, Jupiter, and Saturn in circles concentric with them . . .; but it is not to be conceived that mere mechanical causes could give birth to so many regular motions. . . . This most beautiful system of sun, planets, and comets could only proceed from the counsel and dominion of an intelligent and powerful Being. And if the fixed stars are the centers of other like systems, these, being formed by the like wise counsel, must be all subject to the dominion of One, especially since the light of the fixed stars is of the same nature with the light of the sun and from every system light passes into all the other systems; and lest the systems of the fixed stars should, by their gravity, fall on each other, he hath placed those systems at immense distances from one another.

This Being governs all things, not as the soul of the world, but as Lord over all; and on account of his dominion he is wont to be called "Lord God." . . . The word "God" usually signifies "Lord," but every lord is not a God. It is the dominion of a spiritual being which constitutes a God: a true, supreme, or imaginary dominion makes a true, supreme, or imaginary god. And from his true dominion it follows that the true God is a living, intelligent, and powerful Being; and, from his other perfections, that he is supreme or most perfect. He is eternal and infinite, omnipotent, and omniscient; that is, his duration reaches from eternity to eternity; his presence from infinity to infinity; he governs all things and knows all things that are or can be done. He is not eternity and infinity, but eternal and infinite; he is not duration or space, but he endures and is present. He endures forever and is everywhere present; and, by existing always and everywhere, he constitutes duration and space. . . . We have ideas of his attributes, but what the real substance of anything is we know not. . . . We know him only by his most wise and excellent contrivances of things and final causes; we admire him for his perfections, but we reverence and adore him on account of his dominion, for we adore him as his servants; and a god without dominion, providence, and final causes is nothing else but Fate and Nature.

H. S. Thayer, ed., Newton's Philosophy of Nature: Selections from His Writings *(New York: Hafner Press, 1974), pp. 42–44.*

hope that such natural calamities might be averted or reversed by magical means. In this way they provided an important service and kept village life moving forward.

Possession of magical powers, for good or ill, made one an important person within village society. Not surprisingly, claims to such powers most often were made by the people most in need of security and influence, namely, the old and the impoverished, especially single or widowed women. Witch beliefs in village society may also have been a way of defying urban Christian society's attempts to impose its laws and institutions on the countryside. From this perspective, village Satanism became a fanciful substitute for an impossible social revolt, a way of spurning the values of one's new masters. It is also possible, although unlikely, that witch beliefs in rural society had a foundation in local fertility cults, whose semipagan practices, designed to ensure good harvests, may have acquired the features of diabolical witchcraft under church persecution.

Influence of the Clergy

Popular belief in magic was the essential foundation of the great witch hunts of the sixteenth and seventeenth centuries. Had ordinary people not believed that certain gifted individuals could aid or harm others by magical means, and had they not been willing to make accusations, the hunts could never have occurred. Yet the contribution of learned

Three witches suspected of practicing harmful magic are burned alive on a pyre in Baden. On the left, two of them are shown feasting and cavorting with demons at a sabbat. *[Bildarchiv Preussischer Kulturbesitz]*

society was equally great. The Christian clergy also practiced magic, that of the holy sacraments, and the exorcism of demons had been one of their traditional functions within society. Fear of demons and the Devil, which the clergy actively encouraged, allowed the clergy to assert their moral authority over people and to enforce religious discipline and conformity.

In the late thirteenth century the church declared that only its priests possessed legitimate magical power. Since such power was not human, theologians reasoned, it had to come either from God or from the Devil. If it came from God, then it was properly confined to and exercised only on behalf of the church. Those who practiced magic outside the church evidently derived their power from the Devil. From such reasoning grew accusations of "pacts" between non-Christian magicians and Satan. This made the witch hunts a life-and-death struggle against Christian society's worst heretics and foes, those who had directly sworn allegiance to the Devil himself.

The church based its intolerance of magic outside its walls on sincere belief in and fear of the Devil. But attacking witches was also a way for established Christian society to extend its power and influence into new areas. To accuse, try, and execute witches was also a declaration of moral and political authority over a village or territory. As the cunning folk were local spiritual authorities, revered and feared by people, their removal became a major step in establishing a Christian beachhead in village society.

Role of Women

A good 80 percent of the victims of witch hunts were women, the vast majority between forty-five and sixty years of age and single. This fact has suggested to some that misogyny fueled the witch hunts. Based in male hatred and sexual fear of women, and occurring at a time when women threatened to break out from under male control, witch hunts, it is argued, were simply woman hunts. Older single women may, however, have been vulnerable for more basic social reasons. They were a largely dependent social group in need of public assistance and natural targets for the peculiar "social engineering" of the witch hunts. Some accused witches were women who sought to protect and empower themselves within their communities by claiming supernatural powers.

It may be, however, that gender played a largely circumstantial role. Because of their economic straits, more women than men laid claim to the supernatural powers that made them influential in village society. For this reason, they found themselves on the front lines in disproportionate numbers when the church declared war against all who practiced magic without its blessing. Also, the involvement of many of these women in midwifery associated them with the deaths of beloved wives and infants and thus made them targets of local resentment and accusations. Both the church and midwives' neighbors were prepared to think and say the worst about these women. It was a deadly combination.

Witch Panics

Why did the great witch panics occur in the second half of the sixteenth and early seventeenth centuries? The misfortune created by religious division and warfare were major factors. The new levels of violence exacerbated fears and hatreds and encouraged scapegoating. But political self-aggrandizement also played a role. As governments expanded and attempted to control their realms, they, like the Church, wanted to eliminate all competition for the loyalty of their subjects. Secular rulers as well as the pope could pronounce their competitors "devilish."

Some argue that the Reformation was responsible for the witch panics. Having weakened the traditional religious protections against demons and the Devil, while at the same time portraying them as still powerful, the Reformation is said to have forced people to protect themselves by executing perceived witches.

End of the Witch Hunts

Why did the witch hunts come to an end in the seventeenth century? Many factors played a role. The emergence of a new, more scientific worldview made it difficult to believe in the powers of witches. When in the seventeenth century mind and matter came to be viewed as two independent realities, words and thoughts lost the ability to affect things. A witch's curse was merely words. With advances in medicine and the beginning of insurance companies, people learned to rely on themselves when faced with natural calamity and physical affliction

Why More Women Than Men Are Witches

A classic of misogyny, The Hammer of Witches *(1486), written by two Dominican monks, Heinrich Krämer and Jacob Sprenger, was sanctioned by Pope Innocent VIII as an official guide to the church's detection and punishment of witches. Here Krämer and Sprenger explain why they believe that the great majority of witches are women rather than men.*

✦ *Why would two Dominican monks say such things about women? What are the biblical passages that they believe justify them? Do their descriptions have any basis in the actual behavior of women then? What is the rivalry between married and unmarried people that they refer to?*

Why are there more superstitious women than men? The first [reason] is that they are more credulous; and since the chief aim of the devil is to corrupt faith, therefore he rather attacks them. . . . The second reason is that women are naturally more impressionable and ready to receive the influence of a disembodied spirit. . . . The third reason is that they have slippery tongues and are unable to conceal from their fellow-women those things which by evil arts they know; and since they are weak, they find an easy and secret manner of vindicating themselves by witchcraft. . . . [Therefore] since women are feebler both in mind and body, it is not surprising that they should come more under the spell of witchcraft. For as regards intellect, or the understanding of spiritual things, they seem to be of a different nature from men, a fact which is vouched for by the logic of the authorities, backed by various examples from the Scriptures. . . .

But the natural reason [for woman's proclivity to witchcraft] is that she is more carnal than a man, as is clear from her many carnal abominations. And it should be noted that there was a defect in the formation of the first woman, since she was formed from a bent rib, that is, a rib of the breast, which is bent as it were in a contrary direction to a man. And since through this defect she is an imperfect animal, she always deceives. . . .

As to her other mental quality, her natural will, when she hates someone whom she formerly loved, then she seethes with anger and impatience in her whole soul, just as the tides of the sea are always heaving and boiling. . . .

Truly the most powerful cause which contributes to the increase of witches is the woeful rivalry between married folk and unmarried women and men. This [jealousy or rivalry exists] even among holy women, so what must it be among the others . . . ?

Just as through the first defect in their intelligence women are more prone [than men] to abjure the faith, so through their second defect of inordinate affections and passions they search for, brood over, and inflict various vengeances, either by witchcraft or by some other means. Wherefore it is no wonder that so great a number of witches exist in this sex. . . . [Indeed, witchcraft] is better called the heresy of witches than of wizards, since the name is taken from the more powerful party [that is, the greater number, who are women]. Blessed be the Highest who has so far preserved the male sex from so great a crime.

Malleus Maleficarum, *trans. by Montague Summers (Bungay, Suffolk: John Rodker, 1928), pp. 41–47.*

and no longer searched for supernatural causes and solutions. Witch hunts also tended to get out of hand. Accused witches sometimes alleged that important townspeople had also attended sabbats; even the judges could be so accused. At this point the trials ceased to serve the purposes of those who were conducting them. They not only became dysfunctional but threatened anarchy as well.

Although Protestants, like Catholics, hunted witches, the Reformation may also have contributed to an attitude of mind that put the Devil in a more manageable perspective. Protestants ridiculed the sacramental magic of the old church as superstition and directed their faith to a sovereign God absolutely supreme over time and eternity. Even the Devil was believed to serve God's purposes and acted only with his permission. Ultimately God was the only significant spiritual force in the universe. This belief made the Devil a less fearsome creature. "One little word can slay him," Luther wrote of the Devil in the great hymn of the Reformation.

Finally, the imaginative and philosophical literature of the sixteenth and seventeenth centuries (see below), while continuing to display concern for religion and belief in the supernatural, also suggested that human beings have a significant degree of control over their own lives and need not be constantly fearing demons and resorting to supernatural aid.

Literary Imagination in Transition

The world of the new science developed in the midst of a society where medieval outlooks and religious values remained very much alive. Literary figures of the same period often reflected both the new and the old. In Cervantes one sees a brilliant writer raising questions about the adequacy of medieval values of chivalry and honor and probing the nature of human perceptions of reality. Shakespeare's dramas provide an insight into virtually the entire range of late sixteenth- and early seventeenth-century English worldviews. John Milton could attempt to justify the ways of the Christian God to doubting human beings and in the same work have characters debate the adequacy of the Ptolemaic and Copernican systems. During the same years that Newton reached his deepest insights about nature, John Bunyan could write one of the classic works of simple Christian piety. It is the combination of past and future worldviews that makes the thought of the seventeenth century so remarkable and rich.

Miguel de Cervantes Saavedra: Rejection of Idealism

Miguel de Cervantes Saavedra (1547–1616), the author of Don Quixote, *considered by many to be Spain's greatest writer. [Art Resource, N.Y.]*

Spanish literature of the sixteenth and seventeenth centuries reflects the peculiar religious and political history of Spain in this period. Spain was a deeply Catholic country, and this was a major influence on its literature. Since the joint reign of Ferdinand and Isabella (1479–1504), the church had received the unqualified support of reigning political power. Although there was religious reform in Spain, a Protestant Reformation never occurred, thanks largely to the entrenched power of the church and the Inquisition.

A second influence on Spanish literature was the aggressive piety of Spanish rulers, and this intertwining of Catholic piety and political power underlay a third influence: preoccupation with medieval chivalric virtues—in particular, questions of honor and loyalty. The novels and plays of the period almost invariably focus on a special decision involving a character's reputation as his honor or loyalty is tested. In this regard Spanish literature may be said to have remained more Catholic and medieval than that of England and France, where major Protestant movements had occurred. Two of the most important Spanish writers in this period became priests (Lope de Vega and Pedro Calderón de la Barca). The one generally acknowledged to be the greatest Spanish writer of all time, Cervantes, was preoccupied in his work with the strengths and weaknesses of religious idealism.

Cervantes (1547–1616) had only a smattering of formal education. He educated himself by wide reading in popular literature and immersion in the "school of life." As a young man he worked in Rome for a Spanish cardinal. As a soldier he was decorated for gallantry in the Battle of Lepanto (1571). He also spent five years as a slave in Algiers after his ship was pirated in 1575. Later, while working as a tax collector, he was several times imprisoned for padding his accounts, and it was in prison that he began, in 1603, to write his most famous work, *Don Quixote.*

The first part of *Don Quixote* appeared in 1605. The intent of this work seems to have been to satirize the chivalric romances then popular in Spain. But Cervantes could not conceal his deep affection for the character he created as an object of ridicule, Don Quixote. The work is satire only on the surface and has remained as much an object of study by philosophers and theologians as by students of Spanish literature. Cervantes presented Don Quixote as a none-too-stable middle-aged man. Driven mad by reading too many chivalric romances, he had come to believe he was an aspiring knight who had to prove his worthiness by brave deeds. To this end, he donned a rusty suit of armor and chose for his inspiration a quite unworthy peasant girl (Dulcinea), whom he fancied to be a noble lady to whom he could, with honor, dedicate his life.

Don Quixote's foil—Sancho Panza, a clever, worldly-wise peasant who serves as his squire—watched with bemused skepticism as his lord did battle with a windmill (which he mistook for a dragon) and repeatedly made a fool of himself as he galloped across the countryside. The story ends tragically with Don Quixote's humiliating defeat by a well-meaning friend, who, disguised as a knight, bests Don Quixote in combat and forces him to renounce his quest for knighthood. The humiliated Don Quixote does not, however, come to his senses as a result. He returns sadly to his village to die a shamed and broken-hearted old man.

Throughout *Don Quixote,* Cervantes juxtaposes the down-to-Earth realism of Sancho Panza with the old-fashioned religious idealism of Don Quixote. The reader perceives that Cervantes admired the one as much as the other and meant to portray both as representing attitudes necessary for a happy life.

William Shakespeare: Dramatist of the Age

There is much less factual knowledge about Shakespeare (1564–1616) than one would expect of the greatest playwright in the English language. He married at the early age of eighteen, in 1582, and he and his wife, Anne Hathaway, were the parents of three children (including twins) by 1585. He apparently worked as a schoolteacher for a time and in this capacity gained his broad knowledge of Renaissance learning and literature. His own reading and enthusiasm for the learning of his day are manifest in the many literary allusions that appear in his plays.

Shakespeare lived the life of a country gentleman. There is none of the Puritan distress over worldliness in his work. He took the new commercialism and the bawdy pleasures of the Elizabethan Age in stride and with amusement. He was a radical neither in politics nor religion. The few allusions in his works to the Puritans seem more critical than complimentary.

That Shakespeare was interested in politics is apparent from his historical plays and the references to contemporary political events that fill all his plays. He viewed government through the character of the individual ruler, whether Richard III or Elizabeth Tudor, not in terms of ideal systems or social goals. By modern standards he was a political conservative, accepting the social rankings and the power structure of his day and demonstrating unquestioned patriotism.

Shakespeare knew the theater as one who participated in every phase of its life—as a playwright, an actor, and part owner of a theater. He was a member and principal writer of a famous company of actors known as the King's Men. Between 1590 and 1610, many of his plays were performed at court, where he moved with comfort and received both Queen Elizabeth's and King James's enthusiastic patronage.

Elizabethan drama was already a distinctive form when Shakespeare began writing. Unlike French drama of the seventeenth century, which was dom-

A view of London indicating the Swan Theatre, where many of Shakespeare's plays were performed. [Folger Shakespeare Library]

inated by classical models, English drama developed in the sixteenth and seventeenth centuries as a blending of many forms: classical comedies and tragedies, medieval morality plays, and contemporary Italian short stories.

Two contemporaries, Thomas Kyd and Christopher Marlowe, influenced Shakespeare's tragedies. Kyd (1558–1594) wrote the first dramatic version of Hamlet. The tragedies of Marlowe (1564–1593) set a model for character, poetry, and style that only Shakespeare among the English playwrights of the period surpassed. Shakespeare synthesized the best past and current achievements. A keen student of human motivation and passion, he had a unique talent for getting into people's minds.

Shakespeare wrote histories, comedies, and tragedies. *Richard III* (1593), a very early play, stands out among the histories, although the picture it presents of Richard as an unprincipled villain has been characterized by some scholars as "Tudor propaganda." Shakespeare's comedies, although not attaining the heights of his tragedies, surpass his history plays in originality.

Shakespeare's tragedies are considered his unique achievement. Four of these were written within a three-year period: *Hamlet* (1603), *Othello* (1604), *King Lear* (1605), and *Macbeth* (1606). The most original of the tragedies, *Romeo and Juliet* (1597), transformed an old popular story into a moving drama of "star-cross'd lovers." Both Romeo and Juliet, denied a marriage by their warring families, die tragic deaths. Romeo, believing Juliet to be dead when she has merely taken a sleeping potion, poisons himself. When Juliet awakes to find Romeo dead, she kills herself with his dagger.

Throughout his lifetime and ever since, Shakespeare was immensely popular with both the playgoer and the play reader. The works of no other dramatist from his age are performed in theaters, and even on the screen, more regularly today.

John Milton: Puritan Poet

John Milton (1608–1674) was the son of a devout Puritan father. As a student, he avidly read the Christian and pagan classics. In 1638 he traveled to Italy, where he found in the lingering Renaissance a very congenial intellectual atmosphere. The Phlegraean Fields near Naples, a volcanic region, later became the model for hell in *Paradise Lost*, and it is suspected by some scholars that the Villa d'Este provided the model for paradise in *Paradise Regained*. Milton remained throughout his life a man more at home in the Italian Renaissance, with its high ideals and universal vision, than in the war-torn England of the seventeenth century.

A man of deep inner conviction and principle, Milton believed that standing a test of character was the most important thing in a person's life. This belief informed his own personal life and is the subject of much of his literary work.

In 1639 Milton joined the Puritan struggle against Charles I and Archbishop Laud. Employing his writing talent, he defended the Presbyterian form of church government against the episcopacy and supported other Puritan reforms. After a month-long unsuccessful marriage in 1642 (a marriage later reconciled), he wrote several tracts in defense of the right to divorce. These writings became targets of a Parliamentary censorship law in 1643, against which Milton wrote an eloquent defense of freedom of the press entitled *Areopagitica* (1644).

Until the upheavals of the civil war moderated his views, Milton believed that government should have the least possible control over the private lives of individuals. When Parliament divided into Presbyterians and Independents, he took the side of the latter, who wanted to dissolve the national church altogether in favor of the local autonomy of individual congregations. He also defended the execution of Charles I in a tract entitled *On the Tenure of Kings and Magistrates*. After his intense labor on this tract, his eyesight failed. Milton was totally blind when he wrote his masterpieces.

Paradise Lost, completed in 1665 and published in 1667, is a study of the destructive qualities of pride and the redeeming possibilities of humility. It elaborates in traditional Christian language and concept the revolt of Satan in heaven and the fall of Adam on Earth. The motives of Satan and all who rebel against God intrigued Milton. His proud but tragic Satan, who preferred to reign in hell than to serve in heaven, is one of the great figures in world literature and represented for Milton the absolute corruption of potential greatness.

John Milton (1608–1674). [Courtesy of the Prints Division, Library of Congress]

Milton wanted *Paradise Lost* to be for England what Homer's *Iliad* was for Greece and Vergil's *Aeneid* for Rome. In choosing biblical subject matter, he revealed the great influence of contemporary theology on his mind. Milton tended to agree with the Arminians, followers of the Dutch Protestant theologian Arminius (1560–1609), who, unlike the extreme Calvinists, did not believe that all worldly events, including the Fall of Man, were immutably fixed in the eternal decree of God. Milton shared the Arminian belief that human beings must take responsibility for their fate and that human efforts to improve character could, with God's grace, bring salvation.

Perhaps his own blindness, joined with the hope of making the best of the failed Puritan revolution, inclined Milton to sympathize with those who urged people to make the most of what they had, even in the face of defeat. That is a manifest concern of his last works, *Samson Agonistes*, which

John Milton Defends Freedom to Print Books

During the English Civil War, the Parliament passed a very strict censorship measure. In Areopagitica *(1644), John Milton attacked this law and contributed one of the major defenses for the freedom of the press in the history of Western culture. In the following passage, he compares the life of a book with the life of a human being.*

✦ *Why does Milton think that it may be more dangerous and harmful to attack a book than to attack a person? Was life cheaper and intelligence rarer in his time? Does he have particular kinds of books in mind? What can a book do for society that people cannot?*

I deny not but that it is of greatest concern in the Church and Commonwealth to have a vigilant eye how books demean themselves as well as men; and thereafter to confine, imprison, and do sharpest justice on them as [if they were criminals]; for books are not absolutely dead things, but do contain a progeny of life in them to be as active as that soul was whose progeny they are; nay, they do preserve as in a vial the purest efficacy and extraction of that living intellect that bred them. . . . He who kills a man kills a reasonable creature, God's Image; but he who destroys a good book, kills reason itself, kills the Image of God, as it were. . . . Many a man lives [as] a burden to the Earth; but a good book is the precious life-blood of a master spirit, embalmed and treasured up on purpose to a life beyond life. It is true, no age can restore a life, whereof, perhaps there is no great loss; and revolutions of ages do not oft recover the loss of a rejected truth, for the want of which whole nations fare the worse. We should be wary, therefore, what persecution we raise against the living labours of public men, how we spill that seasoned life of man preserved and stored up in books; since we see a kind of homicide may be thus committed, sometimes a martyrdom, and if it extends to the whole impression, a kind of massacre, whereof the execution ends not in the slaying of an elemental life, but strikes at that ethereal . . . essence, the breath of reason itself; slays an immortality rather than a life.

J. A. St. John, ed., The Prose Works of John Milton *(London: H. G. Bohn, 1843–1853), 2:8–9.*

recounts the biblical story of Samson, and *Paradise Regained*, the story of Christ's temptation in the wilderness, both published in 1671.

John Bunyan: Visions of Christian Piety

Bunyan (1628–1688) was the English author of two classics of sectarian Puritan spirituality: *Grace Abounding* (1666) and *The Pilgrim's Progress* (1678). A Bedford tinker, his works speak especially for the seventeenth-century working people and popular religious culture. He received only the most basic education before taking up his father's craft, and he served in Oliver Cromwell's revolutionary army for two years. The visionary fervor of the New Model Army influenced his work, which is filled with the language of battle.

After the restoration of the monarchy in 1660, Bunyan went to prison for his fiery preaching and remained there for twelve years. During these years, he wrote his famous autobiography, *Grace Abounding*, both a very personal statement and a model for the faithful. Like *The Pilgrim's Progress*, Bunyan's later masterpiece, *Grace Abounding* is Puritan piety at its most fervent. Puritans believed that individuals could do absolutely nothing to save themselves, and this made them extremely restless and introspective. People could only trust that God had placed them among the elect and try each day to live a life that reflected such favored status. So long

Major Works of Seventeenth-Century Literature and Philosophy

1605	*King Lear* (Shakespeare)
1605	*Don Quixote*, Part I (Cervantes)
1651	*Leviathan* (Hobbes)
1656–1657	*Provincial Letters* (Pascal)
1667	*Paradise Lost* (Milton)
1677	*Ethics* (Spinoza)
1678	*The Pilgrim's Progress* (Bunyan)
1690	*Treatises of Government* (Locke)
1690	*An Essay Concerning Human Understanding* (Locke)

as men and women struggled successfully against the flesh and the world, they had presumptive evidence that they were among God's elect. To falter or to become complacent in the face of temptation was to cast doubt on one's faith and salvation and even to raise the specter of eternal damnation.

This anxious questing for salvation is the subject of *The Pilgrim's Progress*, a work unique in its contribution to Western religious symbolism and imagery. It is the story of the journey of Christian and his friends Hopeful and Faithful to the Celestial City. It teaches that one must deny spouse, children, and all Earthly security and go in search of "Life, life, eternal life." During the long journey, the travelers must resist the temptations of Worldly-Wiseman and Vanity Fair, pass through the Slough of Despond, and endure a long dark night in Doubting Castle, their faith being tested at every turn. Bunyan later wrote a work tracing the progress of Christian's opposite, *The Life and Death of Mr. Badman* (1680), which told the story of a man so addicted to the bad habits of Restoration society, of which Bunyan strongly disapproved, that he journeyed steadfastly not to heaven but to hell.

Philosophy in the Wake of Changing Science

By the end of the sixteenth century, many people, weary of religious strife, no longer embraced either the old Catholic or the new Protestant absolutes. The century that followed was a period of intellectual as well as political transition. The thinkers of the Renaissance, reacting against the dogmatic thinking of medieval Scholasticism, had laid the groundwork for this change.

The revolution in scientific thought contributed directly to a major reconsideration of Western philosophy. Several of the most important figures in the Scientific Revolution, such as Descartes and

The microscope of Robert Hooke (1635–1703). The microscope became the telescope's companion as a major optical instrument in the seventeenth century. Several scientists, including Galileo, had a hand in its development, but the Englishman Hooke and the Dutchman Anton von Leeuwenhoek (1632–1723) did the most to perfect it. [Historical Collections, National Museum of Health and Medicine, Armed Forces Institute of Pathology]

Bacon, were also philosophers discontented with the scholastic heritage. Bacon stressed the importance of empirical research. Descartes attempted to find certainty through the exploration of his thinking processes. Newton's interests likewise extended to philosophy; he wrote broadly on many topics, including scientific method and theology.

The new methods of science had a broad impact on philosophers. The emphasis that Galileo placed on mathematics spread to other areas of thought. Pascal, a gifted mathematician, became concerned about the issue of certain knowledge and religious faith. Spinoza would write his ethical discourses in the form of geometrical theorems. Hobbes produced a great political treatise through a mode of rational reasoning resembling mathematics. Locke would attempt to explore the human mind in a fashion that he believed resembled Newton's approach to the physical universe. Virtually all of these writers found a tension that they hoped to resolve between the new science and religious belief.

Sir Francis Bacon (1561–1626), champion of the inductive method of gaining knowledge. [By courtesy of the National Portrait Gallery, London]

Francis Bacon: Empirical Method

Bacon (1561–1626) was an Englishman of almost universal accomplishment. He was a lawyer, a high royal official, and the author of histories, moral essays, and philosophical discourses. Traditionally, he has been regarded as the father of empiricism and of experimentation in science. Much of this reputation is unearned. Bacon was not a scientist except in the most amateur fashion. His accomplishment was setting a tone and helping to create a climate conducive to scientific work.

In books such as *The Advancement of Learning* (1605), the *Novum Organum* (1620), and the *New Atlantis* (1627), Bacon attacked the scholastic belief that most truth had already been discovered and only required explanation, as well as the scholastic reverence for intellectual authority in general. He believed that scholastic thinkers paid too much attention to tradition and to the knowledge of the ancients. He urged contemporaries to strike out on their own in search of a new understanding of nature. He wanted seventeenth-century Europeans to have confidence in themselves and their own abilities rather than in the people and methods of the past. Bacon was one of the first major European writers to champion the desirability of innovation and change.

Bacon believed that human knowledge should produce useful results. In particular, knowledge of nature should be brought to the aid of the human condition. These goals required the modification or abandonment of scholastic modes of learning and thinking. Bacon contended, "The [scholastic] logic now in use serves more to fix and give stability to the errors which have their foundation in commonly received notions than to help the search after truth."[5] Scholastic philosophers could not escape from their syllogisms to examine the foundations of their thought and intellectual presuppositions. Bacon urged that philosophers and investigators of nature examine the evidence of their senses before constructing logical speculations. In a famous passage, he divided all philosophers into

[5]Quoted in Baumer, p. 281.

Bacon Attacks the Idols That Harm Human Understanding

Francis Bacon wanted the men and women of his era to have the courage to change the way they thought about physical nature. In this famous passage from the Novum Organum *(1620), he attempted to explain why it is so difficult to ask new questions and seek new answers.*

✦ *Is Bacon's view of human nature pessimistic? Are people hopelessly trapped in overlapping worlds of self-interest and fantasy imposed by their nature and cultural traditions? How did Bacon expect people to overcome such formidable barriers?*

The idols and false notions which are now in possession of the human understanding and have taken deep root therein. . . . so beset men's minds that truth can hardly find entrance. . . . There are four classes of Idols which beset men's minds. To these for distinction's sake I have assigned names,—calling the first class *Idols of the Tribe;* the second, *Idols of the Cave;* the third, *Idols of the Marketplace;* the fourth, *Idols of the Theatre.*

. . . .

The Idols of the Tribe have their foundation in human nature itself; and in the tribe or race of men. For it is a false assertion that the sense of man is the measure of things. On the contrary, all perceptions as well as the sense as of the mind are according to the measure of the universe. And the human understanding is like a false mirror, which, receiving rays irregularly, distorts and discolours the nature of things by mingling its own nature with it.

The Idols of the Cave are the idols of the individual man. For every one (besides the errors common to human nature in general) has a cave or den of his own, which refracts and discolours the light of nature; owing either to his own proper and peculiar nature; or to his education and conversation with others; or to the reading of books, and the authority of those whom he esteems and admires. . . .

There are also Idols formed by the intercourse and association of men with each other, which I call Idols of the Marketplace, on account of the commerce and consort of men there. For it is by discourse that men associate; and words are imposed according to the apprehension of the vulgar. And therefore the ill and unfit choice of words wonderfully obstructs the understanding. . . .

Lastly, there are Idols which have immigrated into men's minds from the various dogmas of philosophies, and also from wrong laws of demonstration. These I call Idols of the Theatre; because in my judgment all the received systems are but so many stage plays, representing worlds of their own creation after an unreal and scenic fashion.

Francis Bacon, Essays, Advancement of Learning, New Atlantis, and Other Pieces, *ed. by Richard Foster Jones (New York: Odyssey, 1937), pp. 278–280.*

"men of experiment and men of dogmas." He observed:

> The men of experiment are like the ant, they only collect and use; the reasoners resemble spiders, who make cobwebs out of their own substance. But the bee takes a middle course: it gathers its material from the flowers of the garden and of the field, but transforms and digests it by a power of its own. Not unlike this is the true business of philosophy.[6]

[6]Quoted in Baumer, p. 288.

By directing scientists toward an examination of empirical evidence, Bacon hoped that they would achieve new knowledge and thus new capabilities for humankind.

Bacon compared himself with Columbus, plotting a new route to intellectual discovery. The comparison is significant, because it displays the consciousness of a changing world that appears so often in writers of the late sixteenth and early seventeenth centuries. They were rejecting the past not from simple hatred but rather from a firm understanding that the world was much more complicated than their medieval forebears had thought.

Neither Europe nor European thought could remain self-contained. Like the new worlds on the globe, new worlds of the mind were also emerging. Most of the people in Bacon's day, including the intellectuals, thought that the best era of human history lay in antiquity. Bacon dissented vigorously from that view. He looked to a future of material improvement achieved through the empirical examination of nature. His own theory of induction from empirical evidence was quite unsystematic, but his insistence on appeal to experience influenced others whose methods were more productive.

Bacon believed that science had a practical purpose and its goal was human improvement. Some scientific investigation does have this character. Much pure research does not. Bacon, however, linked science and material progress in the public mind. This was a powerful idea and has continued to influence Western civilization to the present day. It has made science and those who can appeal to the authority of science major forces for change and innovation. Thus, though not making any major scientific contribution himself, Bacon directed investigators of nature to a new method and a new purpose.

René Descartes: The Method of Rational Deduction

Descartes (1596–1650) was a gifted mathematician who invented analytic geometry. His most important contribution, however, was to develop a scientific method that relied more on deduction than empirical observation and induction.

In 1637 he published his *Discourse on Method*, in which he attempted to provide a basis for all thinking founded on a mathematical model. The work appeared in French rather than in Latin because he wanted it to have wide circulation and application. He began by saying that he would doubt everything except those propositions about which he could have clear and distinct ideas. This approach rejected all forms of intellectual authority except the conviction of his own reason. He concluded that he could not doubt his own act of thinking and his own existence. From this base he proceeded to deduce the existence of God. The presence of God was important to Descartes because God guaranteed the correctness of clear and distinct ideas. Because God was not a deceiver, the ideas of God-given reason could not be false.

René Descartes (1596–1650) believed that because the material world operated according to mathematical laws, it could be accurately understood by the exercise of human reason. [Erich Lessing/Art Resource, N.Y.]

On the basis of such assumptions, Descartes concluded that human reason could fully comprehend the world. He divided existing things into two basic categories: things thought and things occupying space—mind and body. Thinking was characteristic of the mind, and extension (things occupying space) was characteristic of the body. Within the material world, the world of extension, mathematical laws reigned supreme and could be grasped by reason. Because they were mathematical, they could be deduced from each other and constituted a complete system. The world of extension was the world of the scientist. It had no place for spirits, divinity, or anything nonmaterial. Descartes separated mind from body to banish such things from the realm of scientific speculation. Reason was to be applied only to the mechanical and mathematical realm of matter.

Descartes's emphasis on deduction and rational speculation exercised broad influence. His deductive methodology, however, eventually lost favor to scientific induction, in which the scientist draws generalizations from data derived from empirical observations.

Blaise Pascal: Reason and Faith

Pascal (1623–1662) was a French mathematician and a physical scientist who surrendered all his

Pascal Meditates on Human Beings as Thinking Creatures

Pascal was both a religious and a scientific writer. Unlike other scientific thinkers of the seventeenth century, he was not overly optimistic about the ability of science to improve the human condition. But science and philosophy might help human beings to understand their situation better. In these passages from his Pensées *(Thoughts), he ponders the uniqueness of human beings as thinking creatures.*

✦ *Is this an intellectual's view of human nature? Does the idea that man is a rational creature come from the belief that human reason is more noble than the universe? Does Pascal ignore human will and emotion, selfishness, and destructiveness?*

339

I can well conceive a man without hands, feet, head (for it is only experience which teaches us that the head is more necessary than feet). But I cannot conceive man without thought; he would be a stone or a brute.

344

Reason commands us far more imperiously than a master; for in disobeying the one we are unfortunate, and in disobeying the other we are fools.

346

Thought constitutes the greatness of man.

347

Man is but a reed, the most feeble thing in nature; but he is a thinking reed. The entire universe need not arm itself to crush him. A vapour, a drop of water suffices to kill him. But, if the universe were to crush him, man would still be more noble than that which killed him, because he knows that he dies and the advantage which the universe has over him; the universe knows nothing of this.

All our dignity consists, then, in thought. By it we must elevate ourselves, and not by space and time which we cannot fill. Let us endeavour, then, to think well; this is the principle of morality.

348

A thinking reed—It is not from space that I must seek my dignity, but from the government of my thought. I shall have no more if I possess worlds. By space the universe encompasses and swallows me up like an atom; by thought I comprehend the world.

Blaise Pascal, Pensées and The Provincial Letters *(New York: Modern Library, 1941), pp. 115–116.*

Pascal invented this adding machine, the ancestor of mechanical calculators, around 1644. It has eight wheels with ten cogs each, corresponding to the numbers 0–9. The wheels move forward for addition, backward for subtract. [Bildarchiv Preussischer Kulturbesitz]

wealth to pursue an austere, self-disciplined life. He aspired to write a work that would refute both dogmatism (which he saw epitomized by the Jesuits) and skepticism. Pascal considered the Jesuits' casuistry (i.e., arguments designed to minimize and excuse sinful acts) a distortion of Christian teaching. He rejected the skeptics of his age because they either denied religion altogether (atheists) or accepted it only as it conformed to reason (deists). He never produced a definitive refutation of the two sides. Rather he formulated his views on these matters in piecemeal fashion in a provocative collection of reflections on humankind and religion published posthumously under the title *Pensées*.

Pascal allied himself with the Jansenists, seventeenth-century Catholic opponents of the Jesuits. His sister was a member of the Jansenist community of Port-Royal, near Paris. The Jansenists shared with the Calvinists Saint Augustine's belief in human beings' total sinfulness, their eternal predestination by God, and their complete dependence on faith and grace for knowledge of God and salvation.

Pascal believed that reason and science were of no avail in matters of religion. Here only the reasons of the heart and a "leap of faith" could prevail. He saw two essential truths in the Christian religion: that a loving God, worthy of human attainment, exists, and that human beings, because they are corrupt by nature, are utterly unworthy of God. He believed that the atheists and the deists of his age had spurned the clear lesson of reason. For him rational analysis of the human condition revealed utter mortality and corruption and exposed the weakness of reason itself in resolving the problems of human nature and destiny. Reason properly drove those who truly heed it to faith in God and reliance on divine grace.

Pascal made a famous wager with the skeptics. It is a better bet, he argued, to believe that God exists and to stake everything on his promised mercy than not to do so. This is because if God does exist, everything will be gained by the believer, whereas, should he prove not to exist, the loss incurred by having believed in him is by comparison very slight.

Convinced that belief in God improved life psychologically and disciplined it morally (regardless of whether God proved in the end to exist), Pascal worked to strengthen traditional religious belief. He urged his contemporaries to seek self-understanding by "learned ignorance" and to discover humankind's greatness by recognizing its misery. He hoped thereby to counter what he believed to be the false optimism of the new rationalism and science.

Baruch Spinoza: The World as Divine Substance

The most controversial thinker of the seventeenth century may have been Baruch Spinoza (1632–1677), the son of a Jewish merchant of Amsterdam. His philosophy caused his excommunication by his own synagogue in 1656. During his lifetime, both Jews and Protestants attacked him as an atheist.

Spinoza's most influential writing, the *Ethics*, appeared after his death in 1677. Religious leaders universally condemned it for its apparent espousal of pantheism (a doctrine equating God and nature). Spinoza so closely identified God and nature that little room seemed left either for divine revelation in scripture or for the personal immortality of the soul—a position equally repugnant to Jews and to Christians. The *Ethics* was written, in the spirit of the new science, as a geometrical system of definitions, axioms, and propositions. Spinoza divided the work into five parts, which dealt with God, the mind, emotions, human bondage, and human freedom.

The most controversial part of the *Ethics* deals with the nature of substance and of God. According to Spinoza, there is only one substance, which is self-caused, free, and infinite, and that substance is God. From this definition it follows that everything that exists is in God and cannot even be conceived of apart from him. Such a doctrine was not literally pantheistic because God was still seen to be more than the created world that he, as primal substance, embraced. But in Spinoza's view, statements about the natural world were also statements about divine nature. Mind and matter are thus seen to be extensions of the infinite substance of God; what transpires in the world of people and nature is also an expression of the divine.

Such teaching seemed to portray the world as eternal and human actions as unfree and inevitable. Jews and Christians had traditionally condemned such teachings because they deny the creation of the world by God in time and destroy any voluntary basis for personal reward and punishment.

Although his contemporaries condemned him, Spinoza found enthusiastic supporters among many nineteenth-century thinkers who, unable to accept traditional religious language and doctrines, found in his teaching a congenial rational religion.

Thomas Hobbes: Apologist for Absolutism

Thomas Hobbes (1588–1679) was the most original political philosopher of the seventeenth century. Although he never broke with the Church of England, he embraced basic Calvinist beliefs, particularly their low view of human nature and the ideal of a commonwealth based on a divine–human covenant.

An urbane and much-traveled man, Hobbes enthusiastically supported the new scientific movement. During the 1630s, he visited Paris, where he came to know Descartes, and he spent time with Galileo in Italy as well. He took special interest in the works of William Harvey (1578–1657), famous for his discovery of the circulation of blood through the body. Hobbes was also a superb classicist. His first published work was a translation of Thucydides' *History of the Peloponnesian War*, the first English translation of this work, still reprinted today.

The English civil war made Hobbes a political philosopher and inspired his *Leviathan* (1651). Written as the concluding part of a broad philosophical system that analyzed physical bodies and human nature, the work established Hobbes as a major European thinker.

Hobbes viewed people and society in a thoroughly materialistic and mechanical way. All psychological processes begin with and are derived

A portrait of Thomas Hobbes (1588–1679), whose political treatise, Leviathan, portrayed rulers as absolute lords over their lands, incorporating in their persons the individual wills of all their people. [Bildarchiv Preussischer Kulturbesitz]

from bare sensation, and all motivations are egoistical, intended to increase pleasure and minimize pain. The human power of reasoning, which Hobbes defined as the process of adding and subtracting the consequences of agreed-upon general names of things, develops only after years of concentrated industry. Human will he defined as simply "the last appetite before choice."

Despite this mechanistic view of human nature, Hobbes believed people could accomplish much by the reasoned use of science. Such progress, however, was contingent on their prior correct use of that greatest of human creations, the commonwealth, in which people were freely united by mutual agreement in one all-powerful sovereign government.

The key to Hobbes's political philosophy can be found in a brilliant myth he created about the original state of humankind. According to this account, people in their natural state are inclined to "perpetual and restless desire" for power. Because all people want and, in their natural state, possess a natural right to everything, their equality breeds enmity, competition, diffidence, and perpetual quarreling—"a way of every man against every man." As Hobbes put it in a famous summary:

> In such condition there is no place for industry, because the fruit thereof is uncertain; and consequently no culture of the Earth; no navigation nor use of the commodities that may be imported by sea; no commodious building; no instruments of moving and removing such things as require much force; no knowledge of the face of the Earth; no account of time; no arts; no letters; no society; and, which is worst of all, continual fear and danger of violent death; and the life of man solitary, poor, nasty, brutish, and short.[7]

Whereas earlier and later philosophers saw the original human state as a paradise from which humankind had fallen, Hobbes saw it as a corruption from which only society could deliver people. Contrary to Aristotle and Christian thinkers like Thomas Aquinas, Hobbes did not believe human beings were naturally sociable; they were self-centered beasts and utterly without a master until one was imposed by force.

People escape this terrible state of nature, according to Hobbes, only by entering a social contract, that is, by agreeing to live in a commonwealth tightly ruled by a recognized sovereign. They are driven to this solution by their desire for "commodious living" and fear of death. The social contract obliges every person, for the sake of peace and self-defense, to agree to set aside personal rights to all things and to be content with as much liberty against others as he or she would allow others against himself or herself. All agree to live according to a secularized version of the golden rule: "Do not that to another which you would not have done to yourself."[8]

Because words and promises are insufficient to guarantee this state, the social contract also establishes the coercive use of force to compel compliance. Believing the dangers of anarchy to be always

[7]Thomas Hobbes, *Leviathan* Parts I and II, ed. by H. W. Schneider (Indianapolis: Bobbs-Merrill, 1958), pp. 86, 106–107.
[8]Hobbes, p. 130.

greater than those of tyranny, Hobbes thought that rulers should be absolute and unlimited in their power, once established in office. There is no room in Hobbes's political philosophy for protest in the name of individual conscience, nor for resistance to legitimate authority by private individuals. Contemporary Catholics and Puritans alike criticized these features of the *Leviathan*. To his critics, Hobbes pointed out the alternative:

> The greatest that in any form of government can possibly happen to the people in general is scarce sensible in respect of the miseries and horrible calamities that accompany a civil war or that dissolute condition of masterless men, without subjection to laws and a coercive power to tie their hands from rapine and revenge.[9]

[9]Hobbes, p. 152.

It is puzzling why Hobbes believed that absolute rulers would be more benevolent and less egoistic than all other people. He simply placed the highest possible value on a strong, efficient ruler who could save human beings from the chaos attendant on the state of nature. In the end, it mattered little to Hobbes whether that ruler was Charles I, Oliver Cromwell, or Charles II, each of whom received Hobbes's enthusiastic support—once he was established in power.

John Locke: Defender of Moderate Liberty

Locke (1632–1704) has proved to be the most influential political thinker of the seventeenth century. Although he was not as original as Hobbes, his political writings became a major source of the later

The famous title page illustration for Hobbes's Leviathan. *The ruler is pictured as absolute lord of his lands, but note that the ruler incorporates the mass of individuals whose self-interests are best served by their willing consent to accept him and cooperate with him. [New York Public Library]*

Enlightenment criticism of absolutism. They gave inspiration to both the American and the French revolutions.

Locke's sympathies lay with the Puritans and the parliamentary forces that challenged the Stuart monarchy. His father fought with the parliamentary army during the English civil war. Locke read deeply in the works of Francis Bacon, René Descartes, and Isaac Newton and was a close friend of the English physicist and chemist Robert Boyle (1627–1691). Some view Locke as synthesizing the rationalism of Descartes and the experimental science of Bacon, Newton, and Boyle.

Locke came for a brief period also under the influence of Hobbes. This ended, however, after his association with Anthony Ashley Cooper, the earl of Shaftesbury. Shaftesbury was considered by his contemporaries to be a radical in both religion and politics. He organized an unsuccessful rebellion against Charles II in 1682, after which both he and Locke, who lived with him, were forced to flee to Holland.

In his *Essay Concerning Human Understanding* (1690), Locke explored the function of the human mind. He portrayed it at birth as a blank tablet. There are no innate ideas, he argued; all knowledge is derived from direct sensual experience. What people know is not the external world in itself but the results of the interaction of the mind with the outside world.

Locke also denied the existence of innate moral norms. Moral ideas are the product of people's subordination of self-love to reason—a free act of self-discipline so that conflict in conscience may be avoided and happiness attained. Locke also believed the teachings of Christianity to be identical to what uncorrupted reason taught. A rational person would therefore always live according to Christian moral precepts. Although Locke firmly denied toleration to Catholics and atheists—both of whom were considered subversive in England—he otherwise sanctioned a variety of Protestant religious practice.

During the reign of Charles II, Locke wrote *Two Treatises of Government*. Here he opposed the argument, set forth by Sir Robert Filmer and Thomas Hobbes, that rulers are absolute in their power. Filmer was the author of *Patriarcha, or the Natural Power of Kings* (1680), which compared the rights of kings over their subjects to those of fathers over their children. Locke devoted his entire first treatise to a refutation of this argument, maintaining that both fathers and rulers were bound to the law of nature. The voice of reason teaches that "all mankind [are] equal and independent, [and] no one ought to harm another in his life, health, liberty, or possessions,"[10] inasmuch as all humans are made in the image of God. According to Locke, people enter into social contracts, empowering legislatures and monarchs to "umpire" their disputes, precisely to preserve their natural rights, not to give rulers an absolute power over them. Rulers are "entrusted" with the preservation of the law of nature and transgress it at their peril:

John Locke (1632–1704), defender of the rights of the people against rulers who think their power absolute. [By courtesy of the National Portrait Gallery, London]

[10]John Locke, *The Second Treatise of Government*, ed. by T. P. Peardon (Indianapolis: Bobbs-Merrill, 1952), Ch. 2, secs. 4–6, pp. 4–6.

John Locke Explores the Sources of Human Knowledge

An Essay Concerning Human Understanding *(1690) was probably the most influential philosophical work ever written in English. Locke's fundamental idea, which is explicated in the passage below, was that human knowledge is grounded in the experiences of the senses and in the reflection of the mind on those experiences. He rejected any belief in innate ideas. His emphasis on experience led to the wider belief that human beings are creatures of their environment. After Locke, numerous writers argued that human beings could be improved if the political and social environments in which they lived were reformed.*

✦ *How does Locke explain the manner in which the human mind comes to be furnished? What does Locke mean by* experience*? How does reflection deal with external sensations? What is the role that external environment plays in Locke's psychology?*

Let us then suppose the mind to be, as we say, white paper void of all characters, without any ideas. Whence comes it to be furnished? Whence comes it by that vast store which the busy and boundless fancy of man has painted on it with an almost endless variety? Whence has it all the materials of reason and knowledge? To this I answer, in one word, from experience; in that all our knowledge is founded, and from that it ultimately derives itself. Our observation, employed either about external sensible objects, or about the internal operations of our minds perceived and reflected on by ourselves, is that which supplies our understanding with all the materials of thinking. These two are the fountains of knowledge, from whence all the ideas we have, or can naturally have, do spring.

First, our senses, conversant about particular sensible objects, do convey into the mind several distinct perceptions of things, according to those various ways wherein those objects do affect them. And thus we come by those ideas we have of yellow, white, heat, cold, soft, hard, bitter, sweet, and all those which we call sensible qualities. . . . This great source of most of the ideas we have, depending wholly upon our senses, and derived by them to the understanding, I call SENSATION.

Secondly, the other fountain from which experience furnisheth the understanding with ideas is the perception of the operations of our own minds within us, as it is employed about the ideas it has got . . . and such are perception, thinking, doubting, believing, reasoning, knowing, willing, and all the different actings of our own minds. . . . I call this REFLECTION, the ideas it affords being such only as the mind gets by reflecting on its own operations within itself. . . . These two, I say, viz., external material things as the objects of SENSATION, and the operations of our own minds within as the objects of REFLECTION, are to me the only originals from whence all our ideas take their beginnings. . . .

The understanding seems to me not to have the least glimmering of any ideas which it doth not receive from one of these two.

John Locke, An Essay Concerning Human Understanding, *vol. 1 (London: Everyman's Library, 1961), pp. 77–78.*

> Whenever that end [the preservation of life, liberty, and property] is manifestly neglected or opposed, the trust must necessarily be forfeited and the power devolve into the hands of those that gave it, who may place it anew where they think best for their safety and security.[11]

From Locke's point of view, absolute monarchy was "inconsistent" with civil society and can be "no form of civil government at all."

Locke's main differences with Hobbes stemmed from the latter's negative views of human nature. Locke believed that the natural human state was one of perfect freedom and equality in which everyone enjoyed, in unregulated fashion, the natural rights of life, liberty, and property. Contrary to Hobbes, human beings in their natural state were creatures not of monomaniacal passion but of extreme goodwill and rationality. And they did not surrender their natural rights unconditionally when they entered the social contract. Rather they established a means whereby these rights could be better preserved. The warfare that Hobbes believed characterized the state of nature emerged for Locke only when rulers failed to preserve people's natural freedom and attempted to enslave them by absolute rule. The preservation and protection of human freedom, not its suppression, was government's mandate.

✦

The Scientific Revolution and the thought of writers whose work was contemporaneous with it mark a major turning point in the history of Western thought and eventually had a worldwide impact. The scientific and political ideas of the late sixteenth and seventeenth centuries gradually overturned many of the most fundamental premises of the medieval worldview. The sun replaced the Earth as the center of the solar system. The solar system itself came to be viewed as one of many possible systems in the universe. The new knowledge of the physical universe provided occasions for challenges to the authority of the church and of scripture. Mathematics began to replace theology and metaphysics as the tool for understanding nature.

Parallel to these developments and sometimes related to them, political thought became much less concerned with religious issues. Hobbes generated a major theory of political obligation with virtually no reference to God. Locke theorized about politics with a recognition of God but with little attention to scripture. Both Locke and Spinoza championed greater freedom of religious and political expression. Locke produced a psychology that emphasized the influence of environment on human character and action. All of these new ideas gradually displaced or reshaped theological and religious modes of thought and placed humankind and life on Earth at the center of Western thinking. Intellectuals in the West consequently developed greater self-confidence in their own capacity to shape the world and their own lives.

None of this came easily, however. The new science and enlightenment were accompanied by new anxieties that were reflected in a growing preoccupation with sin, death, and the Devil. The worst expression of this preoccupation was a succession of witch hunts and trials that took the lives of as many as 100,000 people between 1400 and 1700.

[11]Locke, Ch. 13, sec. 149, p. 84.

Review Questions

1. Discuss the contributions of Copernicus, Brahe, Kepler, Galileo, and Newton to the Scientific Revolution. Which do you think made the most important contributions and why? What did Francis Bacon contribute to the foundation of scientific thought?
2. How would you define the term *Scientific Revolution*? In what ways was it truly revolutionary? Which is more enduring, a political revolution or an intellectual one?
3. How did Isaac Newton reconcile his scientific discoveries with his faith in God? Compare his experience with that of Galileo or Pascal. Are reason and faith compatible?
4. Compare and contrast the political philosophies of Thomas Hobbes and John Locke. How did each view human nature? Would you rather live under a government designed by Hobbes or by Locke? Why?
5. How do you explain the phenomenon of witchcraft and witch hunts in an age of scientific enlightenment? Why did the witch panics occur in the late sixteenth and early seventeenth centuries? How might the Reformation have contributed to them?

6. How do the literary works of Cervantes, Shakespeare, and Milton reflect concern about the adequacy of past values and how did they shape the worldview of their own seventeenth century society?

Suggested Readings

R. Ashcraft, *Revolutionary Politics and Locke's Two Treatises of Government* (1986). A major study emphasizing the radical side of Locke's thought.

M. Biagioli, *Galileo Courtier: The Practice of Science in the Culture of Absolutism* (1993). A major revisionist work that emphasizes the role of the political setting on Galileo's career and thought.

H. Butterfield, *The Origins of Modern Science 1300–1800* (1949). A classic survey.

J. Caird, *Spinoza* (1971). Intellectual biography by a philosopher.

H. F. Cohen, *The Scientific Revolution: A Historiographical Inquiry* (1994). Supplants all previous discussions of the history and concept of the Scientific Revolution.

J. Dunn, *The Political Thought of John Locke; An Historical Account of the "Two Treatises of Government"* (1969). An excellent introduction.

M. Duran, *Cervantes* (1974). Detailed biography.

M. A. Finocchiaro, *The Galileo Affair: A Documentary History* (1989). A collection of all the relevant documents and introductory commentary.

S. Gaukroger, *Descartes: An Intellectual Biography* (1995). A major work that explores both the science and philosophy in Descartes's work.

A. Goldgar, *Impolite Learning: Conduct and Community in the Republic of Letters, 1680–1750* (1995). A lively survey of the structure of the European intellectual community.

A. R. Hall, *The Scientific Revolution 1500–1800: The Formation of the Modern Scientific Attitude* (1966). Traces undermining of traditional science and rise of new sciences.

I. Harris, *The Mind of John Locke: A Study of Political Theory in Its Intellectual Setting* (1994). The most comprehensive recent treatment.

C. Hill, *Milton and the English Revolution* (1977). A major biography.

M. Hunter, *Science and Society in Restoration England* (1981). Examines the social relations of scientists and scientific societies.

M. Jacob, *The Newtonians and the English Revolution* (1976). A controversial book that attempts to relate science and politics.

D. Johnston, *The Rhetoric of Leviathan: Thomas Hobbes and the Politics of Cultural Transformation* (1986). An important study that links Hobbes's thought to the rhetoric of the Renaissance.

R. Kieckhefer, *European Witch Trials: Their Foundations in Popular and Learned Culture 1300–1500* (1976). Excellent background for understanding the great witch panic.

A. Kors and E. Peters (eds.), *European Witchcraft, 1100–1700* (1972). Collection of major documents.

A. Koyré, *From the Closed World to the Infinite Universe* (1957). Treated from perspective of the historian of ideas.

T. S. Kuhn, *The Copernican Revolution* (1957). Remains the leading work on the subject.

C. Larner, *Enemies of God: The Witchhunt in Scotland* (1981). Perhaps the most exemplary local study of the subject.

P. Laslett, *Locke's Two Treatises of Government*, 2nd ed. (1970). Definitive texts with very important introductions.

B. Levack, *The Witch Hunt in Early Modern Europe* (1986). Lucid, up-to-date survey of research.

D. Lindberg and R. L. Numbers (eds.), *God and Nature: Historical Essays on the Encounter Between Christianity and Science* (1986). The best collection of essays on the subject.

D. Lindberg and R. S. Westman (eds.), *Reappraisals of the Scientific Revolution* (1990). Important essays pointing the way toward new understandings of the subject.

J. Martin, *Francis Bacon, The State, and the Reform of Natural Philosophy* (1992). Relates Bacon's thought to his political goals.

O. Mayer, *Authority, Liberty, and Automatic Machinery in Early Modern Europe* (1986). A lively study that seeks to relate thought about machinery to thought about politics.

R. Popkin, *The History of Scepticism from Erasmus to Spinoza* (1979). A classic study of the fear of loss of intellectual certainty.

P. Redondi, *Galileo: Heretic* (1987). A controversial work that examines the relationship of Galileo's thought to the church's teaching on the Eucharist rather than to planetary motion.

S. Shapin and S. Schaffer, *Leviathan and the Air-Pump: Hobbes, Boyle, and the Experimental Life* (1985). A study of the debate over the validity of scientific experiment during the age of the Scientific Revolution.

Q. Skinner, *Reason and Rhetoric in the Philosophy of Hobbes* (1996). A major study by one of the leading scholars of Hobbes and early modern political thought.

L. Stewart, *The Rise of Public Science: Rhetoric, Technology, and Natural Philosophy in Newtonian Britain, 1660–1750* (1992). Examines the manner in which science became related to public life and economic development.

K. Thomas, *Religion and the Decline of Magic* (1971). Provocative, much acclaimed work focused on popular culture.

R. S. Westfall, *Never at Rest: A Biography of Isaac Newton* (1981). The major study.

B. H. G. Wormald, *Francis Bacon: History, Politics, and Science, 1561–1626* (1993). The most extensive recent study.

CHAPTER 15

Peter the Great (r. 1682–1725) seeking to make Russia a major military power, reorganized the country's political and economic structures. His reign saw Russia enter fully into European power politics. [The Apotheosis of Tsar Peter the Great 1682–1725 by unknown artist, 1710. Historical Museum, Moscow./E.T. Archive]

Successful and Unsuccessful Paths to Power (1686–1740)

KEY TOPICS

- The decline of Spain and the Netherlands relative to France and England among the maritime powers
- French aristocratic resistance to the monarchy
- Early eighteenth-century British political stability
- The efforts of the Habsburgs to secure their holdings
- The emergence of Prussia as a major power under the Hohenzollerns
- The efforts of Peter the Great to transform Russia into a powerful centralized nation along Western lines

The late seventeenth and early eighteenth centuries witnessed significant shifts of power and influence among the states of Europe. Nations that had been strong lost their status as significant military and economic units. Other countries that in some cases had figured only marginally in international relations came to the fore. Great Britain, France, Austria, Russia, and Prussia emerged during this period as the powers that would dominate Europe until at least World War I. Their political and economic dominance occurred at the expense of Spain, the United Netherlands, Poland, Sweden, and the Ottoman Empire. Equally essential to their rise was the weakness of the Holy Roman Empire after the Treaty of Westphalia (1648), which ended the Thirty Years' War.

The successful competitors for international power were those states that created strong central political authorities. Farsighted observers in the late seventeenth century already understood that in the future those domains that would become or remain great powers must imitate the political and military organization of Louis XIV's France. Strong monarchy alone could impose unity of purpose on the state. The turmoil of seventeenth-century civil wars and aristocratic revolts had impressed people with the value of a strong monarch as the guarantor of minimum domestic tranquility.

Imitation of French absolutism involved more than belief in a strong monarchy. It usually required building a standing army, organizing an efficient tax structure to support the army, and establishing a bureaucracy to collect the taxes. Moreover, the political classes of the country, especially the nobles, had to be converted to a sense of duty and loyalty to the central government that was more intense than their loyalty to other competing political and social institutions.

The waning powers were those that failed to achieve such effective organization. They were unable to employ their political, economic, and human resources to resist external aggression or to overcome the forces of domestic dissolution. Internal and external failures were closely related. If a state did not maintain or establish a central political authority with sufficient power over the nobility, the cities, the guilds, and the church, it could not raise a strong army to defend its borders or its economic interests. More often than not, the key element leading to success or failure was the character, personality, and energy of the monarch.

The Maritime Powers

In western Europe, Britain and France emerged as the dominant powers. This development represented a shift of influence away from Spain and the United Netherlands. Both the latter countries had been strong and important during the sixteenth and seventeenth centuries, but they became politically and militarily marginal during the eighteenth century. Neither, however, disappeared from the map, and both retained considerable economic vitality and influence. The difference was that France and Britain attained so much more power and economic strength.

Spain

Spanish power had depended on the influx of wealth from the Americas and on the capacity of the Spanish monarchs to rule the still largely autonomous provinces of the Iberian Peninsula. The economic life of Spain was never healthy. Except for wool, it had virtually no exports to pay for its imports. Instead of promoting domestic industries, the Spanish government financed imports by using the gold and silver mined in its New World empire. This external source of wealth was uncertain because the treasure fleets from the New World (discussed more fully in Chapter 17) could be and sometimes were captured by pirates or hostile navies.

The political life of Spain was also weak. Within its divisions of Castile, Aragon, Navarre, the Basque provinces, and other districts, the royal government could not operate without the cooperation of strong local nobles and the church. From the defeat of the Armada in 1588 to the Treaty of the Pyrenees in 1659 after Spain's defeat by France, Spain suffered a series of foreign policy reverses that harmed the domestic prestige of the monarchy. Furthermore, between 1665 and 1700, the physically malformed, dull-witted, and sexually impotent Charles II was monarch. Throughout his reign, the provincial estates and the nobility increased their power. After his death, the other powers of Europe fought over who would succeed him in the War of the Spanish Succession (1701–1714).

The Treaty of Utrecht (1713), which ended the war, gave the Spanish crown to Philip V (r. 1700–1746), a grandson of Louis XIV. The new king should have tried to consolidate his internal power and protect Spanish overseas trade. However, his second wife, Elizabeth Farnese, used Spanish power to secure thrones for her two sons in Italy. Such diversions of government resources allowed the nobility and the provinces to continue to assert their privileges against the monarchy. Not until the reign of Charles III (r. 1759–1788) did Spain have a monarch concerned with efficient domestic and imperial administration and internal improvement. By the third quarter of the century, Spain was better governed, but it could no longer compete effectively in great power politics.

The Netherlands

The decline of the United Provinces of the Netherlands occurred wholly within the eighteenth century. After the death of William III of Britain in 1702, the various local provinces successfully prevented the emergence of another strong *stadtholder*. Unified political leadership therefore vanished. During the earlier long wars of the Netherlands with Louis XIV and Britain, naval supremacy had slowly but steadily passed to the British. The fishing industry declined, and the Dutch lost their technological superiority in shipbuilding. Countries between which Dutch ships had once carried goods now traded directly with each other. For example, the British began to use their own vessels in the Baltic traffic with Russia.

Similar stagnation overtook the Dutch domestic industries, such as textile finishing, paper making, and glass blowing. The disunity of the provinces and the absence of vigorous leadership hastened this economic decline and prevented action that might have slowed or halted it.

In the mid-eighteenth century, when this picture of the Amsterdam Exchange was painted, Amsterdam had replaced the cities of Italy and south Germany as the leading banking center of Europe. Amsterdam retained this position until the late eighteenth century. [Museum Boymans-van Beuningen, Rotterdam]

What saved the United Provinces from becoming completely insignificant in European matters was their continued financial dominance. Well past the middle of the century, their banks continued to provide loans and financing for European trade.

France After Louis XIV

Despite its military reverses in the War of the Spanish Succession, France remained a great power. It was less strong in 1715 than in 1680, but it still possessed the largest European population, an advanced if troubled economy, and the administrative structure bequeathed it by Louis XIV. Moreover, even if France and its resources had been drained by the last of Louis's wars, the other major states of Europe were similarly debilitated. What France required was economic recovery and consolidation, wiser political leadership, and a less ambitious foreign policy. It did enjoy a period of recovery, but its leadership was at best indifferent. Louis XIV was succeeded by his five-year-old great-grandson Louis XV (r. 1715–1774). The young boy's uncle, the duke of Orléans, became regent and remained so until his death in 1720. The regency, marked by financial and moral scandals, further undermined the faltering prestige of the monarchy.

The impending collapse of John Law's bank triggered a financial panic throughout France. Desperate investors, such as those shown here in the city of Rennes, sought to exchange their paper currency for gold and silver before the bank's supply of precious metals was exhausted. [Musée de Bretagne, Rennes]

John Law and the Mississippi Bubble The duke of Orléans was a gambler, and for a time he turned over the financial management of the kingdom to John Law (1671–1729), a Scottish mathematician and fellow gambler. Law believed that an increase in the paper-money supply would stimulate France's economic recovery. With the permission of the regent, he established a bank in Paris that issued paper money. Law then organized a monopoly, called the Mississippi Company, on trading privileges with the French colony of Louisiana in North America.

The Mississippi Company also took over the management of the French national debt. The company issued shares of its own stock in exchange for government bonds, which had fallen sharply in value. To redeem large quantities of bonds, Law encouraged speculation in Mississippi Company stock. In 1719 the price of the stock rose handsomely. Smart investors, however, took their profits by selling their stock in exchange for paper money from Law's bank, which they then sought to exchange for gold. The bank, however, lacked enough gold to redeem all the paper money brought to it.

In February 1720, all gold payments were halted in France. Soon thereafter Law himself fled the country. The Mississippi Bubble, as the affair was called, had burst. The fiasco brought disgrace on the government that had sponsored Law. The Mississippi Company was later reorganized and functioned profitably, but fear of paper money and speculation marked French economic life for decades.

RENEWED AUTHORITY OF THE *PARLEMENTS* The duke of Orléans made a second decision that also lessened the power of the monarchy. He attempted to draw the French nobility once again into the decision-making processes of the government. Louis XIV had filled his ministries and bureaucracies with persons from nonnoble families. The regent, under pressure from the nobility, tried to restore a balance. He set up a system of councils on which nobles were to serve along with bureaucrats. The years of idle noble domestication at Versailles, however, had worked too well, and the nobility seemed to lack both the talent and the desire to govern. The experiment failed.

Despite this failure, the great French nobles did not surrender their ancient ambition to assert their rights, privileges, and local influence over those of the monarchy. The chief feature of eighteenth-century French political life was the attempt of the nobility to use its authority to limit the power of the monarchy. The most effective instrument in this process was the *parlements*, or courts dominated by the nobility.

The French *parlements* were different from the English Parliament. These French courts, the most important of which was the *Parlement* of Paris, could not legislate. Rather, they had the power to recognize or not to recognize the legality of an act or law promulgated by the monarch. By long tradition their formal approval had been required to make a royal law valid. Louis XIV had often restricted stubborn, uncooperative *parlements*. In another major political blunder, however, the duke of Orléans had formally approved the full reinstitution of the *parlements'* power to allow or disallow laws. Thereafter the growing financial and moral weakness of the monarchy allowed these aristocratic judicial institutions to reassert their authority. This situation meant that until the revolution in 1789 the *parlements* became natural centers for aristocratic resistance to royal authority.

ADMINISTRATION OF CARDINAL FLEURY In 1726 Cardinal Fleury (1653–1743) became the chief minister of the French court. He was the last of the great clerics who loyally and effectively served the French monarchy. Like his seventeenth-century predecessors, the cardinals Richelieu and Mazarin, Fleury was a realist. He understood the political ambition and incapacity of the nobility and worked quietly to block their undue influence. He was also aware of the precarious financial situation of the royal treasury.

Cardinal Fleury (1653–1743) was the tutor and chief minister of Louis XV from 1726 to 1743. Fleury gave France a period of peace and prosperity, but was unable to solve the state's long-term financial problems. This portrait is by Hyacinthe Rigaud

The cardinal, who was seventy-three years old when he came to office, was determined to give the country a period of peace. He surrounded himself with able assistants who tried to solve France's financial problems. Part of the national debt was repudiated. New industries enjoying special privileges were established, and roads and bridges built. On the whole the nation prospered, but Fleury could never draw from the nobles or the church sufficient tax revenues to put the state on a stable financial footing.

Fleury died in 1743, having unsuccessfully attempted to prevent France from intervening in the

Madame de Pompadour (1721–1764) was the mistress of Louis XV. She exercised considerable political influence at the court and was a notable patron of artists, craftspeople, and writers. This 1763 portrait is by Hubert Drouais (1727–1775) [H. Roger Viollet]

war then raging between Austria and Prussia. The cost of this intervention was to undo all his financial pruning and planning.

Another failure must also be credited to this elderly cleric. Despite his best efforts, he had not trained Louis XV to become an effective monarch. Louis XV possessed most of the vices and almost none of the virtues of his great-grandfather Louis XIV. He wanted to hold on to absolute power but was unwilling to work the long hours required. He did not choose many wise advisers after Fleury. He was tossed about by the gossip and intrigues of the court. His personal life was scandalous. Louis XV was not an evil person but a mediocre one. And in a monarch, mediocrity was unfortunately often a greater fault than vice.

Despite this political drift, France remained a great power. France's army at mid-century was still the largest and strongest military force on the Continent. Its commerce and production expanded. Its colonies produced wealth and spurred domestic industries. Its cities grew and prospered. The wealth of the nation waxed as the absolutism of the monarchy waned. France did not lack sources of power and strength, but the political leadership could not organize, direct, or inspire its people.

Great Britain: The Age of Walpole

In 1713 Britain had emerged as a victor over Louis XIV, but the nation required a period of recovery. As an institution, the British monarchy was not in the degraded state of the French monarchy, yet its stability was not certain.

THE HANOVERIAN DYNASTY In 1714 the Hanoverian dynasty, as designated by the Act of Settlement (1701), came to the throne. Almost immediately, George I (r. 1714–1727) faced a challenge to his new title. The Stuart pretender James Edward (1688–1766), the son of James II, landed in Scotland in December 1715. His forces marched southward but met defeat less than two months later. Although militarily successful against the pretender, the new dynasty and its supporters saw the need for consolidation.

WHIGS AND TORIES During the seventeenth century, England had been one of the most politically restive countries in Europe. The closing years of Queen Anne's reign (1702–1714) had seen sharp clashes between the political factions of Whigs and Tories over whether to end the war with France. The Tories had urged a rapid peace settlement and after 1710 had opened negotiations with France. During the same period, the Whigs were seeking favor from the elector of Hanover, the future George I, who would soon be their monarch. His concern for his domains in Hanover made him unsympathetic to the Tory peace policy. In the final months of Anne's reign, some Tories, fearing that they would lose power under the waiting Hanoverian dynasty, opened channels of communication with the Stuart pretender; and a few even rallied to his cause.

Under these circumstances, George I, on his arrival in Britain, clearly favored the Whigs. Previously the differences between the Whigs and the Tories had been vaguely related to principle. The Tories emphasized a strong monarchy, low taxes for landowners, and firm support of the Anglican Church. The Whigs supported monarchy but wanted Parliament to retain final sovereignty. They favored urban commercial interests as well as the prosperity of the landowners. They encouraged a policy of religious toleration toward the Protestant nonconformists in England. Socially both groups supported the status quo.

Neither group was organized like a modern political party. Outside Parliament, each party consisted of political networks based on local connections and economic influence. Each group acknowledged a few national spokespeople, who articulated positions and principles. After the Hanoverian accession and the eventual Whig success in achieving the firm confidence of George I, the chief difference for almost forty years between the Whigs and the Tories was that one group had access to public office and patronage and the other did not. This early Hanoverian proscription of Tories from public life was one of the most prominent features of the age.

THE LEADERSHIP OF ROBERT WALPOLE The political situation after 1715 remained in flux, until Robert Walpole (1676–1745) took over the helm of government. Walpole had been active in the House of Commons since the reign of Queen Anne and had been a cabinet minister. What gave him special prominence under the new dynasty was a British financial scandal similar to the French Mississippi Bubble.

Management of the British national debt had been assigned to the South Sea Company, which exchanged government bonds for company stock. As in the French case, the price of the stock soared,

Sir Robert Walpole (1676–1745), far left, is shown talking with the Speaker of the House of Commons. Walpole, who dominated British political life from 1721 to 1742, is considered the first prime minister of Britain. [Mansell Collection]

Lady Mary Wortley Montagu Advises Her Husband on Election to Parliament

In this letter of 1714, Lady Mary Wortley Montagu discussed with her husband the various paths that he might follow to gain election to the British House of Commons. Note her emphasis on knowing the right people and on having large amounts of money to spend on voters. Eventually, her husband was elected to Parliament in a borough that was controlled through government patronage.

✦ *What are the various ways in which candidates and their supporters used money to campaign? What role did friendships play in the campaigning? How important do the political ideas or positions of the candidates seem to be? Women could not vote in eighteenth-century parliamentary elections. Is there some other influence they exert?*

You seem not to have received my letters, or not to have understood them: you had been chose undoubtedly at York, if you had declared in time; but there is not any gentleman or tradesman disengaged at this time; they are treating every night. Lord Carlisle and the Thompsons have given their interest to Mr. Jenkins. I agree with you of the necessity of your standing this Parliament, which, perhaps, may be more considerable than any that are to follow it; but, as you proceed, 'tis my opinion, you will spend your money and not be chose. I believe there is hardly a borough unengaged. I expect every letter should tell me you are sure of some place; and, as far as I can perceive you are sure of none. As it has been managed, perhaps it will be the best way to deposit a certain sum in some friend's hands, and buy some little Cornish borough: it would, undoubtedly, look better to be chose for a considerable town; but I take it to be now too late. If you have any thoughts of Newark, it will be absolutely necessary for you to enquire after Lord Lexington's interest; and your best way to apply yourself to Lord Holdernesse, who is both a Whig and an honest man. He is now in town, and you may enquire of him if Brigadier Sutton stands there; and if not, try to engage him for you. Lord Lexington is so ill at the Bath, that it is a doubt if he will live 'till the elections; and if he dies, one of his heiresses, and the whole interest of his estate, will probably fall on Lord Holdernesse.

'Tis a surprize to me, that you cannot make sure of some borough, when a number of your friends bring in so many Parliament-men without trouble or expense. 'Tis too late to mention it now, but you might have applied to Lady Winchester, as Sir Joseph Jekyl did last year, and by her interest the Duke of Bolton brought him in for nothing; I am sure she would be more zealous to serve me, than Lady Jekyl.

Lord Wharncliffe, ed., Letters and Works of Lady Mary Wortley Montagu, *3rd ed., vol. 1 (London, 1861), p. 211.*

only to crash in 1720 when prudent investors sold their holdings and took their speculative profits. Parliament intervened and, under Walpole's leadership, adopted measures to honor the national debt. To most contemporaries, Walpole had saved the financial integrity of the country and had thus proved himself a person of immense administrative capacity and political ability.

George I gave Walpole his full confidence. For this reason Walpole has often been regarded as the first prime minister of Great Britain and the originator of the cabinet system of government. Walpole generally demanded that all the ministers in the cabinet agree on policy, but he could not prevent frequent public differences among them. Unlike a modern English prime minister, he was not chosen by the majority of the House of Commons. The real sources of his power were the personal support of the king, George I and later George II (r. 1727–1760), his ability to handle the House of Commons, and his iron-fisted control of government patronage. To oppose Walpole meant the almost certain loss of government patronage for oneself, one's family, or one's friends. Through the skillful use of patronage, Walpole bought support for himself and his policies from people who wanted to receive jobs, appointments, favors, and government contracts. Such corruption supplied the glue of political loyalty.

Walpole's favorite slogan was "*Quieta non movere*" (roughly, "Let sleeping dogs lie"). To that end, he pursued peace abroad and supported the status quo at home. In this regard he much resembled Cardinal Fleury.

Lady Mary Wortley Montagu (1689–1762) was a famous writer of letters and an extremely well-traveled woman of the eighteenth century. As the previous document suggests, she was also a shrewd and toughminded political advisor to her husband. [National Portrait Gallery, London]

This series of four Hogarth etchings satirizes the notoriously corrupt English electoral system. Hogarth shows the voters going to the polls after having been bribed and intoxicated with free gin. (Voting was then in public. The secret ballot was not introduced in England until 1872.) The fourth etching, "Chairing the Member," shows the triumphal procession of the victorious candidate, which is clearly turning into a brawl. [Metropolitan Museum of Art, Harris Brisbane Dick Fund, 1932. Acc. #32.35.(124)]

THE STRUCTURE OF PARLIAMENT The structure of the eighteenth-century British House of Commons aided Walpole in his pacific policies. It was neither a democratic nor a representative body. Each of the counties into which Britain was divided elected two members. But if the more powerful landed families in a county agreed on the candidates, there was no contest. Most members, however, were elected from a variety of units called boroughs. A few boroughs were large enough for elections to be relatively democratic, but most had few electors. For example, a local municipal corporation or council of only a dozen members might have the right to elect a member of Parliament. In Old Sarum, one of the most famous corrupt, or "rotten," boroughs, the Pitt family simply bought up those pieces of property to which a vote was attached and thus in effect owned a seat in the House of Commons. Through proper electoral management, which involved favors to the electors, the House of Commons could be controlled.

The structure of Parliament and the manner in which the House of Commons was elected meant that the owners of property, especially wealthy nobles, dominated the government of England. They did not pretend to represent people and districts or to be responsive to what would later be called public opinion. They regarded themselves as representing various economic and social interests, such as the West Indian interest, the merchant interest, or the landed interest. These owners of property were suspicious of an administrative bureaucracy controlled by the crown or its ministers. To diminish royal influence, they or their agents served as local government administrators, judges, militia commanders, and tax collectors. In this sense, the British nobility and large landowners actually did govern the nation. And because they regarded the Parliament as the political sovereign, there was no absence of central political authority and direction. Consequently, the supremacy of Parliament gave Britain the unity that absolute monarchy provided elsewhere in Europe.

These parliamentary structures also helped to strengthen the financial position of the British government. The British monarch could not raise taxes the way his continental counterparts could, but the British government consisting of the monarch and Parliament could and did raise vast sums of tax revenue and loans to wage war throughout the eighteenth century. All Britons paid taxes. There were virtually no exemptions. The British credit market was secure through the regulation of the Bank of England, founded in 1693. This strong system of finance and tax collection was one of the cornerstones of eighteenth-century British power.

France and Great Britain in the Early Eighteenth Century

1713	Treaty of Utrecht ends the War of the Spanish Succession
1714	George I becomes king of Great Britain and establishes the Hanoverian dynasty
1715	Louis XV becomes King of France
1715–1720	Regency of the duke of Orléans in France
1720	Mississippi Bubble bursts in France and South Sea Bubble bursts in Great Britain
1720–1742	Robert Walpole dominates British politics
1726–1743	Cardinal Fleury serves as Louis XV's chief minister
1727	George II becomes king of Great Britain
1733	Excise tax crisis in Britain

FREEDOM OF POLITICAL LIFE British political life was genuinely more free than that on the Continent. There were real limits on the power of Robert Walpole. Parliament could not wholly ignore popular political pressure. Even with the extensive use of patronage, many members of Parliament maintained independent views. Newspapers and public debate flourished. There was freedom of speech and association. There was no large standing army. Those Tories barred from political office and the Whig enemies of Walpole could and did openly oppose his policies—which would have been impossible on the Continent.

For example, in 1733 Walpole presented to the House of Commons a scheme to expand the scope of the excise tax, a tax that resembled a modern sales tax. The outcry in the press, on the public platform, and in the streets was so great that he eventually withdrew the measure. What the British regarded as their traditional political rights raised a real and potent barrier to the power of the government. Again in 1739 the public outcry over the alleged Spanish treatment of British merchants in the Caribbean pushed Britain into a war that Walpole opposed and deplored.

Walpole's ascendancy, which lasted until 1742, did little to raise the level of British political morality, but it brought a kind of stability that Britain had not enjoyed for a century. Its foreign trade grew steadily and spread from New England to India. Agriculture became more productive. All forms of economic enterprise seemed to prosper. The navy became stronger. As a result of this political stability and economic growth, Great Britain became a European power of the first order and stood at the beginning of its era as a world power. Its government and economy during the next generation became a model for all progressive Europeans.

Central and Eastern Europe

The major factors in the shift of political influence among the maritime nations were naval strength, economic progress, foreign trade, and sound domestic administration. The conflicts among them occurred less in Europe than on the high seas and in their overseas empires. These nations existed in well-defined geographical areas with established borders. Their populations generally accepted the authority of the central government.

Central and eastern Europe were different. Except for the Baltic ports, the economy was agrarian. There were fewer cities and many more large estates populated by serfs. The states in this region did not possess overseas empires. Changes in the power structure normally involved changes in borders or, at least, in which prince ruled a particular area. Military conflicts took place at home rather than overseas.

The political structure of this region, which lay largely east of the Elbe River, was very "soft." The almost constant warfare of the seventeenth century had led to a habit of temporary and shifting political loyalties. The princes and aristocracies of small states and principalities were unwilling to subordinate themselves to a central monarchical authority. Consequently, the political life of the region and the kind of state that emerged there were different from those of western Europe.

Beginning in the last half of the seventeenth century, eastern and central Europe began to assume the political and social contours that would characterize it for the next two centuries. After the Peace of Westphalia, the Austrian Habsburgs recognized the basic weakness of the position of Holy Roman Emperor and began to consolidate their power outside Germany. At the same time, Prussia emerged as a factor in North German politics and as a major challenger to Habsburg domination of Germany. Most important, Russia at the opening of the eighteenth century became a military power of the first order. These three states (Austria, Prussia, and Russia) achieved their new status largely as a result of the political decay or military defeat of Sweden, Poland, and the Ottoman Empire.

Charles XII of Sweden (r. 1697–1718) led his nation into a number of disastrous wars. These conflicts exhausted the country's resources, preventing Sweden from playing a major role in later eighteenth-century power politics. [H. Roger Viollet]

Sweden: The Ambitions of Charles XII

Under Gustavus Adolphus II (r. 1611–1632), Sweden had played an important role as a Protestant combatant in the Thirty Years' War. During the rest of the seventeenth century, Sweden had consolidated its control of the Baltic, thus preventing Russian possession of a Baltic port and permitting Polish and German access to the sea only on Swedish terms. The Swedes also possessed one of the better armies in Europe. Sweden's economy, however, based primarily on the export of iron, was not strong enough to ensure continued political success.

In 1697 Charles XII (r. 1697–1718) came to the throne. He was headstrong, to say the least, and perhaps insane. In 1700 Russia began a drive to the west against Swedish territory. The Russian goal was a foothold on the Baltic. In the resulting Great Northern War (1700–1721), Charles XII led a vigorous and often brilliant campaign, but one that eventually resulted in the defeat of Sweden. In 1700 he defeated the Russians at the Battle of Narva, but then he turned south to invade Poland. The conflict dragged on, and the Russians were able to strengthen their forces.

In 1708 the Swedish monarch began a major invasion of Russia but became bogged down in the harsh Russian winter. The next year his army was decisively defeated at the Battle of Poltava. Thereafter the Swedes could maintain only a holding action against their enemies. Charles himself sought refuge in Turkey and did not return to Sweden until 1714. He was killed four years later while fighting the Norwegians.

The Great Northern War came to a close in 1721. Sweden had exhausted its military and economic resources and had lost its monopoly on the Baltic coast. Russia had conquered a large section of the eastern Baltic, and Prussia had gained a part of Pomerania. Internally, after the death of Charles XII, the Swedish nobles were determined to reassert their power over the monarchy. They did so but then quarreled among themselves. Sweden played a very minor role in European affairs thereafter.

The Ottoman Empire

At the southeastern extreme of Europe, the Ottoman Empire was a barrier to the territorial ambitions of the Austrian Habsburgs, Poland, and Russia. The empire in the late seventeenth century still controlled most of the Balkan Peninsula and the entire coastline of the Black Sea. In theory the empire existed to enhance the spread of Islam. Its population, however, was exceedingly diverse both ethnically and religiously. The empire ruled these people not on a territorial but on a religious basis. That is, it created units, called *millets,* that included all persons of a particular religious faith. Various laws and regulations applied to the persons who belonged to a particular millet rather than to a particular administrative territory. Non-Islamic persons in the empire were known as *zimmis.* They could practice their religion, but they were second class citizens who could not rise in the service of the empire or profit much from its successes. This mode of government maintained the self-identity of these various peoples and allowed for little religious integration or interaction.

From the fifteenth century onward, the Ottoman Empire had tried to push further westward in Europe. The empire made its greatest military invasion into Europe in 1683, when it unsuccessfully besieged Vienna. In addition, many Christians in the Balkans and on the Aegean islands had converted to Islam. Many of these people had earlier been forced to convert to Roman Catholicism by the Venetians and welcomed the Turks and their faith as vehicles for political liberation. Much of the Islamic presence in the Balkans today dates to these conversions.

By the last third of the seventeenth century, however, the Ottomans had overextended themselves politically, economically, and militarily. From the mid-sixteenth century, the Ottoman rulers spent so much time at war that they could not attend to meetings of governmental bodies in Constantinople. As time passed, political groups in the capital resisted any substantial strengthening of the central government or of the role of the sultan. Rivalries for power among army leaders and nobles, as well as their flagrant efforts to enrich themselves, weakened the effectiveness of the government. In the outer provinces, such as Transylvania, Wallachia, and Moldavia (all parts of modern Romania), the empire depended on the goodwill of local rulers, who paid tribute but never submitted themselves fully to the imperial power. The empire's economy was weak, and its exports were primarily raw materials. Moreover, the actual conduct of most of its trade had been turned over to representatives of other nations.

By the early eighteenth century, the weakness of the Ottoman Empire meant that a political vacuum that would grow during the next two centuries had come into existence on the southeastern perimeter of Europe. The various European powers who had created strong armies and bureaucracies would begin to probe and eventually dismember the Ottoman Empire. In 1699 the Turks

John III Sobieski (1624–1696) was elected king of Poland in 1764. Sobieski led the Polish Army in repulsing the Turkish siege of Vienna in 1683, an event discussed in one of the documents in this chapter. Despite this victory Sobieski failed to establish a strong central monarchy in Poland. [Erich Lessing/Art Resource, N.Y.]

concluded a treaty with their longtime Habsburg enemy and surrendered all pretensions of control over and consequent receipt of revenues from Hungary, Transylvania, Croatia, and Slavonia. From this time onward, Russia also attempted to extend its territory and influence at the expense of the empire. By the early nineteenth century, many of the peoples who lived in the Balkans and around the Black Sea would seek to create their own national states. The retreat and decay of the Ottoman Empire and the scramble of other states and regional peoples to assume control of southeastern Europe would cause political and ethnic turmoil there from the eighteenth century to our own day.

Poland: Absence of Strong Central Authority

In no other part of Europe was the failure to maintain a competitive political position so complete as in Poland. In 1683 King John III Sobieski (r. 1674–1696) had led a Polish army to rescue Vienna from the Turkish siege. Following that spectacular effort, however, Poland became a byword for the dangers of aristocratic independence. In Poland as nowhere else on the Continent, the nobility became the single most powerful political factor in the country. Unlike the British nobility and landowners, the Polish nobility would not even submit to a central authority of their own making. There was

The King of Poland Frees Vienna from the Turks

In 1683 the Ottoman Empire had laid siege to Vienna. The Habsburg monarchy found itself under enormous military pressure. The military forces of John III Sobieski, the king of Poland, rescued the city and repulsed the last great Turkish advance upon central Europe.

✦ *What role did religious sentiments and prejudice play in this description? In that regard, how was the battle portrayed as a conflict between two different religions and two different cultures? How is the ruler of Austria portrayed so as to make the king of Poland the hero of the account? What factors appear to have led the leader of the Ottoman forces to retreat? What were the physical fruits of battle for the victors?*

The Victory which the King of Poland hath obtained over the Infidels, is so great and so compleat that past Ages can scarce parallel the fame; and perhaps future Ages will never see any thing like it. . . . On the one hand we see Vienna besieged by three hundred thousand Turks; reduced to the last extremity; its Outworks taken; the Enemy fixed to the Body of the Place; . . . : We see an Emperor [the Habsburg ruler] chased from his Capital; retired to a Corner of his Dominions; all his Country at the mercy of the Tartars, who have filled the Camp with an infinite Number of unfortunate Slaves that had been forcibly carried away out of Austria. On the other hand, we see the King of Poland, who goes out of his Kingdom, with part of his Army, and hastens to succour his . . . Allies, . . . to march against the Enemies of the Christian Religion willing to act in Person on this Occasion, as a true Buckler of Religion. . . .

The Battle was fought on the 12th, it lasted 14 or 15 Hours; the slaughter was horrible, and the loss of the Turks inestimable, for they left the Field of Battle, besides the Dead and Prisoners, all their Canon, Equipage, Tents and infinite Riches that they had been six Years gathering together throughout the whole Ottoman Empire. . . .

The Night was spent in slaughter, and the unhappy Remnant of this Army saved their Lives by flight, having abandoned all to the Victors; even an infinite Number of Waggons, loaden with Ammunition, and some Field pieces, that designed to have carried with them; and which were found the next Day upon the Road they had taken; which makes us suspect that they'll not be able to rally again, . . .

The King [of Poland] understood afterwards by Deserters, who come every hour in Troops to surrender themselves to him, as well as the Renegadoes, that the Visier [the Turkish leader], seeing the defeat of the Army, called his Sons to him, embraced them, bitterly bewailed their Misfortune, and turned towards the Han of the Tartars [an ally of the Turks], and said, 'And thou, wilt not thou succour me?' To whom the Tartar Prince replied, That he knew the King of Poland by more than one Proof, and that the Visier would be very happy if he could save himself by flight, as having no other way for his Security, and that he was going to show him Example.

The Grand Visier being thus abandoned, took the same way, and retired in Disorder with only one Horse. . . . The Booty that was taken in this Action is infinite and inestimable; The Field of Battle was sowed with Gold Sabres, . . . and such a prodigious Quantity of other things that the Pillage which has already lasted three Days, will scarce be over in a whole Week. . . .

From Polish Manuscripts: or the Secret History of the Reign of John Sobieski, the III of That Name, King of Poland, *trans. by M. Delerac (London: D. Rhodes, 1700), pp. 355–364, as quoted in Alfred J. Bannan and Achilles Edelenyi, eds.,* Documentary History of Eastern Europe *(New York: Twayne Publishers, Inc., 1970), pp. 112–116.*

no effective central authority in the form of either a king or a parliament.

The Polish monarchy was elective, but the deep distrust and divisions among the nobility prevented their electing a king from among themselves. Sobieski was a notable exception. Most of the Polish monarchs were foreigners and were the tools of foreign powers. The Polish nobles did have a central legislative body called the *Sejm,* or Diet. It included only the nobles and specifically excluded representatives from corporate bodies, such as the towns. In the Diet, however, there existed a practice known as the *liberum veto,* whereby the staunch opposition of any single member could require the body to disband. Such opposition was termed "exploding the Diet." This practice was most often the work of a group of dissatisfied nobles rather than of one person. Nonetheless, the requirement of unanimity was a major stumbling block to effective government.

Government as it was developing elsewhere in Europe simply was not tolerated in Poland. Localism reminiscent of the Middle Ages continued to hold sway as the nobles used all their energy to maintain their traditional "Polish liberties." There was no way to collect enough taxes to build up an army. The price of this noble liberty would eventually be the disappearance of Poland from the map of Europe during the latter half of the eighteenth century.

The Habsburg Empire and the Pragmatic Sanction

The close of the Thirty Years' War marked a fundamental turning point in the history of the Austrian Habsburgs. Previously, in alliance with the Spanish branch of the family, they had hoped to dominate all of Germany and to return it to the Catholic fold. They did not achieve either goal, and the decline of Spanish power meant that in future diplomatic relations the Austrian Habsburgs were on their own. The Treaty of Westphalia in 1648 permitted Protestantism within the Holy Roman Empire and also recognized the political autonomy of more than 300 corporate German political entities within the empire. These included large units (such as Saxony, Hanover, Bavaria, and Brandenburg) and scores of small cities, bishoprics, principalities, and petty territories of independent knights.

After 1648 the Habsburgs retained a firm hold on the title of Holy Roman Emperor, but the effectiveness of the title depended less on force of arms than on the cooperation that the emperor could elicit from the various political bodies in the empire. The Diet of the empire sat at Regensburg from 1663 until the empire was dissolved in 1806. The Diet and the emperor generally regulated the daily economic and political life of Germany. The post-Westphalian Holy Roman Empire resembled Poland in its lack of central authority. Unlike its Polish neighbor, however, the Holy Roman Empire was reorganized from within as the Habsburgs attempted to regain their authority. As will be seen shortly, Prussia set out on its course toward European power at the same time.

CONSOLIDATION OF AUSTRIAN POWER While concentrating on their hereditary Austrian holdings among the German states, the Habsburgs also began to consolidate their power and influence within their other hereditary possessions. (See Map 15–1.) These included, first, the Crown of Saint Wenceslas, encompassing the kingdom of Bohemia (in the modern Czech Republic and Slovakia) and the duchies of Moravia and Silesia and, second, the Crown of Saint Stephen, which included Hungary, Croatia, and Transylvania. In the middle of the seventeenth century, much of Hungary remained occupied by the Turks and was liberated only at the end of the century.

In the early eighteenth century, the family further extended its domains, receiving the former Spanish (thereafter Austrian) Netherlands, Lombardy in northern Italy, and briefly, the kingdom of Naples in southern Italy through the Treaty of Utrecht in 1713. During the eighteenth and nineteenth centuries, the Habsburgs' power and influence in Europe were based primarily on their territories outside Germany.

In the second half of the seventeenth century and later, the Habsburgs faced immense problems in these hereditary territories. In each they ruled by virtue of a different title and had to gain the cooperation of the local nobility. The most difficult province was Hungary, where the Magyar nobility seemed ever ready to rebel. There was almost no common basis for political unity among peoples of such diverse languages, customs, and geography. Even the Habsburg zeal for Roman Catholicism no longer proved a bond for unity as they confronted the equally zealous Calvinism of many of the Magyar nobles. The Habsburgs established various central councils to chart common policies for their

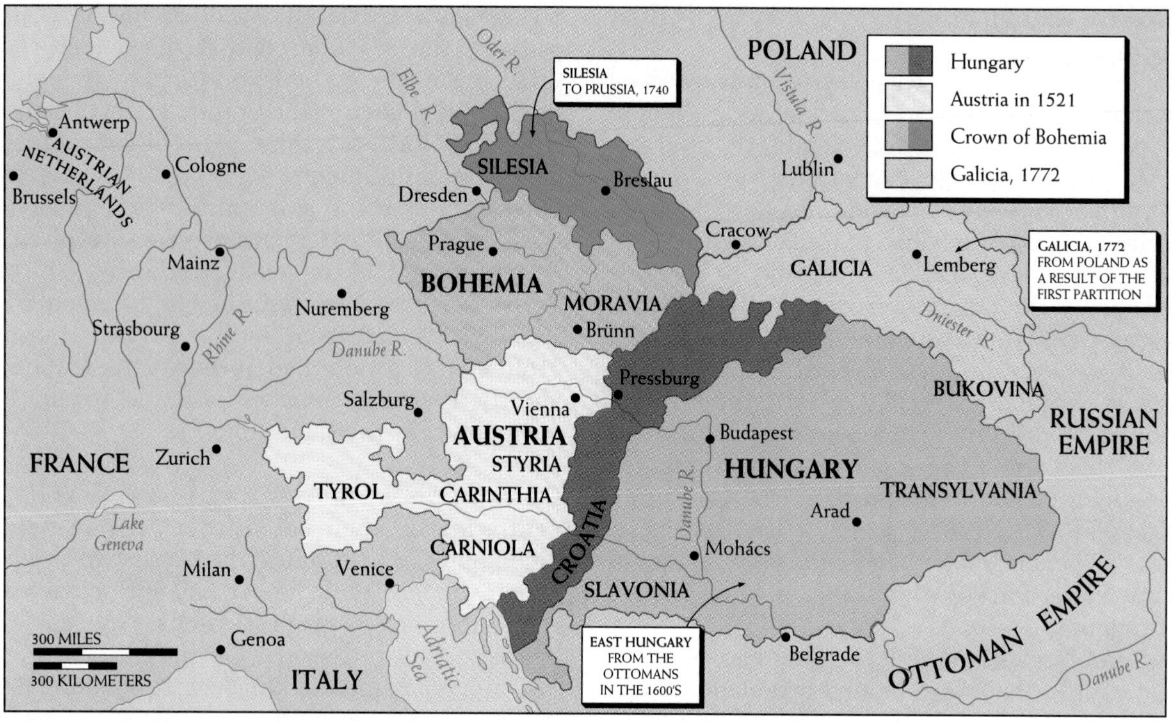

Map 15–1 The Austrian Habsburg Empire, 1521–1772 *The empire had three main units—Austria, Bohemia, and Hungary. Expansion was mainly eastward: East Hungary from the Ottomans (seventeenth century) and Galicia from Poland (1772). Meantime, Silesia was lost, but the Habsburgs retained German influence as Holy Roman emperors.*

far-flung domains. Virtually all of these bodies dealt with only part of the Habsburgs' holdings. Repeatedly, the Habsburgs had to bargain with nobles in one part of Europe to maintain their position in another.

Despite all these internal difficulties, Leopold I (r. 1657–1705) rallied his domains to resist the advances of the Turks and the aggression of Louis XIV. He achieved Ottoman recognition of his sovereignty over Hungary in 1699 and began the suppression of a long rebellion by his new Magyar subjects that lasted from 1703 to 1711. He also conquered much of the Balkan Peninsula and western Romania. These southeastward extensions allowed the Habsburgs to hope to develop Mediterranean trade through the port of Trieste. The expansion at the cost of the Ottoman Empire also helped them to compensate for their loss of domination over the Holy Roman Empire. Strength in the East gave them greater political leverage in Germany. Leopold I was succeeded by Joseph I (r. 1705–1711), who continued his policies.

The Habsburg Dynastic Problem When Charles VI (r. 1711–1740) succeeded Joseph, he had no male heir, and there was only the weakest of precedents for a female ruler of the Habsburg domains. Charles feared that on his death the Austrian Habsburg lands might fall prey to the surrounding powers, as had those of the Spanish Habsburgs in 1700. He was determined to prevent that disaster and to provide his domains with the semblance of legal unity. To those ends, he devoted most of his reign to seeking the approval of his family, the estates of his realms, and the major foreign powers for a document called the Pragmatic Sanction.

This instrument provided the legal basis for a single line of inheritance within the Habsburg dynasty through Charles VI's daughter Maria Theresa (r. 1740–1780). Other members of the Habsburg family recognized her as the rightful heir. The nobles of the various Habsburg domains did likewise after extracting various concessions from Charles. So, when Charles VI died in October 1740, he believed that he had secured legal unity for the Habsburg Empire and a safe succession for his daughter.

Charles VI had indeed established a permanent line of succession and the basis for future legal bonds within the Habsburg holdings. He had failed, however, to protect his daughter from foreign aggression, either through the Pragmatic Sanction or, more important, by leaving her a strong army and a full treasury. Less than two months after his death, the fragility of the foreign agreements became apparent. In December 1740, Frederick II of Prussia invaded the Habsburg province of Silesia. Maria Theresa had to fight to defend her inheritance.

Prussia and the Hohenzollerns

The Habsburg achievement had been to draw together into an uncertain legal unity a collection of domains possessed through separate feudal titles. The achievement of the Hohenzollerns of Brandenburg-Prussia was to acquire a similar collection of titular holdings and then to forge them into a centrally administered unit. Despite the geographical separation of their territories and the paucity of their natural economic resources, they transformed feudal ties and structures into bureaucratic ones. They subordinated every social class and most economic pursuits to the strengthening of the institution that united their far-flung realms: the army. They thus made the term "Prussian" synonymous with administrative rigor and military discipline.

A State of Disconnected Territories The rise of Prussia occurred within the German power vacuum created after 1648 by the Peace of Westphalia. It is the story of the extraordinary Hohenzollern family, which had ruled the German territory of Brandenburg since 1417. (See Map 15–2.) Through inheritance the family had acquired the duchy of Cleves and the counties of Mark and Ravensburg in 1609, the duchy of East Prussia in 1618, and the duchy of Pomerania in 1637. Except for Pomerania, none of these lands was contiguous with Brandenburg. East Prussia lay inside Poland and outside the authority of the Holy Roman Emperor. All of the territories lacked good natural resources, and many of them were devastated during the Thirty Years' War. At Westphalia the Hohenzollerns lost part of Pomerania to Sweden but were compensated by receiving three more bishoprics and the promise of the archbishopric of Magdeburg when it became vacant, as it did in 1680. By the late seventeenth century, the scattered Hohenzollern holdings represented a block of territory within the Holy Roman Empire second in size only to that of the Habsburgs.

Despite its size, the Hohenzollern conglomerate was weak. The areas were geographically separate, with no mutual sympathy or common concern among them. In each, local noble estates limited the power of the Hohenzollern prince. The various areas were also exposed to foreign aggression.

Frederick William, the Great Elector The person who began to forge these areas and nobles into a modern state was Frederick William (r. 1640–1688), who became known as the Great Elector (the ruler of Brandenburg was called an elector because he was one of the princes who elected the Holy Roman Emperor). He established himself and his successors as the central uniting power by breaking the local noble estates, organizing a royal bureaucracy, and establishing a strong army.

Between 1655 and 1660, Sweden and Poland engaged in a war that endangered the Great Elector's holdings in Pomerania and East Prussia. Frederick William had neither the military nor the financial resources to confront this threat. In 1655 the Brandenburg estates refused to grant his new taxes; however, he proceeded to collect the required taxes by military force. In 1659 a different grant of taxes, originally made in 1653, elapsed; Frederick William continued to collect them as well as those he had imposed by his own authority. He used the money to build up an army that allowed him to continue to enforce his will without the approval of the nobility. Similar threats and coercion took place against the nobles in his other territories.

There was, however, a political and social trade-off between the elector and his various nobles. These *Junkers*, or German noble landlords, were allowed almost complete control over the serfs on their estates. In exchange for their obedience to the Hohenzollerns, the Junkers received the right to demand obedience from their serfs. Frederick William also tended to choose as the local administrators of the tax structure men who would normally have been members of the noble estates. He thus co-opted potential opponents into his service. The taxes fell most heavily on the backs of the peasants and the urban classes.

As the years passed, sons of Junkers increasingly dominated the army officer corps, and this practice

The Great Elector Welcomes Protestant Refugees from France

The Hohenzollern dynasty of Brandenburg-Prussia pursued a policy of religious toleration. The family itself was Calvinist, whereas most of its subjects were Lutherans. When Louis XIV of France revoked the Edict of Nantes in 1685 (see the document in Chapter 13), Frederick William, the Great Elector, seized the opportunity to invite into his realms French Protestants. As his proclamation indicates, he wanted to attract persons with productive skills who could aid the economic development of his domains.

✦ *In reading this document, do you believe religious or economic concerns more nearly led the Elector of Brandenburg to welcome the French Protestants? What specific privileges did the Elector extend to them? To what extent were these privileges a welcoming measure and to what extent were they inducements to emigrate to Brandenburg? In what kind of economic activity does the elector expect the French refugees to engage?*

We, Friedrich Wilhelm, by Grace of God Margrave of Brandenburg. . . .

Do hereby proclaim and make known to all and sundry that since the cruel persecutions and rigorous ill-treatment in which Our co-religionists of the Evangelical-Reformed faith have for some time past been subjected in the Kingdom of France, have caused many families to remove themselves and to betake themselves out of the said Kingdom into other lands, We now . . . have been moved graciously to offer them through this Edict . . . a secure and free refuge in all Our Lands and Provinces. . . .

Since Our Lands are not only well and amply endowed with all things necessary to support life, but also very well-suited to the reestablishment of all kinds of manufactures and trade and traffic by land and water, We permit, indeed, to those settling therein free choice to establish themselves where it is most convenient for their profession and way of living. . . .

The personal property which they bring with them, including merchandise and other wares, is to be totally exempt from any taxes, customs dues, licenses, or other imposts of any description, and not detained in any way. . . .

As soon as these Our French co-religionists of the Evangelical-Reformed faith have settled in any town or village, they shall be admitted to the domiciliary rights and craft freedoms customary there, gratis and without payments of any fee; and shall be entitled to the benefits, rights, and privileges enjoyed by Our other, native, subjects, residing there. . . .

Not only are those who wish to establish manufacture of cloth, stuffs, hats, or other objects in which they are skilled to enjoy all necessary freedoms, privileges and facilities, but also provision is to be made for them to be assisted and helped as far as possible with money and anything else which they need to realize their intention. . . .

Those who settle in the country and wish to maintain themselves by agriculture are to be given a certain plot of land to bring under cultivation and provided with whatever they need to establish themselves initially. . . .

C. A. Macartney, ed., The Habsburg and Hohenzollern Dynasties in the Seventeenth and Eighteenth Centuries *(New York: Walker, 1970), pp. 270–273.*

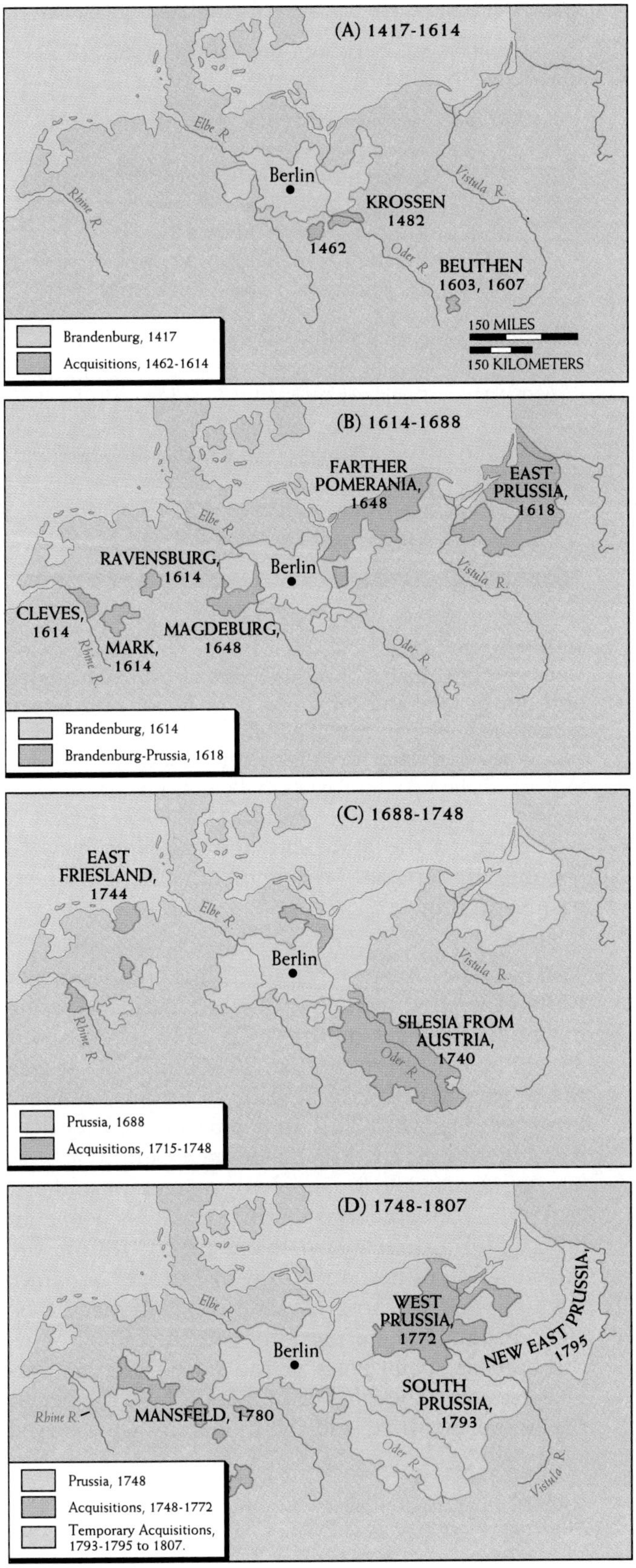

MAP 15–2 EXPANSION OF BRANDENBURG-PRUSSIA
In the seventeenth-century, Brandenburg-Prussia expanded mainly by acquiring dynastic titles in geographically separated lands. In the eighteenth century, it expanded through aggression to the east, seizing Silesia in 1740 and various parts of Poland in 1772, 1793, and 1795.

became even more pronounced during the eighteenth century. All officials and army officers took an oath of loyalty directly to the elector. The army and the elector thus came to embody the otherwise absent unity of the state. The existence of the army made Prussia a valuable potential ally and a state with which other powers needed to curry favor.

FREDERICK WILLIAM I, KING OF PRUSSIA Yet, even with the considerable accomplishments of the Great Elector, the house of Hohenzollern did not possess a crown. The achievement of a royal title was one of the few state-building accomplishments of Frederick I (r. 1688–1713). This son of the Great Elector was the least "Prussian" of his family during these crucial years. He built palaces, founded Halle University (1694), patronized the arts, and lived luxuriously. In 1701, however, at the outbreak of the War of the Spanish Succession, he put his army at the disposal of the Habsburg Holy Roman Emperor. In exchange for this loyal service, the emperor permitted Frederick to assume the title of "King in Prussia." Thereafter Frederick became Frederick I, and he passed the much-desired royal title to his son Frederick William I in 1713.

Frederick William I (r. 1713–1740) was both the most eccentric and one of the most effective Hohenzollerns. After giving his father a funeral that matched the luxury of his life, Frederick William I immediately imposed strict austerity. Some jobs were abolished, and other salaries lowered. His political aims seem to have been the consolidation of an obedient, compliant bureaucracy and a bigger army. He initiated a policy of *Kabinett* government, which meant that lower officials submitted all relevant documents to him in his office, or *Kabinett*. Then he alone examined the papers, made his decisions, and issued his orders. He thus skirted the influence of ministers and ruled alone.

Frederick William I organized the bureaucracy along military lines. He united all departments under the *General-Ober Finanz-Kriegs-und-Domänen-Direktorium*, more happily known to us as the General Directory. He imposed taxes on the nobility and changed most remaining feudal dues into money payments. He sought to transform feudal and administrative loyalties into a sense of duty to the monarch as a political institution rather than as a person. He once described the perfect royal servant as

Austria and Prussia in the Late Seventeenth and Early Eighteenth Centuries

1640–1688	Reign of Frederick William, the Great Elector
1657–1705	Leopold I rules Austria and resists the Turkish invasions
1683	Turkish siege of Vienna
1688–1713	Reign of Frederick I of Prussia
1699	Peace treaty between Turks and Habsburgs
1711–1740	Charles VI rules Austria and secures agreement to the Pragmatic Sanction
1713–1740	Frederick William I builds up the military power of Prussia
1740	Maria Theresa succeeds to the Habsburg throne
1740	Frederick II violates the Pragmatic Sanction by invading Silesia

an intelligent, assiduous, and alert person who after God values nothing higher than his king's pleasure and serves him out of love and for the sake of honor rather than money and who in his conduct solely seeks and constantly bears in mind his king's service and interests, who, moreover, abhors all intrigues and emotional deterrents.[1]

Service to the state and the monarch was to become impersonal, mechanical, and, in effect, unquestioning.

THE PRUSSIAN ARMY The discipline that Frederick William applied to the army was fanatical. During his reign the size of the army grew from about 39,000 in 1713 to more than 80,000 in 1740. It was the third or fourth largest army in Europe, whereas Prussia ranked thirteenth in population. Rather than using recruiters, the king made each canton or local district responsible for supplying a quota of soldiers.

After 1725 Frederick William always wore an officer's uniform. He formed one regiment from the tallest soldiers he could find in Europe. Separate laws applied to the army and to civilians. Laws, customs, and royal attention made the officer corps the highest social class of the state. Military service attracted the sons of Junkers. Thus, the army, the Junker nobility, and the monarchy were forged

[1]Quoted in Hans Rosenberg, *Bureaucracy, Aristocracy, and Autocracy* (Boston: Beacon Press, 1958), p. 93.

into a single political entity. Military priorities and values dominated Prussian government, society, and daily life as in no other state of Europe. It has often been said that whereas other nations possessed armies, the Prussian army possessed its nation.

Although Frederick William I built the best army in Europe, he avoided conflict. He wanted to drill his soldiers but not to order them into battle. Although he terrorized his family and associates and on occasion knocked out teeth with his walking stick, he was not militarily aggressive. The army was for him a symbol of Prussian power and unity, not an instrument to be used for foreign adventures or aggression.

At his death in 1740, he passed to his son Frederick II "the Great" (r. 1740–1786) this superb military machine, but he could not also pass on the wisdom to refrain from using it. Almost immediately on coming to the throne, Frederick II upset the Pragmatic Sanction and invaded Silesia. He thus crystallized the Austrian–Prussian rivalry for control of Germany that would dominate central European affairs for over a century.

Though economically weak and with a small population, Prussia became an important state because it developed a large, well-trained army. Prussian troops were known for their discipline, the result of constant drill and harsh punishment. In this mid-eighteenth-century engraving one soldier is being whipped while another is about to run a gauntlet of other soldiers. [Bildarchiv Preussischer Kulturbesitz]

The Entry of Russia into the European Political Arena

Though ripe with consequences for the future, the rise of Prussia and the new consolidation of the Austrian Habsburg domains seemed to many at the time only another shift in the long-troubled German scene. The emergence of Russia, however, as an active European power was a wholly new factor in European politics. Previously Russia had been considered part of Europe only by courtesy. Geographically and politically it lay on the periphery. Hemmed in by Sweden on the Baltic and by the Ottoman Empire on the Black Sea, the country had no warm-water ports. Its chief outlet to the west was Archangel on the White Sea, which was ice free for only part of the year. There was little trade. What Russia did possess was a vast reserve of largely undeveloped natural and human resources.

Birth of the Romanov Dynasty

The reign of Ivan the Terrible, which had begun so well and closed so frighteningly, was followed by anarchy and civil war known as the "Time of Troubles." In 1613, hoping to restore stability, an assembly of nobles elected as tsar a seventeen-year-old boy named Michael Romanov (r. 1613–1654). Thus began the dynasty that despite palace revolutions, military conspiracies, assassinations, and family strife ruled Russia until 1917.

Michael Romanov and his two successors, Alexis I (r. 1654–1676) and Theodore III (r. 1676–1682), brought stability and some bureaucratic centralization to Russia. The country remained, however, weak and impoverished. The bureaucracy after years of turmoil was still largely controlled by the *boyars*, the old nobility. This administrative apparatus could barely suppress a revolt of peasants and Cossacks (horsemen who lived on the steppe frontier) under Stepan Razin in 1670–1671. Furthermore, the government and the tsars faced the danger of mutiny from the *streltsy*, or guards of the Moscow garrison.

Peter the Great

In 1682 another boy—ten years old at the time—ascended the fragile Russian throne as co-ruler with his half brother. His name was Peter (r. 1682–1725), and Russia would never be the same after him. He and the ill Ivan V had come to power on the shoulders of the *streltsy*, who expected to be rewarded for their support. Much violence and bloodshed had surrounded the disputed succession. Matters became even more confused when the boys' sister, Sophia, was named regent. Peter's followers overthrew her in 1689. From that date onward, Peter ruled personally, although in theory he shared the crown until Ivan died in 1696. The dangers and turmoil of his youth convinced Peter of two things. First, the power of the tsar must be made secure from the jealousy of the *boyars* and the greed of the *streltsy*. Second, the military power of Russia must be increased. In that respect he resembled Louis XIV of France, who had experienced the turmoil of the *Fronde* during his youth and resolved to establish a strong monarchy.

Western Europe, particularly its military resources, fascinated Peter I, who became known as Peter the Great. He was an imitator of the first

Rise of Russian Power

1533–1584	Reign of Ivan the Terrible
1584–1613	"Time of Troubles"
1613	Michael Romanov becomes tsar
1682	Peter the Great, age ten, becomes tsar
1689	Peter assumes personal rule
1696	Russia captures Azov on the Black Sea from the Turks
1697	European tour of Peter the Great
1698	Peter returns to Russia to put down the revolt of the *streltsy*
1700	The Great Northern War opens between Russia and Sweden; Russia defeated at Narva by Swedish Army of Charles XII
1703	Saint Petersburg founded
1709	Russia defeats Sweden at the Battle of Poltava
1718	Charles XII of Sweden dies
1718	Son of Peter the Great dies in prison under mysterious circumstances
1721	Peace of Nystad ends the Great Northern War
1721	Peter establishes a synod for the Russian church
1722	Peter issues the Table of Ranks
1725	Peter dies leaving an uncertain succession

After Peter the Great of Russia returned from his journey to western Europe, he personally cut off the traditional and highly prized long sleeves and beards of the Russian nobles. His action symbolized his desire to see Russia become more powerful and more modern. [The Granger Collection]

order. The products and workers from the West who had filtered into Russia impressed and intrigued him. In 1697 he made a famous visit in transparent disguise to western Europe. There he dined and talked with the great and the powerful, who considered this almost seven-foot-tall ruler both crude and rude. His happiest moments on the trip were spent inspecting shipyards, docks, and the manufacture of military hardware.

Peter returned to Moscow determined to copy what he had seen abroad, for he knew that warfare would be necessary to make Russia a great power. The tsar's drive toward westernization, though unsystematic, had four general goals: taming the *boyars* and the *streltsy*, achieving secular control of the church, reorganizing the internal administration, and developing the economy. Peter pursued each of these goals ruthlessly. His effort was unprecedented in Russian history in both its intensity and scope.

TAMING THE *BOYARS* AND *STRELTSY* Peter made a sustained attack on the *boyars*. In 1698, immediately on his return from abroad, he personally shaved the long beards of the court *boyars* and sheared off the customary long, hand-covering sleeves of their shirts and coats, which had made them the butt of jokes throughout Europe. More important, he demanded that the nobles serve his state.

In 1722 Peter published a Table of Ranks that equated a person's social position and privileges with his rank in the bureaucracy or the army rather than with his position in the nobility. Peter thus intended to make the social standing of individual *boyars* a function of their willingness to

Peter the Great Establishes Building Requirements in Saint Petersburg

By constructing Saint Petersburg on the Gulf of Finland, Peter the Great tried to consolidate his military efforts in the Great Northern War. The city was to provide Russia with a permanent outlet to the West and to be the site of its new capital. The construction of this city consequently served symbolic political ends as well as military and economic ones. In this document, Peter explains how he expected the city to be constructed.

✦ *Why might Peter have been so concerned that the work on the city progress rapidly? What are the difficulties in construction in Russia that this document reveals? What do those difficulties tell you about Russia's society and its economic resources? Why might Peter have been concerned that only houses face on the streets of the new city.*

1. On the City Island and the Admiralty Island in Saint Petersburg, as likewise on the banks of the greater Neva and its more important arms, wood buildings are forbidden, only adobe houses being allowed. The two above-mentioned islands and the embankments excepted, wood may be used for buildings, the plans to be obtained from the architect. . . . The roofs are to be covered either with two thicknesses of turf laid on rafters with cross-ribs (not on laths or boards), or with tiles. No other roof covering is allowed under penalty of severe fines. The streets should be bordered directly by the houses, not with fences or stables.

2. The most illustrious and mighty Peter the Great, Emperor and Autocrat of all Russia, has commanded his imperial decree to be proclaimed to people of all ranks. Whereas stone construction here is advancing very slowly, it being difficult to obtain stonemasons and other artisans of this craft even for good pay; for this reason all stone buildings of any description are forbidden in the whole state for a few years, until construction has sufficiently progressed here, under penalty of confiscation of the offender's property and exile. This decree is to be announced in all the cities and districts of the Saint Petersburg province, except this city, so that none may plead ignorance as an excuse.

3. The following is ordered: no building shall be undertaken in Petersburg on the grounds of houses, between neighboring back yards, until all the main and side streets are entirely built up. However, if after this any person needs more buildings, he may build on his grounds, along the neighbor's lot. No stables or barns may be built facing the street, but only inside the grounds. Along the streets and side streets all the space must be filled by residences, as ordered. In the locations where, as ordered by previous decrees, wooden houses may be built, they must be made of squared logs. If the logs are used as they are, the walls must be faced with boards and coated with red, or painted to look like brick.

From Marthe Blinoff, ed., Life and Thought in Old Russia, *(University Park: The Pennsylvania State University Press, 1961), pp. 16–17.*

Peter the Great built Saint Petersburg on the Gulf of Finland to provide Russia with better contact with western Europe. He moved Russia's capital there from Moscow in 1703. This is an eighteenth-century view of the city. [John R. Freeman]

serve the central state. Unlike Prussian Junkers, however, the Russian nobility never became perfectly loyal to the state. They repeatedly sought to reassert their independence and their control of the Russian imperial court and to bargain with later tsars over local authority and the nobles' dominance of the serfs.

The *streltsy* fared less well than the *boyars*. In 1698 they had rebelled while Peter was on his European tour. On his return, he brutally suppressed the revolt. There were private tortures and public executions, in which Peter's own ministers took part. Almost 1,200 of the rebels were put to death, and their corpses remained on public display to discourage future disloyalty.

Achieving Secular Control of the Church

Peter dealt with the potential independence of the Russian Orthodox Church with similar ruthlessness. Here again, he had to confront a problem that had arisen in the turbulent decades that had preceded his reign. The Russian church had long opposed the scientific as well as the theological thought of the West. In the mid-seventeenth century, a reformist movement led by Patriarch Nikon introduced certain changes into church texts and ritual. These reforms caused great unrest among the Old Believers, a group of Russian Christians who strongly opposed these changes. Although condemned by the hierarchy, the Old Believers persisted in their opposition. Thousands of them committed suicide rather than submit to the new rituals. The Old Believers represented a rejection of change and innovation; their opposition discouraged the church hierarchy from making any further substantial accommodations with modern thought.

In the future Peter wanted to avoid two kinds of difficulties with the church. First, the clergy must not be able to oppose change and westernization. Second, the hierarchy of the church must not be permitted to cause again the kind of controversy that had inspired the Old Believers. Consequently,

Bishop Burnet Recalls the Visit of Peter the Great to England

In 1797 and 1798 Peter the Great of Russia toured western Europe to discover how Russia must change its society and economy in order to become a great power. As this description indicates, English Bishop Gilbert Burnet found the tsar a curious person. He was deeply impressed by the tsar's difficult personality and by his determination to have his subjects learn the ways of western Europe.

✦ *What qualities did Burnet admire and criticize in Peter the Great? How had some of these qualities been manifested in Peter's behavior as ruler of Russia? Why might Peter the Great have been so interested in ships and shipbuilding? What steps did the tsar take to allow his subjects to become familiar with other nations?*

He came this winter over to England, and stayed some months among us. . . . I had good interpreters, so I had much free discourse with him; he is a man of a very hot temper, soon inflamed, and very brutal in his passion; he raises his natural heat, by drinking much brandy, . . . he is subject to convulsive motions all over his body, and his head seems to be affected with these; he wants not capacity, and has a larger measure of knowledge, than might be expected from his education, which was very indifferent; a want of judgment, with an instability of temper, appear in him too often and too evidently; he is mechanically turned, and seems designed by nature rather to be a ship-carpenter, than a great prince. This was his chief study and exercise, while he stayed here: he wrought much with his own hands, and made all about him work at the models of ships. . . . He was . . . resolved to encourage learning, and to polish his people, by sending some of them to travel in other countries, and to draw strangers to come and live among them. . . . After I had seen him often, and had conversed much with him, I could not but adore the depth of the providence of God, that had raised up such a furious man to so absolute an authority over so great a part of the world.

Bishop Burnet's History of His Own Time *(Oxford: Clarendon Press, 1823), vol. 4, pp. 396–397.*

in 1721, Peter simply abolished the position of patriarch. In its place he established a synod headed by a layman, called the Procurator General, to rule the church in accordance with secular requirements. So far as transforming a traditional institution was concerned, this action toward the church was the most radical policy of Peter's reign. It produced still further futile opposition from the Old Believers, who saw the tsar as leading the church into new heresy.

Reorganizing Domestic Administration In his reorganization of domestic administration, Peter looked to institutions then used in Sweden. These were "colleges," or bureaus, of several persons rather than departments headed by a single minister. These colleges, which he imposed on Russia, were to look after matters such as the collection of taxes, foreign relations, war, and economic affairs. This new organization was an attempt to breathe life into Russia's stagnant and inefficient administration.

In 1711 Peter created a central senate of nine members who were to direct the Moscow government when the tsar was away with the army. The purpose of these and other local administrative reforms was to establish a bureaucracy that could support an efficient army.

Developing the Economy and Waging War The economic development advocated by Peter the Great was closely related to his military needs. He encouraged the establishment of an iron industry in the Ural Mountains, and by mid-century Russia had become the largest iron producer in Europe. He sent promising young Russians abroad to acquire technical and organizational skills. He tried to attract West European craftspeople to live and work in Russia. Except for the striking growth of the iron industry, which nevertheless later languished, these efforts had only marginal success.

The goal of these internal reforms and political departures was to support a policy of warfare. Peter was determined to secure warm-water ports that would allow Russia to trade with the West and to have a greater impact on European affairs. This policy led him into wars with the Ottoman Empire and Sweden. His armies began fighting the Turks in 1695 and captured Azov on the Black Sea in 1696. It was a temporary victory, for in 1711 he was compelled to return the port.

Peter had more success against Sweden, where the inconsistency and irrationality of Charles XII were no small aid. In 1700 Russia invaded the Swedish Baltic possessions. The Swedish king's failure to follow up his victory at Narva in 1700 allowed Peter to regroup his forces and reserve his resources. In 1709, when Charles XII returned to fight Russia again, Peter was ready, and the Battle of Poltava sealed the fate of Sweden. In 1721 the Peace of Nystad, which ended the Great Northern War, confirmed the Russian conquest of Estonia, Livonia, and part of Finland. Henceforth Russia possessed warm-water ports and a permanent influence on European affairs.

At one point the domestic and foreign policies of Peter the Great literally intersected. This was at the spot on the Gulf of Finland where he founded his new capital city of Saint Petersburg. There he built government structures and compelled the *boyars* to construct town houses. He thus imitated those European monarchs who had copied Louis XIV by constructing smaller versions of Versailles. The founding of Saint Petersburg went beyond establishing a central imperial court, however. It symbolized a new Western orientation of Russia and Peter's determination to hold his position on the Baltic coast. He had begun the construction of the city and had moved the capital there in 1703, even before his victory over Sweden was assured.

Despite his notable success on the Baltic, Peter's reign ended with a great question mark. He had long quarreled with his only son, Alexis. Peter was jealous of the young man and feared he might undertake sedition. In 1718 Peter had his son imprisoned, and during this imprisonment, Alexis died mysteriously. Thereafter Peter claimed for himself the right to name a successor, but he could never bring himself to designate one either orally or in writing. Consequently, when he died in 1725, there was no firm policy on the succession to the throne. For more than thirty years, soldiers and nobles again determined who ruled Russia. Peter had laid the foundations of a modern Russia, but he had failed to lay the foundations of a stable state.

✦

By the second quarter of the eighteenth century, the major European powers were not yet nation-states in which the citizens felt themselves united by a shared sense of community, culture, language, and history. They were still monarchies in which the personality of the ruler and the personal relationships of the great noble families exercised considerable influence over public affairs. The monarchs, except in Great Britain, had generally succeeded in making their power greater than the nobility's. The power of the aristocracy and its capacity to resist or obstruct the policies of the monarch were not destroyed, however. In Britain, of course, the nobility had tamed the monarchy, but even there tension between nobles and monarchs would continue throughout the rest of the century.

In foreign affairs the new arrangement of military and diplomatic power established early in the century prepared the way for two long conflicts. The first was a commercial rivalry for trade and overseas empire between France and Great Britain. During the reign of Louis XIV, these two nations had collided over the French bid for dominance in Europe. During the eighteenth century, they dueled for control of commerce on other continents. The second arena of warfare was in central Europe, where Austria and Prussia fought for the leadership of the German states.

Behind these international conflicts and the domestic rivalry of monarchs and nobles, however, the society of eighteenth-century Europe began to change. The character and the structures of the societies over which the monarchs ruled were beginning to take on some features associated with the modern age. These economic and social developments would eventually transform the life of Europe to a degree beside which the state building of the early eighteenth-century monarchs paled.

Review Questions

1. Explain why Britain and France remained leading powers in western Europe while Spain and the United Netherlands declined.
2. How did the structure of British government change under the political leadership of Robert Walpole? What were the chief sources of Walpole's political strength?
3. How was the Hohenzollern family able to forge a conglomerate of diverse land holdings into the state of Prussia? Who were the major personalities involved in this process and what were their individual contributions? Why was the military so important in Prussia?
4. Compare and contrast the varying success with which the Hohenzollerns and Habsburgs each handled their problems. Which family was more successful and why? Why were Sweden, the Ottoman Empire, and Poland each less successful?
5. How and why did Russia emerge as a great power? Discuss the character of Peter the Great. What were Russia's domestic problems before Peter came to power? What were his methods of reform? To what extent did he succeed? How were his reforms related to his military ambitions?
6. It has been said that Peter the Great was a rational ruler, interested in the welfare of his people. Do you agree with this statement? Why? Can you make a case for Peter as a bloody tyrant, concerned only with promoting his own glory?

Suggested Readings

T. M. BARKER, *Army, Aristocracy, Monarchy: Essays in War, Society and Government in Austria, 1618–1780* (1982). Examines the intricate power relationships among these major institutions.

J. BLACK, *Eighteenth-Century Europe 1700–1789* (1990). An excellent survey.

J. BREWER, *The Sinews of Power: War, Money and the English State, 1688–1783* (1989). An extremely important study of the financial basis of English power.

R. BROWNING, *Political and Constitutional Ideas of the Court Whigs* (1982). An excellent overview of the ideology of Walpole's supporters.

F. L. CARSTEN, *The Origins of Prussia* (1954). Discusses the groundwork laid by the Great Elector in the seventeenth century.

J. C. D. CLARK, *English Society: 1688–1832: Social Structure and Political Practice during the Ancien Régime* (1985). An important, controversial work that emphasizes the role of religion in English political life.

A. COBBAN, *A History of Modern France*, 2nd ed., vol. 1 (1961). A lively and opinionated volume.

L. COLLEY, *In Defiance of Oligarchy: The Tory Party, 1714–60* (1982). An important study that challenges much conventional opinion about eighteenth-century British politics.

N. DAVIS, *God's Playground*, vol. 1 (1991). Excellent on prepartition Poland.

P. M. G. DICKSON, *Finance and Government Under Maria Theresa* (1987). A definitive work.

W. DOYLE, *The Old European Order, 1660–1800* (1992). The most thoughtful treatment of the subject.

P. DUKES, *The Making of Russian Absolutism: 1613–1801* (1982). An overview based on recent scholarship.

R. R. ERGANG, *The Potsdam Führer* (1941). The biography of Frederick William I.

R. J. W. EVANS, *The Making of the Habsburg Monarchy, 1550–1700: An Interpretation* (1979). Places much emphasis on intellectual factors and the role of religion.

F. FORD, *Robe and Sword: The Regrouping of the French Aristocracy After Louis XIV* (1953). An important book for political, social, and intellectual history.

J. M. HITTLE, *The Service City: State and Townsmen in Russia, 1600–1800* (1979). Examines the relationship of cities in Russia to the growing power of the central government.

H. HOLBORN, *A History of Modern Germany, 1648–1840* (1966). The most comprehensive survey in English.

R. A. KANN AND Z. V. DAVID, *The Peoples of the Eastern Habsburg Lands, 1526–1918* (1984). A helpful overview of the subject.

D. MCKAY AND H. M. SCOTT, *The Rise of the Great Powers 1648–1815* (1983). Now the standard survey.

W. H. MCNEIL, *Europe's Steppe Frontier, 1500–1800* (1964). An interpretive essay on the history of southeastern Europe.

R. K. MASSIE, *Peter the Great: His Life and His World* (1980). A good popular biography.

L. B. NAMIER AND J. BROOKE, *The History of Parliament: The House of Commons, 1754–1790*, 3 vols. (1964). A detailed examination of the unreformed British House of Commons and electoral system.

J. B. OWEN, *The Eighteenth Century* (1974). An excellent introduction to England in this period.

G. PARKER, *The Military Revolution: Military Innovation and the Rise of the West (1500–1800)* (1988). A major work in every respect.

J. H. PLUMB, *Sir Robert Walpole*, 2 vols. (1956, 1961). A masterful biography ranging across the sweep of European politics.

J. H. PLUMB, *The Growth of Political Stability in England, 1675–1725* (1969). An important interpretive work.

N. V. RIASANOVSKY, *The Image of Peter the Great in Russian History and Thought* (1985). Examines the legacy of Peter in Russian history.

N. V. RIASANOVSKY, *A History of Russia*, 5th ed. (1992). The best one-volume introduction.

H. ROSENBERG, *Bureaucracy, Aristocracy, and Autocracy: The Prussian Experience, 1660–1815* (1960). Emphasizes the organization of Prussian administration.

P. F. SUGAR, *Southeastern Europe Under Ottoman Rule, 1354–1804* (1977). An extremely clear presentation.

E. N. WILLIAMS, *The Ancien Régime in Europe* (1972). A state-by-state survey of very high quality.

INDEX

The alphabetical arrangement is letter-by-letter. Page numbers in italic refer to illustrations.

A

B

H

I

J

K

L

S